THE HISTORY OF THORNTON-LE- DALE

by

REGINALD JEFFERY &
KEITH SNOWDEN

BLACKTHORN PRESS

Blackthorn Press, Blackthorn House
Middleton Rd, Pickering YO18 8AL
United Kingdom

www.blackthornpress.com

ISBN 978 1 906259 19 8

CONTENTS

INTRODUCTION

Ever since its publication in 1931, Reginald Jeffery's *Thornton-le-Dale. Being the History of the people of Thornton, Ellerburn-cum-Farmanby, Roxby, Dalby and Thornton Marishes from the earliest times to the present day*, to give the book its full title, has been the standard history of this North Yorkshire village. The style is clear and lacking in the pomposity that bedevils books written in that period. Historical research and fashions might question some of the interpretations but the book remains sound.

The opportunity has been taken with the issuing of this paperback version to bring the story down to the end of the twentieth century with the addition of a chapter by local historian Keith Snowden. The chapter first appeared in his book *Thornton Dale Through the Ages* published in 2000. The opportunity has also been taken to add photographs wherever suitable and particularly in the last chapter. Special thanks are due to John Garbutt and Bob Hill for the use of photographs from their collections and to all the inhabitants of Thornton le Dale who have contributed to this book.

Pickering 2009

THORNTON-LE-DALE.

Being the History of the People of
Thornton, Ellerburn-cum-Farmanby,
Roxby, Dalby, and Thornton
Marishes from the
earliest times to
the present
day.

By

REGINALD W. JEFFERY, M.A.,

Fellow and Tutor, Brasenose College, Oxford.

AUTHOR OF

" *The Manors and Advowson of Great Rollright.*"
' *The Industries of Oxfordshire* " (*V.C.H. Oxon. II*),
&c.

Printed and bound in Great Britain by
CPI Antony Rowe, Chippenham and Eastbourne

Dedication.

———

To the Memory of
EDWARD WILLIAM HESLOP,
to whom I am ever indebted
for Many Happy Days in these
wide moorland spaces.

Contents.

Some abbreviations frequently used in the footnotes.

Arch. Jour.	Archaeological Journal.
Cal. B. of F.	Calendar Book of Fees.
Cal. Char. R.	Calendar of Charter Rolls.
Cal. Close R.	Calendar of Close Rolls.
Cal. Cttee. of Comp.	Calendar of Committee of Compounding.
Cal. Feud. Aids.	Calendar of Feudal Aids.
Cal. Fine R.	Calendar of Fine Rolls.
Cal. Inq.	Calendar of Inquests *post mortem*.
Cal. Pap. Reg.	Calendar of Papal Registers.
Cal. Pat. R.	Calendar of Patent Rolls.
Camb. Al.	Cambridge *Alumni*.
Charlton	Charlton, *History of Whitby*.
C. R.	Registers of All Saints' Church, Thornton.
D. and C. of W.	Dean and Canons of St. George's Chapel, Windsor.
D. N. B.	Dictionary of National Biography.
Eastmead	Eastmead's *Rievallensis*.
F. Y. in M. P.	Canon Atkinson, *Forty Years in a Moorland Parish*.
G. F. G. H.	Documents in the possession of George F. G. Hill, Esq., kindly lent to the writer.
Hist. MSS. Com.	Historical Manuscripts Commission.
J. L. W.	Documents in the custody of J. L. Whitehead, Esq., kindly shown to the writer.
N. R. Rec. S. N.S. or O.S.	North Riding Record Society, New Series or Old Series.
Rev. A. H.	Documents kindly lent to the writer by the late Rev. A. Hill.
Sur. Soc.	Surtees Society.
V. C. H.	Victoria County History.
Y. A. J.	Yorkshire Archaeological Journal.
Y. A. S. Rec. S.	Yorkshire Archaeological Society Record Series.
Y. G. S.	Yorkshire Geological Society.
Young	Young, *History of Whitby*.

Introduction.

I do not suppose for a moment that the pleasure of reading this book will be comparable with the pleasure I have had in compiling it. The history of 'Thornton-le-Dale' is, so to speak, the return to an old love, for I began making my first notes in 1899. Owing to circumstances, over which I had no control, my thoughts with regard to village history were carried south for some years; but as soon as I could, I returned to my former interest in the story of Thornton. Ever since 1894, when I first stayed with my cousin, the Rev. E. W. Heslop, the village has been to me 'the beloved village,' and during part of the last thirty-six years I occupied a house in it, and had a good opportunity of an intimate acquaintance with many of its inhabitants. The old days and old memories are passing away, and I have been fortunate in not only having documents put at my disposal; but also many of the older generation have assisted me by word of mouth. I have, in the past, often chatted with those who remembered very different days now a hundred years ago.

The Civil Parish of Thornton-le-Dale, comprises, to-day, the different Manors that go to make the titles of some of these chapters. Its total area is 9,689 acres, of which 2,680 ac. are arable and 2,620 ac. are permanent grass, 233 ac. woodland, and the rest mainly moor. The village, adjudged 'the most beautiful in Yorkshire,' is situated in Pickering Lythe Wapentake, on each side of its picturesque Beck, at the crossing of the Malton-Whitby and Pickering-Scarborough roads. Its subsoil is Kimmeridge Clay and Corallian Beds, the soil, gravel and limestone.

As in my other village history, I have tried to show in this, how its records may illustrate in miniature the history of the nation; but, in the case of Thornton, to show also that it was more than a typical example of an ordinary village throughout the centuries, because of it being within the important Forest of Pickering. I trust that, however barren the narrative, I have, at least, partly fulfilled these objects. If I have failed to convey the true historic interest of Thornton, and I quite realize that I have indeed failed entirely to convey its glorious charms of sparkling beck and purple-clad moor, I must bear the full blame. It is not for want of devotion to the place, nor for lack of assistance and kindness on all sides.

CHAPTER ONE

Early History.

"Methinks it were a happy life,
To be no better than a homely swain."

SHAKESPEARE.

"How blessed is he who leads a country life."

DRYDEN.

IN prehistoric times the district of Thornton was occupied by bears, elephants, hyenas and rhinoceroses, remains of all of which have been found in the neighbourhood.[1] These wild beasts were driven south during the Ice-Age; and it was this glacial epoch that created the chief beauties of Thornton, for the action of ice and water caused the innumerable 'riggs' and dales, and carved the 'slack ends', all of which are such features of this parish. After the melting of the ice, the Vale of Pickering, of which the dale of Thornton is an offshoot, was at one time a huge lake, and into this, water-courses worked their way, until, blocked by the slowly dissolving ice-sheet of what is now the North Sea on the east, they found an exit by the gorge at Kirkham Abbey on the west.[2]

With the retreat of the ice human beings appeared.[3] Centuries later there were two main invasions; the earlier, or Gadhelic,[4] left scarcely any traces, but the men of the second, or Celtic, settled in the neighbourhood, and remains of their habitation are still to be found. These are to be seen in the parish of Thornton, first, in the fourteen tumuli; one on Pexton Moor,[5] two between

[1] In Kirkdale Cave, one and a half miles west of Kirkby Moorside. *Vide* Buckland, *Reliquiae Diluvianae*, and H. Schroeder, *Annals of Yorkshire* I. p. 229. For elephant's tooth and tusk at Robin Hood's Bay and Scarborough, *cf.* Young p. 786.

[2] G. Home, *The Evolution of an English Town*, p. 23. Dr. J. L. Kirk considers the north shore of this lake to have been at Thornton about the level of Low Mill Garth.

[3] For existence of Preglacial Man *cf. The Times*, 2nd September, 1929; but on 13th September, 1929, Mr. Frank Elgee said that the earliest men in these parts lived approximately 4000, B.C.

[4] G. E. Morris, *The North Riding of Yorkshire*, p. 19.

[5] On 11th February, 1911, pieces of an ancient wheel were dug up here, where previously the gamekeeper, J. Green, had found a small portion, while ferreting.

Howldale[1] and the Whitby road, two in fields above Dalby, one
on Dalby Warren, three south west of Red Dyke and five on
the west of the Adder Stone.[2] Secondly in the Brythonic[3] dykes
or entrenchments, such as those along the top of the north-west
edge of the dale above Ellerburn Banks and above the old Dalby
nut-wood, or again above Ellerburn Wood near Whitbygate, or
between Howldale and Kingthorpe Lane, or between Seive Dale
and Swair Dale, beyond High Dalby. Thirdly in the flint and
stone weapons which have been frequently unearthed, as an
unbarbed arrow-head found in Nabgate, or an ash-leaved arrow-
head in Sand Flats, or a spear-head, below the station. And lastly
in the old flint workings[4] on the top of Flainsey Warren, or in,
the possible, iron workings in circular pits, such as three on Pexton
Moor, regarded by some as pit-dwellings,[5] by others as entrenchments abandoned as soon as begun,[6] and by others as natural
sink holes.

Besides these traces of very early inhabitants, there is the
pottery, found in the garden of Low Mill Garth, which dates a
little nearer modern times, possibly fifty years before or fifty
years after the birth of Christ.[7] This pottery[8] consists of
some almost whole cookery pots[9] mostly *vesicula*, (a few with
notches in the brim), some isolated pieces of La Tène type with
incised design, several scraps of Terra Sigillata, a clay object,
possibly a spoon or a toy or a votive boat, perhaps a model of a
coracle, and a crutch shaped pottery handle said to be from a

[1] On 11th February, 1911, one of these barrows in Monklands was found
to contain a human skeleton and an earthern vase. The latter was like a round
jar with straight sides curving to the base. It was ten inches high. Although
broken it was skilfully restored by Dr. Kirk of Pickering.

[2] Probably the ashes of important men only were interred in these
'Howes' or *tumuli*, *cf.* F. Elgee, *Moorlands of North-East Yorkshire*, p. 24.

[3] F. Y. in M. P. p. 259.

[4] *Cf.* Ibid. p. 157. 'Where the chippings, *spiculae*, remnants of flint
of divers characters as plainly showed that flint implements and weapons
had been manufactured there, as the matters commonly lying about a blacksmith's shop show the vicinity (past or present) of the forge.'

[5] Ord, *History of Cleveland.* Ord's view is strongly attacked F. Y. in
M. P. pp. 162-166.

[6] Compare the pits above Ebberston, *vide* Arch. Jour. LII. p. 266.
Mediaeval references to iron-works speak of *fossas* which suggest open-cast
workings or a very elementary type of bell-pit. *cf.* Y.G.S. XIII. p. 456, and
G. Barrow, *Geology of North Cleveland*, p. 59.

[7] R. G. Collingwood, Fellow of Pembroke College, Oxford, kindly gave
me this date. These discoveries were made between 1922 and 1923, by L. G.
Rowland, of Goathland, Esq. In January 1930 it was hoped to find remains
of a house in Low Hall Garth on the west side of Maltongate. Dr. J. L. Kirk
had trenches dug without any more result than a few pieces of Roman pottery.

[8] Some pottery of the *vesicula* type was turned up when Low Mill Garth
was being built in 1913.

[9] These are now in the Pickering Museum.

house urn such as those found in Italy. Two Roman bronze brooches have also been discovered, one, with red enamel, of the *Aucissa* pattern, but without the signature, which points to a native copy of an imported type common on the continent about 43 A.D., in use under Claudius and even later.[1] From this evidence it is clear that there must have been Romano-British in, what is now Thornton, in the very early days of the Roman occupation[2] after the ferocious Brigantes had been either massacred or reduced to law and order; and it is not altogether surprising considering how near Thornton lies to the Roman Derventio [?] or Malton and to the Roman camp of Delgovitia [?] or Cawthorne,[3] which is known to have been a military centre in the first century A.D.[4]

After the Roman legions left this island, about 406, the Picts probably burst through The Wall, and, with fire and sword, swept down from the north;[5] though the sparse population of this particular district, being far from any main route leading south and being sheltered on the north by a rampart of moorland, may have escaped desolation. A century later, about 520, the Angles came, and their leader Aella marching northward from the Humber, may have gazed from Settrington Beacon on these parts; but seeing no advantage in floundering through the marshy valley of the Derwent, almost certainly turned west in his conquest, and sought the wealth of Malton and of York, rather than the bleak poverty of the wild moorlands of the north-east. After his establishment of the Kingdom of Deira, Angles would settle in Thornton where the land had already been prepared by the Romano-British and had been partially reclaimed from moor and fen.[6]

One of the first known excitements for the people of this district was in 664, when King Oswy of Northumbria, with Bishops Colman and Wilfred, made their way with their enormous

---

[1] I am indebted to Dr. J. L. Kirk for this information.

[2] Possibly as early as the arrival of Ostorius Scapula, c. 50 A.D. Dr. J. L. Kirk would place the occupation of the site at 70 A.D.

[3] R. G. Collingwood, Esq. considers that Cawthorne only shows signs of first century occupation.

[4] Young, p. 733 suggests, with no evidence, that Thornton was a post on the Roman road between Scarborough and Cawthorne. But as Cawthorne was limited to the first century, and as Scarborough has no proof of existence earlier than the fourth century and as there is no sign of a road between the two, [*cf.* F. Elgee, *Early Man in North-East Yorkshire*], Mr. Collingwood feels unable to agree with this view. To call Malton 'Derventio' is still a doubtful point but Messrs. Corder and J. Kirk in '*Antiquity*' II. 5 p. 51 are in favour of it.

[5] After writing the above I see that the same suggestion is made in Arch. Jour. LXXI. p. 44. *Cf.* 'Antiquity' IV. 15, p. 315.

[6] *Cf.* Seebohm, *English Village Community*, p. 436.

retinues from York to Whitby, to take part in the famous ecclesiastical synod of that town, when it was decided that English Christianity should be according to the teaching of Rome and not according to that of the Northumbrian Church. It may be imagined that the villagers flocked to the junction of the Pickering and Thornton roads,[1] near the present Crossdale Head, and watched the procession of King, princes, prelates, priests, thegns and slaves cantering by, all on horseback for vehicular transport was then practically unknown. The sturdy priest of Thornton, if there were one,[2] may even have joined the band and tramped the rough track through the heather, down Saltersgate Brow, splashing through Ellerbeck, stumbling down the steep hill to the Esk, and keeping no doubt on the east bank, for the river would be difficult to cross, and coming at last into the little land-locked harbour town of Streanaeshalch, as Whitby was then called, and so up the precipitous hill-side to the abbey, where the royal lady, St. Hilda, held sway, and where not only the gulls, are said, to have swooped down to do her obeisance, but even the snakes were turned to stone when she prayed.[3]

But dark days were to come; for the sparse population[4] of Thornton and its neighbourhood was destined to bear the burden and terror of the Danish inroads. News would gradually filter through, first of coast raids, then talk of the rough Norsemen actually settling along the shore; and one can imagine the horror and consternation of the Thornton folk when they heard of the destruction of the abbeys at Lastingham and at Whitby *c.* 867. The news of the latter would, no doubt, be brought by flying monks, who had, perhaps in happier days come on pilgrimage, called at the little Anglo-Saxon Church at Ellerburn, and then passed across the moor to St. Hilda's second ecclesiastical foundation at Hackness.[5] Nor would the villagers in 1066, feel very safe or happy, when refugees came pouring in from the ravaged and

---

[1] It is possible that there was no road on the east side of the valley. They may have been obliged to take the Roman Road known, to-day, as 'Wade's Causeway'. '*Antiquity*' II. 5 p. 77, shows that in Roman times there was no road from Malton to Pickering as the district 'must have been too marshy to be traversable.' *Cf.* map in F. Elgee's *Early Man in North-East Yorkshire.*

[2] There may have been a priest, but it is not very likely as East Yorkshire was mainly converted at a slightly later date, when Wilfred, was at York.

[3] *Cf.* Sir Walter Scott, *Marmion* II. xiii; Drayton, Polyolbion. Pt. II. p. 146; Camden, *Britannia*, and *Charlton, History of Whitby.*

[4] The country was probably not very fully settled before the Danish irruptions. *Cf.* F. Y. in M. P. p. 423.

[5] There were nuns at Hackness in 680 when St. Hilda died; but the inhabitants of Whitby Abbey were probably monks.

utterly destroyed town of Scarborough, hoping to find, inland, some salvation from the bloodthirsty Harold Hardrada.[1]

All this, however, is speculative. Even the origin of the name of Thornton is a matter of doubt. It has been suggested by some writers that it is derived from the name of the old heathen god, Thor, others have said that it means Tower-town,[2] others again assert that it was a settlement surrounded by thorn-bushes.[3] The word in its earliest form is 'Torenton'[4] and it might mean the settlement-near-the-stream of a man called Tor, probably of Norwegian extraction. It may, indeed, be a case of the village having had one name in very early times, and having adopted another in the later Anglo-Saxon period.[5] It is, at least, significant that the holder of the main manor immediately before the Norman Conquest was named Tor.

There are no historical documents that tell anything of Thornton until the great Norman record of Domesday Book, in 1086. Then, at last there begin to be some solid facts to work on. Thornton as a complete unit was within the royal soke or jurisdiction of Pickering, but the village of Thornton was divided into three separate manors, while, in addition, now within the civil parish, there were the manors of Ellerburn-cum-Farmanby, Roxby, Dalby, Chigocemers or Theockemarais, that is the modern Thornton Marishes. All these manors suffered the great devastation of William the Conqueror, in 1069, and the Chronicler[6] asserts that

---

[1] Freeman, *The Norman Conquest*, III. p. 347. This might be compared with the influx of refugees on 16th December, 1914, when Scarborough was bombarded by the Germans.

[2] Eastmead, p. 316.

[3] A. H. Smith, *Place Names of the North Riding*.

[4] *Domesday Book.*

[5] *Cf.* the case of Whitby which in historic times has been Streanaeshalch, Prestebi and Whitby. But in the case of Thornton there is an eponymous lord. *Cf.* Stenton, *Types of Manorial Structure in the Northern Danelaw*, p. 91. He writes 'We may minimize the significance of the eponymous lord; we may refuse him the ownership of the village lands; we may believe that a village of free settlers co-existed from the beginning beside his dominant homestead; but we cannot explain him away; and it is probable that for a long time yet he will remain to complicate the earliest phase of the local history of the Danelaw.'

[6] 'Ab homine usque ad pecus periit quicumque repertus est ab Eboraco usque ad mare orientale.' Alured. *Beverl.*, p. 129 ed. Hearne; *cf.* Symeon of Durham, *Op. Hist.* Rolls Ser. II. p. 188. V.C.H. *York* III. p. 397, says 'the Norman forces marched through the forests harrying the land, killing all who came in their way, guilty or innocent, destroying the villages, and burning the crops and the implements of husbandry. Yorkshire was left a wilderness, its blackened fields covered with dead bodies which there was none to bury. Famine followed, and for the next few years the scanty survivors....were driven to live on horses, dogs and cats, and even, it was rumoured to resort to cannibalism.' It should be remembered that the total population for the North Riding in 1086 has been estimated as less than the present (1928) population of the civil parish of Thornton. *Cf.* Y.A.J. XIX.

not a human being was left alive between York and the Eastern Sea. This must not be taken as literally true, but practically true, as Domesday Book definitely records that before the devastation, the soke of Pickering, including the manors of this neighbourhood, was worth to King Edward the Confessor, £80 p.a.; but that after the devastation the whole district, sixteen *leugae* long and four *leugae* broad, only produced for the Crown £1. 0s. 4d. p.a.[1]

At this time the few miserable families which escaped butchery or starvation, found strange masters placed over them.[2] Their old lords, Gospatric, Tor and Torbrand were evicted, and in their place, King William received the main manor of Thornton,[3] and passed it to his sister (or niece), the Countess of Albemarle, the other manors[4] being granted to such great barons as Robert de Brus and Berenger de Todeni, and in one instance to the Norseman, Torfin, descendant of Gospatric, and ancestor, through the female line, of the family of Hastings.[5]

The style of life and the surroundings of the people in these numerous manors were poor and mean.[6] Their houses were built of wattle-and-daub[7] on a wooden frame, with no windows and no chimneys: a hole in the roof let out the smoke and let in the light. There was only one room: the bare earth formed the floor, and a hob of clay in the centre of the house was the only hearth.[8] They were entirely subordinated to the lord of the manor in which they dwelt,[9] and would pay so many hens and eggs at certain seasons,[10] and work so many days a week under the superintendence of a reeve.[11]

---

[1] Domesday Book.

[2] William of Malmesbury III. p. 245, says the change from an Anglo-Saxon lord to a Norman was often very much for the better.

[3] *Cf.* Young, p. 77.

[4] *Vide* Chs. XII-XIV.

[5] J. H. Round in V.C.H. *Hants* I. pp. 427-8, suggests that the English holders were mainly dispossessed entirely. This seems to be the case in Thornton, Ellerburn and Dalby but not in part of Chigocemers or the Marishes. *Cf.* on this question of dispossession, W. Farrer, in V.C.H. *Lancs.* I. p. 283.

[6] The inhabitants would be mostly 'villani' or 'nativi'. *Cf.* Vinogradoff *Origin of the Manor*, pp. 74, 340.

[7] These cottages were held 'at the will of the lord'. *Cf.* Pollock and Maitland, *History of English Law* I. p. 352 and Bracton, *De Legibus Angliae* p. 207.

[8] Ballard, *The Domesday Inquest*, p. 260.

[9] For the lord's power over villeins, *cf.* Glanville, *Tractatus de Legibus* (1780) V. c. 5; *cf.* Seebohm, *ut supra*. p. 89, *cf.* Petit-Dutaillis, *Studies Supplementary to Stubbs' Constitutional History*, I. p. 21; *cf.* Traill, *Social England*, (1893) I. p. 372.

[10] Neilson, *Customary Rents*, pp. 21, 68, 98; *cf. Custumals of Battle Abbey*, p. 30.

[11] The reeve would certainly be of the servile class, *cf.* J. H. Round, V.C.H. *Hereford* I. p. 287.

Professor Maitland once wrote 'to describe a typical *manerium* is an impossible feat.' Despite his words, as far as can be judged, Thornton in early times was a typical manor,[1] or rather three typical manors,[2] excluding, for the moment, the other manors of Ellerburn-cum-Farmanby, Roxby, Dalby and the Marishes. Not that this split[3] into three makes the story of the village any more easy to understand, for it produced exactly the complications described by Professor Vinogradoff when he said 'The plain and most usual cause of manorial complications lay in the fact that the manor being originally a unit of property and not of settlement or husbandry could stand in all sorts of relations to the organic unit of the township; it could include one or several, but could also share with another manor or several the basis of a single township. Quite apart from subinfeudation which produced well-known results in the parcelling-up of mediaeval estates, they appear from the very first, in innumerable instances as fractions of townships.'[4] In the case of Thornton there were three such 'fractions' controlling different portions of the village, and probably the owners of all three were absentees.

The manor-houses, and there were four in the parishes of Thornton and Ellerburn-cum-Farmanby, besides being dwellings,[5] would also serve by the reign of Edward I., as places for the holding of the courts,[6] where the 'villagers bond and free had to report

---

[1] Maitland, *Domesday Book and Beyond*, p. 120 says 'A manor is a house against which geld is charged.' Pollock and Maitland *ut supra* I. p. 586, say that it is not necessary that the house be occupied by a lord.

[2] *Vide* Chs. XI-XIII.

[3] A. Hamilton Thompson in *Parish History and Records*, p. 25 says 'The word "manor" even in its more extended sense is not geographical; the lord of the manor is not lord of a definite territory, but of rights customarily attached to a certain house which is or has been the *caput maneri*.'

[4] Vinogradoff, *Society in the Eleventh Century*, pp. 394-5. His statement entirely refutes that of Ordericus Vitalis II. p. 223, 'villas quas manendo manerios vulgo vocamus.' Bland, Brown and Tawney, *English Economic History Select Documents*, p. 53, say 'the typical manor exists only in theory, actual manors being continuously modified by the inevitable changes due to the growth of population and commercial expansion.' Jeudwine, *Tort, Crime and Police in Mediaeval Britain*, p. 199, says 'all that can be safely said about the manor is that it was very probably a former tribal division generally identified with the township or vill, and that it was the unit for fiscal and agricultural purposes.' *Year Books* 14-15 Ed. III. p. 320, says 'a manor may extend into divers vills and into divers counties.'

[5] The main one would be on the site of the present Hall; another was by tradition and from the appearance of the ground in the field bounded by Whitbygate on the west and the Ellerburn road on the north, the third was probably in Maltongate; and the fourth, known as the Low Hall was in the field bounded on the north by Westgate and on the east by Maltongate.

[6] Maitland, *ut supra*, p. 94 says concerning the period of Domesday Book 'The term *curia* is in use but it seems always to signify a physical object, the lord's house or the court yard around it, never an institution or tribunal.' In the reign of Edward II., the word 'court' is used in this sense in the poaching case of John son of Alan of Thornton *vide infra*.

themselves and tell tales one of another.'[1] If the lord of each manor was not present, his steward[2] sat in the court in his place. The house of the priest would be the next most important and this, in the case of Thornton would be on the site of the present rectory, while at Ellerburn from the most ancient times, it was the cottage nearest to the Church gate. It should be remembered that 'through his endowment with a common holding the priest was a regular member of the village community, and it is only natural that he was made to appear as one of its representatives on all occasions when it was called up for police, judicial or administrative duties.'[3] The tenants and villeins would have their houses along the way leading from the Church to Scarborough and Malton, and behind each would be a little garden, and in later times in many cases what was called a hemp-yard.[4]

Far more important, however, was the land of the manor and the method of its tillage. The system of agriculture from Anglo-Saxon times to the middle of the eighteenth century changed very little, though 'any theory that would paint all England as plotted out for proprietary and agricultural purposes in accordance with a single pattern would be of all theories the least probable.'[5] The *demesne* land of the lord of each manor would be the ground immediately surrounding the manor house,[6] and tilled under the

[1] Pollock and Maitland, *ut supra* I. p. 568.

[2] Ibid. p. 580. *Cf.* Vinogradoff. *Origin of the Manor*, p. 364. *Cf. Fleta* (Selden, 1647).

[3] Vinogradoff, *Society in the Eleventh Century*, p. 374.

[4] The 'hemp-yard at the end of the eighteenth century was a most important appendage to the better sort of cottages.' W. H. R. Curtler, *The History of Agriculture*, pp. 250-1, says 'whenever a cottager had 10 or 15 perches of land...., with the aid of his wife's industry it enabled him to pay his rent. A peck of hempseed, costing 2s. sowed about 10 perches of land, and this produced from 24 to 36 lbs. of tow when dressed and fit for spinning. A dozen pounds of tow made 10 ells of cloth, worth generally about 3s., an ell....The hemp was pulled a little before harvest, and immediately laid on grass land, where it lay for a month or six weeks. The more rain there was the sooner it was ready to take off the grass. When the rind peeled easily from the woody part, it was on a dry day, taken into the house, and when harvest was over well dried in fine weather and dressed, being then dressed for the tow dresser, who prepared it for spinning....Since 1815 little hemp or flax has been grown in England.' Hemp was so much in demand in the eighteenth century that Dr. Johnson wrote :—

    'Scarce can our fields, such crowds at Tyburn die,
    With hemp the gallows and the fleet supply.'

[5] Maitland, *ut supra*, p. 366.

[6] A glance at the 6 in. Ordnance Survey will give a very good idea of the old demesne of the main manor. It would be bounded on the north and west by the beck, on the south by Botton's Lane and on the east by Peaslands Lane. Owing to the building of the railway it is more difficult to imagine the demesne of the Low Hall, but presumably it must have extended over Dor Croft. Another manor demesne may have reached from Whitbygate on the west to the beck on the east and bounded on the south by Brock Lane. If Maltongate was the site of the other manor it is not easy to visualize the exact size or boundaries of the demesne.

superintendence of the lord or his bailiff. Outside the *demesne* were the *arable* lands held by the tenants in the common three fields. These were known in Thornton east of the beck, as (i) Botton field,[1] near the present Botton's Lane, including Peaslands, and probably bounded by Hurrell Lane: it was sometimes known as Harrowcliff Field; (ii) the East Field, a little east of Utgang Lane with Nabgate on the north, and New Ings Lane on the south: it was sometimes called Farfield; and (iii) Townsfield, sometimes called Middlefield, from Buffit Wood on the north west across Utgang Way till it bounded with East Field. These three contained by computation 800 ac.[2] In Farmanby there were clearly (i) Highfields on the same spot as the fields so named to-day; (ii) West Fields south of the Pickering Road, bounded on the east by the demesne of Roxby, and then again south of Westgate, and bounded on the west by the parish of Pickering; and (iii) an unnamed field probably the Carrs. These common fields were divided by balks[3] into strips known as broadlands,[4] oxgangs,[5] roodlands,[6] and lands,[7] and are not to be confused with garths,[8] crofts,[9] ings[10] and intacks.[11] The reason why the strips were scattered was that no particular tenant might have any advantage. In these fields the lords of each of the manors and the priest would also have strips. After harvest the cattle were turned out,[12] or, to use the older expression 'turned up', to feed on the stubble which before the introduction of machinery was often knee-deep.[13] Besides this there was common *pasture*; but each tenant was restricted or *stinted* in the number of cattle he might turn out.[14] Meadow-land

---

[1] Botton not Bottom. It is from the Icelandic *botn*. *Cf.* F. Y. in M. P. pp. 397, 425.

[2] The Award of 1780. G.F.G.H.

[3] Maine, *Village Communities*, p. 89. For the origin of the word 'balk' *cf.* Seebohm *ut supra*, p. 382.

[4] More than the average allotted share.

[5] The carucate was divided into eight oxgangs or bovates. *Cf.* Ballard, *ut supra*, p. 40 and Maitland, *Domesday Book and Beyond*, p. 395.

[6] *Cf.* Maitland, *ut supra*, pp. 372, 382.

[7] Lands equal the acre land or strip, the average allotted share.

[8] A close; a little backside; *cf.* Warde Fowler, *Kingham, Old and New*.

[9] Much the same as a garth.

[10] An enclosed pasture or meadow near water.

[11] An enclosure from the waste of the manor of early date, and not by a decree of Chancery or an Act of Parliament.

[12] This right was limited and not necessarily open to all the inhabitants.

[13] This made excellent manure when it rotted, and in living memory afforded splendid cover for partridges, but it was a great waste of straw. At the beginning of the nineteenth century, the reaping was mainly done by women. *Cf.* Young, p. 823.

[14] *Cf.* Vinogradoff, *Origin of the Manor*, p. 181, and Maitland, *ut supra* p. 76.

was either distributed,[1] or belonged to the lord and was let out to tenants at a fixed rate which could only be paid by the more well-to-do. This was also the case with the *crofts* consisting of definitely marked off patches let separately. The lord would have several of these and the better class tenants one or two. Such would be 'West Crofts' sloping up to the old wall of Roxby Castle; or 'Incroft Bank' on the south of Botton's Lane. In some manors there was what was called *waste*. This consisted of land which was not regarded as sufficiently fertile for cultivation, but on which *some* of the inhabitants had the rights of *turbary*, or turf cutting and *estovers*[2] or fuel and litter collecting. This would be done on Thornton Common, which appears to have been both on the Pexton and Nabgate sides of the valley; and on Farmanby common which according to a map of 1729, is now Ellerburn Wood. But as all the manors were within the Forest of Pickering these rights were much restricted.[3]

The land under cultivation was therefore divided according to the ancient three-field system,[4] which was carried on century after century. According to the agricultural methods of very early times each portion in turn would be suffered to lie fallow, and the two remaining portions would be distributed among the cultivators, who were obliged 'not through the personality of the lord....but through chosen or customary representatives of a community,[5] each on his own share to grow a certain kind of crops.' The system,[6] with slight modifications, lasted generation after generation[7] in Thornton, and dating back, as it did, to a period long before the Conquest,[8] it is interesting to find it reproduced in the seventeenth and eighteenth centuries. In fact it might be said that the methods of the people of Thornton were those of their Danish and Norwegian forefathers until ended, partly in the case of Farmanby in 1678,

---

[1] *Cf.* Vinogradoff, *Society in the Eleventh Century*, p. 287.

[2] Williams, *Rights of Commons*, pp. 186-7. *Cf.* W. H. R. Curtler, *The Enclosure and Redistribution of Our Land*, pp. 245 and 257. 'The commons were not common property, but the subject of a privilege which had to be paid for.'

[3] *Vide infra.*

[4] Barnard, *Companion to English History, Middle Ages*, p. 225, says 'There will be a regular routine for all; no experiments will be possible. There is no chance for the men with ideas under the system of open fields.'

[5] Vinogradoff, *Origin of the Manor*, p. 361.

[6] The three-field system is fully explained in Traill, *Social England* (1894) II. p. 95.

[7] For little change in the condition of the rustic from the middle of the thirteenth to the beginning of the nineteenth century, *vide* Thorold Rogers, *Six Centuries of Work and Wages*, p. 84, and W. H. R. Curtler, *ut supra*, p. 45.

[8] *Cf.* Seebohm, *ut supra*, p. 439.

and in the cases of Thornton by the Enclosure Act of 1780, and of Ellerburn-cum-Farmanby, Thornton and Kingthorpe by the Act of 1795.[1]

[1] *Vide* Ch. VI.

CHAPTER TWO.

Mediaeval Poachers.

"And when he [the hunter] is comen home he shall doon him of his clothes, and he shall doon of his shoon and his hosen, and he shall wash his thighes and his leggs, and peradventure all his body."

'THE MAISTER OF THE GAME.' c. 1399.

THE very fact that Thornton was situated within the Forest of Pickering[1], helped to lead men astray from the rigid paths of virtue and many of the inhabitants, lords, priests and labourers alike, were tempted to do a certain amount of poaching of game and stealing of timber. At first the records are very brief indeed as to these trespasses on the royal forest. As early as the autumn of 1190, Geoffrey de 'Tornton', son of Alan the Forester of King-thorpe, was fined half a mark because he had acted as bail for a trespasser who did not appear.[2] In 1230 Walter Blaber of 'Thorneton' owed 12d. for the same offence, and Robert, the miller of 'Thorneton', owed a similar sum for vert[3], and these two

[1] G. J. Turner, *Select Pleas of the Forest*, Selden Soc. XIII. pp. ix, x, says 'In mediaeval England, a forest was a definite tract of land, within which a particular body of law was enforced, having for its object the preservation of certain animals, *ferae naturae*. Most of the forests were the property of the Crown, but from time to time the Kings alienated some of them to their subjects. Thus the forest of Pickering in Yorkshire and all those in the county of Lancaster were in the fourteenth century held by the Earls of Lancaster, who enforced the forest laws over them, just as the King did in his own forests. But though the King or a subject might be seized of a forest, he was not necessarily seized of all the land which it comprised. Other persons might possess lands within the bounds of a forest, but were not allowed the right of hunting or cutting trees at their will.' Manwood, *Treatise of the Lawes of the Forrest* (1598), f. 1 says 'A forrest doth chiefly consist of these foure things, that is to say, of vert, venison, particuler lawes and priviledges, and of certen meet officers appointed for that purpose to thend that the same may the better be preserved and kept for a place of recreation and pastime meet for the royall dignitie of a prince.' Coke, *Fourth part of the Institutes of the Laws of England* (1644), p. 289 says 'A Forest doth consist of eight things, *videlicet* of soil, covert, laws, courts, judges, officers, game and certain bounds.'

[2] *Pipe Roll.* New S. I. p. 65. 'Galfridus de Tornton' debet dim. m. quia non habuit quem plegiauit.'

[3] Ibid. 4 p. 285. '*Walterus Blaber de Thornet*' debet xij.d. quia non habuit [quem plegiauit]....*Robertus molendinarius de Thorneton* debet xij.d. pro viridi.'

seem incorrigible, for their names again appear in 1241.[1] In the same year, Alan, brother of Alan son of Geoffrey of 'Tornton', was fined 2s. for vert,[2] though Alan, son of Reginald of 'Farmanneby', was only fined 1s.[3] Roger Brun,[4] a member of a well-known family in Thornton, was caught pasturing his cattle in the forest without licence from the agistator,[5] and for this offence he was fined 2s. Then darkness comes upon the records for half a century.

On 18 June, 1292, Alan, the son of John de Thornton, grandson of a former rector, and great-nephew of the already mentioned Geoffrey, evidently had for a moment one glorious hour of life in chasing a hart and slaying it in Troutsdale, which then, without any enclosures, would be even lovelier than to-day. Much, however, as he and his companions, William Archer, Ralph son of Peter Martin and Robert Westerdale,[6] had enjoyed their break-neck race down into the valley, Nemesis followed; and as they remained contumacious,[7] they were declared outlaws, a terrible penalty for any unfortunate enough to receive this judicial sentence.[8]

One night, less than a year after Alan's escapade, there was a most picturesque scene, in what is now called Howldale,[9] but which in those far off days, was known as Langathoudale Wood. The night in question was that of 5 April, 1293. It was a lovely moonlight night,[10] so clear and bright that the forest keepers could

---

[1] *Great Roll of the Pipe*, pp. 27, 30.
[2] Ibid. p. 33.
[3] Ibid. p. 32.
[4] Ibid. *'quia pavit pecora.'*
[5] Petit-Dutaillis, *ut supra*, p. 159 says 'Each forest had as a rule four *agistatores* charged with the oversight of the *agistment* of the cattle and swine in the woods and fields, and with the collection of the rents exacted for pasturage.' *Cf.* G. J. Turner, *ut supra*, pp. xxiv.-xxvi.
[6] N. R. Rec. S. N.S. II. p. 90.
[7] Petit-Dutaillis, *ut supra* p. 163 says 'In the thirteenth century convicted delinquents were fined, and if they did not pay, were sent back to prison till they found the money. If anyone cited failed to appear, he was summoned in the county court, and if he remained contumacious, was outlawed.'
[8] To be declared an outlaw, a crime or a misdemeanour must have been committed. A demand for justice of a purely civil character by the plaintiff was not enough. *Cf.* Bracton, Rolls S. II. p. 330, *'Item videtur nulla esse utlagaria si factum, pro quo interrogatus est, civile sit et non criminale.'* *Fleta*, 1. ch. XXVII. says that a woman outlaw was a 'weyve whom no one will own....an outlaw and a weyve bear wolves' heads which may be cut off by anyone with impunity, for deservedly ought they to perish without law who refuse to live according to law.'
[9] The Parish boundary runs down the centre. The west side still belongs to the Duchy of Lancaster: the east is in the possession of G. F. G. Hill, Esq.
[10] *'infra vesperam luna lucente tenuit duos leporarios unum album et unum nigrum, infra coopertum de Langhoudale juxta Lydeyate.'*

see well, and, as one of them, Alan Godrickneve by name, crept quietly forward, possibly down the narrow 'Shakersty',[1] he saw a man holding two greyhounds, the one white, the other black, and he realized that the man was William de 'Everle',[2] a gentleman of good position, a forester of the Forest of Whitby, an important person in Ugglebarnby, a small landowner in Thornton and a relative of a future rector of Thornton. Besides the gentleman there was another man, clad all in russet, and the latter, suddenly seeing the keeper, slipped into the wood. Afterwards, it was discovered that the man in russet, was John de Rouceby, a man of some position in Kingthorpe.[3] Of course they had to appear before the Court of Attachment.[4] Then years went by, and they must have felt that all was well; they had probably forgotten their evil deeds. The law, however, worked slowly but surely, and at last in 1334, when the great Eyre of the Forest was held, and as they were contumacious, they were outlawed for a crime committed forty-one years before.[5] It is true that their crime had always been regarded as particularly serious. The Assize of Woodstock, of Henry II., stated that 'no one shall hunt to take beasts *by night* within the forest or without, in any place which the King's beasts frequent, or where they have their peace, on pain of imprisonment for a year and of making fine at the King's pleasure.' Richard I. had gone so far as to threaten the loss of eyes and castration. These terrible mutilations had ceased to be put into operation long before the days of William de Everley. The imprisonment, however, still continued, and it is conceivable that William and his companion, knowing something of the horrors of prison life, and that the discipline, being what it was, caused the death of most of those incarcerated,[6] preferred to fly and bear the burden of outlawry. In any case, both of them had run considerable risk when discovered by the keeper, for the very year of their

[1] Shakersty or Shakerstile is a very anciently named path still known by that title. It carries us back in thought to the Norse settlers of this district.

[2] N. R. Rec. S. N.S. IV. p. 42. He must have been a relation of the William de 'Everlee' who on 20th May, 1260, together with Adam de Rouceby and John le Campion [? of Farmanby] gave evidence as to the unrepaired state of Scarborough Castle, *cf.* Y.A.S. Rec. S. XII. p. 72.

[3] *Cf.* Lay Subsidies of 1327 and 1333., N. R. Rec. S. N.S. IV. pp. 143, 156.

[4] Petit-Dutaillis, *ut supra* pp. 160, 161, says 'There were really only two kinds of tribunals—the court of attachment, *attachiamentum*, held as a rule in each forest every six weeks, and the court of the itinerant justices of the forest, *justiciarii itinerantes ad placita foreste*, who held an Eyre in each forest every few years. The functions of the court of attachment were rather administrative than judicial....important cases concerning the vert and all concerning the venison went before the justices in Eyre.'

[5] N. R. Rec. S. N.S. II. p. 110.

[6] *Cf.* Jusserand, *English Wayfaring Life in the Middle Ages*, p. 266.

adventure (1293) Parliament had ordained that no proceedings should be taken against foresters, parkers and warreners if they killed poachers who would not suffer themselves to be arrested.[1]

A less sporting incident was that of John Burmer, who, on Monday 22 February, 1305,[2] 'hurled such large stones at a stag that he killed it, and afterwards he and his lad, Ralph Rook, carried it away to the barn in his cart. He was arrested and let out on bail,[3] and there the record ends for the moment. Afterwards John Burmer appeared and was fined 30s. But a far worse fate befell John, son of John, son of Austin of Pickering, and Alan, son of John the neatherd [or cowtenter, as he would now be called] of Farmanby. They slipped into the forest one fine Monday, 13 June, 1306, and took a fawn in Haincliff beck. But they were not clever enough, and were caught by the keepers in the act and carried to Pickering Castle with their game. They were let out on bail to await the Great Eyre of 1334. Then they and their bail failed to appear, and the usual verdict of outlawry was declared.[4]

An extraordinary thing about these forest delinquencies is that the offenders did not seem to learn wisdom. John, son of Alan of Thornton, forgetting the danger that still threatened his father, got himself implicated on 23 October, 1311.[5] It was a Saturday night, and William, son of Henry, and Adam, son of Ralph Raffat, set a snare in John's court-yard,[6] and caught a 'soar.'[7] John must have known of their tricks; at any rate, he was a participant, because he had both the flesh and the skin. The latter he sold in York, and with the proceeds bought some fur for his overcoat.[8] Vain man! he was caught, and like his father was outlawed in 1334.[9]

In the first twenty years of the thirteenth century, two most persistent poachers were Hugh and William Yeland, or Eland. The latter was, for a short time, lord of the manor of Ellerburn;[10] but neither his responsible position there, nor the fact that his

---

[1] '*Statutum de malefactoribus in parcis.*'
[2] N. R. Rec. S. N.S. II. p. 110.
[3] His bail were William de Bergh, parson of Thornton, Edmund, Hugh and Herbert Hastings of Farmanby, John de Rouceby of Kingthorpe and others.
[4] N. R. Rec. S. N.S. II. pp. 84-5. III. p. 69.
[5] Ibid. II. p. 107.
[6] '*posuerunt laqueum in Curia.*'
[7] A soar was a buck of the fallow deer of the fourth year, *vide* N. R. Rec. S. N.S. I. p. 140.
[8] '*ad supertunicam suam.*'
[9] N. R. Rec. S. N.S. II. p. 107.
[10] *Vide* Ch. XIV. *Cf.* V.C.H. N.R. II. p. 469.

brother was a guardian of the Forest in the east ward of Pickering,[1] prevented them from trespassing in vert and venison alike. On Thursday, 23 June, 1309, William Yeland took a 'soar' in Staindale Greens and carried it to the house of his old poaching friend Sir Nicholas Hastings, at Allerston. But he was marked down for that offence, and he was also known to have received three harts from John de Dalton, the disloyal Seneschal at Pickering.[2] Nor did he improve his chances of obtaining mercy, when it was found, that he was a rebel against Edward II., and had championed the cause of the traitorous Thomas of Lancaster, at Boroughbridge, in March, 1322. His goods were seized and sold to Robert de Bordesdene, of Thornton, and John de Hutton.[3] Hugh Yeland had been a companion with William in the abortive rising, but he appears to have bought his liberty by compounding for £50.[4] It is almost certain that William was dead when the Great Eyre was held in 1334, but, nevertheless, he was charged with many offences, such as illegal enclosures in the forest,[5] stealing a green oak in Kingthorpe,[6] and slaying one hind, three prickets[7] and one soar with bows and arrows in Langdale.[8] His daughter Catherine,[9] had to appear for him, and she was pardoned.[10]

William Latimer, lord of the main manor in Thornton, was no less guilty than the poaching Yelands, for he was to be found in all parts of the Forest stealing timber, destroying underwood and taking venison, when ever opportunity arose. On Wednesday, 25 September, 1329, he, with others unknown, at St. Hilda's Cragg, within the forest took a hart with his hounds and carried it off to his own use.[11] Again, on Tuesday, 27 June, 1333, he took a sorrel[12] and two hinds[13] and brought them, either to Thornton, or to his other manor at Sinnington.[14] Although in 1334, he was,

---

[1] N. R. Rec. S. N.S. II. p. 52.
[2] Ibid. pp. 121-2.
[3] Ibid. IV. p. 203.
[4] Ibid. II. p. 261.
[5] Ibid. p. 153.
[6] Ibid. III. p. 41.
[7] A pricket is a buck of the fallow deer of the second year; *vide* N. R. Rec. S. N.S. I. p. 139.
[8] N. R. Rec. S. N.S. II. p. 118.
[9] Ibid. IV. p. 27.
[10] '*condonatur per Justiciariis.*'
[11] N. R. Rec. S. N.S. II. p. 63.
[12] A sorrel is a buck of the fallow deer of the third year, *vide* N. R. Rec. S. N.S. I. p. 139.
[13] Hinds are the females of the red deer.
[14] N. R. Rec. S. N.S. II. p. 63.

himself, a verderer,[1] he seems to have committed numerous thefts of wood. It was found, on the testimony of the Regarders,[2] that Brymbleclif wood was wasted of old and had lately been despoiled by the township of Sinnington and by its lord, William Latimer.[3] And when he acted as bail for Peter Walnut, who had taken some small oak branches without the demesne without licence, he with the other bail, including Alexander de Bergh[4] never appeared.[5] Nor did he produce the rolls of his predecessor, as verderer, Robert del Cliffe of Thornton[6], and for this he was heavily fined.[7] But worst of all, was what happened in the parish of Thornton. Hindslackside[8] wood was declared to have been wasted of old and, just before October, 1334, to have been despoiled again, to the amount of 3s. 4d., by the Township of Thornton on the east side of the beck, to which township it was appurtenant. The Justices decided that the township was to be amerced and the wood forfeited; but later Thomas Brett replevied the wood for 6s. 8d. his sureties being Geoffrey de Kingthorpe and John Campion of Farmanby. In addition to this the woods of Ekkedale[9], Flaxdale[10] and Willerdale[11] on the north, had also been wasted by the late William Latimer,[12] by the present William Latimer[13] by the late William de Bergh, rector of Thornton,[14] by Richard Russel of Thornton, and by the townships of Thornton and Wilton. The woods were declared to be in socage tenure in the fees[15] of John

---

[1] The verderers were as a rule of the rank of Knights or at least landowners holding property within the bounds of the forest. There were generally four for each forest and were elected in the County Court, usually holding office for life. *Cf.* G. J. Turner *ut supra* p. xix.

[2] Petit-Dutaillis *ut supra* p. 161, says 'as early as the twelfth century.... there took place every three years the *visitatio nemorum* or "regard". The regarders were twelve knights appointed by the Sheriff at the instance of the King. This commission of enquiry had to visit the Forest and investigate any offences that had been committed, basing their procedure on a list of questions which were called "chapters of the regard".

[3] N. R. Rec. S. N.S. II. pp. 174-5. IV. p. 40.

[4] Heir and executor of William de Bergh, rector of Thornton.

[5] N. R. Rec. S. N.S. III. p. 26.

[6] Ibid. IV. p. 29.

[7] Ibid. p. 39.

[8] I have not been able to identify this wood.

[9] Marked on Ordnance Map as Heck Dale. A. H. Smith, *ut supra*, p. 89 says it means the dale by the hatch at a ford, from *haecc*.

[10] Still the same name.

[11] Unknown to-day, probably Sieve Dale.

[12] William Latimer died June, 1335.

[13] William Latimer who succeeded 1335. This must mean by those acting for him, because he was only a small child in that year.

[14] It is almost certain that he had died in 1323.

[15] This was certainly not true in 1334. 'Eston's' manor had passed to Latimer. This branch of the Brus's was extinct in the male line in 1272; and John Mowbray had been hanged at York in 1322.

'Eston,' Peter Brus and John Mowbray.[1] In 1334, for Hindslackside - wood, Thornton had to pay 3s. 4d. damages and a fine of 6s. 8d.;[2] but for the other woods William Latimer, Richard Russel[3] and the townships had to pay 10s. damages, and fines, consisting of 2s. from Latimer, 2s. from Wilton, 1s. 6d. from Thornton and 1s. from Richard Russel, which in the last case, considering he had at one time been an official of the very forest he had helped to despoil, seems mild enough.

The bad example of so important a person as William Latimer was readily copied by his neighbours the Hastings of Farmanby and their tenants. On 22 June, 1309, Sir Nicholas Hastings took part in the trespass of William Yeland,[4] already described, and was as far as can be ascertained outlawed in 1334.[5] A Hastings again broke the law, on 6 October, 1311, when Hugh Hastings with Reginald Pippinhead, shepherd of Sir Nicholas, brother of Hugh, came poaching in Stockland and Hipperley. In answer to the charge at the Great Eyre, Hugh produced a letter, dated 17 August, 1317, from Thomas, Earl of Lancaster, containing the words 'whereas Hugh Hastings is indicted of offences of venison....in the company of Sir Nicholas his brother....we willing to show to him especial favour....have absolutely released him and pardoned his offence.'[6] On Midsummer Eve, 1316, another brother, Edmund Hastings, hunted a hart in Howldale, and carried it to his castle of Roxby, and, though not very far, he was caught in the act. Once again, in 1334, Edmund produced a pardon by letter patent from Thomas, the late Earl, saying 'we have pardoned all offences committed by Edmund Hastings up to the date of these presents ....26 October, 1316.'[7]

But, like master like man, and on Saturday, 4 December, 1322, William Ashby, and William, son of Robert Todd of Kingthorpe, went up into the moors. They doubtless took the loneliest route. To have gone by the way of the valley and Dalby would have been better walking, but, also, more dangerous as they might so easily have fallen in with the Forester of Dalby. They, probably, went

---

[1] N. R. Rec. S. N.S. II. pp. 179-80. It should be remembered that FitzNeal in the time of Henry II., had laid it down in the *Dialogus de Scaccario* I. XI. that 'Those who dwell within the Forest do not take of their own wood, even for the necessities of their house, except under the view of those who are appointed to keep the Forest.'

[2] N. R. Rec. S. N.S. IV. p. 41.

[3] Ibid. p. 68.

[4] *Vide supra.*

[5] N. R. Rec. S. N.S. II. p. 86. He had been dead for many years.

[6] Ibid. pp. 103-4.

[7] Ibid. pp. 73-4.

round the old pound at 'Town End', then by Utgang Lane and along Nabgate. Even now it would be strange to meet anyone: then it would have been practically impossible. The surface of the track is very rough to-day: at that time the path would have been almost non-existent. They would pass over the old earth-work of Red Dyke and rest, perhaps, by the Adder Stone, and then drop down into Crosscliffe; and there, somewhere near Newgate Foot,[1] they slew a hind. The return had now to be made, and it is difficult to imagine what their labours must have been up 'rigg' and down 'slack,' staggering under their burden in the pitch dark-ness of a winter's night, until they managed to deposit the carcase in the house of Richard Campion of Farmanby, whose son and his wife, Alan and Juliana, received it, with his knowledge and consent, for the use of the lay brother of Rievaulx Abbey, Austin Stalwardman,[2] the granger of 'Kekmarsh' or the Marishes.[3] Their secrecy and care had been of no avail, they had been tracked down; and they had to find '*manucaptores*,' such as Robert Trutcok, Alan the Fisherman, Ralph Banaster, William Itory,[4] William the Shepherd and William the Weaver of Lockton, until the coming of the Justices in 1334.[5]

William Page of Farmanby,[6] was also indicted for poaching, but as he was 'out' in the rebellion of Earl Thomas, and his possessions confiscated and sold to Hugh de Whitenere, Richard Russel and Robert de Boresdene of 'Thorneton,' Robert 'Campyoun' and William, son of Alice of Farmanby, for £8. 14s. 0d.,[7] he had little or nothing wherewith to pay a fine. It is extremely likely that he was either dead, or had fled the district, but which ever had happened, his bail, John de Rouceby and John de Holm, had, in 1334, to produce a fine of 5s.[8] This same John de Holm had at first failed to appear and was fined 1s.; so, too, Robert de Wygane of Farmanby, who was a forest official, paid the same for absence; but another Farmanby man, Thomas de Backy, for a similar offence, was only fined 6d.[9] Robert de Wygane was, evidently, rather a disreputable character. He was first accused

---

[1] The account says 'the north end of Crosscliffe.'
[2] *Vide* Ch. XVII.
[3] N. R. Rec. S. N.S. II. pp. 95, 217. *Cf.* Close R. 17 Ed. II. m. 39.
[4] William Itory lived in Thornton 1327. *Cf.* N. R. Rec. S. N.S. IV. p. 140.
[5] Ibid. II. p. 143. IV. p. 36.
[6] Ibid. IV. p. 140. He is mentioned in the Lay Subsidy of 1327 but not in that of 1333.
[7] N. R. Rec. S. N.S. IV. p. 29.
[8] Ibid.
[9] Ibid. p. 27.

of taking some oxen into Dalby meadow, without the leave of
the agistator. This was innocent enough: even the clergy played
that kind of game.[1] He appears to have been a fairly well-to-do man,
for he was a tenant both of William de Everley and of the late
John de Foturer. At the same time, he was a verderer, and yet,
in 1334, he was fined 6s. 8d. for offences in the Forest under colour
of his office,[2] and another 2s. for taking fees[3] and making a collection of sheaves, wool and hay, and receiving bribes for putting
others under him in his bailliwick[4] and 'haia.'[5]

The greatest person of all to be indicted in Farmanby was
the Lady Beatrice Hastings, who had taken a 'green oak without
the demesne without livery of the forester or warrant.'[6] The
good lady, however, had been dead some time before she was
charged, and so her son, William, now tenant of her lands in
Farmanby, had to pay 6d. for vert.[7] But this was not the worst
offence of Lady Beatrice. She seems to have had a share in wasting
Langatdale wood (Howldale) on the east side, and in these misdoings
she was in alliance with her neighbour, William Latimer, and
supported by her own people, the inhabitants of Thornton West,
Farmanby and Roxby 'to which it is appurtenant.' The offenders
were ordered, in 1334, to be amerced and the wood forfeited; but
the latter was replevied for 6s. 8d. by Sir Ralph Hastings.[8] Nor
did Langatdale wood escape on the west, for about the same time,
it had been wasted and despoiled in three places to the amount of
3s. 4d., by sales of wood made by William Eure [?Evers], the
bailiff, for the lord's use, and in respect of faggots given to several
men of Pickering, and by the Dean's men,[9] residing in the townships of Thornton-in-the-west, Farmanby and Roxby.[10] In this
case the men of Pickering were fined 2s.: the Dean's men 2s.: and
Thornton and Farmanby 1s. each.[11] William Hastings does not seem
to have cared, one way or the other, and, actually while the Eyre

---

[1] Ibid. p. 47.
[2] Ibid. p. 59.
[3] *'quia cepit mercedem.'*
[4] *'accepit de aliis diversa dona ut poneret alios sub se in balliva de haia.'*
Dr. J. E. Morris in *Berks. Bucks. and Oxon. Arch. Jour.* Autumn 1927, says
hagae equals haughs or closes. *'Haia'* probably means very much the same.
At Pickering to this day there is the Haugh. For an interesting article on
these words, *Vide* Y.A.J. XX. pp. 66 7.
[5] N. R. Rec. S. N.S. IV. p. 69.
[6] Ibid. III. p. 41.
[7] Ibid. II. p. 52.
[8] Ibid. II. p. 182.
[9] The Dean of York, i.e., Robert de Brus or Pickering, 1312-32.
[10] N. R. Rec. S. N.S. II. p. 188; *cf.* IV. p. 67.
[11] Ibid. IV. p. 42.

was still sitting, on 2 December, 1336, was caught hare-coursing, and fined 2s.;[1] while, on 31 March, 1338, both Edmund Hastings senior and junior, together with William, again coursed hares in the precincts of the forest, and were fined, between them, 7s. 6d.[2]

Sir Ralph Hastings,[3] relative of Edmund and Lady Beatrice, now all powerful at Pickering, made a most daring assertion before the Justices in 1334. He claimed in 'a wood in "Farmandby" called 'Langatdale' in all that part to the east of the *Howe*, the right of taking vert, according to the assize of the forest for house-bote and hedgebote, and to take, sell, give away and do what he liked with the dry wood; and also the right of common pasture for his goats in all the woods and moors....of Allerston as of Farmandby....and also the right of hunting the fox and hare within the Acredikes of Allerston and Farmandby; and also of presenting (at the Attachment Court) a woodward for his moors and woods of Farmandby.' The jury gave a verdict in his favour about the goats and the woodward; but as to Langatdale wood 'they say that the only right Sir Ralph or any of his ancestors ever had therein was that all their woodwards from ancient time were accustomed to take from men, women and children, who had no common of estovers[4] and carried dry wood away on their heads, sometimes a penny and sometimes a halfpenny a week, saving all rights of common, and if the men, women or children did not pay they were summoned to Sir Ralph's court and fined there for the offence.' The jury also said 'that Sir Ralph and all his ancestors and the tenants of the manor of Farmandby have from ancient time had heather and bracken and cut turves for their own use only and not for sale or gift.' As to the hunting they said 'that judgement was given in the last Eyre....against the claim of the ancestors of Sir Ralph to hunt fox and hare in the Acredikes of Allerston and Farmandby.'[5]

If such men as Sir Ralph Hastings endeavoured to get complete control over a whole wood within the Forest, it is not surprising to find more humble persons taking a few trees. In 1334, Robert

---

[1] Ibid. p. 58.
[2] Ibid. p. 66.
[3] For Sir Ralph Hastings, *vide*. Ch. XIV. He was succeeded by his son Sir Ralph who received 40 marks a year out of the Honor of Pickering. He bequeathed 40s. each to Ralph and William Yeland and to John and Robert Chymney. *Cf*. Sur. Soc. IV. p. 216. This Sir Ralph sometimes lived at Allerston for on 22 October, 1391, he sent a receipt for his pension, dated at Allerston, Sunday before the Translation of St. John of Beverley. *Cf*. Hist. MSS. Com. Rawdon Hastings. MS. Vol. I. p. 191.
[4] *Vide* Ch. I.
[5] N. R. Rec. S. N.S. III. pp. 113-6.

'Tan' of Ellerburn was accused of taking eight green oaks in Sully Hay[1] and William Stut[2] of taking one. 'Ralph Tann' was fined 8s. 8d. and William Stut 1s.[3] Eldred of Ellerburn,[4] also carried off a green oak valued 7d.; but in this case the fines were heavier than in the case of Stut, for Edmund Hastings, who was responsible, had to pay 7s. fine and 7d. the value of the timber.[5]

Such was the condition of life in the Forest in the fourteenth century. The economic effects of the forest system upon such places as Thornton, Farmanby and Ellerburn were not good, sometimes they were intolerable. A great French historical writer has said 'We can imagine the result of the state of things just described. The forests swarmed with game, and even in time of famine it was unlawful to touch it. It had freedom and protection, and might ravage the crops without fear of arrows. The very owners of the soil were forbidden to make clearings, on pain of fines and yearly compositions. A tenant was not allowed to follow his own wishes in the development of his land, even to the extent of making a hedge or ditch. The ancient customary rights which had formerly ensured to the Saxon peasant many advantages and some prosperity, were now pretexts for the infliction of fines; at a time when the cultivation of forage-crops was seldom practised, the law forbade the use of grass-land and woods for the feeding of cattle; and one might not cut down a tree or a bough on one's own property, except under the surveillance of the all-powerful forester, with his vexatious restrictions and demands. It was within his power to make a family's lot intolerable, and in the event of opposition, to summon its members time after time before the court of attachment and ruin them by countless fines.... From a legal and political standpoint the forests were a dangerous anomaly. They were withdrawn from the operation of the common law and of the custom of the realm, and governed by the rules laid down in special assizes and ordinances. In them, too, there lived troops of royal officials, who alone were allowed to bear arms and who were pledged by oath to serve the interests of the King. The Forest was the stronghold of arbitrary power'.[6]

[1] Ibid. p. 27. Can this be Solley Wray?
[2] In 1301 there was a William Stut in Kingthorpe; *cf.* Y.A. Rec. S. XXI. p. 64. He does not appear in the Lay Subsidies of 1327 and 1333 and he is stated to have been dead in 1334. *Cf.* N. R. Rec. S. N.S. III, p. 27.
[3] Ibid. IV. p. 50.
[4] Eldred or Elered de Ellerburn is said to have had lands which in 1334 were in the hands of Edmund Hastings, junior, *cf.* N. R. Rec. S. N.S. IV. p. 50.
[5] Ibid. III. p. 32.
[6] Petit-Dutaillis, *ut supra* pp. 164-5.

CHAPTER THREE.

The Hermits of Thornton.

RICHARD ROLLE AND WILLIAM OF DALBY.

——————

'A solitari here: hermit life i lede
For ihesu love so dere: all flescli lufe i flede.'
THE DESERT OF RELIGION.——
Cotton, MS. Brit. Mus.

IN very recent years Thornton-le-dale has become well known, at least among Yorkshiremen, for the wonderful natural beauty of the village itself and of its immediate surroundings. But it has earned some notoriety in a far wider world as being the supposed birthplace of Richard Rolle,[1] the famous mystic, poet and hermit. This notoriety is mainly due to certain zealous modern writers, according to whom, particularly to Miss G. E. Hodgson, (*The Sanity of Mysticism*, 1926), Miss H. E. Allen (*Writings ascribed to Richard Rolle*, etc., 1927), and Miss F. M. M. Comper (*The Life of Richard Rolle*, 1928), it was during the late thirteenth century that the parents of Richard Rolle lived in Thornton-[-le-dale]; and according to Miss Allen, in one part of her very painstaking work and to Miss Comper as a main fact of her interesting story, Richard Rolle was not only born in Thornton-[-le-dale], but came back there after a course at Oxford.[2] The question to be considered is whether the evidence for Thornton-[-le-dale] being Rolle's birthplace is historically satisfactory.

The Dictionary of National Biography conjectures that Richard Rolle was born about 1290; Dr. Horstmann, on one occasion, says 'his earlier life belongs to the thirteenth century',[3] and, on another, remarks 'I fix 1300 as the most appropriate date'.[4] Miss Hodgson is in favour of 1300, Miss Allen would place his birth a little before that date, and Miss Comper is also in favour of a

---

[1] Dr. Horstmann, in his '*Yorkshire Writers, Richard Rolle of Hampole,*' 2 vols. pub. 1895-6, accepts Thornton-[-le-dale] as the birthplace of the mystic without much verification.
[2] Miss Allen, p. 442.
[3] Horstmann, II. p.v.
[4] Ibid. II. p.v. n.

'few years earlier.'[1] All agree, however, in placing his death in September, 1349.[2]

There is no evidence of Rolle's birth or birthplace or where he resided before he went to Oxford, except that it is stated, in the *'Office'*,[3] that he 'received the origin of his propagation in the village of Thornton in the diocese of York.' But to which of the score of Yorkshire Thorntons is reference made? It would be quite possible to assume, especially from the narrative of Miss Hodgson, that the place of his birth was Thornton-le-Street, three miles north of Thirsk. But Miss Allen points out that, in an early Bodleian Manuscript about 1400, there are added to the word 'Thornton,' the words *'iuxta Pickering.'*[4] Now these words were interpolated in a handwriting the date of which is accepted by experts as somewhere between 1450 and 1475, or more than one hundred years after Rolle's death. The term *'iuxta Pickering'* is somewhat suspicious in itself. In the numerous references to Thornton-[-le-dale], from the time of Domesday to the Stuart period, when the name is used alone, it is generally 'Torenton,' 'Torinton' and 'Thorneton'; but it is seldom used alone, and in the cases where it is not, it is commonly 'Thorneton in Pickering-lithe.' If the combined 'Thornton iuxta Pickering' means anything, it could mean 'Thornton Riseborough' just as easily, if not better than Thornton-[-le-dale];[5] and it was in Thornton Riseborough that Rolle's later patrons, the Nevilles of Raby obtained a mesne-lordship in 1284-5.[6]

It has been argued from the above and from the fact that in later life Richard Rolle was in touch with the Priory at Yedingham, that as Yedingham is only six miles from Thornton-[-le-dale] he must have been born there. But Yedingham is also only twelve miles from Thornton Riseborough, so that he might just as well have been born there. Though, logically, the first proposal is as fallacious as the second.

[1] Miss Comper, p. 4.
[2] 'anno domini 1349 in festo S. Michaelis.'
[3] Written 35 years after his death and 84 years after his birth by persons who could have had little or no first hand knowledge.
[4] This fact does not appear to have been known to Miss Hodgson, and is certainly not mentioned by Miss Comper. The latter boldly says 'was born at Thornton near Pickering' but does not explain that *'iuxta Pickering'* is a late interpolation.
[5] The distance of Thornton Riseborough from Pickering is about half a mile more than the distance of Thornton-[-le-dale] from Pickering. It is, perhaps, worth noting that after 1323 the Dalton family, supposed friends of Rolle, became possessed of an estate at Kirby Misperton about 3½ miles from Riseborough. *Cf.* Miss Allen, p. 450.
[6] V. C. H. N. R. I. p. 542. This point seems to have evaded all three of these ladies.

Miss Hodgson gives many pages to 'Scenes of Rolle's Birth and Early Life'; but as she completely fails to prove anything historically connected with Rolle as to birth or birthplace, these 'scenes' are entirely irrelevant, and her statements about his school life, and still more concerning a song-school at Thornton-[-le-dale], verge upon the purely imaginary. The more Miss Hodgson writes the more one is persuaded to favour as the place of origin Thornton [-le-Street][1] not far from Topcliffe and to disfavour Thornton-in-Pickeringlithe.

Is it possible to rely for historical information on these statements? Miss Hodgson, for example, describes Thornton-[-le-dale] Church and says that 'it has not been much ruined by restorers.'[2] She forgets that the main Chancel arch was rebuilt at least a hundred years after Rolle died, and that the Church was restored in the late seventeenth century (when the pitch of the roof was considerably lowered), and again in the mid-nineteenth, and that the present appearance of the Church is very different from that shown by pictures previous to 1866. She lays stress on the east window and the windows in the choir, but all the windows in the Church were remade in 1866, when the Chancel was completely rebuilt from the ground (the roof being once again raised), and having little or no resemblance to its predecessor. And yet she definitely asserts that the present Church was the same as 'the Church where Rolle's boyish prayers were said [and] where the foundations of his spiritual life were laid.'[3] No one knows the exact date of the fourteenth century rebuilding of the Church, and experts agree that the Tower, at any rate, was completed towards the end of the century; but Miss Hodgson dogmatically states that 'In his youth Rolle must have watched its restoration.'[4] This assertion, however, necessitates the belief that the period of the restoration was 1300 to 1310, of which there is no proof.

Miss Allen is equally led astray by her imagination. She says 'The stream comes curving down into the village from the high wooded moors which closely overhang the settlement at the back. The appearance of the stream and moors can hardly have changed since Rolle's time, and a short distance up the course of the stream on the moor is a very primitive small church.'[5] But what is the

---

[1] Miss Hodgson, p. 57.
[2] Miss Comper, p. 5 speaks of 'the old Norman Church' at the present time as 'a much restored building,' and she may well, for the only 'Norman' thing about it is the bowl of the font.
[3] Miss Hodgson, p. 34.
[4] Ibid. p. 33.
[5] Miss Allen, p. 442.

All Saints Church, Thornton Dale

truth? The present stream through the village is known to have had a different course in 1729,[1] and altered again since 1830. The high-woods closely overhanging Thornton were planted in 1797, and 'the moors beyond' were in Rolle's time covered in parts with oak,[2] and not, as when Miss Allen wrote, with heather and bracken. Nor can anyone, who knows, describe the 'primitive small church' as 'on the moor,' for it is nothing of the kind, nor is there any reason to think that since the Norman Conquest Ellerburn Church was 'on the moor.' It certainly was not in Rolle's day, when the village had its bleaching mill and was surrounded by cultivated land.

Miss Comper[3] evidently does not agree with Miss Hodgson and Miss Allen in thinking that all the surroundings in Thornton have remained the same. She says the road on the west of the Bridge has been widened for motor traffic, and that 'the modern eyesores would have filled Richard with alarm.' As a matter of history, the road was widened more than sixty years ago,[4] and at a time when the motor question had not arisen. Miss Comper does think that some things were the same in Rolle's time. She seems to infer that the market cross was standing in 1300. There may have been a market cross, for the grant was given in 1281,[5] but the present cross though ancient, is not as old as that. She speaks of the 'Black Hole' as an '*old* prison,' and as if it might have been seen by Rolle, but it cannot be older than 1734, when it was first used. But is it possible to take any of these statements seriously? Miss Comper says 'Pickering lies about four or five miles *east* of Thornton,' when, as a matter of fact, from Thornton Church to Pickering Church is exactly three miles, and Pickering is as due *west* of Thornton as it possibly can be. She is also wrong in stating that Thornton is ten miles from the Derwent, because the parish boundary touches the Derwent at a point three miles from the centre of the village. It is equally difficult to accept Miss Comper's remark that the names of the Thornton vicar (1282-1304) and rector (1267-1323), de Amcotes and de Everley, 'appear to be Norman.'[6] Considering they are both place-names, in existence

---

[1] Tithe Survey of 1729 *vide* Ch. VI.
[2] N. R. Rec. S. N.S. II. pp. 179-80. For the causes of the disappearance of trees *cf.* F. Elgee, *ut supra*, p. 130. For the existence of trees, *cf.* F. Y. in M. P. p. 452.
[3] Miss Comper, p. 5.
[4] By the destruction of a blacksmith's shop which stood by the beck and on what is now part of the road.
[5] Cal. Charter R. II. p. 257.
[6] Miss Comper, p. 6.

before the Conquest, it seems a remark that is not only completely unnecessary but entirely erroneous. It might also be noted that Thomas de Amcotes, the vicar, was instituted on the presentation of the rector Robert de Everley in November, 1271, and that he had left Thornton in 1282, i.e., eighteen years before the supposed date of Richard Rolle's birth. Miss Comper has been misled as to the period of de Amcotes' residence by an error in the Rector's list in the Church porch. She is also incorrect in saying that Robert de Everley was rector until 1323, as he was succeeded by William de Bergh in or before 1305. She has confused Robert with John de Everley who was appointed in 1323. In particular, however, one must draw the line at her statement 'I was told at Thornton-le-dale that the tradition[1] that Richard Rolle was born there is strong among the oldest inhabitants of the village.' To use a vulgarism 'the oldest inhabitants' must have been pulling the leg of Miss Comper. One can say emphatically that there is no *tradition* whatsoever. Until a year or two ago there were not half a dozen persons in Thornton who had ever heard the name of Richard Rolle of Hampole.

Miss Allen, quite rightly, considers that the name Rolle is very rare in Yorkshire. Dr. Horstmann says[2] 'The name, probably Norman, is not found in northern registers of the time.' But what 'registers' in the ordinary sense, were there in 1300 ? If the word 'registers' means 'documents,' in a general sense, or Lay Subsidy Rolls, then Miss Allen refutes him. She points out that about 1300-1 there was a Hugo Rol at Slingsby. She then states that 'there is at least a strong chance that he also "took his origin" from Thornton Dale,'[3] because 'The principal landowners in Slingsby were de Wyviles....and they at the time of Kirkby's Inquest owned land in Thornton Dale. Their claim.... was opposed by the abbot of Rievaulx and an action was brought on the subject in 1278-9.'[4] But Miss Allen fails to point out that, although it is true that William de Wyvile held three carucates of Roger de Mowbray, he, in turn, had subinfeudated the heirs of Roger Morant[5] and that they were the sitting tenants, and that there is no evidence that William de Wyvile or any of his Slingsby tenants were in Thornton-[-le-dale] in their lives. Why then, because

---

[1] It should be remembered that the late J. Horace Round said that "To some 'tradition' is a sufficient warrant....although there is, perhaps, no 'authority' so unworthy of credit." *Cf. Family Origins*, p. 13.

[2] Horstmann, II. p.v. n. 2.

[3] Miss Allen, p. 433.

[4] Y.A.S. Rec. S. XXI. p. 6. *Cf.* Sur. Soc. LXXXIII. p. 402.

[5] Cal. Feudal Aids. VI. p. 82.

a man called Hugo Rol appears in Slingsby, fifteen miles away, in 1300, he should necessarily be a late resident in Thornton is beyond imagination. And if Richard was born in Thornton in 1300, it would be reasonable to suppose that his parents would be present at the event. But in any case why refer to Hugo Rol? No one supposes that he is the same as the father, William Rolle. Nor is he likely to have been the grandfather, as Miss Allen, herself,[1] gives reasons for thinking that he had no children in 1316.

If there were a family called Rolle in Thornton-[-le-dale] at the beginning of the fourteenth century, it is somewhat remarkable that in none of the Lay Subsidies does the name occur. There is nothing like it in Thornton or in Farmanby either in 1301, or in 1327 or in 1333.[2] Miss Allen points out that in the Subsidy Roll for 1327 there is a gap where there has been a name beginning with 'W,' and she suggests that this may have been William Rolle. But she does not show that some way from the 'W' is a 'b,' and that, in the Roll of 1301, there is 'Willelmo de Hokelbardi,' otherwise William de Everley, a small landowner in Thornton and who was alive as late as the subsidy of 1327. She has a faint hope the 'William son of Robert,' in the 1333 list, might be William Rolle, but after examining the Lay Subsidy of 1327, it is almost certain that this William is the son of Robert the village blacksmith. The absence of the name is also noticeable in a list of about one hundred and forty inhabitants collected by the present writer for the years 1154 to 1301.

Miss Allen thinks that she has found an ancestor of Richard Rolle in a Charter of Rievaulx Abbey, a document which Professor Hamilton Thompson told her was about 1160.[3] One of the witnesses to the grant of the Marish land was 'Ricardus Rollevilain,' which Miss Allen at once reads as 'Richard Rolle villein' and assumes that this man *must* be an ancestor. For this there is no proof whatever, and there are several objections. In the first place the reading is very difficult. Mr. Turton reads 'Ricardus filius Rollemylans,' and the reading of the editor of Dugdale's *Monasticon* is 'Rollevylani.' Miss Allen attempts, but does not satisfactorily explain another name, in the same document, of a similar character, *viz.*, 'Stephanus Maungevylayn' as read by Mr. Turton, or 'Mangevilam' as read by the editor of Dugdale, or 'Maungevileyne' as

---

[1] Miss Allen, p. 433.
[2] *Cf.* Y.A.S. Rec. S. XXI. and N. R. Rec. S. N.S. IV. pp. 140, 156.
[3] No one would doubt a date suggested by Professor Hamilton Thompson. *Cf.* Dugdale, *Monasticon* V. p. 282.

the word appears in 1284-5, when the man so-called was not a
'villein' at all, but holding one of the manors of Thornton-[-le-dale]
from William Percy of Kildale, who had held from Peter Brus
of Skelton.[1] Miss Allen persists in her view of having found the
ancestor of Richard Rolle, although Professor Hamilton Thompson
has pointed out to her that a 'villein' would not be called upon
to witness a charter; this does not deter her, and she says that as
the charter was a kind of 'perambulation' a villein's evidence
would be most valuable.[2] But what did the gentry on the inquest
think of having among their number a villein ? In any case the
charter did not say 'Richard Rolle, villein of Thornton' or of
anywhere else, and even if it had done, there would be no evidence
of relationship, as one hundred and forty years intervened between
the two. A little later, Miss Allen makes the startling statement
that 'the abbot of Rievaulx was the principal landlord in Thornton
Dale,'[3] whereas he was nothing of the kind. She also says that
because the name 'Ricardus Rollevilain' occurs in the charter it
'would indicate that the person was in the service of the monks,
or lived on their estates.' Considering that the charter was only
just transferring the property to the abbey which had held nothing
in Thornton Marishes before, it is an astounding assumption that
a person mentioned in the charter of conveyance, must be 'in the
service of the monks,' who had not, as yet, any ownership in the
land. So that the discovery of 'Ricardus Rollevilain' does not
seem to have thrown any real light on the ancestry or birthplace
of Richard Rolle.

Although Miss Allen clings to the idea that Richard Rolle
was born in Thornton-[-le-dale], she suddenly gives evidence of a
William Rolle living at Aiskew, near Bedale, and another William
Rolle at Yafforth, near Northallerton. Now these two appear in
the Lay Subsidies of 1327 and 1333, and Miss Allen says that it is
very possible that one or the other was the father of Richard
Rolle.[4] But two pages before she had explained that the probable
reason why William Rolle did not appear in the Lay Subsidy of
1333 for Thornton-[-le-dale], was because he was dead. Her own
words are that 'Rolle's parents seem to have been dead by the
time he wrote the *Job* (that is when he was probably about thirty,
which if he were born about 1300 would fall between the dates of

---

[1] Cal. Feudal Aids. VI. p. 82.
[2] Miss Allen, p. 434.
[3] Ibid. p. 479.
[4] Ibid. p. 435.

the two subsidies).'[1]   But if William Rolle was not in Thornton
in 1333 because he was dead, then the William Rolle of Aiskew and
the William Rolle of Yafforth, being alive in 1333, hardly come
into the story. Perhaps, however, Miss Allen has found Richard's
father, if we throw up all idea of Richard being born at Thornton-
[-le-dale], and if we reject the death of his parents in 1330. The
William Rolle of Aiskew near Bedale, would live 7 miles from
Thornton-le-Beans,[2] 7 miles from Thornton-le-Moor,[3] 9 miles
from Thornton-le-Street,[4] 5 miles from Thornton Watlass,[5] 8
miles from Thornton Steward,[6] and only 12 miles from Topcliffe.
While the William Rolle of Yafforth would be, from the same
places, 4 miles, 6 miles, 8 miles, 9 miles, 13 miles, and 14 miles.
If therefore, as the '*Office*' says, Richard Rolle 'received the origin
of his propagation' at Thornton, not meaning that he was born
there, but that his family sprang from *a* Thornton and moved
elsewhere, then either the Aiskew or the Yafforth William Rolle
had many more Thorntons from which to migrate in their neighbourhood, than if William Rolle had migrated from 'Thornton iuxta
Pickering,' meaning either Thornton-[-le-dale] or Thornton Riseborough. In fact at one point Miss Allen appears to speak strongly
in favour of William Rolle of Yafforth as the parent of Richard.[7]
She points out that no one of the name of Rolle appears in the
Lay Subsidy of 1301 either in Aiskew or in Yafforth. This would
be natural, if the family in Richard's youth, migrated into
Richmondshire. Yafforth would be in Richmondshire, and his
father could easily have come from any of the neighbouring
Thorntons. If either Aiskew or Yafforth is considered as a place
of Richard's youthful residence he would then be in touch, first
with Raby Castle, the home of his University patron, and secondly,
with John Dalton of Topcliffe.

Miss Allen's firm belief in Richard Rolle's connection with
Thornton near Pickering is, partly, because his father was a friend,
or possibly a member of the household, of a John Dalton; and she
is sure that this John Dalton was the same man as the Keeper of
Pickering Castle 1306 to 1322. In this, she has little support from
Miss Hodgson, who shows a John Dalton in the neighbourhood

---

[1] Ibid. p. 433. She refers for this to Dr. Horstmann.
[2] In Allerton Wapentake. V. C. H. N. R. I. p. 208.
[3] Ibid. p. 209.
[4] Ibid. p. 205. N.B. The Bishop of Durham had tenants in Thornton-
le-Street, V. C. H. N. R. II. p. 50.
[5] In Richmondshire, *cf. A. H. Smith, ut supra*, p. 235.
[6] Ibid. p. 248.
[7] Miss Allen, p. 437.

of Topcliffe.[1] Miss Hodgson fails to prove that the two Daltons were one and the same. She says that in Rolle's two autobiographical works, the *Melum Contemplativorum* and the *Incendium Amoris*, he 'tells next to nothing of his family and gives no help in solving the problem of this "Squire Dalton's" relation, if any, to the Keeper of Pickering Castle.'[2]

If it be pressed that Rolle's father was a 'member of the household' of John Dalton, then it may safely be assumed that William Rolle did not live in Thornton, because, most certainly, John Dalton, whether of Topcliffe or of Pickering, never dwelt there at all. Against the idea of the friendship being with John Dalton of Pickering is a point made by Miss Allen herself. She suggests that the Rolle family had moved in Richard's youth to Richmondshire. If this is so, the move was (being in his youth) before or about 1306. But if John Dalton only came to Pickering that year, how could William Rolle of Thornton-[-le-dale], who does not appear in the Lay Subsidy of 1301, have been a great friend or 'a member of the household'[3] of Dalton of Pickering Castle ? If he were a friend of this avaricious Seneschal, it is rather remarkable that Miss Comper should say 'in all probability Richard's parents were poor,'[4] though Dr. Horstmann says that William Rolle 'was apparently of respectable position.'[5] On the other hand if William Rolle had lived in or come from, one of the numerous Thorntons in central Yorkshire, for example, Thornton-le-Street, he could have been either a 'friend' or a 'member of the household' of John Dalton at Topcliffe, and about 1306, have moved to Yafforth in Richmondshire.

Whether from Richmondshire or from some other part of Yorkshire, there is little doubt that Richard went to Oxford. The *'Office'* says that 'when he was of adult age, Master Thomas Neville, at one time Archdeacon of Durham,[6] honourably maintained him in the University of Oxford, where he made progress'; and where, apparently, he studied with the young Daltons whose home was, possibly, near Topcliffe.[7] Miss Comper[8] finds the reason for the patronage of Thomas de Neville, as a Durham man,

[1] Rev. H. R. Bramley in *'The Psalter of Richard Rolle of Hampole'*, p. vi. note, holds the view that Rolle met John Dalton at Topcliffe.
[2] Miss Hodgson, pp. 48-49.
[3] Miss Allen, p. 443.
[4] Miss Comper, p. 6.
[5] Horstmann, II. p.v.
[6] Meaning long after Richard's time at Oxford: in 1334.
[7] Miss Hodgson, p. 57.
[8] Miss Comper, p. 8.

in the fact that, 'parts of the North Riding were in those days under the ecclesiastical jurisdiction of Durham'; but she has forgotten that the all-important statement[1] about Rolle's 'origin' at Thornton says that it was '*Eboracenis diocesis.*'[2] She then states 'The Neville and Percy families were practically the owners of all that district of Yorkshire.' If she means Thornton-[-le-dale] this is not correct, for the owners of what is now the civil parish, at the time of Rolle's birth were Roger Mowbray, William Percy of Kildale, Roger Bigod, the abbot of Rievaulx and the Earl of Lancaster. If, on the other hand, she means Richmondshire, then as already shown, Yafforth is not very far from Raby Castle.

The question arises, how old was Rolle when he went to Oxford? Miss Hodgson[3] and Miss Comper[4] agree that he was between fourteen and sixteen years of age. Miss Hodgson says 'when he was nineteen or so, the call of spiritual things won his mystical love.'[5] She is sure that he gained much from Oxford; he must therefore have stayed sometime, and yet the '*Office*' states that he returned at the age of eighteen.[6] But can any reliability, on a point like this, be placed on a work which cannot be earlier than 1383 or 1384, or thirty-five years after Rolle's death? If he had gained anything from Oxford, even though no degree, one would imagine him to have been not less than twenty-one or twenty-two when he returned to what Miss Allen calls 'the new family home' in Richmondshire, and from which he goes to the old home i.e., Thornton-[-le-dale], 'which he would have known well to be suitable for a hermit.'[7] If then he were born about 1300, this return to Thornton must have been between 1318 and 1322, though why he should have known it to be suitable for a hermit, considering he left it as a child, it is difficult to see. Nor do any of the three writers prove that Richard Rolle was a hermit in Thornton-[-le-dale] at any time in his life.

Miss Allen has shown, at this point, that he started his flight as a hermit from Richmondshire to Thornton-[-le-dale]. But, later, she speaks of Rolle starting to fly from Thornton-[-le-dale], and that 'in no direction could he have hoped to find solitude and

---

[1] Miss Allen, p. 431.
[2] This would be an argument against his place of origin being Thornton-le-Street for that village would be under the ecclesiastical control of Durham.
[3] Miss Hodgson, p. 65.
[4] Miss Comper, p. 9.
[5] Miss Hodgson, p. 76.
[6] Miss Allen, p. 109.
[7] Ibid. p. 436.

escape from his father nearer than' Foulbridge.[1] But Miss Comper
is much more definite. She says, that after making his long journey
from Oxford, 'when he reached his native *wolds*, and looked *down*
upon the squat Norman Tower[2] of the old Church at Thornton
he must have hesitated before he descended the hill.'[3]   But is
this statement historically true ?   In the first place Richard could
only have been out of his senses if he went anywhere near 'the
Wolds': certainly Thornton-[-le-dale] is not in 'the Wolds.'   And
secondly, Richard would not have any hill to descend in returning
from the south, because Marishes Lane and Maltongate rather
rise into the village than fall, though very slightly, about 60 ft.
in a mile. Miss Comper in imagining his return has thought that
he must have come down Roxby Hill into the village from Pickering.
If he really knew Thornton-[-le-dale], which is extremely doubtful,
it would not have entered his head to add extra miles by going
round by Pickering, after tramping close on 200 miles. Her story
is picturesque, but it lacks historical proof, as indeed does every
point in Rolle's early life. Miss Comper champions the idea of
Rolle's return to Thornton; Miss Allen first says Richmondshire,
and then says Thornton; Miss Hodgson is more cautious and says
that he 'returned to his father's house in Yorkshire.'[4]

Miss Allen, like Miss Hodgson, refers to 'Thorntondale Wood'[5]
as being mentioned in a document of 1335,[6] and says this may have
been the *'nemus vicinum'* where Richard met his sister on his
abrupt return from Oxford. But she seems to forget that she has
shown that the home of the Rolle family had been transferred to
Richmondshire. Besides, it should be noted, that 'Thorntondale'
wood does not necessarily refer to Thornton-[-le-dale] for, from
the context, it was contiguous to Brompton and Sawdon, and in
no other known mediaeval document is such a wood mentioned
at Thornton-[-le-dale], though there are several references to woods
such as Hindslackside, Skeathwood and others. In addition, a fact
which Miss Allen and Miss Hodgson do not consider sufficiently,
might be pointed out. The term 'Dale' as applied to Thornton
is not common previous to the building of the railway between

[1] Miss Allen, p. 459.
[2] The top of the Tower is, if anything, higher than the highest point
of Roxby Hill; and Miss Hodgson has decided that it was already Early English!
[3] Miss Comper, p. 55.
[4] Miss Hodgson, p. 78.
[5] Unfortunately I have not been able to see the original manuscript
but from the context I suggest that 'Thorntondale' is a misreading for
'Troutsdale.'
[6] N. R. Rec. S. N.S. IV. p. 42.

1879 and 1882, and does not seem to occur earlier than the second decade of the nineteenth century, except in this one document; and if, by a remarkable chance, it does refer to Thornton-[-le-dale] it has not the faintest connection with the story of Richard Rolle, and serves in no way to elucidate the place of his birth.

Miss Hodgson regards Richard Rolle as 'our sane, very human and truly English mystic.'[1] His own sister, however, would not have borne out this statement. She must have been pondering on him, at least, for some weeks, because his ultimate flight as a hermit was 'many weeks after the end of term.'[2] Wherever the incident took place, whether at Aiskew, or Yafforth, or Thornton Riseborough, or Thornton-[-le-dale], his wild and hysteric actions must have very much surprised her. He took from her two of her dresses, the one white and the other grey, cut off the sleeves of the grey and fitted them to the white, and having stripped his other garments, put one dress on the top of the other and his father's 'rainhood' on his head, and these he regarded as a suitable hermit's garb. When he returned to her arrayed like this, the sister, very naturally, at once exclaimed 'My brother is mad!' Whereupon he 'drove her from him and fled straight away from home.' Whether the sister, who was on the spot and had known him from childhood, or whether twentieth century writers who have merely studied his works are the best judges of his mental condition at the moment of his flight, it is, perhaps, difficult to say.

If then he fled away from 'home' which Miss Allen in one place[3] decided might have been Thornton, and the 'nemus vicinum' might have been the Thorntondale wood already referred to, it is clear that he had left Thornton and was not there as a hermit. Miss Hodgson tells us that 'he did not travel very far though he probably crossed rough country. It is impossible on the evidence to determine his stopping place. It is generally thought to have been Topcliffe in the Vale of York.'[4] If this were so, then it would not have been far for him to have walked from Thornton-le-Street; but it certainly would have been a good tramp if he had left Thornton-[-le-dale] after the incident with his sister, and stumbled across 'rough country' to Topcliffe, a distance of thirty miles. Miss Comper prefers to think that the distance is only twenty-four miles, and describes the journey in some detail. She

---

[1] Miss Hodgson, p. 81.
[2] Miss Allen, p. 109.
[3] Ibid. p. 442.
[4] Miss Hodgson, p. 80, *cf.* Miss Comper. pp. 36, 57 who is convinced that the place was Topcliffe.

speaks of 'Stape Cross above Newton Dale,' and says 'as the sun drew near its setting and the arms of the cross were outlined against a blood-red sky, Richard must have felt some premonition of the fire of love which he was to experience later....We may picture him in his uncouth dress, kneeling at the foot of the rough granite cross.'[1] If this narrative had any elements of historic facts in it, no greater proof of the truth of his sister's exclamation, 'My brother is mad,' could be found. For a man with a journey due west to go anywhere near Newton Dale and Stape Cross, which would be practically due north from Thornton-[-le-dale] and add at least eight miles outward and as much again to get into the right direction, must have been out of his mind. And if the sun set when he was at Stape, and, being the middle of August,[2] it would do so about 7.23 p.m., no earthly power could have brought him to Topcliffe in time for 'vespers,' even though he were a 'boy bounding over the moors exultant in his freedom.'[3]

At any rate whether at Topcliffe or at Pickering or at Foulbridge, Richard came first to the Church and then to the house of John Dalton, and the sons of the house recognized him at once as Richard, son of William Rolle, with whom they had been at Oxford. On the other hand, although John Dalton had been such a friend of the elder Rolle, he did not know his son. The next day, though probably not in holy orders, Richard preached in the Church, and Miss Allen says 'Whether Rolle preached his first sermon at Pickering or at Snainton, and met the Daltons at Pickering or at Foulbridge, it seems likely that when he settled under their protection it was at Pickering.'[4]   Miss Hodgson, however, is equally convinced that when John Dalton 'prevailed on him to accept a solitary dwelling on his estate, together with the bare necessaries of life' it was at Topcliffe,[5] and Miss Comper supports this view.[6] All three agree therefore that it was not at Thornton-[-le-dale].

Miss Allen thinks that John Dalton welcomed Rolle, arrayed in his astounding costume, as one who would give him prestige. She assumes that Rolle was with the Dalton family either at Pickering or at Foulbridge, at the latter of which Dalton had a

---

[1] Miss Comper, p. 57.
[2] Miss Allen definitely states that the 'flight' was in the middle of August, basing her assertion on the *'Office'* which gives as the day the Assumption of the Blessed Virgin Mary.
[3] Miss Comper, p. 58.
[4] Miss Allen, p. 459.
[5] Miss Hodgson, p. 81.
[6] Miss Comper, p. 57.

manor,[1] and in which may have been, what Rolle describes as 'a dilapidated and ancient room.'[2]   One would conclude, that the words of the *'Office'* must inevitably rule out Pickering.   No writer would have described Dalton, the Keeper of Pickering Castle, as 'the aforesaid squire,' and as a person who had a *'manerium'* near 'a church.'   Such a description might apply to a small lord of a manor at Topcliffe, but it seems inapplicable to one who was not a landowner himself in Pickering, but an official acting for a relative of the sovereign.   Nor does Miss Comper's description of John Dalton as 'a devout man' at all tally with the character of John Dalton at Pickering, who seems to have been a 'ruffianly soldier of fortune.'

As to the length of time Richard Rolle stayed with the Daltons at some completely unknown place, Miss Allen shows that he met the young Daltons in August, and that it was two years and nine months later, 'when the discomfort of his cell became unbearable to him' he took his departure.   If then Richard became a hermit in August, 1318, he would leave the Daltons in May, 1321, or, if as is quite possible, the date of his frenzy should be August, 1319, then he would leave in May, 1322.   Miss Allen speaks of the 'special events which tore Rolle's world in 1322 from March on,'[3] referring to Dalton's traitorous connection with Earl Thomas of Lancaster, and the collapse of their schemes at the battle of Boroughbridge. Gradually, while under the Dalton's hospitable roof[4] disagreement began to crop up between Richard and John Dalton.   Miss Allen seems to find great difficulty in suggesting a cause for this, but having read her account, it might be that John Dalton became jealous because of the attention his wife paid to the hermit.   Miss Comper[5] suggests it was undue familiarity with a maidservant in the Dalton household.   That there was trouble of some kind is shown by Rolle himself writing 'not that I have unlawfully desired anything of them with whom I have some while taken my bodily sustenance.'[6]   Miss Allen prefers to suggest as a reason for Rolle's ultimate departure that 'a rival is perhaps hinted at,' and this rival, she thinks, was William, the hermit of Dalby, whom she

---

[1] This had been granted by Earl Thomas of Lancaster to John Dalton for life.   It had belonged to the Templars before their dissolution in 1308, and probably ultimately passed to the knights of St. John.

[2] *'domus abiecta et antiqua.'*

[3] Miss Allen, p. 112.

[4] Rolle himself said 'some do not fear to assert impudently that I am not a hermit.'

[5] Miss Comper, p. 52.

[6] Cf. *'non pertinet ad statum suum scilicet heremeticum ludere cum mulieribus.'*

calls, because of his grant from Edward II., 'a very practical sort of hermit, probably very different from Richard Rolle.'[1]

If, however, it is correct to allow that Rolle came upon the scene either at Pickering or at Foulbridge or at Topcliffe between 1319 and 1322, one wonders why the hermit at Dalby should have been a rival in any sense. In that period there were plenty of hermits,[2] and the one at Dalby was evidently a complete recluse and would neither have interfered with another at Pickering, five miles away, with a most precipitous hill in between and no house, by the direct route, other than the manor of Kingthorpe, nor with one dwelling at Foulbridge, the nearest route to which, from William's cottage, was nine miles across very marshy country, still less with one at Topcliffe, thirty-three miles away across the Hambledon Hills. It is quite clear from the grant to William, in August, 1323, that sometime previously he had had another grant, at what date it is now impossible to say; and that, therefore, there was no question of a new hermit coming on the scene, for William had probably been up the Dalby valley before the arrival of Richard in the vicinity, if, indeed, he were ever in these parts. What is very noticeable is, that John Dalton, at the date of the grant, was no longer guardian of the Castle of Pickering for it was under the control of John de Kylvyngton,[3] John Dalton having been dispossessed by William Latimer in 1322. So that Miss Allen's idea of a rival in William of Dalby in 1323 collapses, because John Dalton was not at Pickering and therefore Richard was not there either.

Once more Miss Allen seems to put Richard in three places at one time, for having mentioned his 'rival' in 1323, at Dalby, and having said that between 1320 and 1326 she imagined him to be living in the district of Byland and Rievaulx,[4] later in her work, she says 'so far as the dates go[5].... Rolle might have been in Paris in the latter part of 1320.'[6] Against this view it should be noted that Horstmann says that Richard Rolle never 'excepting the years of his studentship, left the precincts of Yorkshire.'[7] If a 'mystic' is also a 'mystery' certainly the whereabouts of Richard Rolle at any given moment are mysterious indeed. Miss Comper

---

[1] Miss Allen, p. 464.
[2] Miss Clay, *The Hermits and Anchorites of England*.
[3] N. R. Rec. S. N.S. II. p. 256.
[4] Miss Allen, p. 480.
[5] Are there any dates ?
[6] Miss Allen, p. 494.
[7] Horstmann, II. p. xxxix.

states 'It is not possible to say where Richard lived from the time
he left the Daltons until he went to Hampole';[1] but it *might* be
significant, as pointed out in the *'Office,'* that when he left the
Dalton estate, which Miss Comper is positive was at Topcliffe,
he went to some place 'twelve miles' from Ainderby Steeple. This
could not have been Yafforth, his possible Richmondshire home
in the past, for that is only two miles away. It is impossible to
suggest the exact spot it might have been, but Richard had
apparently, according to the wording of the *'Office'* come back to
his own countryside to be near the recluse, the Lady Margaret
Kirkeby. And here again we are confronted with the difficulty
of knowing which of the authors has judged rightly. Miss Hodgson
says 'he had found an understanding and wise friend' in the Lady
Margaret;[2] while, Miss Comper quotes the Rev. L. W. Grensted,
who says 'she was a typical hysteric and a much more unhealthy
one' than even those of modern times.[3] But after all it does not
matter, for it is now proved that the *'Office,'* the basis of what is
known of Richard Rolle's life, is misleading in using the term *'olim'*
for Margaret Kirkeby's period as a recluse at Ainderby, because
Miss Clay has found from the registers of Bishops Zouche and
Thoresby that Lady Margaret Kirkeby 'did not reach Ainderby,
till some years after Rolle's death,'[4] probably in 1357.[5] If then,
the *'Office'* is unreliable on this point, can any historic reliability
be placed on the other pieces of information given? Even Miss
Allen says both the *Psalter* and the *'Office'* 'were written years
after the event and evidently mixed up the periods in the lives
of the persons involved.'[6]

There is apparently no agreement as to Rolle's birth, his birthplace, the place of his early life as a hermit, the character of his
associates, nor even whether those associates were in a particular
place before or after his death. There is, however, one point on which
all the writers agree, and that is, that after his departure from the
Daltons, Rolle never had any connection whatsoever with
Thornton-[-le-dale]. Nor does it seem to the present writer to have
been proved that either he or his parents ever had any historical

[1] Miss Comper, p. 184.
[2] Miss Hodgson, p. 131.
[3] Miss Comper, p. 177.
[4] Miss Allen, p. 502, Miss Comper, p. 174 says 'she was still at Ainderby
when Richard died.' Miss Hodgson, p. 131 shows that she is also unaware
of Miss Clay's discovery.
[5] Miss Allen p. 52 says that Margaret Kirkeby may have supplied the
details concerning herself, and yet on p. 517 she thinks the main incident
a fiction.
[6] Miss Allen, p. 188.

connection at all with that village. The whole story is based on a doubtful interpolation, a century after his death, in a manuscript containing a short, but proved fallacious,[1] account of his life, written by some person, unaccustomed to weigh evidence, and who, as far as is known had never conversed[2] with the man of whom the record was made, because a great many years had passed since Richard Rolle was probably swept away, with thousands, when England was ravaged by the Black Death. Such material for an infallible biography cannot be regarded as either historical or conclusive.

The supposed rival of Richard Rolle, William of Dalby, was evidently a saintly man, at least he desired to be far away from the men and women of the world. He perched his little cot on the gentle slope of the valley side, and was there content to live with his two cows and their calves, or, perhaps not quite content, because we only know of his existence, by the fact that on 20 August, 1323, he obtained a grant from Edward II., that he should have three cows with their issue for three years,[3] and that he should have pasturage for a third cow as long as he remained a hermit.[4] He had chosen a perfect spot. His tiny cot was at the foot of Flaxdale, at that time covered with oak trees,[5] and on the northern side was a little spring, which still gushes into the beck flowing a few yards away on the west; and in the early months of the year the short and steep banks, on either side of the spring, were covered, as to-day, with bright primroses. His complete solitude would only be disturbed by the gentle caw of rooks that he perhaps attracted to the spot.[6] It was here that the pious man spent his lonely life,

[1] Miss Allen, p. 61, allows that in the *'Office'* 'the facts are being stretched a little.'

[2] There is no reasonable proof that the *'Office'* was the work of William Stopes, the personal friend of Richard Rolle, towards the end of his life. Even if it were the work of Stopes, he had allowed so long a period to pass that his memory might easily have failed him on many points. Miss Allen, p. 517 says 'In the frightful emotions of the year 1349 we can imagine that memories were deeply disturbed, and that in years to come imagination had more than ever free play over incidents of this period.'

[3] Cox, *Royal Forests of England*, p. 108.

[4] N. R. Rec. S. N.S. II. p. 256. *'Rex dilecto sibi Johanni de Kylvynton custodi castri et honoris de Pykeryng salutem. Volentes dilecto nobis in Christo Willelmo de Daleby heremite de Daleby gratiam facere specialem, concessimus quod ipse ultra pasturam ad duas vaccas et earum exitum duorum annorum quam habet in foresta nostra de Pykeryng, habeat ex nunc quamdiu vixerit ut heremita ibidem sit pasturam in foresta predicta ad unam vaccam cum exitu duorum annorum. Et ideo vobis mandamus quod ipsum heremitam pasturam ad tres vaccas cum earum exitu trium [sic] annorum ex nunc in foresta nostra predicta habere permittatis juxta tenorem commissionis nostre predicte. T.R. apud Pykeryng xxdie Augusti per ipsum Regem.'*

[5] N. R. Rec. S. N.S. II. pp. 179-80.

[6] To-day there is a fairly large rookery close by.

tending his cows, supplementing his spare meals with a trout from the stream, and passing his days in deep and holy meditation. There is no record of this worthy's death, but it must have been before 1351, when his little house was let by the Honor of Pickering to the Forester of Dalby.[1] Generation after generation, different persons rented the site from the Duchy of Lancaster. The original cot may have been destroyed hundreds of years ago; but to-day the place is still visible, and some of the cumbersome stones that mark the foundations of a ruined hut may be the same that were used to make his home, in the early fourteenth century by William of Dalby.[2]

[1] G. F. G. H.
[2] Documentary search enabled me to trace the site to the present day. It is marked on the 6 in. Ordnance Survey as 'Harwood House' at the bottom of Flaxdale; *vide* Ch. XVI.

CHAPTER FOUR.

Mediaeval Violence.

"In every shire with Jakkes and Salades clene
Myssereule doth ryse and maketh neyghbours werre;
The wayker gothe benethe, as ofte ys sene,
The myghtyest his quarell wyll preferre."

HARDYNGE'S Chronicle, 1457.

O N the whole the ordinary villagers' lives were placid ones.
Sometimes wars and rumours of wars would be discussed; but,
for the most part, the few inhabitants of Thornton would tend
their moorland sheep and sow and reap their crops, with little
knowledge of what was going on in the outside world. Of course,
the fact that Thornton lay between Pickering and Scarborough,
would occasionally bring to the villagers tidings of great events,
such as the visit of Henry I., a Yorkshire-born King, to Pickering
about 1122; or again, in February, 1201, they would congregate,
where now there is the Cross, and stare in amazement at the
procession from Wykeham Abbey, marching to Pickering Castle,
to obtain a Charter from King John;[1] and again, would do the same
when that King, with his immense and gorgeous retinue clanked
through on his way to Scarborough Castle. Then, too, once a year,
after about 1248, the abbot of Whitby had to send to the Master
of St. Leonard's Hospital at York, 1500 red and 1500 white
herrings. The place where the abbot had to hand over this tribute
was at the four cross roads in Thornton, and many a yokel would
watch with interest the Hospitallers taking over this huge load.[2]

---

[1] G. Home *ut supra*, p. 104. King John was also at Pickering in August,
1208, and March, 1210. He would probably have been in a vile temper when
he left Pickering in the latter year for he is stated to have lost 10s. to the
Earl of Salisbury in playing at backgammon. *Vide* Y. A. J. XXII. p. 370.

[2] There seems to be some confusion as to this tribute. Young, in his
History of Whitby, p. 333, says that the payment was in exemption of tithes,
and adds that it was continued as late as 1813 (when he wrote) though paid
to the Archbishop at Bishopthorpe and not at Thornton. Charlton, in his
History of Whitby, p. 207 does not agree with Young in dating the first
instance in 1225, but gives 1248, which seems to be correct. Both writers,
however, appear to be wrong in stating that the payment was to the Archbishop instead of to the Master of St. Leonard's Hospital. Even the original
documents seem doubtful about the number of the herrings, for one says
2000 and the other 3000. *Cf.* Whitby Chartulary, Sur. Soc. LXIX. pp.
213, 236. Possibly the V. C. H. *N.R.* II. p. 512, is correct in stating that the
number was originally 2000 and increased to 3000 in 1248.

All these, however, were peaceful events and the villagers, like others of the time, were destined to witness, and be connected with, acts of violence. In 1252 Thornton would be agog with the news that a well-known local gentleman, Roger son of Stephen of Kingthorpe, had been charged with the murder of his cousin Astinus,[1] son of John of Thornton and grandson of Gilbert the parson. It would be a relief, no doubt, when it was heard that the great judge, Roger de Thurkill, had decided that the death was due to misadventure.[2] But William Laweys of Thornton was not so fortunate in 1289, for he was incarcerated in York Castle, for the murder of Emma, daughter of John 'le Prevost'[3] of Thornton. It is hardly likely that he went unpunished, though history does not record his execution.[4] And yet another Thornton man in the early fourteenth century, Alan, son of Richard de la Hou, managed to procure a pardon from the King, on 21 November, 1310, for the death of Adam de Folkyngton in Hardfordlithe.[5]

One great excitement was when the siege of Scarborough Castle took place in 1312, and it is probable that some of the men of Thornton, Farmanby and Roxby were in the band of those 'three hundred all clad in green jackets,' arrayed and led by John Dalton the Keeper of Pickering,[6] and who strenuously kept up the siege until Piers Gaveston, or the Earl of Cornwall as he was called, surrendered himself to such great noblemen as the Earls of Pembroke and Warenne.[7] Even if the Thorntonians held back from this act of violence, which was indeed an act of treason, for Gaveston held the castle at the command of the King, they must have stood agape at seeing that green-coated company march down Roxby Hill and up, passed the Church which was old even then,[8] and so 'Up-Street' and on to the east.

It is probable, however, that the exceptionally wet summers of 1315 and 1316, which brought about an almost total failure of crops, and which produced very bad murrain among the deer in

---

[1] It is rather curious that Young, pp. 336-7, mentions an Astinus de Thornton as proctor for Whitby in 1262 and as appearing at the court at Rome in 1263; and that Cal. Pat. R. 1272-8, p. 278 shows an 'Astinus de Thornton' as a monk at Winceby.

[2] Cal. Pat. R. 1247-58, p. 155.

[3] 'The agricultural tenants and labourers on a manor were accustomed to elect from among themselves a 'Provost' to be head over them and to stand between them and their lord, whom they were pledged to obey in all things.' *Vide* Mrs. J. R. Green, *Town Life in the Fifteenth Century*, I. p. 170.

[4] Cal Close R. 1288-96, p. 7.

[5] Cal. Pat. R. 1307-13, p. 296.

[6] N. R. Rec. S. N.S. II. p. 243.

[7] Tout, *Political History of England* (pub. Longmans), III. p. 250.

[8] There was a Church certainly before 1200. The present font is Norman.

the Forest,[1] would be of far greater interest to all at Thornton than any swashbucklering deeds of the Keeper of Pickering; and the older members of the village would compare these famine years with their memories of the scarcity period of their youth between 1256 and 1258. But agriculture, good or bad, could not have been the only source of village conversation, and arguments and disputes must have raged when the people heard of the defeat of Earl Thomas of Lancaster, Lord of the Honor of Pickering, at the battle of Boroughbridge and of his hasty execution at Pontefract, on 22 March, 1322. William Latimer, one of their own lords, had for a time, been of the Earl's party, and had been present at the battle, to see his old friend's capture. They knew that men had been hastily despatched under the command of Latimer to seize Pickering Castle into the King's hands immediately after the battle, and some would know that a lord of another manor in the village, John de Mowbray, had fought by the side of Earl Thomas, had been taken prisoner and hanged in chains at York.[2] Lesser men than these had gone from the village itself to take part with the rebel barons, such as William Page of Farmanby,[3] William Yeland, lord of the little manor of Ellerburn,[4] and Hugh, his brother.[5]

Although Pickering Castle and the powerful house of Lancaster were near at hand, Boroughbridge and rebel fights were far away, and were soon forgotten. There was, however, a more dangerous foe, often in the neighbourhood, and one obviously much feared. Ever since Edward I. had stirred up the wasps' nest in Scotland, in the late thirteenth century, Scottish raids upon Yorkshire were a perpetual dread. That such inroads, whether great or small, were a reality is to be found in the fact that, in February, 1323, it was stated that the chief messuage at Kingthorpe was worth 2s. per annum and no more 'on account of the invasion of the Scots.'[6] This, no doubt, was due to the fact that in August, 1322,[7] Bruce had once again devastated the northern counties and the Earl of Winchester was powerless against him.[8] Then followed the disgrace, disaster and despair of Edward II.'s precipitate flight from Byland; and it is not surprising that in that very October, on the 13th of the month, John Topcliffe, rector of Seamer and others, purchased

---

[1] N. R. Rec. S. N.S. IV. p. 200.
[2] Ibid. II., p. xxii.
[3] Ibid. IV., p. 29.
[4] Ibid. IV., p. 203.
[5] Ibid. II., p. 261.
[6] Ibid. II., p. 242.
[7] Tout, *ut supra*, p. 284.
[8] Cal. Pat. R. 1321-4, p. 187.

from the Scots the immunity of the Forest of Pickering from the river Seven on the west to the sea on the east. For this reason Thornton escaped devastation for the moment; but the inhabitants showed little gratitude to the men who had saved them. On October 17th Nicholas Haldane, William Hastings of Farmanby,[1] and John Manneser delivered themselves to Bruce as hostages, at Rievaulx Abbey; but the community of the Forest refused to pay what they had promised, and the three gallant men were still prisoners in Scotland, as late as July, 1325.[2]

The Scottish peril vanished for the time after the battles of Halidon Hill in 1333, and Neville's Cross in 1346, in the latter of which, Sir Ralph Hastings,[3] chief lord of Farmanby, received the wounds from which he died. Liar and poacher he may have been, but he was evidently a trusty servant of Edward III.

By the victory near Durham, a temporary respite came from the Scots, but the perpetual warfare against France flooded the country with unruly disbanded soldiers, and fourteenth century England witnessed a remarkable wave of lawlessness both in the north and south, and from end to end the land was full of riotous outlaws.[4] Even as early as 1304-5, so-called Commissions of Trailbaston had been issued to cope with this violence.[5] There are no early instances in Thornton history of these burglarious attacks on manor-houses, breaking of gates, doors and windows, and driving off of horses, mares, oxen, sheep and even swans.[6] It may have been that during the years 1348, 1349, and 1351, the inhabitants of these parts had enough to do to resist the ravages of the Black Death. Certainly it is remarkable that there seems to be no documentary evidence of good or ill deeds, of business or of pleasure, in Thornton, during the period that the plague is known to have been at its worst in Yorkshire. But, as the century grew older, cases began to arise; and on 14 July, 1362, a Court of Oyer and Terminer was held because John, 'Earl' of Lancaster and Richmond,[7] complained that evil doers had broken his parks and

---

[1] Son of Edmund Hastings and the Lady Beatrice.

[2] It is uncertain whether the Scots kept their word. It looks as if they did not because in 1325 the manor of Thornton was stated to be only worth £10. 'owing to destruction by the Scots.'

[3] *Vide* Ch. XIV.

[4] Bright, *History of England,* I. p. 195.

[5] *Cf.* Jeudwine, *ut supra,* p. 151.

[6] Cal. Pat. R. 1321-4, p. 169.

[7] Henry, nephew of Earl Thomas of Lancaster had died with his wife from bubonic plague on 24 March, 1361-2. He was the first Duke of Lancaster and famous throughout Europe for his chivalry. His daughter Blanche married John of Gaunt, was created Duke of Lancaster in 1362 so that it is curious that in this commission he should be called 'Earl.'

closes in Pickering, Thornton and Dalby,[1] and again in January, 1364, there is the same complaint.[2] One of the chief ruffians of the day was Robert Greteheved of Thornton, against whom on 10 February, 1366, the neighbouring magnate, 'Peter de Malo Lacu le sisme' [Peter Mauley][3] charged this scoundrel with having broken into his property in 'Clivelande.'[4] Very soon after, on 8 November, 1367, an Oyer and Terminer was held on complaint of the avaricious William Latimer that many men had broken down his closes at Thornton in 'Pykerynglith,' and had stolen hares, conies, pheasants and partridges, and trodden down and 'consumed' corn and grass, and assaulted his servants.[5] He evidently got no redress, for he brought a similar action two years later, on 6 March, 1369.[6] He was, as a matter of fact, a very unpopular man, of low morality, a slave to avarice, proud, cruel, irreligious, deceitful and untrustworthy;[7] so that he is undeserving of sympathy.

Nor were the Hastings' family more peaceable. As early as 1368, Edmund Hastings of Roxby was badgering the Prior of Malton, William de Bentham, concerning certain titles to property.[8] Then, two years later, William Latimer, John Bigod and the abbot of Rievaulx, William IX., and the abbot of Byland, Robert de Helmeslay, complained that their lands had been damaged by the overflow of the waters of the Derwent owing to the mismanagement of the Mill Ponds of the Priory. They demanded settlement by arbitration, but the Prior did not trust the arbitration of Sir Ralph Hastings, Lord of Allerston and Farmanby, and his opponents were determined to have Sir Ralph and no one else. The Prior refused to submit. Whereupon 'on Sunday after the feast of St. Luke,' that is 20 October, 1370, Sir Ralph Hastings 'came in force with two hundred armed men and archers and wrecked the mills [at Malton] and diverted the water from its ancient water-course through the Priory.' The terrified monks declared that they did not dare 'to pass their door for fear of their lives'; and 'In this plight the Prior was forced by Monsieur Ralph to bind himself......to submit to his arbitration in the matter of dispute and damage.' It may have been very annoying for the

---

[1] Cal. Pat. R. 1361-4, p. 286.
[2] Ibid. pp. 367, 454.
[3] For the Mauley family *vide* V. C. H. N. R. II. *passim*, and a short note in Rev. S. L. Ollard, *Notes on the History of Bainton Church and Parish.*
[4] Cal. Pat. R. 1364-7, p. 280.
[5] Ibid. 1367-70, p. 63.
[6] Ibid. p. 264.
[7] D.N.B.
[8] *Vide* Ch. XV.

landlords to have their estates unnecessarily flooded, but because the Prior did not agree to receive the arbitration of Sir Ralph immediately on demand can hardly be an excuse for the violent and high handed conduct of that turbulent Knight. It is not surprising that the Prior petitioned the King that he and the monks should be freed from the bond of £40 which they had been forced to enter, that their ancient course should be restored and that they should have redress concerning their mills.[1] But, as Sir Ralph Hastings was evidently a favourite of John of Gaunt,[2] and as that royal Duke was not too friendly towards the Church, it is not likely that Sir Ralph suffered any severe punishment, nor that the Prior gained much by his piteous appeal.

Murders were apparently common, and Walter Lofthouse, bailiff of Thornton in 'Pykerynglithe,' on the supplication of William 'Latymer,' the King's chamberlain, was a lucky man to be pardoned on 1 September, 1372, for the death of Robert Tagg of Barneby Bossall.[3] And Nicholas Bogo, shoemaker[4] of Louthe, was equally fortunate when pardoned on 30 April, 1373, for the death of John Barkere[5] of Thornton 'of Pykerynglythe' dwelling[6] in Louthe.[7] A little later in the century, the mantle of Robert Greteheved seems to have fallen on the shoulders of William Dodemore[8] of Thornton. Both carried their attacks upon property outside their own village, and just as Greteheved had infuriated Peter Mauley, so Dodemore aroused the wrath of Sir Robert de Hilton, by attacks on his estates particularly on that of 'Baynton,' near York, that Sir Robert obtained a Commission of Oyer and Terminer on 4 June, 1394.[9] It seems to have had little effect, as far as William Dodemore of 'Thornthon in Pykeringlythe' was concerned, for if it had, it would not have been possible for the rogue to have obtained on 3 May, 1396, a pardon of outlawry[10] for not appearing to answer Robert de 'Wylughby' lord of Eresby,[11] touching a debt of £40.

---

[1] Hist. MSS. Com , Rawden Hastings MS. I. pp. 189, 190.
[2] Ibid. p. 191.
[3] Cal. Pat. R. 1370-4, p. 196.
[4] '*Sutori.*'
[5] i.e., the tanner.
[6] '*manentes.*'
[7] Cal. Pat. R. 1370-4, p. 272.
[8] Probably an ancestor of Henry 'Dodmer' of Pickering, who was father of Ralph 'Dodmer,' mercer, Lord Mayor of London in 1521. *Cf.* Fuller, *Worthies.*
[9] Cal. Pat. R. 1391-6, p. 444.
[10] Ibid. p. 679.
[11] *Vide* Ch. XI.

These, however, are minor matters and the people of Thornton must have had some knowledge of what was happening in the great political world at the end of the fourteenth century. When it is remembered that Pickering is hardly an hour's walk from Thornton, all that happened in that important ducal town would be repeated amongst the gossips of the village. No one, of course, in this isolated spot would understand the rights or wrongs of the quarrel between Henry Bolingbroke, Duke of Lancaster, and his cousin Richard II.; probably no one in Thornton had ever heard that the former had been banished by the latter. But after Henry had landed at Ravenspur on 4 July, 1399, and marched forthwith to the castle at Pickering, the fact that it had been quickly handed over to him would make the people of Thornton wonder what these great barons were about. And remembering human curiosity it is not too much to imagine that when the tide of events turned against Richard II. and for a brief time before his murder at Pontefract, he was incarcerated in Pickering,[1] many a villager must have walked those short three miles and stared with wondering eyes at the massive walls that 'hedged in' one of the first to claim 'the divinity' of Kings.[2]

The next century was quite as troublesome, although in the early part the records are not so complete. On 5 June, 1467, a pardon was granted, why it is impossible to imagine, to John Kirkeby, 'yeoman' late of Thornton, and Alexander 'Botcher', webster, of the same, for assaulting Ralph Eyre [? Eure or Evers] Esq. at Kirby Misperton, and for taking him and imprisoning him at Kirkby Moorside.[3] These kinds of attacks on property and on individuals are well known to all lovers of the *Paston Letters*; and it is clear, from many sources, that the Wars of the Roses created havoc in the manners and morals of the period. These Wars brought armed bands to Pickering Castle on the side of the House of Lancaster, which did not help to produce peace and quiet in the district. We read of disguised and masked brigands

---

[1] Hardynge's *Chronicle* (Harl. MSS. No. 61, Brit. Mus.) says,
  'The Kyng then sent the Kyng Richard to Ledes
  There to be kept suerly in privete
  Fro thence after to Pikerynge went he nedes
  And to Knaresburgh after ledde was he
  But to Pountefracte laste, where that he did dee.'
[2] Shakespeare 'Richard II.' Act III. Sc. II.,
  'Not all the water in the rough rude sea
  Can wash the balm from an anointed King;
  The breath of worldly men cannot depose
  The deputy elected by the Lord.'
[3] Cal. Pat. R. 1467-77, p. 2.

stealing the royal deer and murdering the gamekeepers.[1] Poaching seems to have been as bad as ever, and when the wars had died away, after the battle of Bosworth in 1485,[2] many servants[3] of Sir Roger Hastings of Roxby, such as William Thornley, Richard Todd[4] and Richard Solett,[5] were accused of venison offences.

The misdemeanours of the servants are not surprising when it is remembered that their master was violent and law-breaking. There is one good story told of this man in the year 1497. He had a bitter quarrel with Ralph Joyner or Jenner,[6] his tenant, in the autumn of that year. The quarrel seems to have been concerning a 'relief' payable by Sir Roger, but possibly, by the terms of his tenure, Ralph Joyner was bound to satisfy this duty. And so Sir Roger sent 'his servantes [who] came to the sayed Joiner and demaunded the rent [26s. 8d.] and he refused they payment.'[7] Whereupon Sir Roger endeavoured to recover the sum by distrain assisted by 'the wyeff of the said Sir Roger Hastynges, Riotously and agayns the Kinges peas, the Vth. day of October....with Force and armys causy it diverse of hys servantes to breke the house....of Rauff Joynnor purposyng there to have caryed away from hys lath[8] certayn cornez....and then they entred the house ....and bare away a payer Sheres, called Walkar Sheres,[9] price xxs. and in money iis. iiiid. Wherefore the said mysdoers ere indited as apperith be the Kynges bookes,'[10] and the case was brought 'afore my lord of Surre' when Sir Roger promised to return the 'Sherys' [Shears]. All this time, apparently, Ralph Joyner[11] was in ignorance as to the cause of his landlord's wrath. He asserted, possibly falsely, that Sir Roger was angry because he had shown 'misplaced zeal in rescuing his master's cattle distrained for not

---

[1] *Cf.* I. Hen. VII. c. 7.

[2] Richard III. was almost certainly at Pickering in 1484. *Cf.* Camden, *Britt.*

[3] This was contrary to the statute of Richard II. 1390, which forbade on pain of a year's imprisonment 'every layman who did not possess landed property worth forty shillings a year, and every clerk with an annual income of less than ten pounds to keep hunting-dogs or to use ferrets or any snares whatsoever to catch deer, hares, rabbits, or any other game. This, said the Act, was 'the sport of the gentle.' *Cf.* Petit-Dutaillis, *ut supra*, pp. 247-8.

[4] Probably of Kingthorpe.

[5] N. R. Rec. S. N.S. I. p. 151.

[6] He held Joyner's Garth or Jenner's Garth now corrupted into China Garth and owned by Miss M. L. Heslop.

[7] N. R. Rec. S. N.S. I. pp. 190-1.

[8] Lath means barn.

[9] i.e., fuller's shears.

[10] N. R. Rec. S. N.S. II. pp. 187-8.

[11] Ralph Joyner's descendants continued in Thornton until about 1740. The last two were James and Roger Joyner.

paying the King's taxes.'[1] In favour of this view is the fact that after Ralph Joyner had made his attempted rescue, Sir Roger 'put hym from his servis whom nowe Sir Richard Chamle[2] kepes and maynteyns.'[3] It may have been because Ralph Joyner had found this patron, a man so hostile to Sir Roger, that he became fiercer than ever. But the real origin of the fury was, almost certainly, because of the failure of Ralph to supply the 'relief,' and Sir Roger's temper was blown to white heat when he was compelled to pay the tax himself.[4]

By this time nothing would satisfy Sir Roger but the blood of Ralph Joyner, who 'comme to Roger Chamley[5] and compleyned to hym that every day he stode in Jeopardy of his liff: and how that he was diverse tymes chased by diverse of the menyall servantes of the said Sir Roger Hastynges, whereuppon the said Roger Chalmley sent to....Sir Roger....in curteyse waise desyring hym to kepe the Kinges peax, whiche he effectually promysed to doo, uppon truste wherof upon Christemas day....the said Rauff Jenore cam to his parisshe chirche called Elborne [Ellerburn] chirche, as belonged to a christen man to doo....Howbeit soon after that comme thedir the said Sir Roger accompenyed with the numbre of xx persons....arrayed with bowes, bills and other weponz....and in a great fury wolde have entred the said churche ....How be it he was by the great labor....of the Vicarie of the ....churche [Sir Robert Sawdane], knellyng upon his kneez.... tarried, and thereupon the wif of....Sir Roger....cam into the said Churche and said unto....Rauf "Woo worthe man this day! the churche wolbe suspended and thou slayn without thou flee awey and gette the oute of his sighte": Whereupon....Rauf....flede oute of the churche by a bakke doore[6] and cam to Pykeryng and Petyously desired of....Roger Chalmley....that he might have suertie of the peax. And then....Roger Chalmley remembred[7] the good day suffred for that day; Howbeit upon the morowe.... ther was a precept of the peace....direct to the said Roger.... whereyn....Sir Roger should be bounde....to the Kinges use in the summe of an c.li. to bere the Kinges peax....inesspecial against the said Rauff Jenor.' Sir Richard Cholmley then tried to

---

[1] N. R. Rec. S. N.S. *ut supra*.
[2] *Vide* Ch. XV.
[3] N. R. Rec. S. N.S. I. p. 190.
[4] Ibid. p. xxvii.
[5] Brother and deputy of Sir Richard Cholmley.
[6] This door is still visible, but has been built up.
[7] This is a beautiful touch. Sir Roger Cholmley would not have been so Christian had the matter really affected himself.

get Sir Roger to seal this bond; but being of 'great myghte havyng many Riottous personez aboute hym,' the Cholmleys failed to get admission to Roxby Castle. They, therefore gathered more men, 'in peasible maner,' but found, when they came for the second time, that Sir Roger had 'goone and departed from his dwelling place.' And so they, too, withdrew.[1]

As soon as possible, Sir Roger Hastings wrote to 'the Ryght Honorable Ser Raynold Bray, Knyght Chaunceller of the Douche[2] of Lancastur,' and said, that instead of 'more men in peasible maner,' there were 181 men, who were, as a matter of fact, all of note and importance in the Honor of Pickering. They were 'arraied in maner of warr with Cures,[3] Cirsettes,[4] Brygendens,[5] Jakkys,[6] Salettes'[7] etc., 'and there to have murdered and slayn your said Besechor....and with blowyng of hornes and showttes escryed hym in his said maner.' What a day for the Thornton people, and how they must have flocked up Roxby hill to gaze upon the howling mob of Sir Roger's enemies! According to Sir Roger, the Cholmleys did not stop here, for on 'xxvith. day of Aprell [1498] ....Riotusly with force and armys' they laid in 'wayte to have murdered and slayn' him, supposing him to have returned to his 'maner of Ruksby....Where he cam nott, but....his wieff with vi of her servantes with her, Appon whom the....misdoers made assaut and her vyolently custe downe from her horse, and her sayd servantes bett and greivously wounded and there puttyng them in Jopardy of there lyves.' The rioting still continued, for Sir Roger wrote again and said that when he 'came home unto his owne maner of Rousby the iiijth. day of June....Sir Raif Ivers [Evers] and Roger Chamley....came Ryottously with the naombre of xii persons....in....furme of warre....which....Sir Roger and his wyfe perceyvyng....departed the morowe....unto Skarburgh in Pylgrimage.' Sir Ralph Evers, having ascertained the date of his return, waited for him at Brompton to murder him. But Sir Roger had sent his servants in advance. Coming out from concealment, Sir Ralph cried 'ye false hirson Kaytyffes, I shall lerne you curtesy and to know a gentilman,' and thereupon set an arrow in his bow saying 'And your Master were here I wolde stoppe

[1] N. R. Rec. S. N.S. I. pp. 180-1.
[2] Just as it is pronounced in the neighbourhood to-day.
[3] Cuirass.
[4] Body armour.
[5] Pliable armour on leather.
[6] Garment of quilted leather.
[7] Salette or Sallet or Salade was a light globular headpiece, with or without vizor, and without crest. The lower back portion was curved outwards.

hym the wey.' The servants managed to get to Snainton, when out of the house 'of one Avery Shinney [? Chymney] servant to ....Sir Rauf,' there rushed another band of twenty hoping to murder Sir Roger, 'In profe wherof ii of the servantes of the seid Sir Roger, of guod and sad disposicion, are here redy to depose the premises to be trewe.'[1]

Needless to say that all these stories were denied by Sir Ralph Evers and by Roger Cholmley.[2] Sir Roger Hastings then accused the Cholmleys of using their powers beyond the common law and of pretending that their actions were according to ancient custom, 'by color of wyche custome they oftentymes have comytted this and many other grett Riottis and extorcians, as of latte in puttyng in execution one Ruddoke[3] to the dethe under the color of the sayd mysused custome wyche is an haynos morder. The wyef of the sayd Ruddok beyng of no pouer to sue her Appell of Murder[4] att the comen lawe, to the utter undoyng and oppressyng of the Kynges people dwelling there.'[5] There may have been a great deal of truth in this charge, for it closely resembles the Star Chamber Case, of 1523, where a certain Alice Taylour accused Roger Cholmley of riotous seizure of cattle and of murder.[6]

The Cholmley party fell back on poaching accusations against Sir Roger and Lady Hastings. They accused her of being in 'Blandesby Park....and with dogges toke....a fat Stott.... and slowe hym and ete hym and no mends [amends] will' she or he make. They also said that without licence, Sir Roger 'hath enclosed within the Fields of Thornton and Farmanby....ij acres and more of arrabill grownde and annexed it to a Cunnyng yerthe [Rabbit warren] to the gret hurt and distruccion of the Kynges tenantes.' And that he had enclosed 'a nother close between Rouceby and Farmonby.' But the worst charge of all was that he and his men came to Pickering Castle, on 13 October, 1498, 'abowt mydnyght with lothus [? ladders] clame ore the walles and then and there brake the kinges prison and toke owt with them oon John Harwod, the which was set there for diverse Riottes by hym made agayns the Kinges peas.'[7] In the end the Cholmleys won and

---

[1] N. R. Rec. S. N.S. I. pp. 172-7.
[2] Ibid. pp. 181-3.
[3] There was a William Ruddocke connected with Thornton as late as 1620. *Cf.* Y. A. S. Rec. S. LVIII. p. 149.
[4] For the form of an Appeal of Murder, *vide* Jacob's *Law. Dict.* (1782) under Appeal.
[5] N. R. Rec. S. N.S. I. pp. 183-4.
[6] Y. A. S. Rec. S. LXX. pp. 62-68.
[7] N. R. Rec. S. N.S. I. p. 189.

Thornton knew the Hastings' family no more.[1]

Such were the wild doings in Thornton at the end of the fifteenth century, and similar scenes of outrageous disorder were witnessed by the people occasionally in the sixteenth. There were two instances in May and June, 1546, that must have long been remembered by the villagers. For some unknown reason John Gresham[2] and Frances his wife had earned the hatred or jealousy of the turbulent Anthony Hunter.[3] The story of his attack upon the peaceful John Gresham is best told in the delightful old wording of the petition to the Court of Star Chamber. 'Humbly shewithe unto your maiestie....John Gresham, esquire, and Fraunces his wyffe, as for and in the right of his said wyffe....John Gresham is lawfully seased in his own demeane as of fee....of and in the manor of Thornton....and alwayes....peacably possessed of the saide manor....So it is nowe, most drad soueraigne lorde, that certaine riotusse and ildisposed persones....Antony Hunter, Roger Hunter, Cristofer Hunter, Robert Smythe, John Smythe, Thomas Allane, otherwyse called Rowlynson, and Gefferey Barghe [Barugh][4] assemblyng themselffes....to the nomber of xvj persones....in maner of warre, withe bowes, billes, arrowes, staffes, clubbes and other waypens indefenseable at two severall daies....the xij daie of Maie and the xvj daie of June, in the xxxviij year of your....reigne, into two severall messuages, parcell of the manor, did unlawfully and most cruelly....enter....and the said yldisposed persones....did riotusely bete and ill entrete one William Thirtelby, servante to Stephane Holford, receyvour of the said manor, than and there beyng in Godes peace and yours, in doyng his said maisters businesses, gyffyng to them, the said riotuse persones, none occasion so to doo by wordes, actes, or otherwyse, And further the said wrongfull doweres....haithe given, unto the said Stephen Holford....many seditouse wordes of thretyes, by reason wherof the said Stephen Holford[5] cannot quietly go boute his said masteres affayrys according to his office, withe oute helpe and reformacion of your Highnes'e'.[6]

No decision was recorded, but as John Gresham and his wife

---

[1] *Vide* Ch. XV.

[2] *Vide* Ch. XII.

[3] Ibid.

[4] *Vide* Ch. VII.

[5] It is almost certain that Stephen Holford lived in Thornton because of the references to his children in the Register. In 1544 'Barbara Holford dowght' of Stephē Holford was cristened the viii day of August.' In 1547 'George Holford son of Stephen Holford was cristened the xvij day of May.' He was buried the following August.

[6] Y. A. S. Rec. S. XLI. pp. 148-9.

continued to hold the manor until conveyed to Roger Hunter in 1564,[1] it may be presumed that the violent actions of Anthony and his relatives were restrained.

With this outburst, mediaeval violence concluded, and the village of Thornton gained that quiet, restful peace that has for so long added to its natural charms. That a change had come is shown by the fact that when the Great Eyre of the Forest was held in 1560, it is stated that 'there is nothing charged for the Profits arising from the Goods and Chatells of ffelons and ffugitives happening withn ye Liberty....this yeare ffor that no such Casualties have therein happened upon the Oath of the Accomptant.'[2]

Not that Thornton was allowed to be unprepared for untoward events for, as in the case of every village, there had to be a supply of arms and armour under the Statute of Winchester of 1285,[3] which had been very much elaborated in the reign of Queen Mary.[4] 'The effect of this, however, was short-lived; for under James I. the repeal of the Statute of Winchester did away with the special obligations to possess arms, though not of course with the common law obligation of defence.'[5] Up to the time of James I.'s Statute, the armour was almost invariably kept in the Church, but, by that act, magazines of arms were established in one place in each county. The Church Register of 1605 records the village arms as follows :—

'A note of the Armer laid up in the Revistrie

Ao Dni 1605 Feb: primo, and delivered

to Robte Simpson & Cuthbert Browne[6] constables.

of Thornton and Farmanby

Imp"mis   5 corsletts[7] & 5 pikes

Item   two muskets,[8] 2 murrions 2 bandeberres[9] two vests.[10]

[1] *Vide* Ch. XII.

[2] Rev. A. H.

[3] 'And further it is commanded that every man have in his house harness for to keep the peace after the ancient assize.'

[4] 4 & 5 Phil. and Mar. c. 2.

[5] Medley, *English Constitutional History* (edit. 1894) p. 421.

[6] Cuthbert Browne died 1611. His son Cuthbert Brown died in 1619; his three daughters Elizabeth, Agnes and Ellen had predeceased him, in or before 1618; his son Thomas died 1623.

[7] The corslet was of leather and was the only armour of pikemen. *Cf.* Cox, *Churchwardens' Accounts*, pp. 326-7.

[8] The musket was a heavy gun on a forked support.

[9] Bandeberres or bandoleers were small wooden or tin cases covered with leather containing a single charge for the Caliver, and fastened to a broad band of leather over the shoulder.

[10] Leather waistcoats with metal thigh pieces.

Item   two calevers[1] 2 Flaxe & touch Boxe two morions.[2]

Item   9 swords 9 dagers 6 girdles

Item   one Bow and a sheffe of arrowes, a sword and a dagger.

Item   a sleeke [?] Cape

Item   a paire of mouldes for a Callever & two wormes two rammer heads for the musket.

Barwick a muskett	John Robinson[3] a cal.
Rob[t]. Hunter[4] a muskett	William Skelton[5] a cal.
Rob[t]. White[6] a cal.	Andrew Skelton a cal.
	Will[m]. Eggleford[7] a muskett.
	Mr. Steven Miller[8] [blank].

[1] The caliver was the regulation firearm of Elizabethan days, so called from the calibre being of a certain standard.

[2] A kind of helmet without beaver or vizor.

[3] Probably the future rector before his ordination. *Vide* Ch. IX.

[4] *Vide* Ch. XII.

[5] Afterwards Churchwarden.

[6] He and his son were evidently landowners and always described as 'gentlemen.'

[7] William Ecclefield.

[8] Stephen Milnes or Mills. His will was proved 10 January, 1626. *Cf.* Y. A. S. Rec. S. LXXIII. p. 61. The C. R. says under 1562/3 'Steven Mylles son of Rauffe Mylles' was christened on 26 January.

CHAPTER FIVE.

Village Life in the Seventeenth Century.

---

*'The Justices of the Peace, be those in whom at this time
for the repressing of robbers, thieves and vagabonds of
privy complots and conspiracies, of riots and violences
and all other misdemeanours in the commonwealth, the
prince putteth his special trust.'*

THE COMMONWEALTH OF ENGLAND, 1589.

*'When the feuds ran high between Roundheads and
Cavaliers.'* ADDISON, 1711.

DESPITE the struggle made in the north of England in the
Pilgrimage of Grace in 1536, in which a lord of a Thornton
manor took a minor part,[1] despite the Rising of the Northern Earls
in 1569, the Reformation had been effected and radical changes
had been made. The ancient vestments of the priests had disappeared, the old church service had been abolished, and by the
beginning of the seventeenth century everyone had become
accustomed to the Prayer Book as enjoined by Queen Elizabeth.[2]
For some weeks after the old Queen had passed away, on 24 March,
1603, Thorntonians would be completely ignorant of the fact;
but, by the middle of April, tidings of the procession south of the
new King and his principal nobility, would reach the village by
means of those who had relatives in York, and had seen the dirty
and unattractive Scottish monarch pass through.[3] It is impossible
to imagine that the villagers were affected very seriously by the
world events that were taking place outside their borders. They
continued to live their simple lives, and, as already said, the
vagaries of the English climate were of far greater importance
to them than any dynastic problems.

Thus, in 1607, the farmers had to contend with a severe

---

[1] John, fifth Baron Latymer 1490-1543: second husband of Catherine
Parr; *vide* Ch. XI.
[2] 1 Eliz. c. 2.
[3] James I. spent 16 and 17 April in York. The latter was a Sunday
'and after much feasting, speech making and giving of presents, he was
escorted on the Monday to the southern limits of the city.' *Cf.* V. C. H.
York III. p. 417.

frost beginning in January and lasting for four months, and which seriously delayed all agriculture.[1] Eight years later, in 1614/5 their efforts were paralysed, first, by a long series of very heavy snow storms, that swept from end to end of Yorkshire between January and March;[2] secondly, by a drought so that everything was parched, as there were only two showers between 25 March and 4 August;[3] and thirdly, by the deer breaking out of the Forest.[4] The latter caused the men of Thornton to make the bitter complaint that the 'Deares have recourse day & night into the Peticioners cornfields and doe not only feed but also doe make such great waste as the Peticioners are thereby damnified.'[5] Sir Thomas Posthumous Hoby[6] and Sir John Gibson, were ordered by James I. to take steps to remedy this state of affairs, but there is no proof of what was done.

During the seventeenth century the inhabitants of Thornton, as dwellers in a normal rural parish, would find their lives and actions ordered and controlled to an extent which, under modern conditions, would be regarded as intolerable. From contemporary records we can see the working of the paternal legislation of the period, and there are numerous examples of the good and ill accomplished by the Poor Law of Elizabeth, the Highway Acts, the Tippling Acts, the laws of Bastardy and the Recusancy Acts. The justices of the peace in the seventeenth century were kept very busy indeed, and have well been called the 'State's men-of-all-work.' They looked after every branch of rural life and guided and controlled the destinies of the villagers from the cradle to the grave.

Under the Poor Law Acts of 1597[7] and 1601,[8] the justices of the peace had very considerable powers, and these they exercised with regard to a Thornton man, at the Quarter Sessions at Thirsk, on 5 April, 1608, when it was ordered that 'James Iveson, a verie poore man be provided for by two justices next unto Thornton in Pickeringlith as they in their wysdomes shall thinke fitt.'[9] It would

---

[1] Cox, *Parish Registers*, p. 205.
[2] Ibid. p. 206.
[3] Ibid. p. 217.
[4] The people complained that the deer in Blandsby Park broke out because the Park was not 'Stanch.' Parks were distinguished by the fact that they were enclosed by a wall or fence. *Cf.* G. J. Turner, *ut supra*, p. 40.
[5] G. F. G. H.
[6] For a full account of this man *vide* D. M. Meads, *Diary of Lady Margaret Hoby.*
[7] 39 Eliz. c. 3.
[8] 43 Eliz. c. 2.
[9] N. R. Rec. S. O.S. I. p. 117.

seem that James Iveson was not only 'verie poore' but also impotent, and so would be entitled to assistance under both acts. But for the non-impotent, particularly for the sturdy vagabond, there was the House of Correction, where after whipping, employment had to be found. It was with this idea of employment that the magistrates at Thirsk, on 27 April, 1652, ordered that Lieu. Colonel Nicholas Battersby, Master of the House of Correction at Pickering, shall see that manufactures of spinning and knitting be carried on, and for this purpose he shall 'sette and imploy jersey spinners and knitters both in the towne of Pickeringe and Thorneton.'[1] This evidently cost money, and the assessments did not come in with promptitude. In fact the inhabitants of Farmanby petitioned against the rate, but the justices at Malton, on 11 July, 1654, ordered 'the occupiers of the lands for the time they occupy the same to pay their just proportions for soe much as they occupied towards the making of the sum in arrears.'[2]

Later in the century, however, after the Law of Settlement had been passed in 1662,[3] parish authorities became more drastic. No parish desired the poor of another, and the act allowed the removal of any stranger within forty days, back to his own parish where he had obtained a settlement, which was a continuous residence of forty days, unless the newcomer could give sufficient security that he would never become chargeable to his new place of settlement.[4] This was one of the problems with which the magistrates had to deal at Quarter Sessions at Helmsley, on 12 January, 1674/5. They ordered that 'a man with his wife and children....be permitted to remain at Thornton, and to be settled there for the future unless the inhabts of Thornton should show good cause' why he and his family should be removed.[5] Apparently they did show 'good cause,' or the man and his wife failed to show that they 'would never become chargeable.' Which ever way it was, on 13 April, 1675, at the Quarter Sessions at Thirsk, the Parish Officer of Thornton was given leave to remove the man and his wife and children 'to Middleton the place of their last legal settlement.'[6] It was owing to such laws as these that 'the iron of

---

[1] Ibid. V. pp. 107, 117.
[2] Ibid. p. 162. Ibid. pp. 12, 28, show that in July, 1648, the parish officers of Thornton were not very prompt in paying over the £20 they had received as poor rate. The magistrates at Malton ordered them to pay £2 to a poor woman of Ellerburn.
[3] 14 Car. II. c. 12.
[4] Medley, *ut supra*, p. 367.
[5] N. R. Rec. S. O.S. VI. p. 228.
[6] Ibid. p. 234.

slavery entered into the soul of the English labourer.'[1]

In the same spirit of paternal government the justices enforced the practically useless Highway Acts. At Quarter Sessions at Helmsley on 8 July, 1612, when Robert Hunter[2] was one of the Chief Constables of Pickeringlithe, Valentine Story[3] and William Skelton, Churchwardens of Thornton, were summoned for 'not appointing Surveyours for the highe waies,[4] according to the Act.'[5] The old levy of actual labour, under the Act, was gradually commuted for a money payment or assessment. No distinctions were made between ownership and occupation, residence and non-residence.[6] The inhabitants of Farmanby evidently did not approve of these rural assessments, and were indicted before Quarter Sessions at Malton, on 11 July, 1650, 'for not repairing their common pynfold.'[7] Under the Acts, on 8 July, 1651, at Quarter Sessions at Helmsley, 'the inhabts of Thornton and Farmanby' were indicted for not repairing the highway between 'Farmanby Gate and Thorneton';[8] and it was also decided that 'Roger Hunt[er] and Wm Skelton ought to pay their assts towardes the repair of Thorneton Bridge,[9] over the water called Thorneton Beck.'[10] This bridge was evidently in very bad condition, for at Quarter Sessions at Thirsk, on 17 April, 1652, £13. 6s. 8d. was allowed for its repair.[11]

Far harsher laws were those dealing with bastardy. An act of 1572,[12] had enjoined that, in order that the support of illegitimate children should not defraud the aged and impotent poor of their relief, the justices should place the burden of such a child's support upon its parents. Subsequent legislation made an attempt to

---

[1] Fowle, *History of the Poor Law*, p. 63.

[2] *Vide* Ch. XII.

[3] The Church Register says 'Old Valentine Story haveing been Parish Clarke 55 years [was buried] aged 89 years' on 31 December, 1663. A relative of his 'old John Story of Pickeringe was perished in ye way to the Marish and was buried ye ninth of Novemb.' 1658. The will of Robert Story 'linnen weaver' of Farmanby was administered by Margaret Story relict, on 20 April, 1657. *Cf.* Y. A. S. Rec. S. I. p. 175.

[4] N. R. Rec. S. O.S. I. p. 261.

[5] Under Mary (2 & 3 Phil. and Mary c. 8) a surveyor of highways was to be elected by the vestry, who could levy on all individual owners in the parish a rate in kind, such as the loan of a cart or actual manual labour for the repair of the local highways. *Cf.* Medley, *ut supra*, p. 361.

[6] Ibid.

[7] N. R. Rec. S. O.S. V. p. 84. The pinfold still stands in Maltongate. It might be noted that a Farmanby man was fined 10s. at Malton, on 15 July, 1653, 'for breaking the pinfold.' *Cf.* N. R. Rec. S. O.S. V. p. 136.

[8] Ibid. p. 76.

[9] A foot bridge until about 1830.

[10] N. R. Rec. S. O.S. V. p. 78.

[11] Ibid. p. 105.

[12] 18 Eliz. c. 3. sec. 2.

punish the parents. Thus, under an act of James I., the mother was to be imprisoned with hard labour,[1] but this was not passed till 1623.[2] The magistrates, therefore at Malton, on 12 January, 1607/8, had no such act to guide them, and they ordered 'John Collyson of Thornton his recogs be respited till the next sessions, and that a warrant be made directed to the Constable of Farnaby [Farmanby] and Richard Dale to apprehend the said Collison and bring him....to answere....touching a bastard child begotten [as alleged] by him on Agnes Preston, and in the meantime Richard Dale of Farnaby, being Collison's suretie, shall paie 8d. weekly towards the relieff of the said child.'[3] In much the same way, the jury[4] at Quarter Sessions at Helmsley, on 9 January, 1622/3, considered the case of two Thornton men, and the magistrate ordered that 'Fr Horsley of Thornton, gentn., and Tho. Lodge of Farmanbie, glover, shall enter bond with verie good sureties to appear at the next Easter Sessns to answer &c for begetting of a bastard child on the bodie of Kath. Longe.'[5] These moral questions very much exercised the justices, particularly in the time of the Commonwealth. Thornton seems to have been remarkably free from offences in this way, and there is only one case, during this period, of a Thornton woman having to appear before Quarter Sessions at Kirkby Moorside on 9 January, 1654/5, 'for fornication'; and the sentence was that she be 'committ to gaole.'[6] Had this charge been brought at any time, other than the Commonwealth period, the unfortunate would have had to do public penance in Thornton Church, standing either on a form or in the middle aisle, with bare feet, clad in a white sheet and holding a taper. At that day, however, the sanctity of the Church was little respected, and the harsh treatment in gaol was regarded as more likely to be efficacious.

Brewing offences were very numerous. The sale of beer had been somewhat restricted by Parliament in 1606.[7] Thus, acting within their powers, the justices at Pickering, on 12 April, 1611, fined Roger Horsley of 'Fermanby' for selling ale above the assize, and John Shawe of Ellerburn, Peter Metcalfe of 'Dalbie,' Thomas

---

[1] Medley, *ut supra*, p. 370.
[2] 21 Jac. I. c. 27.
[3] N. R. Rec. S. O.S. I. p. 103.   The Church Registers show a John Collinson married Kateran Barughe, 26 September, 1590.
[4] On this jury was James Dale of 'Farmanbie' yeoman. *Cf.* N. R. Rec. S. O.S. III. p. 155.
[5] Ibid. p. 159.
[6] Ibid. V. p. 173.
[7] 4 Jac. I. c. 4.   Repealed 9 Geo. IV. sec. 35.

Browne and Christopher Boyes, both of Thornton, for brewing contrary to the Act.[1] Under the same statute the justices at Helmsley, on 10 July, 1611, ordered that 'William Preston of "Ellerborne" having, by his own confession brewed without licence since Michaelmas last, be fined 20s. and that he be imprisoned in York Castle for three daies....and be not there discharged until he enter recognces &c., not to offend again in the same way.'[2] On 28 April, 1615, at Special Sessions held at Snainton, when Robert Hunter was Chief Constable, and one of the jurymen was John Story of Thornton, the jury presented two ale-house keepers in Farmanby and Thornton, for brewing contrary to the assize.[3] Other Thornton men also got into trouble for drinking too much of the good malt liquor. So on 12 January, 1609/10, at Richmond it was ordered 'that Edw. Robynson of Roxby near Pickering, confessinge himself once drunken at a meeting, be fined 5s.'[4] Again, on 8 January, 1612/3, at Helmsley Quarter Sessions, the worthy churchwarden 'Will. Skelton of Thornton, yeoman' got into a sad scrape 'for absenting himself from the church on the Saboath day and sitting drinking in the ale-house.'[5] This was a terrible lapse from the straight and narrow way, and also a breach of trust, for it was his duty to see 'that all the parishioners duly resort to their church upon all Sundays and Holy days,' and how could he act as the mentor of the parish being convicted as a backslider? It was a bad example, as seen on 4 April, 1616, when George Smales, the village constable of Thornton, had to appear at Special Sessions at Hutton Bushel. Here he was confronted with several fellow-villagers on the jury, such as Robert Hunter, junior, of Thornton, Roger Keddey, yeoman of Farmanby and 'George Smales, Thornton yeoman.' The latter it is to be presumed was his relative and not the accused himself. The jury presented him for keeping an ale-house and selling 'ale in scales [bowls] and pottes not sealed above 4d. &c.'[6] This was a particularly heavy day for Thornton, for after dealing with the case of George Smales, there were two presentments of Thornton men for brewing contrary to the act, two men were charged with distempering themselves 'with drinkinge,' a Farmanby man and four others were charged with the same offence as George Smales, and one of the four was

[1] N. R. Rec. S. O.S. I. p. 223.
[2] Ibid. p. 193.
[3] Ibid. II. p. 94.
[4] Ibid. I. p. 179.
[5] Ibid. II. p. 7.
[6] Ibid. p. 111.

also charged with wanting 'stable and lodging,' two other Farmanby men were said to have been 'sitting drinking in the house of one of the other five.' A Thornton man was also brought before the justices 'for abusing himself with drinking having gott too much ale,' and another for 'drinking till he laid drunke at the townes end.'[1]

To many good people, of those days, play acting savoured too much of the devil, and a Statute of Queen Elizabeth[2] was aimed against 'common players in interludes and miustrees, not belonging to any baron of this realm.' The Puritans looked upon these players[3] as 'drunken sockets and bawdye parasits as range the cuntreys, ryming a singing of vncleane corrupt and filthie songs in tauernes, ale-houses, innes and other publique assemblies.'[4] It was in this way that these players were regarded by the North Riding magistrates. The justices of Thirsk, on 12 April, 1616, ordered 'Richard Hudson of Huton Bushell, weaver, 49 years of age' to be whipped in the town of Thirsk, and that other punishment should be meted out to 'Will. Hudson, 12, George Hudson, 11, Chr. Hutchinson of Hutton Bushell, 16, Edw. Lister of Allerston, weaver, 46, Roger Lister of the same, 7 and upwards, and Robert Skelton of Wilton, near Pickering, 7 and upwards, as players of Enterludes, vagabundes and sturdy beggars &c.,' and Will. West of Buttercrambe for harbouring them and supplying them with food.[5] They not only got themselves into trouble, but also their friends, for already, on 4 April, 'An' Shaw, an Ellerburn widow, had been charged at Hutton Bushel with 'entertayninge' Edward Lister and his company to 'act a stage play or interlude in her house.'[6] Several of these players were incorrigible, for the following were again charged at Thirsk, on 7 April, 1619, 'Edw. Lister, aged 52, of Allerston, Roger Lister of Buttercramb, Tho. and Luke Birdsall[7] of Thornton in 'Pickering lieth,' all weavers. . . .all above

---

[1] Ibid. pp. 117, 118. Towne's end or Town End is where the four roads from Pickering and Scarborough, and Hurrell's Lane and Utgang Way cross.

[2] 14 Eliz. c. 5. sec. 5.

[3] *Cf.* how Gilbert Theaker, the piper of Thornton, was fined at Special Sessions at Snainton, 1 July, 1614, 'for a meeting of young people.' N. R. Rec. S. O.S. II, p. 51.

[4] Philip Stubbes in *Anatomy of Abuses*, pub. 1583.

[5] N. R. Rec. S. O.S. II. p. 122.

[6] Ibid. p. 119. What this play 'in her house' could have been like is beyond imagination for there can have been no room in any of the tiny cottages at Ellerburn in which, to use an old expression 'you could swing a cat.' For the smallness of the Cleveland cottages, *cf.* F. Y. in M. P. pp. 24-25.

[7] An old Thornton family. The first appeared about 1499, and the last died 13 April, 1909, aged 88.

the age of 7, as Common Players of Interludes &c. playing at New Malton and divers places.[1]

Assaults were fairly common during the period; nor were these always confined to the rougher elements of society. On 8 October, 1606, Ralph Hassell and Thomas Hassell[2] (shortly afterwards to be connected with Thornton), with their companions, were presented at Quarter Sessions at Malton, 'for riotously assembling with many others to the number of twenty persons and assaulting at Cony-stropp on Sept. 5, 1606....collectors or deputies of the High Sheriff.'[3] In 1611, there must have been a fine to-do at Ellerburn, as afterwards appeared at Quarter Sessions at Malton, on 3 October, when 'Ralph Watson yom[n] and Rich. Watson, Jun[r] of Ellerborne ....Rob. Shawe and Roger Watson of Ellerborne, Edw. Elrington, yeom[n], and Margery Watson, spinster of the same, [were indicted] for an assault and affray on Richard Wiles,[4] and at a place in Ellerborne called le Bothome Close, making a rescue of three oxen seised and distrained to the great loss of the said Wiles.'[5] It is clear that the magistrates regarded the assault a very serious one, for considering the then value of money the fines were heavy. Ralph Watson was fined 20s. Richard Watson and Robert Shawe 6s. 8d. each and Margery Watson 12d.[6] The 'godliness' of the Commonwealth period did not check these assaults and affrays. 'A Thornton gentleman' was charged with assault, on 11 January, 1652/3, at Kirkby Moorside, but nothing seems to have come of it.[7] A year later, a Thornton yeoman, for the same offence was fined 1s.;[8] while, on 27 April, 1652,[9] at Thirsk, 'four yeomen of Farmanby' were charged and fined 3s. 6d. each, for 'forcible entry.'[10] On 14 July, 1657, at Malton 'a fellmonger of Thornton' for 'assault and affray' was mulcted 6s. 8d.;[11] and a 'Thornton tailor,' at Helmsley, for a similar misdemeanour, got off with a fine of 5s.

---

[1] N. R. Rec. S. O.S. II. p. 197.

[2] *Vide* Ch. VII.

[3] N. R. Rec. S. O.S. I. p. 49.

[4] In 1635 Richard Wiles of Farmanby is described as a gentleman. He is charged with being a recusant *vide infra*. One imagines that he must have been a member of the family Wyles mentioned in 1334 when Ralph Hastings was bail for poaching offences for William Wyles son of Peter Wyles. But neither of the latter were residents in Thornton though residents in the district.

[5] N. R. Rec. S. O.S. I. p. 227.

[6] Ibid. p. 239.

[7] Ibid. p. 123.

[8] Ibid. p 147

[9] Ibid. p. 102.

[10] *Cf.* 21. Jac. I. c. 15.

[11] N. R. Rec. S. O.S. I. p. 242.

because he submitted himself to the Court on 22 January, 1657/8.[1]

As to thefts there were a fair number of these, but not as many, perhaps, as might have been expected, when poverty was great, property was not respected and life was held very cheap. At Quarter Sessions at Malton, when one of the jurymen was Richard Wait,[2] yeoman of Thornton, the jury presented, on 12 January, 1607/8, 'Matilda Wilkinson, late of Thornton in "Pickering-lith," spinster, for stealing at Thornton a pair of stockins of the value of 3d. of the goods of George Clarke; also for stealing "unam tunicam *Anglice* a petty cote" of the value of 4d. belonging to Anne Boyes; also for stealing "unam peciam linei panni *Anglice* a neckerchief" valued 3d. from Jas. Jennyson.' The judgement on these three charges,[3] was that 'the saide Mawde to be whipped in Malton presently, and from thence to be conveyed from Constable to Constable to Thorneton, there to be whipped upon a holly day (it not being a Sonday) after Evening prayer tyme from the Church Stile to the place of her late dwelling there.'[4] On 26 April, 1609, the magistrates ordered at Thirsk that 'as Tho. Blackborne of Thornton has confessed to stealing of a goose....he be sett in the stocks at Thirsk and whipped.'[5] Elizabeth Browne,[6] late of 'Farmanby in Pickering-lith,' must have been a daring woman, for she committed a burglary in the house of William Lee of 'Wickham' [Wykeham], and stole a pewter-basin valued 10d., for which crime she appeared before the justices at Malton, on 3 October, 1611,[7] and they handed her over 'to the Sheriff, and a *mittimus* was to be made to convey her to gaole.'[8] There is only one case of timber stealing in the period which is reminiscent of the forest trespasses of the fourteenth century. Thomas Robinson[9] of 'Thorneton,' in 1618 'cut downe and caryed awaye one oke in Newton dale at a place called Hollenheade worth vjs. viijd.'[10] A year after the event the jury reported the fact to the authorities at Pickering, but little or nothing seems to have happened. A much more common cause of theft was the desire to obtain yarn, material or

[1] Ibid. p. 258.
[2] Ibid. p. 101.
[3] A side note says 'Judicium de hiis tribus.'
[4] N. R. Rec. S. O.S. I. p. 103.
[5] Ibid. I. p. 155.
[6] Was she the daughter of Cuthbert Browne ? *Vide* Ch. IV.
[7] N. R. Rec. S. O.S. I. p. 237.
[8] Ibid. p. 239.
[9] Probably Thomas 'Robynson' son of John, baptised 22 January, 15923/: married Elizabeth Hicke, 30 November, 1626: died 27 February 1660/1. Evidently a respectable member of society as he was a trustee in a conveyance in M. T. 1617. *Cf.* Y. A. S. Rec. S. LVIII. p. 98.
[10] N. R. Rec. S. N.S. I. p. 30.

goods that would assist in weaving. This was John Marshall's temptation, for which he was punished at Malton, on 9 January, 1621/2, being charged as a 'Thornton in Pickering lieth lab^r,' who had 'stolen 17 pounds of wollen yarne value, 10s.'[1] The same kind of thing was the undoing, on 8 January, 1623/4, of a man called 'Bothrode,'[2] 'a fuller of Thornton near Pickering,' who stole 'a pair of fullours sheeres from a shop,' valued at 16s.[3] It was probably grinding necessity, rather than trade interests, that persuaded the unnamed 'lab^r of Thornton' to steal in the autumn of 1652 'two pecks and a half of wheat and rye' valued at 2s. He was found guilty of stealing sixpennyworth and ordered to be whipped.[4] It must have been the same necessity of starvation that drove another 'Thorneton lab^r.' to steal 'three quarters of mutton'[5] valued at 16d., and 'three quarters of honey' valued at 18d., 'the goods of whom not known.' The poor man 'putts himself not guiltie,' and it is to be hoped that the magistrates found him so, on 11 January, 1652/3.[6] But there can have been little excuse for the son of the Rector, 'Sam Robinson of Thorneton,' to seal 'a lease of ejectment under pretence of searching for stolne goods.' This was mere high-handedness, and the magistrates, on that same January day, fined him 40s.[7] Nor is it possible to have any sympathy with another Thornton man, tried at the same time, 'and committed to the custody of the Shirrif till he finde securities to be of good behaviour for seaven years, he being a person that hath committed severall felonyes, often committ to the gaole and a person of dissolute life.'[8]

Another breach of the law, for which a few unfortunate people had from time to time to appear before the magistrates, was solely because of their religion and sturdiness of conscience. The Statutes they disobeyed were known as the Recusancy Laws, and were, in some parts carried out very harshly, and in others there was little or nothing to fear. Ever since 1559, the Churchwardens

[1] N. R. Rec. S. O.S. III. p. 129.

[2] This man's name may have been 'Boothroyd'; but it is noticeable that in the village at the time there was a Richard Butteroyde and Elizabeth his wife. *Cf.* Y. A. S. Rec. S. LVIII. p. 98.

[3] N. R. Rec. S. O.S. III. p. 188.

[4] Ibid. V. p. 117.

[5] This reminds one of the poor labourer at 'Kinthorpe,' who for 'stealing' one ewe sheep, valued at 3s. 4d. was found guilty at Malton, on 13 January, 1651/2. He evidently pleaded 'benefit of clergy' and was ordered 'to be burnt in the hand.' *Cf.* N. R. Rec. S. O.S. V. p. 90; and for 'benefit of clergy' and 'being branded' *cf.* Holdsworth, *History of English Law*, VI. p. 406.

[6] N. R. Rec. S. O.S. V. p. 123.

[7] Ibid.

[8] Ibid. p. 127.

had been given large powers to force the population to attend Church and they were directed to levy 12d. on all absentees;[1] which fine, in the reign of James I., could be enforced by a justice of the peace.[2] Those who naturally refrained persistently from Church attendance were those who could not accept the Elizabethan *via media*—the Roman Catholics and Dissenters. The former were commonly known as recusants,[3] and were perpetually harried. They were liable after 1581, to a very heavy fine and to suffer one year's imprisonment.[4] All persons over sixteen years of age who refused to attend Church were to be fined £20 for every month so offending, or, if the sovereign so desired, two-thirds of their land could be withheld from them until they should conform.[5] All recusants were barred from the legal and medical professions;[6] nor could they act as magistrates, or municipal, civil or military officials.[7] Thus the laws against them were many and severe. The first of this district to appear in a list, that shames one for its intolerance, were 'Richard Dutton, gentleman and his wyf [of Dalby] for not receying the holie comunion at Easter last [at Pickering],' on 6 September, 1591.[8] The next in the hateful record was 'Isabell Sympson' of Thornton, aged 66, who was declared a recusant in 1611.[9] Quite a number were presented both from 'Farmanby in Ellerburne,' on 30 September, 1624, including Mary, wife of Richard Wyles, gentleman, and from Thornton, Ralph Salvin[10] Esq. and Ursula Hebton, spinster, his servant, together with Mary Kildale, spinster and Ann Hodgson, widow.[11] Richard Wyles was presented on 8 October, 1634,[12] and Hildah Hunter, spinster,

[1] 1 Eliz. c. 2. sec. 14. H. Prideaux, *Directions to Churchwardens*, p. 5 considers that the fine could be exacted if a person refrained from staying to the end of the service.

[2] 3 Jac. 1. c. 4. sec. 27.

[3] Burn, *The Justice of the Peace* (1769), III. pp. 181-2 shows that the term recusant need not necessarily apply only to Roman Catholics.

[4] 23 Eliz. c. 1. sec. 4. One lady connected with Thornton to suffer, was the Roman Catholic wife of Sir Henry Cholmley, but this was more during the time they lived at Whitby. Her grandson Sir Hugh Cholmley in his *Memoirs* says that she harboured numerous 'seminary priests coming from beyond seas. . . . all which Sir Henry connived at, being a little then in his heart inclining that way, though he went to church. . . . she was often carried to and kept long in prison, as were most of the eminent Papists in those times.'

[5] Ibid. sec. 5, and 3 Jac. I. c. 4 sec. 8.

[6] 3 Jac. I. c. 5 sec. 8.

[7] 13 Car. II. stat. 2 c. 1 and 25 Car. II. c. 2. It was not until 31 Geo. III. c. 32 that Roman Catholics were legally released from the obligation of attendance at Church.

[8] Y. A. J. 1905, p. 219.

[9] N. R. Rec. S. O.S. III. p. 81.

[10] Of the old Yorkshire family and a relative of the Cholmleys. He was baptised in Thornton Church on 3 May, 1590. *Vide* C.R.

[11] N. R. Rec. S. O.S. III. pp. 211, 225.

[12] Ibid. IV. p. 21.

daughter of Anthony Hunter, gentleman, together with Robert Rogerson of Farmanby were similarly charged on 5 October, 1636.[1] Richard Wyles and Robert Rogerson were again presented on 2 October, 1639.[2] The latter was evidently a stout adherent of the old faith, for on 13 July, 1658,[3] a warrant was issued for him to appear before the next justice of the peace,[4] to answer 'wherefore he continueth to teach a school' in Farmanby, 'being a convict Recusant.'[5] These non-conformists were always liable to trouble from unkind neighbours and from common-informers, so that it is some satisfaction to hear that one of the latter, William Spavin of York, tailor, claiming to be a common informer, was trapped and punished. He was accused at Helmsley, on 9 January, 1615/6, of 'receiving divers sums, varying from 1s. to 9s. 6d. from seven different persons living in Thornton near Pickering, and making a composition with them without authority. He submitted himself to the mercy of the court and was fined 10s.[6] Amongst dissenters who were reported and fined for 'not repairing to the parish church' in July, 1670 were Robert and Elizabeth Gamble, Robert and Sarah Smales, Richard and Anne Todd, John Mayman and Jane Chapman [7]

Another unhappy body of non-conformists treated, at first, severely by the magistrates, was that of the Quakers. They were heavily penalised by what is generally called the Clarendon Code; but, in particular, by the Conventicle Act of 1664.[8] By this any person over 16 years of age attending a meeting other than that of the Church of England, 'where five persons more than the household were present,' was liable to three months imprisonment on the first conviction; and in 1670, persons convicted of preaching at a conventicle were to forfeit £20 for the first offence, and a similar forfeiture was the penalty for permitting a conventicle

---

[1] Ibid. p. 60.
[2] Ibid. p. 123.
[3] Ibid. VI. p. 8.
[4] This brave old schoolmaster reminds us of another who was buried on 14 January, 1648/9. The Thornton Burial Register says 'Richard Throssell buried the 14th. of Januarie att Allastone [Allerston] hee dyed at Crosscliffe where hee taught children.' It does not appear that he lived in Crosscliffe, and if not what buffetings of wind and weather this gallant man must have experienced in the interests of education and for the sake of isolated moorland farm children. All honour to him.
[5] Rogerson had broken two main acts. By 23 Eliz. c. 1 sec. 6 a schoolmaster must attend Church: and by 1 Jac. I. c. 4 sec. 9 a schoolmaster must be licenced by the ordinary.
[6] N. R. Rec. S. O.S. II. p. 111.
[7] Ibid. VI. p. 148.
[8] 16 Car. II. c. 2.

in a house.[1] Such was the persecution accorded to those who, for conscience sake, withdrew from the Church. Of these Quakers the Priestmans were the most important family in Thornton.[2] The name first occurs in the Registers as early as 1544, and from that date there are regular entries until 1672, when they ceased to appear, save very exceptionally, because the family had become, by that time, members of 'The Society of Friends.' The Priestmans were, therefore, some of the earliest to join that body, founded by George Fox, in or about 1650. One can imagine that one of them had been drawn to Pickering, when George Fox preached there in 1665, in what he called the 'Steeple-house,'[3] and that his words produced conversion. For forty years, perhaps, they suffered much, but in 1700, the house of John Priestman,[4] that is Beck Hole,[5] was licensed for 'devine' worship for Quakers,[6] and they ceased to be troubled by the Anglican magistracy.[7]

All these checks on individualism whether religious, moral, just or unjust, were, in a sense, more tiresome than calamitous. The worst disaster of all that could fall on a village in the seventeenth century was an outbreak of infectious disease, and the terror of the plague was destined to burst upon Thornton and Ellerburn. The loathesome bubonic plague, originally imported from the East, was never out of England from 1348 to 1679; but, in the first half of the seventeenth century it was particularly common, and though by no means so virulent as it had been either in the fourteenth or fifteenth centuries, was bad enough. Villagers tried to combat its entry by employing night watchmen, and chains were drawn across the roads[8] to keep out strangers who might possibly carry the infection. In 1624 there was a severe outbreak at Scarborough,[9] and the Thornton people probably began to take precautions. Two years later, owing to the import

[1] 22 Car. II. c. 1 sec. 1.
[2] *Vide* Ch. VII.
[3] Fox's *Journal*.
[4] N. R. Rec. S. O.S. VII. p. 176.
[5] Another 'John Priestman in the becke hole' was buried 14 September, 1658.
[6] There is an interesting reference in the Thornton Baptismal Register to Quakers. 'Elizabeth Robinson born at Pickering having neither father nor mother living, brought [up] by a Quaker, aged nineteen or thereabouts, was baptised 21st. of May 1682.'
[7] Perhaps the magistrates were not as harsh as the laws they were supposed to administer, as State Papers Domestic, 225 doc. 131 shows that 'the magistrates do not put the least check on conventicles.' F. Y. in M. P. p. 223, shows that Quakers were numerous in North-East Yorkshire at the end of the seventeenth century.
[8] 1 Jac. I. c. 31.
[9] N. R. Rec. S. O.S. III. p. 227.

of infected goods from London, there were numerous cases in Malton, Huttons Ambo, Wykeham and Hutton Bushel.[1] But still Thornton was free until at last, in May, 1638, it reached the village which it struck with great force considering the small population. In seven weeks 19 persons died, while the average number of deaths per annum for the six previous years was $8\frac{1}{2}$.[2] The best and most speaking account is to be found in the Church Registers, written by the Rev. John Robinson, who must have been sorely shaken by this blow to his little flock. 'Roger Sawer buryed the 16th. day of May, whose house was the first house that was suspeckted to have the plague in it after a child died in the house. Hee was a man well beloved soe that all the tyme of his sicknesse his nighbours did much use his house, untill his death and wente to the Church wth him, yet blessed be God for his preventinge mercie few of them take any hurt by it.'

'Elizabeth Cowltus buryed the 19th day of May. She died in the house of Roger Sawer, her bodye, being spotted, wrought greate feare that it was the plague.

Henrye Robinson sonne of Thomas Robinson, a child buried the 25th. day of May dyed of of [*sic*] the plague.

Elizabeth Marshall, an old blynd woman was buryed the 9th day of June, it was thought she dyed of the plague by her daughter cominge into the house to her, and the plague on her, but dyed not.

Elizabeth Sawer, wife of John Sawer, was buried the 10th. day of June dyed of the plague.

Robert Westwood, son of Richard Westwood, a suckling child, was buryed the 3 day of June, dyed of the plague wch. came (as it was thought) by his mother frequenttinge Tho. Robinson's house.

---

[1] Ibid. p. 275.

[2] The following selected statistics may be of interest :—

Christened	1539—18	1540—11	1541—13	1542—17	1543—13
	1544—17	1545—20	1547—14	1548—14	1549—20
	1550—27	1624—11	1625—11	1627—19	1628— 6
	1632—13	1633—11	1634—12	1635—11	1636—11
	1638— 8	1639—15	1640—13	1641—13	1642—13
	1643— 2	1644— 6	1645—11	1646—17	
Married	1623— 5	1624— 4	1625— 4	1626— 2	1627— 4
	1628— 1	1629— 1	1631— 2	1633— 3	1634— 4
	1635— 2	1636— 3	1637— 2	1638— 6	1639— 7
	1640— 4	1641— 7	1644— 1	1645— 1	1646— 7
	1647— 4	1649— 1	1650— 6	1652— 4	1675— 4
Buried	1606—13	1607—12	1608— 8	1622—23	1623—15
	1624— 9	1625—14	1626—18	1627—24	1628— 9
	1631—14	1632— 2	1633— 5	1634—13	1635—10
	1636—15	1637— 6	1638—33	1639—12	1640—14
	1642— 7	1644— 5	1645—10	1646— 4	1647—12
	1648—13	1649—10	1650—17	1651—12	1652—21
	1653— 7	1675—10			

John Stevenson buryed the 4th. day of June dyed of the plague, hee was of the p̄ish of Ellerborne.

Anne Throssell buryed the 5th. day of June, dyed of the plague.

Tho. Robinson, sonne of Tho. Robinson buryed ye 5th. day of June, dyed of the plague.

Margritt Cowllom, doughter of Richard Cowllom, buryed the 10th. day of June, she was of the p̄ishe of Ellerborne, it was thought by those that viewed her she died not of the plague.

John Sawer buried the 11th. day of June, dyed of the plague.

Margrett Bankes, doughter of Jayne Banke buried the 11th. day of June, dyed of the plague.

Elizabeth Petch, servant to Margritt Wilkinson buryed the 12th. day of June, dyed of the plague.

Tho. Watson, sonne of Tho. Watson buryed the 16th day of Julye [*sic* ? June] an infant, the house was not infected with the plague.

Richard Cowllom and Anne Cowllom his wife, buried 22nd. day of June, they weare of the parish of Ellerborne dyed at the pest houses of the plague.

Margritt Wilkinson, widow buryed the 25th. day of June dyed att the pest houses of the plague.

Marye Greene of the p̄ish of Ellerborne buryed the 29 day June dyed att the pest houses of the plague.

Easter Bankes doughter of Jayne Bankes buried the 29th day of June, dyed att the pesthouses of the plague.

Henrie Marshall, an infante sonne of Willm Marshall buried the 6th. day of Julye died att the pest houses.

Isabell Green, widow of Ellerborne parish buryed the 7th. day of Julye, dyed of the plague at the pest houses, after this thayr was was [*sic*] not one dyed of the plague in both parrishshes until the 27 day of August nor any one after of the plague (blesse be God.)'[1]

There had been numerous acts passed concerning the plague, particularly in the sixteenth century; but there was one act of 1603,[2] peculiarly applicable to this outbreak, which authorized mayors and other local officials to tax the inhabitants of any city, borough, etc. for the relief of those in it, sick of the plague; and if the means of the place itself were inadequate, then to tax the county within a circuit of five miles from the place, in which the infected were to be put under the strictest laws of quarantine.[3] The powers given under this act were now put in operation, though the

[1] C. R.
[2] 1 Jac. I. c. 31.
[3] N. R. Rec. S. O.S. I. p. 3.

justices did not hesitate to go beyond 'the five mile limit.' On
10 July, 1638, the justices at Quarter Sessions at Malton, agreed
that 'whereas £25 was Ordered to be assessed for the relief of
the inhab[ts] of Thornton in Pickering lieth, nowe infected with the
plague, within five miles thereof, and the infection still continues
[to quote the parson, 'blesse be God' it had ceased], £100. be
levied throughout the N. R. for the relief of the inhab[ts] of the said
town, and Roger Wivell and John Caley Esq[res] are requested to see
the same carefully applied.'[1] It was found, however, at Helmsley,
on 8 January, 1638/9, that the £100 were unnecessary 'for the
relief of Thornton near Pickering, infected with the plague,' and
only £46. 0s. 8d.,[2] had been expended. And so Thornton passed
through its hour of agony and survived.

Soon after the prosperity of the parish was again checked by
a very severe winter in 1641-2, and the roads in the neighbourhood
were rendered impassable from November to February.[3] This, a
purely local and agricultural disaster,[4] was followed by the terrible
national disaster of the Civil War.

On the whole, Thornton escaped many of the horrors of the
Great Rebellion; but the villagers must have seen the comings
and goings of armed men to and from Scarborough; they must
have heard of Sir Hugh Cholmley's fight near Malton,[5] and they
must have seen his messengers dashing through occasionally to
other commanders in the district. The Church Registers show
that soldiers were billeted[6] in the village without improving
its morality, so, for example, it is recorded[7] that 'Elday Willyamson
al[ia]s Shepheard d. of Elizabeth Wilyamson [was] baptized the
10 day of Julye 1647. She fathered the child at the bearth of it
of one Nicholasse Shiphard, a Troper that was quartered in the

---

[1] Ibid. IV. p. 99.

[2] Ibid. p. 110.

[3] *Memoirs of Sir Hugh Cholmley*.

[4] 'The century was distinguished.... for the curious number of cycles
of good and bad seasons: 1646-50 were years of prolonged dearth, wheat
reaching an enormous price, and 1661-2 were famine years, while the end
of the century was long famous for its barren years.' *Cf.* W. H. R. Curtler,
History of Agriculture, p. 115.

[5] *Vide* Ch. XV.

[6] This illegal billeting, illegal because of the Petition of Right of 1628,
seems to have started before the outbreak of the Civil War. It was complained
of at Quarter Sessions at Malton as early as 11 January, 1641/2, where it was
said 'for as much as the countrie hath beene very sore oppressed and put to
griate charge by reason of souldiers billeted in most partes of the N. R. soe
that diverse poore men and others have been forcte [? forced] by meanie of
the saide souldiers to break the law.' This must refer to the Bishop's War.
Cf. N. R. Rec. S. O.S. IV. pp. 214-5 and Y. A. J. I. p. 91.

[7] C.R.

Town.'[1]   The Quarter Sessions Records also prove that a few
Thorntonians lost their lives. At Thirsk it was stated, on 3 October,
1648, that 'whereas Rob. Dawson of Thornton in Pickering lythe
was slain in the service of the Parliament and has left a widow and
divers small children in distressed circumstances, and whereas there
is an Ordinance of Parliament providing for the releife of the said
wife and children, the Court requests the two next Justices to
attend to the matter according to their discretion.' On 3 April,
1649, it was agreed that the Treasurer for Lame Soldiers should
pay to Dawson's widow '40s. in hand and 25s. quarterly till further
order.'[2] Another instance came before the magistrates at Kirkby
Moorside, on 10 July, 1649, when it was decided that 'Richard
Marshall of Farmanby parish, a souldier under Capt. Wade, having
been slain in the Parliament's service before Pontefract Castle,[3]
and having left a widow and three children, one of which children
is lame and necessitated to be relieved of the almes of the parish,
Mr. Marm. Norcliffe Thre[r] for L.S. [Lame Soldiers] to pay Alice
Marshall[4]....20s. as a gratuity for her and her children, and the
H.C.[8] [High Constables] for Pickering Lythe to pay her 2s. 6d.
a week till further Order.'[5]

There is no information, however, as to the royalists. The
parliamentarians had won when Naseby had been fought and lost
by the King in June, 1645, and still more triumphant were they
when Charles' head fell beneath the axe on that snowy winter's day,
30 January, 1649. There was no chance for benefactions for the
widows and orphans of those who had adhered to their sovereign.
And yet there must have been some. Is it possible that Sir Hugh
Cholmley drilled the militia on Pexton Moor for the Bishop's War

---

[1] This means that the wretched mother before the child had been
delivered had been brow-beaten by the midwife to confess. At that period
midwives were licensed by the Bishop, not only because in emergency they
might be called upon to baptise the child, but also that they might report
to the Ecclesiastical Court any one suspected of being unmarried, and before
assisting in bringing the child into the world they were to do their best to
persuade the poor mother to declare the name of the father. This grim
piece of work had evidently been done.
[2] N. R. Rec. S. O.S. V. pp. 16, 30. The first statutes for sick and maimed
soldiers were 35 Eliz. c. 4 and 39 Eliz. c. 21. These were repealed and
re-enacted 43 Eliz. c. 3.
[3] On Christmas Day, 1644, the parliamentarians under Fairfax occupied
the town of Pontefract and began to siege the castle defended by Sir Richard
Lowther. There was a second siege begun on 21 March, 1644/5. For these
sieges *cf.* Sur. Soc. XXXVII.
[4] This widow lost her son in 1651 as the Register says 'Thomas Marshall
buried the 29th. of Januarie [1651] his father was slayn att Pomfritt beinge
in the Parlant service.'
[5] N. R. Rec. S. O.S. V. p. 34.

in 1639,[1] and that not one followed him to Edgehill, to York, to Malton and above all to the Castle at Scarborough where he sustained such a memorable siege ? It is impossible to believe that, in a village where the rector took up arms for the King and lost for a time at least his rectory[2] and much of his fortune, that no Thorntonian fought for Charles I. There were royalists who had landed interests in the Marishes,[3] did none of the labourers throw down their tools and march into York ? Perhaps not in the Marishes, for Robert Hunter was the all important person at Newstead Grange, and he was a parliamentarian,[4] but in other parts of the parish there must have been a few at least. Whether royalists or parliamentarians, the blood of the people must have been stirred by the news of the surrender of Sir Hugh Cholmley, in July, 1645:[5] and of his exile abroad. Nearer at home throughout the period there was, however, no excitement with regard to Pickering Castle, once so formidable, because it was too ruined even then to be of any real military value.[6]

When the wars were over and England was converted into a Commonwealth, men had to take an oath of obedience to the new government, or, as was said, 'take subscription to the Engagement,' in these words, 'I do declare and promise that I will be true and faithful to the Commonwealth of England as it is now established without a King[7] or House of Lords.'[8] Certain magistrates of this district, including 'Mr. Leonard Conyers, clerk, of Lastingham' and 'Robert Hunter, gentleman,' lord of one of the manors in Thornton,[9] saw an ingenious way of making money, for that 'the said gentl^n did in the month of January, 1650, at Kirby Misperton and other places, for their own covetous ends, and to procure money to themselves, and to oppress the said inhab^ts, publiquely and falsely devulge, to the great scandal of the Commonwealth, that

---

[1] *Vide* Ch. XV.
[2] *Vide* Ch. IX.
[3] *Vide* Ch. XVII.
[4] Ibid.
[5] *Vide* Ch. XV.
[6] It was said as early as 1599 'Pickering Castle if not repaired likely to be ruined.' Rev. A. H. Hinderwell in his *History of Scarborough* contradicts the view that no fighting took place at Pickering Castle during the Civil War. He asserts that it was besieged by the Parliamentary forces, and that a large breach was made on the west side 'and after it was taken great quantities of papers and parchments several of which had gilt letters on them were scattered about the street.' The story is very doubtful. But I have been informed that a woman, in recent years, claimed to have seen some of these papers collected by an ancestor, and handed down in her family until she was a child, when they were lost. But hearsay is no evidence.
[7] The act abolishing the office of King was passed 17 March, 1648/9.
[8] The act abolishing the House of Lords was passed 19 March, 1648/9.
[9] *Vide* Ch. XII.

there was a necessitie of all persons having subscribed, should have certificate from them testifying such subscription, and in case such persons had not certificate to produce, that they could not travaile above five myles from home or go to the markett, but any persons might take them prisoners, and take away their horses, cloathes or other goods from them, and the persons soe taken prisoners, and having their goods soe taken away could obtain noe remedy in that behalf, and that, by which false and indirect dealings, they persuaded the inhab[ts] that there was a necessity of having their certificate, and yett not withstanding would not give or signe any such certificate under 6d. each, all which is contrary to law, to the scandall of the Commonwealth, and contrary to the public peace, and deceipt of the people.' It is most pleasing to find the outrageous tricks of these so-called 'gentlemen' were discovered, and that Mr. Conyers, who was regarded as the worst offender, and so he was, being in holy orders, was fined £6. 13s. 4d., Mr. Robert Hunter £3. 6s. 8d., and the others £1 each.[1]

Among those connected with Thornton who suffered loss[2] owing to the Civil War, was Lord Lumley, lord of the main manor in right of his wife, Elizabeth, granddaughter of the fourth Baron Latymer.[3] Towards the end of the Commonwealth period, having no offspring of her own, she determined to help the children of others. It was, because of this maternal sorrow[4] that in October, 1657, she executed a deed by which were founded not only the Grammar School, but also the Almshouses, both of which have played such a part in the history of Thornton, and are such features of charm and beauty in the village to-day. The buildings were not completed until 1670.[5] During the last thirty years of the seventeenth century many a Thornton boy must have blessed the name

---

[1] N. R. Rec. S. O.S. V. pp. 96, 97, *cf.* p. 90.

[2] He had to pay a fine of £1925, to the Commonwealth Government.

[3] *Vide* Ch. XI.

[4] Eastmead, p. 267, draws on his imagination when he says that Lady Lumley, in April, 1657, 'had been deprived of her only child and heir and whilst still suffering under this recent and heavy affliction' made her bequest. The 'child' to whom reference is made was a full grown man, 'Henry Lumley, Esq.' son of Lord Lumley by a former marriage, and Eastmead seems to have forgotten that when Lady Lumley drew up her deed of gift she was over 80 years of age.

[5] The fly leaf of the Church Register has these words 'The Lady Lumley's ffrue schoole & hospitall was builded Anno Domini 1670.' The next reference to the Charity is for the year 1675 'Cicily Miton a hospitall woman buried ye 17 of Oct.' In 1743 Archbishop Herring's Visitation Return says 'There is in this Town an Hospital, built & endowed by the same Lady Lumley: 7 or 8 Trustees were lately appointed by ye present Lord Chancellor [Lord Hardwicke] for managing the revenue of it, & all being Gentlemen of estates, no fraud or abuse can be suspected in ye management of it.' *Cf.* Y. A. S. Rec. S. LXXV.

of Lady Lumley for having started him on the first rungs of the ladder of education.[1]

Thus the century closed with great changes in progress. A new family had been established at the Hall,[2] which had been much enlarged. A good school had been created for the benefit of the young. Comfortable almshouses had been erected for the deserving and aged poor. A new rectory had been built and a much restored church had been evolved from the ancient pile that dated from the fourteenth century.[3] Even a new spirit in religious thought had been caused by the passing of the Toleration Act of 1689[4] by which Dissenters and Quakers[5] had a little more freedom. So that Thornton, unchanged in many ways, and even more beautiful than it is to-day, was ready to enter the eighteenth century far better equipped than when the Latymers, the Hunters, and the Robinsons had controlled the village a hundred years before.

[1] *Vide* Ch. VIII.
[2] *Vide* Ch. XI.
[3] *Vide* Ch. IX.
[4] 1. Will. & Mar. c. 18.
[5] In 1743 the only dissenters were two families of Quakers, who attended a meeting house in Pickering, where the teacher, Robert Pearson, lived. He ministered for sixty-nine years, and died 30 March, 1748. *Cf.* Y. A. S. Rec. S. LXXVII., p. 238, and G. Baker, *Unhistoric Acts*, p. 46.

CHAPTER SIX.

The Village in the Eighteenth and Nineteenth Centuries.

'But we have bid farewell
To all the virtues of those better days,
And all their honest pleasures.'

COWPER.

'For now I see the true old times are dead.'

TENNYSON.

IT is hardly likely that the people of Thornton, at the beginning of the eighteenth century, would worry very much about the wranglings of the newly-formed parties of Whigs and Tories; and the shouts of joy over the victory of Blenheim, or the later cries of 'Sacheverell for ever,' and, 'Down with the Duke,' would scarcely be heard in the quiet solitude of this northern village. The death of Queen Anne and the accession of George I., would pass by without comment. No one, save perhaps the parson and the squire, would have heard of Harley and St. John, and certainly not even they would have understood the constitutional importance of Shrewsbury's *coup d'état* in 1714. The John Hill of that day[1] thought far more of the excellency of his breed of hounds than of the legitimacy of Prince James, Chevalier de St. George, 'The Old Pretender'; and Jacobitism would leave the village untroubled. One might have imagined the first two John Hills of the eighteenth century, to have been the typical Jacobite squires of the day, but it happens there is proof that they were not. First, in the fact that the elder took the oaths to the Hanoverian sovereign on 26 April, 1715,[2] just as he had done to Dutch William in 1696 and in 1700;[3] and secondly, because his son John, the Commissioner of Customs, received very short but friendly letters from General Wentworth[4]

---

[1] *Vide* Ch. XI.
[2] N. R. Rec. S. O.S. IX, p. 45.
[3] Ibid. pp. 20, 26, 28.
[4] I imagine this to be a relative of Charles Watson-Wentworth, afterwards second Marquis of Rockingham, who served as a volunteer in 1746, and who was a friend of the Hill family.

throughout the Forty-Five Rebellion, keeping him *au fait* with the state of affairs. The villagers, therefore, would occasionally hear, through leakage from the servants' hall, as to whether Bonnie Prince Charlie was advancing or retiring, and would remain unperturbed, for to them he would seem so far off; and the last of the Stuart forlorn hopes would pass unheeded, except for a Sermon preached in the Parish Churches of Thornton and Pickering 'on occasion of the present Rebellion' by the Rev. John Samuel Hill, called '*False Zeal and Christian Zeal distinguished, or The Essentials of Popery describ'd.*'[1]

Nor is it likely that the bulk of the population were in any sense keen on political questions of any kind, though, that Squire Hill was, is evident enough. At that time there would be a fair number of freeholders in the village, probably between fifty and sixty, but they would be supremely indifferent, as a general rule, and quite ready to vote either way. They would, perhaps, be excited about Walpole's Excise Bill, for that, in 1733, generally roused an ignorant people to extremes of wrath against a very wise measure.[2] An election followed immediately in Yorkshire, when Mr. Turner opposed Sir Rowland Wynne, of Nostel. In those days vast sums were spent by candidates in bribery, but it was impossible for them to visit every village in the county to offer these gifts. Their friends therefore assisted them by giving entertainments to the freeholders hoping to win their promise to vote the right way. So John Hill commissioned his steward, Sam Tetley, to do what he could. His account book shows, taking one day as an example, the following :—

'Mar. 16. [1733/4] To Expences with the freeholders abt the Election

To ale for the freeholders at Newton	0—12—0
To Ditto at Lockton	1— 9—6
To Ditto at Middleton	0—19—2½
To Ditto at Aislaby	0—11—3
To Ditto at Wrelton	1— 4—8
To Ditto at Cropton and Cawthorne	1—19—5
To Ditto at Rosedale and Hartofft	0— 0—0.'

And on the 30 July there is the total entry,

---

[1] Kindly lent by Miss M. L. Heslop.

[2] The late Rev. Arthur Hill showed me in 1915 two remarkable silk handkerchiefs which had been preserved in the family, and had been woven to commemorate Walpole's withdrawal of his bill. They contained the coats of arms of all the members who had opposed the measure. No doubt an Excise Bill would not be approved by a Commissioner of Customs.

'To Sam Tetley's Bill of Disbursements relating to Sir Rowland Wynn's & Mr. Turner Ellection 072—16—05½.'[1] If all the candidates' friends spent proportionately, the freeholders of Yorkshire, in 1734, must have had a lively time. In the great Yorkshire Election of 1807 the three candidates for the two seats poured out money like water. It is said that the famous William Wilberforce champion of the 'Abolition of Slavery,' spent £25,000, Lord Milton, son of Earl FitzWilliam, spent £150,000, and Mr. Lascelles £160,000.[2] The first two were elected, and it is extremely probable that a small part of this vast expenditure found its way into the pockets of the 48 freeholders[3] residing in Thornton, Ellerburn and Farmanby.[4] But real excitement could not exist until the franchise had been widened. In an agricultural district, like Thornton, the Great Reform Bill of 1832, would be of no interest at all; nor would the people be stirred by the act of 1867. It was only when the agricultural labourer got the vote in 1885 that interest in politics began to show itself. From that date to the present politics have been an absorbing topic, and an important feature of village history.[5]

But politics were not all: they did not give a man his daily bread. The background of life was agriculture, and for many years not only in Thornton but all over England it had been deteriorating, so that, at the end of the seventeenth century, before the remarkable improvements of Tull, Townshend and Bakewell, the actual productivity of the soil was at a minimum. In many parts of the country an improvement had been attempted by breaking up the three field system into Quarters,[6] but Thornton did not adopt this. The wasteful method of the scattered strips in the three fields, with no possibility of proper drainage or experiment, and

---

[1] Sam Tetley's *Account Book*, G. F. G. H.   S. Tetley ceased to be steward in 1746.

[2] *The Poll of the County of York*, 1807.   Kindly shown to me in 1928 by Mrs. George Skelton.

[3] The freeholders would be rather fewer in number than in 1734, for some freeholds had been purchased by the Hill family.

[4] The figures quoted as to the cost of the election are in manuscript on the fly-leaf of *The Poll*, etc. and do not agree with those given by C. G. Harper, *The Great North Road II*. p. 31, who says, that Lord Milton spent £107,000, and Mr. Lascelles £102,000, and that £64,455 was subscribed for William Wilberforce, a large part of which was returned. These vast sums were spent, when only thirty-four thousand voted.

[5] *Vide* Ch. VII.   This political enthusiasm is evinced in a small degree in Parish Council Elections.   The excitement concerning the first was considerable and was the cause of a poetical effusion.   *Cf.* Appendix D.

[6] This change began in the late seventeenth century but it was not common before 1750.   *Cf.* W. H. R. Curtler, *The Enclosure and Redistribution of Our Lands*, p. 67.

very little chance of rotation of crops, continued for many years into the eighteenth century. Some change, however, was inaugurated, as far as Farmanby was concerned, as early as 1675. It evidently occasioned desperate tussles amongst some of the villagers, and there were many who argued for and against. Those desiring an enclosure[1] of Farmanby and West Thornton open fields were :—John Hill, gentleman, Richard Walmsley Esq.,[2] Elizabeth Browne, widow, William Brown and Sarah Smales, widow. Those against it were the Dean and Canons of Windsor,[3] Isaac ffairfax,[4] Samuel Robinson,[5] Robert Hunter, gentleman,[6] Thomas Skelton the eldest, Thomas Skelton the younger, Thomas Skelton the youngest, William, Robert and Edward Skelton, William Maw, James and John Todd, William and Robert Egglefield, Anthony Dynham;[7] Robert Slee the elder, Robert Slee the younger, John and William Clarke, Jane Clarke, Simon and Robert Smythson, John Watson, Thomas Dinham, Thomas Smales the elder, Thomas Smales the younger, John Smales, Richard Smales the elder, Richard Smales the younger, Jane Smales, Thomas [?] Roger Joyner, George Denison, James Dixon, Robert Champley, George Wilkinson, Christopher and John Baker, Christopher Bradley, clerk, Richard Jackson, John Buttery, Margaret King, Thomas Robinson, Ralph Kay, Elizabeth Browne, Marmaduke Wikes, clerk,[8] [of Ellerburn] Richard Sollatt, John Horton, Roger Widd, ffrancis Godall, Henry Sympson the younger.[9]

Despite the strong opposition of so many, the advocates of the scheme won, and by means of a decree in Chancery,[10] dated 19 October, 1678, the greater part of Farmanby was enclosed. The 'Extract of yᵉ Exemplification of yᵉ Decree to inclose Thornton

[1] The Commissioners were John [?] of Malton, Thomas 'hutchinson' of Pickering and Robert Hunter of *Wilton*.
[2] *Vide* Ch. XV.
[3] *Vide* Ch. XIV.
[4] *Vide* Ch. VII.
[5] *Vide* Ch. XIII.
[6] *Vide* Ch. XII.
[7] *Vide* Ch. VII. The will of Robert Dynham of 'Farmanbye' was proved on 22 October, 1627; of Stephen Dynham on 24 April, 1635: of Thomas Dynham on 4 May, 1641: of Henry Denham 7 May, 1664: of Thomas Denham 10 June, 1 07: of Anthony Denham 23 March, 1712. *Cf.* Y. A. S. Rec. S. LXXIII. pp. 43, 45. The will of Anthony Denham was proved by his nearest of kin, George Wilkinson in 1692. Denham Farm or Denham by the Syme was sold by G. F. G. Hill, Esq. to Mr. Morley in 1927.
[8] *Vide* Ch. IX.
[9] G. F. G. H.
[10] Enclosures were sometimes made by Acts of Parliament in this period; but they were not usual. The ordinary method was authorization by either the Court of Exchequer or the Court of Chancery.

& Farmanby Fields &c on the west side of the Beck' shows the following arrangements.[1]   Pexton Moor and Green Cliffe[2] were excepted from the enclosure. The King got about 20 ac.: the Dean of York 3 or 4 ac. in Cow Carr: the Dean and Canons of Windsor 20 ac. in West Wandales,[3] and 50 ac. 34 per. in Highfields: Richard 'Walmesley' 11 ac. 27 per. in the West Field in a place called 'Botton.'

John Hill had next to Botton 'the Nine Oxgang Close' and 25 ac. 2 ro. in West Field called West Croft next to the Street leading 'to Pickering on the north and adjoynnye on Roxby on the East,' and 16 ac. in Brecondale[4] 'being part of the common of Thornton.' As tenant of the Dean of York, he got 10 ac. 2 ro. 2 per. in West Ends, and as tenant of the Dean and Canons of Windsor, 43 ac. in West Ends and 10 ac. in 'Dawcroft[5] laying next Boot Close Flatt.'[6]

Robert 'Egglefield' obtained 2 ro. 30 per. in the Low Field 'next Mr. Hill's with Pannierman's Pool on the north'; while William 'Egglefield' got 11 ac. 3 ro. 2 per. in 'Ingdales from a New Lane[7] extending from Malton Way to Oxcar Hedge.'[8]

John Welburn got 4 ac. 2 ro. 36 per. in Ingdales. Isaac Fairfax got 20 ac. in Wisperdales[9] and West Ends. Samuel Robinson got 20 ac. from Malton Way to Cow Carrdyke; and Thomas Priestman got 3 ac. in Ox Carr.[10]

Important as this was, the village had to wait another century before the really valuable move was made. In 1780 an act was passed as far as Thornton, east of the Beck was concerned 'for

[1] G. F. G. H.

[2] Immediately above White Cliffe Quarry. In the map of 1729 above the Whitby Road there were three enclosures called Lower, Middle and Upper Fawcus.

[3] Wandales or Wandles. Canon Atkinson thinks that *vandela* is a single division a *deal* or *dale* or *dole* in the open arable field from the A. S. *wang* a field and *dal* a share. *Cf.* N. R. Rec. S. O.S. IV. p. 136. *Cf.* also *The Antiquary*, March, 1886.

[4] This name still continues; it is on the north side of Green Gate Lane and east of Howldale. It is mentioned in 1575 as Brackendell.

[5] Dorcroft is the field opposite the Broats on the west side of Maltongate.

[6] This must not be confused with the modern 'Tony Booth's Sand Flat' next to the Canada allotments on Sand Flats just before the Corpse road leads to Wilton. It is sometimes spelt 'Bout' or 'Booth' and is between High Riggs and Westgate.

[7] Now known as Swallow-me-crack Lane leading to Grundon House.

[8] A field in 1928, running down to the Syme.

[9] It is not from 'whisper' but, according to Canon Atkinson, from the Cleveland *weeze* that is English *ooze* meaning a boggy locality where the water oozes out under pressure of the foot. *Cf.* N. R. Rec. S. O.S. IV. p. 208. In 1928 it runs from Maltongate near 'America House,' by an oak tree, to High Riggs Lane. I am indebted to Mrs. Richard Hill for its position.

[10] In 1729 this is known as Priestman's Carr.

Deviding and Inclosing the Open and Common Fields, Common, Meadows, Common Pastures, Commonable Closes, Common Grounds, Heath and Waste Grounds.' And this was followed almost immediately after, in 1795, by a similar act referring to Thornton, Farmanby, Ellerburn and Kingthorpe. Thus the whole agricultural system of the village was revolutionized, and the manorial system collapsed.[1] The old scattered strips in the three fields disappeared for ever; the curious relics of a communal system which dated back so far and which had in detail changed so little from century to century were swept away;[2] farms were concentrated and lands were redistributed; so that the slothful, wasteful and unscientific methods of the past vanished in the face of the needs of the country for increased production.[3] Marketing farming was what was needed on a wide scale. The population was increasing with great rapidity, and the country was soon to be faced with a twenty-two years war. Much has been said about the iniquity of Enclosures, but it should be remembered that 'the settlement of such innumerable claims as the commissioners were called upon to decide, opened up an immense field for individual dissatisfaction and grumbling, of which we may be certain full use was made by all those who fancied themselves wronged, but we may be quite certain that a far greater number falsely imagined they were.'[4] Again, 'Few will have any sympathy with those who represent English landowners as engaged in a long Machiavellian plot to deprive the poor man of his land, for such a charge shows ignorance both of history and of the character of Englishmen.'[5]

The commissioners who were appointed to carry out the Act of 1780, were 'Wm Willmott, S. Milburn and R^t Dunn gents.' It

---

[1] Marshall, *Rural Economy of the West of England*, I. p. 22 advocated the revival of manorial Courts 'as the most natural guardians of the rights of the villagers and the most prompt and efficient police of country parishes.'

[2] Seebohm, *ut supra*, p. 439.

[3] *Cf.* Dr. Grundy in *Berks, Bucks, Oxon Arch. Jour.* Autumn 1927, pp. 113-4. 'People do not as a rule realize that the Enclosure Acts of the latter part of the 18th and earlier part of the 19th century completely revolutionized both the system of land-holding in this country, and also the system of cultivation. Also from the name "Enclosure Acts" they are apt to conclude that the main object of them was to bring common and waste land into cultivation. That was one object, and a very important one, too. But the most important was the concentration of single holdings, so that the holder might have his plot, as it were, in order that he might work it economically. This was effected by a process of exchange. The expenses of working a farm under the old system must have been at least double that under the new.'

[4] W. H. R. Curtler, *The Enclosure and Redistribution of Our Lands*, p. 439.

[5] Ibid. p. 245.

would be impossible to go into the details of the Award, but it might be noted, that the Dean and Canons of Windsor had the steep field between Buffit and the Beck, and the equally steep field between Nabgate and the Low Paper Mill; the Priestmans had from the Church corner to the ford by the Mill; the Rector had the Broats;[1] Richard Johnson [Hill] had Musdale Quarry ground, but not the quarry;[2] Robert and John Champley had the next two enclosures northward.[3] Amongst others who had shares in the redistribution were Mrs. Catherine Hill,[4] the Lumley Charity, Robert Gibson, William and James Read, Robert and John Birdsall, John, Samuel and William Baker, John and Richard Jennison, James and Anne Smales, John Audus, James Marflitt, William Spendley, William Bolton, John 'Nateriss,' Thomas Maw, John Dixon, William Harland, John Crosby, John Boyes, George Pickering, William Harrison, Mathew Crosier, Samuel Skelton, Mr. Walmesley, John Berriman, Mrs. H. Bland, Mrs. Ann Warren, Miss M. Scafe, and Miss E. Ness.[5]

In 1795, as already said, Parliament passed another very important Enclosure Act; and in the following year, the three Commissioners, William Whitelock, John Hall and Timothy Parke made their award for Thornton, Farmanby, Ellerburn and King-thorpe. It would be impossible to give this enormous Award in anything like detail. Its size as preserved to-day is portentous. In the first place the Commissioners insisted that all the public drains, that is dykes and ditches, on the east side of the Beck should be repaired. That this was necessary for the good working of other drains, ditches and sewers is obvious in a country that sloped gently to the Marishes, the Syme and the Derwent. It is not uninteresting to find that the banks and course of the Syme were also to be repaired from certain specified points, and that, that notorious trap for the hunting man, was 'to be well and sufficiently cleansed and scoured to the middle of the stream by the respective owners of the Lands in Thornton and in ffarmanby'; and the same order was also made to apply to the Beck. The importance of this drainage scheme is shown elsewhere, but it may be said here that in the Award of 1796, the matter is considerably stressed, and the following drains or dykes, most of which are

---

[1] 'Broats' derived from the old Norse 'brote' meaning 'a heap of trees felled in a wood,' and therefore a clearing in a wood. *Cf.* A. H. Smith, *ut supra*, p. 86.
[2] This was reserved for the freeholders on the east side of the Beck.
[3] Now owned by Mrs. Whitney.
[4] *Vide* Ch. XI.
[5] The Map of the Award. G. F. G. H.

marked on the modern Six-Inch Ordnance Map, were definitely ordered to be kept clear and cleansed by their respective land-owners :—East Field, Carrs, Hunter Carr, Row Dyke, Bottons, Elliker, Blakeland, Hurrell's Lane, New Ings, Woolness, Nine Oxgangs, Ing Dales, Ings, Pickering Carr, New, Broadmires, Hill's Dyke, West Field, Little, and West Ends.

A change in agricultural methods is evidenced in the Award by the action of the Commissioners with regard to the Town Bull. From time immemorial there had been such an animal the use of which had been inimical to the good breeding of cattle. The commissioners now proceeded to compensate for the 'depasturing of a Town Bull,' and to 'award the Yearly sum of Three Pounds and three shillings as an Equivalent and full satisfaction for the ....privilege of depasturing a Bull from the twelfth day of May to the tenth day of October in every year in some part of Cow Carr or Noble Carr within the townships.' And that the same yearly sum 'be charged upon....all that close situate in Noble Carr belonging to' the Rev. John Ward as trustee for Richard Hill, and be paid 'to the Churchwardens and Overseers of the Poor.... to be by them applied for the Keeping and depasturing of the said Bull....for the benefit of the Proprietors and Their Tenants for ever.'

For the general good of the community the Commissioners also dealt with the all-important 'Herbage' by the public road-sides, now known as 'Cowgates.' For ten years after the Award[1] this 'Herbage' was only to be mown and was to be let to the highest bidder; but after that time it was to be offered to the highest bidder to be eaten by beasts, and many a villager until recent years found the enormous advantage which was provided by renting a cow-gate and leaving his beast to the care of the cow-tenter.[2]

Having solved these problems the Commissioners undertook the task of rearranging with meticulous care the burden of the tithes, and also the allotting, awarding and exchanging the lands. In general the Commons of Thornton and Farmanby were divided up amongst the freeholders. The pieces of land were very numerous and often minute, and of such a character that it is quite impossible to deal with them in detail. In some cases, however, there are allotments and redistributions that have some interest. Apparently the Vicar of Ellerburn from the long past had possessed a piece of

---

[1] This was ordered until the hedges had had time to grow up. Gerard Hill, Esq. kindly informed me of this.
[2] This system has been given up for all practical purposes, I presume because of the increase of motor traffic.

land of 1 acre, 29 perches, called by the unaccountable and strange
name of 'Saint Iles.' On enquiry no present inhabitant knows this
name; but fortunately the Commissioners numbered this patch
in the Award and on the accompanying plan, and it lies at the
northern end of the narrow line of trees known as 'The Stray' on
the eastern side. In 1796 'Saint Iles'[1] was exchanged with Richard
Hill's trustee and it became the property of that family. Lord
Petre, owner of the Roxby estate, also exchanged for Vasey Ings,
near the Syme, and a few other small pieces of property 'all that
close called Walmesley Carr' on the west and north of Cow Carr,
together with the two closes called Burtons with Netherhead[2]
to the north.

Perhaps the most important changes were those connected with
the Dean and Canons of Windsor. They were allotted a portion
of Common (168 acres, 2 roods, 39 perches) above Dalby Wood,
and this was immediately purchased from them by the Hill trustee,
who also acquired by exchange Millholme, Buttery Close, Dean's
flatt,[3] several portions of High Fields, 'Selly Rea'[4] in the Marishes
and 'Bleaching Yard Close' at Ellerburn. From the Rector, the
Rev. J. Hill Webb, the trustee obtained certain tithe rents from
Boot Close Flat on the west side of Dean's Flatt and from
Broadmire Close north of Cow Carr and south of West Wandles,
together with Mill Close or Dale Bank, Skelton's Garth, and a
cottage and garth in Brock Lane bounded on the west by
Whitbygate. The Rector got certain other cottages, including
one that stood on what is now the Rectory kitchen garden, and
also a piece of land called Pannierman's Pool.[5]

Such in brief outline were the important Enclosure and Redistribution Awards in Thornton, Farmanby and Ellerburn.

The obvious result of these Acts was that the very aspect of
the land was changed. Where, hitherto, Thornton Common on the
western and eastern heights had been wide open spaces running
up into the heather, there now came into existence what is such
a feature of this countryside—the stone wall. Where now, on the
right-hand side of Sand Dale, one can see walls or remains of walls,
before 1780, there would have been none; and it was evidently

---

[1] I suggest that as it belonged to St. Hilda's Church, it was first known
as St. Hild's, then St. Ilds and finally Saint Iles.

[2] Burtons and Netherhead are marked on the map of 1729, and are on
the extreme west of the parish with Hagg Farm on the north and the
Pickering road on the south.

[3] On the west of Maltongate.

[4] The Six-Inch Ordnance spells it 'Selley Wray.'

[5] This is close to the Broats.

some vagary of the act that produced what is still known as 'the Double Wall,' beyond the little copse, 'The Shoulder of Mutton.' Along Nabgate there would be planted the quick set hedge; and on the south-east of Nabgate and the east of Utgang Lane, the great open field, broken only by balks, was now divided and redivided, by fences. And it was the same in Caulklands, in the West Field below the Pickering Road, and in Botton field south of the Hall. The Enclosure Acts did really bring about enclosure, in the true sense, and much that had been completely open was restricted.

Such was the most vital change that was effected in the eighteenth century, and in many ways the most drastic change that Thornton had or has ever experienced. But the time of change had come all over England, the Industrial Revolution was beginning to make itself felt, and, although Thornton has remained unbesmirched by the unlovely results of that great mechanical outburst that has made, and, at the same time, marred the West Riding, the village did begin to experience other changes besides those produced by the Enclosure Acts.

On the other hand, although the ancient methods of agriculture had been swept away, the manorial courts and time-honoured customs still survived. The Court Rolls of Thornton, however, have not proved of very great interest nor are there any left[1] of any considerable antiquity. The villagers were under a double jurisdiction for they were bound to their own manorial lord, either of Thornton proper or of Farmanby, and also were connected in a more general way, like all the villages within the bounds of the Forest, with the Honor and Manor of Pickering. At this court the Constable and four lawful men, from both Thornton and Farmanby, were obliged to attend. The earliest record of this, that the present writer has found, is that of 1707, where it is stated that 'upon the oathes of the Constable and four men of ffarmanby wee finde and present that John Buttery dyed sized of a house and garth in Thornton-cum-ffarmanby of about the yearly value of ten shillings and that John Buttery is his son and heire who ought to pay the Lord for his Reliefe a fine of 6s. 8d.' The same is said of Thomas 'Dinham' and his son and heir Anthony; but in this case the relief is fixed at 13s. 4d.;[2] and, as he had not paid in 1713, the fine was raised to £1. 6s. 8d. In the Rolls of 1711 it is recorded that 'on oath of ye four men of Thornton we present

---

[1] Most unfortunately many documents were burnt in 1910. I was informed of this by James Green in 1928.

[2] For the value of these, *cf.* Marshall, *The Rural Economy of Yorkshire* I. p. 28 (1796 ed.).

John White of Thornton for his Browdyke being not sufficient. Therefore he is amerced 1s. 4d.' At the same time for the same offence Robert Hunter and John Read were fined 6d. each. In all the Rolls from 1711 to 1715, there is the complaint, 'on oath of four men of ffarmanby we present ye Town of Pickering for their Newgate being out of repair'; and in the latter year they added that they presented Thomas Hick 'for his fence lyeing down next ye south side of ye Newgate.'[1] These charges no doubt referred to the fact that the boundary hedge between the open fields of the two parishes was inadequate. The gate was probably across the road on the Pickering side of West Wandles.[2]

Besides these annual representative attendances at the court in Pickering, courts were also held in Thornton and in Farmanby. The existing records for these only date back to 1792, but they are complete to 1926.[3] The ancient formula was used and the oaths solemnly exacted. The proclamation was to 'All manner of persons that do owe Suit and Service to the Court of [Mr. George Francis Gordon Hill] now holder in and for the Manor and Honor[4] of Thornton (or Farmanby) draw near and give your attention and answer to your names.' Then followed the list of freeholders and tenants in the respective manors. The oath administered to the Homage was 'A.B. You as Foreman of this Homage shall inquire and true presentments make of all such things as shall be given you in charge, and of all such other matters as shall come to your knowledge presentable at this court and this you shall do without fear, favour, affection, hatred or malice to the best of your understanding. So help you God.' The other members of the Homage were sworn, four at a time, with the words, 'The like oath which your Foreman hath taken on his part you and every of you shall well and truly observe and keep on your respective parts. So help you God.' The Affeerors had also to swear that 'you and each of you shall well and truly affeer and affirm the several amerciaments here made and now to you remembered. You shall spare no one through fear, favour or affection, nor enhance any one from hatred or malice, but shall impartially act herein. So help you God.' The next proceeding was to elect a Pindar to look

---

[1] In 1790, according to the Award, the gate on the Pickering road bounding the Thornton and Pickering fields was called 'Mule gate.'

[2] J. L. W.

[3] The stewards of the Manors since 1792 to the present day have been in succession John Piper, John Watson, James Dove Whitehead, James Loy Whitehead.

[4] This is of course an incorrect term which has crept in with the passage of time. Thornton never was an 'Honor.'

after, in the case of Thornton, the Pinfold on the north side of the
Scarborough road opposite the High Hall, and at the foot of Utgang
Lane; and in the case of Farmanby, the Pinfold which still stands
in Maltongate.[1] He had to swear 'You shall well and truly serve
our Sovereign Lord, the Lord of this Manor in the office of Pindar
in and for the manor of Thornton (or Farmanby) until you be
thereof discharged according to the course of law. You shall well
and truly do and execute all things belonging to your office
according to the best of your knowledge. So help you God.' As
the nineteenth century progressed another village official, the
Bellman, was solemnly elected and he was bound to affirm that
the bell was the property of the lord of the manor.

After 1792 the work of these courts was very small. They did
act, however, as a kind of Drainage Board, and viewed the drains,
dykes and sewers and presented defaulters and fined them. In
1793 John Bellerby was fined 2s. 6d. for a defective 'bridge and
suer,' which caused a block in the Beck. At the same court William
Hodgson was fined 5s. 'for Leading Stones from a Quarre whore
he had no wright.' In 1799 and again in 1801 Stephen Dixon was
fined 3s. 6d. for not cleansing the Beck near Ing Closes, and
similar fines for similar offences were exacted from many others.
Apparently the next year everyone had done his duty for the
jury stated 'we have no presentments.' But in 1805, 1815, and
1823 there were several instances of persons being fined for not
cleansing their ditches. From that date onwards this work of
superintending the Beck continued, but it became very much
a matter of routine and the chief feature of the Court was a dinner
held alternately at the two Inns. An interesting point arose in 1905
of a somewhat different character. For some time many persons
had been taking stone from Musdale Quarry, which was on the
land of the lord of the manor of Thornton, but restricted in the
Award of 1781, and was not open to the use of the freeholders in
Ellerburn. Quite unwittingly, one of the most serious offenders
was the vicar of Ellerburn, who used the stone for the restoration
of the Church. In December, 1905, the Court Leet and Court Baron
of Richard Hill, Lord of the Manor of Thornton, passed a resolution
asking the Lord of the Manor to notify any offenders, who contrary
to the Award, took stone for building either from Caulklands or
Musdale, to the west of the Beck. This is probably the last act

[1] In July, 1926 it was thought by some that the Pinfold in Maltongate
was the property of the Duchy of Lancaster, but it was concluded that this
was not so, and it was the property of the Lord of the Manor of Farmanby.

of the slightest importance that the manorial courts of Thornton will ever perform.[1]

One of the most noticeable differences between the early eighteenth and the early twentieth centuries is the stupendous alteration in the value of money.[2] In 1734,[3] in Thornton, prices were very low, food was cheap, the cost of living was small. At that time a snipe cost 2d.: a partridge, 4d.: a pheasant, 1s.: butter was never above 4½d. a pound: Cheshire cheese was 3d. a pound: a chicken or a duck was 6d.: a goose, 1s. 8d.: mutton was 2½d. a pound: veal, 2d.: 50 pounds of beef cost 9s.: 3 turkeys were 3s. 4d.: rabbits were 8d. a couple: 141 eggs cost 1s. 11½d.: 6 quarts of brandy were 6s.: 6 quarts of 'Rumm' were 9s. 3d.: 5 dozen 'orringes' 5s.: 6½ pounds of 'Ruswarp trout,' including carriage, cost 2s. 8d.: and 26 Lobsters were 10s. 2d. What are really more astounding are the prices of cows, bulls, ewes and rams in 1743.[4] In restoring and improving the farm at Dalby,[5] John Hill III, paid Thomas Parke for cows 45s. each, and John Priestman, for the same 46s. each: for a bull for breeding 35s.:[6] for ewes 6s. apiece and for rams 7s. 6d.: and as the farm was on the Warren, for a 'Rabit Dogg' 4s. 6d.

They sound happy times, and yet they were not so happy for those who had to earn their daily bread by the sweat of their brows. An ordinary labourer earned 8d. a day,[7] a haymaker 10d.[8] a thatcher[9] or ditcher or mason,[10] 1s., a charwoman[11] or a sempstress[12] 4d. a day. The grooms[13] received £1 p.a., the housemaid and

---

[1] The above material is from Court Rolls, J. L. W.
[2] 'From 1715 to 1765 was an era of good seasons and low prices generally; in that half-century Tooke says there were only five bad seasons.' *Cf.* W. H. R. Curtler, *History of Agriculture*, p. 179.
[3] Sam. Tetley's *Account Book.* G. F. G. H. These prices are still more remarkable when compared with those in London fixed by proclamation a century before in 1633. Turkey cock, 4s. 4d.: fat goose, 2s.: duck, 8d.: 1 lb. of butter in winter 6d., in summer 5d.: 3 eggs a 1d.: pullet, 1s. 6d.
[4] Ibid.
[5] *Vide* Ch. XV.
[6] In 1734 Mr. Hill paid 'Richd Baker for a milch cow £3-4-6,' and 'John Dobson for a bull £2-15-0.' The prices for horses were, 'the Black Gelding' £2-2-0: 'the Walpole Gelding' £7-0-0: and 'the Halifax mare' £10-0-0.
[7] Such as 'Wm Harland 1 day cuting thorns for Hurrell 0-0-8.'
[8] Two men, Gill and Doyoo, were only paid 10d. a day between them for stacking hay.
[9] William Read was thatcher in 1734, and buried 27 September, 1748. He was succeeded by William Banks, buried 22 November, 1764.
[10] R. Gilbanke.
[11] 'Mary Hoggard 6½ days in Laundry 00-02-02.'
[12] 'Barbara Foster for 3 days making sheets 0-1-0.'
[13] John Hardwick and William Keddey.

the dairymaid[1] £2 p.a. each, the housekeeper[2] and the butler[3] £4 p.a. each, the coachman,[4] £6 p.a. and the gardener[5] £9 p.a. Nor could any of them comfort themselves with a cup of tea, for tea varied from 12s. to 17s. 6d. a pound,[6] equivalent to about £3 to £4. 10s. of present-day money.

Prices, at any rate for sound cattle, would rise, very rapidly, soon after 1743. Between that year and 1754, England was ravaged by the cattle plague. Remedy after remedy was suggested[7] without effect.[8] The farmers of Thornton and Ellerburn suffered very heavily;[9] and a most interesting record of this calamity has been preserved in the Ellerburn Registers in these words, 'In the year 1748 a distemper amongst horned cattle (believed to be infectious) carried off more than a third part and not quite half the horned cattle in this parish. It broke out in January and raged above six months; no human skill being able to stop its rapid progress. It has prevailed above five years in this Kingdom, and several places abroad much longer. In the township of Wilton it was more fatal and of longer continuance, they lost upwards of two-thirds of their cattle. Oswald Langwith,[10] then curate of Ellerburn and Wilton, willing to transmit so signal a visitation from the hand of God to future ages, made this memorial in the year 1750, the Rev. John Samuel Hill[11] being vicar.'

Low wages, few comforts and poor houses did not produce any great unhealthiness in the village. A random selection of years shows that in 1710 there were only 3 burials; 1730, 5; in 1789, 4; in 1792, 4; in 1809, 8; and in 1811, 5. Like all other places in the

---

[1] These were Ann and Jane Hoggard. In 1726 maids were paid 30s. and 35s. was reckoned extravagant. *Cf.* Young, p. 635.

[2] Mrs. Elizabeth Husband was housekeeper and cook. She could not sign her own name and had to make her mark. She was succeeded by Isabell Lunn in 1736 and Ann Hind from 1737 to 1748.

[3] Thomas Plummer.

[4] Symon Hartley [? Hardy].

[5] George Sherwood.

[6] Hist. MSS. Com., Rawden Hastings MS. I. p. 413 shows that in 1705 tea was in Oxford 48s. a lb.

[7] *Cf. The Gentleman's Magazine* for the period.

[8] W. H. R. Curtler, *History of Agriculture*, pp. 185-6 says 'The cattle plague of 1745 was so severe that owing to the scarcity of stock great quantities of grassland were ploughed up....The cattle plague also raged in 1754 in spite of an Order in Council that all infected cattle should be shot and buried 4 ft. deep, and pitch, tar, rosin and gunpowder burnt where infected cattle had died, and cow-houses washed with vinegar and water. Such were the sanitary precautions of the time.' *Cf.* the pamphlet *An Exhortation to all People to Consider the Afflicting Hand of God*, p. 6.

[9] Eastmead, p. 329.

[10] *Vide* Ch. IX.

[11] Ibid. He was at Cambridge in 1734. Sam Tetley records 'To Mr. John Sam¹ Hill for his journey to Cambridge 015-15-00.'

eighteenth century, Thornton suffered from smallpox, to a slight extent. The first reference to it was in 1742-3, when at least 9 persons died from that disease. Between 1747-8, there were only 2 cases;[1] but in 1773, a note was made in the Burial Register, 'N.B. The small-pox were very fatal this year,' and 28 deaths were recorded, but the rector did not notify whether they were all due to small-pox or not. After this there is no recurrence of epidemic disease, until an outbreak of typhus in the late 'sixties, and the scourge of influenza at the end of the nineteenth and beginning of the twentieth centuries.[2] Up to the middle of the nineteenth century the population steadily rose, and reached its zenith just before the outbreak of the Crimean War, when agricultural prices were very high; but it is interesting to note, that as agricultural prospects grew gloomier and gloomier, the population fell off not merely gradually, but, in the 'eighties, with immense rapidity. The following census returns for Thornton, Ellerburn and Farmanby combined[3] will illustrate this point.

1801 1811 1821 1831 1841 1851 1861 1871 1881 1891 1901
1227 1380 1485 1560 1572 1581 1541 1439 1426 1267 1163.[4]

It is true that since the beginning of the twentieth century the population has increased once again, but this is not due so much to a return of agricultural labourers, as to an influx of residents who have come to enjoy the moorland air and the natural beauties of the village.

It is worthy of remark that the most noticeable point of the decline in population corresponds with the coming of the railway. In the early nineteenth century the means of transport to and from Thornton were somewhat restricted. Once a week, on Thursdays, about 1820,[5] there was what was called the 'Boat Coach' which after 1840,[6] was under the proprietorship of Joseph Garbutt of Pickering, and which, setting out from that town at 6 a.m. for Scarborough, took up passengers at the Cross at Thornton. And that was all! About that time there had arisen in the minds of

---

[1] In Ellerburn parish between May and November, 1748, there were eight deaths, six being due to smallpox.

[2] *Vide* Ch. VII.

[3] By Local Government Order, 1866, Ellerburn was amalgamated with Thornton. Bulmer, *North Riding of Yorkshire*, pp. 1124-6, says that in 1887 the limits of the Civil Parish of Thornton were rearranged at Michaelmas when the parish of Ellerburn (minus Wilton) was incorporated. The total area of the Civil Parish is in Bulmer 10,059 acres, but in V. C. H. N. R. II. p. 492, 9,609 acres.

[4] V. C. H. *York*, III. pp. 519-20.

[5] G. Home, *ut supra*, p. 245.

[6] *East and North Ridings*, p. 465.

some a desire for trains, although as early as 1833 the Pickering
and Whitby Railway was opposed by the authorities of the Duchy
of Lancaster.[1] In 1836, however, this railway[2] was working as a
coach running on lines and drawn by horses.[3] About the same
time a Company, known until 1844 as the North Midland Railway,
connected York and Scarborough.[4] One can imagine how even
these distant lines would worry the Tory propensities of Richard
Hill, and he bitterly complained of them to the Duchy Office, on
30 December, 1844, adding the words, 'Railway Compainys become
armed with such powers that they ride over us poor squires with
impunity.'[5] Thornton people had, at any rate now, a chance of
seeing the outside world, for after walking to Pickering they
could reach Rillington by train, and, either proceed via Malton
to York, or by changing, could get to Scarborough, without relying
on the somewhat uncertain journeys of the 'Boat Coach.' With
these new possibilities, or by driving between any desired points,
they had to be content for the next forty years; but, at last in
1879[6] the North-Eastern Railway began to construct the Pickering-
Scarborough branch, which passed through the parish, and which
was opened in 1882.[7]

Throughout the two centuries the aspect of the village has gone
through some transformations. The Hall was changed in appearance in the reign of Queen Anne, when it was enlarged. Parts of
it are, of course, far older, being Tudor in character, and to this
day there are a Tudor chamfered plinth and mullioned windows
in the basement. It is, in fact, possible that part of the lower outer
walls are Elizabethan. The very charming fish ponds, mediaeval
in origin, most likely owe their present appearance to a builder
of the period of William III. The high 'Palisadoe' Wall outside
was probably built at the beginning of the eighteenth century,
though it may be a little earlier, especially as it needed repair in
1734;[8] and the sunk fence which surrounds the gardens was made

---

[1] Rev. A. H.
[2] Morris, *The North Riding of Yorkshire*, p. 15 says the railway was *not*,
as sometimes stated, constructed by George Stephenson.
[3] Belcher, *Pickering and Whitby Railway* (1836).
[4] Rev. A. H.
[5] Ibid.
[6] Church Terrier shows the sale of a piece of land to the Company
this year.
[7] It is commonly thought that Thornton became Thornton Dale after
the N.E.R. opened the station. But in Cary's Atlas for 1816 and Lewis'
Topographical Dictionary for 1842 it is called Thornton Dale and the parish
is so marked on the 6 in. Ordnance Map of 1854.
[8] Sam. Tetley, *ut supra*.

The Hall

in 1739.[1] At the end of the eighteenth century a very beautiful change was inaugurated by the trustees of the minor, Richard Hill, on the outskirts of the village, by the planting of Ellerburn Wood on the bare hillside in 1797.[2] Those splendid beeches, somewhat thinned in the Great War, but still very lovely, have been a glorious addition to the charms of the village.

As late as 1830,[3] Robinson's farm at Ellerburn[4] and T. Darrell's farm at Millholme were bleaching mills, and the Tanyard was still in full work. Up to the same date, the Bridge at Thornton was a footbridge,[5] with two wide stone bulwarks on either side, and when the drummer in the village band was marching up to Church at 'Club-Feast,' he had to lift his drum, quite independently of the tune, and carry it over, as there was no room for it.[6] At the side of the footbridge was a ford, and the carriages making for the Hall splashed through, and then, in what is now called Cherry Garden,[7] swung round a gravelled sweep, and so into the gates at the sides of which were chained foxes.[8] The story goes that the first Baron Feversham had, one day, to pass in his carriage through the ford, and the Beck had the impertinence to come into the carriage and wet his lordship's feet. Whereupon there was such a hullabaloo that the bridge was widened and the old ford abolished.

Even the Beck and some of the roadways have changed their appearance. Apparently the Beck ran in early days from the footbridge and as a stream along the south side of the road as far as the Smithy, there it turned as it does to-day, washing by the edge of the house, as shown by the map of 1729 and passed into 'The Walks.' The map is minute in detail, but it shows no Beck, not even a runnel, down the left-hand side of Maltongate. The original stream was therefore on the east of the houses and not on the west. In 1729, as to-day, the course by 'The Walks' was much the same

[1] Letter of Sam. Tetley to Commissioner Hill, Normanby Documents. J. L. W.
[2] Told me by the late Rev. Arthur Hill.
[3] Ibid.
[4] *Vide* Ch. VII.
[5] Eastmead, p. 318, says in 1824, 'the proposed addition of a handsome bridge across the stream, and the removal of several unsightly appendages promise to render it one of the most beautiful villages in Yorkshire.'
[6] Told me by Miss Jane Hill, died 1915, aged 90. 'Club-Feast' was omitted for the first time in July, 1915.
[7] Told me by George Pickering, who died 1927. After the Bridge was widened the curve, in Cherry Garden, was not so much used. Some horse-breakers took to training colts in the circle to the annoyance of Richard Hill, whose property it was, so that he had it enclosed and planted as it is now, about 1850.
[8] The present writer can remember chained foxes about 1902.

as far as Low Mill. A later map, perhaps one hundred years later, shows that at the Smithy a new channel had been made, with sluice gates, and was artificially embanked down Maltongate, so that the land to-day, from the Smithy to Low Mill is a sort of island. At the time that the railway station was built, a hundred yards to the north, the course of the Beck was again diverted and made to pass more to the east, the older course being roughly where Maltongate crosses the Scarborough and Pickering line.

As far as can be ascertained the main roads have not changed very considerably. The alterations with regard to the High Street as far as the Church and Rectory are concerned have been dealt with elsewhere. During the eighteenth century the general aspect of the street must have been very much as to-day, except that tiles have been substituted for thatch. No very safe deduction can be drawn from the survey of 1729 as there are signs that the indications of buildings in this street have been tampered with in a different ink, at a later date. If it is to be trusted there was a building where the High Hall stands to-day, and a cottage at the corner of the street and Hurrell's Lane. The survey shows no buildings between the street and the Mill, along what is now called Priestman's Lane, but does show the present cottages from Dog Kennel Lane to the Rectory.

Some suppose that the old road to Whitby was up a narrow lane off the Pickering Road, through the High Nursery and above the present Whitbygate. This may be so, but there is no sign of such a thing in the map of 1729, and the lane, now known as Prospect Place, is definitely and clearly ended long before the High Nursery is reached and in 1729 buildings extended up Whitbygate to the same extent as now except for 'Ganstead.' It is interesting to notice that some lanes like Hungrellway, now Hurrell's Lane, and Harrowcliff had identically the same courses two hundred years ago as to-day. But this is not the case with some others. The present Ellerburn road is at a very much higher level above the Beck than the original route. The old road was on the north-west side of the mill, and its track can still be followed by the eye not far from the bank of the stream. The modern road probably dates from the end of the eighteenth century when the wood was planted.

Two lanes in particular are no longer roadways. In 1729, there was a 'Clay Pit Lane' which led on the left to the Aunums, and on the right emerged in 'Apple Garth Lane,' which entered the Pickering Road opposite Lewis's Plantation or just south-east of

Green Lane.[1] Clay Pit Lane would in the old days be reached from Maltongate by a narrower lane, possibly named Key Lane, and now Roxby Terrace. The two joined in what was called, in 1729, 'Bacside Lane,' but which for many years was known as 'Back Lane' until in recent times it became Roxby Road. Clay Pit Lane was in the past always marshy and may have had something to do with the Clay Pits belonging to the Robinson property[2] in the late seventeenth century. The track of Apple Garth Lane is still to be seen, but a fence has been swept away and it is now part of the field. Parallel with Clay Pit Lane to-day, as well as two hundred years ago, and probably many more, there is an ancient causeway running up Apple Garth, or the field now called 'Garth End.' The flag-stones that mark the track are large but deeply embedded. Two suggestions have been made concerning these: either that it was a foot-track leading from an archway in Maltongate to Roxby Castle; or that, as tradition has it, a stone track laid for the women going to milk the cows in the Aunums.[3] In the early eighteenth century survey the track does not go beyond Apple Garth Lane,[4] if it had, it might have been possible to suggest that it was a pack horse track from the village to the Castle at a more convenient gradient than the Pickering Road;[5] but as it does not one is tempted to doubt the footpath to the Castle. And yet the thoughtful care to preserve the milkmaids from wet feet is somewhat unusual either in the past or at the present; and the line of the track is certainly castlewards. The Roxby Road of to-day, or the Back Lane of earlier times, has the appearance of a new road. Certainly there are new houses on it, but the road itself dates far back, and its shape in 1930 is exactly that of two hundred years ago.

When the passage of time is considered Maltongate might also be referred to as changing extraordinarily little, except for the already mentioned cutting of the Beck. On the west there was in the early eighteenth century a somewhat smaller building where now stands the New Inn. Even in living memory there were, southward, two thatched cottages, but except for the new vicarage and two new houses the actual sites covered were the same two hundred years ago as now. The field known as Herry Dy, of curious undulations, giving the appearance of grass-grown foundations

---

[1] This has had several names. In 1729 it is called Breckondell Way. It is now commonly known as Greengate Lane.

[2] *Vide* Ch. XIII.

[3] I am indebted for this to Mr. Joseph Watson.

[4] On the Six-Inch Ordnance of to-day a footpath does lead to the site of Roxby Castle.

[5] This in the last year or two has been reduced for motor traffic.

was as free from buildings under George I. as it is under George V.
Box Tree farm house stood where it does now, and the old barn
just off Maltongate in Back Lane was there then as to-day, built
without mortar. Beyond Box Tree farm, what at present is a
potato garth had a small building on it, but on that side, except
what has been indicated the sites seem little changed. On the east
side there is, as far as buildings go, almost less. The road itself has
owing to the making of the Beck been shifted a little to the west;
but where the Beck to-day widens out from the artificial restriction
there was a similar enlargement of the old road. The building sites
are very much the same, except for 'Rookwood'; very few of the
open sites of 1729 have been built on; and the fact that Darrell's
farm house was not in alignment with the other buildings seems to
have been true even then.

In the eighteenth century the Pickering road from the west
side of Prospect Place to the Hagg Farm was without a house,
just as it was on the south from the New Inn until Pickering was
reached. The corner site now covered by The Buck had buildings
on it in 1729; but what was very different from to-day was a group
of erections on the north and south of the 'Cross', so that it must
have been almost invisible from these two points, though open
to view from east or west.[1]

A most important change, and a vast improvement in recent
years has been at the 'Cross.' Where now there are the trees and the
enclosed ground, made by the Rev. John Richard Hill, there were,
in 1874, a shop and a stable, in the centre, abutting on to, but on the
south-east side of, the ancient cross and stocks.[2] These buildings
were swept away that year, and some of the stones were used to
build the present village school, for which thanks are due to the
same benefactor. It might be added here that this year, 1874[3]
witnessed the last occasion on which a village royster was actually
placed in the stocks.[4]

Another form of punishment for vagrants and thieves in the
old days was the 'Black Hole' at the Poor House. In the third
decade of the eighteenth century, the Poor House, now consisting

---

[1] All the references to the map or survey of 1729 are from 'Plans of the
several parts of the Lordship of Farmanby.....copy'd from a plan of a Survey
made in October 1729' kindly shown to me by the Rev. Godfrey Marshall.
[2] The present stocks are not old. They were made by William Wray
and Son.
[3] Told me by the late Rev. Arthur Hill.
[4] It was a cruel punishment. Jusserand, *Wayfaring Life*, etc. p. 269,
says 'people when released felt so benumbed that they were scarce able to
stand, and experienced great difficulty in getting away.'

of two delightful cottages, was known as 'French wife's house.'[1] It was old, even then, and was put in a state of repair, in November, 1733, and leased in the next year to Thomas Robinson and John Birdsall, as Overseers of the Poor, at a rent of 10s. p.a. It must have been at this time that the unpleasant underground cell was made, and here, in the 'Black Hole,' refractory tramps were placed, until sent before the magistrate sitting in the North Parlour of the Hall, where judgement would be given. As late as about 1850, this horrible 'Black Hole' was used as a village prison, and old Richard Birdsall, who lived in the Almshouses until 1909, used to say that the last prisoner was a woman, released by four men who forcibly broke their way in to effect her rescue.[2]

Village tradition says that John Wesley once preached in Thornton at Box Tree Farm. The fact is not recorded in his *Journal*; but it is certainly possible, as he passed through from Scarborough to Middleton, on Wednesday, 16 July, 1766;[3] and the time taken over the journey would allow him to be able to do so. Whether it was due to the personal appeal of John Wesley or not, by the beginning of the nineteenth century Wesleyanism was very strong in Thornton, the first chapel being the old house at the corner of Roxby Terrace and Maltongate,[4] and, as early as 1813, a Chapel capable of holding 400 persons was erected at a cost of £1500.[5] Three years later a large Methodist Sunday School was founded with a regular attendance of 180.[6] It is noticeable that in the early years of the century there was no Church Sunday School.[7] Thornton, however, was not left without other philanthropic institutions, for it had a most flourishing Friendly Society of 400 members with an accumulated Capital Fund of £4000 in 1824,[8] and besides this, there was a Cow Club, which proved invaluable to its members for a time, but having died out was resuscitated in 1908.

The cottage-like rectory, built by Dean Comber at the end of

---

[1] Sam. Tetley, *ut supra*. It may have had this name from 'Mrs. Anne Barney, a Frenchwoman,' whose illegitimate child 'Rowland John' was baptized in Ellerburn Church, 7 April, 1692. *Vide* Ellerburn Register.

[2] G. Home, *ut supra*, p. 279.

[3] Wesley's *Journal*, III. p. 261. *Cf. Wesleyan Methodist Record, Christmas*, 1900. I am indebted to Mrs. William Croft of Box Tree.

[4] This is the house dated 1721 at the north side of Roxby Terrace and Maltongate and once the property of W. Wilmott.

[5] Bulmer, *ut supra*, pp. 1124-6.

[6] Young, p. 873, says that the Methodist ministers, in 1817, for Thornton and district were Henry Anderson and Charles Ratcliffe.

[7] Ibid.

[8] Eastmead, pp. 318-9.

the seventeenth century,[1] was destroyed by the Rev. J. R. Hill in 1839, and the present comfortable rectory-house was completed the next year.[2] By the middle of the century the fabric of the Church again required attention, and was restored at considerable cost in 1866.[3] Since 1870 several buildings that had stood along Beck Isle for more than a century[4] have been destroyed. About 1888 the appearance of the lower part of Maltongate was slightly altered by the building of Ellerburn Vicarage on an open site, but requiring for its garden the destruction of two ancient whitewashed and thatched cottages[5] abutting on the main road, and making the south corner of the modern Roxby Terrace.[6] The two chapels in Pickeringgate and Maltongate were built in October, 1900 and August, 1909, respectively; and the century-old Chapel in Whitbygate was converted into a private house some years ago.

Since 1895, in addition to the already mentioned chapels, there have been numerous changes.[7] A different type of house came into existence at the end of the century, when building began in Roxby Terrace and was followed by Holbeck Terrace and Jessamine Villas. 'The Lodge' and 'Farmanby' gave a new appearance to the land adjoining the old Roxby fields, and the spirit of Sir Hugh Cholmley, returning to his ancient haunts, would hardly recognise Roxby Hill with its smaller houses on the south, and 'Roxby,' built about 1910, on the north. Towards Scarborough additions have also been made, and four or five houses have been erected during the last thirty years that have extended the village eastward. The most complete alteration, however, is in the centre of the village. The tiny post-office[8] of the 'nineties kept by Mrs. F. A. Garbutt, who deputised for her father, and the small general shop owned by the village factotum, photographer, stationer, carriage-proprietor, rate collector, registrar, postmaster, and churchwarden, Thomas

[1] *Vide* Ch. IX.
[2] Ibid.
[3] Ibid.
[4] Shown on map of 1780. G. F. G. H.
[5] Richard Wray kindly gave me an old photograph of these two cottages.
[6] As late as 1888 the present Roxby Terrace was known as 'Key Lane.'
[7] The village street obtained a different aspect after the establishment of stand pipes. The water works were created in June, 1901, and were enlarged with a new ram below 'Jinny Trout' in the autumn of 1928.
[8] The earliest postmaster I have been able to find is Matthew Labron in 1759. In the mid-nineteenth century old Bennet Dow was postmaster and for many years the post-office stood where the house with its Adam's door is divided between Ingle's Café and T. Coverdale's Boot Shop. At one time in the eighteenth century, this must have been one of the best houses in the village.

Wardill,[1] son of John Wardill, carpenter, have now blossomed into two quite separate concerns; the one the large modern post-office under the present postmaster, Alfred Garbutt, on the east side of the Beck, and the other, the much extended premises, still on the old site on the west under the able management of 'Tom' Wardill's grandsons, Messrs. H. and W. Garbutt. These, together with 'The Institute,' erected in memory of the late Rev. J. R. Hill, in November, 1897,[2] have transformed this part of the village. But they have not deprived it of its old world beauty; and the ancient Cross still stands, horrified, perhaps, at the influx of chars-à-bancs and the accompanying litter, but after so many centuries of watchfulness, it must have learnt that nothing will prevent the changes effected by time, though all such changes are not necessarily for the better.

[1] I cannot let this opportunity pass without a word as to Thomas Wardill's sister, Alice Ann Wardill. Possessed of one of the kindest hearts in the village, 'Nana' had the affection of everyone. To her we all turned for village lore and history. Her memory was unfailing; her goodwill unbounded; and her faithfulness well-proved as housekeeper and friend of the family of R. A. Scott, Esq. for thirty years. She died 4 May, 1923, aged 77.

[2] The Rev. Edward W. Heslop, by will, proved 14 March, 1900, bequeathed £100, the income of which was to be applied for the benefit of this institute. *Cf.* V. C. H. *N.R.* II. p. 497.

CHAPTER SEVEN.

The Inhabitants and their Industries.

'But a bold peasantry, their country's pride,
When once destroyed can never be supplied.'
> OLIVER GOLDSMITH, D.D. 1770.

'Local history has its roots in the distant past, but it
often helps us to understand the origins of present-
day life.' W. CUNNINGHAM, D.D. 1919.

TO ardent lovers of the past all change presents a melancholy aspect. It seems strange that in Thornton, to-day, there are no resident members of certain families, which in earlier times, took such an active part in village affairs. The Atkinsons, the Barughs, the Champleys, the Ecclefields, the Fairfaxes, the Hassells, the Horsleys, and the Priestmans have all gone.

The Atkinsons appear in Thornton records as far back as the beginning of the sixteenth century and continued to reside until the late eighteenth. The earliest to be mentioned is Robert Atkinson, son of Christopher, who was buried on 25 November, 1542. The first male to be married was Richard 'Atkynson' who espoused Annas Johnson, on 16 November, 1570; and their child 'Kateran' was baptized on 23 March, 1571/2. And so they continued until the 24 May, 1731, when Roger Atkinson[1] received from John Hill a piece of land called Harrowcliff in Botton Field, and gave to him, in exchange, one broadland in Hurrell, consisting of 1 ac. 1 ro. 20 per., with glebe land on the west, John Hill's land on the east, Charity land on the south and Harrowcliff on the north, and 3 roods more and another small piece reaching to Hungerill gutter on the south.[2] By 1769 financial difficulties[3] had set in, for all the Atkinson land had been mortgaged to Mrs. Ann Croft; it then passed into the hands of the Hill family; and on 25 April, 1788, 'Josiah Maynard[4] handed over to Richard Johnson

---

[1] Buried and paid a mortuary of 10s. on 6 January, 1735/6.
[2] G. F. G. H.
[3] Up to 6 January, 1735/6 all must have been well, for Roger Atkinson when buried was charged a mortuary of 10s. This was supposed to be measured by a man's worth or 'stability' as the Church Terriers say.
[4] Richard Johnson Hill's land agent.

Hill all Roger Atkinson's property.'[1]

The Barughs, or Barghs or Barghts or Burges appear in the Registers on 10 February, 1539/40, when 'Rycherde Barugh' was buried; but from other sources they are known to have been in the village before 1458.[2] The family remained in Thornton until the reign of Charles II, when it probably moved to Wilton. The last to be married was 'Jane Bargh' to Edward Sellar[3] on 25 June, 1668; the last to be baptized was Anne 'Burge' daughter of John on 2 February, 1674/5, and she was the last to be buried in Thornton on 12 August, 1677. One member of the family, Agnes 'Burgh' or 'Bergh' is named in a somewhat inexplicable grant of James I, inexplicable in the sense that it is the only document, so far discovered, that seems to show that the Priory of Wilberfoss ever held any property in Thornton. Whether the wording of the grant is erroneous, and for 'Wilberfoss' we should read 'Rosedale,' or whether the Priory of Wilberfoss did really hold a small property in the village is very difficult to say. It is, perhaps, as a document requiring explanation, worthy of being quoted in full.

'King James in x[th] yr. granted to John Eldred and his heirs all that p̄cel of land in the tenure of Agnes Burgh in Thorneton in Pickeringlithe, p̄cel of the late Priory of Wilberfosse.

in xv[th] yr. granted to John Grey and his heirs a p̄cel of meadow vo[c] The Kirke or Churching[4] in Thorneton in Pickeringlithe.

in xxii[nd] yr. granted to John Hewet and his heirs all that p̄cel of land & all ten[ts] & in occ. Agnes Bergh viḋ. in Thorneton in Pickeringlithe & in Farmanby in the p̄ish of Ellerburn late p[arcel] of the Priory of Wilberfosse.'[5]

There is no reason why the Priory of Wilberfoss should not have held some land in Thornton, but at present where it was and when it was conveyed have evaded discovery.

The first Champley to appear in Thornton history was George 'Champay,' father of Roger 'Champnay,' as the name was occasionally spelt, who was baptized on 13 September, 1539.[6] From that time forward until well into the nineteenth century some members

---

[1] G. F. G. H.

[2] The will of Richard Barugh, 'Thornton in Pickerynglith,' Esq. was made on 1 June, 1457 and proved 7 April, 1458. The will of another Richard Barghe of 'Thorneton in Pykerynglith' was proved 27 October, 1512. *Cf.* Y. A. S. Rec. S. VI. pp. 12, 193.

[3] They were possibly the parents of the bellmaker E 'Seller' in 1710.

[4] I am informed by Mrs. Richard Hill that there is no piece of land known by this name in 1930.

[5] G. F. G. H.

[6] 'Roger Champnay ye son of George Champay [*sic*] was crystynde ye xiij day of September' 1539.

of the family were resident in the village. In the reign of Charles II, Robert Champley bought four oxgangs of arable in Thornton from John and William Monkman of Allerston, and on two occasions, exchanged land with John Hill, I. On 13 January, 1669,[1] John Hill gave Robert Champley, yeoman, land on Dudda Hill,[2] extending to the ditch called Outgang Ditch,[3] to the way called Wilton way on the south, between the lands of Christopher Bradley,[4] on the east, and the lands of Roger Browne on the west, in the East Field, in exchange for 4 acres of meadow lying in 'ffarmanby Ings.'[5] The second exchange was on 15 May, 1674,[6] when John Hill again gave to Robert Champley a piece in 'Buttery Stub' extending from Bottons Way, in exchange for 2 broadlands in Botton Field. The names of Robert and John Champley occur on the Enclosure maps of 1780 and 1796. They tilled their own land, but were also, possibly, tenants of the Dalby farm for a short time. Robert Champley, farmer, was again mentioned as a freeholder, in the '*Poll of the County of York*,' in 1807; but once again, in error, the name is spelt 'Champney.' They have left their memorials outside the Church in the shape of tombs to Robert Champley of Dalby, 1759 to 1827, and to others; and inside, to 'John Champley of Thornton and Scarborough' 1791-1864, and to John Champley Rutter, 1798-1870. Their present representative,[7] who has not forgotten the home of her ancestors, is Mrs. Whitney, wife of the eminent historian, Professor Whitney, Fellow of Emmanuel College, Cambridge.[8]

The family of Ecclefield may date back to the fifteenth century, when Richard Ecclefield was lord of one of the manors in Thornton for a short time.[9] But if the later family came of this stock its fortunes went down hill. A 'Frauncis Aglefield' [Ecclefield]married

---

[1] G. F. G. H.

[2] Sometimes spelt Dodohill: *vide infra.*

[3] Utgang Way below Nabgate.

[4] The Rector. *Vide* Ch. IX.

[5] It is possibly out of these Ings that the charity of 6s. 8d. known as 'Samuel Skelton's dole' arises. It was to come from Carr Field and an adjoining field called 'the Ings.'

[6] G. F. G. H.

[7] V. C. H. *N.R.* II. p. 497; refers to a charity founded by Robert Champley in 1895 to be applied by the incumbent and churchwardens of Thornton in the distribution of money and coal.

[8] For a full pedigree of this family *vide* Foster, *Pedigrees of Yorkshire*, III.

[9] *Vide* Ch. XII. Foster's *Visitations of Yorkshire* is unsatisfactory on this family. It is stated that Thomas Eglesfield of Barton-in-the-Willows, had as his second son Bryan who married Ann, daughter of ? Watson and widow of ? Cleyburgh. They had a son, William of Farmanby, who married Ann daughter of ? Browne, and they had three sons: Bryan, b. 1608, William and John.

Annas Burton on 11 November, 1584.[1]   William 'Eggleford'
[Ecclefield] was evidently a man of substance in 1605.[2]   A Robert
'Eglefield' owned, about 1660, two broadlands of arable in Botton
Field, and these he sold to Roger Browne, who, in turn, on 1 March,
1674 exchanged them for another piece in 'Botton' with John Hill
I.[3]   Possibly this same Robert, and his brother William 'Egglefield,' were freeholders in Farmanby in 1675.[4]   A Robert 'Ecclefield,' joiner, was buried in August, 1697;[5] and it may have been
his daughter Diana who is mentioned in 1711.   There was a 'widow
Egglefield' whose house was burned down in 1734.[6]   In the latter
part of the eighteenth century there was one Robert 'Ecclefield'
who had numerous children between 1790 and 1812; there
was another Robert, who had a daughter Miriam in 1844; and there
was a Peter Ecclefield, who had several children, one of whom was
William Ecclefield, born 26 March, 1794.[7]   He became, as years went
by, a village character.   He was always known as 'Old Willie
Ecclefield,' and lived in Brock Lane.   His duties were those of
kennel man and hound feeder at the Hall, and when going to be
married he asked the Squire, Richard Hill, if there was anything
that he wanted done, especially that day, with regard to the
hounds, for if so, he would put off *'getten wed,'* until convenient.
Tradition says that he once cooked a fox and ate it, to see what
it tasted like; but there is no record of the eccentric old man's
comments.   He used to play the piccolo in the Church band before
an organ was introduced.[8]   When it was proposed that there should
be an organ, 'old Willie' asked *'Will she gang to ma fluett?'*   He was
told that he must play his flute no more.   This he could not, or
would not, understand; and on one or two of the Sundays when
the organ was first played, the old man burst in with a tootle from
'ma fluett.'   The rector remonstrated on the first occasion in vain,
but when it happened a second time, and 'Willie' was forbidden

---

[1] C. R.   He may be the Francis who sold the manor of Barton-in-the-
Willows in 1607.   *Vide* V. C. H. *N.R.* I. p. 117.

[2] List of Armour, *vide* Ch. IV.   The will of Brian Egglesfield of Farmanby
was proved on 9 September, 1616: of Richard Egglesfield on 27 August, 1610:
of William Egglesfield on 5 September, 1614: and of Richard 'Eglefield of
Farmonby' on 20 May, 1681.   *Cf.* Y. A. S. Rec. S. LXXIII. p. 45.   A Jane
'Ecclesfield' lived in Allerston in 1691.   *Cf.* Y. A. J. I.

[3] G. F. G. H.

[4] Ibid.

[5] C. R.

[6] Sam. Tetley, *ut supra.*

[7] C. R.

[8] I was told this by Miss Mary Hardy.   The piccolo was given by 'old
Willie' to the Rev. Arthur Hill who had it for years at the High Hall and
gave it to Harold Robinson of Thornton.

sternly to play, he ceased to come to Church and never came again.[1] He died in March, 1872, much regretted as being one of the last of the real old village characters.

Another family that was of some importance in Ellerburn-cum-Farmanby for a short time during the seventeenth century was that of Fairfax. By the end of the century the name is known no more. They were descended from Cuthbert, the third son of Sir Nicholas Fairfax of Gilling Castle and of the manor of Dunsley. Cuthbert Fairfax died in 1606 and was soon followed to the grave by his son Nicholas in 1609, who had married Jane, eldest daughter of Ralph Hungate.[2] He left two sons, Hungate, who died in 1637,[3] and Thomas, lord of Sand Hutton and Dunsley and who, in 1665, lived in Dunsley.[4] But in later years he evidently lived in Farmanby for he was buried at Ellerburn in 1680.[5] His son Isaac was born in 1633[6] and lived part of his time, at any rate, in Farmanby being declared in 1670 to be an occupier of 'Calverts House and 1 Oxgang of Francis Dale's land.'[7] This holding gave him common rights and in 1678 he was mentioned in the Farmanby Award as being allotted 20 ac. in 'Wisberdales' and West Ends.[8] He was buried at Ellerburn on 1 August, 1687.[9] Of two of his daughters nothing is known, except that with their mother Katherine, they held the manor of Sand Hutton in 1688;[10] a third, Catherine, married Samuel Hassell, of [Sand] Hutton, in Ellerburn Church, on 19 April, 1683;[11] and the youngest, Dorothy was buried at Ellerburn on 27 September, 1681.[12] Isaac Fairfax had numerous brothers and sisters. There are no local records concerning Thomas, Nicholas, George and Elizabeth. But of the three youngest something is known. Melior was baptized at Bossall on 16 December, 1641,[13] and at some suitable period married a man called Hird.[14] She married secondly, as his second wife, Samuel Robinson, son of the rector of Thornton. The

---

[1] I was told this by R. A. Scott, Esq. who had heard the story from his father-in-law, the Rev. E. W. Heslop.

[2] V. C. H. *N.R.* II. p. 94.

[3] Ibid. p. 519.

[4] Ibid.

[5] *The Genealogist*, N.S. pp. 174-5.

[6] Ibid.

[7] White vellum MS. folio 'Accounts of the Honor of Pickering,' G. F. G. H.

[8] G. F. G. H.

[9] *The Genealogist, ut supra.*

[10] V. C. H. *N.R.* II. p. 94.

[11] *The Genealogist, ut supra.*

[12] Ibid. *The Genealogist* does not agree here with either Foster, *Yorkshire Pedigrees*, or V. C. H. *N.R.* II. p. 94.

[13] Ibid.

[14] Conveyances, G. F. G. H.

marriage could not have taken place before October, 1669, when Helen the first wife of Robinson died;[1] but it must have been before April, 1673, as her name began at that date to appear in the mortgage documents of the family.[2] Samuel Robinson is shown, from these business papers to have been dead by 1683; Melior, however, is stated to be alive as a widow in 1691, but her name does not occur in a mortgage of 1692.[3] Her sister Lucretia was baptized on 11 January, 1645,[4] and probably while staying with the Robinsons came in contact with George Jackson, of Whitby, draper, and they were married at Thornton, on 8 September, 1672.[5] The youngest sister, Anne, was married in Thornton Church on 1 June, 1675,[6] to William Smith, clerk in Holy Orders, but whether he was curate to Christopher Bradley in his declining years or not, is not shown.[7]

The Hassells also appear in the seventeenth century. The first name of this family in the baptismal register is 'Thomas Hassell son of Thomas,' on 1 April, 1635.[8] The first to be buried is Philip Hassell on 10 December, 1645. He is followed by Ralph Hassell 'gent' on 7 September, 1655,[9] and his will, dated 4 February, 1654/5, was administered by 'Isabel Harison [*sic*] relict' in 1657.[10] Presumably she was the same as 'Mrs. Isabell Hassell, widow,' who was buried on 13 September, 1658.[11] John Hassell married Mary Hunter, daughter of Bethell Hunter, lord of one of the Thornton manors,[12] on 22 February, 1657/8, and died on 12 October, 1670.[13] The family was particularly connected with Dalby, and some members of it held a lease for many years.[14] The last, however, to be mentioned in the Registers, is the Rev. Thomas Hassell, vicar of Seamer, who was buried at Thornton, on 11 February, 1706/7.

[1] C. R.
[2] G. F. G. H.
[3] Ibid.
[4] *The Genealogist, ut supra.*
[5] C. R.
[6] Ibid.
[7] A Mrs. Catherine Fairfax of the parish of Cottingham is mentioned in the Ellerburn Registers 24 February, 1693/4.
[8] C. R.
[9] Ibid. V. C. H. *N.R.* II. p. 447 says that Robert Gere of Great Barugh conveyed that 'Manor to Thomas Hassell, apparently as a marriage settlement, on the marriage of Thomas his son and Mary, daughter of Ralph Hassell of Thornton.' According to the Church Register the marriage took place 27 November, 1656.
[10] Y. A. S. Rec. S. I. p. 167.
[11] C. R.
[12] *Vide* Ch. XII.
[13] C. R.
[14] *Vide* Ch. XVI.

The Horsley family was at one time closely associated with Farmanby and Ellerburn.[1] Between 1591 and 1601 Christopher, William, Frank, and Roger Horsley were all churchwardens in Ellerburn. In 1623 Francis Horsley is described as a 'gentleman' of Thornton;[2] and on 17 November, 1664, William Horsley married Helen Barugh.[3] Between 1710 and 1711, the family was still dwelling in Farmanby, represented by Richard Horsley;[4] and in 1711, Robert Horsley had the water mill called Millholme. As late as 1807, Thomas Horsley was a freeholder and farmer at Ellerburn; but soon after that date the name of the family appears no more,[5] except for the fact that there was a Grace Horsley in the Almshouses as late as 1867.[6]

Members of the Priestman family have been continuously resident in Thornton from before 1544 to 1928. The first to be mentioned was George 'Prestman,' who was buried 9 August, 1544.[7] He had made his will on 22 June, and is therein described as 'husband man.'[8] The first to be baptized was John 'Prestman' on 26 August, 1548, and the first marriage is that of John 'Presmande' to 'Ellyng Thomson' on 5 November, 1563. At the end of the sixteenth and beginning of the seventeenth century the family was an increasing one. The most frequent male christian names were John, Richard, Thomas, and once Roger. They evidently had a liking for somewhat peculiar female names. Thus we find in the Registers, Annas, Sissalayne, Sissalaye, Issabell and Mehetabell. A John 'Preistman' married Alice Smales on 30 November, 1641, and was buried on 21 September, 1657.[9] His widow administered the will in 1659.[10] His sons were George, baptized 2 October, 1642, John, baptized 7 April, 1647, and Richard, baptized 25 February, 1653/4.[11] The will of Richard Priestman,[12] dated 8 February, 1684/5, shows him to have been a carpenter and mariner at Scarborough, but closely connected with Thornton. He gave to his wife, Mary, a piece of land in Thornton, then in

---

[1] Y. A. J. XVIII. pp. 211-13.
[2] N. R. Rec. S. O.S. III. p. 159.
[3] C. R.
[4] G. F. G. H.
[5] *Poll of the County of York*, 1807.
[6] Document of Lady Lumley's Charity, J. L. W.
[7] C. R. It might be of interest to note that there was a William 'Prestman' at Flamborough in 1297, a Ralph 'Prestman' of Bootham, York in 1327 and a Simon 'Prestman' at Seamer in the same year.
[8] Y. A. S. Rec. S. VI. p. 91.
[9] C. R.
[10] Y. A. S. Rec. S. I. p. 250.
[11] C. R.
[12] Copy of the will, G. F. G. H.

the hands of his brother John, together with the house in Farmanby given to him by his uncle, Robert 'Smailes.' To his mother he left 40s. p.a. for life. His daughters, Elizabeth and Alice were, no doubt, at the time infants, but ultimately succeeded to what property there was. By the beginning of the eighteenth century, they had moved from Thornton and resided at Barking in Essex, and while there, sold on 20 May, 1712, to John Hill two and a half acres, in the Low Carr,[1] probably Priestman's Carr, which in 1729 is shown to abut on 'Priestman's Farm called Cottage Carrs' near the Syme.[2] Long before this, as already shown,[3] the family had become Quakers, and in 1700 'devine' service was conducted in the house of John Priestman.[4] In 1743 John Priestman was a tenant of John Hill, III., holding the New Close called Hurrell.[5] John and Samuel Priestman are registered as freeholders on the Enclosure Map of 1780;[6] and the former on 23 January, 1787, rented the Corn Mill.[7] He was in touch with the famous Quaker, William Allen,[8] who used to correspond with him on large foolscap sheets, written in the most marvellously minute hand, telling him, for example in 1791, all the news of the French Revolution and what were the chances of victory in the Slave Trade question.[9] Jonathan Priestman,[10] (died 1816) held the Tan Yard, at the end of the eighteenth century,[11] and it was carried on by Joshua and John Priestman as late as 1861.[12]

The will of Joshua Priestman, senior,[13] proved 22 January, 1845, shows him as a yeoman while other documents give evidence that he was a corn-miller and tanner. He had a large family

---

[1] G. F. G. H.

[2] From a volume of about 1774 based on a survey of 1729, kindly lent by the Rev. Godfrey Marshall.

[3] *Vide* Ch. V.

[4] Thomas Priestman was probably not a Quaker as he is entered in the Thornton Register as being buried, 6 July, 1699.

[5] Sam. Tetley, *ut supra.*

[6] G. F. G. H.

[7] Ibid.

[8] Allen, William, 1770 to 1843; quaker, scientist and philanthropist. *Cf.* D. N. B. I. p. 322.

[9] This interesting letter was kindly shown me by Miss Ethel Priestman.

[10] In 1807 he is described as a farmer.

[11] G. F. G. H.

[12] It may have been even later but Documents of Lady Lumley's Charity (J. L. W.) show that they were at the Tan Yard in April, 1861. The Rate Books prove that they had ceased to occupy the yard in 1869; and a document in the possession of J. H. Fraser, Esq. states that the Rev. J. R. Hill purchased the Tan Yard on 16 December, 1882.

[13] Son of John Priestman (Will. 14 March, 1807) and nephew of David Priestman. Joshua's wife's name was Hannah.

including three sons and three daughters Samuel,[1] Joshua, John, Rebecca,[2] Jane, and Mary.[3] The most conspicuous of the three brothers was John, born in 1805[4] at Thornton. He was educated at the Friends School, Ackworth, and afterwards apprenticed to an uncle at York as a tanner. But as early as 1824 the call came to the rising industrial centre of Bradford, where John Priestman joined his brother-in-law, James Ellis, in the Old Corn Mill. Both of them were men who were guided by the highest philanthropic principles and as such founded, and financially supported, the first ragged schools in Bradford. John Priestman, however, did more than this, for his name is remembered as one of the creators, in 1832, of the Friends Provident Institution, a society which obtained as years went by immense success, partly because he remained on the board of direction until his death, and partly because of sound economic management and the self-abnegation of the members. John Priestman was well-known too, for his support of the Anti-Corn Law League and his resistance to the collection of church rates. It was not until 1838 that he began the manufacture of woollen goods, and so satisfactory did this prove that he ultimately resigned the millstone in favour of the weaver's shuttle. It is said that owing to his sympathetic and enlightened treatment of his mill-hands, chiefly women, 'their tone grew so refined that his works obtained the title of "Lady Mills." '[5] Like other members of his family he was devoted to the causes of peace[6] and temperance; and, until his death on 29 October, 1866, he sternly adhered to the Quaker principles of his forebears.[7] His two nephews, Alfred and John Priestman, sons of Joshua Priestman, junior,[8] were also connected with the Bradford manufacturing trade, but ever kept in very close touch with Thornton owning

---

[1] Joshua in his will of 1845 left his dwelling-house (the present Brook Cottage) to his son Samuel, who appears to have lived at Sutton, near York. Samuel Priestman and Mary Anne his wife, conveyed the house, on 6 April, 1846, to Joshua Priestman, junior.

[2] Named after her aunt, Rebecca Hopkins, daughter of John Priestman.

[3] Married James Ellis of Bradford. She died before 1845.

[4] D. N. B. xlvi, pp. 377-8.

[5] Ibid.

[6] He was a great supporter of Richard Cobden in his condemnation of the Crimean War.

[7] He married first on 28 November, 1833, Sarah, daughter of Joseph Burgess of Beaumont Lodge, Leicester, who died 1849, leaving two sons, Edward and Frederick, and a daughter, who married Joseph Edmondson of Halifax. Secondly he married in 1852, Mary, daughter of Thomas Smith, miller, of Uxbridge, Middlesex, by whom he left Arnold, a landscape artist, and Walter.

[8] He died 22 February, 1874.

until well into the present century two[1] of the most charming
houses in the village on what is called Priestman's Lane and other
properties such as Dale Bank Closes, Priestman's plantation,[2]
certain cottages[3] in Kirk Lane and fields called Duddy Hill,[4]
Town End close[5] and Common close.[6] The widows of Alfred and
John Priestman survived them for a short time, and after their
deaths, the last member of the family to reside in Thornton was
Miss Ethel Priestman,[7] who always took the keenest interest in
the welfare of the village, particularly of the little children.
Generation after generation for four hundred years the Priestman
family has played its part in the life of Thornton, but now, long
respected and full of good works, it has passed from the ancestral
home.

Of families which have dwelt in Thornton for centuries and
which still remain, there are many. A few may be selected. The
name of the family of Boyes, derived from *bois* is perhaps a natural
one to find in a great forest district. The first one to be found in
the neighbourhood, at Kingthorpe, is mentioned as early as the
reign of Henry III;[8] though the family does not appear in the
Thornton Registers until 1568, from which date to the present day,
it repeats with regularity. The family of Skelton obtained its
name, not from Skelton, near York, but from the ancient Brus
Castle at Skelton in Cleveland, and it was the Brus connection
with both Thornton and Pickering, that brought the first Skeltons
into this district in the fourteenth century. The family appears in
the Thornton Registers in early Tudor times, and was closely
connected with a family of the same name in Sinnington.[9] The
Bakers date from the reign of Henry VIII. 'Roger Baker, ye son

---

[1] The one on the north, Brook Cottage, was bought by J. H. Fraser,
Esq. from the executors of Henry Brady Priestman, son of the John Priestman above. The one on the south, now known as Beck Hall or Beckside
was formerly occupied by Alfred Priestman and at a much earlier date, as
shown by a conveyance of 1888 by his great uncle, Joseph Priestman.

[2] Now part of Woodland Farm.

[3] Two of these (in one of which Matthew Grimes, the Waterloo veteran,
resided) were converted by Alfred Priestman into the present 'Kirkbrow,'
now owned by Mrs. Richard Hill.

[4] This was bought by Joseph Priestman, son of John Priestman (will, 1807)
from John Dixon.

[5] This was bought by Joseph Priestman from William Spendley.

[6] This is mentioned in the will of Joshua Priestman, senior, as 'my close
of land called the common close in Thornton,' and was left by him to Joshua
Priestman, junior, and in 1888 was tenanted by John Bolton, James Hornsey
and another.

[7] She migrated to the south of England in 1928.

[8] 1241-2. *The Great Roll of the Pipe*, p. 25.

[9] Y. A. Rec. S. LV. *passim*.

of John Bakar was crystynd the fourte day of November' 1538. Roger Baker has the honour to be the first named in the new register called into being by the order of Thomas Cromwell, Vicar-General. The Whites follow closely on this, for the next entry is 'Wyllm Gwhytte ye son of Rycherde Gwhytt was crystynede ye xxvi[th] day of January' 1538/9; and they come, one after the other, with the most wonderful spelling, such as Gwyt, Whyte, Whytt, Whiet, Whitt, Whit,[1] until, about 1607 there is the usual form of White. The earliest appearance of the family of Roger or Rogers is in 1540. The first Robinson is 'Marie Robynson,' buried 21 June, 1546.[2] Of other familiar names there are between 1540 and 1580, those of Maw, Watson, Birdsall,[3] Harland, Read, Smith, Green and Smales, or Smailes or Smayles. In 1580 there are such names as Raw, Nellis and Merser or Mercer, but they lack continuity. The Dixons are registered for the first time when Matthew Dixon, son of Jacob, was baptized on 23 September, 1607. On 2 June, 1692, James Dixon, 'ffellmonger' and Elizabeth his wife sold to John Hill, I. a parcel of pasture or meadow in Whitgate lands in the High Fields of Farmanby of 2 roods 18 perches. On 4 June, 1739, and in Trinity Term, 1740, Robert Dixon and Margaret his wife exchanged with and sold to John Hill, III. certain messuages in Thornton.[4] The Gambles are mentioned first, when 'Marie Gamble' daughter of Matthew Gamble, was baptized on 26 June, 1623. The first Buttery was in 1640, the first Hoggard in 1643, the first Marfitt or Marflitt in 1646.[5] About 1663 the names of Wray and Widd both begin to be entered,[6] followed in 1669, by Cockerill,[7] in 1672, by Wood, in 1692, by Croft, in 1700, by Cross and in 1717, by Hardy.

Throughout the centuries, agriculture, though by far the most

---

[1] The spelling here is very peculiar, but after all, Raleigh, Shakespeare, and Pepys and many others had the same idiosyncrasy.

[2] A family still in the village to be distinguished from the Robinsons who became lords of one of the Thornton manors in the latter part of the sixteenth century and remained so till the beginning of the eighteenth. *Vide* Ch. XIII.

[3] The first date in which I have found this name at Thornton is 1499. The name was sometimes pronounced 'Bossle' and occasionally in the eighteenth century spelt this way.

[4] G. F. G. H.

[5] The spelling of this name varies very much. The Churchwarden in 1765-6 spelt his name James Marfitt. The tombstones up to 1875 show Marfitt, e.g., Thomas Marfitt, Senr. of the City of York died 11 September, 1771; another Thomas Marfitt died 24 February, 1837. In many mediaeval documents the spelling is Marflet. In the *Polling Register* of 1929 it is spelt 'Marflitt.'

[6] In 1655 the Widds lived in Wilton.

[7] This name can be found in this district as far back as 1334, but not in Thornton.

important, was not the only industry in Thornton. Corn-milling, fulling, bleaching, wool, hemp and linen weaving, straw-hat making,[1] gloving, tanning,[2] lime-burning, building, butchering and game-preserving were carried on year after year.

As to farmers their name is legion. It would be impossible to go back previous to 1700, to give the names of those who tilled the soil for profit. Before that date, most men[3] had some share in the great village fields, but gradually farms, not in the modern sense, for they were still split up into strips until 1780, and even to 1796, but still, farms of many scattered strips, let on lease by the land-lord, began to come into existence. In 1702, Henry Joyner and John Kirby were farmers. In 1711, in Farmanby, there were Richard Horsley, Richard 'Natress,' Robert Marshall and Robert Champley. In 1717 a man called Dobson farmed 'Monklands';[4] and died, as of 'Hag House' in 1722.[5] In 1734 the following were tenants of the Hill family, some as farmers and others as cottagers— Robert Maw, William Pinkney, George Champley, Roger Coates, John Eaman, John Boyes, Robert Watson, John Priestman, William Gill, Richard Baker, John Croft, John Skelton, John Buttery, Robert Smales, John Thompson, Robert White, William Read, Richard Birdsall, Robert Dixon, William Allanson, Edward Kitching, Richard Webster, Thomas 'Marfett,' Elizabeth 'Hawsome,' Elizabeth Hunter and 'widow Egglefield.'[6] In 1741, John Marshall is mentioned as continuing to hold the farm at Ellerburn, including the bleaching mill,[7] Mallison's Close,[8] 'Buffit Close' and 5 acres in 'Kyrkdale.'[9] Two years later John Todd had 'pannierman's Stable,'[10] and ground about the Low Hall.[11] 'He is abated 5s. of what his rent was last year in Consideration of a great part of the ground about Low Hall being planted with trees.'[12] At the same period, William Postgate[13] rented a small farm, and amongst names that did not

---

[1] About 1837, George Smith was a straw-hat maker in a thatched bonnet shop at the south corner of Brock Lane, from whom the Misses Hill purchased their best and gayest bonnets.

[2] Under Jonathan and Joshua Priestman. Two tanners, Thomas Reynolds and George Allanson died in 1817.

[3] But by no means all.

[4] G. F. G. H.

[5] Ellerburn Ch. Reg.

[6] Sam. Tetley, *ut supra.*

[7] *Vide infra.*

[8] Named after the previous holders in 1711, 'widow Mallison' and Thomas Mallison.

[9] G. F. G. H.

[10] *Cf.* Pannierman's Pool of to-day.

[11] At the south corner of Westgate.

[12] G. F. G. H.

[13] This family was in the village for some time.

occur in 1734, there is that of John Barnes. John Robinson tenanted Flainsey Warren[1] and a relative was at Dalby. In 1743, Richard Marshall paid £30. 0s. 0d. p.a. for a house, garth, Ellerburn Warren, one 'Wandall' and '2 Broads and a Gore on Dodo hill.'[2] 'Dinham Lands'[3] were held by Robert Champley, 'Landon Sandy Banks' by William Read the thatcher, the Incrofts[4] by John Gilbank, 'Broad Wandles' by Mary Hoggard and 'Narrow Wandles'[5] by Thomas Maw.[6] By 1785 the Marshalls seem to have left Ellerburn farm, for Richard Kirk in that year paid £6. 4s. 0d. for 'Buffit Wood, Buffit Close, the Bleaching Ground on the North side of the beck and Kirkdale Close.' Thomas Smales had 'Wisberdales' and 2 Closes, and William Spendley had 'Lark flatt Close'[7] and Champley Garth.[8] The effect of the Enclosure Act began to be seen by 1787, when William King rented Deerholme Farm at £50, William Smales paid £150 for Ringrose Farm[9] and Robert Lythe held Hagg House.[10] In 1807, there were the following farmers in the village, all of whom must have owned some freehold of their own, worth at least 40s. p.a. John Boyes, William 'Hawson'[11] Edward Jackson, George Pickering, Robert and Samuel Skelton, Robert Smithson, Richard Todd, John Watson, John Belt[12] and William Belt of Farmanby, Robert 'Champney,' William King, Jonathan Priestman, William Spendley, John Tweedy, George Crosby, Stephen Dixon, Thomas Horsley at Ellerburn, William Rogers, William Read, Richard Smailes, John Storr, Michael Wailes,[13] William Wilmott,[14] Jonathan

[1] *Vide* Ch. XVI.
[2] Now known as 'Duddy Hill' on the right-hand side of Utgang Lane. Doda is an old English personal name. *Cf.* A. H. Smith, *ut supra*, p. 332.
[3] *Vide* Ch. VI.
[4] At Ellerburn, known now as Elliot's Banks.
[5] *Vide* Ch. VI.
[6] G. F. G. H.
[7] [?] 'Larban flatt' mentioned in 1685.
[8] G. F. G. H.
[9] I made many inquiries with regard to this farm, but no one seems to remember it now. At last I found it in a survey of 1729, bounded on the west and south by Midsyke drain, on the north by Noble Carr and on the east by 'Priestman's Farm called Cottage Carrs.'
[10] G. F. G. H.
[11] His mother 'widow Hawson' had been a tenant of the Hill family in 1787.
[12] He held Thornton Common farm; and the present name 'Belt Common' is not, as often thought, from the belt of trees, but because of the name of the farmer. His daughter married James Elliot and was the mother of John Elliot, usually known as 'Lord John' of 'Ragby Castle' a nickname for his farm-house in the village 'up street.'
[13] Probably the same as 'Wyles.'
[14] William Wilmott succeeded Sam. Tetley, as steward to the Hill family in 1746. He resigned after 40 years in 1786. By that time he had acquired property in the village, mainly in Farmanby. He died 20 April, 1817, aged 95, leaving one daughter Hannah, who died 12 May, 1820, aged 58 years. The property or some of it is said to have passed to a Mrs. Craven. The memorial in Ellerburn Church says that William 'Willmott' was born at 'Bridgenorth in the County of Salop.'

Briggs and Jeffrey Nicholson of the Marishes. In 1814, some of the chief farmers were John Gamble, Joseph Croft, George Allanson, John Boyes, Matthew 'Reeviley,' William Hodgson and John Coates. Thirty-five years later there are the names, Benjamin, John and Samuel Baker, George Gamble, William Beilby, John Booth, Stephen Burden, Thomas Cross senior and junior, James Elliot,[1] Thomas Frank, John Lambert, Francis Mallory, Richard Miller, James Nichols, George and William Pickering, Hessel Robinson, Isabel Robson and Richard Smales.[2] Between 1840 and 1890 many changes took place. Farming went through two distinct phases. About 1840 to 1874, it boomed; but from the latter year it declined.[3] Some succeeded: some did not, and though many of the old names are still to be found, some have gone and their places have been taken by newcomers. The following were farming in the district in 1890. Philip Abbey, 'Low Newstead,' Simpson Allanson, 'Common Ellers,' Samuel Armstrong, 'Church Street,' William Brisby, 'Marishes,' Thomas Brisby, 'Newstead,' John Buttery, 'High Paper Mill,'[4] Joseph Coulson, 'Summertree Bridge,' Henry Coverdale, 'Hagg Farm,' William Croft, 'Box Tree,' John Cross, 'Low Dalby,' William Dennison, 'Church Street,' Thomas Dixon, 'Brock Lane,' John Elliot, 'Ragby Castle,' Mrs. Ann Gamble, 'Church Street,' Benjamin Gamble,[5] 'Maltongate,' Charles Grayson, 'Marishes,' George and Thomas Grayson, 'Carrs,' Thackray Green, 'Manor Farm,' William Green, 'Church Street,' Francis Hill, 'Church Street,' Robert Hill, 'High Grundon House,' Robert S. Marflitt, 'Westgate,' Thomas N. Marr,[6] 'The Hall Farm,' John Morrill, 'Westgate,' Mrs. Parker, 'Marishes,' Mrs. Alice Pearson, 'Low Grundon House,' Thomas Pearson, 'Newstead Grange,' Charles Pratt, 'Marishes,' Mark and Thomas Rex, 'Westgate,' George Robinson, 'Highfields,' Hessel P. Robinson, 'Ellerburn,' Thomas Robson, 'Newstead,' John Rodgers, 'Maltongate,' Thomas W. Sedman, 'Maltongate,' Alfred Smith, 'Brock Lane,' George Smith [?], John W. Spanton, 'Newstead,' William Walker, 'Todd Bridge Farm,' George Wharrick, 'Newstead,' Goodwill Weetman,

---

[1] Died 1861, aged 70.
[2] *East and North Ridings*, pp. 490-1.
[3] From 1854 to 1865 there were ten good harvests from 1874 to 1882 there were only two good crops; in 1893 there was a prolonged drought and in 1894 the average price of wheat was 22s. 10d. a quarter which was the lowest for more than one hundred years.
[4] Died, aged 84, June, 1915.
[5] When dying he could not be persuaded to make a will. His sister being annoyed at last said 'Get on with thi deeing an' tak bit with yer.'
[6] Was born at Kingthorpe and was a farmer in Thornton for 29 years.

'Church Street,' and Robert White, 'Maltongate.'[1]

In 1930 the only man still farming the same land as in 1890 is Alfred Smith of Brock Lane. Amongst the present farmers in the civil parish are— Fred. Allanson, 'The Carrs Farm,' Samuel T. Armstrong, 'Church Street,' Messrs. Avison, cattle dealers, Henry Barnes, 'Church Street,' Charles James Beauvais, 'The Hagg,' Johnson Beswick, 'Selleybridge,' John R. Bowes, 'High Paper Mill,' John Arthur Coulson, 'High Dalby,' William Croft, 'Box Tree,' Edward Darrell, 'Thornton Common,' Thomas Darrell, 'Maltongate,' George Elliot, 'Low Paper Mill,' Mrs. John Elliot, 'Ragby Castle,' Philip Abbey Hall, 'Low Newstead Grange,' Simon Hardy's trustees, 'Fir Tree Farm,' Henry Hill,[2] 'The Hall Farm,' Robert Hill,[2] 'Brock Lane,' Reginald Green, 'Brock Lane,' William Green, 'Manor Farm,' Charles Kirkby, 'Woodland Farm,' R. Marflitt, 'Westgate,' James Albert Robinson, 'Charity Farm,' Hessel Robinson, 'Ellerburn,' George Robinson, 'Grundon,' George Skelton, 'Maltongate,' F. E. Stonehouse, 'Willow Grange Farm,' Frank Weetman, 'Church Street,' George Wharrick, 'Rookwood,' John White, 'Maltongate,' Robert White, 'Westgate,' Robert White, 'Maltongate,' — Hirst, 'Newstead Grange,' A. Robson, 'Summertree Bridge,' William T. Barnby, 'Westgate.'

It is disappointing to find such poor records concerning corn-milling in the village, when it must always have been of very considerable importance. Perhaps it is because the mill was so essential to the people, and because in early times it would be a feudal property at which the tenants were bound to grind, that very little is said of it. It is certain that there was a corn-mill at Thornton as far back as the reign of Henry II,[3] but no miller is mentioned. The first known miller was called William, and flourished about the year 1200.[4] His successor was Robert '*molendinarius*,' about 1230,[5] and though he was somewhat of a trespasser in the Forest, he lived till 1245.[6] About the same period there was a corn-mill at Ellerburn, where now Robinson's farm stands. It probably dates back long before there is documentary evidence of it, in 1227.[7] It no doubt remained a corn-mill for some time, but by 1335, it had become a fulling mill.[8] There were two

---

[1] Bulmer, *ut supra*.
[2] No relation of the Hill family who own the property at the present time.
[3] Dulton, *Monasticon*, p. 363.
[4] *Whitby Chart.*, Sur. Soc. LXIX., p. 131. *Cf.* Charlton, *ut supra*, and *vide* Ch. IX.
[5] *Pipe Roll*, N.S. IV. p. 283.
[6] *Great Roll of the Pipe*, p. 30.
[7] Cal. Pat. R. 1225-32, p. 160.
[8] N. R. Rec. S. N.S. II. pp. 273-4.

millers in Thornton in 1301, Simon and Hugh;[1] but none are mentioned in the Lay Subsidies of 1327 and 1333, and no further references to mills or millers are to be found for many generations, except that there was a water corn-mill in Farmanby in 1618.[2] In 1733 William Rogers, son of William Rogers was paid £8. 0s. 0d. p.a.,[3] to act as miller, and he was still so doing in 1739, his faithful carter being John Atkinson.[4] Whether Rogers was succeeded by Richard Porret it is difficult to say, but he was certainly miller before 1777.[5] On 23 January, 1787, John Priestman[6] rented the Mill and closes at £61. 10s. 0d. p.a.; and in 1841, John Frank, one of a family of farmers, was miller. About 1857, Henry Hill[7] tried his hand at milling, and lived in the mill house,[8] and afterwards, in what is now called, Manor Farm. In 1867 William Gilson was miller. He was followed by John Priestman. In later years, John Boyes took over the business, before 1887 and died at the mill in 1896. Herbert Marr succeeded, and later John P. W. Cussons worked the mill from 1901 to 1910, being followed by his father for a short time.[9] Messrs. Sam. Cook and Son were there from 1911 to 1913, when the business was taken over by Charles Stonehouse.[10] In 1919 the picturesque building was practically re-built, and has been tenanted by Messrs. Burgess and Sons for the last ten years.

Spinning, weaving and the allied trades of fulling and bleaching, have been carried on in Thornton for centuries. The bleaching mills at Ellerburn and 'Millholme,'[11] where now T. Darrell's farm stands, date back to a very early period. Both, as said, were originally corn-mills, but Millholme is recorded as a fulling-mill in 1335,[12]

[1] Y. A. Rec. S. XXI. p. 60.
[2] Ibid. LVIII. p. 114.
[3] Sam. Tetley, *ut supra.*
[4] Sam. Tetley mentioned him as a labourer in 1734. He was buried 16 February, 1757.
[5] C. R.
[6] *Vide supra.*
[7] Youngest son of Richard Hill and Jane, daughter of James Walker: born 11 May, 1835, married 1870, M. Fanny, daughter of the Rev. H. Pixell, died 27 April, 1907.
[8] He bought the High Hall and lived there for many years as the agent for his eldest brother, the Rev. John Richard Hill, in which post he was succeeded by his nephew the Rev. Arthur Hill, who died on 20 January, 1923. The present (1929) agent is W. Holgreaves, of Ebberston, Esq.
[9] *Yorkshire Post,* 9 April, 1929.
[10] Information kindly supplied by George Hardy who worked at the mill, 1887 to 1914.
[11] There is still an old building behind the Darrell's and White's houses in Maltongate, said to have been the mill. The field it stands in was full of holes, at one time called British huts, but really bleaching holes; these were filled in August, 1929. This land was bought from Capt. Laye by the Rev. J. R. Hill about 1880. I am indebted to Mrs. Richard Hill.
[12] N. R. Rec. S. N.S. II. pp. 273-4.

and the mill at Ellerburn had become the same. 'William the Weaver' lived in Farmanby in 1301,[1] and thirty years later, 'Ralph the Weaver' resided in Thornton.[2] In the fifteenth century weaving was carried on in Thornton by Alexander Botcher in 1467,[3] and fulling by the already mentioned Ralph Joyner in 1497.[4] Presumably this domestic industry was so common in the sixteenth century that there was no occasion to call attention to it. No names, at any rate, have been found. In Stuart times, nearly every house would have its loom in the chamber opposite the living room, and in such, Christopher Oates of Farmanby would ply his trade in 1613.[5] Thomas and Luke Birdsall were weavers, in name, in 1619, but obviously idlers, 'as players of interludes.'[6]   John Marshall[7] was a weaver, and a man called Boothroyd[8] was a fuller, in 1624. The short wool from the fells was supplied in 1657[9] by an unnamed Thornton man, who may have been the James 'Dixson' who is described as a fellmonger in 1692.[10] John Skelton, Robert Gamble of Newstead Grange and William Robinson,[11] were all engaged in the woollen trade during the period of the Commonwealth; and a little later in the century, Andrew Horsley of Ellerburn,[12] and Robert Story of Farmanby were linen weavers. Robert Horsley, in 1711,[13] had Millholme in Farmanby, and this, passing through different hands remained a fulling mill until the beginning of the nineteenth century; and, by means of this, or some other, William Keddey in 1733,[14] Richard Harding in 1756,[15] and John Leaf[16] and William Westerman,[17] between 1760 and 1766, were able to carry on their tasks of bleaching. John Marshall[18] was a fuller and bleacher at Ellerburn mill in 1741, and in his work he was succeeded by Richard Marshall about 1743,[19] and the mill was rented, after 1785, by Richard Kirk, who also kept

[1] Y. A. S. Rec. S. XXI. p. 63.
[2] N. R. Rec. S. N.S. IV. p. 156.
[3] Cal. Pat. R. 1467-77, p. 2.
[4] *Vide* Ch. IV.
[5] N. R. Rec. S. O.S. II. p. 7.
[6] Ibid. p. 197.
[7] Ibid. III. p. 129.
[8] Ibid. p. 188.
[9] Ibid. V. p. 242.
[10] G. F. G. H.
[11] Ibid.
[12] Y. A. S. Rec. S. I. pp. 169, 175.
[13] G. F. G. H.
[14] Sam. Tetley, *ut supra*.
[15] C. R.
[16] Ibid.
[17] Ibid.
[18] G. F. G. H.
[19] Ibid.

up the bleaching grounds.[1]   In 1818 Thomas Rogers was a bleacher
at Ellerburn, but he died in 1819.[2]   William Hodgson as a weaver
in 1827 was allowed to take an apprentice by the Lumley trustees.[3]
As late as 1830,[4] there was a bleaching mill at Ellerburn, and as
many as forty webs at a time were stretched in the fields, where
still remains of the water courses are to be found, and where
within the memory of the oldest inhabitants was the ancient
water-wheel.[5]   In Thornton itself, 'Elin' Vesey was a linen weaver
in 1734,[6] and Thomas Skelton[7] in 1743, Mathew Smales in 1752,
John Todd in 1754,[8] Richard Barker and William Harland in
1768, Thomas Hustlar in 1774, Isaac Rogers in 1805, Robert
Harland in 1807 and William Scales in 1813 were all weavers, and
William Burnett was a flax-dresser in 1817.[9]   By this time the
domestic industries were rapidly on the decline; and the introduction of power machinery, driven by steam, dependent on the
coal-mines of the West Riding, gradually brought to an end, in
Thornton, the old system that had, for so long, been an additional
means of livelihood in so many homes.

At exactly what date paper-making became an industry at
Ellerburn it is impossible to say.   It was a new trade in England
in Tudor times.[10] Certainly it was in full operation up the valley at
the two Paper Mills in the late seventeenth century.   The first
reference to it in March, 1680/1,[11] gives the impression that it was
by no means new at that time.   The two mills were being worked
at the same period, the one occupied by William Warren, and the
other by William Long.[12] As early as November, 1733, the High
Paper Mill near the Pond[13] was rebuilt, and both mills, in 1734,
were rented by William Warren, at £60 p.a.;[14] and he continued

[1] Ibid.
[2] Documents of Lady Lumley's Charity, J. L. W.
[3] Ibid.
[4] Told me by Miss Jane Hill.
[5] Told me by George Pickering.
[6] Sam. Tetley, *ut supra*.
[7] G. F. G. H.
[8] Ellerburn Ch. Reg.
[9] C. R.
[10] Cunningham, *Alien Immigrants to England*, p. 242.
[11] The Church Register reads 'Richard Warren son of William Warren of
the Paper Mill, baptized 6 March, 1680/1.'
[12] 'Jane yᵉ daughter of Will. Long of yᵉ White Paper mill' was baptized
31 May, 1696.   The Registers show that William Long was still at the
Paper-mill in 1700.
[13] The Pond had nothing to do with the mill, and the Rev. John Richard
Hill has recorded that he could remember a wheel connected with the water-
fall above the mill in his early youth.   In his opinion the Pond was far
older than any paper-works.
[14] Sam. Tetley records that 170 oaks were purchased from William
Robinson of 'Kirby' for £22. 0s. 0d. for re-building the mill.

to rent them until his death in 1748.[1] His son, William Warren, junior, carried on the mills until his death on 28 March, 1778, and during the period employed, before 1760, Christopher Postgate[2] at the High Paper Mill. In 1762 John Hodgson was one of his workmen, but afterwards he became a 'ragman' and sold what he collected to William Warren.[3] Between 1769 and 1778, Joseph Andrews, William Holmes, John Jackson, James Nelson, James Mason, William Hall and Joseph Whitaker were employed making paper at the mills, and all lived in Thornton.[4] After the death of William Warren, junior, the mills were again leased separately, and in 1778, the tenant of the upper Mill was Thomas Campion,[5] a descendant, possibly, of the Campions of Farmanby who had been prominent in the reign of Edward II. He occupied the premises till about 1811.[6] James Nichols[7] was Warren's successor at the Low Paper Mill, which was completely restored by the village millwright and blacksmith, William Stephenson, in 1789.[8] It would appear to be at that time in a flourishing condition, and James Nichols,[9] about 1817, produced 80 cwt. of paper per annum,[10] while he also utilized the adjoining meadows to do a certain amount of bleaching for the weavers of the village. His tenancy was continued by Richard Nichols as late as 1833,[11] and possibly a little later. During this period the paper makers residing in Thornton were John Spenley, Thomas King, Robert Yeoman[12] and John Maw. But John Maw seems to be the only one of these left in 1840,[13] their places having been filled, for a short time only,

---

[1] The Church Register records 'Mr. Warren, Senior interred at Ellerburn aged 73,' 15 February, 1747/8. He had married 24 November, 1699, Elizabeth Jeffery.

[2] Christopher Postgate died 1760.

[3] C. R.

[4] Ibid.

[5] G. F. G. H.

[6] There are still persons of the name of Campion to be found in Pickering.

[7] G. F. G. H.

[8] Accounts and bills, G. F. G. H.

[9] Documents of Lady Lumley's Charity, J. L. W., show an interesting relic of the apprenticeship days. 'We the minister and Churchwardens of the parish of Thornton....and James Nicholls of Thornton aforesaid, Farmer and Paper-maker, Do Certify that John Hill aged Fifteen years a poor Child belonging to Thornton....bound an apprentice to the said James Nicholls until he should attain the age of Twenty-one years, by Indenture bearing date the Fifth day of February one thousand eight hundred and sixteen, is now and actually has been one year in his said Master's service and is likely to serve the Remainder of the said Term.' This was so the poor lad could obtain £10 for clothes from the Charity.

[10] Young, p. 819.

[11] G. F. G. H.

[12] C. R.

[13] *East and North Ridings*, p. 490.

by Richard Guffick and John Birdsall.[1]   When John Bellerby[2] had this mill, in the mid-nineteenth century, the dye used in the paper was said to have poisoned the trout in the Beck, so a filtering bed was made by the landlord, Richard Hill, which is still visible surrounded by fir trees, on the west side of the Beck. About 1865, George Pickering[3] was one of the last to be employed, as a lad, at the Low Paper Mill, and the present loose-box on the right side of the road going up the valley was a shed where a machine tore up the linen rags and at which he worked, under the foreman, Isaac Spendley.[4] It was, at this time, that Thomas Marsden, who also had works at Sheffield, rented the Low Paper Mill, and lived in what is now Brook Cottage, Priestman's Lane, and carried on the business to 1869.[5] The waggons carried the paper to Pickering and waited for a return load of rags; but the distance from the railway, improved machinery run by steam, the fact that each sheet of paper had to be dried separately, and the tendency to concentrate industries in towns, brought the paper mills of Thornton slowly down in the world and the day came when these isolated factories became farms.[6]

Even the blacksmith's job is not what it used to be, and there are fewer smiths in Thornton to-day than there were 'in the good old times.' The first blacksmith recorded in the village was Hugh, the Smith of Thornton, who, in 1301 had a rival in Alan, the Smith of Farmanby.[7] By 1327 both seem to have died; and their places were taken by John and Robert, each of whom lived in Thornton.[8] They were alive in 1333, and a fresh competitor started a business lower down the street, in the person of another John of Farmanby.[9]   At the beginning of the seventeenth century William Robinson was the village blacksmith; but he died on 20 July, 1626.[10] Contemporary with him were William Boyes and John Wilkinson who were at smithies in Thornton in the reigns of

[1] C. R.
[2] A John Bellerby is first mentioned as a tenant of 'Caulklands' in 1787.
[3] George Pickering died 1927.
[4] James Green told me this, and stated that Isaac Spendley lived at the most northern of the cottages in Ellerburn. No doubt he was a descendant of the 'Spenley' who gave his name to 'Spenley Close' first mentioned in a document of 1670, and of Roger 'Spenlaye' who married 'Elsabethe Robynson' on 9 February, 1594/5.
[5] Document in the possession of Wilfred Garbutt.
[6] The High Paper Mill was a farm in 1869 in the hands of Thomas Buttery, about 1900 it was rented by Robert Watson, and about 1920 by J. R. Bowes.
[7] Y. A. S. Rec. S. XXI. p. 63.
[8] N. R. Rec. S. N.S. IV. p. 140.
[9] Ibid. p. 156.
[10] C. R.

James I. and Charles I.[1]   A hundred years later, in 1734, the blacksmiths were Richard and John Birdsall,[2] and the millwrights, Michael and William Rogers.[3]   For some years before his death in 1766, William Maw had been a blacksmith.[4]   His son, in 1785, had two smithies,[5] and William Stephenson had one.   But in 1789 the latter had also acquired two shops,[6] and his son John carried on, as he is mentioned as a smith in 1840[7] and died as a 'veterinary surgeon' on 5 March, 1881, aged 83.[8]   About 1813 three new names appeared as blacksmiths: Thomas Cook, Robert Green and William Burnett.[9]   Despite these rivals, William Maw continued his farriery work, but, by 1836, preferred to call himself a veterinary surgeon.[10]   The Burnett family carried on as blacksmiths till about 1895.[11]   The Rogers however, have the longest tradition of all, and Dawson Rogers, following his father, grandfather and other members of his family remains a smith to the present time.[12]

The earliest carpenter to be mentioned in Thornton was one Bartholomew, who flourished in 1327.[13]   From that time to 1597, there is a complete blank, when William Sollett had to assist in the repair of a bridge.[14]   In 1618, John Gill, carpenter, sold a broad-land to John Spenley.[15]   Exactly eighty years after Robert Ecclefield[16] is referred to as 'joiner,' but there are no more entries until 1734 when the gatemaker and joiner was William Allison or Allanson,[17] and the carriage-builder John Brewster.[18]   Allanson's descendants carried on his work, for William Allanson, joiner, was living in

[1] Ibid.
[2] Sam. Tetley, *ut supra.*
[3] Ibid.
[4] C. R.
[5] G. F. G. H.
[6] Ibid.
[7] Ibid.
[8] As shown by tombstone in Thornton Churchyard.   He had the smithy near the Cross.
[9] C. R.   Possibly this man was also a flax-dresser.
[10] Ibid.   At the end of the nineteenth and at the beginning of the twentieth century the two properly qualified veterinary surgeons were James Best and Robert Robertson.
[11] There were a Thomas Burnett and a Jonah Dobson blacksmiths in 1860, and Thomas Burnett died aged 81 years in August, 1900.   Between the Grammar School and the Beck, on the Beck side, there stood a blacksmith's shop until about 1860.   There was another, at the bottom of Back Church Lane until about 1870, and a third in Dog Kennel Lane until about 1900.
[12] It is somewhat remarkable that members of this family have been smiths in Wilton, Allerston, Ebberston and Snainton as well as Thornton.
[13] N. R. Rec. S. N.S. IV. p. 140.   A different reading is given to this name in Y. A. Rec. S. LXXIV. p. 111.
[14] N. R. Rec. S. O.S. I. p. 223.
[15] G. F. G. H.
[16] C. R.
[17] Sam. Tetley, *ut supra.*   William Allison spent a day and a half mending Mrs. Hill's bed and his bill was 1s. 9d.
[18] Ibid.

1778[1] and his son James Allanson was a wheelwright in Farmanby in 1814.[2] At the beginning of the nineteenth century Thomas Readshaw was a carpenter in Farmanby and Joseph Pearson and William Brewster were the same in Thornton.[3] In 1814 besides Allanson there were three joiners in the village, George Evers, Thomas Moody and Robert Simpson;[4] and a little later there were Richard Hesslewood[5] and Peter Dennis. In 1830 there was still Robert Simpson,[6] and Richard Bolton seems to have had good employment.[7] Ten years later John Wardill[8] appears to have had most of the trade though there was a competitor in 1848 in Harrison Maw.[9] In 1867 there were George Barnes, John Bolton and Robert Dennis.[10] Towards the end of the nineteenth century there were Alfred Bolton, Benjamin and Arthur Robinson, William Wray and Son and J. T. Bielby. The last two are carrying on their business to the present time; and there are also Alfred Thorsby and A. Cousins.

There are only two stone-masons mentioned before the eighteenth century, George Rand and Gyles Raunde who were employed by Sir Richard Cholmley in 1562.[11] Masonry work was required at the Hall in 1734, and it was done by Robert Gilbank and James Joyner.[12] From that date until 1801, there is a blank, but in that year John Houldsworth having died is entered in the Burial Register as 'a stone mason.' In 1814 William Wallis was a mason in the parish of Ellerburn,[13] and in 1815 there were William Hardy and William Spendley.[14] Thomas Barnes had been a mason for

---

[1] C. R.
[2] J. L. W.
[3] Ibid.
[4] Ibid.
[5] C. R.
[6] J. L. W.
[7] Ibid.
[8] *East and North Ridings*, p. 491. To John Wardill was apprenticed about 1850 William Willerton son of John Willerton, gardener and sexton. John Willerton thought nothing of walking to Whitby and back for the purpose of clipping a horse for which he was much sought after. William Willerton after working in York migrated in 1858 as a joiner to the U.S.A. He married well and became a farmer and was joined by his brother Alfred. Information from Mrs. Sedman, William Willerton's daughter.
[9] J. L. W.
[10] White's *Directory*.
[11] N. R. Rec. S. N.S. I. p. 207.
[12] Sam. Tetley, *ut supra*.
[13] John Gilby in a letter written in 1814 to Richard Hill says 'W. Wallis, mason, was killed by a fall from his horse in the village of Ganton and that he has left behind him 5 small children & his Widow far advanced in Pregnancy. I attended the funeral at her Request yesterday morning.' The Ellerburn Registers show that W. Wallis was buried at Ellerburn.
[14] J. L. W.

William Wardill, 1855 - 1938 was born in Thornton Dale and was five times mayor of Gateshead

some time, in the village, before 1840.[1] He was succeeded by William Barnes who was actively employed in the last decade of the nineteenth century, and his work has been carried on by some of his descendants to the present day. About 1856 Alfred Willerton was a stone-mason for a short time in the village and so also were John Mercer and Thomas Skelton. There were for many years, too, Thomas Widd[2] and his son Richard, the latter only giving up his work shortly before his death on 19 April, 1925; and Reuben Charles, who following in the footsteps of his father, John Charles, has executed much good masonry work in Thornton and its neighbourhood, and continues to do so.[3]

The demand for regular quarrymen in Thornton has never been great enough to create a definite class of labourers. The middle calcareous grit of the district furnishes plenty of freestone of varying quality;[4] but no industry has been evolved. As required, the stone has been taken from either the field[5] west of the newly built 'Roxby' on the Pickering road, or from Whiteways for those on the Farmanby side; or from Musdale Quarry for those dwelling on the east side of the Beck. Lime-burning has also been a somewhat sporadic industry. At one time there were large lime-kilns on the west of Utgang Lane and in Caulklands. The first reference to a kiln is in the spring of 1615, when Christopher Boyes and Jane, his wife, and Thomas Boyes and Elizabeth Salmon *alias* Boyes, conveyed to John Noble, senior, 'a messuage and a Kiln situate in Thornton and Farmanbye.'[6] In 1807 William Bolton was a free-holder and a lime-burner,[7] and in 1817, when lime was much used as a manure, lime-kilns are said to have been worked on an extensive scale in Thornton.[8] As late as 1867 several lime-kilns are mentioned,[9] remains of which are still to be seen.

The two industries that seemed to flourish particularly, in the eighteenth and nineteenth centuries, were shoemaking and tailoring. Richard Jackson of Farmanby was shoemaker in 1727.[10] In 1762 the work was carried on by Harry 'Cordukes,'[11] and two years later,

---

[1] *East and North Ridings*, p. 490.
[2] He died March, 1910, aged 81 years. He was full of interesting reminiscences. For 20 years he was parish clerk of Ellerburn, where he used to play the 'cello before the introduction of a harmonium.
[3] A more recent mason in Thornton is Edwin Manby.
[4] V. C. H. *York* II. p. 380.
[5] Now called Cow Pasture.
[6] Y. A. Rec. S. LVIII. p. 30.
[7] *Poll of the County of York*, 1807.
[8] Young, p. 818.
[9] White's *Directory*.
[10] G. F. G. H.
[11] Son or grandson of William 'Cordux' who had a messuage in Beck Hole.

John Smailes is mentioned.[1] In 1767 there was Thomas Daisley,[2] and, in 1780, William Storr.[3] George Beal on 16 September, 1789, made 'Master Richard[4] morrocky pumps' for 3s.,[5] and he was still alive in 1807. He was succeeded at the beginning of the nineteenth century by Robert Maw in 1818[6] and Robert Beal, Thomas Creaser, Robert Ecclefield, John Jackson and John Hodgson.[7] In 1826 there was Charles Wray,[8] in 1840, Richard Bower,[9] and in 1861 Richard Birdsall.[10] Later in the century the work was carried on by James Metcalf and William Lumbard, the second having, as a lad, been apprenticed to Richard Bower;[11] and during the twentieth century, H. W. Ogle and Henry Coverdale and Son have been actively employed.

As to tailors, they seem to have been as numerous as the shoemakers. William Read is the first tailor recorded in 1724.[12] Ten years later Henry Jackson did a great deal of work for the Squire at the Hall.[13] In 1764 John 'Natris' was tailor at Ellerburn, which seems a curious spot to have resided if he desired custom.[14] His rival, Thomas Walker, was at Thornton in 1777;[15] but there were two others in 1780, John Mann and John Hustlar;[16] and the latter was still working in 1789, and charged 4s. 6d. for '2 sutes clothes making,' and, even allowing that his employers supplied the cloth, he could hardly be called an expensive tailor.[17] George Skelton was a tailor before 1807 and was alive in 1823,[18] when

[1] C. R.
[2] Ibid.
[3] Not to be confused with the Master of the Grammar School.
[4] The son and heir of Richard Johnson Hill.
[5] Accounts and papers, G. F. G. H.
[6] Documents of Lady Lumley's Charity, J. L. W.
[7] C. R.
[8] Ibid.
[9] *East and North Ridings*, p. 490.
[10] Documents of Lady Lumley's Charity, J. L. W.
[11] J. L. W.
[12] G. F. G. H.
[13] Sam. Tetley, *ut supra*. Some of the tailor's charges are rather startling for 1929. 'To Henry Jackson & his 2 men, each 3 days making Mrs. Hills bed' 3s. 9d. 'for mending Miss Kitty coate' 6d. 'for making a coate for Miss Kitty & a wastecoat for Master Jacky' 3s. 6d. 'for making Miss Kitty 2 coates' 4s. 'for making Mrs. Hill Jackett & Peticoate' 4s. 'for making Miss Kitty a hoop and mending her bed' 1s. 2d. 'for making Mrs. Hill a Goun' 2s. 'for altering Mrs. Hill a Goun' 6d. 'a waisticoate making for my master' 6d. 'for making Coachman great coate & a suit of cloaths' 11s. 'Bill for making & mending Cloathes for Mr. John Samuel Hill' 17s. 6d. 'for making a suite of cloathes for my master' 9s.
[14] C. R.
[15] Ibid.
[16] Ibid.
[17] G. F. G. H.
[18] In a book in her possession shown to me by Mrs. George Skelton.

Robert Richardson, John Mackley[1] and Thomas Hardwick[2] were also working in the village. In 1855, Thomas Skelton, who had been a tailor for many years, received through the Lady Lumley Charity, John Ecclefield, nephew of 'Willie' Ecclefield as an apprentice.[3] In 1867 William Dixon was a tailor,[4] and so also John Barnes, John Guffick, Thomas King, William Nawton and Robert L. Parkin.[5] Towards the end of the nineteenth century Mark Johnson and William Leaf were the same, and the work of the latter was carried on until recent years by Peter Owston and now by C. Mercer.

In early times, every farmer would be his own butcher, and as the villagers themselves eat little or no meat the trade would hardly exist. By the mid-eighteenth century, however, butchers begin to appear, the first being Thomas Allanson, who died in 1760; and the second Stephen Dixon who died in 1768.[6] Robert Holmes was a butcher in 1787,[7] and so also was Robert Smailes in 1814.[8] The Dixon family, however, still continued the business for Robert Dixon was a butcher in 1840;[9] and George and Thomas Dixon were butchers in 1867, and a little earlier Thomas 'Marfitt' also engaged in the business. Shortly before the middle of the nineteenth century the Cross family took up the trade, and as late as 1874, had a shop abutting on 'The Cross.' After that for more than twenty years, Tom Cross, of portentous size, carried on the business, which of recent years has been in the hands of another family of the same name. Harry Hill was a butcher in or before 1882, John Croft in later years had a small shop off Maltongate, and C. Robinson has a shop in the Pickering road.

Grocers are even more rare than butchers. In 1733[10] Mrs. Beale was probably a grocer as she sold tea, and a Miss Foord and a Miss Mason[11] did the same; but there is no proof that the two latter lived in the village. Mrs. Walker[12] was a village grocer dispensing 'soape and candles,' for which the bill, £11. 0s. 0d., seems very heavy. William Jackson[13] also sold soap for which £2. 4s. 0d. was

[1] Documents of Lady Lumley's Charity, J. L. W.
[2] C. R.
[3] Documents of Lady Lumley's Charity, J. L. W.
[4] Ibid.
[5] White's *Directory*.
[6] C. R.
[7] Ibid.
[8] Ibid.
[9] *East and North Ridings*, p. 490.
[10] Sam. Tetley, *ut supra*.
[11] Ibid.
[12] Ibid.
[13] Ibid.

paid. A Mr. Harrison[1] sold soap at 5d. a pound, and prunes at 3d. a pound. George Todd and Robert Smithson[2] both sold coffee, the former at 5s. 6d. a pound, the latter for 4s. Mr. Wilson[3] may have been a grocer, for he sold almonds at 1s. a pound, and Mrs. Hayley sold chocolate for 5s. but the weight is not specified. There are no other references to a grocer until John 'Nuttrass' in 1807,[4] and William Humphreys in 1832.[5] In the middle of the century there was Francis Parkinson's shop at the corner of Pickering Road, continued into the twentieth century by Parkinson's Executors and afterwards by T. S. Cattle and at the present time by L. E. Wood. In 1867 there were John Linfoot, William Pennock and Robert Scales, and in the latter part of the nineteenth century there were also Messrs. William, Alfred, and Robert Garbutt, and John W. Clarke.[6] The business of the former, no longer a grocery, is that of Alfred Garbutt, and that of the latter was taken by G. E. Pickering and Son some twenty-five years ago and still continues.

Of innkeepers the first to appear is William 'Hawsome,' who received in 1743, £1. 7s. 0d. 'for Eating & ale at Thornton & Farmanby Court-Keeping Dinner';[7] but whether he held the Buck, the New Inn, or the Pack Horse it is impossible to say. In 1807 and in 1820 John Parkin[8] and Francis Wardell were innkeepers;[9] while in 1840 the host of the New Inn was John Mercer[10] and he was succeeded some years later by his widow Susannah Mercer until 1870, when it was held by Thomas Bulmer afterwards followed by Thomas Johnson,[11] who was still holding it in the late nineteenth century. At the beginning of the twentieth century it was in the hands of John Marflitt, and later in those of A. Jobson, and at the present in those of W. W. Gill. Richard 'Boulton' kept the Pack Horse in 1840,[12] which afterwards changed hands several times, being in 1867 in those of Mary Wood,[13] later it became the

[1] Ibid.
[2] Ibid.
[3] Ibid.
[4] *Poll of the County of York*, 1807. This name has many forms of spelling.
[5] Document of Lady Lumley's Charity, J. L. W.
[6] He was a life-long resident in Thornton, and died 3 January, 1902 aged 70 years.
[7] Sam. Tetley, *ut supra*.
[8] *Poll of the County of York*, 1807.
[9] C. R.
[10] *East and North Ridings*, p. 490.
[11] Mrs. Widd told me this. Mr. T. Johnson was the father of Mrs. Dennison (Mrs. Johnson, later) the first Mrs. Reuben Charles, and Mrs. Richard Widd.
[12] *East and North Ridings*, p. 490.
[13] White's *Directory*.

'Temperance Hotel' and to-day is a private house. The Buck in 1840 was held by Thomas Richardson;[1] in 1869 by Robert Hall and in 1890 it was under John Charles Hopper,[2] and shortly after under John Grey. In 1901 it was occupied by G. G. Weetman, and during the War by George R. Judson. In recent years it has been conducted by Thomas Steel. The 'off licence' in 'Up Street' or Church Street, very recently known as 'The Fox and Hounds,' seems to have been managed by the family of Robinson since about 1840[3] to the present day.

The story of the village gamekeepers can, with many blanks, be traced back to the fifteenth century. It would appear that Sir Roger Hastings had as his keepers, William Thornley, Richard Todd and Richard Solett.[4] But of these men, little or nothing is known, except that a gamekeeper is sometimes 'a poacher turned outside in, and a poacher a keeper turned inside out'; and these men, rather disgracefully, bore out Charles Kingsley's definition.[5] It is not until the eighteenth century that there is any clear information. On 13 January, 1735/6, William Beilby was 'appointed gamekeeper by John Hill, jun[r]., Esq., Lord of the Castle Mannor and Liberty of Pickering, for which Mannor and Liberty he is appointed and authorized pursuant to the statute.'[6] This appointment would authorize William Beilby 'to kill game for' the use of his employer, 'and to take seize all such Guns, Grey hounds, Setting Dogs and other dogs, fferetts, snares or Engines, for the taking killing and destroying of Hares Pheasants and Partridges or other game, and further to act and to do all and everything and things which belong to the office of a Gamekeeper.' Beilby was followed on 13 January, 1739/40, by Roger Coats of Thornton;[7] and he, in turn, on 24 July, 1744, by Richard Barker of Kirkby Moorside.[8] He held the post a brief five years and then on 30 October, 1749, George Brown of Dalby was appointed.[9] From that date for many years there is no reference to keepers. Richard Hill had for his keeper (and huntsman) John Booth. He became keeper in 1797, and remained so, in name, at least, until his death

---

[1] *East and North Ridings*, p. 490.
[2] Bulmer, *ut supra*.
[3] *East and North Ridings*, p. 490.
[4] N. R. Rec. S. N.S. I. p. 151; but they lived at Pickering and at Kingthorpe and not in the village.
[5] *Water Babies*, p. 20, edit. 1886.
[6] N. R. Rec. S. O.S. VIII. p. 210. Ibid. p. 218 shows that John Hill, 17 April, 1737, appointed Richard Barker as gamekeeper 'for his Mannors of Normanby and Welbourne.'
[7] Ibid. p. 231.
[8] Ibid. p. 247.
[9] Is this the George Brown of Dalby who was churchwarden after 1755 ?

in 1853 in his 85th year.[1]   He was succeeded by Thomas Cockerill, who was still keeper in 1867.[2]   In the latter part of the nineteenth century John Brewster was a keeper of the old sort, autocratic, and perhaps domineering, but a really loyal servant to the Hill family.   When navvies were engaged on the railway line, between 1879 and 1882, his work was very hard, and night after night old Brewster was out, assisted by the under-keepers, George Pickering, who then lived at Ellerburn,[3] and John Smithies.   On one occasion, in 1880, they had a real and dangerous struggle with poachers,[4] in the fields on the west side of Maltongate, just below the present station.[5]   Many years afterwards, in 1894, Brewster, with the help of the police, made a fine capture of poachers with very valuable nets in Howldale.   George Pickering did not remain an under-keeper for long;[6] but Brewster and Smithies went on for many years. Brewster[7] was succeeded as head-keeper in 1900, by James Green[8] who remained so until 1926, when he was followed by George Craig.

It has not been possible to find the name of an eighteenth century huntsman.   It may be said that this is natural, because it is always asserted that the present pack in this neighbourhood,

[1] *Vide* Ch. IX.

[2] White's *Directory*. His son, Robert Cockerill, aged 88, died 26 December, 1929 and was buried at Thornton.

[3] George Pickering told me this.

[4] The 'Old Squire,' the Rev. J. R. Hill, always spoke of poachers as 'pilgrims of the night.'   He liked his little joke, and was particularly fond of Hymn 223 *Hymns Ancient and Modern*.

[5] Told me by George Pickering a few weeks before his death in 1927.

[6] He was a very fine old Yorkshireman, of a type now fast disappearing: well educated and remarkably well-read.   A delightful conversationalist. He was not a native born, but came, I believe, with his parents as a small boy.   After being a footman in Lord Lansdowne's house, he returned as butler to the Hall, and on retirement became a farmer and lived, until his death at the house opposite the Hall Gates.

[7] Brewster had a garden of herbs in Ellerburn Wood at the top of Kirkdale which now (1929), a neglected open patch in the wood, full of wild thyme and sage, is called 'Brewster's Garden.'   He had an idea that an ancient roadway passed this point on to the moor, and he thought that he had found a stone basis.   John Brewster died December, 1899.

[8] A man of the most remarkable power of eyesight that has ever been known.   He could see the least movement below a hedge many hundreds of yards away.   In several things he resembles 'Old' Brewster, but is far better educated, has seen men and cities, and has a keen interest in the history of his village.   But more than that, he is a botanist and ornithologist of very considerable knowledge and ability.   A man of great native wit, and very quick at the uptake.   On one occasion a would-be sportsman, who generally blew the birds to smithereens, fired with both barrels at a covey that got up from beneath his feet and not a bird dropped. The sportsman let fly a volley of sulphureous language.   The keeper very quietly said, 'Nay, nay, Mr....... There's noa nead for woords sich as yon. Burds are nea wuss.'   A wonderfully gentle rebuke for his habit of firing too quickly.   At another time when a poor shot missed very badly an un-usually fine hare, he said, 'Aiam sorry, sur, Aiam, for Ai haven't a bigger un i'parish.'

now called 'The Derwent,' was founded by Richard Hill in 1808. This, however, is not true, as shown by an old letter,[1] which proves that John Hill, II., had a pack of foxhounds in Thornton as early as the reign of Queen Anne, if not earlier. The letter was written by Sir William Hustler, Bart., to John Hill II., on 22 February, 1713/4, and says 'I am become a Great Hunter by assistance of my Good Friends having picked eight couple of Dogs. I have a Whelp about two months old that I doubt will be too large & goe to [sic] fast, which if you please is at your service for when I was att Thornton [I] remember you was for having your Dogs goe as fleet as you could get them, he is extraordinary well breed.' As there were not many genuine packs[2] before the reign of Charles II., and as John Hill's hounds evidently existed for some time before the letter was written, this pack must have been one of the earliest in the country. Whether some member of the Hill family kept them up during the middle portion of the eighteenth century it cannot be said. It is not likely that there were any foxhounds at the Hall during the long minority of Richard Hill.[3] But the name 'Dog-kennel Lane,'[4] probably dates back to the days of Queen Anne (if not earlier), rather than to the resuscitation of the pack in 1808. The Rev. John Richard Hill wrote, in 1890, 'Perhaps I had better point out that before his [Richard Hill's] country was formed—the Sinnington, said to be the oldest Pack of Foxhounds in England—hunted at will over the whole district.'[5] It has been said[6] 'There is a tradition that Mr. Richard Hill hunted the carted deer before' he founded his pack of foxhounds; and it has also been suggested that there had been a trencher fed pack. But the Rev. J. R. Hill writes,[7] that Richard Hill 'I believe in his teens and Oxford days amused himself with a few couple of old Beagles.' The carted deer was probably earlier than Richard Hill, for his son says 'It is quite probable that my grandfather Richard Johnson Hill kept a small pack of staghounds at Thornton, for there was a tradition in my younger days of some kennels in the Grounds and I can remember

[1] G. F. G. H. It was first shown to me by the late Rev. Arthur Hill some twenty years ago.
[2] Foxes had been regarded as vermin to be slain at sight. This is shown in Sir Walter Scott's *The Lady of the Lake.*
'Whoever recked where, how, or when
The prowling fox was trapped or slain ?'
Under 8 Eliz. c. 15, there was a reward of 1s. for every fox's head.
[3] 1793-1807.
[4] Leading from the High Street to Peaslands.
[5] MS. of Rev. J. R. Hill kindly lent me by R. A. Scott, Esq., to whom it was given by the author.
[6] V. C. H. York II. p. 481.
[7] MS. of Rev. J. R. Hill.

myself a kind of oat-house box standing where 'the Deer' were said to have been kept, and also an old Deer cart tumbling to pieces.'[1] But Richard Hill was the true founder of the pack of foxhounds, and he took the deepest interest in their breed partly from his own stock and judicious crosses from the pack of 'Sir Tatton Sykes that grand old King of our Yorkshire wolds.'[2] About 1820 the pack was said to be perfect, having been 'carefully bred for nose and music, paramount desiderata in our wild and sometimes impassable country.'[3] At this time the hounds could hardly be equalled, and certainly not excelled. Eleven years later they suffered a very heavy blow, for in 1831 the pack was terribly stricken with hydrophobia. 'We did not know how the disease originated, but we lost 12 couples of hounds and other dogs'[4] between June 1831 and June 1832. Richard Hill died in 1855 'having hunted his own hounds for forty-seven years successively[5] and with great success as the old stable doors [at the Hall] ornamented with the yearly strips of noses amply testify to this day.'[6] John Richard 'being a Parson'[7] did not follow his father but the hounds were taken over by his half-brother 'Jack' Hill,[8] who 'then carried on the old pack, with a subscription and pioneered them himself for seven seasons to the year 1862 when he sold them on his retirement (as was understood) to Colonel Pennant for his Grace the Duke of Grafton, then Lord Euston.'[9] By this time, however, Thornton had ceased to have the hounds kennelled in the village, though the inhabitants have never ceased to show themselves keen followers of this sport.

In the illiterate and lethargic eighteenth century, Thornton, not having experienced the benefits of education, probably did without a village schoolmaster. What little education there was

---

[1] Ibid.

[2] Ibid.

[3] Ibid.

[4] Ibid.

[5] John Booth was huntsman the greater part of this period.

[6] MS. Rev. J. R. Hill.

[7] Ibid.

[8] He was the son of Richard Hill: born 1821, married Elizabeth Bower who died 1877; he died 1906. He lived for many years at the Low Hall, Brompton. His second son, Robin Hill, has been one of the most ardent supporters of foxhunting in the neighbourhood for nearly fifty years, and has acted as huntsman to Sir Everard Cayley and whipper-in to P. C. Sherbrooke, Esq.

[9] MS. Rev. J. R. Hill. There is a good story recorded of one of these hounds 'Old Truelass.' The famous huntsman, Ben Morgan, of Lord Middleton's pack said to 'Jack' Hill 'I'll tell you what. If you'll give me that bitch, I'll lead her on my hands and knees back with me to Birdsall.' As this would be a distance of 13 miles it shows what an opinion he had of the hound.

would be given by the curate in the Grammar School to a select number of scholars. No one, except the Squire, would ever buy a newspaper.[1] We know that he did, at any rate in 1733-4, because he paid on 23 July, 1734, 'To Mr. Preveran for 2 yrs. News papers Ending at Midsummer 1734,' the sum of £5. 0s. 0d.[2] No doubt the Rector and the Squire's agents would borrow the paper; as for the rest it is very unlikely that more than a few could read, and certainly quite a number could not write.[3] It is true that as early as 1806 Elizabeth Brewster kept a dame's school so as to earn enough to support her old mother who was too infirm to live alone in the Almshouses, but that was all.[4] With the dawn of modern times, however, when the old order began to change, there seems to have been a village schoolmaster before 1817 in the person of William Teal;[5] his successor being Robert Storr[6] who died in 1840; and he was followed by Samuel Clark who was teaching in Thornton in the next year.[7] One followed another, such as Albert Bell from 1856 to 1864, and George A. Taylor from 1864, until Thomas Anderson became master on 10 January, 1870,[8] and for more than forty-five years did marvels with the village children. Helped as he was, during part of the time by his excellent wife, capable daughter and others, nevertheless it is to Thomas Anderson's education that many to-day—men and women who are now grandparents— owe much of the pleasure they have had in life. After a strenuous career he retired on 30 September, 1914, looking as fresh as a young man, and was succeeded by Robert Parratt, who still retains control of the school.

How the people of Thornton managed before about 1820, when anyone was ill or had an accident it is difficult to imagine. It is conceivable that there was a doctor in Pickering, almost certainly there would be one in Malton, and there were three or four in

---

[1] In 1861 and 1862 the inhabitants read *The Pickering and Thornton Mercury*, published by William Heseltine of Pickering, containing practically no local news. Copies of these were kindly shown to me by James Green.

[2] Sam. Tetley, *ut supra*.

[3] I remember two cases in 1909 of comparatively young men, between thirty and forty who could not write. And in 1918 two young Scotch soldiers detailed for agriculture came into the village and neither of them could write. *Cf.* on this subject F. Y. in M. P. p. 6.

[4] Lady Lumley's Charity documents, J. L. W.

[5] C. R.

[6] Grave in Churchyard.

[7] C. R.

[8] All three of these men married Thornton women. Albert Bell married Rachel Skelton daughter of Thomas Skelton, the tailor, George A. Tailor married Mary E. Brewster, niece of John Brewster, the keeper, and Thomas Anderson married Mary Martha Baker.

Scarborough.[1] But in the eighteenth century roads were impassable, and for a doctor to be fetched from Scarborough would have meant a messenger from Thornton, struggling through the boggy road, and reaching Scarborough in perhaps six hours. The doctor would drive in his 'chariot,' arrayed in a bag wig, black cut-away coat-tails, and carrying a gold headed cane, all symbols of his profession. By the time he arrived, having to travel even slower than the messenger on horseback, the patient would almost certainly be dead. Accidents[2] might happen at any time, and many persons in the eighteenth century died solely for want of immediate medical assistance. But perhaps there was no call for a doctor in a village where the 'old gossip,' or 'good wife' could act as midwife to bring babies into the world, and the others had to shuffle out of it as best they could. About 1820, however, William Sheffield was in Thornton as surgeon and was there for twenty or more years, being succeeded by Dr. Robertson (who married Sheffield's daughter), from 1834 to 1889.

The present doctor, Richard Arthur Scott, came to Thornton in 1888, and it is the general desire of the inhabitants that he should go on for ever. To him, more than to any man living or dead, Thorntonians owe an immense debt. He has helped to bring many into the world; he has tended them in their sickness; he has guided and befriended them with advice and has never spared himself for his relatives, his friends, the man next door, or for the most unfortunate invalid in the wildest and most distant part of the moor. In wintry blasts or in summer heat, by night or by day, he has ever readily answered the call of duty. When he took Thornton under his wing he arrived at the exact moment to help the people professionally, and to instruct them in the new political rights which so many had recently acquired. He came to the village just before the return of the influenza scourge which reached its height in the great snow and frost year of 1895, when this neighbourhood 'down below' and 'up above' was ravaged. Out all the morning in the low country, with one set of horses, wet through himself time and again, he would seize a mouthful of food, and then, with fresh

---

[1] There was no resident doctor in Whitby before 1764. *Cf.* Young, p. 635.

[2] The sort of accidents referred to are those mentioned in the Church Registers.

13 March, 1645	'Henrie Skelton child buried 13th March it received hurt by fire wch. was the death of it.'
23 July, 1769	'George Storr killed by a fall from a waggon, aged 51.'
28 Nov., 1774	'Ann Nicholson killed by a brick falling from the chimney, aged 73.'
12 Sept., 1798	'Joseph Peirson killed in a stone quarry, aged 78.'

horses away to Lockton or Levisham, or beyond. His horses were worn out, the roads were so buried in drifts that they had to be cut out by the farmers, who readily did it, to get a visit from him; but he never spared himself, with the result that he contracted a long illness. Having, after many months, made a marvellous recovery, he once more helped, pacified, soothed and amused those he visited, until his malady returned. Thanks to surgical skill, in 1910, he again recovered.[1] In the great outburst of influenza towards the end of the War, history almost repeated itself. If anything, his district was wider than ever, for he had to take the work of younger medical men called to the Front. Ebberston and Allerston and that side of the neighbourhood learnt to know him and appreciate his cheeriness and self-sacrifice as Thorntonians had long done. As a magistrate, for many years he has had the friendship of his colleagues, and the respect of the unfortunate who appear before him. As Chairman of the Thornton Conservative Association, for twenty years, from 1905 to 1925, he retained the friendliest relations with all his political opponents. The successful candidates of his own party of recent years, Sir Gervase Beckett and Captain S. Herbert, have found in him a loyal supporter, and Sir Gervase Beckett said in 1925, that 'he thought of Thornton Dale in terms of Doctor Scott.' No other man in Thornton has been what Richard Arthur Scott has been, a Father to the people, a Friend in adversity, a bracing and invigorating companion, a man to whom, both rich and poor alike have gone for advice, whether it be medical, legal, domestic or personal. A thorough sportsman, a splendid shot, a keen fisherman, he stands out as a fine example of a true Yorkshireman.[2]

[1] His two assistants during these periods were Dr. Martin Loy and Dr. H. G. Pesel.

[2] His father was the Rev. George Scott, for many years vicar of Coxwold. He married Mary, elder daughter of the Rev. Edward Heslop, rector of Thornton, and has one daughter, Dorothy.

CHAPTER EIGHT.

The Grammar School.

*'Moved....to raise and beget unto her selfe in vertue
and learning many children.'*

ANCIENT BENEFACTION.

IT has already been shown[1] that Elizabeth, Viscountess Lumley,
in the distress of soul caused by leaving no children of her own,
determined to assist others in the education of their offspring;
and for this reason Thornton Grammar School came into being.
In October, 1657, Lady Lumley executed a deed which stated that
she was the wife of the Right Hon. Viscount Lumley, and had been
the wife of Sir William Sandys, Knight, of Montisfont, co. Southampton. Reference was then made to her lands and these were
placed in the hands of trustees who were ordered, within six years
of her death, to build first, 'in manner & forme of an Hospitall, or
in such other manner as Sir John Mayne and John Penrice & their
heirs....shall thinke fitt' in Sinnington or in Thornton, for '12
poore people men and women'; secondly similar almshouses in
London;[2] and thirdly another structure for the habitation of a
schoolmaster in Sinnington or in Thornton 'for the schooling,
instructing and teaching of the said parrishes & reading of prayers
morning and evening in the ....chappell[3] so to be erected.'[4]
There was also to be set on one side a sum of £10 per annum for
five scholars at Oxford and five at Cambridge.[5] Under the terms
of this benefaction the appearance of the village of Thornton was
gradually changed, and by 1670[6] the Almshouses and Grammar

---

[1] *Vide* Ch. V.

[2] These were afterwards known as Lady Lumley's 'hospitall of St. But-
tolphs, Aldgate and St. Buttolph's, Bishopsgate.'

[3] Eastmead, p. 327, says that the chapel was never built because as the
school and almshouses were so near the Church 'It was considered unnecessary,
and prayers are read in the Schoolroom on Thursday afternoons.'

[4] Copy of the Trust Deed of 1657 made on 14 July, 1741.

[5] G. F. G. H.

[6] Fly-leaf of Church Register.

131

Lady Lumley's Grammar School and Hospital

School were completed and have remained externally the same to the present day.[1]

The story of the Grammar School has been somewhat chequered. As early as 1679 the good Dean Comber, then rector[2] and trustee, 'found himself called upon to correct the abuses that had crept in; and again in 1690, to bring an action in the Court of Chancery against Sir Anthony Mayne, one of Lady Lumley's trustees, for a misappropriation of the funds; which suit depending 3 or 4 years wasted above £40 (a large sum in that day) which had been saved out of the improved rents, and which had been designed for repairs and other uses. The Court of Chancery upon a full hearing of the cause, compelled the intruders to quit the receipts and Sir Anthony his trust, which he had so shamefully betrayed; and as Dr. Comber was about to leave this part of the country, he got a decree to settle those chantries in the hands of 6 or 7 of the neighbouring gentry:[3] who were likely to take care of them for the time to come.'[4]

The first master must have undertaken the work before the completion of the buildings, for a certain 'Mr. Grey' did the necessary teaching before 1670, and one of his earliest pupils was John Hill the eldest son of the new Squire.[5] Information is lacking as to who this 'Mr. Grey' was; but as the Hills were owners of the advowson of Normanby and as 'Nicholas Gray' became the rector of Normanby in 1671 and remained such till 1701 it may be safely assumed that the Normanby rector had been the first Thornton schoolmaster. Little or nothing is known of him[6] except that he was born at Pocklington, and, like so many of that day and district, attended the administrations of Robert Sidgwick at Pocklington School. Thence he passed to Sidney Sussex College, Cambridge where he matriculated on 20 June, 1657, proceeded to his B.A. degree in 1660 and his M.A. in 1664.[7] Who succeeded Grey is by no means

---

[1] Tradition says that both the Master's House and the School were kept as low as possible, by the influence of the Squire, who did not want the Hall to be overlooked. But as the buildings must have been designed and almost completed before the arrival of John Hill I., and as there is no reason to think that any other Squire had lived in the Hall since the death of Lady Lumley, one must, once again, discard 'tradition.'

[2] *Vide* Ch. IX.

[3] The trustees at the end of the seventeenth century were Sir William Hustler, Sir Thomas Worsley, Sir Thomas Strangways, barts., ? Gibson John Hill, junior, Edward Hutchinson, Thomas Langley, junior, and Christopher Percehay, Esquires. *Vide* J. L. W.

[4] Comber, *Life of Dean Comber*, pp. 126, 289.

[5] Camb. Al.

[6] Probably a relative of the Rev. Nicholas Grey, vicar of Sinnington during the Commonwealth.

[7] Camb. Al.

clear,[1] but it may possibly have been the Rev. Thomas Wilson.[2]
He was certainly the master when appointed vicar of Ellerburn
in 1690;[3] and must have been followed as schoolmaster by the
Rev. Henry Hunter. The tenure of office of the latter can have
been but very short as he is said to have died on 9 April, 1691.[4]
His successor was, undoubtedly, the Rev. John Garnett who was
also the curate of Thornton,[5] and acted as master till 1700, when
he probably became rector of Cowlom-on-the-Wolds.

It must have been during the mastership of Grey or of Wilson
that the Grammar School was destined to have its most illustrious
pupil, in the person of John Leng, afterwards bishop of Norwich. He
was born at Thornton[6] in 1665,[7] and would be a pupil at the School
in about 1673. He afterwards went to St. Paul's School, and
obtained an exhibition at Catharine Hall, Cambridge, where he was
admitted a sizar 26 March, 1683.[8] It was about this time that Robert
Clavell, the bookseller,[9] wrote to Dean Comber, who may have been
Leng's guardian and said 'This, sir, is Mr. John Leng's account
before he went to Cambridge; I lent him many books which he
makes use of and returns. He delights in nothing more than study,
which he is at early and late; and indeed deserves a better character
than any young man I ever knew.'[10] Leng graduated B.A. in 1686.
'His subsequent degrees were M.A. 1690, B.D. 1698, D.D. 1716.
He was elected fellow of his college 13 September, 1688, and
subsequently became a very efficient tutor. He obtained great
distinction as a Latin scholar. In 1695 he published the *"Plutus"*
and the *"Nubes"* of Aristophanes with a Latin translation, and in
1701 he edited the magnificent Cambridge *Terence* adding a

---

[1] The Church Register shows that a 'Mr. Frank Parkinson, Cler.' was
resident in December, 1684, but it does not describe him as either curate
or schoolmaster.

[2] 'Mrs. Maggy Hunter and Mr. Thos. Willson' were married with Licence
on 28 June, 1697. *Vide* C. R.

[3] Ellerburn Register.

[4] Eastmead, p. 326, infers that he was the first master. In this he is
obviously wrong.

[5] Canon Ecclesiastical 78 says 'In what Parish Church....there is a
curate....well able to teach youth, and will willingly so do, for the better
increase of his living....we will and ordain, That a decree to teach the youth
of the parish where he serveth be granted to none by the Ordinary of that
place, but only to the said curate.'

[6] D.N.B.

[7] I have failed to find the entry in the Baptismal Register.

[8] D.N.B.

[9] Robert Clavell was a famous London bookseller. Dunston describes
him as 'a great dealer who has deservedly gained himself the reputation
of a just man.' Dr. Barlow, bishop of Lincoln used to call him 'the honest
bookseller.'

[10] Comber, *Life of Dean Comber*.

dissertation on the metres of the author....In 1708 he was presented....to the rectory of Beddington, Surrey, which he held *in commendam* to his death.'[1] He was Boyle Lecturer in 1717, chaplain to George I., shortly after, and in 1723 was consecrated bishop of Norwich. He held the see barely three years as he died of smallpox on 26 October, 1727, and was buried in St. Margaret's, Westminster.[2] He was not only 'a good and learned man,'[3] but he was also remarkably modest and diligent. He published his *Boyle Lectures* which were regarded as 'solid and weighty, clear and concise in statement, well-reasoned throughout, enriched with the fruit of much learning, gracefully but not pedantically exhibited.'[4]

Who the master was at the beginning of the eighteenth century it is impossible to say.[5] Presumably he must have been a good teacher if it is true that John Clarke, afterwards so famous for his classical learning, particularly Greek, was first educated at this Grammar School.[6] He was the clever son of an honest and industrious mechanic of Kirby Misperton, where he was born in 1706,[7] and after Thornton proceeded to Wakefield. Having obtained the Lumley exhibition he was entered as a sizar at Trinity College, Cambridge, where he took his B.A. in 1726, was made a fellow in 1729 and a Master of Arts in 1730. When he left the University he was appointed to the living of Nun Monkton, Yorkshire, and was afterwards a schoolmaster, at different periods, at Skipton, Beverley and Wakefield.[8] He died at Scarborough in the house of his brother, Francis Clarke, and was buried at Kirby Misperton 11 February, 1761, 'where an elegant monument has been erected to his memory at the expense of not less than 148 of the sons of the principal gentry in the county of York, as well as those of other counties, all his pupils. A plain marble tablet is also placed in each of the schools over which he presided with inscriptions by D[r]. Zouch.'[9] He was undoubtedly a very great Greek scholar and was the second most famous pupil that the old Grammar School at Thornton ever produced.

[1] D.N.B.
[2] Walcot, *History of St. Margaret's*, p. 19.
[3] Whiston, *Memoirs*, p. 347.
[4] Quoted in D.N.B.
[5] C. R. shows that a Thomas Kirby, B.A. was resident in January, 1701/2, but it does not describe him as either curate or schoolmaster.
[6] T. Langdale, *Yorkshire*, p. 60.
[7] Langdale, *ut supra*, says 1703. D.N.B. says 1706.
[8] D.N.B. *Cf.* Dr. Whitaker, *Loidis and Elmete*, ed. 1816, p. 261.
[9] Langdale, *ut supra*, p. 60. *Vide* Dr. Zouch, *The good schoolmaster exemplified in the character of the Rev. John Clarke, M.A.*

In 1722[1] John Dowbiggin was curate and master and amongst his pupils were William Ward and Robert Hunter, both of whom were born in Thornton. The former was the son of William Ward, gentleman, and proceeded after his schooldays in the Grammar School to Sidney Sussex College, Cambridge, at the age of eighteen in 1727. He took his B.A. in 1730, and was ordained in the diocese of Lincoln on 4 June, 1732, and was ordained priest in the diocese of Chichester on 6 October, 1734.[2] Two years later he returned to his old school, on the death of its master, John Dowbiggin, in April, 1736. How he managed to do his work efficiently it is a little difficult to say, for he was vicar of Scalby and curate of Thornton, Yedingham and Cloughton. Between 1738 and 1741 he came to loggerheads with the trustees of the Lady Lumley Charity.[3] It was probably as well that he did because it led to a useful decree in Chancery on the 17 July, 1741, which made certain important alterations in the Trust. Evidently the income was increasing and it was decided to invest £400 in land. It was also pointed out that under Lady Lumley's bequest there was a sum of £10 per annum for 10 poor scholars of the school at either Oxford or Cambridge; but that since 1702 very few scholars had applied, and that those that there were went to Cambridge as being so much nearer. The authorities now declared 'and for ye method of Living both in Cambridge and Oxford is become more expensive then it was when ye said charity was given the said Trustees do therefore propose that only five Schollars in ye whole may be Elected by ye said Trustees.' It was also decided that if there were not five Thornton boys then the Trustees might nominate other scholars up to that number. Each of these were now to receive £5 per annum until graduates; while the schoolmaster was to have £20 per annum.[4] After this victory Ward remained master for another ten years,[5] only retiring in 1751, to become the head master of Beverley School which post he held until 1768. He married Elizabeth, daughter of John Watson of Malton, and died 5 November, 1772, and was buried at Beverley.[6]

The other scholar of this period, Robert Hunter, was a little

---

[1] The C. R. shows that Christopher Storr, Usher of the School was buried on 4 September, 1724, and a mortuary of 10s. was paid.

[2] Camb. Al.

[3] G. F. G. H. *Cf.* Eastmead, p. 325.

[4] J. L. W.

[5] Archbishop Herring's Visitation Return in 1743 describes the School, saying that it 'has been for some time, & is now in a flourishing Condition.' *Cf.* Y. A. S. Rec. S. LXXV., p. 168.

[6] Camb. Al.

junior to William Ward as a pupil at the Grammar School. He was admitted a sizar, aged 21, at Sidney Sussex College, Cambridge, on 3 April, 1735.[1] He took his B.A. in 1738 and was ordained by the Bishop of Chester on 17 June, 1739. He must have kept on friendly terms with Ward as in later years he became his curate at Scalby.

While William Ward was the master, he had as his assistant or 'usher,' William Storr, a layman, who is first mentioned in 1740.[2] He succeeded Ward as head master, and actually taught in the school for forty-six years, as he died[3] in harness and was buried 18 March, 1786, aged 73.[4] During the last years of his life, at any rate from 1773,[5] he had as his usher his son Thomas.[6] The younger Storr[7] was not appointed to succeed his father, and the new master in 1786 was the Rev. Michael Mackereth and remained such until his death in 1829. By 1809 he had to have assistance from an usher called John Wardell who came from the Wold country; and during his last few years, when he was also vicar of Ellerburn, he was assisted by the Rev. R. B. Scholefield,[8] curate of Thornton. It was at some period between 1786 and 1796 that Thomas Bateman, son of a Whitby surgeon, was educated at the Grammar School. He afterwards earned fame as a doctor of medicine and as author of *Synopsis of Cutaneous Diseases.*[9]

At the end of the eighteenth century,[10] the trustees were all men of substance in the district such as Josiah Maynard, Richard Johnson Hill,[11] Thomas Hayes,[12] William Strickland, Charles Duncombe, junior, Rev. William Comber,[13] and the Rev. John Robinson. It was, no doubt, through these trustees that an

---

[1] Ibid.

[2] C. R.

[3] A document of 1785 (G. F. G. H.) shows that 'Mr. Wm. Storr pd. 6d. for a Fronstead & Garth called Strangers Garth inclosed within the walls of the Schoolhouse Garden.'

[4] C. R.

[5] Ibid.

[6] A John Storr was Richard Hill's agent in Thornton in 1814.

[7] The family of Thomas Storr seems to have gone down hill. In 1832 George Storr aged 60 years petitioned the Trustees for an Almshouse and said 'my grandfather William was master of the school at Thornton and lived to the advanced age of 90 years (note the discrepancy) and also my Father assisted him as a Teacher for 30 years and upwards.' (J. L. W.)

[8] Eastmead, p. 326.

[9] He died at Whitby, 9 April, 1821.

[10] J. L. W.

[11] In 1803 Sir George Cayley was appointed in the place of Richard Johnson Hill.

[12] In 1810 the Rev. Cutts Rudston Read of Sand Hutton succeeded Thomas Hayes deceased.

[13] In 1810 John Robinson 'ffoulis' of West Heslerton succeeded the Rev. William Comber deceased.

important exchange was made in the Award of 1796 when
'Stranger's Garth,' that is the present garden on the east side of
the dwelling-house, which hitherto belonged to the Hill family,
became the property of the School Trustees.[1]

On the whole the school did not do badly under the superintendence of Michael Mackereth.[2] It is clear from bills and accounts
that the buildings were kept in good repair and that the roof was
rethatched from time to time, as for example in 1815, when it was
done by William Scales at the extremely moderate cost of £7. 13s.[3]
It was about this time that Joshua Priestman and others petitioned[4]
for a change in the regulations of the Charity.[5]   The case was
carried to Chancery where it was asked whether the school ought
to be a grammar school only or a free school[6] for reading, writing
and arithmetic as well as classical learning. The Vice-Chancellor,
Sir Thomas Plumer, decided that it was a grammar school only,
and that the school at Sinnington was not a grammar school and
could have no share in the University scholarship.[7]

During the early years of the nineteenth century the numbers
of scholars, free boys and boarders varied very considerably. There
were never in any year more than 13 scholars, 5 free boys and
13 boarders. The total numbers for selected years are as follows :—

1806	1808	1810	1812	1814	1818	1824[8]
26	17	27	16	16	13	31

It is interesting to notice that when over eighty years of age
Michael Mackereth had more pupils than ever before, but it may
be due to the fact that Rev. R. B. Scholefield had been called in
to do the main work. It is equally interesting to find in Mackereth's
own careful handwriting the names of the books that these boys,
day by day, fingered and dogeared in their struggle to imbibe a
little learning. How some of these particular works were applicable
to students for a University education it is difficult to understand.
All of them at some period had to work at a volume, we hope aptly

[1] Thornton, Farmanby, Ellerburn and Kingthorpe Award, 1796.
[2] Young, p. 874 says that Michael Mackereth was, in 1817, incumbent
of Middleton, Lockton and Cropton. Eastmead, p. 327, shows that in 1824
the stipulated income of the Schoolmaster was £52 and a house; but that
the actual income was £100 and a house.
[3] J. L. W.
[4] Ibid.
[5] The income of the Charity on 12 March, 1818, was £563. 2s. 0d.
[6] In 1820 a certificate was signed by a few villagers including a member
of the Priestman family, stating that rich and poor children alike paid five
shillings a quarter.
[7] Eastmead, p. 325.
[8] J. L. W.

named, '*Pleasing Instruction*,' and also at the Old and New Testaments and at a '*Spelling Book*.' Some studied '*Telemachus*,' '*Cornelius Nepos*,' '*Grotius*,' '*Heathen Gods*,' '*Hutton's Arithmetic*,' '*Goldsmith's History of England*' and the Greek Testament. Some others were supposed to enjoy '*Mrs. Trimmer's Fabulous Histories*' and '*Doddridge's Rise and Progress*.'[1] It is not surprising that from such a grounding as the above that there were not many applications in Michael Mackereth's time for the Lumley exhibition. Only two have been found, both for the year 1803. The first exhibitioner was William Christopher Paul, member of St. John's College, Cambridge, and the second William Berwick, member of Pembroke Hall, Cambridge.[2]

The Rev. Thomas Irvin was elected in 1829 to succeed the old schoolmaster; but for some unknown reason he was unable to come into residence immediately, and the rector of Thornton, the Rev. Hill Webb was therefore paid £12 for teaching in the school during the vacancy.[3] At this time it was proposed by the trustees to rebuild the school house completely, but fortunately this extravagant plan fell through and the old thatched house, with its high wall and gates shutting it out from the road, remained, and was merely drastically repaired in 1831 by Richard Bolton, the carpenter, at a cost of £31. 11s. 0d.[4]

It is evident that Squire Hill thought well of the teaching capacity of the Rev. Thomas Irvin as he entrusted two of his sons to his care, as shown in Irvin's report on his pupils to the trustees in 1830, where he states that John Hill, aged 8 years, son of Richard Hill, Esq. is reading classics, Valpy's *Latin Delectus*, writing Latin Exercises and Latin Verse, also learning Arithmetic, Geography and History; while his younger brother Thomas, aged 7 years, is reading Valpy's *Latin Delectus*, writing Latin Exercises but not Verse, and is also learning Arithmetic and History but not Geography.[5] No figures have been found as to the number of scholars instructed by Thomas Irvin,[6] between 1830 and 1840, but the following received the Lumley exhibitions and held them at Cambridge. In 1834 R. B. Scholefield, son of the curate of Thornton, who went to St. John's College; in 1835 John Glaves, exhibitioner of Catherine Hall; in 1839 John Barry, exhibitioner of Caius College;

---

[1] Ibid.
[2] Ibid.
[3] Ibid.
[4] Ibid.
[5] Ibid.
[6] He was probably a relative of the Rev. Thomas Irvin, curate of Hackness in 1817.

in the same year, Robert John Thomas Bulmer of St. John's College; in 1840 C. Hardwicke, exhibitioner of Catherine Hall, who had acted sometime as usher at the School; and in 1841 Joseph Henry Thompson,[1] exhibitioner of Queen's College.[2]

In 1840[3] Thomas Irvin was succeeded by the Thornton curate the Rev. George Thomas Terry, LL.D. A contemporary account makes the somewhat startling statement that in this year there were 20 boarders and 30 day boys.[4] If this were really so, George Thomas Terry cannot be regarded as a very successful master, as in 1844, by his own returns to the trustees,[5] there were only eight boys doing reading, writing and arithmetic, one boy studying classics, and no boarders. The following year there was still further decline as one had retired from reading, writing and arithmetic.[6] It is not surprising to find, therefore, that on 6 April, 1846, the Rev. George Thomas Terry left the village. The Rev. R. B. Scholefield of Great Saxham, near Bury St. Edmunds, late pupil of the school, had already been unanimously appointed[7] to the post on 19 December, of the previous year.[8] R. B. Scholefield did not remain long, nor does he seem to have done anything to restore the waning fortunes of the school. In 1847 and again in 1848 there were only six pupils in all. In 1850 he was followed by Edward Firmstone, and in his first year three boys were studying classics and eight were doing reading, writing, and arithmetic, and, remarkable to relate, when he left in 1855[9] there were five classical scholars and twenty-five engaged in the humbler studies.

From that date for over thirty years the School took on a new

---

[1] He was only at Thornton Grammar School for one year.

[2] J. L. W.

[3] *East and North Ridings*, p. 490 says that this year the estates belonging to the Charity produced a yearly rental of £407. 16s. 0d.; and consisted of 209a. 3r. 17p. of land in Thornton: 189a. 25p. at Thirsk, Sowerby and Bagby: 5a. at Wilton: 20a. at Kirklevington: exclusive of 11a. occupied by the Schoolmaster, together with £1249. 11s. 10d. three per cent. consols.

[4] Ibid.

[5] The Trustees in 1840 were Lord Feversham, Richard Hill, Sir William Worsley, George Cholmley (resigned 7 August, 1844), Mark Foulis, Sir James Walker (resigned July, 1868), Thomas Mitchelson.

[6] J. L. W.

[7] A certain William Heslop, vicar of East Witton, Bedale applied for the mastership as early as 4 October, 1845. He is not known to have been any relation of the rector, Edward William Heslop of later years.

[8] J. L. W.

[9] On 27 February, 1856, the late head master, Edward Firmstone, signed a certificate for a Lumley exhibition stating that Dale John Welburn had been a scholar at Thornton Grammar School for two years and was now a member of Sidney Sussex College, Cambridge. The same kind of certificate was signed on 22 August, 1862 by the Rev. Thomas Simpson for William Dennis of Lutton who had been one year and was now a member of St. Catherine's, Cambridge.

lease of life under the very able Rev. Thomas Simpson, D.D. and his admirable wife who did much to assist him in educational restoration in Thornton. He has been described by one who knew him well, as very painstaking, a splendid worker and a stern disciplinarian. During his period of office he produced some good scholars. At the same time he was a gifted preacher and, not holding the curacy, took much clerical work on Sundays throughout the neighbourhood.[1] In 1856 he had 29 pupils in all.[2] Two years later there was a slight diminution, for the records show only 24, but this was probably due to the fact that he suffered very severely from ill health, and the school was closed for three months while he recuperated at Whitby.[3] But from the moment of his return the numbers rose rapidly. In 1859 there were 51 including 19 boarders, and the climax was reached in 1865 with a total of 59.[4] At the same time the buildings were kept up-to-date; in 1867 the school house was rethatched; in 1868 very considerable repairs were made; and in the next year—wonder of wonders, considering the period—a bathroom was added at the cost of £26.[5] So the school continued until Thomas Simpson's death in February, 1887, when his end, no doubt, was hastened by anxiety owing to rash speculation in Egyptian Bonds.

Simpson's successor was, for a short time, the Rev. Francis Read[6] and he, in turn, was followed by the Rev. John Church Frank Hare of Docking, Norfolk, who had taken his B.A. from Exeter College, Oxford, in 1879. Whatever the cause, from Simpson's death, the numbers of the school began to decline. When Hare left[7] in 1890,[8] there are stated to have been only 16 pupils; and when the Rev. Robert Hyde took the post in 1891 fewer still and when he went to Cottingham in 1900 the days of the old school were obviously numbered. Among the last of the pupils taught, in the early stages of their education, in the Lumley School were the son of old John Cross, who galloped each day on his pony down

[1] Thomas Anderson kindly told me this.
[2] J. L. W.
[3] Ibid.
[4] Ibid.
[5] Ibid.
[6] His son is Captain Herbert Read, author of '*Ambush,*' '*Collected Poems* 1913-1925,' '*Reason and Romanticism,*' and '*In Retreat.*' In the latter, he writes, 'The sight of beaten, frightened men plunging into the water effected one of those curious stirrings of memory that call up some vivid scene of childhood; I saw distinctly the water rats plunging at dusk into the river dam at Thornton-le-Dale where I had lived as a boy of ten.'
[7] From 1894 until recently he was rector of Bircham Newton, Norfolk.
[8] The trustees at this time were Lord Feversham, Sir William Worsley, Sir George Cayley, Hon. C. Duncombe, Rev. J. R. Hill, Rev. James Hill, Henry Hill, Robert Lesley (appointed trustee September, 1872).

from Dalby, Douglas Arthur Scott, nephew of the master, afterwards educated at Jesus College, Cambridge, where he took his B.A. in 1908 and has been rector of Thormanby since 1915, and George Arthur Hyde, son of the master, who afterwards distinguished himself as a gallant airman in the Great War and won the M.C., and having taken his B.A. at St. Peter's College, Cambridge, in 1920, was ordained and is now rector of South Milford.

When the Rev. Robert Hyde left the village the questions that faced the trustees were, either the appointment of a new master or a radical change in the administration of Lady Lumley's Bequest. On 15 April, 1902, an inquiry was held at the Court House, Pickering, with a view to the production of a scheme for the school. In January of the next year, the Board of Education announced that it had established such a scheme; and in 1905 the Lumley Grammar School was amalgamated with the School at Pickering. A new school was built on the outskirts of that town at a cost of £5000. In 1909 the Board of Education made this foundation a secondary public school for boys and girls with a preference for those born or resident in the parishes of Sinnington, Thornton and Pickering; and since the amalgamation to the spring of 1930, it was under the mastership of E. G. Highfield, B.A. Meanwhile Richard A. Scott had purchased the school house at Thornton, pulled down the unsightly wall and gates, and converted the somewhat prison-like building into a pleasant-looking dwelling. The School itself, with its fine window, stands out as a piece of architectural beauty, as it has done since 1670, and still serves a useful purpose as a hall for meetings of one kind and another.

CHAPTER NINE.

The Church and Rectors of Thornton.

' *A good man was there of religioun,*
And was a poure parsoun of a town;
But riche he was of holy thought and werk.
He was also a lerned man, a clerk,
That Christe's Gospel trewely wolde preche,
His parischens devoutly wolde he teche.
But Christe's lore and His Apostles twelve
He taughte, but first he folwede it himselve.'

CHAUCER, C. 1395.

NO one can fail to admire the natural and commanding position of Thornton Church. From the bridge the main road runs due east, and, below the Church, divides into two, the north wing passing into a back lane, the south continuing the main route to Scarborough. At the fork is a mound, resembling a small cliff jutting out between the lane and the road, and perched on this is the Church of All Saints, surrounded by its churchyard, and approached from the west by a steep flight of stone steps. The external view of the building is very attractive, and internally one is struck by its quiet dignity and its impression of being large, possibly larger than it really is, for its total length is less than 96 feet. The glass in the windows is for the most part in good taste; the memorial brasses are beautifully kept, and there is a feeling of restfulness to the mind as soon as one enters. There are, however, no salient features of mediaeval architecture to attract the connoisseur, except, perhaps, the tomb in the north wall of the Chancel, and the Norman font. Despite what some writers have said, it must be acknowledged that the Church has suffered much from restoration.

That there was a Church here in the remote past may be surmised, first from the fact that the bowl of the font is Norman, and has been dated as late twelfth century; and secondly because, as will be shown, there was a parson[1] in Thornton about the same

---

[1] Cardinal Gasquet, *Mediaeval Parish Life*, p. 71 writes 'The word "parson" in the sense of a dignified personage—"the person of the place" was applied....in the eleventh century, in its Latin form of "persona" to any one holding the parochial cure of souls....In ecclesiastical language, at any rate in England, according to Lyndwood (the great Canonist) the word "parson" was synonymous with "rector."'

time. The Norman Church has, however, except for the font, entirely disappeared, and in the fourteenth century a new Church, with a porch,[1] was erected from Chancel to Tower. The latter, with its buttresses and crocheted pinnacles, was completed at a period far nearer the end than the beginning of that century. The Tower, perhaps, might be described as unfinished as it can clearly be seen, on examination, that there was every intention of adding a spire, but this was never done. It is said that the piscina on the south wall of the Chancel and that in the south aisle, together with parts of the triple sedilia and a low side window[2] in the choir, are all of considerable antiquity. The fourteenth century rebuilding does not seem to have been entirely satisfactory, and other restorations had to be done, for the present much-repaired Chancel arch cannot be dated earlier than the fifteenth century, though the arcades of four bays, separating the nave from the north and south aisles, are contemporary with the re-building of the century before.

There are no records to show whether any restoration work was undertaken between the fifteenth and the seventeenth centuries. One can understand that by the close of the latter, some repairs were needed, and these were done by the Rector, Dean Comber. It is fairly easy to surmise that he made drastic alterations to the fabric, for in April, 1681, he had completed the repairs which included the roof,[3] floor and windows, and had replaced the old altar rails with new ones.[4] He left a quaint-looking little Church, with a flat-roofed Chancel, very much below the level of the original nave roof, but above that made by himself, and with, proportionately, a large and somewhat squat porch on the south-west side. One hundred and ninety years later this building was again in a serious condition. The Chancel was thick in ivy, the strands of which had penetrated the masonry. Thanks, mainly to the Rev. John Richard Hill and the Rev. Edward W. Heslop, the building was taken in hand, and restoration was started on 21 May, and the corner stone was laid on 20 June, 1865.[5] The

---

[1] An old picture of the Church before its restoration shows a porch with what looks like a Norman arch. I am indebted to Miss M. L. Heslop.

[2] This must have been built up at some period as it is not shown in the old picture and is said to have been discovered when the walls were destroyed 1865-6.

[3] The roof pitch was very considerably lowered. The line of the old pitch was still visible on the Tower as late as 1866 when the new roof was restored to the old level.

[4] Comber, *ut supra.*

[5] Edward Hill, then a young son of the Rev. John Richard Hill placed in it a bottle with coins, etc.

architect, E. W. Tarn, insisted on the Chancel and the Vestry being completely rebuilt[1] and the roof of the former was raised a considerable height, and is now rather higher than that of the nave.[2] A very thorough restoration was made in the nave, all the windows were renewed, and the gallery removed.[3] The old square pews were abolished, and the Church reseated with oak. The lead on the roof was replaced by Westmorland slates. The whole work was completed at a cost of £2500; and though much of the old beauty and quaintness were swept away, and the loss is regrettable, yet the Church has undoubtedly gained in dignity.

The almost new Church was first used for service in October, 1866, when consecrated by the Archbishop of York.[4] In 1900, after being without for nearly forty years, a porch[5] of a more elegant design than that destroyed in 1865, was built as a memorial to the Rev. Edward W. Heslop by his parishioners and friends. The last change in the external appearance of the Church was made in 1920 when the clock was placed in the Tower, as a thank-offering for peace after the Great War.[6] Inside the Church from 1866 to the beginning of the twentieth century, there was little change,[7] the organ still remained at the west end, and there was no surpliced choir, the stalls being occupied by the rector's household on the south side, and that of the lord of the manor and patron on the north.[8] In 1905 this old-world custom ceased. New stalls were made, the level of the Chancel was raised, a fine organ was placed on the north of the choir, and in 1910, new altar rails took the place of those of 1866.[9]

[1] Church Terrier.
[2] It is a curious fact that twenty-four hours before the swallows migrate in September, hundreds collect on this roof with the effect that the whole roof appears to be quivering.
[3] White's *Directory*.
[4] William Thomson.
[5] The architect was Hodgson Fowler, Esq.
[6] This is stated on a tablet in the Church.
[7] A brass pulpit desk was given by Coulson Fowler in December, 1881; the carved oak reredos was the gift of the Rev. Edward W. Heslop at Easter, 1892; and an oak credence table was given by Mrs. Fowler and her sister, Mrs. Spencer in remembrance of their mother, Mrs. Jelly, at Easter, 1896; two churchwarden's staves and some glass vases were given by R. A. Scott in May, 1901; two hammered metal candlesticks were given by Mr. and Mrs. H. Fraser in May, 1921; an oak lectern was erected to the memory of the Rev. A. Hill in January, 1925; and two hymn boards were given by the Misses Miles in July, 1928.
[8] This custom was not directly contrary to the prohibition of Simon Langham of Ely in 1364, which stated that 'lay persons are not to stand or sit with the clerks in the chancel during the celebration of divine service, unless it is done to show reverence (to some particular person) or for some other suitable and obvious reason; but this is allowed for the patrons of churches only.'
[9] The generosity of the Rev. Godfrey Marshall helped these changes to be made.

In the meantime the surroundings of the Church had also undergone some alterations. Up to 1853 the churchyard was very small and circumscribed. On the east side it was bounded by a lane, a hundred yards west of the present one running from the main road to Back Church Lane; and abutting on this were a cottage, a garden and a joiner's shop. These were purchased from the patron, Richard Hill, and levelled to the ground. The new space was enclosed and planted with yews; and consecrated by Bishop Spencer in 1854.[1] After a time the churchyard again required enlargement, and in 1890, the Rev. John Richard Hill gave the land to the parish; the lane was then moved to its present site, and the utmost limits of the churchyard were reached. The new portion was consecrated by the Bishop of Beverley on the 18 September, of that year.[2] No further burials can now take place, and a cemetery was purchased on the east side of Peaslands and consecrated by Bishop Crosthwaite on 5 September, 1922.[3]

The most interesting monument in the Church is the fine wall-tomb with gabled canopy of crocheted pinnacles, dating back to the very early fourteenth century. The figure is that of a slim lady, and on either side are six carved shields alternately of St. Quintin and of Hastings.[4] This dame of the early Edwardian period is commonly known as 'The Black Knight of the North,' solely because the Register states that Sir Richard Cholmley, the real 'Black Knight,' was buried 'in the Chancel' in May, 1583. It is extremely likely that the recumbent figure represents Lady Beatrice Hastings,[5] who flourished in the reign of Edward II. The next oldest memorial is a fine brass, with a well engraved coat of arms,[6] to the memory of Mr. John Porter 'late of London, merchant' who died in October, 1686. Near by is another brass to his widow, who died in

---

[1] Church Terrier.

[2] Ibid.

[3] From information supplied by Herbert Garbutt.

[4] The V. C. H. *N.R.* II. p. 497 states that the arms are those of the families of St. Quintin and Conyers. But the Conyers had nothing to do with Thornton, whereas the Hastings had. In an ancient carving it would be practically impossible, without external evidence to differentiate between the coat of Conyers and of Hastings. The Conyers was *azure a sleeve or*, and the Hastings was *argent a sleeve sable*. *Cf.* Y. A. J. XXVIII. pp. 46-7 where the arms are clearly shown to be St. Quintin and Hastings. I suggest that the Lady Beatrice was the daughter of Sir Herbert St. Quintin who died in 1303, and was named after her grandmother Beatrice or Beatrix daughter of the lord of Sutton-in-Holderness who was married to William St. Quintin, and who flourished about 1241. *Vide* Foster, *Pedigrees of Yorkshire*.

[5] If she were a St. Quintin, it might be noted that Beatrice or Beatrix was evidently a family name at this time. *Cf.* V. C. H. *York*, III. p. 179.

[6] The coat is (sable) three church bells (argent) a canton ermine (Porter) impaling (argent) a chevron ingrailed between three moorcocks (sable) (More).

1705. On the south wall is a good brass, dated 1744, to the memory of the Rev. Thomas Mason and his wife, and stating that '*in a Life of 40 years seldom seperate, in Death but 10 days devided.*' There are five other brasses of more modern date. The first, on the south wall of the Chancel, to John Champley Rutter, who died 30 December, 1870; the second, on the north wall of the Chancel, to Harriet, widow of John Richard Hill, who died 5 November, 1899: the third, on the same wall, to Captain Lionel George Hill, who fell in action on 17 February, 1915; the fourth to Jane, second wife of Richard Hill, who died March, 1890; and the fifth in the north aisle, to the 24 men of Thornton who laid down their lives in the Great War. There are two typical eighteenth century urn-ornamented memorials in marble, on the south wall of the Chancel, the one to John Hill, who died aged 63 years, on 1 March, 1773; the other to Richard Johnson Hill, who died aged 32 years, on 28 July, 1793, of whom, so states the inscription, '*His Integrity and private Worth render'd him respected thro' Life and at his Death lamented by all who knew him.*' Three other marble slabs commemorate the Rev. John Hill Webb '*50 years the Benevolent Rector of Thornton,*' who died aged 81, on the 21 July, 1837; Helen Turville Terry, wife of the Rev. George Thomas Terry, 'Master of the Grammar School,' who died on 19 September, 1842; and Richard Hill who died on 21 January, 1855. The west window is to the memory of John Champley who died in 1864; the south-west to Major Francis H. J. Hawley of the Scots Greys,[1] who died on 27 April, 1900; the east window of the south aisle to the Rev. Edward W. Heslop, who died on 8 December, 1899; the south window of the Chancel to Lucy, wife of the Rev. Edward W. Heslop, who died on 2 March, 1860, and to John Rutter, who died in 1843; the east window to Eliza, mother of Richard Hill, who died 1830, to Richard Hill who died 1855, and to Anne, first wife of Richard Hill, who died 1815; the north window to John Richard Hill, who died on 21 December, 1896. And lastly there is an oak-framed illuminated parchment recording the names of the 164 Thornton men who strove in that 'great adventure,' in the unforgettable years 1914-18.[2]

Outside the Church there are the memorials of many, and amongst them the graves of two Thornton worthies who were among the lesser stars that go to make English history. The first

---

[1] Not a native of the place but a friend of the Hill family.
[2] *Vide* Appendix.

is that of the gallant old soldier, Matthew Grimes,[1] who died in 1875, aged 96 years, who had fought in India and in the Peninsular War, and who had guarded Napoleon I. in St. Helena and helped to carry that monarch to his grave in May, 1821.[2] The second is that of John Booth, who died, aged 85, in 1853, after having been fifty-six years gamekeeper and huntsman to Richard Hill, and on whose tomb his employer placed the words, '*Well done, good and faithful servant.*'

Of the treasures of the Church there is not much to record. In the nave, near the south door there is a Jacobean alms-box of quaint but rather rough workmanship and design. The three bells can claim little antiquity. The third is marked 'S.S. Ebor. 1663. Jesus be our speed'; the tenor was cast by E. Seller, and is inscribed 'Gloria in excelsis deo. 1710'; and the second was cast by E. Seller[3] (II.) of York, and is inscribed 'Soli deo gloria, 1758.' As to the communion plate, it is of ordinary pattern and design.[4] 'Roger Hunter, of Newstead Grange in the Marish, gentleman, [gave the chalice] to the use of the parish Church of Thornton in Pickering lythe, wherein he lies buried.' He died 28 April, 1659; and the cup was evidently bought after his death, as it was made in York the following year. The silver Paten was given by John Hill I. in 1689; and the flagon was presented by the Rev. John Gilby, stepfather of Richard Hill, in 1804. The Registers are particularly interesting as they date from so early a period—for baptisms and burials, 1538, and for marriages, 1560—but unfortunately for the two former there are serious blanks between 1553 and 1558, and for all three between 1608 and 1622.

The Terriers of Church property are, from some points of view, almost as interesting as the Registers. The first three of 1727, 1764, 1770, are very much alike and agree with that of 1777, except that, in the case of the Terrier of 1764, there is the following memorandum made by the Rev. Oswald Langwith on 22 November,

---

[1] The jacket worn by M. Grimes at Waterloo passed to a blacksmith at Middleton and from him to Dr. Kirk and is now in the Pickering museum.

[2] This is recorded on his tombstone.

[3] V. C. H. *York*, II., p. 452 says A 'foundry was started in York 1710 by Edward Seller, by whom we have some fifteen bells in Yorkshire and also two in Lincolnshire. He was Sheriff of York in 1703-4, and died in 1724, being buried in St. Sampson's Church. He was succeeded by his son, Edward Seller (II.), whose career was longer, and his bells more numerous. In Yorkshire there are over sixty. . . . He lived in Silver Street and was Sheriff in 1731-2; he died 20 November, 1764.

[4] A second Chalice and Paten were presented by the Rev. Godfrey and Mrs. Marshall, and dedicated on 2 February, 1927. The design of this Chalice is not ordinary for it was copied from one in York Minster which had been found in the tomb of Archbishop Melton, who died in 1340.

1758 :—'When Mr. Hill enclosed his Langlands in Botton Field he took in two broad Arable lands which are part of the Glebe of the Rectory of Thornton. They lie next the South Hedge which Hedge now stands upon the Further of the said lands.' A review of the Terrier of 1777 reveals some old field names and some interesting customs with regard to Tithes. First of all the rectory, built by Dean Comber, is described as a thatched stone house. There was not much accommodation for the rector, except in a stone hall and a 'wainsatted parlour.' In the servants' department there was a hall, a kitchen and a butler's pantry and two cellars. Upstairs there were four bedrooms and garrets. Outside there were stables, coach-house and cowhouse, and on the south, as now, was a garden, on the west of which was an orchard. The glebe consisted of four oxgangs dispersed in the Three Fields on the east side of the Beck. In the 'Town End Field' there were on the north of 'the King's Street' 2 broadlands, and 2 broadlands called Caulklands,[1] with Buffit Hedge on the north; south of 'the King's Street' were 4 broadlands, two known as 'Lands in the Hole' and two as 'Longlands.'[2] In 'Far Field,' with 'the King's Street' on the south, 2 broadlands called 'Dimans Lands' and 2 called 'Graystone lands'[3] and with 'the King's Street' on the north 2 broadlands called 'Langlands' bounded on the south by Charity 'Woolnest.'[4] In 'Botton Field' there were 2 broadlands in Harrowcliff bounded on the south by 'Charity Carr', 1 narrowland called 'Horrel land' with 'West Horrel' on the north and 'Charity Carr' on the south; 2 broadlands called 'Wandles' with Hungrel Way on the east, Botton Way on the west, Mr. Hill's land on the north and south; 2 broadlands called 'Buttry Stubs,'[5] Botton Way on the east, Mr. Hill on the west, John Priestman on the north; 2 broadlands called Botton Lands and a 'narrow land' called 'Flattends.'[6] Besides these there were, one Carr, with Mr. Hill's Carr on the east, a large

[1] Still so called.
[2] *Cf.* 'Langlands Lane,' Six-inch Ordnance Map.
[3] Up Utgang Lane. This Grey Stone which is referred to several times has now disappeared.
[4] The spelling of this word varies; in 1670 and in 1729 it is 'Woolness,' in 1756 'Woof Nest,' in 1777 'Woolnest,' and in 1780 'Woolness's.' 'Woolness' is now a lane turning east off Hurrell Lane just below where the railway crosses the road.
[5] A field now cut in two by the railway at Harrowcliff Bridge; the name is first found in a document of 1692. In the will of Joshua Priestman, proved 22 January, 1845 it is referred to as 'all that my close of land called Buttry Stubbs.'
[6] A flat or flatt according to Canon Atkinson, is a fairly level piece of land devoted to agricultural purposes.

pasture, divided into three, called 'Broats'[1] with the Beck on the east [? west]; and the New Ing of ten acres, with Dean's New Ing[2] on the east, 'Horrel' lane on the west, New Ing Lane on the north and Charity Carr on the south.

The Terrier then proceeds to give the customs concerning tithe. The whole tithe of 'Corn and Hay growing on the East side of the Beck' went to the rector.[3] The west side presented greater complications, for Thornton and Farmanby were, and are, inextricably intermingled.[4] The rector, however, states 'on the West, Thornton and Farmanby Tythe is interspersed but it is well known what Falls belongs to each parish.' The tenth Fleece of wool 'is paid at Shearing Time' and the custom 'is for the owner to take Three Fleeces' and the agent of the rector a fourth. 'On St. Peter's day Tythe Lambs are taken,[5] for five, half, for six or more a whole one, for four and under the Rector's agent takes nothing in regard the owner pays one at six.' Pigs are paid when three weeks old, for half a pig in money as the rector and owner can agree, for six a whole one, for four nothing. 'Geese, Turkies, Ducks are Tytheable at Mich^ms, for five the prices of half a one, for six or more a whole one. Every house inhabited pays a hen on St. Thomas' Day every year.' Every swarm of bees 'pays a penny: the old Stock that are taken in Summer are to pay the tenth part of Honey & wax: of Six Hives or more' the rector has one. A cow with calf pays two pence at Easter: 'a Dry Cow a penny. He that hath 5 calves in the year pays ten groats, for six or more a noble, for a Foal is paid a penny for ever'.... 'Hearth money was taken formerly (wch is half-pence). But the Rev^d. Thos. Mason, some years ago, Rector of this parish, never received it, but waved [*sic*] his right, for peace sake, since wch it has never been demaunded, these with the offerings, wch is twopence for every person above sixteen years of age, make up the Easter Book.' Tithe was also due in kind from the two Dalby Farms, and, in money, from the farms into which

---

[1] According to the Terrier of 1727 the Broats were divided into three by the Rev. Thomas Mason. A. H. Smith, *ut supra*, p. 86, says the word means 'a clearing in a wood.'

[2] Now known as New Ings.

[3] For all the different kind of things titheable, as corn, honey, butter, cheese and so on *vide* Capes, *History of the Church of England*, III. p. 268.

[4] *Vide* Ch. XIV.

[5] Selden, *Tithes*, p. 222 says 'the tithe of yong cattell to be paid at Whitsontide and of fruits of the earth at All Hallows.'

the old Newstead Grange had been divided.[1] Mortuaries[2] were due by custom and paid according to 'stability.'[3] For opening ground in the Chancel the rector was to have ten shillings and the same fee for reading the Burial Service, these fees were halved if the burial was in the body of the Church. 'For a Burial in the Church Yard with a coffin a shilling, without a coffin eightpence.'[4] Marriage by licence was ten shillings, by banns, one shilling; and churching was eightpence. 'Twenty shillings is paid yearly out of the Rectory of Thornton to the Rector of Thorp Basset (as tradition has it) for not burying there';[5] and ten shillings were paid to the Ringers on 5 November, 'charged (as tradition has it) upon a part of the Broats.' This was, of course, for the Curfew, or as the Terrier says, 'The Eight o'clock bell is rung from 5 Nov. to Shrove Tuesday.'[6]

The Terriers of 1781 and 1786 are much the same and so also that of 1809, except that it says 'in lieu of Rector's Common Right & all the tythe of the Common & Waste on the East side of the Beck' there was an allotment of 120 acres with Allerston Common on the east, Robert Champley on the west, Mr. Hill on the north, and the Wilton lordship on the south. The Broats still belonged to the rector, but there is an additional statement that 'one little

[1] *Vide* Ch. XVII.

[2] Mortuaries are ecclesiastical heriots being customary gifts claimed and due to the minister in many parishes on the death of any of his parishioners *vide* Blackstone, *Commentaries* IV. ii. ch. iii. That the mortuary system was a constant source of friction *vide* G. C. Coulton, *ut supra*, p. 348. Miss Neilson, *ut supra*, p. 192 says '*Soulscot* was in origin the Anglo-Saxon mortuary due, paid at the open grave, if a man were buried in his own parish, and if he were buried elsewhere still paid to the minster to which he had properly belonged.' *Cf.* Seebohm, *Tribal Custom in Anglo-Saxon Law*, p. 461. An important statute on mortuaries was 21 Hen. VIII. c. 6. which was re-enacted 28 Geo. III. c. 6.

[3] According to a man's financial position. Thus on 6 April, 1720, at the burial of James Dixon, junior, there was a mortuary of 10s.; again on 27 September, 1727, when James Dixon 'in ye 77 year of his age' was buried, there was a similar sum.

[4] The custom of burying in coffins is a comparatively modern one save among the wealthy classes. The wording of the Burial Service anticipates uncoffined burial. The word coffin is never used. Up to 1860 uncoffined burials were still very common in Derbyshire. 'It was the custom for each parish to provide a shell or coffin to rest on the bier for the carrying of the corpse to the edge of the grave, when it was lifted out and lowered into the grave in its shroud which was wrapped round with strips of canvas.' *Vide* Cox, *Parish Registers*, pp. 120-1.

[5] It should be noted that Dugdale, *Monasticon* II. p. 220 states that Berenger de Todeni and Albreda his wife gave the Church of Thorpe Basset and the tithes of Settrington to St. Alban's Abbey.

[6] Cardinal Gasquet, *ut supra*, p. 162 says 'The Angelus bell, the Ave bell, or the Gabriel bell, as it was variously called in England probably grew out of the Curfew, which originally was a civil notification of the time to extinguish all lights; but in the thirteenth century it was turned into a universal religious ceremony in honour of our Lord's Incarnation and of His Blessed Mother.'

Close in Exchange from Mr. Hill to Rector of Thornton called
Pannier Man's pool adjoining west of the said Broats & containing
2 roods and 30 perches, Malton road on the west, Mr. Hill on
South, Robert Smithson on North, and now the only way into the
Broats, the old way being lost thro' long disuse, which lay formerly,
as I have heard, through Robert Smithson's Ellicar.'[1] This Terrier
also explains that, since the Enclosure Award in 1781, a money
payment has been made in lieu of Tithes, viz. £100. 2s. 4¼d. paid
by the proprietors of lands for old enclosed lands, and £81. 18s. 0d.
for old enclosed lands in the parish of Ellerburn. There had also
been an allotment to the rector of 35 ac. 2 ro. 19 per. of land
adjoining the Whitby Road on the west, Isaac Rogers on the
north, Mr. Hill on the east 'and a Lane leading to Dalby on the
South.'[2]

The Terriers of 1817 and 1825 show little change, but that
of 8 June, 1849, has some points of interest. It describes the new
rectory house completed in 1841, and speaks of a garden of ¾ of
an acre with a garden and orchard, east of the house, walled with
stone.[3] It also shows that an improvement had been made at the
north-east corner of the rectory grounds, as an old barn and
cowhouse had been destroyed and on the site a dwelling-house
had been built.[4] The service is evidently improved for 'There is a
sermon preached every Sunday in the forenoon and prayers afternoon throughout the year.' In addition it gives the information that,
in 1840, the Rev. John Richard Hill gave 'Two Common Prayer
Books & a Bible containing the Old & New Testaments with yᵉ
Apocrypha & Two Books of Altar Services for the Communion
Table.'

The Terriers of 1853 and 1890 record the enlargement of the
Churchyard, already mentioned; and that of 1866 contains the
story of the restoration of the Church. That of 1879 is interesting
as it specifies the date of the coming of the railway. The North
Eastern Railway Company, in that year, bought ¾ of an acre of
grass land from the rector, known as East Field Allotment, for
£200, which sum was invested partly in 3 per cent. Consols and
partly in a small grass field on the south side of Back Lane behind

---

[1] *Cf.* Baptismal Register where in 1733 there is the same statement that
Pannierman's Pool is the only entry, and that any other had been lost thro'
long disuse.

[2] This is the lane that leads from the Whitby Road to Belt Common
and Pexton Moor, and generally known as Belt Lane.

[3] This means that a cottage that stood here in 1796 had been destroyed.

[4] Formerly tenanted for many years by Alfred Bolton, carpenter, and
now by J. T. Bielby.

the rectory, bounded on the east by land of the Rev. John Richard Hill, and on the west and south by land belonging to the rector.

Finally with regard to the possessions of the Church, reference must be made to the very complete set of 'briefs'[1] which are recorded on the fly-leaves of the registers. During the period 1660 to 1768, there were frequent briefs for fires, rebuilding of churches, rescue of Christian slaves and losses from inundations, shipwreck and storms. The places affected were not confined to the British Isles. During the eighteenth century the briefs for the restoration or rebuilding of churches were particularly common, which fact would seem to refute the usual charge of the period being a godless age. The reading of these briefs, by the rector, must have been in some ways a method of conveying the news to the villagers. It would appear from the sums subscribed that the people were more generous towards outlandish places, and less generous towards the needs of their immediate neighbours. The numerous references to serious and destructive fires were no doubt due to the fact that nearly all villages were at that time thatched. It would be impossible to give a complete list, here, of all the briefs. The following will serve as examples. 'Collected on a brief':—

		s.	d.
16. Dec. 1660.	'For a fire in the City of London in S. Bartholomew's Exchange'	3	1
22. June. 1662.	'for his losse at sea, for Tho. Welby'	2	1
24. June. 1666.	'for Hartlepool pier'	1	1
10. Oct. 1666.	'for the fire at London'[2]	3	4
21. May. 1671.	'for the Captives under the Turkish Pyrates'	15	0
20. Oct. 1671.	'for a fire at Oxford'	2	6
22. Sept. 1672.	'for the sugar houses at London'	5	4
14. Sept. 1690.	'for ye irish Protestants'	19	9
(blank) 1692.	'for ye redemption of captives'	1 8	0

---

[1] *The Dictionary of English History*, p. 189 ed. 1896, says Church Briefs 'were letters addressed by the sovereign to the archbishops, bishops and clergy, empowering them to raise voluntary contributions for....charitable purposes generally. They do not appear to have been issued before the Reformation, and may possibly be derived from the briefs given by the papal court to the mendicant friars, empowering them to collect contributions. The granting of briefs appears to have led to great abuses. It was regulated by 4 and 5 Anne cap. 14, and practically abolished by 9 Geo. IV. cap. 42, though briefs have been issued for special purposes since the date of the latter Statute.'

[2] The Great Fire of September, 1666.

		£	s.	d.
15. Oct. 1700.	'for redeeming ye slaves at Mackanes'[1]	1	11	5
27. Feb. 1703.	'for ye French Refugees'	2	17	6
7. May. 1704.	'for ye widows & orphans of those seamen who perished in ye late dreadful storm'[2]	1	2	0
25. Nov. 1705.	'for rebuilding All Saints Church in Oxford'[3]		5	10
4. April. 1708.	'for erecting & building a Protestant Church at Ober-barmen in ye Duchy of Berg'		5	6
? May. 1717.	'for ye Reformed Episcopal Churches in great Poland & Polish Prussia'	4	0	0
15. Oct. 1727.	'for rebuilding St. Peter's Church in Oxford'[4]		3	4
13. May. 1730.	'for ye Protestants at Copenhagen in Denmark'		16	6
15. July. 1739.	'for ye sufferers by Inundations at Bobi & Villar in ye valley of Lucerne in Piedmont'		7	0
26. May. 1742.	'for ye oyster dredgers of Medway & in Com: Kent'		5	0
27. June. 1762.	'for Saarbruch Church & School in Germany'		5	0
(?) 1763.	'towards the founding of two Colleges in America, viz Philadelphia & New York'		9	6
24. March. 1765.	'for the benefit of the Phillipan Colony in Turkish Moldavia'		3	4
24. Aug. 1766.	'for losses by fire at Montreal in the Province of Quebec'		8	10
8. May. 1768.	'the Vaudois protestants'		14	7½

To chronicle such points as these with regard to Thornton
Church has been an easy matter, but the task of attempting to
disentangle the story of the descent of the advowson has proved
well-nigh impossible. The following account, with some hypothesis,

[1] G. H. Wakeling, Esq., Fellow of Brasenose College, kindly suggests
that this is a mis-spelling for Mekines or Mekinez, a large town near Fez in
Morocco.

[2] This was the Great Storm of 26-27 November, 1703. 1500 seamen of
the Royal Navy were drowned: the damage in London was over £1,000,000,
and in Bristol £200,000; the Eddystone lighthouse was destroyed.

[3] This had been burnt. It still has a flame as a weather vane.

[4] St. Peter-le-Bailey, but not the present one.

is, as far as the present writer can make it, historical. It has been said, by an authority on ecclesiastical law, that 'all our parochial churches were at first rectories, possessed of the tithes, glebe and offerings.'[1] Presumably, in the earliest times, the church of 'All Hallowes' was a rectory in the patronage of the family of Brus of Skelton Castle.[2] It was, therefore, connected with the manor in Thornton held by the Brus's for two centuries. If this were so, the patronage would be what is called an advowson *appendant*, and would become an advowson *in gross*, if ever alienated from that manor,[3] which, in years to come, it certainly was. After the death of Gilbert, the first known parson,[4] there seems to have been a dispute as to the right of presentation, and as the quarrel between the two parties lasted so long, it fell, for the occasion, to the Archbishop of York, who was, at that time, Walter de Gray; and in August, 1225, he issued a notice that 'we collate Adam de Insula to it'; the said vicar to have the whole alterage and four bovates of land,[5] with the manse, and all the tithes of crofts in Thornton, "Farmarneby" and "Elreburn"; reserving to Galfridus (Geoffrey) de Twenge, the parson (i.e., the rector) a rent of twenty marks, *'quem ei in decimis bladi tantum tanquam personae fecimus assignari.'*[6] It is clear, therefore, that at the time there were both a rector and a vicar. In the period of the middle ages many rectors were absentees, resident vicars taking their duty at an annual stipend of five marks or sometimes £5.[7] But in this case the benefice was divided into two parts, one mediety being held by a rector, the other by a vicar. The actual disputants as to the possession of the advowson were Nicholas de Yeland and Eustachia, his wife, and John, son of Alan the Forester, who was the brother of Gilbert the recently deceased parson. The dispute was decided on 13 October, 1225, at Westminster, before five judges;[8] and Nicholas and Eustachia quitclaimed for themselves and the heirs of Eustachia to John and his heirs, and for the advowson John gave ten marks of silver.[9] By a document dated 23 December, 1282, it appears as if the right of presentation to 'the vicarage' was in the hands of the rector, Robert

---

[1] A. Gibbons, editor of *Liber Antiquus de Ordinationibus vicariarum tempore Hugonis de Wells.*

[2] Rev. Godfrey Marshall.

[3] *Cf.* Blackstone II. p. 22.

[4] *Vide infra.*

[5] *Cf.* the four oxgangs in the Terrier of 1777.

[6] *Archb. Gray's Reg.* Sur. Soc. LVI. p. 5.

[7] V. C. H. *Oxford* II. p. 12.

[8] Martin of Pateshull, Thomas of Muleton, Thomas of Haiden, Robert of Lexinton, Geoffrey Savage.

[9] Y. A. S. Rec. S. LXII. p. 63.

Ellerburn Church

de Everley;[1] but this is not certain, because on one occasion it is said that Robert de Everley presented, with 'the consent of the patron.'[2] Who then was the patron? Not the family of Brus, for that was extinct in the main branch of the male line on the death of Peter Brus in 1272. One difficulty, at any rate, was got over in 1308, by the union of the rectory and vicarage, and henceforth all alms, oblations, tithes and profits were to go to the rector.[3] But this does not clear the mystery as to the owner of the advowson. It has been suggested[4] that the Stephen Mangevilein, who appears in the charter to Rievaulx Abbey concerning property in the Marishes in 1158,[5] had a great-grandson, Robert Mangevilein,[6] who was the sub-tenant of Sir William Percy, who in turn had held from Brus,[7] and that this Robert had a daughter Alice, who carried her rights as heiress to her husband, Alan de Everley, and they had a son, the already mentioned William de Everley of Ugglebarnby.[8] In favour of this view it may be pointed out that Robert de Everley was presented in 1267.[9] This family must have died out in the male line, leaving a female, named Joan, who married John de Wandesford about 1361, as his second wife, when the advowson was passed by trustees, Burton Amneys, chaplain, and Robert Rodheram of 'Whyteby,' to John de Wandesford and Joan, and the heirs of their bodies with remainder to the right heirs of Joan.[10] It seems that the advowson with the Brus manor,[11] remained with the Wandesfords until about 1437, when they ceased to hold the manor which for the moment possibly escheated to Sir William Brus of Pickering.

The advowson was evidently divided into three moieties between the three daughters and coheiresses of Sir William Brus and of Margaret, daughter of Walter Hawyke, his wife. This is shown by a series of documents now in the possession of the Countess of Loudoun.[12] On 9 February, 1437/8, Robert Browne and Maud,[13] his wife, daughter of William 'Bruys' and one of the

---

[1] *Archb. Wickwane's Reg.* Sur. Soc. CXIV. p. 128.
[2] Rev. Godfrey Marshall.
[3] Ibid.
[4] V. C. H. *N.R.* II. p. 497.
[5] *Vide* Ch. XVII.
[6] *Vide* Ch. XII.
[7] Cal. Feud. Aids VI. p. 82.
[8] *Vide* Ch. II. and XII.
[9] *Archb. Giffard's Reg.* Sur. Soc. CIX. p. 44.
[10] Y. A. S. Rec. S. LII. p. 80.
[11] *Vide* Ch. XII.
[12] Hist. MSS. Com., Rawden Hastings MS. I. p. 192.
[13] Maud must have married secondly William Marshall, son of William Marshall, lord of Empingham, alive in 1418 and Katharine, daughter of George Tamworth, his wife. The V. C. H. *N.R.* II. says that 'William' Marshall, husband of Maud, was 'John.'

heirs of his land, granted to Sir William Eure, no doubt in trust, the advowson of a third part of the Church of Thornton, and on 1 August, 1439 the same granted to the same a third part of one messuage in Thornton called 'le Kyrkhous,' and again repeated the grant of a third part of the advowson. On the same day the second daughter of Sir William Brus[1] came into the agreement, for a grant was made by William 'Appulby' and Isabella, his wife, one of the coheirs of Robert [William] 'Bruys' to William Eure of the same premises. On 10 August of that year William Eure, Knight, appointed Thomas Stokeslay his attorney to receive 'seisin of two parts of a moiety of the Church of Thornton in Pickering Lythe according to the form and effect of certain charters made to him by William "Appylby" and Isabella[2] his wife, one of the coheirs of Robert [William] "Brusse," and Richard "Hekylfeld" [Ecclefield, lord of the manor] and Elizabeth his wife, the other [alteram] coheir of the said Robert [William] "Brusse".' On 11 October, of the same year, conveyance was made by the first two daughters and their husbands of all their rights in the same premises. It would appear, therefore, that two sisters resigned through a trustee their shares in the advowson to the third sister, Elizabeth, who had married the man who had recently followed[3] the Wandesfords as holder of the Brus manor in Thornton. It is clear that Richard Ecclefield did not remain lord for long and it is equally clear that on the resignation of the rector, William de Morton, the living was vacant in 1461.[4] Possibly Richard Ecclefield was dead, possibly his heir, perhaps a son, but probably a daughter Joan,[5] was under age. At any rate the appointment to the living was not made by an Ecclefield, because, for an unknown reason, on 20 July, 1461 the Crown granted the right of the next advowson and patronage of Thornton Church to William 'Hastynges', Knt.[6] and

---

[1] The editor of the Rawden Hastings MS. says that 'William' is probably an error for 'Robert'; but I think 'Robert' is an error for William for no 'Robert' is shown in the descent of this family at this time in the article on Barton-le-Willows, *cf.* V. C. H. *N.R.* II. p. 117, where William Brus is shown to be alive as late as 1428.

[2] A third daughter of William Brus is mentioned, V. C. H. *N.R.* II. p. 117, but is not named. It must be this Isabella. Glover's *Visitation* quoted in the Y. A. J. VII. p. 89 shows 'Isabell' daughter of William Brus, married William 'Appelby,' and died without issue.

[3] He held other lands in right of his wife *cf.* V. C. H. *N.R.* II. p. 117.

[4] Rector's List.

[5] *Vide* Ch. XII. It is very likely that their daughter would be called Joan as it was common to christen children after their grandparents. Elizabeth's grandmother was Joan Brus, a widow in 1415. *Cf.* V. C. H. *N.R.* II. p. 117.

[6] This was six days before the special writ of summons was issued to William Hastings. Attention is called to this writ by J. H. Round, *Family Origins*, p. 194.

John Hudleston, Esq.[1] This again may have been a form of trust for a minor; in any case they availed themselves of the grant for the living was filled on 10 November.[2]

It would appear, therefore, that up to 1461 the advowson had remained *regardant* to the Brus manor, and it might have continued to remain so after this one exception, had not William, Lord Hastings, on 1 May, 1467,[3] specially reserved the advowson when making certain land grants to William Marshall[4] and Agnes his wife.[5] Thus the advowson passed from the Brus manor into the hands of the lords of the manor of Farmanby and so became an advowson *in gross*. From William, Lord Hastings, after his execution on 13 June, 1483, the right of presentation passed to his son, Sir Edward, second Lord Hastings[6] and from him to George Hastings, created first Earl of Huntingdon in 1529, and again from him to Francis the second Earl.[7] It is strange that when Sir Edward conveyed the manor of Farmanby to the Dean and Canons of St. George's Chapel, Windsor in 1506,[8] he did not grant with it the advowson of the Church of Thornton. But that he evidently did not do so is proved by the fact that it was in the hands of his grandson as late as Hilary Term 1548/9, when it was transferred with the Hastings' property at Allerston to 'Stephen Holforde and Eleonora his wife.'[9] It must not be supposed that this was more than a conveyance in trust.[10] Stephen Holforde was 'the receyvour of rents' and steward, of Sir John Gresham,[11] and it is certain that he did not obtain the advowson of Thornton as a possession for himself, but as a trustee for some other party. This is shown by his re-conveyance of the Allerston lands and the advowson of Thornton Church as early as Easter Term 1551, to John Forbye, James 'Phyllyppe,' Ralph 'Phyllype,' and Christopher Wykeclyff.[12] It is noticeable that in 1555, when there was a conveyance of the

---

[1] Cal. Pat. R. 1461-7, p. 123.

[2] *Vide infra.*

[3] Hist. MSS. Com., Rawden Hastings MS. I. p. 194.

[4] He was the son of Maud by her second marriage with William Marshall. This document proves his name to be 'William,' though some authorities give it as 'Robert.'

[5] She is said to be (from a somewhat unreliable source) daughter of John Browne of Kingston-upon-Hull.

[6] Born 1466.

[7] Francis married Katherine, daughter of Henry, Lord Montague and died 23 June, 1560.

[8] *Vide* Ch. XIV.

[9] Y. A. S. Rec. S. II. p. 139.

[10] I am afraid I disagree with the V. C. H. *N.R.* II. p. 497, on this point.

[11] *Vide* Ch. XII.

[12] Y. A. S. Rec. S. II. p. 155.

manor of Sir John Gresham,[1] there is no reference to the advowson; nor again when the manor is finally transferred to the family of Hunter[2] does it receive the advowson. Nor did any member of that family, as far as is known, ever exercise rights of presentation. The advowson must have been transferred to Sir Richard Cholmley, the Black Knight of the North, at some date previous to the marriage of his sister, Margaret, to Sir Henry Gascoigne, when arrangements were made concerning it; and when she, before May, 1561,[3] quite illegally married her deceased sister's husband, Henry, fifth Earl of 'Westmerland'[4] further trusts with regard to it were created. During that period, it is not likely that, except for marriage and family settlements, the advowson was in the possession of any other than the family of Cholmley. Sir Hugh Cholmley, in later years, definitely stated that the Black Knight 'was the patron' of Thornton Church, when he died in May, 1583.[5] In 1609, Sir Henry 'Slingsbie' and others were granted, as trustees, the advowson because Sir Richard Cholmley was left a widower and his children were under age.[6] Again in 1613 the advowson was passed by the Cholmley family to others, but this must have been a settlement[7] at the time of Sir Richard's second marriage to Margaret Cobb. There was a similar arrangement in 1622,[8] and from that time the Cholmleys seem to have been the patrons in the seventeenth century. They were certainly so in February, 1678/9, when Dr. Comber's presentation was entered in the register '*Hon. verum D. Hugonem Cholmly indubitatum ejus Patronum*'; and, in December, 1699, the Register records that the Rev. Thomas Mason of Sidney Sussex College, Cambridge, was presented by '*Dominam Mariam Cholmley indubitatam ejus Patronam*.'[9] Before the death of the Rev. Thomas Mason in September, 1744, John Hill

---

[1] Ibid. p. 184.
[2] Ibid. p. 296.
[3] Doyle, *Peerage and Baronage of England.*
[4] The Earl died August, 1563, the Countess in 1570.
[5] *The Memoirs of Sir Hugh Cholmley.* He erroneously says for the death of Sir Richard, 1579. The Church Registers show May, 1583.
[6] Y. A. S. Rec. S. LIII. p. 112.
[7] *Vide* Ch. XV.
[8] Y. A. S. Rec. S. LVIII. p. 201.
[9] V. C. H. *N.R.* II. p. 497, says that John Hacker presented in 1700. As there was no presentation that year and as the Register shows that in 1699 Lady 'Mary' Cholmley presented, this must be an error. This Lady Cholmley was Lady Ann Compton (not Mary) the eldest daughter of the Earl of Northampton. She died 26 May, 1705. Archbishop Herring's Return, 1743, states 'The present Rector was instituted by John Lord Arch Bishop of York the 24 day of December, 1699, [14 Dec. *cf.* Reg. York] & inducted by John Garnet, Curate, ye 12 day of January following.' *Cf.* Y. A. S. Rec. S. LXXV. p. 168.

III. had acquired the advowson, and from that date to the present time the right of appointing the rector has been in the hands of the Hill family.

One of the regrettable features of village history is that it is very seldom possible to find any information about the rectors of the parish in the early days. Sometimes it is even impossible to find the names, apart from any facts. Any point, therefore, however small, is of value to connect the man with the place; but in Thornton, as elsewhere, such information has in many cases evaded all efforts to find it.

The first known rector was not discovered from an ecclesiastical source, but in a legal record, for he, like many other landowners of the neighbourhood, made a conveyance to the great abbey of Whitby. Had it not been for this there would have been no trace of 'Gilbert, parson of Thornton, son of Alan the Forester,' who was in residence at Thornton in the early days of King John.[1] His father was a man of considerable importance, not only as a forester in fee of the Royal Forest of Pickering, but as a mesne lord in Thornton, and as lord of the manor of Kingthorpe.[2] Some readers may be surprised that this mediaeval cleric, Gilbert, was a married man, his wife being Ysolda;[3] but the English did not take kindly to the celibacy laws of Hildebrand, Pope Gregory VII., and, although Archbishop Lanfranc ordered their enforcement after 1074, secular priests did not obey the command, in many cases, until the later years of the thirteenth century.[4] Thus John de Thornton was the son of Gilbert and Ysolda,[5] and he it was who disputed the ownership of the advowson, already referred to,[6]

---

[1] c. 1200, Gilbert....grants to Whitby all the land that he had bought of Ralph Bardolph [son of Hugh Bardolph of Farmanby] 'quam Willelmus Claudus (the lame man) tenuit quae jacet inter toftum Walterii filii Reginaldi et Will de Milne.' Cf. *Whitby Chartulary*, Sur. Soc. LXIX. p. 131. N.B. about the same time Ralph son of Hugh Bardolph of Farmanby grants to Whitby 'duo tofta et quandam particulam prati cum pert. suis in Farmanby—scil.—duo tofta, quorum unum jacet ex meridionali parte viae, inter toftum quod fuit Willelmi filii Roberti et fossatum, et alterum jacet ex aquilonali parte viae, inter toftum monalium de Rossedale et toftum quod fuit Willelmi de Swyntona, et pratum quod jacet inter praedictum toftum et culturam quae vocatur le Ovenham [Ofnam, Ovenam, or Avenham, or Aunam, or Hornum]. Cf. *Whitby Chart., ut supra*, p. 459.

[2] Cf. 'Alanus filius Galfridi tenet in Kinthorp per seriantiam foreste iii carucatas valencie carucatarum xxx*s*.' in 1198. Cal. B. of F. I p. 4. But Ibid. p. 248, in the year 1219, says 'Alanus de Kintorp tenet tres carucatas terre per seriantiam nesciunt per quod servicium valet xlij*s*.' Ibid. p. 356, in 1226, places the value at 1xs.

[3] *Whitby Chart., ut supra*, p. 86.
[4] *Enc. Brit.* V. p. 603.
[5] *Whitby Chart., ut supra*, p. 86.
[6] *Vide supra*.

in 1225. At some date before August, 1225, Gilbert 'the parson' had died, because in the settlement of Archbishop Gray,[1] it is quite clear that the rector of Thornton was 'Galfridus de Tweng.' The particular dispute, however, was not about the appointment of the rector, but concerning the vicar, and Archbishop Gray instituted Adam de Insula,[2] who, in August, 1231,[3] was also nominated clerk of Ellerburn.[4] As already explained, the benefice was divided, and whoever may have been vicar in the last years of the reign of Henry III., it is clear that 'Dns.[5] Robertus de Overleye vel Everley, presbyter' was the rector on 17 November, 1267.[6] It would be natural to expect that there must have been a vicar of the mediety besides Adam de Insula, before the appointment of 'Sir Thomas de Amcotes' on 18 November, 1271. At that period life did not tend to be long, and for Adam de Insula to have been vicar for forty years was, of course, possible, but extremely unlikely. There is, however, no evidence of any other, until de Amcotes was created vicar of 'Thorneton in valle de Pikering' on the presentation of 'Sir Robert de Everley' and admitted and instituted by Archbishop Giffard.[7] It is to be hoped that he was not of the ordinary type of the priest of the day, for Roger Bacon has left it on record that at this particular period, 'country priests recite the Church Services (of which they understand little or nothing) like brute beasts.'[8] Whether learned or unlearned it was decided that de Amcotes was to have the whole of the alterage[9] excepting the tithes of lands and of sheaves and the Church lands which shall entirely belong to the rector.[10]

De Amcotes successor was 'Magister Thomas de Burton' instituted on 23 December, 1282.[11] It was during the years that he

---

[1] *Archb. Gray's Reg.* Sur. Soc. LVI. p. 5.

[2] Ibid.

[3] Ibid. p. 47.

[4] *Vide* Ch. X.

[5] 'Dominus' was the title of a man in holy orders with a University degree. 'Sir' was the title of one without a degree; but 'Sir' became the equivalent of our modern 'Rev.' until the end of the sixteenth century.

[6] *Archb. Giffard's Reg.* Sur. Soc. CIX. p. 44.

[7] *Archb. Thomas de Corbridge's Reg.* Sur. Soc. CXLI. p. 162. The Rector's list in the Church Porch is in error about the appointment of de Amcotes and Burton. De Amcotes was instituted '14 Kal. Dec. anno 5' of Giffard, i.e., 18 November, 1271. Giffard is described in Corbridge's Register *'miseracione divina Ebor. archiepiscopus Anglie primas.'*

[8] *Cf.* G. C. Coulton, *Social Life in Britain from the Conquest to the Reformation*, p. 260.

[9] Neilson, *ut supra*, p. 193 says *'Alteragium* or *Altelagium* were fees of one kind or another made at the altar for services and the maintenance of vestments.'

[10] *Archb. Thomas of Corbridge's Reg.* Sur. Soc. CXLI. p. 162.

[11] *Archb. Wickwane's Reg.* Sur. Soc. CXIV. p. 128.

was in office that there is the first reference, in 1291, to Thornton's connection with the rectory of Thorpe Basset :—[1]

'Ecclia de Thorneton p' t pens'		13	6	8
'Pens' R'coris Ecclie de Thorp Basset				
	in eadem	1	0	0
Vicar' ejusdem		5	0	0[2]

Whether the Thornton rector of the period had made a mistake in giving way to this demand from Thorpe Basset in the thirteenth century, or whether there was a genuine legal claim to this 'superiority,' it is impossible to say now; but it is interesting to note that the claim was very definitely acknowledged in the seventeenth century,[3] and recognised in the Terriers of the eighteenth, and the sum paid regularly to the end of the nineteenth century.[4] If it were a new claim at the end of the thirteenth century the Rev. Thomas Burton might rightly be annoyed, if it actually affected him, but probably the annual sum would be paid by the rector and not the vicar. By 1301 the vicar was assisted by one Geoffrey as his curate, but nothing is known of him or his work.[5] Thomas de Burton may have lived until 1308, when changes were made with regard to the benefice, but the date of his death has not been recorded. Like so many others of his time, he was guilty of forest offences and was charged with 'vert' in 1334, when Thomas 'Vicarius ecclesie de Thornton' was said to have taken 'within the demesne a green oak, value $\frac{1}{2}$d.' Even the original bail, John de 'Chimyne' was dead by that time, and his successor, William 'de la Chymine,' had to pay the fine of 6d.[6]

The long-lived Sir Robert de Everley—he first appeared as rector in 1267—must have died before the end of 1305, for in that year William de 'Bergh,' 'persona ecclesie de Thorneton,' was bail for John Burmer a poacher in the Forest of Pickering.[7] It is impossible to imagine this rector as the usual uneducated priest described by Bacon. He was, evidently, a man of well-known family, probably a relative of the Prior of Bridlington, and certainly no nonentity, for in 1306, he was chosen as clerical proctor in the parliament of that year.[8] It is generally thought,[9] that the members of the

---

[1] *Vide* V. C. H. *N.R.* II. p. 497.
[2] *Taxatio Nicolai*, pp. 301, 335.
[3] V C H N R II p 497
[4] The Rev. Godfrey Marshall.
[5] Y. A. S. Rec. S. XXI. p. 60. Geoffrey of Thornton was ordained priest September, 1270. *Cf. Archb. Giffard's Reg.* Sur. Soc. CIX. p. 198.
[6] N. R. Rec. S. N.S. III. p. 25.
[7] Ibid. II. p. 78.
[8] Rot. Parl. I. p. 191.
[9] Sir James Ramsay, *The Dawn of the Constitution*, p. 510.

Parliament of 1306 were so excited about granting subsidies for the new war with Scotland, that they did not notice Edward I.'s revocation of the forest concessions, but if William de Bergh were present, from the very centre of forest difficulties, and of which he had personal experience, it is not likely that he would fail to appreciate what the King had done, and to view his action with strong disapproval. It was, one may suppose, due to William de Bergh's common-sense that in November, 1308, the old difficulty of the divided benefice was abolished, and the vicarage mediety disappeared, and henceforth, the rector was to be entitled to all oblations, tithes and profits.[1] He was, evidently, a determined upholder of individual rights, and, in his opinion, the rectors of Thornton were being deprived of their privileges of pasture. At an unknown date, shortly after March, 1322, and before October, 1323, this self-reliant man petitioned the King in Council, stating that 'he and his predecessors in the Rectory [of Thornton] ought and were wont to Common with all manner of beasts as appurtenant to his glebe, at all seasons of the year, in Dalby, Clenfield[2] and Haverbergh,[3] which are places adjoining Thornton and within the parish. These places, since Earl Thomas's death [March, 1322], have been in the King's hands.' The Rector prayed the King that he might have his common rights as in the past.[4] The fact of the matter was, that William de Bergh had been caught by the Forester of Dalby turning out 'six pigs valued 2s.....unagisted.' Long before the question came before the Great Eyre in 1334, the rector had died, and Alexander de Bergh, the nephew and executor of William, must have been very much annoyed at having to appear before the Justices for an offence, however trivial, and committed eleven years before, and being obliged to pay the fine of 6d.[5] There can be little doubt that William de Bergh had died before 11 October, 1323, as once again a member of the family of Everley appears as rector in the person of 'Dⁿˢ. Johannes de Everley, presbyter,'[6] who was appointed on that date,[7] probably by a relative who owned the advowson. It is obvious that John was rector in 1334, as he was fined 1s. for not appearing on the first day of the Eyre of the Forest; and it is certain that he resigned the rectory of Thornton in

---

[1] Rev. Godfrey Marshall.
[2] This name is still in use at High Dalby.
[3] I have failed to identify this.
[4] N. R. Rec. S. N.S. III. p. 252.
[5] Ibid. p. 48 and IV. p. 46.
[6] Rector's List.
[7] Y. A. S. Rec. S. LXXIV. p. 111 shows Hugh the vicar and Bartholomew 'capellanus' as paying the subsidy in Thornton in 1327; but in N.'R. Rec. S. N.S. IV. p. 140, the reading for *capellanus* is *carpentarius*.

1345, when he accepted the living at 'Skyrpenbeck.'[1] His successor was 'D^ns. Johannes de Ampleford, capellanus.'[2] In 1346 he is recorded as holding as glebe one carucate of land in perpetual alms,[3] of that fee which the Earl of Albemarle[4] had formerly held.[5] As far as can be ascertained he was an exemplary character, for there are no poaching records to go to in which stories of hunting escapades might be found. During his period of office, under an order from Archbishop Zouche, every Wednesday and Friday, 1348-9, the Litany would be sung in Thornton Church and collects would be said daily at Mass for the cessation of the plague and for the welfare of the King, the Church and the realm.[6] John de Ampleford was almost an exception, amongst Yorkshire clergymen, to have escaped the Black Death,[7] but there can be no doubt that he did survive as he is mentioned in 1352, in the 'Regista' of Pope Clement VI., as John de 'Ampisford,' rector of 'Tornton' in the diocese of York;[8] and in 1354, it is known that he resigned the rectory to accept the benefice of 'Tyverington.'[9]

Of the next incumbent, 'D^ns. Willelmus de Appilton, capellanus' little or nothing is known except that he was appointed on 21 April, 1354, and died in 1372.[10] It was during his rectorship that the advowson was conveyed in 1361, as already explained,[11] to the

[1] Ibid. Skirpenbeck is near Stamford Bridge.
[2] This term 'capellanus' is not easy to define. The Rev. P. H. Ditchfield in *The Old-time Parson*, would consider him a curate (p. 30). He says 'Sometimes he was known as chaplain or *capellanus*, one who served a chapel in connection with the mother-church of the parish.' If this is so, then John de Ampleford was not rector, but acting for a possible future member of the Everley family. But in 1352 there seems to be little doubt that he was rector. Mr. Ditchfield looks upon a *capellanus* as a chantry-priest, but, as far as one knows with regard to the history of Thornton, there was no chantry or chapel or aisle 'erected by the founder and endowed by him, wherein prayers were to be offered for himself, his family and friends and all faithful souls.' (p. 31).
[3] This means tenure in 'frankalmoin,' or 'in liberam eleemosinam' i.e., in free alms. Petit-Dutaillis, *ut supra*, p. 56, says 'It is theoretically the land given to the Church, without any temporal service being demanded in return; it is agreed or understood that the community will pray for the donor. In practice, the tenure in frankalmoin admits of certain temporal services and its clearest characteristic, at the end of the twelfth century, is that judicially it is subject only to the ecclesiastical forum.' *Cf.* Maitland, *The Constitutional History of England*, pp. 25, 157.
[4] *Vide* Ch. XI.
[5] Cal. Feud. Aids VI. p. 258.
[6] Arch. Jour. LXXI. p. 103.
[7] Ibid. p. 113, says that this district embracing the Vale of Pickering and the moorland of Cleveland suffered less than some parts.
[8] Cal. Pap. Reg. III. p. 442.
[9] Rector's List. Tyverington is possibly Tytherington in Gloucestershire. At this period Gloucester, by a grant of Henry I., was in the diocese of the Archbishop of York. It is more probably Terrington in E. R.
[10] Rector's List.
[11] *Vide supra.*

family of Wandesford, and held by them for nearly a century. William de Appilton was succeeded by 'Dominus Ricardus de Malton, presbyter,'[1] about whom, up to the present, nothing has been found, beyond the fact that he was rector for nearly thirty years, and that it was probably during his time that the fourteenth century restoration of the Church was completed. He was not, apparently, a member of the family of the patron,[2] but his successor undoubtedly was. 'Dominus Walterus de Wandesford, presbyter,'[3] became rector on 20 March, 1403/4. It is not certain whether he died or resigned; nor is there a definite date attached to the entry of his successor. The Wandesfords, as far as can be ascertained, had ceased to hold their manor in Thornton in 1437.[4] The question arises, did Walter de Wandesford retire to some other parish or die about that time?

The next incumbent was William de Morton, 'presbyter.' He could not have been rector before 1446, but he might well have been in that year, or at least, before 1452. William Morton of the city of York[5] was ordained subdeacon at York on 7 March, 1442/3.[6] It is thought that he was the same person who was proctor at Oxford in 1445, being a member of Balliol College.[7] It is difficult to know whether, having been made a subdeacon, he was presented to the living of Thornton, or whether he continued to pass some years at Oxford, and, after his proctorship, came to the north. He may, of course, have resided in Oxford until he took his B.D. degree on 6 June, and his D.D. on 15 October, 1452.[8] At least by that time he was in touch with Yorkshire, as on 26 October, he had granted to him by the University a supplicatory letter to the Archbishop of York.[9] The letter seems to have had a remarkable effect, for on the following 24 July, he was collated to the Chancellorship of York on the death of John Kexby.[10] By this time he was certainly rector of Thornton, and this benefice he resigned on 9 November, 1461, and on the following day was instituted to the rectory of Scrayingham,[11] on the presentation of the King.[12] He held,

[1] Rector's List.
[2] The will of Sir Richard Malton, rector of 'Thorneton' was proved 17 April, 1404. *Cf.* Y. A. S. Rec. S. VI. p. 109.
[3] Rector's List.
[4] *Vide* Ch. XII.
[5] *Test. Ebor.* Sur. Soc. LII. p. 52n.
[6] *Archb. Kempe's Reg.*
[7] Le Neve, III. p. 482.
[8] O. H. S. Reg. of the Univ. I. p. 18.
[9] Ibid.
[10] *Reg. of Archb. William Booth.*
[11] On the river Derwent, N.E. of York.
[12] *Reg. of Archb. William Booth.*

after 3 July, 1465, the stall of Bole,[1] with his rectory of Scrayingham, until his death.

With startling rapidity, the very day that William Morton was instituted to Scrayingham, 'Magister' John Rede, Bachelor of Law and presbyter, was appointed rector of Thornton. This man was apparently widely read for the period. He had studied both at Cambridge and at Oxford, and had obtained his degree of Bachelor of Canon Law at the latter University on 17 December, 1450.[2] He was only rector for about six years, as he resigned on 22 March, 1467/8,[3] and was succeeded by 'Magister' William 'Leybron,' Bachelor of Law, chaplain and registrar to the Archbishop of York. This rector had been, as William 'Laybron,' a student of Civil Law and an undergraduate member of Broadgates Hall, in the parish of St. Aldate's, Oxford,[4] and had obtained his degree in 1451.[5] It is very uncertain that he ever resided in Thornton, for as Archbishop's chaplain, his duties would require him elsewhere, but he held the living to his death in the early part of 1481. The next rector, 'Dominus Rolandus Huddam, capellanus,' could hardly have settled in the rectory before he died. He was appointed on 24 March, 1480/1[6] and was dead before the following 21 November, when succeeded by Richard Bartholomew, who certainly died in 1507.[7]

It was on 4 May, 1508, that the Thornton benefice was presented to the most remarkable rector who ever held it; but it must not be imagined that the village gained in any way, because there is every reason to believe that the new rector, John Chambre, Chamber, Chambar, Chambyr, or Chambers,[8] never resided and never even put his foot inside the parish.[9] His life exemplifies the scandal of

[1] *Reg. of Archb. George Neville.*

[2] O. H. S. I. p. 12.

[3] Rector's List. According to R. C. Fowler, *Episcopal Registers*, p. 23, 'this short period of incumbency in comparison with modern times' was very common in the middle ages.

[4] *Munimenta Academica*, Rolls Ser. 1. p. 590. It is necessary to state the parish in which this Broadgates Hall was situated, as there were in mediaeval times, eight halls with this name.

[5] O. H. S. I., p. 12.

[6] Rector's List.

[7] Ibid. As the will of 'Sir Richard Barthilmew, rector of Thorneton in Pykerynglith' was proved on 17 December, 1507, he must have died before 1600. *Cf.* Y. A. S. Rec. S. VI. p. 11.

[8] D.N.B.

[9] How different was this from what was laid down at the Synod of Exeter in 1257, 'avoiding all negligence, parish priests shall be watchful and thoughtful in the charge committed to them, and that without reasonable cause they must never sleep out of their parishes and that if they do so, they must procure some fitting substitute who knows how to do all those things required in a cure of souls.'

early sixteenth century pluralities, as well, if not better, than that of any other clergyman of the time. He was born in Northumberland, and educated at Merton College, Oxford, where he obtained a fellowship in 1492. According to custom, he entered holy orders, and may have been appointed immediately to the living of Tichmarsh in Northamptonshire. Being a non-resident he had leisure to go on a long visit to Italy, where he obtained the degree of Doctor of Medicine, at Padua, and on the strength of which was appointed physician to both Henry VII. and Henry VIII. But doctors, even royal doctors, need some form of revenue, and if the practice of medicine did not produce it, in those happy days there was always the Church. Between 1494 and 1509, John Chamber was Prebend of Corringham in Lincoln Cathedral, and about the time that he acquired the living of Thornton, he was also instituted to Bowden in Lincolnshire. For forty years, from 1509 to 1549, he was rector of Leighton Buzzard, and for twenty-four years of this period, 1525 to 1549, he was drawing a stipend as Archdeacon of Bedford. Not content with these sources of income, between 1510 and 1543, he was Treasurer of Wells Cathedral, between 1524 and 1549, precentor of Exeter, between 1525 and 1544, Warden of Merton College, Oxford, in 1537 a canon of Wivelscombe, and between 1540 and 1542, Archdeacon of Meath and dean of the Collegiate Chapel of St. Stephen's, Westminster, where he built the cloisters and lived to see them demolished. All this time he seems to have acted as a royal physician. His name appears in the first Charter of the College of Physicians in 1518 and in the Charter to the Barber Surgeons in 1541. The portrait of this remarkable man shows a person with a short straight nose, thick eyebrows and a clean-shaven, severe face. He died in 1549 and was buried in St. Margaret's, Westminster.[1]

But what did John Chamber do for Thornton? The answer must be, nothing. For forty-one years he took the income of £20 per annum,[2] and came no more frequently to Thornton than to any other of his benefices. Of course he did not make a clear profit of £20, for, as it was stated shortly after his time, 'of a benefice of twentie pounds by the yeare, the incumbent thinketh himself well acquited, if all ordinarie paiments being discharged, he may reserve thirteene pounds, six shillings, eight pence, towards his owne sustentation and maintenance of his familie.'[3] In Dr. Chamber's

[1] D.N.B. *Vide* H. E. Salter *Reg: Coll: Mertoniencis*, and B. W. Henderson, *History of Merton College*.
[2] 'Mr. doctor Chambar, rector de Thornton xx".' *Cf.* Y. A. J. XXI. p. 244.
[3] Parker Soc. *Zurich Letters*, II. p. 24.

case there would be no family, as at that date celibacy was still
in force. What he did was to pay some poor curate, to carry out
the work, £4 per annum, and the rest, swelled with the similar
receipts from his other benefices, would help to keep him in comfort
in London attending on the King, or in Oxford within the walls of
Merton College. It has been impossible to find the names of his
curates before 1525, but in that year Brian Spofford is said to have
acted for him at £4 a year.[1] It may be surmised that the next of
his curates was 'Syr John Pynder [who] was buryede the thyrde
day of Februarye,' 1538/9.[2]

'Dominus Marmaduke Atkinson, presbyter,' became rector on
2 November, 1549.[3] As far as is known he peacefully held the
benefice during very troublous times. Before his appointment to
Thornton he would have got accustomed to Edward VI.'s first
Book of Common Prayer, because that had been in use in all
Churches since the previous Whit-Sunday.[4] He, no doubt, as
readily accepted the Second Book of 1552. He must have bowed
before the dictates of Mary, and again given way to the Act of
Uniformity of 1559.[5] Had he declined to accept the Elizabethan
version of the Prayer Book, he would have been severely punished,
and for his third offence, suffered deprivation and imprisonment for
life.[6] As in the case of hundreds of others he was obliged to recog-
nize the superiority of the State.[7] Like his predecessor, Marmaduke
Atkinson was a pluralist, though of a less distinguished kind.
As early as 28 April, 1540 he had been vicar of Wharram Percy;
and after the death of John Hastings at Bainton in 1554, Atkinson
had had that rectory, but the exact date of his institution is not
known,[8] though it is known that the presentation was by the
Black Knight of the North, Sir Richard Cholmley, acting as
trustee for the young Ralph Salvin.[9] The date must have been
somewhere between September and December, 1554, because he

---

[1] Y. A. J. XXI. p. 247.
[2] C. R. The will of Sir John Pynder, Thornton, priest, was made on
2 January, 1538/9 and proved on 14 March, 1538/9. *Cf.* Y. A. S. Rec. S.
XI. p. 140.
[3] Rector's List.
[4] The act was passed in January, 1549, and ordered to come into use
on the evening of Whit-Sunday. *Cf.* 2 & 3 Ed. vi. c. 1.
[5] 1 Eliz. c. 2.
[6] Ibid sec. 2
[7] Canon Ollard in his *Notes on the History of Bainton Church and Parish,*
p. 31, considers that Marmaduke Atkinson did not see 'in the religious changes
made respectively under Henry VIII. and Elizabeth any reason to believe
that the English Church had ceased to be part of the Holy Catholic and
Apostolic Church.' I am indebted to Mrs. Richard Hill for this.
[8] The Archbishopric was vacant.
[9] *Vide* Ch. XV.

paid his annates to the Crown on 11 October, and his successor, William Firbye was instituted to the vicarage of Wharram Percy on 1 December. After a somewhat protracted suit in the Court of Common Pleas as to the right of presentation, which ended in 1558, Marmaduke Atkinson remained rector of Bainton, and, somewhat curiously, was also instituted to the rectory of Huggate on 21 October, 1569. He thus held the three rectories of Thornton, Bainton, and Huggate at the time of his death on 8 September, 1572.[1]

The exact date of the appointment of John Richardson, 'clerus,'[2] has not, as yet, been ascertained. It is known that he was also vicar of Ellerburn, but the Visitations show that he was not there until 1591.[3] His character as vicar of Ellerburn was not a good one,[4] and presumably he was as lazy and as much given to absenteeism at Thornton as in the neighbouring parish.

The next rector was a Thornton man, bred and born, John Robinson. He was the second son of Henry Robinson and Agnes his wife,[5] owner of the Mowbray manor in Thornton.[6] He was presented to the benefice by Sir Henry Cholmley on 14 July, 1609. As a young man he matriculated at Trinity College, Cambridge about 1596, and took his B.A. degree from St. John's in 1600-1, and his M.A. in 1604. He was ordained at York in September, 1607, and proceeded to priest's orders a year later.[7] For many years his life was peaceful enough. When his father died, his elder brother Henry succeeded to the small property, and the rector would have few anxieties, except when, as shown,[8] the village was ravaged by the plague. He married, first, in 1613, Grace Moore of Guiseley,[9] and secondly in 1619 Jane, the daughter of Christopher or William Ives of Gilling,[10] and had five daughters and four sons,[11] one of whom only, Samuel, survived.[12] His youngest child was born in the village, at the end of July, 1641:[13] the last summer, for ten long years, in which Thornton or any part of England knew a period of calm.

[1] Rev. S. L. Ollard, *ut supra*.
[2] The Curate in 1582 was James Stainclyffe. He presumably had gone in 1584 as there is a different style of entry in the Registers.
[3] Y. A. J. XVIII. pp. 211-13.
[4] *Vide* Ch. X.
[5] Y. A. S. Rec. S. V. p. 44 shows the name 'Agnes.' She was presumably the daughter of ? Greaves, Lord Mayor of York.
[6] *Vide* Ch. XIII.
[7] Camb. Al. III. p. 470.
[8] *Vide* Ch. V.
[9] Camb. Al. III. p. 470.
[10] Possibly the same as Christopher 'Ive,' *vide* Ch. XVII.
[11] C. R.
[12] *Vide* Ch. XIII.
[13] C. R.

As in thousands of other cases, the Civil War caused an upheaval in the somewhat hum-drum life of the rector of Thornton. The actual clash of arms came after the raising of the King's standard at Nottingham in August, 1642. As early as April, 1643, 'an ordinance was passed for the sequestering of delinquents' estates, and local committees were appointed in all parts of the country, under the obedience of the Parliament, to carry it into effect. It was through the action of these local committees that the bulk of the Clergy suffered.[1] After September, 1643, the Covenant was usually offered to each incumbent as a test, and if he refused to subscribe he was treated as a delinquent, ejected from his benefice and deprived of his goods....the work was pushed on with unrelenting zeal and considerable acrimony. Informers were invited to give evidence against the Clergy, and the smallest pretexts were taken hold of to effect the desired change.'[2] In addition to this, it is to be remembered that 'the Parliament' quite illegally abolished the Book of Common Prayer, on 13 March, 1644, and substituted for it, '*A Directory for The Publique Worship of God*,'[3] and if an incumbent could not bring his conscience to worship according to this new-fangled order of service he was driven from his benefice. One would imagine that John Robinson did not stop at refusing to obey this order, but, from the accusations afterwards brought against him, went very much further. On 9 July, 1645, he was ejected, and Christopher Bradley, M.A., of Peterhouse, Cambridge, was instituted in his place.[4] If the charges of the Parliamentarians are to be believed, John Robinson may have gone so far as to take up arms on behalf of the King.[5] It is a picturesque thought, the by no means youthful rector—for he must have been about sixty years old at least—marching into York to join whatever band he could for Charles I., who, at the moment, had lost his throne at Naseby in June, and was wandering from place to place. But perhaps the charge of 'taking up arms,' means as said in another document, 'adhering to the forces raised against

---

[1] The Committees were directed to 'take and to seize into their hands as well all the Money, Goods, Chattels, Debts and personall Estate, as also all and every the Manors, lands, Tenements and Hereditaments, Rents, arrerages of Rent, Revenues, and profits of all and every the said Delinquents or persons before specified, or which they or any other in trust for them, or any of their use or uses, have, hath, or shall have.'

[2] H. O. Wakeman, *Church and Puritans*, pp. 162-3.

[3] J. C. Cox, *The Parish Registers of England*, p. 37.

[4] C. R. where Bradley himself enters the fact. Christopher Bradley matriculated as a sizar at Peterhouse, Cambridge in the Lent Term 1626/7: B. A. 1630-1. M.A. 1634. Ordained priest (Peterborough) 20 May, 1638. Author of *Sermons*. *Cf.* Camb. Al. I.

[5] Y. A. S. Rec. S. XX. p. 33. *Cf.* XVIII. p. 207.

the Parliament,'[1] and this may be interpreted that he would not bow down in the house of Rimmon. His case must have been, at any rate, a very hard one, for it is recorded 'that he was imprisoned for his Zeal and Loyalty.'[2] It is shown elsewhere, how he was fined for his lands in the Marishes,[3] and for his brother's manor in Thornton after that brother had died.[4] Then came an inexplicable incident in his career. If he had been ejected for his royalist beliefs, and even if he had compounded for his offences, how came it that he was restored in 1653, and Christopher Bradley was, in turn, ejected ?[5]

It was during the period of John Robinson's rather peculiar restoration to office, that great changes were made in Thornton in the methods of marriage registration. The Commonwealth was nothing if not thorough. The old methods of performing and registering marriages were abolished, for marriages in the past had been celebrated by 'a priest' in 'a church,' and this smacked too much of Popery. After the act of 1653,[6] marriages were to be no longer by the rector, but in the presence of magistrates, and the Thornton Registers illustrate the practice very clearly. It is possible that John Robinson was so convinced by his sufferings that the Cromwellian party was likely to remain in power, that he acquiesced in the records appearing in the Church Registers, for the duty of registration was no longer incumbent upon the clergy, but was in the hands of a popularly elected lay 'Register.'[7] This is first shown by the words in the *Church* Register, 29 December, 1653, and signed by Luke Robinson.[8] 'I having received Certificate from the inhabitants of Thornton and Ellerburne signifying that they have elected Robert Hunter of Thornton, gentleman, to bee the parrish Register within the said parrishes of Thornton and Ellerburne abovesaid do hereby approve and allow of the said Robert Hunter to bee parrish Register accordingly, given in pursuance of an Act of Parliament in that behalf made, Given under

---

[1] Cal. Cttee. of Comp. p. 1906.
[2] Walker, *Sufferings of the Clergy*, p. 349.
[3] *Vide* Ch. XVII.
[4] *Vide* Ch. XII.
[5] C. R. There was a very momentary Episcopal toleration, but this would hardly account for the restoration. *Cf.* Ranke, *History of England in Seventeenth Century*, vol. III.
[6] '*An Act touching Marriages and the Registring therof,*' published Wednesday, 24 August, 1653, and printed by John Field, Printer to the Parliament of England.
[7] The word 'Registrar' is modern, and does not occur in Johnson's *Dictionary*. The abbreviation of the Latin 'Registrarius' was 'Registrar' and in a generation ignorant of Latin it was taken for the official designation.
[8] *Vide infra.*

my hand att Pickering the nine and twentieth day of December, 1653.' Evidently there was no hurry, and in those days of no haste, it was not until 8 June, 1654, that 'the said Robert Hunter was sworn to execute the office of Register according to an Act in that behalf made.' In the meantime, however, there had been a marriage on 16 May, which may be taken as an example of others. 'Thomas Reade of Thornton and Elizabeth White of the same town, the consent of matrimony having been three several Lords dayes by me Robert Hunter register of the said parrish published in the said parrish church of Thorneton upon the sixteenth, three and twentieth and thirtieth day of April last past immediately after divine service, and consent of Anthony Reade, father of the said Thom: Reade, and Ann Brough [? Barugh] mother of the said Elizabeth White having first been acknowledged unto me, the said register, were married together by Christopher Percehay, Esquire, a justice of the peace within this Commonwealth for the North riding of the County of York, the day and year in the margent written in the presence of Roger Mawe and George White the Younger of Thornton, aforesaid.' Similar marriages occurred between 2 July, 1654, and 10 May, 1658.[1]

Before this system ceased,[2] old John Robinson's sufferings ended in death, and he was buried on 1 February, 1656/7.[3] The very next day, by whom one does not know, Christopher Bradley was reinstated. It certainly could not have been by the rightful patron, Sir Hugh Cholmley, for he, after eating his heart out in exile at Rouen and being imprisoned on his return, was on his death bed, and died that year.[4]

---

[1] The magistrates were Luke Robinson of Thornton Riseborough, son of Sir Arthur Robinson of Dighton, on 23 Nov., 1655, 22 April, 1656, 18 March, 1656/7, 31 March, 1657, 6 April, 1657, 14 Dec., 1657: Arthur Nooll on 7 Dec., 1655: Christopher Fawcet,' baliffe of Skarborough' on 20 Dec., 1655, 7 January and 5 February, 1655/6: William Weddall on 27 May, 1656: Thomas Styringe, on 5 July, 1656: Richard Etherington on 27 Nov., 1656 and 1 January, 1656/7: Justice Stafford of Thwinge on 16 Dec., 1656: William Robinson 'one of the bailiffs of Skarbrough' 2 Dec., 1656: Christopher Percehay on 18 July, 1657, 22 February, 1657/8, 17 April, 1658, 10 May, 1658. In one case, Thomas Storr of Cloughton married Ann Denham of Farmanby in the presence of 'John Kay, shoomaker, one of the bailiffs of Skarborough for the time being.' N.B. These civil marriages before justices were legalised by Act of Parliament, 12 Car. II. c. 33.

[2] It is noticeable that on 23 July, 1658, James Dixon and Margery Storye 'were married by Christopher Bradley, Clerk' and from that date the marriages were normal. In 1697 there is the first entry concerning marriages 'after 3 publications.' This was due to 7 & 8 Will. III. c. 33, repealed 33 & 34 Vic. c. 99.

[3] C. R. No names of Churchwardens during his rectorship have been found except, 1662, Valentine Story and William Skelton. *Cf.* N. R. Rec. S. O.S. I. p. 261.

[4] After writing the above I am not so sure. In any case I ought to point out that Sir Hugh Cholmley and Elizabeth his wife were living in Whitby in 1652 as shown by an engraved stone of that date, *cf.* Young, p. 639.

Christopher Bradley seems to have been a typical 'Vicar of Bray.' He himself records, in the Church Registers, that he was baptized on 8 January, 1606/7, at Haram in the parish of Helmsley. How he went to Peterhouse at Cambridge, or why he ever came to Thornton, in 1645, is not explained. It is possible that his sister, Mary, was some kind of relative by marriage of the Robinsons, for she died as 'Mary Robinson' at Pocklington.[1] Bradley was a married man before he came to Thornton, for his son, John, went to school at Pocklington on 27 September, 1651, at the age of ten;[2] and, therefore, must have been about four years old when the father first succeeded John Robinson. In the early period of his ministry, he does not seem to have been popular. He was evidently regarded by the villagers as a 'skin-flint,' for in depositions taken in 1647, it is said that he 'was never a good paymaster.'[3] As a typical 'Vicar of Bray' it behoved him, posing as a godly Puritan, to walk as they walked, and he is to be found as 'the Minister of Thornton in Pickering Lythe,' with other neighbouring ministers, presenting a petition to the Quarter Sessions at Kirkby Moorside on 10 July, 1649. They expressed repugnance 'of the great profanation of the Lord's Day in the North Riding.' They stated that 'the Ordinance of Parliament for the suppressing of vice and punishing of offenders' was 'neglected by the Constables and Churchwardens....to the great Dishonour of God and Discouragement of painfull and laborious Ministers.'[4]

What Christopher Bradley really felt when Charles II. was restored, on 29 May, 1660, is impossible to know, but when the Uniformity Act[5] was passed in 1662, he was not the one to suffer on any 'St. Bartholomew's Day,' and meekly submitted to the orders of the Cavalier Parliament. The old incumbent was no longer in this world to claim anything, and the Thornton 'Vicar of Bray' settled down happily to nearly a score of years of quiet comfort. He watched the gradual rise of the Almshouses and the Grammar School;[6] and just before he died, he had to record in the Registers the first case of a person 'buried in woollen,' on 22 August, 1678. An act had been passed on this subject as early as 1666,[7]

---

[1] C. R. The will of Mary Robinson, of Pocklington, widow, was proved on 2 November, 1677. *Cf.* Y. A. S. Rec. S. LXXIII. p. 68.

[2] Y. A. J. XXV. p. 59. The Church Register shows that Bradley's other sons were 'Gregorie' 1647; 'Henrie,' 1652; Francis, 1656; Samuel, 1658; Robert, 1660.

[3] Exch. Dep. Trin. 23 Chas. I. No. 2.

[4] N. R. Rec. S. O.S. V. p. 33.

[5] 14 Car. II. c. 4.

[6] He himself entered the building of these in the Church Register.

[7] 18 and 19 Car. II. c. 2. Repealed 26 and 27, Vict. c. 125.

but the more important legislation was in the later year.[1] The purpose of the new act was to encourage not only the woollen trade of England, but also to depress the linen trade of Ireland, which was regarded as injurious by the cloth-manufacturers in this country. At the same time, it was hoped that it would stimulate the paper trade, for by the accumulation of old linen there came to be large stocks of linen-rags, estimated at the time, at 200,000 lbs. per annum, which were essential, in the late seventeenth century, for the manufacture of paper. The act, no doubt, helped in the paper industry of Thornton;[2] though it is hardly likely that Christopher Bradley, now seventy-two years of age, appreciated the economic point attached to the words 'buried in woollen.' He was almost the next to have those words entered against his name in the Register, for he was buried on 3 January, 1678/9.[3]

If Dr. John Chamber may be regarded as the typical absentee rector of early Tudor times, so Dr. Thomas Comber[4] may be regarded as the same, in the late Stuart period. But the medical doctor, Chamber, did nothing for Thornton, whereas the Doctor of Divinity, Dean Comber, did a good deal. Hardly a month had passed after the burial of Christopher Bradley, than Sir Hugh Cholmley appointed Thomas Comber, M.A., of Sidney Sussex College, Cambridge, on 11 February, 1678/9;[5] and he held the benefice with that of Stonegrave, and others until his death. He had taken his Bachelor's degree in 1663, and proceeded to his Master's three years later. He became rector of Stonegrave in 1669, prebendary of York in 1677 and precentor in 1683. When he became Dean of Durham in 1691, he took the degree of Doctor of Divinity[6] from Lambeth. In many ways he was a great and good man, but like the clerics of his day, it cannot be denied that he was a pluralist, and that his benefices saw very little of him. It is indeed a marvel that belief in the doctrines of the Church of England survived in the hearts of simple-minded rural parishioners, when the complete neglect of their rectors is remembered; and it can only be due to the unswerving perseverance of poorly-paid curates, who did the work for their absentee pastors and masters. Thomas

[1] 30 Car. II. c. 3. Repealed 54 Geo. III. c. 108, sec. 1.
[2] *Vide* Ch. VII.
[3] What a series of changes old Valentine Story might have recorded, having been Parish Clerk for 55 years and dying, aged 89, in December, 1663. The sexton, William Robinson, was buried 24 January, 1670/1.
[4] No names of Churchwardens during his rectorship have been found except, 1696, Thomas Smith, who died that year.
[5] Son of James not John as in D.N.B. He was born at the home of his mother at Westerham, Kent.
[6] D.N.B.

Comber seldom, if ever, resided in Thornton, nor did he give much more personal attention to Stonegrave. He lived for the most part on his estate at East Newton, four miles from Helmsley, having acquired that property by marriage with Alice Thornton.[1] Not that he wasted his time, intellectually, for he published '*Companion to the Temple*' between 1672 and 1676, and other works on the liturgy, and against Roman Catholic doctrines. He even launched into the political world, and issued pamphlets in favour of William III., between 1689 and 1692.[2] But none of these things comforted the souls of the Thornton people, who, after such experiences as the Civil War, the Protectorate and the wild excesses of the period of Charles II., must have wondered, sometimes, where they exactly stood in a supposed Christian land. But, if Thomas Comber did not minister to the souls of the parishioners he never knew, at least he had the material welfare of the benefice at heart. He fought the battles of the Grammar School and he ousted fraudulent trustees;[3] he did a great deal to restore the battered old church in 1681,[4] and his restorations lasted till 1865; and he rebuilt the rectory in 1695, and though his house may not have been an ideal home, it was evidently better than that which had existed before, and it sufficed till 1840.[5] For these things Thornton can, indeed, be grateful to him; and the people of his own day would, no doubt, feel real regret when he died on 25 November, 1699.

It is probable, however, that the ancestors of many of the present inhabitants owed far more to Dean Comber's curates, who lived on the spot, tended the poor, visited the sick, taught in the Grammar School and fulfilled the duties of village clergymen. If they did their duty in this northern village, it was not the same as the clerical duties in a snug southern or midland village. A curate at Thornton had a parish of wellnigh ten thousand acres; and up in the wild moorland parts, even then, there would be scattered farms that needed visitation. At the present time, in the depths of a bad winter, for anyone to bear comfort to the sick and dying at High Dalby Farm, requires more than physical strength; it needs a spiritual enthusiasm. At that period, the so-called road was more a morass than a road; and whether by Whitbygate and across Pexton Moor, or by Ellerburn, on either the right or left

---

[1] His son was Thomas Comber of East Newton, and his grandson was the Rev. William Comber, Vicar of Kirkby Moorside, and who died in his 85th year, in 1810.
[2] D.N.B. and *cf.* Camb. Al. I. p. 377.
[3] *Vide* Ch. VIII.
[4] *Vide supra.*
[5] *Vide supra.*

of the Beck, the parson would, in wintry weather, need a brave heart.[1] This being so, it is good that there have been left on record some of the names of the curates that did the work of the absentee rector. Probably the first of these was William Walker. It is not clear that he was in Thornton as early as 1679, but he was certainly there in 1682, and remained at his post till 1694.[2] He was followed in that year, by John Garnett, and he resided till 9 January, 1699/1700, as is shown by the fact that he took the oath to William III. at Helmsley on that date.[3] He must have felt, after a period of personal responsibility, that he did not wish to serve under a new master, and it is clear that he had gone later in the year, as the new curate was the Rev. Thomas Wilson,[4] who had ceased to be vicar of Ellerburn in 1695.

It may be quite erroneous but one surmises that the Rev. Thomas Mason,[5] who succeeded Dr. Comber, on 14 December, 1699, being presented by Lady Mary Cholmley,[6] and who was, like his predecessor, of Sidney Sussex College, Cambridge,[7] was not an absentee, though from 1724 to 1745 he was a pluralist as rector of Normanby.[8] At the beginning of his rectorship there is evidence of a curate, as shown above, but there are no further signs of such clerical assistance until 1722 when John Dowbiggin took up the work of curate and schoolmaster and remained as such until just before his burial on 8 April, 1736.[9] He was succeeded by the Rev. William Ward, who was a considerable pluralist as in 1743[10] he was not only curate and Grammar School Master of Thornton but also curate of Cloughton and Yedingham, and vicar of Scalby. From that date onwards he assisted Thomas Mason in his parochial work until the

---

[1] It might be said here that within the last thirty years there have been occasions when a rider to Dalby did not know when he crossed a gate or hedge because of the depth of the snowdrifts, but he reached the house, to which he came as a much-needed medical man. On 27 April, 1919, such was the wind, sleet and snow that no one except the vicar got to the evening service at Ellerburn. The vicar recorded this as the first time in more than twenty years experience.

[2] N. R. Rec. S. O.S. IX. p. 20, shows that he took the oaths to William and Mary on 13 January, 1690/1.

[3] Ibid. p. 27.

[4] The actual date of the Rev. Thomas Wilson is a little uncertain. He married by licence 'Mrs. Maggy Hunter' on 28 June, 1697.

[5] N. R. Rec. S. O.S. IX. p. 30, shows that 'Tho. Mayson' rector of Thornton took the oath to Queen Anne at Helmsley, on 14 July, 1702.

[6] *Vide supra.*

[7] This fact is shown on the brass in the Chancel, though the list in the Porch says, St. John's College, Cambridge.

[8] Y. A. S. Rec. S. LXXII. p. 201. *Cf.* also Y. A. S. Rec. S. LXXV. p. 169, where it gives the date 11 May, 1724, for the dispensation for Normanby.

[9] C. R.

[10] Y. A. S. Rec. S. LXXI. p. 160.

good rector died.[1] The long and loving lives of the rector and his
wife,[2] recorded in the Chancel, give the impression that they were
spent very largely in Thornton, where the two were ultimately
buried with less than a fortnight between their deaths.[3] One
pictures the two, as the ideal rector and his wife in rural surroundings,
doing what they could for their people,[4] seldom, as the memorial
says 'seperated' and only for so short a time 'devided.'[5]

The first occasion on which John Hill, Commissioner of Customs,
and 'Squire' of Thornton, exercised his right of presentation to the
living, was after the death of Thomas Mason, when he appointed
his nephew, John Samuel Hill, on 29 March, 1745.[6] He was the son
of John Hill's younger brother, Richard, who had been rector of
Normanby for some years, and had died in 1734.[7] After Richard's
death, it appears as if John Samuel lived at the Hall, Thornton;
for he went from there to Cambridge in June, 1734, and his clothes
were paid for by John Hill's steward.[8] John Samuel was born in
1714, and was educated under the celebrated Greek scholar, John
Clarke, at Skipton and afterwards matriculated at St. John's College,

[1] Eastmead, *ut supra*, says that Oswald Langwith was curate in 1742.
This is quite impossible as he only matriculated at University College,
Oxford, in 1741, aged 19. *Cf.* Foster *Alumni* 2nd Ser. III. p. 818.

[2] Martha, daughter of Andrew Perrott of York, married 1704, in York
Minster.

[3] Thomas Mason's will was proved at York, 15 March, 1744/5.

[4] The following Churchwardens served him during his long rectorship:—
1701, William Poade, John Skelton; 1702, William Maw, John Skelton;
1706, James Atkinson, Christopher Welborn; 1708, William Birdsall; 1713,
George Todd; 1716, James Boyes, Thomas Plumer; 1717, Simon Nicholls,
James Dixon; 1718, William Kirk, William Spendley; 1719, John Read, Robert
Skelton; 1720, Robert Gilbank; 1721, William Warren; 1722, Robert Smithson;
1723, John Skelton; 1724, John Barker, M. Body; 1726, John Alleson,
William Harland; 1727, William Harland; 1728, Christopher Smales, Richard
Birdsall; 1729, Same; 1730, Robert Dixon; 1731, John Birdsall, Roger Coats;
1734, John Read, William Smales; 1735, Same; 1736, John White, Thomas
Eman; 1737, Same; 1738, John Parke, Thomas Petch; 1739, Thomas Forster,
Philip Read; 1740, Robert Forster, Robert Smithson; 1741, Roger Atkinson,
William Storr; 1742, Same; 1743, Thomas Marflitt, John Wilson; 1744,
Thomas Shotten, James Maw; 1745, William Warren, William Hawson.

[5] Archbishop Herring's Visitation Return states that Mason from 12
January, 1699/1700 to 1743 'has resided constantly & in ye Parsonage House
wch is now, & will be found at his death, in a much better condition than
when he came to it.' *Cf.* Y. A. S. Rec. S. LXXV. p. 168. The poor old
man evidently did his best, but he became very deaf and could not hear the
answers given to the Catechism. In 1743 he presented William Smailes
and Christopher Smailes for following their callings publicly on the Lord's
day, and Robert Smailes, senior, for not paying Church Rates.

[6] Rector's List. The following Churchwardens served him during his
rectorship :—1746, Mark Staines, Bartholomew Pickering; 1747, Same;
1748, John Ripley, Thomas Nicholson; 1749-50, Same; 1751, Thomas
'Plummier' junr., John Champley; 1752, William Hoggard, William Harrison;
1753, Same; 1754, Francis Allance (?Allanson), Francis Boddy; 1755, Same;
1757, George Brown, and John Birdsall.

[7] Sam. Tetley, *ut supra*.

[8] Ibid.

Cambridge, of which he became a Fellow. In September, 1738, he was ordained in the diocese of Lincoln and on 12 April, 1740, proceeded to priest's orders[1] and was appointed Vicar of Pickering,[2] and held that benefice with the vicarage of Ellerburn, till his acceptance of Thornton, when he resigned the former, but continued to hold the latter. It is evident, as shown elsewhere,[3] that his residence in Pickering between 1740 and 1745, was not by any means acceptable to the Churchwardens of Ellerburn, who complained of his absenteeism,[4] though they may have become more resigned when he came to dwell in the old rectory at Thornton. Of course, his work was done by a curate, but even he seems to have been something of a pluralist, for it is recorded that John Walker was not only the curate at Ellerburn, but also did duty at Pickering, Newton and Wilton, but not at Thornton.[5] After 1745, John Samuel Hill was assisted, at Thornton and at Ellerburn, by the Rev. Oswald Langwith, son of James Langwith of York. He was born in 1722, matriculated at University College, Oxford, in 1741 and took his Bachelor's degree in 1745. It was during this period, as already mentioned, that Oswald Langwith registered the outbreak of cattle plague. John Samuel Hill, having proceeded to the degree of Doctor of Divinity, was not destined to enjoy the dignity for long, as he was buried at Thornton on 10 September, 1757, aged 43 years.[6] In the following spring, Captain John Hill, first cousin of John Samuel Hill,[7] presented Oswald Langwith to the rectory on 24 February, 1758, which he held for nearly ten years, being buried on 25 January, 1768.[8]

There was no member of the Hill family at the time, in holy orders, and so John Ward, B.A., was appointed on 20 July, 1768, and he resigned in August, 1781, when John Robert Hill Webb,

---

[1] Camb. Al.

[2] G. Home, *ut supra*, p. 292.

[3] *Vide* Ch. X.

[4] Y. A. S. Rec. S. LXXI. pp. 187-8. This was not surprising as like many others he was a pluralist. He was Prebendary of York 1745-8, Rector of Easington, 1745-57, Rector of Hollinbourne 1751-7, and Prebendary of Ely, 1751-7.

[5] Ibid.

[6] Rector's List.

[7] Captain John Hill was son of William Hill of Antigua. He married Catherine, daughter of Rev. Richard Hill, on 21 October, 1758.

[8] Foster, *ut supra*, p. 818, says that he died rector of Thornton on 23 February, 1768. The following Churchwardens served him during his rectorship :—1757, George Brown, John Birdsall; 1758, Same; 1759, Matthew Nicholson, Christopher Posgate; 1760, Mathew Nicholson, Robert Birdsall; 1761, Mathew Nicholson, Richard Jennison; 1762, James Smailes, Richard Jennison; 1763-4, Same; 1765, James Marfitt, John Hodgson; 1766, Same; 1767, Robert Skelton, William Marfitt, junr.; 1768, Same.

B.A., LL.B., of Clare College, Cambridge, was presented. He was the grandson of William Hill of Antigua, his mother, Elizabeth Hill, having married Charles Webb. John Robert Hill Webb was born in 1757, so that he was only twenty-four years old, when he became rector, and such he remained for fifty-six years as '*The Benevolent Rector of Thornton,*' and was buried on 28 July, 1837. During his tenure of office he was assisted by curates such as W. Walmsley in 1786, Christopher Wilkinson in 1800, Michael Mackereth from 1804;[1] and between 1819 and 1838 by Richard Brown Scholefield.[2] It is interesting to notice that the 'Benevolent' rector apparently did little parochial work after 1785 as his name hardly ever occurs in any of the Registers up to his death. The entries are made either by the above-mentioned curates, or by non-resident 'officiating ministers,' who came from the neighbouring parishes.

On 10 February, 1838, Richard Hill presented his eldest surviving son, John Richard Hill, B.A., to the living. He was born 29 October, 1811, and was educated at University College, Oxford, taking his B.A. in 1834 and his M.A. in 1847.[3] During the years 1839 to 1841, he was busy in rebuilding the rectory as already shown. From 1838 to 1840, his curate was the Rev. Thomas Irvin,[4] and he was succeeded in the latter year, by the Rev. George Thomas Terry, who married Helen Turville, a memorial to whom is in the Church. He left Thornton on 6 April, 1846.

It is not clear whether R. B. Scholefield, junior, was curate between 1846 and 1850, or only the Grammar School Master, but it is certain that in the May of 1852, the curacy was given to the Rev. Edward William Heslop, third son of the Rev. John Heslop, of Haxby, Yorkshire. He was born on 29 December, 1828, and was educated at St. Peter's School, York, and at Queen's College, Oxford, where he matriculated on 10 June, 1847, and proceeded to his Bachelor's degree in 1851, and his Master's in 1855.[5] He was

---

[1] Registers of Ellerburn Church.

[2] C. R. Only the following names of Churchwardens have been found during his rectorship :—1769, Robert Skelton, William Marfitt, junr.; 1770, Roger Atkinson, Stephen Dixon (died 1818, aged 87); 1771, Same; 1772, Stephen Dixon, William Harrison; 1773, Same; 1774, William Allanson, William Harrison (died 1816); 1775, Same; 1776, William Harrison, William Staines; 1777, Mathew Labron, William Staines; 1778, Mathew Labron, John Champley; 1779, Same; 1780, Richard Jennison, William Spendley; 1781, Same; 1786, Robert Harland, James Marfitt; 1803, John Marshall, John Watson, John Boulton; 1809, Hugh Berwick, John Coates; 1817, Hugh Berwick, William Hodgson; 1825, Hugh Berwick.

[3] Foster, *ut supra*.

[4] C. R.

[5] Foster, *ut supra*. As a curate he lived in what is now called Manor Farm, then tenanted by the Booths.

a good sportsman and a very keen cricketer; and it was to play in a cricket match at the Hall, that he first visited Thornton,[1] having just left Oxford. The rector at once liked him and offered him the curacy. He became a friend of the family, and a great love sprang up between him and the rector's half-sister, Lucy. After Richard Hill died at the Hall, his son, the rector, became the 'Squire'[2] and resigned the living to Edward Heslop in March, 1857,[3] who, very shortly after, married Miss Lucy Hill.[4] The great proof of the affection in which the Rev. E. W. Heslop was held was shown by the villagers on his return from his honeymoon in December, 1857. The young married couple were met on the Pickering road by a number of tenants and Thornton farmers, bearing torches, the horses were taken from the carriage and it was drawn by hand into the village. The shopkeepers, to show their joy, did what was then the most unusual thing, of closing their shops for four days round Christmas. The rectorship of the Rev. Edward Heslop is looked back upon, by all who knew him, as a Golden Age in Thornton. He was a man of unostentatious kindness and unbounded generosity, of simple faith and piety, a friend to all, the best type of country clergyman. He lived in Thornton, as curate and rector, for forty-seven years, having the deep affection of all his parishioners and being sincerely mourned, when he died on 8 December, 1899.[5] One who knew him well, rightly said 'few men have been more loved or have better deserved to be loved.'

For the last twenty-nine years the rectory has been held by the Rev. Godfrey Arthur Marshall, M.A., grandson of the Rev. John Richard Hill. He took his B.A. from Trinity College, Cambridge, in 1891. He was ordained in 1894 and was curate at Swinton, Lancs., from 1897-1900, when he became rector of Thornton, after induction in York Minster on 20 April, and institution in the Church on 10 May. He married, on 10 June, 1914, Zoe A. M., daughter of the Rev. C. H. V. Pixell of Stoke Newington. Between 1917 and 1918, he served in one of the Military Hospitals

[1] It is more than thirty years ago that he told me this.
[2] John Richard Hill, or 'The Old Squire' continued to live at the Hall, doing many good works, until his death on 21 December, 1896.
[3] Rector's List.
[4] She died March, 1860, leaving two daughters, Mary (afterwards Mrs. R. A. Scott, died 1913) and Margaret Lucy.
[5] I am indebted to Miss M. L. Heslop for the names of the following curates: Rev. William Serjeantson, who lived at the Mill, 1865, Rev. H. P. Bainbridge, c. 1869-1874, afterwards vicar of Ganton, Rev. Robert Hyde, September, 1891, to March, 1900, afterwards curate of Cottingham and vicar of Riccal, married Julia, daughter of the Rev. George Scott of Coxwold; buried at Thornton, 23 August, 1916.

in Oxford, during which period the services of the Church[1] were conducted by the Rev. James Thornton, vicar of Ellerburn.

In the spring of 1930, after much debate, a commission decided that the rectory of Thornton should at last, when a suitable time came, absorb the vicarage of Ellerburn. Thus the territorially interlocked parishes will, at a future date, become equally ecclesiastically united.

[1] Amongst the documentary losses of this village are the Churchwardens' Books: apparently, in 1930, there are none in existence of any period. For this reason, for fear of a complete disappearance of names, I give the following Churchwardens of recent years as far as I have been able to collect them :—

Hugh Berwick (1804-36); John Boulton (1804-6); John Coats (1809); John Dixon (1811-14); Robert Skelton (1815); Henry Hodgson (1816-19); Wilfred Sadler (1821); William Pickering (1824); Thomas Cross (1825); Thomas Walker (1827); John Boyes (1830-1); James Elliott (1832); Thomas Richardson (1833-6); Thomas Cross (1839-44); Thomas Booth (1839-56); James Elliott (1848-9); Thomas Skelton (1850-3); Samuel Baker (1856-60); Thomas Buttery (1858-71); John Wardill (1861-6); Francis Hill (1867-71); John Elliott (1872-86); Richard Birdsall (1879-87); Coulson Fowler (1888-99); Joseph W. Clarke (1888-93); Richard A. Scott (1900-1); John Read (1894-1926); Alfred Smith (1902-6); Richard Hill (1907-10); Clement Briggs (1911-14); George F. G. Hill (1915-16); W. Wilson (1917-30); T. Taylor (1927-30).

CHAPTER TEN.

The Church and Vicars of Ellerburn.

'Matrons and Sires—who, punctual to the call
Of their loved Church, on fast or festival
Through the long year the House of Prayer would seek:
By Christmas snows, by visitation bleak
Of Easter winds, unscared, from hut or hall
They came to lowly bench or sculptured stall,
But with one fervour of devotion meek.'

WORDSWORTH, 1827.

THE little Church of St. Hilda, of the parish of Ellerburn-cum-Farmanby, is situated in one of the most delightful spots in this countryside. Unlike the Church at Thornton, St. Hilda's does not hold a commanding position, but nestles below the slopes of Kirkdale on the north and the wooded hillside of Buffit on the south. Outside the Churchyard the Beck follows its winding course; and, on a still, fine day, few places surpass in peaceful restfulness that which is to be found here. It would be a satisfaction to all lovers of beauty and of antiquity if it could be known how long, in these quiet surroundings, there has been a church and, indeed, why there ever was a church, so far from a real village, because there never seem to have been any more than the three or four houses that still cluster near it. But answers to such questions are not likely to be found.

The Church itself must tell its own tale, for there are no documentary records. As far as can be ascertained, parts are pre-Norman, but the main fabric dates from after the Conquest. This has been restored from time to time, and in the fifteenth century some considerable rebuilding was undertaken. The first window in the south wall is usually dated as thirteenth century, and so also the Chancel arch.[1] The pillars of the arch may be pre-Norman, and they have St. Hilda's serpents engraved upon them. At the east end of the south wall there are the remains of an arch but writers fail to agree as to whether it was built in the fourteenth or fifteenth

---

[1] In December, 1904, the architect, W. D. Caröe, decided that over this Chancel arch there had been a fresco of the 'Last Judgement.'

centuries. The late vicar, the Rev. James Thornton, was much interested in this, and was convinced that it marked the entry into a side-chapel, now entirely lost, but which extended in former times considerably into the Churchyard.[1] Above this archway on the inside, are the remains of a Norman window, which may possibly have been blocked up when the side-chapel was built. The ugly buttressed bell-cote, seriously spoiling the effect of the west window, was erected in the early nineteenth century, and the south porch is of very recent date.

The walls of the Church contain many pieces of pre-Conquest sculpture, but there seems to be some uncertainty as to their exact period and character. One writer speaks of them as Anglo-Danish,[2] while another is convinced that some of them, at least, are of Norwegian workmanship much influenced by Irish culture.[3] Fine stone has been used for somewhat rough work, part of which was executed by the chisel and part by the pick. The most important piece is the cross head built into the outer surface of the south wall of the nave. It is composed of close-grained cream-coloured freestone, and is 29½ inches long and 18 inches wide. The centre of the head is flat, and it is thought that this is the reverse side and that on the other there may have been an inscription on the neck, where on the outer side is the representation of a gagged dragon. The want of symmetry is remarkable, and the whole has been hacked with a hammer and rather deeply cut.[4] A small stone, showing demi-human figures is also interesting. In Mr. Collingwood's opinion they represent ecclesiastics,[5] probably priests;[6] the workmanship, however, is not finely but rather rudely executed. Besides these there is a Swastika, or emblem of well-being[7] and two hog-backs built into the east wall of the porch.

The font is a rough bowl, and though not beautiful has the attraction of antiquity, as it dates from the twelfth century and possibly before. But the most interesting relic of the past, discovered in 1905, is the enormous pre-reformation stone altar top. It is probable that this was made at the time of the first establishment of a Church at Ellerburn, possibly in the ninth century. The vicar obtained a faculty so that this massive block, placed on

[1] In 1904 this was found to be 16½ft. long and 9ft. wide.
[2] W. G. Collingwood, Y. A. J. XIX. p. 209.
[3] A. H. Smith, *ut supra*, p. xxvi.
[4] Y. A. J. XIX. p. 316.
[5] Ibid. p. 280.
[6] Ibid. p. 316.
[7] The Rev. J. Thornton recorded that he had been informed by Mr. W. Collingwood that it was 'characteristic of the Viking period as opposed to the Anglian, though it occurs in the Bronze Age relics of Yorkshire (Ilkley).'

trestles, should serve to-day, as the communion table. The pulpit has considerable charm, being a very fine specimen of Jacobean work. The whole Church was repaired under the careful attention of the vicar in 1905,[1] and there can be no question that he loved every stick and stone.

The possessions of the Church are not as historically valuable as those of Thornton. The chalice is marked 'Ellerburn,' and dated 1756. The paten was presented as recently as 1888, and there is a pewter flagon. The Registers are disappointing as they are comparatively modern, as none of them are older than the last decade of the seventeenth century. Neither the marriages nor the burials are quite complete.

The Terriers are not of any great interest. The first is of 1764 and records the existence of a vicarage house twelve yards long and six yards wide. This is the cottage near the Church and is still the property of the vicar. The glebe was said to consist of 41 ac. 3 r. 2 p., but all this has been sold except 8 ac. of pasture in Upper Kirkdale. The tithe in Farmanby is fully described and amongst numerous points it shows that the parishioners in Farmanby paid tithe of hay, herbage, small seeds, wool and lambs. Tithe was also due from occupiers of Roxby and of Benson's Close. Thus 6s. was to come from Great Aunums, 2s. from 'Lille' Aunums, and 2s. from Low Hall Garth. The vicar must have been overwhelmed with poultry at the end of the year for he was entitled to one hen from every house in Farmanby on Christmas Day. The Terrier of 1778 is a repetition of the former one, and a copy of it was stated to have been delivered in 1786. The only noticeable addition in that of 1809 is a reference to certain payments arising in Wilton and payable by Sir Charles Hotham and John Baker. In 1817 the pewter flagon, the silver cup, the Bell and the large Bible are all added to the usual notifications. The terrier of 1853 is much the same but on the back is a statement that in 1883 the Ecclesiastical Commissioners agreed to pay £150 per annum towards the stipend. There is also the entry that on 23 January, 1888, the Commissioners purchased from the Rev. J. R. Hill the present site of the vicarage and handed it over to the incumbent.

Of the memorials it is regrettable that they are few and not old. On the south side of the west wall is a marble slab to the memory of William Willmott, died 21 April, 1817, and to his daughter Hannah, died 12 May, 1820. On the north wall, in stone and gilt,

---

[1] In August, 1902, 'Two foundation walls were found whilst excavating for the vestry, each running northward and parallel with the east and west walls of the Church.'

is a tablet[1] in memory of the Rev. James Thornton, vicar 1898 to 1926. On the north wing of the reredos is a bronze tablet to the Rev. Richard Shawcross, vicar 1866 to 1886, and on the south wing, a similar design, to Richard and Evereld Ellen Hill of Thornton Hall. On the font there is a memorial to Robert and Minnie Champley in 1905.[2] In the churchyard there are several quaint eighteenth century box-tombs recording the burials of the families of Staines, Smithson, and Smailes. There is an almost obliterated tomb to Thomas Stonehouse and family, several stones to the Buttery, Skelton, and Watson families, one to John 'Nattress' who died in 1794, and another to John Harding who died the same year. There is, unfortunately, a hideous pink marble obelisk, erected in the worst of taste, and which jars upon the eye and mind of every visitor; and finally there is a stone to the memory of George Robertson, who died 1 February, 1889, after having been fifty years the village doctor. The lych gate[3] was presented in September, 1908, by W. A. Meek, Esq., K.C., Recorder of York, as a thank-offering for being allowed a plot in the churchyard as a family burial ground; and his ashes and those of his wife were placed there 24 April, 1929.

If little is known about the rectors of Thornton, still less can be ascertained concerning the vicars of Ellerburn. In early times the benefice was a chapelry of Pickering, and it is possible that some of the vicars of Pickering may have held the chapel with the vicarage. Of this, however, there is no proof. The first known person to administer the sacred rites in St. Hilda's, was Adam de Insula, *vicar* of Thornton, where he had been appointed in 1226,[4] and was confirmed, as clerk of 'Ellerburne,' in August, 1231, with the Corn tithe of 'Faremanby,' by Roger de Insula, Dean of York, and with the consent of the Chapter.[5] A very great change, however, was made with regard to Ellerburn, in 1252, when Archbishop Gray ordained that all the Chapelries of Pickering,[6] including

---

[1] The designer of the tablet and the architect for the restoration of the Church was W. D. Caröe, of Westminster. The builder employed was H. W. Barnes, of Thornton.

[2] In 1904 Mrs. Thomas Scoby of York (formerly of Whitbygate, Thornton) presented a solid brass cross with Passion steps. In 1905 many friends gave an oak lectern in memory of the late Mrs. Garbutt, who had for many years been organist, and died in 1904. In September, 1926, a brass ewer with oak stand was presented by relatives in memory of John and Ann Rodgers. In March, 1927, there was an anonymous gift of an altar cruet. In 1929 a silver wafer-case was given in memory of William Beaumont.

[3] The architect was W. D. Caröe, of Westminster.

[4] *Vide* Ch. IX.

[5] *Archb. Gray's Reg.* Sur. Soc. LVI. p. 47.

[6] Y. A. S. Rec. S. LXXIII. p. xi.

that of Ellerburn, should be converted into vicarages.[1] As the records of the diocese of York are missing for some years,[2] it is not certain how long Adam de Insula continued to administer the spiritual affairs of the two parishes.

Ellerburn is mentioned in the celebrated Taxatio Nicolai of 1291, and it is clear that the officiating cleric had only the poor sum of £6. 13s. 4d. per annum, for all his wants.[3] As no vicar appears in any of the Subsidy Rolls of 1301, 1327, and 1333, it may be presumed that he was an absentee, though the vicar of 1301 had a 'servant' Alan, who evidently had some personal possessions,[4] and may have been Alan the 'capellanus,' or curate, mentioned in a late thirteenth century Thornton document; but no such person appears in either of the subsequent Rolls. And then follows nearly one hundred and thirty years of darkness until it is stated, in 1428, that the vicars of Ellerburn, Pickering, Allerston, and Ebberston were all to be taxed five marks.[5] In 1497, the vicar, 'Sir Robert Sawdane,'[6] had the unpleasant experience already recorded, connected with the story of Sir Roger Hastings and Ralph Joyner. In 1527, 'dns Richardus Bruster vic. de Ellerburn' is said to have had to struggle along on the princely sum of £7 per annum.[7] Though this is not accurately the sum, for the *Valor* shows in 1535, that he received £7. 4s. 8d., but had to pay in tax, 13s. 5¼d.[8]

All this time Ellerburn had been in what is known as the Dean of York's 'Peculiar.' It might be well to explain here that very often within the area presided over by the archdeacon, who dealt with ecclesiastical cases within his district, all churches were not necessarily under archidiaconal supervision. Some parishes were exempt and were stated to be within 'peculiar jurisdictions,' which term was frequently curtailed into the word 'Peculiars.'

[1] *Archb. Gray's Reg.* Sur. Soc. LVI. pp. 211-13, 1252. 'In capellis vero de Ellerburn et Wilton sit unus vicarius, qui ministros utrique capellae inveniat necessarios, et habeat nomine vicariae decimam trium culturaram de Ellerton, et totum alteragium utriusque capellae, cum foeno, praeter mortuaria in vivo averio et praeter decimam lanae et agnorum de Wilton. Dictus autem vicarius solvat matrici ecclesiae suae de Pyk' annuatim nomine subjectionis ad festum Pentecostes et ad festum Sancti Martini in hyeme, duos solidos per partes aequales.'
[2] The registers begin in 1225, and are complete except for a gap 1255-1266. *Cf.* R. C. Fowler, *Episcopal Registers of England and Wales*, p. 31.
[3] '*Vicaria de Ellerburn que est de Decanatu Ebor.* 6-13-4.'
[4] Y. A. S. Rec. S. XXI. p. 64. N. R. Rec. S. N.S. IV. p. 46, shows that the vicar of Ellerburn was recently dead in 1334.
[5] Cal. Feud. Aids. VI. p. 312.
[6] *Vide* Ch. IV.
[7] Y. A. J. XXI. p. 244.
[8] *Valor Ecclesiasticus*, 1535.

Amongst these, which included subjection to royalty, archbishops, bishops, and others, there were certain parishes, like that of Ellerburn, that were under the jurisdiction of a dean or a dean and chapter; and in this particular case, the Dean of York exercised 'peculiar' jurisdiction over the little parish. From time to time the Dean, and not the archdeacon, made 'Visitations' to enquire into the morals and general welfare of Ellerburn.

Thus, in 1568, when John Waddington, or Wallington, was clerk in holy orders at Ellerburn, there was such a Visitation; and the vicar, evidently not an absentee, attended personally,[1] and showed his letter of ordination; which fact goes to prove that he had just recently been appointed. But the work that he did must have been small enough, for the record also shows the personal presence of the curate (a native, one supposes), Robert Todd. The Churchwardens[2] were questioned as to the state of affairs, and they replied that 'all is well' 'saving there churche is in some decaie in leades and glasse windowes,' and they are warned to repair the premises before St. Martin's Day[3] next.[4] In 1570, John 'Wallington' and Robert Todd were still the pastors in Ellerburn. Their Churchwardens had, naturally, changed,[5] and perhaps the incomers were severer moralists than their predecessors, or, at least, their charges give this impression. They presented 'all the inhabitants of Wilton for not contrybuting to there parishe churche of Ellerburne. *Item* William Butler *alias* Fisher and Margaret Cook lyveth to geither as man and wif offensyvelie and not maried. *Item* John Shawe for fornication with Elizabeth Birdsall of the parishe of Thorneton.'[6] This was the last time 'Sir' John Wallington appeared at these Visitations, for he was buried at Thornton on 4 August, 1573.[7]

It may be supposed that the Deans of York lost interest in the morals and welfare of Ellerburn for twenty years. At any rate there is no other Visitation recorded until 1590, when Ralph Hunt was the vicar, and was present. The Churchwardens[8] do not seem

---

[1] *'vicarius ibidem personaliter.'*

[2] The Churchwardens were:—William Preston and George Boyes.

[3] *'Moniti sunt ad reparanda premissa citra festum Sancti Martini Episcopi in yeme proximum.'*

[4] Y. A. J. XVIII. pp. 211-13.

[5] There seem to have been four churchwardens at the same time in 1570. But it probably means the two out going and the two in coming. They were John Haggett, Henry 'Kiddye,' Robert Skelton and Robert Beryman.

[6] Y. A. J. *ut supra.*

[7] Thornton C. R. There seems to have been some kind of collection at his funeral service for the Register records 'at hys offering when he was buried, vijd.' Perhaps this was his minute mortuary.

[8] William Preston and George Boyes.

to have had the same conscientious scruples of those of the earlier date, in any case they confined themselves to the statement 'that the vicaredge is in some decaie. To the rest all is well.'[1] To make up for past indifference a Visitation was made the very next year, and Ralph Hunt had apparently gone, and the new vicar was the already mentioned John Richardson, rector of Thornton.[2] He was not in person, at the Visitation, and was represented by his curate, Henry Jackson. The out going[3] and the in coming wardens[4] were both present. They seem, like some of their predecessors, to have felt the burden of their position, as not only guardians of the Church, but also of village morals, and so they charged 'Cisse Robinson of the Marrys gotton with child by one William Sleight-holme of New Malton and was born at "Formanbye" in one Robert Craven his house.' But these tiresome village problems and scandals were stilled in the next year when the Churchwardens '*dicunt omnia bene*.'[5] In 1593, John Richardson attended the Visitation in person. It may have been that this was a special occasion to look into a particular question. The Churchwardens[6] at any rate, 'saie they have none [i.e., no recusants] within there parishe.'[7] John Richardson was excused the next year, and no curate was present, and so the Churchwardens,[8] had a free hand and seized their opportunity to state that 'Mr. John Richardson is not resident vpon his vicaredg but his curate dothe diligentlie instruct the youthe. Jane Gryme for fornicacion with William Gill. But whether the curate did churche hir or no they cannot tell. To the rest they saie all is well.'[9] At the next Visitation in 1595, John Richardson and his curate, Henry Jackson, were both present. The Churchwardens[10] said 'that there queare is in decaie in glasse and also in poynting of the slate. Thomas Walker dothe not come to the Churche but haithe absented himself....a yeare and more.'[11] They then proceeded to say that 'there vicar, John Richardson is not resident vpon his vicaredg, but what he bestoweth vpon the poore they know not. All the rest is well.' Three years later, John Richardson and Henry Jackson were still there. The

---

[1] Y. A. J. *ut supra*.
[2] *Vide* Ch. IX.
[3] William Browne and Christopher Horsley.
[4] William Horsley and Robert Kirkby.
[5] Y. A. J. *ut supra*.
[6] William 'Ratclif' and John Calvert.
[7] Y. A. J. *ut supra*.
[8] Robert 'Goodale' and John 'Fairwether.'
[9] Y. A. J. *ut supra*.
[10] John Collinson (*vide* Ch. V.) and Francis Horsley.
[11] This has been struck through with a pen and may not refer to Ellerburn.

Churchwardens[1] have even now got their knives into their absentee vicar. They said 'that they have not had there quarter sermons this last yeare. There vicar is not resident nor kepethe hospitalities, neither distributethe any parte his benefice emongest the poore.' They also presented 'John Dow for adultery with Emmott Kyng of Ellerburn.' They were, however, able to say 'all the rest is well.'[2] From this time forward it was not altogether surprising, after these attacks, that John Richardson ceased to attend the Visitations, and relied upon the representation of his curate. When George Bucke was curate in 1598, the Churchwardens,[3] said that all was well. In the next year, Bucke's place had been taken by Francis Lawson, and the service seems to have been better conducted for the Churchwardens[4] reported 'that they had iiij [sermons] the last year preached preached [*sic*] by Mr. Richardson, the vicar.' They also said that 'Francis "Lowson" is vnmaried'; and they concluded on the happy note 'All the rest is well.'[5] The report of the year 1600 was very much the same. That of 1601 showed Francis 'Lowson' still curate. The old Churchwardens had been changed,[6] and the new ones[7] presented Peter Boyes, John Prowde, William Browne, Robert 'Goodaill,' Axor Lodge, Thomas Godson and Anne Robynson for not paying the clerk his wages 'as the clerke dothe enforme theme.' But this, evidently, is a light matter, for 'To the rest all is well.'[8] In 1602, vicar and curate were still the same. The Churchwardens[9] had changed as usual, but their clamour for more clerical work did not cease. They presented 'that there haithe beyne a want of catekesing the youthe, but here after they will diligently present the offenders therein.' Then they stated, coldly and without sympathy, that 'Anne Robinson, widowe, now remayning in York [? gaol] for not paying cessment towardes the churche. For the rest all is well.'[10]

John Richardson had ceased to be the vicar of Ellerburn by the year 1609, and one may imagine that his successor was not always present in his cure of souls, because the Thornton Registers show that in January, 1615/6, John Robinson occasionally took a service 'the minister of Ellerburne beinge absent.' The vicar, if

[1] Roger Hobson and Richard 'Eglesfield.'
[2] Y. A. J. *ut supra.*
[3] Thomas Watson and Henry Kirby.
[4] John 'Daile' and Thomas Reade.
[5] Y. A. J. *ut supra.*
[6] Henry 'Slie and Robert 'Dynam.'
[7] Roger Horsley and George 'Smayles.'
[8] Y. A. J. *ut supra.*
[9] Richard 'Daile' and John Browne.
[10] Y. A. J. *ut supra.*

in residence at the little cottage, near the Church, in 1638, must have felt the same heart rendings as the rector of Thornton, when the plague brought death so rapidly to his parishioners. During the Commonwealth period it may be supposed that the curate or vicar doing the work was 'Mr. Francis Catley, of Ellerburn, cler.'[1] Presumably, from the record, he was alive in the spring of 1657, his son died in April of that year, and his wife, 'Jaine', in the following August.[2]

It must have been during Catley's administration that a piece of vicarage property was alienated. Henry 'Osburne' of Chicksands, Beds., Esq., had come to be possessed of a small tenement, cottage, garth and yardland at Ellerburn lying between 'the vicaridge garthe on the west and one garth in the occupation of Robert Rogerson on the east wch said premises were parcell of and belonging to the Rectory [*sic*] of Ellerbourne.'[3] These he sold on 26 May, 1655, to Robert. Harding, John Browne, and Richard Wetherill of Pickering, John Monkman of Allerston and William Mawe of . Thornton, yeoman. The last on 2 October, 1658, sold to John Harland of Ellerburn, yeoman.[4] What became of this property is very uncertain, but the probability is that as the land was Church property it reverted to the vicar of Ellerburn at the time of the Restoration.

It is possible that Marmaduke 'Wikes, clerk,'[5] succeeded Francis Catley, but it is not known for certain that he was vicar of Ellerburn until 1678 when he is mentioned in the Farmanby Award. He was undoubtedly vicar on 16 July, 1689, when he took the oaths to William and Mary at 'Stoxley' [Stokesley].[6] He was buried on 31 January, 1690/1 and was succeeded in February[7] by the Rev. Thomas Wilson, Master of the Thornton Grammar School. The latter did not remain for long as the Rev. Joshua Newton, who had been vicar of Pickering since 1691, was instituted vicar of Ellerburn by the Dean of York in 1695,[8] and continued to hold the

---

[1] A Francis Catley or Catlye matriculated as a sizar at Jesus College, Cambridge, at Easter, 1602, and took his B.A. 1605/6.
[2] C. R.
[3] G. F. G. H.
[4] Ibid.
[5] According to Baring-Gould, *Yorkshire Oddities*, the Rev. Marmaduke Wykes was on a certain Sunday proceeding to the Church when he saw a man ill-treating his wife, whereupon he endeavoured to bring about peace, with the result that the two laid violent hands on the vicar and soused him in the Beck. History does not record whether the service was held that day or not.
[6] N. R. Rec. S. O.S. IX. p. 40.
[7] Ellerburn Registers.
[8] Ibid.

two in plurality[1] until his death in 1712.[2] Robert Hargreaves followed Joshua Newton in both vicarages, being appointed to Ellerburn on 4 April, 1713,[3] and ten days later took the oath to Queen Anne.[4] For twenty-seven years he lived a peaceful and somnolent existence, and died unknown to fame in 1740.[5] John Samuel Hill was then appointed vicar of Pickering[6] and was collated vicar of Ellerburn in the same year,[7] having as his curate, in 1743, the Rev. John Walker. It was during this period that Archbishop Herring's Visitation took place, and the answers to the questions give some picture as to the condition of ecclesiastical affairs in the little hamlet. The returns state :—

'I.   There are abt. Eighty Families in the parish—of which there are Four Families called Quakers.

II.   There is not any Meeting House licens'd in the parish or without License.

III.   There is no publick or Charity School maintained in the Parish.

IV.   There are no Alms House—Hospitals or other charitable Endowmt in the Parish.

V.   The Curate has for many Years resided in Pickering—and does at this Time.

VI.   The Curate is resident at Pickering qualifyd according to the Canons and proportional Allowance made him.

VII.   I know not of any unbaptized Person that comes to church or of any unconfirmd of a competent Age that is baptizd.

VIII.   The publick service is performed once every Lord's Day in the Afternoon according to Custom.

IX.   The Children have been very carefully instructed in the Ch. Catechism in order for Confirmation &c.

X.   The Sacramt is administr'd in the Church Three Times according to the Canons in the Year, generally there are more Comunicants at Easter than in any other Time.

XI.   I always give Notice and sufficient Warning of the Administration of ye Sacramt the Week before, as for giving in their Names, it is not according to Custom among us.'

This report was signed by John Walker; and he stated that the

---

[1] He must have had a dispensation. The Rev. H. E. Salter, Fellow of Magdalen College, Oxford, kindly tells me that a man might hold a vicarage and a rectory, but not two vicarages or two rectories except by dispensation.
[2] G. Home, *ut supra*, p. 292.
[3] Ellerburn Register.
[4] N. R. Rec. S. O.S. IX. p. 41.
[5] G. Home, *ut supra*, p. 292.
[6] Ibid.
[7] Ellerburn Register. *Vide* Ch. IX.

vicar was John Samuel Hill, and the Churchwardens were Thomas 'Stanes' and John Longburne.[1]

John Walker must have left about 1745, when Oswald Langwith became curate of both Thornton and Ellerburn, on behalf of John Samuel Hill;[2] and it was during his curacy that he made the interesting entry in the Ellerburn Register concerning the cattle plague already recorded.[3] He succeeded Dr. Hill at Thornton as rector, but not at Ellerburn as vicar. The new vicar in 1757 was the Rev. Samuel Harding,[4] who laboured under the terrible affliction of being blind. He like others was a pluralist as he was vicar of Pickering from 1764 for twenty years, when he died.[5] During the years 1782 to 1784, he was assisted at Ellerburn by a resident curate, William Walmesley,[6] and in 1784 by his son Samuel Harding junior, who, afterwards in 1786,[7] became the vicar of Pickering and was buried there on 27 January, 1804.[8] His successor at Ellerburn was the already mentioned John Gilby.[9] He was the son of William Gilby of Winterton, co. Lincoln, and matriculated at University College, Oxford, on 14 June, 1775, aged eighteen. He took his B.A. four years later, and proceeded to the B.C.L. in 1796. He was appointed J.P. and D.L. of Yorkshire E. Riding, and became rector of Barmston which he remained until his death on 26 June, 1829.[10] He married Elizabeth, widow of Richard Johnson Hill in 1797 and had two daughters, Elizabeth and Jane, both of whom died in 1830. After Gilby's appointment to Ellerburn on 29 February, 1804, he had as his curate the Rev. Henry Thomas Laye who was also vicar of Pickering from that year till his death in 1809.[11] Henry Thomas Laye was the son of Francis Laye of Doncaster, and, after being educated at Westminster School, matriculated at Christ Church, Oxford, on 29 May, 1797, aged nineteen. He was vicar of Rampton, Notts., in 1802[12] and came from there to Pickering. He married Nancy Maynard, niece of Richard Johnson Hill and had several children.[13]

John Gilby resigned the vicarage of Ellerburn on 23 March,

---

[1] Y. A. S. Rec. S. LXXI. pp. 187-8.
[2] *Vide* Ch. IX.
[3] *Vide* Ch. VI.
[4] Ellerburn Register.
[5] G. Home, *ut supra*, p. 292.
[6] Ellerburn Register.
[7] The Rev. John Robinson was vicar of Pickering from 1784 to 1786.
[8] G. Home, *ut supra*, p. 292.
[9] *Vide* Ch. XI.
[10] Foster, *Alumni*. Miss Heslop tells me that he was known as 'His Honour.'
[11] G. Home, *ut supra*, p. 292.
[12] Foster, *ut supra*.
[13] Information from the Rev. A. Hill.

1809, and his place was taken by the already elderly Thornton Grammar School Master, the Rev. Michael Mackereth.[1] Between 1816 and 1817 he was assisted by the Rev. Thomas Brown, who married his daughter Ann:[2] in 1818, and again from 1825 to 1829 by the Rev. Charles Macereth,[3] afterwards vicar of Middleton:[4] in 1824 by the Rev. R. B. Scholefield, curate of Thornton.[5] All this time Michael Mackereth lived in the Grammar School house, where he died about eighty-five years of age in 1829.[6]

For a very short time the vicarage was in the hands of the Rev. W. Cockburn, D.D., Dean of York,[7] who had as his resident curate the Rev. G. A. Cockburn, B.A.[8] But in 1830 the Dean resigned and on 28 January, 1831, G. A. Cockburn was instituted vicar. The tiny cottage between the Church and the Beck was quite unsuitable for residence, and the incumbent obtained a licence to live outside his parish because of the 'unfitness of the vicarage house.'[9] In 1832 he appointed the Rev. Thomas Irvin, the Grammar School master, his curate at Ellerburn; but Cockburn did not remain long as his place was taken in 1838 by the Rev. John William Watson,[10] B.A., who like his predecessor preferred to live out of his parish and resided, until 1842, at the High Hall, Thornton.[11] In that year the Rev. James Parker became vicar,[12] and for fifteen years was much beloved in the parish being generally and affectionately known as 'little Jimmy Parker.' No names of curates have been found during the first nine years he held the living, but in 1851 he appointed the Rev. Edward Firmstone.[13] He was the third son of William Firmstone of Highfield, Staffs., and matriculated

[1] Ellerburn Register.
[2] Ibid.
[3] Ibid.
[4] It might be noted that the Rev. William Mackereth, vicar of Middleton was a freeholder in Thornton in 1807 (*vide* Poll Book), and that Mark Anthony Mackereth, Chaplain to His Majesty's Forces, died in Farmanby in 1822. (*Vide* Thornton Registers). Eastmead, *ut supra*, p. 253, says that the Rev. Mark Anthony Mackereth was curate of Salton in 1824, which is impossible. The Thornton Register shows the Rev. George Mackereth, as 'officiating minister.'
[5] Eastmead, *ut supra*, p. 326.
[6] *Vide* Ch. VIII.
[7] Ellerburn Register.
[8] He was afterwards vicar of Pickering from 1858 to 1863.
[9] Ellerburn Register.
[10] Ibid. He wrote an 'Ode to Ellerburne' in 1841 which ended with the lines

> 'Oh! vale of peace, where'er I be
> In years to come
> My heart with joy will turn to thee
> Sweet Ellerburne.'

[11] *East and North Ridings*, p. 457.
[12] Ellerburn Register.
[13] Ibid.

at Lincoln College, Oxford, on 4 June, 1842, aged eighteen. He took his B.A. in 1846, and his M.A. in 1849.[1] He remained curate at Ellerburn until he gave up his work at Thornton Grammar School in 1855.[2]

Two years after Firmstone's resignation,[3] William Henry Hugall was instituted and lived in what is now called 'the Old Vicarage,' Maltongate. It must have been a great change for him to come to the tiny rural parish after his bustling life as incumbent of Paddington. His health, however, was very poor, and after a long illness he died and was buried at Scarborough in 1866.[4] His first curate, in 1859, was the Rev. W. Macdowall,[5] and he was succeeded about 1864 by the Rev. Frederick Shum,[6] and he again in 1865 by the Rev. Henry B. Beedham.[7]

The Rev. Richard Shawcross when he came to Ellerburn in 1866 first resided in the 'old Vicarage,'[8] and later until his death in 1886 at East Hill, Thornton. His curate from 1872 to 1874 was the Rev. H. P. Bainbridge,[9] who was at the same time curate to the Rev. Edward Heslop at Thornton. In 1887 the Rev. A. J. Durrard was appointed vicar of Ellerburn and from his coming until 1890, lodged at the Thornton Mill, but in that year became the first occupant of the new vicarage in Maltongate. During the last few years of his life he failed in health[10] and in 1896 the work of the parish was done by a curate, the Rev. Colin Graham.

When A. J. Durrard died on 4 September, 1897, his place was taken in the following year by the Rev. James Thornton. He had taken his B.A. at the University of Durham in 1882, and was ordained in 1883. He was curate of St. James's, Kingston-upon-Hull, from that year to 1885 when he transferred to Drax until 1889 and was at Brayton until 1898.[11] He remained vicar of Ellerburn

---

[1] Foster, *Alumni.*

[2] *Vide* Ch. VIII.

[3] Probably the same man as William Henry Hugall, second son of Thomas Hugall, of Sculcoats, Yorks., who matriculated at St. Mary's Hall, Oxford, 22 April, 1826, aged seventeen.

[4] Ellerburn Register.

[5] Ibid.

[6] A Frederick Shum matriculated at Brasenose College, Oxford, in 1811. He was ordained and held several curacies and died 24 December, 1877. It is not certain whether the curate at Ellerburn was the same man. Madeline (died 1874), daughter of the Ellerburn curate, married John Elliott (died 1910) and was the mother of Frederick and George Elliott.

[7] Ellerburn Register. The Rev. J. M. Raines kindly tells me that the burials registered in 1863 were 18; 1864, 17; 1865, 18; 1866, 16; 1867, 16; 1868, 13, proving that there was no serious epidemic.

[8] Mrs. Hugall owned the 'Old Vicarage' as late as 1869, *vide* Rate Books.

[9] Afterwards vicar of Ganton: a devoted lover of cricket, died 1904.

[10] He forgot to recognise his parishioners, and one old villager, being hurt, said to me 'he ganged paast wi' his t'ead oop i' t'elements.'

[11] Crockford's *Clerical Directory.*

to the day of his death in 1926, by which time he had become an enthusiastic lover of the old church and of everything connected with the parish.

The present incumbent is the Rev. John Marshall Raimes who took his B.A. at Lincoln College, Oxford, in 1908 and his M.A. in 1912. He was curate at St. James's, Upper Edmonton, in 1909-13, at Monk Bretton 1913-15, at Newington, Kingston-upon-Hull 1915-19 and at St. Mary's, Lowgate, in the same place 1919-26.

As has already been stated,[1] a commission sat in 1930, and decided that the smaller vicarage of Ellerburn shall at some future and convenient time cease to be separated from the larger rectory of Thornton, thus producing an ecclesiastical union of Thornton, Ellerburn, and Wilton.

[1] *Vide* Ch. IX.

Part II.

———

The History of the Manors

CHAPTER ELEVEN.

The Tor-Albemarle-Eshton-Latimer Manor.

———

'It often happened that the township included one or more manors.'

HONE, 1906.

IT has already been shown that the whole district of Thornton was terribly ravaged by William the Conqueror in 1069.[1] So great was the devastation caused that the lands at Thornton were barely worthy of mention in Domesday Book, but, in that 'greatest legal monument of the Conqueror's reign,'[2] it was very briefly stated that in the village there were three manors in Anglo-Saxon times, held by Torbrand, Gospatric, and Tor, and that they had three carucates[3] for geld. It was, in the Recapitulation, recorded that in 'Torentun the King has five and a half carucates.'[4] These statements produce two problems. The first is, which of these manors was kept in the hands of a member of the royal house? And the second, why had William the Conqueror five and a half carucates when only three were entered previously? In answer to the first question, by a process of elimination, it may be shown that the later owners of two of the manors, Brus and de Todeni, did not in any part of Yorkshire receive the land of Tor, nor did de Todeni in any part receive the lands of Gospatric. Therefore the latter must have held the manor of Torbrand, and that of Gospatric must have passed to Brus. It has already been suggested that 'Torentun' is not an early and long continuous name, but a late one associated with its chief owner,[5] and it may be fairly safe to assume that it was Tor's manor that was the main one in the 'township' of Thornton, and was reserved by William for a relative.

---

[1] *Vide* Ch. I.

[2] Maitland, *Constitutional History of England*, p. 8.

[3] The original hide or hiwisc was sufficient land for the maintenance of a warrior and his family, and it consisted of no definite area. In later times, for fiscal purposes, it was 120 acres arable. In the north its equivalent was the Danish-named carucate from '*caruca*,' a plough. After the reign of Richard I., the Anglo-Saxon term hide begins to decline, and carucate takes its place both in the north and the south.

[4] Domesday Book.

[5] *Vide* Ch. I.

As to the variation of the number of carucates a possible solution may be that the extra two and a half carucates were found before the Recapitulation was drawn up and the record was finally completed.

Soon after the Conquest, Tor's manor was granted by William I. to his sister,[1] Adelaide, or Adeliz, named in Domesday Book, 'Comitissa de Albarmarla,'[2] and thus Thornton came to be in the fee of Albemarle. It is unnecessary to investigate all the marriages of this much-married lady; but it may here be stated that she married, thirdly, the Count of Champagne, and by him had a son, Stephen, Count of Aumale or Albemarle, Lord of Holderness, about 1070. He married Hawise, daughter of the well-known Ralph Mortimer, and had three children. The first, Agnes, married Adam de Brus, and died about 1143.[3] The second, William le Gros, is supposed to have built Scarborough Castle about 1134,[4] founded the Abbey of Meaux in 1150,[5] and his nickname gives some idea of the man. He married Cicely, Lady of Skipton, daughter of William Fitz-Duncan, and by her, had a daughter, Hawise, named after her grandmother, and who married twice. Her first husband was in 1180, William de Mandeville, Earl of Essex, son of the notorious Geoffrey de Mandeville, and who, through his wife, claimed the title of Count or Earl of Aumale. It is during his life that there is the first reference to the manor of Thornton, since Domesday Book.[6] He died at Rouen in November, 1189. Her second husband was William de Forz, and, again through his wife, Count of Aumale. They were married about 1190; and had a son William, Earl of Aumale or Albemarle and lord of the manor of Thornton, who married Aveline, daughter of Ralf de Montfichet. She died in 1239, but he did not die until 1241, when he succumbed to starvation in crossing the Mediterranean Sea.[7] He left an heir to the Albemarle estates in his son, William, born 1237, who married secondly, Isabel, daughter of Baldwin de Rivers. He died on 23

---

[1] T. Stapleton, *Archaeologia* XXVI. p. 357 says that Adeliz was not the sister but the niece of the Conqueror.

[2] Domesday Book.

[3] Their child was Adam Brus who married Ivetta, granddaughter of Osbert de Arches, sheriff of York, and whose name is perpetuated in Thorp Arch.

[4] Eastmead, *ut supra*, p. 348.

[5] Chron. Mon. de Melsa. Rolls Cer. I., p. xlii.

[6] Cartulary of Rievaulx. Sur. Soc., LXXXIII. p. 118. His tenants do not seem to have been above reproach for the Pipe Roll XXXVI., p. 95, records for 1185-6, '*Homines ville de Toriton' de parte comitis Willelmi reddt. comp. de ij. m. pro. virdi foreste et pro bosco vastato. In Thesauro liberaverunt.*'

[7] '*In marie Mediterraneo peregrinans, cum nullo modo posset comedere et octo diebus jejunando martirium protelasset, die veneris proxima ante Pascha.*' M. Paris, IV., p. 174.

May, 1260,[1] leaving three children: Thomas, who died in 1269, Avice, who died the same year, and Aveline, who married Edmund Crouchback, son of Henry III., and lord of Pickering. But she died without issue on 10 November, 1274.[2] Who then was heir to the fee of Albemarle?

It has been stated above, that Stephen, Count of Albemarle had a third child. This was Simon and descended from him— probably his great-grandson—was one Philip de Wivelsby or Wivelby. He petitioned, in 1276, for various manors, including that in Thornton, against a certain John de Eston, Eshton, or Ashton.[3] This John de Eshton derived his name from Eshton, in the parish of Gargrave, in the West Riding; and he alleged that he was descended from Avicia, daughter of William le Gros, and half-sister of Hawise, who had married William de Forz.[4] But Avicia was, almost certainly, the daughter of a nun, and was there- fore illegitimate. Sir C. G. Young[5] thinks that John de Eshton's claim was a fiction,[6] 'to give the King a colourable pretence for retaining the Honour in his own hands, as by admitting the fictitious claim and then purchasing it from him, he shut out all that claim that might have been justly made by Wivelby, who afterwards proved his descent.' And it certainly does look as if there were something peculiar in the whole circumstances of the case, as proved by the fact that the King gave John de Eshton land to the value of £100 per annum in Thornton and in Skipton,[7] 'in lieu of the hereditary right which he claimed in the Cty. of

---

[1] During the period of William de Albemarle, it would appear that Levisham was subordinate to the manor of Thornton. On 31 March, 1276, the jury had to decide, 'if Roger le Bygot [*sic*], Earl of Norfolk and Marshal of England, or his ancestors, tenants of the manor of "Leviscam," used at any time to do suit at the court of Thorneton in Pykeringlithe (formerly of William Earl of Albemarle, and his heirs, and now in the King's hands) for the said manor or not. They say that neither Roger le Bygot nor his ancestors ever did suit at the Court of Thorneton for the manor of "Levescam," but one, Osbert de "Bolebake," who formerly held the manor in the time of William de Fortibus, Earl of Albemarle, last deceased [1260], did suit at the said court, until Hugh de Bygot [*sic*], father of the said Earl, was enfeoffed of the manor, but how and by what warrant the suit for the manor was afterwards withdrawn the jurors know not.' *Cf.* Y. A. S. Rec. S. XII., p. 166. V. C. H. *N.R.*, II., p. 450 says that Osbert de 'Bolebec,' son of Ralph, sold his land at Levisham and elsewhere to Hugh Bigod about 1255. Ralph de Bolebec had already granted some land and the mill to the Priory of Malton. But this Hugh Bigod acquired by exchange.
[2] *Complete Peerage*, I., pp. 356-7.
[3] Cal. Char. R., II., p. 208.
[4] A Coram Rege Roll. M.T. 4 Ed. I. (1276) quoted by Dodsworth CXLIV. 22 gives the pedigree of the claimants.
[5] Coll: Top: et Gen: VI. 261.
[6] *Complete Peerage*, I., pp. 356-7.
[7] Y. A. S. Rec. S. XXXI., p. 146.

Aumale etc....and for the same the said John performs the service of one Knight.'[1]

John de Eshton was evidently in favour with Edward I. On 12 November, 1281, he and his heirs had a grant of a weekly market on Tuesday, at his 'manor of Thorneton,' and two yearly fairs, one on the vigil, the feast, and the morrow of Holy Trinity, and the other on the same occasions[2] of All Saints.[3] It must not, however, be supposed that all the lands inside his manorial jurisdiction were his actual possessions, for there were certain lands held from the King-in-chief by Henry de Edlingthorp of 'Thorneton in Pickering-lithe.' When this man died, John de Eshton 'claimed a right because Henry died without a lawful heir of his body,' and John entered upon these lands. Edward I., continuing his generous treatment, on 20 October, 1282, instructed the escheator, Thomas de Norman-vill, to deliver the lands to Eshton.[4] The matter, however, was evidently not settled, for on 8 February, 1290, the escheator was ordered, from Westminster, to replevy to 'Hugh de Luchre,'[5] until a month from Easter next, his lands which had been taken into the King's hands, at the suit of the heir of Henry de Edling-thorp, tenant-in-chief, on the condition that Hugh answered for the issues, if the King wished to have them.[6] In the meantime, John de Eshton held his court at Thornton 'de tribus septimanis in tres septimanas,'[7] et capiunt emendas de pistoribus et bracia-tricibus.'[8] On 28 June, 1283, he had still further proof of the King's good-will as he was acquitted from paying the ancient tallage of twenty marks which was formerly exacted from Thornton.[9] At this period his mesne tenants in the manor were Alan, son of John, holding 6 bovates, Hugh Brown, 2 bovates, Stephen, son of Alan, 2 bovates, Robert de Caishliffe, 3 bovates, Alan the chaplain, 1 bovate, William de 'Everle,' 1 bovate, Henry de 'Eston,'

---

[1] Cal. Char. R. II., p. 208.

[2] Ibid., p. 257.

[3] Till the time of Edward I. the fairs were frequently held in the churchyard. *Cf.* Hone, *The Manor and Manorial Records*, p. 121.

[4] Cal. Fine R. I., p. 170.

[5] Rot. Parl. I., p. 34 spells the name 'Louther.'

[6] Cal. Fine R. I., p. 270.

[7] Lyttleton's *Tenures*, p. 108, says 'suit service is to come to the court from three weeks to three weeks by the whole year, and for that a man shall be distrained but not amerced. Suit real is to come to the court leet, and that is but two times in the year, and for that a man shall be amerced and not distrained.' In practice the free tenants were amerced for non-attendance at the court baron.

[8] Cal. Feud. Aids. VI., pp. 83-4.

[9] Cal. Close R., 1279-88, p. 211.

1 bovate,[1] and James de Mora, 10 bovates.[2] At the same time John de Eshton was himself a tenant of some freehold land in Thornton which belonged to Bigod, Earl of Norfolk. As early as 12 December, 1234, this question of tenancy had been decided between Roger, Earl of Norfolk, and William de Forz, Earl of Albemarle;[3] and long after, in 1284, it was stated to be the fact by local jurators.[4]

How the Bigods obtained this particular piece of land in Thornton is not clear; but as they were lords of the manors of Wilton, Levisham, and Settrington, they obviously had considerable interests in the neighbourhood.[5] Hugh Bigod, the justiciar, and younger son of the third Earl of Norfolk, would know the country well, for in 1256, he was appointed governor of Pickering Castle, from which he was transferred to Scarborough in 1260, and reappointed to Pickering four years later.[6] The family was evidently desirous of rounding off its possessions in Yorkshire, and Roger Bigod, the fifth Earl, negotiated with John de Eshton to alienate[7] the Thornton manor to him. To find whether such alienation was legal, a writ was issued on 11 June, 1294, and an inquisition was held at 'Thorneton,' on Friday, 9 July, to see 'whether or not it be to the damage or prejudice of the King if he grant to John de Eston that he may enfeoff the manor of Thornton near Pyk' with the appurtenances, which he holds of the King in chief, Roger le Bygot [*sic*] ....to have and to hold of the King and his heirs to him [the earl], his heirs and assigns for ever.' The jurators[8]

[1] Henry de 'Eston' was John's brother. The other brothers were, Robert, who had a son John, born about 1276: James, alive in 1299: and Richard, who married Juliana, and had a son William, who was alive in 1332.

[2] Kirby's Inquest, Sur. Soc., XLIX. p. 145.

[3] Y. A. S. Rec. S. LXVII., p. 29.

[4] Cal. Feud. Aids. VI., p. 82.

[5] Osbert, son of Ralph Bolbeck resigned all his rights to the King who, 27 May, 40 Hen. III. gave all rights in Levisham, Lockton, Newton and Pickering to Hugh Bigod. *Vide* a seventeenth century copy of Patent Roll, G. F. G. H. This differs from V. C. H. *N.R.* II. p. 450.

[6] He died November, 1266.

[7] Pollock and Maitland, *History of English Law*, I., p. 316, write 'Britton states that earls, barons, knights and serjeants, who held of the King-in-chief cannot, without his licence, alienate their fees, but the King may eject the purchasers, no matter how ancient the alienation, since time does not run against the King. Fleta states that no tenements held of the King can be given without his assent. This becomes the law of after times. Before the end of Edward's reign, both theory and practice draw a marked distinction between the King and other lords, and the King is making a considerable revenue out of licences to alienate and fines for alienations effected without licence.'

[8] Those on the inquisition were mainly of local importance. They were, Sir William Malkake, Thomas de Edbriston, William de Nevile, William de la Chymene, John White [*blundum*], John son of Robert of Alverstain [Allerston], John son of Odo of the same, Alan Pye of 'Thorneton,' Adam son of Isabel of the same, Alexander de Percy, Robert de Vall' of Loketon [Lockton], and Robert de Rostan [Ruston, near Wykeham].

said 'that it is not to the damage or prejudice of the King' to do so. 'The said manor is worth by the year in all issues £31. 18s. 6½d.'[1]

Everything seems to have been satisfactory, for on the following 17 October, an order was sent to the escheator to permit Roger 'le Bigod' to enter and hold the manor of Thornton near 'Pikeryng as the King learns....that it is not to his damage or prejudice to grant to John de Aston [Eshton] power to enfeoff the Earl of the said manor, which John holds of the King-in-chief.'[2] As far as is known, Roger Bigod was, up to this time, a loyal subject of the King. But after 1295 quarrels arose, and when in 1297, the King ordered Bigod and Bohun, Earl of Hereford, to Gascony, while he himself intended to go to Flanders, there came the celebrated outburst on Bigod's refusal to serve except in person with the King. 'By God, Sir Earl, you will either go or hang,' shouted Edward I. To which Bigod replied 'By God, Sir King, I will neither go nor hang.'[3] The quarrel waxed hot and furious, but so long as Bohun lived, with his support, Bigod held his own; but after his coadjutor's death in 1298, everything went against him; and in 1301, Bigod so much collapsed that he made the King his heir.[4] On 12 April, 1302, Roger gave into the King's hand his Marshal's staff, and granted all his lands to Edward, except 'the manors of Setrington, Wylton, Thorneton and Levesham.'[5] On the same day Edward granted to Bigod a licence to alienate these manors,[6] to whomsoever he wished. The mesne holders in the Thornton manor in this year were, Hugh 'de Luther'[7] with 10 bovates, Henry de 'Eston' with 1 bovate, and William de Ormesby with an amount not definitely specified.[8]

William de Ormesby,[9] was a knight and judge of the King's Bench; and the first step that Bigod took to alienate the manor of

[1] Y. A. S. Rec. S. XXIII., p. 164.

[2] Cal. Close R. 1288-96, p. 370.

[3] Hemingburgh ii., p. 121, records, 'Et iratus rex prorupit in haec verba, ut dicitur; "*Per Deum, Comes, aut ibis aut pendebis.*" Et illi "*Per idem juramentum, O rex, nec ibi nec pendebo.*'

[4] D. N. B. *Cf.* Jenks, *Edward Plantagenet*, p. 276.

[5] Cal. Close R. 1296-1302, p. 581.

[6] Y. A. S. Rec. S. XXXIX., p. 170 says that the grant included the advowsons of the three; but as Wilton was under Pickering at the time, and Pickering was under the Archbishop of York, it could not be true. It is not very likely that Bigod ever had the advowson of Thornton. *Vide* Ch. IX.

[7] *Cf.* for Hugo de 'Luther' Cal. Chanc. R. I., p. 73, which says 17 November, 1303, 'The Earl of Lancaster, the King's nephew, has....letters to the Justices of the Bench for an assize of novel disseisin that Hugh de "Louthre" arramed against him for common pasture in Est Thornton in "Pykeringlith" co. York until Easter.'

[8] Cal. Feud. Aids. VI., p. 136.

[9] D. N. B.

Thornton was to enfeoff him. From what happened afterwards, it is certain that this was merely a stage in the legal process of transfer; but, for the moment, Sir William de Ormesby was the lord of the manor, and was badgered for the debts of the late lord, the Earl of Norfolk. This, however, was not for long, for an order was sent to the Treasurer and barons of the Exchequer, on 11 March, 1303, saying 'whereas William de Ormesby holds the manor of "Thorneton near Pykering," of the gift and feoffment of Roger Bigod....and they cause William—to be distrained in that manor for the debts due from the Earl to the Exchequer, omitting the lands of the Earl himself, the King orders them to desist from distraining William de Ormesby, and to cause the Earl to be distrained on his own land, since he has sufficient.'[1] On the next day after this order the manor was transferred to Sir John de Drokenesford,[2] 'clerk,' as he is described, 'to Sir Edward[3] the King's son';[4] and he in turn conveyed to Sir William 'le Latymer'.[5] About the same time, but the date is unknown,[6] Sir William 'le Latymer,' lord of Scampston, received from John de Lythe of 'Whitteby,' 'a messuage in Thornton in Pikering-lythe lying in breadth between the land of Cecily,[7] daughter of Alan of Thornton, and that formerly belonging to William de Shirburne, and in length from the Highway of Thornton to the land of John,[8] son of Alan.'[9]

The family of Latimer had been settled at Billinges, Yorkshire, since the reign of Richard I. William Latimer was sheriff of Yorkshire between 1253 and 1259, and succeeded Hugh Bigod as Keeper of Pickering Castle in 1266. His son, William, was first baron Latimer, a brave but needy and avaricious soldier and a comrade in arms of Edward I. He married Alice, Amicia, or Agnes,[10] eldest daughter and coheiress of Walter Ledet, baron Braybroke,

---

[1] Cal. Close R. 1302-7, p. 19.

[2] Sir John de Drokenesford had charge of the Great Seal for a short time in 1302, and was appointed Bishop of Bath and Wells in 1309. He died 1329. *Cf.* Tout, *The Place of Edward II. in English History*, pp. 78, 344-5.

[3] Afterwards, Edward II.

[4] Y. A. S. Rec. S. XXXIX., p. 170.

[5] Ibid. The witnesses were, Sir Brian son of Alan, Sir Edmund Deyncourt, Sir John de Sothull, Sir Thomas le Latymer of Warden, Sir Warin de Insula of Kyngeston, Sir John de Wygton, Sir Henry de Bosco, Sir John de Barton of Friton, Sir Gerard Salvayn, and Sir John de Heselerton.

[6] But it is after the Statute of Quia Emptores in 1290.

[7] Great-niece of Gilbert 'the parson'; *vide* Ch. IX.

[8] John was either brother or cousin of Cecily.

[9] Y. A. S. Rec. S. XXXIX., p. 171. The witnesses were, Edmund de Hastynges, John Morin, William de Yeland, William de Everle, Thomas Brette, William Thornef, William de Wyerne, Russet de Thornton, and William Tenelby.

[10] She died in 1316.

who represented the Ledets, lords of Warden.[1] They had two sons, John, who died without issue in 1299, and William, who was born about 1276, and was lord of Scampston and of Sinnington. He married in August, 1294,[2] Lucy de Thweng, or Tweng, at that time fifteen years and five months old. 'She was the only child of Sir Robert Tweng (ob. 1279), of Kilton Castle, N.R., by his wife Matilda, daughter and coheir of Sir Roger Merley, of Morpeth Castle, Northumberland, and was heir to her grandmother Lucy,[3] one of the sisters and coheirs of the last of the powerful Brus barons of Skelton Castle. She thus became the ward of the King, who, against the wishes of her relatives,[4] gave her in marriage to William Latimer. . . . The marriage was an unhappy one, partly because of the unpleasant character of Latimer, partly because of the frivolous and lively character of the wealthy heiress.'[5] From the first, Lucy both hated and despised her husband. She had already given 'ample proof of the laxity of morals for which she subsequently became so notorious,' and at the time of her marriage, was likely soon to become a mother by her cousin Marmaduke.[6] The son was born in December, 1294, and in the next few months Lucy deserted her husband and openly lived as the mistress of Marmaduke Tweng at Kilton. William Latimer took part in the Scottish wars between 1297 and 1304,[7] and during this period his wife became first the mistress of young Peter de Mauley, 'afterwards the notorious Peter V';[8] and secondly of Lord Meynell, by whom she had a son Nicholas, born in 1303.[9] It was while she was living with Lord Meynell that William Latimer obtained a divorce in the Consistory

[1] D. N. B.
[2] Y. A. J. XXII., pp. 85-91.
[3] The four sisters of Peter de Brus III., had been claimants of the Albemarle manor of Thornton, when granted to John de Eshton.
[4] Her uncle was much opposed to this marriage.
[5] Y. A. J. XXIX., p. 19. The V. C. H. N.R. II., p. 336, gives a slightly different account of the wardship. It says 'In 1285 the custody of Danby and other lands during the minority of Lucy daughter and heir of Robert eldest son of Marmaduke and Lucy (G. E. C., Peerage VII., p. 400) was granted to William le Latimer, sen., Lord Latimer, Robert FitzWalter and William de Leyburn. (Cal. Pat. R. 1281-92, pp. 179-80).'
[6] Y. A. J. XXII., pp. 85-91.
[7] In 1300, it is clear that William and Lucy had not parted legally, for Y. A. S. Rec. S. XVII., p. 224 shows William le Latimer, junior and Lucy his wife complained of William, Abbot of 'Whitoby' and William de Roscles, for forcibly abducting Alexander, son and heir of William de Percy at 'Aselby,' the said Alexander being a minor whose marriage belonged to the plaintiffs.
[8] Y. A. J. XXII., pp. 85-91.
[9] Ibid. XXIX., p. 19, says 'Lord Meynell settled his estates on this boy, in the event of having no legitimate issue, and the barony of Meynell passed to him to the exclusion of Meynell's legitimate heir, his brother, Sir John Meynell, (ob. 1337) of Castle Levington, N.R.'

Court of York, and the son, born in 1294, was declared illegitimate.[1]

William Latimer continued to serve the King in Scotland, and after Edward II. came to the throne, took part in his disastrous attempt to reconquer the northern Kingdom, and was taken prisoner, on 24 June, 1314, at Bannockburn.[2] He was liberated the next year; and in 1316, was definitely mentioned as lord of the manor of Thornton.[3] At this period England was rent by the trouble existing between the misunderstood King and the Lords Ordainers, and for a time William Latimer ranged himself on their side, and was a friend of their leader, the turbulent and treacherous Thomas, Earl of Lancaster. But, in 1319, Latimer was pardoned for his perfidious conduct, and in March, 1322, was present at the battle of Boroughbridge, where his erstwhile friend, Thomas of Lancaster, was carried off an ignominious prisoner to Pontefract. Latimer was despatched with all haste to occupy Lancaster's stronghold at Pickering; and the 'Ministers Accounts' of the period show 'expenses of the men of William Latimer residing at Pickering for 4 days to seize the Castle into the King's hands ....8s. 10¾d.'[4]

When John de Eshton transferred his manor in Thornton to the Earl of Norfolk, it seems that a small portion had already been alienated elsewhere. This is made clear during the lordship of William Latimer, and is stated in an inquest *post mortem* dated 4 December, 1325. The document concerns 'Henry le Chaumberlayn'[5] who had in 'Thornton in Pykeringlithe,' a messuage, a toft, 1 bovate, 12 acres, 1 rood of arable land and 3 acres of meadow held jointly with his wife, Alice, who survived her husband. These lands were 'held of the King-in-Chief, as of the honour of

---

[1] From this time Lucy Tweng disappears out of the history of the Latimers; but it might be noticed that in 1313 she married Sir Robert de Everingham, great grandson of Robert de Everingham, who died 1246; and in 1320 she again married, and this time probably an old love, Sir Bartholomew de Fanacourt, who had been page to her first husband. She died 8 January, 1346.

[2] D. N. B.

[3] Cal. Feud. Aids. VI., p. 177.

[4] N. R. Rec. S. N.S. IV., p. 206.

[5] Hist. MSS. Com., Rawden Hastings MS. I., p. 192 shows that on 6 March, 1316/7, Henry 'Chaumburlayne' made a grant of a small quantity of land. It states that he was the brother of Sir John de 'Eston' 'chaplain.' The document is witnessed by Thornton residents, Edmund de Hastinges, John son of Alan, Adam son of Isabel, William Hert and Alan 'Souer' [? Gower]. Another untraceable little bit of land of this period was granted by Robert de Joueby, son and heir of Thomas de Joueby and Joan his wife, to his two sisters Nicholaa and Joan. This is witnessed by Edmund de Hastinges, John de Cliff, John son of Alan. *Cf.* Hist. MSS. Com., *ut supra.*

Albemarle,[1] by service of 1/40 of a knight's fee.'[2] On the same
day a command was sent to the escheator, Simon Grymnesby, to
take these lands into the hands of the King;[3] and there they remained
for more than a year. But on 6 February, 1327, the escheator was
ordered 'to cause Alice, late the wife of Henry le Chaumberlayne
....to have seisin of certain lands in Thornton in Pykeringlith
and to deliver the issue thereof to her....and the King has taken
the fealty[4] of Alice.'[5] Whether Alice really lived until 1392, or about
that date, it is impossible to say, but her lands appear again on
5 February, 1392, when a pardon was granted by Richard II.,
after payment of one mark 'by Nicholas son and heir of William
de Hastynges of Thornton in Pykerynglith' for the trespass
'committed in the acquisition in fee simple *without licence* by the
said William from Alice, late the wife of Henry Chamberlayne....
of land in Thornton....and grant to the said Nicholas of the
premises in fee simple.'[6]

In the meantime there was a likelihood of trouble about the
Thornton manor when 'William le Latymer,' died in February,
1326/7. The inquest on his property was held on 3 March,[7] but
the document as far as the Thornton property is concerned has
been defaced. 'An old copy, found in the Tower [of London] is,
however, extant. It states that at one time he held (amongst other
manors) the manors of Thornton in Pickeringlith and of Sinnington,
but that before his death he granted them to his son, William
le Latimer in tail with remainder to his son Thomas in tail with
remainder to his son Warin in tail male, with remainder to his
own right heirs.'[8] An inquest had already been held to see
if the King would be endamaged and it concluded that he would

---

[1] *Dictionary of English History*, p. 574, says the term honour was used
'especially of the more noble sort of seignories on which other inferior lord-
ships or manors depend by performance of some customs or services to those
who are lords of them'....'Though each of the various manors composing
the honour had its own separate jurisdiction, yet only one court was held
for the whole....under the Norman Kings the number of these greater
franchises or honours increased largely.'

[2] Cal. Inq. VI. Ed. II., No. 649.

[3] Cal. Fine R. III., p. 368.

[4] *Cf.* Pollock and Maitland, *ut supra*, II., p. 412.

[5] Cal. Close R 1327-30, p. 33.

[6] Cal. Pat. R., 1391-6, p. 22.

[7] Cal. Inq. VII. Ed. III., No. 56.

[8] N. R. Rec. S. N.S. II., p. 265. The editor says 'this shows a little
doubt in the accuracy of the copy. It is difficult to see why the limitation
to the youngest son should be in tail male and to the two elder in tail general.'
The copy has missed out the remainder to Thomas le Latymer of Warden.

not.[1] This being the case on 8 March, a pardon was granted to William Latimer for acquiring in fee tail from his father the manor of Thornton and entering thereon without licence, and restitution was made to him.[2] The whole question of his succession is somewhat curious, for, shortly after his birth, he had been declared illegitimate, but immediately after the death of his father, he was accepted as legitimate,[3] though everyone who knew anything about it, would be convinced that he was the son of Marmaduke Tweng. His birth, however, having been satisfactorily settled, he married Elizabeth, daughter of John, lord Botetourt.[4]

Unlike other lords of the manor this William, third baron Latimer, was frequently in the village of Thornton, and if he did not actually reside where now stands the Hall, he lived near by at Sinnington, and on his poaching expeditions was often in the place.[5] It was fortunate for him that he died at the beginning of June, 1335, for otherwise he would have suffered imprisonment for a year, if he had dared to face the court, or outlawry if he did not appear. He was, however, dead by Monday, 19 June,[6] as his inquest *post mortem* was held that day. This inquest is a particularly interesting one as giving a full description of his Thornton manor. It was decided that 'William Latimer held in demesne as of fee.... the manor of Thornton in Pickeringlith with certain tenements in Ayton of the King in-chief as of the honor of Albemarle, then in the King's hands, by the service of one knight's fee charged with the payment of a quit rent of 6s. 5d.[7] payable on St. Andrew's day, Palm Sunday, Midsummer and Michaelmas, at Pickering Castle, which is in the possession of Henry of Lancaster.[8] The yearly values are as follows:—In the manor there is a chief messuage[9]

---

[1] Y. A. S. Rec. S. XXI., p. 30. At this time the manor of Thornton was said to be only worth £10 per annum owing to destruction by the Scots. *Cf.* Inq. *ad quod damnum*, file 180, No. 14, 18 Ed. II.

[2] Cal. Pat. R., 1327-30, p. 30.

[3] Y. A. J. XXII. *Cf.* F. Y. in M. P., p. 286.

[4] D. N. B.

[5] *Vide* Ch. II.

[6] Cal. Inq. VII. Ed. III., No. 689 says 'Monday before S. Thomas the Apostle,' but *cf.* N. R. Rec. S. N.S. II. p. 273 which contains the Inquest and says 'Monday before the feast of S. John the Baptist.'

[7] *Vide infra.*

[8] Henry, brother of Thomas, b. c. 1281: d. 1345.

[9] The chief messuage is stated (Chan. Inq. p.m. 4. Ric. II. no. 35) to have been in ruins in 1380. This probably accounts for the fact that the Latimers preferred to stay at Sinnington when in the north of England. (Cal. Pat. R., 1401-5, p. 482). It is interesting to notice that in this summary of the manor there is no reference to an '*aquarium*' or manorial fish-pond. To-day these ponds at the Hall are very picturesque, the general character of the walls etc. being Dutch. They probably acquired their present appearance in the reign of William III., but they must have been in existence for many generations before that. *Vide* Ch. VI.

worth in garden produce and herbage 13s. 4d.; twenty-five oxgangs in demesne worth 13s. 4d. an oxgang: total £16. 13s. 4d. Demesne lands called Avenames[1] containing twenty-four acres, worth 8d. each, total 16s. two and a half acres of meadow in demesne called the Newfirth, worth 18d. an acre, total 3s. 9d.; one oxgang of arable in demesne, which ought to be in the hands of tenants-at-will worth 10s.; a water-mill,[2] worth and paying 53s. 4d.; a fulling-mill,[3] worth and paying £1; a common oven[4] in the hands of a tenant-at-will paying 3s.; rent of freeholders 13s. 4d.; rents of bondmen and tenants-at-will, £17; rents of cottars £4. 15s. 8d.; twenty-one days' work in reaping corn to be provided by the tenants, each day's work worth beyond the food, which the lord provides, 1d., total 1s. 9d.; at Ayton rents of freeholders, worth 3s., pleas and perquisites of the Court 13s. 4d. Total £46. Deduct 6s. 5d. rent to Pickering Castle. Net value £45. 13s. 7d.[5]

William, fourth baron Latimer, succeeded his father at six years of age, and was not granted livery of his lands until 1351.[6] Five years later he married Elizabeth, daughter of Richard FitzAlan, Earl of Arundel, and his daughter Elizabeth was born the following year. In 1359 he was away fighting in Gascony, and, after the celebrated Treaty of Bretigny, was made a Knight of the Garter in 1361. He was obviously very unpopular in Thornton both in 1367 and 1369,[7] as seen by the attacks on his property. Nor was he any more favourably regarded by Parliament, for he is famous in constitutional history as the first man to be impeached by the House of Commons at the bar of the House of Lords. The Good Parliament of 1376 declared him to be an evil adviser, but being a great personal friend of John of Gaunt, Duke of Lancaster, and lord of Pickering, the attempt to bring him to justice failed. John of Gaunt, after the death of Edward the Black Prince, was all-powerful in 1377, and Latimer was rewarded for his evil deeds with the governorship of Calais.[8] After some fighting in France in 1380, he died on 28 May, 1381, of paralysis, and was buried in

---

[1] A. H. Smith, *ut supra*, p. 144 says that the word is from O. Eng. *haefen*, a refuge, a shelter; but on p. 329 says 'Afnam' i.e., land taken from common land from O. Norman 'afuima, to seize.' In the Whitby Cartulary (1190-1227) there is the word 'ofnames': at Middlesborough in the twelfth century there is Houenam. *Cf.* in Roxby document, 1580, Hornums, spelt in 1710 Anham and in 1796 Aunums.

[2] *Vide supra.*

[3] *Vide supra.*

[4] The lord's oven was a matter of legal controversy as late as the reign of James I. *Cf.* Mrs. J. R. Green, *ut supra*, I., p. 199.

[5] N. R. Rec. S. N.S. II., pp. 273-4.

[6] D. N. B.

[7] Cal. Pat. R., 1367-70, pp. 63, 264 and *vide* Ch. IV.

[8] This had been captured thirty years before.

the Priory of 'Gisburn en Cliveland.'[1] He was not a man of estimable qualities, but rather a despicable person, 'a man of very lax morality and a slave to avarice. His luxurious habits made him no use in war. He was proud, cruel and irreligious, deceitful and untrust-worthy. He had enough eloquence but a lack of wisdom.'[2] His widow survived him for three years and died in 1384.

The lordship of Thornton, and all that appertained to the barony of Latimer, passed to William's daughter and heiress Elizabeth. She married first, about 1380, as his second wife, John, Lord Neville of Raby.[3] Their child was born in 1381, as shown in later years by a proof of age, 'taken at "Midelham".' He 'was born in Midelham Castle in the tower called Barountoure, and baptized in the Church of St. Mary in the same town, 12 June' 1381. His nurse was 'Eufemia de Ketiwell.'[4] Elizabeth Neville became a widow on 17 October, 1388, and married secondly, Robert, Lord Willoughby de Eresby, as his second wife and apparently had a child by him. After her death on 5 November, 1395, an order was given on 14 February, 1396, to Peter de Bukton, escheator of Yorkshire, to take the fealty 'of Robert de Wilughby, Knt. and to give him livery of the manors of Danby and Thornton in Pikeryng-lith, Synelyngton and Lyverton and the issues....; as the King has learned by inquisition....that Elizabeth who was the said Robert's wife at her death held the manors of Danby and Thornton in chief by Knt service,....and that he has issue between them begotten, wherefore the same pertain to him for life to hold by the *curtesy of England*';[5] and 'for one mark paid in the hanaper[6] the

---

[1] William Latimer said in his will, made just before his death, 'et mon corps d'estre en l'esglise de Prioralte de Gisburn en Cliveland, devant le haut auter nostre Dame.' *Cf.* Test. Ebor. Sur. Soc., IV., I., pp. 113-4.

[2] D. N. B.

[3] The arms of this nobleman are conspicuous both on the Castle of Danby and the old bridge below the castle. *Cf.* F. Y. in M. P., p. 292.

[4] Y. A. S. Rec. S. LIX., pp. 42-3.

[5] Reeves, *History of English Law*, I., p. 298, writes 'Bracton says, the husband should have the land if he married a woman *habentem haereditatem, vel maritagium, vel aliquam terram ex causa donationis*....He agrees with Glanville that the second husband was equally intitled with the first.' Sir Robert de Willoughby would establish his title to Elizabeth's possessions by this curtesy; and it is possible to imagine him, according to the custom of the time, outside his wife's chamber, at the hour of birth, listening for the wail of the child, which must be audible within the four walls, (*cf.* Pollock and Maitland, *ut supra*, II., p. 345) and which would inform him that he had acquired 'his curtesy.' This somewhat remarkable right arose from the idea that 'the law of England' was a courteous law (Ibid. p. 414). It gave to the husband very liberal privileges. Reeves, *ut supra*, p. 299, says 'The tenant *per legem Angliae* was to have all incidents that happened, whether in service, wards, reliefs or the like during his life.'

[6] Originally a kind of hamper for carrying the King's money when on a journey, and so came to be considered the King's treasury and thus a department of State.

King has respited his homage[1] until the quinzaine[2] of Easter next.'[3]

Presumably Robert, Lord Willoughby de Eresby, died about 1403, and the possessions of Elizabeth reverted to her son by the first marriage, who had already succeeded to the barony on his mother's death. An inquest was held on 2 January, 1403/4, because he claimed the livery of his inheritance as 'heir of Elizabeth who was the wife of John de Nevyle of Raby, chivaler, deceased.'[4] For legal or financial reasons John Neville, now Lord 'Latymer,' obtained a licence, after paying 100 marks into the hanaper, on 24 July, 1405, 'to enfeoff Gerard Braybroke, chivaler, Baldwin Pygott, chivaler, Edmund "Hastynges," chivaler, John Hervy, Henry de Nesfield and John Lovell of his manors of Danby and Thornton in Pykerynglythe, co. York, except an acre of land in the manor of Danby.[5] It is clear as late as 25 March, 1428, that the ownership of the manor in Thornton is a little uncertain for at the time of a collection of a subsidy an inquest had to be held at Brompton, and it was there declared that the holders of the manor were, the Earl of Westmorland, Robert 'Bruys,'[6] Robert Barde[7] and William Gower.[8] A very unusual thing had happened, for John Neville had transferred the barony to his half-brother, Ralph Neville, first Earl of Westmorland; and when John died in December, 1430,[9] the manor of Thornton passed to George, son of the Earl, by his second marriage with Joan, daughter of John of Gaunt.[10] In February, 1431, George was created first Lord Latymer of the new creation and was regularly summoned to the House of Lords as such until September, 1469.[11]

There is no reason to think that this Lord Latymer ever spent much time in Thornton. He married Elizabeth, the daughter of Richard Beauchamp, Earl of Warwick.[12] As a chief commander against the Scots in 1435, he earned some fame; but, what was

[1] For this question of when a person should pay homage after having married an heiress cf. Blackstone, *Comm.* II., p. 126, and Pollock and Maitland, *ut supra*, II., p. 412.

[2] The Quindene or Quinzaine was a fortnight after the feast, cf. R. L. Poole, *Mediaeval Reckonings of Time.*

[3] Cal. Close R., 1392-6, p. 452.

[4] Y. A. S. Rec. S. LIX., p. 42.

[5] Cal. Pat. R., 1405-8, p. 212.

[6] Probably 'Robert' is an error for 'William' de Brus of Pickering, *vide* Ch. IV.

[7] Robert Barde of West Lutton, son of William Barde, was born at West Lutton on S. Mark's Day, 1384. *Cf.* Y. A. S. Rec. S. LIX., p. 63.

[8] Cal. Feud. Aids VI., p. 311.

[9] His will was dated 8 December and proved 14 December, 1430.

[10] The marriage took place 3 February, 1396/7. She was the widow of Sir Robert Ferrers.

[11] Burke's *Peerage*, 1915 edition, p. 1196.

[12] Her will was dated 22 September, 1480.

more important as far as local history is concerned, was that he came to an arrangement with Maud,[1] Countess of Cambridge, divorced wife of his uncle John, sixth Lord Latimer of the first creation, as to the division of the Latimer estates, and as to what share, to avoid litigation, should be granted to Sir John Willoughby, the next heir in blood to the late sixth Lord Latimer.[2] The outcome of the agreement was that the lordship of the manor of Thornton remained with George, first Lord Latymer. His son Henry married Joanna, daughter of John, first Baron Berners, and was slain, in his father's lifetime, at the battle of Edgcote, near Banbury, on 14 July, 1469;[3] but he left an infant son, Richard, born in 1468, who succeeded his grandfather George (who had become insane), on 30 December, 1469, and thus became the second Lord Latymer of the new creation.

If Richard, Lord Latymer, did not occasionally reside in Thornton itself, he was, in his young manhood, frequently in the neighbourhood. Sinnington was still the favourite dwelling place of the family, and there it may have been that he always stayed when in the north; but it is probable that from time to time, Thorntonians also saw his face, and recognized him as their lord. On 27 March, 1470, he was declared not to be of age, being as a matter of fact, not quite two years old. This being the case, on 31 March, William Blesdale was appointed to the office 'bailiwick' of Thornton during his minority.[4] At the remarkably early age of nineteen, Richard held a command at the battle of Stoke on 16 June, 1487, against the rebels; and at twenty he married Anne, daughter of Sir Humphrey Stafford of Grafton, co. Worcester.[5] It is, therefore, not surprising that on 8 May, 1491, special livery and licence of entry, without proof of age, was allowed to him 'with respect to his possessions....in Thornton, Danby and in the town of Pykeryng.'[6] He was summoned to Parliament for the first time on 12 August, 1492, and continued to receive such summons until 3 November, 1529. He had a very large family, and his eldest son, John, was born on 17 November, 1493.[7] It was during these early years of domestic anxieties that Richard became a forest poacher, and on 4 July, 1491, entered the preserves of Pickering and killed a stag at Cheesebeck, and thirteen months

---

[1] Daughter of Thomas Clifford, married Richard, Earl of Cambridge, who was executed in 1415.
[2] Burke, *ut supra.*
[3] Ibid.
[4] Cal. Pat. R., 1467-77, p. 206.
[5] Burke, *ut supra.*
[6] Cal. Pat. R., 1485-94, p. 339.
[7] Burke, *ut supra.*

later,[1] on 10 August, 1492, killed two stags and a doe at Grind-stonewath.[2] According to Eastmead,[3] there were more than domestic troubles at this time, for in the reign of 'Henry VII. there was a contest between Richard, Lord Latymer and Sir Robert Willoughby, Lord Brooke for the 'Barony of Latimer.' The said Lord Brooke challenged the barony as....heir of Elizabeth, his great-grandmother; who was sister and heir of John Neville.' That there evidently was trouble there can be little doubt, because on 3 April, 1500, a licence was granted, with the inevitable fee (on this occasion £30), that 'Richard Nevile of Latymer and Anne his wife, Robert Willoughby [of Broke] Esq. and Elizabeth, his wife,' should 'alienate the manors in Daneby in Blakhommore and Thornton in Pikeringlight and the chace of Danby' to numerous persons including the Archbishop of Canterbury, Robert Constable and Richard Empson.[4] But this was all part of the necessary legal process of the time.[5] The facts were that the second Lord Willoughby de Broke contested Lord Latymer's title; but he was unsuccessful, as it was proved that while Lord Willoughby was, as heir of blood, entitled to the ancient baronies of 'Latimer' created by Edward I., Sir Richard Neville was entitled to the barony of 'Latymer,' conferred by writ upon his grandfather, Sir George Neville, in 1431.[6] Thus, amongst other of the estates of the barony, Thornton remained in his hands. In the meantime Richard Neville had gained a name for himself as a soldier in the relief of Norham Castle in 1496, and, afterwards, in the battle of Flodden on 9 September, 1513. In 1522, he was made a lieutenant general and two years later a commissioner of the north, an office which he held for six years, until his death in 1530.[7]

The second Lord Latymer was succeeded by his eldest son, Sir John Neville, who was summoned to Parliament from 5 January, 1533/4, to 16 January, 1541/2. He took a small part in 'The Pilgrimage of Grace' in 1536, and, with Lords Scrope, Lumley and Darcy of Templehurst, negotiated with the Duke of Norfolk, the King's deputy, at Doncaster. He seems to have escaped any serious

---

[1] N. R. Rec. S. N.S. I., p. 153, says 'Itm dic. qd Ricus Dns de latymer nuper de Sevellyngton in Pykerynglith iiij^to die Julie a regni dni Regis nunc vj^to interfecit unum Cervum apud Chesbek infra Forestam dicti dni Regis.'

[2] Ibid. says 'Itm idm Ricus dns de latymer x^mo die Augusti a dni Regis nunc vij interfecit apud Grynstoynwath duos Cervos et unam Cervam.' (A Hart of the fifth year and a Hind of the third year of Red Deer, *vide* N. R. Rec. S. N.S. I., pp. 139-40).

[3] Eastmead, *ut supra*, p. 108.

[4] Cal. Pat. R., 1494-1509, p. 198.

[5] Y. A. S. Rec. S. II., p. 14.

[6] Burke, *ut supra*.

[7] D. N. B.

consequences for his rebellious conduct, and died on 2 March, 1542/3.[1] He was a much-married man. He married first, Dorothy, sister and coheiress of John de Vere, fourteenth Earl of Oxford, by whom he had his son and heir, John; secondly, Elizabeth, daughter of Sir Edward Musgrave; and thirdly, in 1533, Catherine, daughter of Sir Thomas Parr of Kendal, already a widow, and later the wife of Henry VIII. With her, Lord Latymer is said to have spent some of his time at Sinnington, but there is no mention of any residence at Thornton.

The next lord of the manor was John Neville, fourth baron Latymer, who must have been born before 1527,[2] and who was summoned to Parliament on 14 June, 1543. He married Lucy, daughter of Henry Somerset, second Earl of Worcester, and by her had four daughters. When he died on 22 April, 1577,[3] the barony of Latymer fell into abeyance between his four daughters and coheiresses, and so remained till 1913.[4] As to the property, however, there was a settlement amongst the daughters who had all married. The eldest, Katherine, married about 1562, Henry Percy, ninth earl of Northumberland;[5] the second, Dorothy, married on 27 November, 1564, Thomas Cecil, first earl of Exeter;[6] the third, Lucy, married before 1577, Sir William Cornwallis; and the fourth, Elizabeth, married before her father's death, Sir John Danvers.[7] In Trinity Term, 1579, arrangements were made by which the properties were handed over by Henry, Earl of Northumberland, and Katherine his wife, Thomas Cecil, Knt. and Dorothy his wife, John Danvers, Knt. and Elizabeth his wife, and William 'Cornwallys,' esq. and Lucy his wife, to Thomas Somerset, esq., Michael Lewes, esq., Robert Freke, gent., and William Seres, gent.[8] The

---

[1] His will was signed on 12 September, 1542 and proved on 15 March, 1542/3.

[2] His mother Dorothy Vere died 7 February, 1526/7. She is commemorated by a brass plate in the church of St. James at Well.

[3] V. C. H. *N.R.* I., p. 353 states that below the east window of the south chapel in St. James's Church, Well 'is an altar tomb with the effigy of Sir John Neville, fourth....Lord Latimer....He is in full plate armour with a sword and poniard, a ruff about his neck and his hands in prayer. The date on the tomb is 1596 and it has on the front four shields the alliances of his daughters and coheirs with Percy, Cecil, Cornwallis and Danvers.' His widow died 23 February, 1582/3 and was buried at Hackney. *Cf.* Y. A. S. Rec. S. L., p. 130.

[4] The abeyance of the barony of Latymer was terminated in favour of Francis, Burdett, Thomas, Coutts-Nevill, Esq., who was summoned to Parliament by writ 8 February, 1913. *Cf.* J. H. Round, *Family Origins,* pp. 184-5.

[5] The ninth earl died 21 June, 1585. The widow, who married secondly Francis Fitton of Binfield, died 28 October, 1596.

[6] The earl died 7 February, 1621/2: she died 23 March, 1608.

[7] Sir John Danvers died 10 December, 1594: his widow married Sir Edward Carey: she was buried 24 June, 1630.

[8] Y. A. S. Rec. S. V., p. 138.

outcome of the Final Concord was that the manors of Thornton and Sinnington passed to Lucy and her husband, until her death on 30 April, 1609. A fresh arrangement had to be made between her two daughters, Frances, wife of Sir Edmund Withipool, of Christ Church, Ipswich, and Elizabeth, wife of Sir William Sandys, of Montisfont, co. Southampton,[1] in Easter Term, 1610, by which the two manors passed to Elizabeth Sandys.[2]

It was during the period when Sir William Sandys was lord of the manor, in right of his wife, that there was another reference to the fee paid to the Honor of Pickering, first mentioned in 1335. In Norden's *Survey*, about 1619, there are the words—

'Sir William Sandes, Knt, for Latimers landes vis. vd.'[3] In the same *Survey* there are to be found the bounds of the lordship of Thornton.[4] 'The boundes of the Lordship.... Incipiunt ad quoddam fossatum vocat *fryerdike* juxta le Caufe Coatgarth et inde per Holosike, inde per gravium[5] inter dominium de Thornton et dominium de Wilton, Inde usque ad locum vocatum Robhow et inde ad locum vocat Mauslacoate, Inde usque le Howledike, usque ad caput de Stoneygate, inde usque ad inferiorem partem de Stonygate, Inde ascendendo usque *le Howe* de Hawdale, usque ad aquam cadentem in superiore parte de Hawdale, et inde ad petram Saxosam[6] in Waytemeare, Inde recta linia usque ad tres puteos in australi parte de Langdale qui limitant terras principis, Willi Sandes, militis, et Rici Egerton, militis.[7] Et a tribus puteis predictis usque ad superiorem partem de Flaxdale, Et inde descendendo usque ad le Howle in Flaxdale, usque ad rivulum de Dalbye, et per rivulum predictum usque ad locum vocatum Keldehouse warth,[8] Inde in cacumen montis usque ad le howle *dike* inter Dalby *browe* et *Peckstone Moare* et inde aquilonem versus per fossam usque ad fossam vocatam Midledike, et inde usque le slate feilde, Inde descendendo le Howle de Easingdale[9] usque ad locum vocatum Cheesmarr. Et inde usque ad lapidem vocatum *marshestone*[10] in le Howle de Langandale,[11] et a dicto

---

[1] They married in 1592.
[2] Y. A. S. Rec. S. LIII., p. 125.
[3] N. R. Rec. S. N.S. I., p. 43.
[4] Ibid., pp. 23-4.
[5] Modern translation 'grove': old translation 'hillock.'
[6] Presumably the Adderstone on Adderstone Rigg.
[7] Sir Richard Egerton was lord of the manor of Allerston at this period.
[8] *Vide* Ch. XVI. A wath or warth means a ford.
[9] On Six-Inch Ordnance it is Orchandale. In the Award of 1796 this word is spelt Hirkendale. In modern times it is pronounced Hawkendale.
[10] This stone was removed in living memory.
[11] The modern Howldale.

lapide, usque ad locum vocatum *Holie maydens grave*,[1] Et inde inter campos et Thornton et Pickeringe usque ad le Carr *dyke*. Et inde per le Cundits *sewer to the fryer dike* ad salicem curvatum.'[2]

For some unknown reason, in 1625, Sir William Sandys and Elizabeth his wife conveyed the manor to trustees in the persons of her two cousins, Henry, Lord Danby,[3] and Sir John Danvers,[4] and Sir Anthony Mayne.[5] Sir William Sandys died before 1630, and on 11 May of that year, Elizabeth married Richard Lumley, first Viscount Lumley. To him she carried her Thornton and Sinnington estates. He was the grand-nephew of John, fifth[6] Baron Lumley, who died about 1544. He gained the favour of Charles I. and was elevated to the peerage of Ireland, as Viscount Lumley of Waterford on 12 July, 1628. During the Civil War he adhered faithfully to the King, and made the yellow sandstone pile of Lumley Castle, which had been left to him by a relative in 1609, a garrison for the royalists. Later, being a principal commander under Prince Rupert, he took part in the siege of Bristol until its surrender in 1645.[7] In 1651, it is stated that he paid to the Honor of Pickering the usual quit rent of 6s. 5d., for the manor of Thornton.[8] Four years later the Committee for Compounding[9] fined him £1925.[10] In the meantime, Elizabeth, Viscountess Lumley, lived mainly on her manor at Sinnington,[11] and it was while there that in October, 1657, she determined to dispose of her lands for charitable purposes.[12] On 2 February, 1657/8, she was buried in Westminster Abbey.

Throughout England, at the time of the restoration of Charles II. to the throne, there must have been very much the reverse of a restoration to many country estates. The old manorial lords had gone and new ones took their places. What exactly happened in Thornton between the death of Lady Lumley and the sale of the manor is not clear. That the manor was in the hands of trustees is evident, and in Trinity Term 1669, these trustees, Henry, Marquis

---

[1] Eastmead, *ut supra*, says that in Anglo-Saxon times Malton was called Meldum pronounced 'maiden' and 'Maiden Greve Balk is at this day [1824] one of the boundaries of Malton.' This view is probably erroneous.
[2] Old translation is 'notched willow.'
[3] Born 1573: died 1643, *vide* D. N. B. XIV., p. 37.
[4] Born 1588 ? died 1655, *vide* D. N. B. XIV., p. 40, and *vide* Ch. XV.
[5] V. C. H. *N.R.* II., p. 494.
[6] The D. N. B. shows the difficulty of calling this man fifth or sixth.
[7] Clarendon, *History of the Great Rebellion*, VII., 123-4.
[8] G. F. G. H. Parl. Survey.
[9] Cal. Com. Comp. Pt. II., 920.
[10] Lord Lumley died about 1662. His eldest son John, by his first marriage, had died in his father's lifetime.
[11] Eastmead, *ut supra*, p. 267.
[12] *Vide* Chs. VI., VII.

of Dorset,[1] Sir Geoffrey Palmer,[2] Sir John Mayne and John Penrice conveyed the manor to a certain John Hill;[3] and so the Hill family entered upon their heritage. It has been ascertained that no present member of the family can supply anything vitally important about this first John Hill. Family tradition, for what it is worth, states that he was a retired silk merchant of London, who had made a fair fortune, and like others of his kind at the period, wished to acquire land.[4] But why did he choose Thornton? There must have been hundreds of estates on the market at that particular time. Had he any connection with the village? It now seems likely that he had. His father[5] was almost certainly a Thomas Hill, of 'Hilltopp,' in the county of York,[6] gent., who held Farmanby as chief tenant from the Dean and Canons of Windsor in 1620. John Hill held from them in 1663, and in 1669, this same John Hill was lord of the manor of Thornton. It is, also, worth noting that John Hill and his wife were in the district before he purchased the Thornton estate. His eldest son John, was born at York in 1654,[7] and John Hill was the owner of the advowson of Normanby as early as 1661,[8] and in a document of 1663, he is described as 'of Normanby, Yorks.'[9]

John Hill was not a young man at the time, for he was fifty-eight years of age, and had been married for at least sixteen years, to one Sarah,[10] but who she was is not known. In 1670, there is a reference to the fact that, like his predecessors from early times, he paid the quit rent of 6s. 5d. to the Honor of Pickering,[11] and one can imagine that he must have had some satisfaction in doing so, feeling that it marked his actual lordship of the manor of Thornton.[12] At the time of the Declaration of Indulgence in 1687

[1] Henry Pierrepont, first Marquis of Dorset, 1606-1680. D. N. B. XLV., p. 264.
[2] Sir Geoffrey Palmer, 1598-1670. D. N. B. XLIII., p. 126.
[3] Feet of Fines. Trin. Term. 21 Car. II.
[4] *Cf.* Defoe, *Complete Tradesman*, edition 1839, p. 74, Boswell, *Life of Johnson*, 7th edition, II., pp. 106, 107; and Toynbee, *Industrial Revolution*, pp. 61-4, who have some interesting remarks on this subject.
[5] D. and C. of W. XV., 18, 20.
[6] Possibly a township in the parish of Wragby, 5 miles from Barnsley.
[7] Camb. Al. II., p. 371.
[8] V. C. H. *N.R.* I., p. 544.
[9] D. and C. of W. xv., 18, 22. The manor of Normanby was ultimately sold by Commissioner John Hill in 1739, but not the advowson, which remained with the direct family until passed to the Rev. James Hill and from him to his son the Rev. Reginald Hill and sold by the latter in 1896, who spent the proceeds on the restoration of the present church.
[10] She was buried 7 September, 1680, *cf.* C. R.
[11] As the act 12 Car. II. c. 24 for the abolition of feudal tenures had been passed it might have been expected that this payment was obsolete.
[12] G. F. G. H.

certain questions were propounded to the Yorkshire Magistrates to discover if they were in favour of James II.'s attempt to introduce 'toleration' or rather 'Roman Catholicism' under the disguise of so-called toleration. John Hill answered the questions in favour saying 'I am resolved to observe his Majesties' Declaration'; but evidently he was looked upon as a trimmer for in the margin of the Attestation there are the words 'Mem: has since given another answer to the Lord Lieut.'[1] It is not surprising then that as a magistrate he took the oath to William and Mary at Thirsk on 6 October, 1691.[2]

Not satisfied with the extent of the manor, from time to time, he added little bits of property to the original purchase, which conveyances have retained both the names of fields and villagers of a bygone time. Thus in 1669 and 1674, he made exchanges with Robert Champley already referred to.[3] In March and April, 1674, he obtained from Roger Browne, Robert 'Jennyson' and Mary Story, widow, some small portions of land in 'Botton-field'; and in the following May, he was evidently desirous of still further rounding off his property, so that he made an exchange with the rector, Christopher Bradley, and gave to him, 20 'lands' of arable and meadow in 'Botton Field' 'in a pcell of ground called North Peaslands,' and 6 broadlands extending to 'Bastan's ditch,' [?] and lying between glebe land on the east and land of Christopher Hunter on the west in exchange for 3 oxgangs of freehold of 30 acres lying in 'Townsfield.' In 1677, and again in 1692, he made some exchanges with William Parke,[4] yeoman of Thornton, and Jane his wife, by which he ultimately obtained 2 broadlands in 'Botton Land.' In 1680 William Skelton, who was at this time contemplating a move to Sinnington, where he had relatives,[5] sold his house to John Hill, with the street on the north and west and the Beck on the east. Between 1692 and 1693, John Hill also acquired from 'Symon' Smithson and Ann his wife, a piece of pasture of 1 acre 16 poles in 'Whitegate' lands in the Highfields of Farmanby, lying between his own land on the north and the land of James Dixon on the south, together with a cottage[6] and 3 roods of arable lying in 'a field called Botton field in A place

---

[1] Y. A. J., V., p. 468.
[2] N. R. Rec. S. O.S. IX., p. 20.
[3] *Vide* Ch. VIII.
[4] There were members of this family residing in Pickering in the seventeenth century.
[5] For the intermixture of these families, *cf.* Y. A. S. Rec. S. LV. A relative of his, Ann Skelton of Thornton was married in York Minster on 3 April, 1683, to Simon Nicholl of Folkton, *cf.* Y. A. J., I.
[6] There is no cottage there to-day.

called Buttery Stubb,' and 5 acres 3 roods on what was called 'old Build Rigg.' And after July, 1692, he acquired from John Kirby, who had them from his wife Elizabeth, coheiress of Roger Browne, 'a parcell of meadowe or pasture ground in the Highfield in a place called Batter Scrambs,[1] one close in the Ox Carr, one close in the Beckends in the lowe field, six beast gates in the Common pasture called Boodall Carre.'[2] On 23 July, 1695, Robert Gilson, of Allerston, sold to John Hill a messuage, cottage and 'one ffouldgarth & Garden Platt' between the lands of Christopher Hunter, gentleman, on the west and the 'Rectory or parsonage' on the east, in the tenure of Henry Wilson. In the following September, Thomas Vasey of the Marishes and Henry Dickinson of Ayton sold to the new lord a messuage, cottage and three roods of arable on [?] Banke together with 1 rood in 'Middlefield[3] of Thornton called Dudda Hill' and 1 rood above 'Wilton Highway,' 'neare A great Gray stone, the gleabe on the East'; and 1 rood extending from the highway to 'the brow dyke.'[4] When John Hill passed away in November, 1695, he must have felt that he had built up a compact estate and founded a family of country gentlemen.

John Hill I.[5] was followed by John Hill II.[6] The latter as already stated was born in York in 1654. He was a boy of fifteen when his parents transferred to Thornton, where he had his early instruction in the newly-created Grammar School under Mr. Grey until, for a short time, he was taught by Mr. Singleton at Pickering. After two years in the village he was admitted a scholar at Sidney Sussex College, Cambridge, on 2 January, 1671/2, but did not proceed to a degree.[7] In those days men lived quickly and were soon men of the world and fathers of families. He married first, Grace, daughter of Sir John Legard, first baronet of Ganton.[8] Apparently on marriage, John Hill II. left the paternal roof at Thornton Hall and resided in the other family mansion at

---

[1] In 1729 this is spelt 'Scambs.'

[2] This is Boodhill Carr near Charity Farm.

[3] *Vide* Ch. I.

[4] G. F. G. H. There is no trace of this 'great Gray stone' at the present time.

[5] His daughter Rebecca married J. Gibson of Welburne, whose relative was Thomas Gibson of 'Loathbury', London, scrivenor. *Cf.* G. F. G. H.

[6] He may have had a brother Robert, because Robert son of John Hill, of York, aged 11 was admitted at Pocklington School on 2 February, 1665/6.

[7] Camb. Al. II., p. 371.

[8] Sir John Legard was a Parliamentarian. He married first, 18 October, 1655, Grace, third daughter of Conyers Darcy, first Earl of Holderness, by whom he had a daughter Grace as above. She was born in 1656. He died in 1678.

Normanby.[1] By Grace his wife, he had three children, Anne, born 11 December, 1677,[2] John, baptized 9 June, 1681, and buried on 12 January, 1681/2, and Sarah, baptized 3 February, 1682/3, and buried on the following 1 March. It was probably on account of these losses that Grace Hill pined away and died on 14 October, 1683.[3] John Hill II. married again, before 1687, Elizabeth,[4] daughter of Sir William Hustler of Acklam.[5] By this wife he had numerous children, Elizabeth, born 1687, died 1693; James, born 1695, and presumably died young: Sarah, born 1699, died 1757; and Catherine, born 1704, and died young.[6] The children who survived to be married and have offspring of their own, were:—John, baptized 2 June, 1689, William, baptized 12 March, 1690/1,[7] and Richard, born in 1694.

In the meantime, John Hill II. lived the ordinary life of the country gentleman and justice of the peace, but he did rather more than that, because in May, 1697, he became a most important official of the Duchy of Lancaster, for at that date there was an assignment to him of the Castle and Manor of Pickering for a sum, which is illegible,[8] and thus began a connection between the family and 'The Duchy,' of two hundred years.[9] As a magistrate he was required to take the oath to the sovereign on several occasions, and he did so, to William III. on 6 October, 1696, at Thirsk,[10] and again in 1700, at Kirkby Moorside.[11] On 6 October, 1702, he did the same to Queen Anne, at Thirsk,[12] and on 26 April, 1715, to George I.[13] By 1717 he had evidently acquired more than the manor in Thornton for in addition to the historic 6s. 5d. to the Honor of Pickering for the manor, he paid for lands in Farmanby, 1s. 7d.[14] The last of his public acts seems to have been the appointment of William Beilby as his gamekeeper,[15] at Quarter Sessions at Easingwold, when he is described as 'Lord of the Castle, Manor and Liberty of Pickering.'[16] He died in 1738.

[1] G. F. G. H.
[2] C. R.   This is the first reference to the Hill family in the Registers.
[3] C. R.
[4] She died 1732.
[5] William Hustler had a daughter Catherine and a son James, of Scampston. *Cf.* G. F. G. H.
[6] C. R.
[7] Ibid.
[8] Many documents of the family were seriously injured by an unprecedented flood in May, 1910.
[9] G. F. G. H.
[10] N. R. Rec. S. O.S. IX., p. 26.
[11] Ibid., p. 28.
[12] Ibid., p. 34.
[13] Ibid., p. 45.
[14] G. F. G. H.
[15] *Vide* Ch. VII.
[16] N. R. Rec. S. O.S. VIII., p. 210.

Like his father he did his best to add to the manorial property. On 1 March, 1696/7, William Skelton, now of Sinnington, sold to him a messuage house 'wherein William Skelton's family dwelt in the township of Thornton or ffarmanby,' and now in the occupation of 'Enos Rithard, barber.' A little later, on 3 March, 1701/2, John Clarke and Mary his wife transferred to him a close called Hill's Dyke,[1] near Cow Carr; and in the following October, Henry Joyner sold a close, probably 'Joyner's Garth' now known as China Garth.[2] On 1 January, 1704, George Cooper of Coddenham, Suffolk, and Margaret his wife, sold 1 balk of meadow ground of $2\frac{1}{2}$ acres in 'the flat or ffall of Peaslands in the ffield called or known by the name of Bottonfield on the east side of the Beck.' In the May, of the same year, James Smith of Bemfield [?] Essex sold 2 arable closes, and on 20 May, 1713, Elizabeth Priestman, now of Barking in Essex, and Alice Priestman, daughters of Richard and Mary Priestman, sold $2\frac{1}{2}$ acres in Cow Carr.[3] On 27 February, 1717/8, Richard Burrow of Pickering, shoemaker, transferred to John Hill 'that ffronsted[4] where a house had once stood in Thornton' consisting of 1 rood of land. Two years later, in March, 1720, John Mery of Thornton, yeoman and Elizabeth his wife sold to John Hill a cottage, barn and garth. In 1730, he bought a piece of ground in 'Harrowclif' from Richard Jennyson, and in 1732, a cottage from someone whose name is illegible. On 4 December, 1734, another cottage was added, being acquired from Christopher Harland to whom it had come from his wife.[5]

John Hill III. was the eldest surviving son of John Hill II. and was baptized at Thornton on 22 June, 1689.[6] Even to this day, he is known in the family as 'The Commissioner,' and that is what he became, for during the greater part of his manhood, he held what was then the lucrative post of Commissioner of Customs.[7] As everyone knows the office was somewhat of a sinecure, and although many letters were addressed to him at 'the Custom

---

[1] G. F. G. H. shows that on 2 March, 1697/8 John Clarke, yeoman, the tenant, and Anthony Hunter of the 'Marrishes' leased, with purposes of sale ultimately to John Hill II. and conveyed to John Burdett of 'ffurnival's Inn', a close called Hill's dyke in 'the premises, ffields & territories of ffarmanby.'

[2] Now in the possession of Miss M. L. Heslop.

[3] Is this possibly the 'Priestman's Carr' of the survey of 1729 ?

[4] N. R. Rec. S. U.S. V., p. 198 says concerning 'ffrontstead' that it is the site on which a house stands or has formerly stood, but the term is limited to the site of a house of sufficiently ancient date to carry with it what are called 'common rights.'

[5] From numerous documents, G. F. G. H.

[6] C. R.

[7] Their position, duties and necessity of oaths to the sovereign are laid down in an act 6 Will. & Mar. c. 1. sec. 5.

House, London,' it did not deprive him of the pleasure of living at Thornton, and exercising from that place all the bents of a typical eighteenth century gentleman, squire and justice. He appointed gamekeepers[1] in 1739/40,[2] 1744,[3] and 1749.[4] He improved and stocked the farm at Dalby in 1743;[5] and like his father and grandfather did his best to add acre to acre in the consolidation of the estate. In June, 1739, he made an exchange with Robert Dixon[6] and Margaret his wife, by which he acquired a messuage and a stable abutting on the 'King's highway on the north' and with Barwick Lane on the south and west. In the same month, he received from John Bell of Scarborough, a cottage[7] in 'Thornton cum ffarmanby,' with a garth and a croft, his own land on the north and Thornton Beck on the east. Or again in Trinity Term, 1740, by a Final Concord, Robert Dixon and Margaret his wife conveyed to him 1 messuage, barn and garden, 5 acres of meadow, 2 acres of pasture and common rights. On 11 December, 1742,[8] Frank Stephens and Mary his wife of New Malton sold him a cottage garth and orchard in Maltongate, and in the next year, on 20 June, Thomas Skelton, weaver, sold him his house and garth near the 'Grinclif' i.e., 'bounded on the north by a common called Green Clyf,'[9] or on the west side of the present Whitbygate, possibly the site of the house now called 'Ganstead.'

All this time he must have been nursing political ambitions for in July, 1747, he suddenly resigned his post as Commissioner of Customs,[10] in order to become Member of Parliament for Higham Ferrers,[11] which he continued to be until his death.[12] Nothing is

1 *Vide* Ch. VII.
2 N. R. Rec. S. O.S. VIII., p. 231.
3 Ibid., p. 247.
4 Ibid., p. 290.
5 *Vide* Ch. VI.
6 G. F. G. H. shows that a James Dixon bought on 25 March, 1717, a close of 4½ acres in the West Field from Richard Browne of Scampston, who had received it from his uncle the late William Browne of 'ffarmanby.'
7 In a bundle of papers concerning the Normanby manor [J.L.W.], I unexpectedly found a letter from Samuel Tetley on the subject of this cottage. Writing on 13 May, 1739 to the Commissioner at The Custom House, London, he says 'Mr. Bell has just put up a paper at the Cross in this Town giving notice that his House and Garth adjoyning on John Boyes house and orchard, is to be sold, this is the house you was once desirous of having. If you have a mind to prevent its falling into the hands of a Tanner or Skinner, now is your time to do it, for it is so convenient for either that in all probability one that is of those proffessions will buy it.'
8 In this conveyance John Hill is called 'The Honourable John Hill of Thornton.'
9 From numerous documents G. F. G. H.
10 Presumably he would have to take the step because of the Statute 15 Geo. II. c. 22.
11 Gentleman's Magazine, 1747, p. 343.
12 Ibid., 1753, p. 344.

known of his political life except that he was not a Jacobite; but, in the next six years, he must have been in London occasionally and he probably heard the debates on the change of the calendar and on Lord Hardwicke's Marriage Act.[1]

As far as is known Commissioner John Hill never settled down to married life. Like many others he may have imagined that his brothers would carry on the name, and it certainly looked as if they would have done so. His brother William left the quiet of Thornton, and launched into the world, and was a planter in the West Indies in Antigua,[2] and died there in 1723.[3] But he left two children, one Elizabeth, who married Charles Webb, and had a son, John Robert Hill Webb, rector of Thornton for many years;[4] and a son, Captain John Hill, who married on 21 October, 1758, his cousin Catherine Hill, daughter of Richard. This Richard, brother of John and William, was born, as already said, in 1694. He was educated at Beverley School and matriculated at Sidney Sussex College, Cambridge, on 6 March, 1712/3. Here he seems to have been caught, very young, by one Martha, of unknown parentage, and their first child was born at Cambridge in 1714. His wife died and was buried at Thornton 12 January, 1724/5.[5] By that time Richard was rector of Normanby,[6] and had been since 1719. From 1723 to 1734 he was vicar of West Heslerton, where he died on 26 March, 1734.[7] One of his sons, Richard, had died young, in November, 1723, at which time he also lost his daughter, Sarah.[8] His eldest son, John Samuel, born in 1714, survived till 1757, and was rector of Thornton.[9] His youngest child Catherine, who was born in 1722, lived as a widow at Middleton near Pickering,[10] and died long after her husband,[11] in 1786.

The 'old Commissioner' made every preparation for his family, before he died in 1753. But man proposes: God disposes. He must have been very far-sighted because he went even beyond the limits of ordinary forethought. He left his property in trust to

---

[1] 25 Geo. II. c. 30, and 26 Geo. II. c. 33.

[2] Named after the Church of Santa la Maria la Antigua at Seville.

[3] The Hill family evidently kept up the connection with the West Indies because the Church Register records on 21 November, 1755 'George Thornton an adult negroe servant to Capt. Robert Hill of Jamaica, baptized.' Up to the present I have failed to identify this Capt. Robert Hill.

[4] *Vide* Ch. IX.

[5] C. R.

[6] John Hill I. purchased the advowson of Normanby.

[7] Sam. Tetley, *ut supra*.

[8] C. R.

[9] *Vide* Ch. IX.

[10] Y. A. J., XIV., p. 71.

[11] He died 1 March, 1773 *vide* Memorial in Thornton Church.

Charles, Marquis of Rockingham,[1] unto the use of his nephew, Captain John Hill of the Royal Regiment of Artillery,[2] during his life (he died in 1773), with remainder to the first living son and sons of the body of the said John Hill (there were none), with remainder to his nephew, Dr. John Samuel Hill (died 1757), and to his first surviving son (he had no children), with remainder to Lieutenant John Johnson ('The Commissioner's natural son') of Colonel Trelawney's Regiment in Jamaica, he changing his name to Hill, with remainder to his sons. Lieutenant John Johnson died in the lifetime of Captain John Hill, but left three children, John, Richard, and Ann.[3] John enjoyed the estate from 1773 to 1776, when he died a batchelor in Lisbon,[4] and Richard succeeded.

Richard Johnson, or as he afterwards became, Richard Johnson Hill, was a man of taste and education.[5] He was typical of his age.[6] He loved good books and beautiful bindings, he liked to have around him furniture that was both artistic and useful, and he filled a lovely Chippendale bookcase with eighteenth century folios gloriously bound, that made the modern book-lover's mouth water. His representation of his age, however, was not only to be found in these directions, but in less attractive ones. No period in English History is so marked by the prevalence of gambling, and Richard Johnson Hill was no exception, and followed the example of such men as Charles James Fox and Colonel Dennis O'Kelly.[7] The tradition is, that before he inherited Thornton he was well-to-do, but all that he had before went into the hands of others, until, about 1793, he actually staked the manor of Thornton to George

---

[1] This is the famous Marquis of Rockingham, for a short time 'Prime Minister.' The basis of friendship with the Hill family has so far evaded research, but as John Samuel Hill was at St. John's College, Cambridge, and so also was the Marquis, it may lie here.

[2] Gentleman's Magazine, 1773, p. 155, but it is interesting to notice that the Church Register says he was a Captain in the Royal Navy.

[3] Ann was born in 1758 and died in 1812. She married Josiah Maynard and had four children: Josiah, who died in the West Indies; Fanny, who married the Rev. R. Cottam; Nancy, born in 1782, and who married the Rev. H. T. Laye, vicar of Pickering; and Harriet, who married the Rev. Procter Robinson.

[4] Gentleman's Magazine, 1776, p. 530.

[5] Already in 1780, when not of age, he was living in some style as he paid taxes for 4 male servants. *Cf.* Y. A. J., XIV., p. 7.

[6] The Rev. John Richard Hill, his grandson, wrote "he was chronicled in old hunting lore as a sportsman and especially in an old song as '*Squire Hill of Thornton*,' '*where chestnut brave he will not save*,' and as '*The Preserver of our game*' (*viz.*, foxes)."

[7] He was the owner of the famous race-horse 'Eclipse,' and made a fortune by gaming and horse-breeding.

Osbaldeston,[1] his neighbour, on one game of billiards. Thanks to the Lord Middleton of the day,[2] the game was stopped, and Thornton manor was saved for his descendants.[3] This spendthrift *'was cut off in the Prime of Life at Broomsgrove in Worcestershire, on the 28th day of July in the Year* 1793.'[4] And although the marble memorial goes on to record that *'His Integrity and private Worth render'd him respected thro' Life and at his Death lamented by all who knew him,'* there are those who think that had he not departed this life when he did, there would have been little for his widow and child.

On the other hand it is only fair to say that his tutor, brother-in-law and agent, Josiah Maynard,[5] and Richard Johnson Hill, himself did add to the estate. On 6 April, 1779, Maynard purchased from Richard Parke, a messuage with Town Street on the south, 'now in possession of Edward Crosier.' About the same time William Spendley sold a piece of allotment of common; and on 5 April, 1781, James 'Marfit' sold a 'common right,' i.e., an allotment of common under the Enclosure Award. On the same day Matthew Crosier also conveyed to Maynard as agent for Richard Johnson Hill, a parcel of land in the 'Eastffield.' Richard Hill, however, made a far bigger purchase from the same vendor on 6 April, 1787, when he acquired a messuage and 42 acres 3 roods 3 perches, known as Fox Farm [? Box Farm], together with Vasy Ings, a messuage known as Hay [Hagg] House, and a garth called Freehold Oxgang, Broadmires field and Three Highfields [late Tweedy's], Becondale [Brecondale or Brackendell], Swincroft Hill,[6] Deerholme, West End, Booth [Boot] Close, Beck End, the two

---

[1] This was George Osbaldeston, son of the Rev. Dr. and Mrs. Wickens who assumed the name Osbaldeston when they acquired the property, but not Hunmanby nor Hutton Bushel. The latter property went to this George who married Jane, daughter of Sir Thomas Head. Their son George was the famous 'Squire' Osbaldeston, educated at Eton and Brasenose Colleges, born 1786, died aged 66, having married shortly before, Elizabeth, widow of Thomas Williams. *Cf. 'Squire' Osbaldeston: His Autobiography,* pop. edition.

[2] Henry, fifth Baron Middleton.

[3] This was told to me by my friend, Richard Hill, who died in 1906. Thanks to him I had a free use of his books, particularly between the years 1900 and 1905. I have spent many happy hours in a long passage lined with books on the south-west side of the North Parlour, now swept away by modern building improvements.

[4] Memorial in the Church.

[5] *Vide supra.*

[6] Swincroft Hill abuts on the Pickering Road west of Long Batter Scrambles, and is opposite West Fields and south of Brackendell. I have reason to suppose that it had belonged to the Dean and Canons of Windsor.

Wisperdales[1] and 3 parcells called Carrs. A year later, on 25 April, 'Josiah Maynard handed over to R. H. all Roger Atkinson's property,' whatever that might be. On 1 December, 1789, Sir George Osborn, of Chicksands, co. Bedford, fourth baronet, sold to Richard Johnson Hill, 1 oxgang of glebe within the lordship of 'ffarmanby,' and a 'Cottage House in Ellerburn.' This Sir George Osborn was descended from Sir John Danvers, who had married Elizabeth, daughter of Sir John Neville, fourth baron Latymer. Their daughter, Dorothy, had married Sir Peter Osborn, of Chicksands. Some member of the Osborn family possibly Sir Danvers (died 1753), had acquired the property though not having any other territorial interest in the parish,[2] and held it until Sir George Osborn was persuaded to convey it to the Hill family.[3]

Richard Johnson Hill married, about 1785, Elizabeth,[4] daughter of John Johnston[5] and Elizabeth his wife, daughter of John Rogers.[6] The spendthrift's only surviving child,[7] Richard, was born on 4 June, 1786. This child was, therefore, seven years old when his father died. Whatever faults Richard Johnson Hill may have had, at least, he had taken precautions for the future, and by his will, dated 23 May, 1790, had appointed excellent trustees for his son.[8] They were, Dr. John Johnston, doctor of medicine of Beverley, his father-in-law, the Rev. John Ward, vicar of Yedingham and John Bell[9] of Scarborough. Of these, John Ward remained the surviving trustee. Richard Johnson Hill's widow, Elizabeth, as Mrs. 'Eliza' Hill, married again in 1797,[10] the Rev. John Gilby, and owing to her marriage settlement, made a deed of settlement of the manor of

---

[1] Wisperdales or Masdales are on the west side of Malton gate just before Ordmerstones Lane, and Beck Ends are on the east side of the road between it and the Beck. I prefer the spelling 'Odmiston' Lane.

[2] Sir Danvers Osborn seems to have been lord of the manor of Middleton as shown by a map of 1729. J. L. W. He also leased from the Dean of York part of the Tithes of Farmanby as shown by a survey made in October, 1729.

[3] From many documents, G. F. G. H.

[4] She was born 21 November, 1757.

[5] John Johnston, born 19 August, 1727, was son of Samuel Johnston, born 3 August, 1685, died 2 February, 1767. Samuel had married on 3 August, 1717, Sarah Tadman, born 14 November, 1695 and died 1 July, 1770. Samuel was the son of Samuel Johnston, baptized 22 December, 1628, and died 3 December, 1718. He married Anne Seaman, 4 August, 1670, who had been born 22 March, 1647/8 and died 18 July, 1697. I found these facts in an old Prayer Book, G. F. G. H.

[6] She was married 19 August, 1755.

[7] There was another child John, born in 1788 but he died the same year.

[8] G. F. G. H.

[9] On 30 July, 1805, John Bell sold to the Rev. John Ward, as trustee, the Highfield Close in Farmanby.

[10] She died in 1830.

Thornton upon herself and her infant son Richard, then about eleven, during her life. The trustees in this case were Dr. John Johnston and the Rev. John Ward.[1]

Richard Hill after a short period of education at University College, Oxford, came of age in 1807, and, as already recorded,[2] became the Master of Hounds, soon after. He was also a keen preserver of partridges, and concerning this sport, Squire Osbaldeston records 'shooting with my neighbour, Richard Hill of Thornton, on his ground, I killed 20 brace of partridges at 40 shots, never missing one. I did this with a flint and steel of 18 bore made by the celebrated Joe Manton.'[3] Richard Hill married in July, 1807, Anne,[4] daughter of the Rev. Luke Yarker, of Leyburn Hall, and by her had three children: Eliza, born 21 February, 1809, and died 22 March, 1883; secondly, Richard Luke, born 1810 and died 1812; and thirdly, John Richard, born 29 October, 1811. Richard Hill married a second time in 1819, Jane,[5] daughter of James Walker of Sand Hutton, Esq., by whom he had a large family.[6] Richard died on 21 January, 1855.

He was succeeded by his eldest surviving son by his first wife, John Richard Hill. As stated[7] he was educated at University College, Oxford, and was rector of the parish until after the death of his father. It is not always easy to write of those one has known, but it may be said, as the ideal squire of a north country village, John Richard Hill fitted the part exactly. A kindly man, devoted to his friends, a true benefactor to the village, and one of the old school that is so rare to-day. He married on 19 June, 1842, Harriet, daughter of Joseph Robinson Pease, of Hesslewood, Esq. They happily celebrated, surrounded by their children and grandchildren, their Golden Wedding in 1892; and he died on 21 December, 1896, and she on 5 November, 1899.

The 'Old Squire' was succeeded by his eldest son, Richard, born 14 May, 1843, and married on 5 September, 1872, to Evereld Ellen, daughter of Rev. George Hustler, late of Weald Manor, Oxon. During his parents' lifetime, after his marriage, he lived near Whitby and later at Sinnington and at York, but took up his residence at Thornton in 1900. He, like his grandfather, father

[1] G. F. G. II.
[2] *Vide* Ch. VI.
[3] *Squire Osbaldeston: His Autobiography*, pop. edition, p. 25.
[4] His wife towards the end of her life could not live at Thornton and passed many months at Sidmouth. She died of consumption, 15 July, 1815.
[5] She died 1890.
[6] *Vide* Appendix.
[7] *Vide* Ch. IX.

and brother Arthur, was educated at University College, Oxford, and following the family tradition, had the kindest heart, was a true Conservative, a good sportsman and, in his prime, a fine shot. He died on 1 April, 1906, and was followed within a few days by his wife.

Richard Hill, born 14 November, 1877, succeeded his father. He was educated at Repton School, and was a keen officer in the Militia, spending much of his time at headquarters at Richmond. He married on 16 August, 1911, Gertrude Mary, daughter of Edward Rymer of London, Esq. On the outbreak of the Great War he was a Major in the 3rd Battalion, A.P.W.O. Yorkshire Regiment, and was in the trenches at West Hartlepool when bombarded by the German fleet on 16 December, 1914. Shortly after, he contracted pneumonia from exposure, and died on duty, 17 February, 1915, and was buried at Thornton with full military honours.

His successor was his brother, George Francis Gordon Hill, the present owner. He was also educated at Repton School. He married on 25 February, 1911, Monica, daughter of J. P. Crosland of Scarborough, Esq. and has a surviving child, Evereld Monica.

CHAPTER TWELVE.

The Gospatric-Brus-Gresham-Hunter Manor.

'Domesday Book....shows us that the Norman landowners were conceived as slipping into the exact place of the English owners whose forfeited lands had come into their hands; the Norman represents an English antecessor whose rights and duties have fallen upon him.'

MAITLAND, 1887.

AFTER the completion of the great survey of Domesday Book, Robert de Brus was given certain lands, including 11 bovates in 'Torentona.'[1] If it is correct to believe that the first manor in Thornton was that of Tor,[2] and, as it is known, that the third manor was that of Torbrand, these 11 bovates must have been the holding, in the village, of Gospatric. Many years before the Norman Conquest, 'a certain Yorkshire thane Kilvert, son of Ligulf, married Ecgfrida, daughter of Aldun, Bishop of Durham (who flourished 990-1010), by whom he had a daughter Sigrida, who became the wife of Archil and mother of Gospatric.'[3] At first Gospatric was friendly with William the Conqueror, but later, quarrelled irrevocably with him, and his lands were confiscated and granted to numerous Normans.

The smallness of this manor does not invalidate its manorial character, because, as has been said, 'to the size of a manor we can set neither an inferior nor a superior limit.'[4] According to the latest view, the fact that Gospatric's land had the letter M against it like the others, may not mean all that Professor Maitland urged as to complete manorial adjuncts, and may only intend to convey that there was 'the former existence of a "hall" on the property'[5] or 'a thegn's residence situate upon an estate to which services were rendered, and at which dues were paid.'[6]

[1] Domesday Book.
[2] *Vide* Ch. XI.
[3] R. H. Skaife, *The Domesday Book of Yorkshire*, p. 15.
[4] Pollock and Maitland, *ut supra*, I., p. 391.
[5] Stenton, *Types of Manorial Structure*, etc. Oxf. Soc. Leg. Stud. II., p. 57.
[6] Ibid., p. 59.

Large or small, however, this manor continued to be held by the Brus family, lords of Skelton Castle,[1] amongst whom, perhaps, the most famous was Peter de Brus, who assisted in producing Magna Carta in June, 1215, and died in 1222. By 1272,[2] with the death of Peter III., this branch of the Brus stock died out in the male line, but, for some time before this, William Percy de Kildale had held the manor from the lords of Skelton, and had in turn subinfeudated, the already mentioned,[3] Robert Maungevileyn.[4] The Percys remained as lords, and it was not until long after 1290, and the passing of *Quia Emptores*, that they made a final and complete alienation, when, it is conceivable, that in some, at present, inexplicable way the manor had fallen into the overlordship of the Brus family of Pickering.

The William Percy de Kildale referred to in 1284, was a somewhat pathetic figure. He was the son of Walter de Percy and grandson of William and Agnes de Flammarville, his wife. At an inquest held on 11 February, 1284/5, it was said that he was insane. The fact was, from the account, that William was suffering from, amongst other things,[5] neurasthenia, but that particular disease had not been 'invented' in the reign of Edward I. The jurators pointed out that William had given to his younger son, William, the manors of Ormesby and Kildale, although they ought to have gone to his elder son, Ernulf or Arnald. They then showed that upon examination, the poor old man could explain nothing, but was always crying softly (*tenere lacramento*).[6] Naturally the two brothers quarrelled, and there was much unpleasantness between them, but Arnald, though he carried the matter to the Court of King's Bench, and complained bitterly of the outrages of his brother, could get little or no redress.[7] At last, in 1288, William Percy, junior, went to Jerusalem, and ten years later acknowledged his fealty to his brother,[8] the estates being divided, and William became the ancestor of the Percys of Ormesby. Arnald married Christiana, and had four children, the second of whom, John,

---

[1] Three miles south-west of Saltburn. According to Y. A. J., XXII., p. 280, Richard de Surdeval and Nigel Fossard founded Skelton Castle.
[2] Guis Chart. Sur. Soc., LXXXIX., II., p. 119n and Fine R. 56 Hen. III., m. 4.
[3] *Vide* Ch. IX.
[4] Cal. Feud. Aids, VI., p. 82.
[5] Y. A. S. Rec. S. XXIII., p. x., quotes '*infirmabatur quadam infirmitate, que dicitur paralasis.*'
[6] Y. A. S. Rec. S. XXIII., pp. 19-23.
[7] Ibid. *Cf*. Anct. Pet. 3254.
[8] Y. A. S. Rec. S. XXXI., p. 11.

married Mary, daughter of John Mautalent,[1] and on the death of his father Arnald in 1323/4, succeeded to the estates. In 1346, he was declared to have held 3 carucates in Thornton for the fourth part of one knight's fee.[2]

It has already been said that Robert Maungevileyn was the sub-tenant of the Percys in the latter part of the reign of Edward I., and it has been suggested[3] that Alice, the female descendant of the sub-infeudated Maungevileyn family, came to be regarded as the lord. She probably married Alan de Everley, and again, through a female, the manor was carried to a Wandesford, and in 1361, like the Everley manor of Ugglebarnby, it was in the hands of John de Wandesford holding by the *curtesy of England*,[4] in right of Joan his wife,[5] presumably great-great-granddaughter of Alice Maungevileyn. And it was probably their son or grandson, Thomas, who is mentioned as lord of the manor in a collection of a subsidy on 25 March, 1428, at an inquest held at Brompton.[6] But the heir of Thomas was not destined to hold for long, for in 1441 the three carucates had passed to Richard 'Eglesfield,'[7] who was the husband of Elizabeth, daughter of Sir William Brus of Pickering.[8] They are said to have had two sons, John and Robert.[9] But what became of these, and why did not one or the other inherit? That they did not, is clear from the fact that the next lord was a certain Edmund Thwaites, and it is equally clear that he was lord by the *curtesy*

---

[1] Whitby Chart. Sur. Soc. LXIX., p. 702*n*. Guis. Chart. Sur. Soc. LXXXVI., p. 272*n*.

[2] Cal. Feud. Aids, VI., p. 258.

[3] *Vide* Ch. IX.

[4] *Vide* Ch. XI.

[5] Y. A. S. Rec. S. LII., p. 80.

[6] Cal. Feud. Aids, VI., p. 312. '*Heres Thome Wandesford tenet in Thorneton iij car. terre pro iiij*ta *parte j.f.m. quas Johannes Percy de Kildale quondam tenuit. Et solvit subsidium xxd.*' It might be noted that there was a Hugh 'Wandsford' in Scarborough in 1337, and an Alice 'Wandsford' in Pickering in the same year. A Thomas 'Wandesforth' was on a jury at Malton in 1407 and in 1418. *Cf.* Y. A. S. Rec. S. LIX., pp. 68, 143.

[7] V. C. H. *N.R.* II., p. 495 says that the three carucates had apparently escheated to the Lord of Pickering, for Richard Eglesfield was distrained to do homage there. This may be true, but all the manors were in the superior soke of Pickering as shown in Domesday Book, and it may be that he was called upon to pay the usual fee attached to his lands, just as the Latimers, Lumleys and Hills had to pay 6s. 5d. for the main manor *ut supra*. In fact in 1619 Norden's Survey shows that there was such a fee attached to 'Eglesfield lands,' *vide infra*

[8] Foster, *Visitations of Yorkshire*, p. 130. Foster gives the two sons John and Robert, but the Provost of Queen's College in his monumental history I., p. 312 says 'a pair of brothers John and Robert appear about the same time in Mr. Stenhouse's pedigree of Eglesfield but he gives their father as Robert and makes him brother of Provost Thomas.'

[9] There was, in the neighbourhood, as early as 1334, one 'Eustace Eggesfield' *cf.* N. R. Rec. S. N.S., IV., p. 43.

of England through Joan, his wife. Was Joan the surviving daughter and heiress of Richard Eglesfield? Edmund Thwaites was the son of Henry Thwaites, who was in Pickering in 1448,[1] and died in 1480. Edmund himself died in March, 1502, and it was stated in the inquest that he was 'seised in his demesne or of free tenement the day he died, by the curtesy, after the death of Joan his wife, of 20 messuages, 500 acres of land, 40 acres meadow and 200 acres pasture in Thornton in Pykerynglith,[2] Snaynton, Eberston, Leberston and Westhorp, which before his death described' etc. The next words are practically incomprehensible, but sufficient be it to say, that Edmund and Joan Thwaites had three children. First, Eleanor, who married Sir John St. Quintin, secondly, Henry who died before 1500, and thirdly, Edmund, who was still alive in 1504. Henry did not die without an heir,[3] for his son was Sir Henry Thwaites of Lound-in-the-Wolds, who married one Agnes. He made his will in 1520, and died that year, seised of this manor of Thornton, leaving two daughters Katherine and Frances. As far as is known the elder never married, but the younger married, about 1538, John Gresham, who, again by the *curtesy of England* became lord of this manor in right of his wife.

The Gresham family was one of those which succeeded by worldly-wise marriages, steady industry and commercial acumen. Sir Richard Gresham,[4] who married Audrey Lyne, was the grandson of John Gresham of Holt.[5] Sir Richard had three sons: John, born in 1517,[6] Thomas, probably born in 1519,[7] and William. It would be interesting to know how John Gresham, of London, met his wife, the lady of a small north country manor. Had he married her after his father had acquired the property of the dissolved abbey of Fountains in 1540, one might have reasoned that a visit to Yorkshire to view the new possessions had brought about a meeting; but there seems no doubt that the marriage had taken place two years before Sir Richard Gresham was lord of Fountains. Sir John Gresham was a citizen and alderman of London, and when he

---

[1] N. R. Rec. S. N.S., I., p. 245.

[2] Cal. Inq. H. VII. II., pp. 384-5. Probably this amount of property is mere legal verbiage. A hundred years later this was quite common, and no truth must necessarily be attached to the figures.

[3] Henry Thwaites also had a daughter, 'Elyn', who married William Killinghall of Middleton St. George, co. Durham.

[4] Sir Richard Gresham was born about 1485: Lord Mayor of London: died 1549.

[5] John Gresham of Holt married secondly, Margaret, daughter of William Billingford, of Norfolk, and had a son John, who married Alice, daughter of Alexander Blyth.

[6] D. N. B.

[7] Thomas Gresham was the celebrated founder of the Royal Exchange. He died 1579.

married Frances Thwaites was, somewhat remarkably, declared as next of kin and heir to Edmund Thwaites.[1]

Sir John Gresham did not hold his Thornton property in complete peace. In May and June, 1546, the manor and the 'receyvour of the manor,' Stephen Holford,[2] were violently attacked by members of the family of Hunter.[3] No reason for this assault was offered in the account sent before Star Chamber, and so far it has remained a mystery. But that affairs were not altogether right, either financially or legally, is clear by the number of conveyances made at this period. As early as Michaelmas Term, 1545, 24 messuages with lands in 'Thorneton Farmondby and Ellerburne' were conveyed by 'John Gresham Esq. and Frances his wife'[4] to 'Stephen Holforde and Eleonora his wife.' The recipients in Michaelmas Term, 1548, conveyed to William Robson, senior, Johanna, his wife, and William Robson, junior, his bastard son, the same lands.[5] In the following Hilary Term, Francis, Earl of Huntingdon and Katherine, his wife, conveyed certain lands and the advowson of the Church in Thornton to Stephen Holford.[6] And so it went on, for the same lands were reconveyed in Easter Term, 1551,[7] to a number of men unconnected with Thornton. In Trinity Term, 1555, John and Frances Gresham conveyed to Wilfred Brand and John Wharffe this manor of Thornton and 8 messuages and 2 cottages with lands;[8] and there is a still further conveyance in Easter Term, 1558.[9] It may be supposed that all these were a long and complicated series of mortgages. By 1564 Sir John Gresham was dead, and in the Michaelmas Term of that year, there was another conveyance when Sir Henry Neville and Elizabeth his wife, and Frances Gresham, widow, conveyed the manor and 8 messuages, etc. to Roger Hunter.[10] Sir Henry Neville had married Elizabeth, who was the daughter and only child of Sir John Gresham and Frances his wife. Presumably all parties were anxious to get rid of a manor that had caused so much trouble.

In this way the aforetime Brus manor passed into the hands of the Hunter family which held it for the next one hundred years. The first reference to the family is to Robert Hunter 'valect. dni

[1] Y. A. S. Rec. S. II., pp. 84, 124.
[2] *Vide* Ch. XIV.
[3] *Vide* Ch. IV.
[4] Y. A. S. Rec. S. II., p. 119.
[5] Ibid., p. 138.
[6] Ibid., p. 139.
[7] Ibid., p. 155.
[8] Ibid., p. 184.
[9] Ibid., p. 215.
[10] Ibid., p. 296.

Regis ad coronam,'[1] in 1494. He was, at this period, of 'Staun-nestoon' and Scampston, and must also have resided at Scarborough because on 12 April, 1497, he had six oaks from the forest of Pickering 'for building of an hous of his in Scardburgh.'[2] The tracing of this family has proved most difficult and the suggested line of succession is open, no doubt, to many criticisms. Robert the 'yeoman,' who had married one, Agnes, was followed by his son Robert, who is mentioned as being at Newstead Grange, the Marishes, in 1534.[3] He had two sons, Robert and Roger.[4] The elder, Robert, paid £100 subsidy in Thornton in 1544,[5] and was buried at Thornton on 14 May, 1560,[6] having had three children: Anthony, buried on 14 March, 1560;[7] Christopher, who took part in the riot at the Gresham manor in 1546, and who lived until April, 1603;[8] and Roger, probably the eldest, and who married twice. His first wife was Kateran,' but of what stock is not known: she was buried on 2 January, 1550/1.[9] His second wife was 'Dorithe Laurance,' and they were married on 13 October, 1564.[10] From the first wife he had a large family[11] including Robert, and from the second an equally large family including Anthony of 'the Marish.' Robert, born in 1546, married first, in 1569 Cecilia 'Vavisors,' but she died in 1575.[12] Whereupon he married secondly, on 28 August, 1576, at Bridlington,[13] Anne, daughter of John 'Carleill' of Sewerby,[14] 'a man of importance and large possessions.'[15] Their child was Robert, who was an infant when his grandfather, Roger, died, and was buried on 9 June, 1583.[16]

Robert Hunter, son of Roger, took some part in the public life of Thornton. In October, 1597, he was commissioned by the

[1] Valect. = Valettus, a yeoman, and it is possible that this man was one of the Yeomen of the Guard created by Henry VII. His will, signed on 24 February was proved 14 March, 1508/9. The will of a Robert Hunter of Scarborough was proved on 3 January, 1406/7. *Cf.* Y. A. S. Rec. S. VI., p. 91.

[2] N. R. Rec. S. N.S. I., pp. 140, 166, 200, 202, and II., pp. 201, 206, 210.

[3] *Vide* Ch. XVII.

[4] Roger Hunter of this period according to the Church Registers had a large family.

[5] Lay Subs. R. bdle., 212, No. 161.

[6] C. R.

[7] Ibid.

[8] Ibid.

[9] Ibid.

[10] Ibid.

[11] Ibid.

[12] Ibid.

[13] Burke, *History of Commoners*, III., p. 588.

[14] The will of John 'Carlill' senior of Thornton in Pickeringlithe, gent. was signed on 11 January, 1596/7, and proved on 11 March. *Cf.* Y. A. S. Rec. S. LXV., p. 140.

[15] Burke, *ut supra*.

[16] C. R.

magistrates to see that William Sollett, carpenter, repaired the
North Riding section of New Malton Bridge. Evidently it was not
a period of bustle for it was not until 12 July, 1602, that it was
recorded that Robert Hunter 'did procure the said work of the
said bridge to be done.'[1] On 8 January, 1611/2, and again on 28
April, 1615, Robert Hunter was elected 'Head Constable for
Pickering lithe.'[2] He was also on juries at Snainton in April, 1612
and 1615, at Helmsley in July, 1612, and at Hutton Bushel in
April, 1616.[3] Three years later, in Norden's *Survey* he is mentioned
as holding this manor in Thornton with 540 acres and paying to
the Honor of Pickering £2.[4]

Robert Hunter died sometime before 1620, when his son, Robert,
made a conveyance of lands in Thornton.[5] He had married, at an
unknown date, but about 1601, Ellen or Helen, daughter of William
Spacye, of Brackton. Like his father he was active in the services
of the district. In 1641 and 1642, he was Treasurer of the Hospital;[6]
and on 6 October, 1646, a 'Head Constable.'[7]   But he was not a
scrupulously honest man, as has been shown, by trying to cheat
the villagers into paying illegal fees.[8]   He did not long survive[9]
this disgrace and was buried on 28 March, 1653.[10]   He had had many
children, including, his eldest son, 'Bethoelys,' 'Betheill', or Bethell,
born in 1602, a daughter Helen, who married Samuel Robinson
in 1654, and a very much younger son, Robert, born in 1618.
Bethell Hunter, after matriculating at Christ's College, Cambridge,
at Easter, 1620, had married at Kirby Misperton in 1630,[11] Magdalen,[12] daughter of Thomas Percehay of Ryton, and they had
three children, Ann, born in 1640, Christopher, baptized 26 April,
1646, and Mary, who married John Hassell[13] in 1657/8. Bethell
Hunter was buried at Thornton, on 28 November, 1660,[14] leaving
his son Christopher aged fourteen years.

[1] N. R. Rec. S. O.S. I., p. 223.
[2] Ibid., p. 243, and II., p. 94.
[3] Ibid., I., p. 257.
[4] Ibid., N.S. I., p. 51.
[5] Y. A. S. Rec. S. LVIII., p. 149. *Cf.* D. M. Meads, *ut supra*, p. 170.
[6] N. R Rec. S. O.S. IV., pp. 203, 206.
[7] Ibid., p. 260.
[8] *Vide* Ch. V.
[9] The Church Register says 'Mr. Robert Hunter senior dyed at Yorke
in the Assize week, and was buried there in Gotheramgate Church the 28th
day of March, 1653.'
[10] C. R. I think V. C. H. *N.R.* II., p. 495 gives an incorrect date.
[11] Camb. Al. II., p. 435.
[12] She died 1657/8.
[13] He died 1670.
[14] All these dates are from the Church Register. His will was proved
in February, 1660/1.

It is not very clear who was the owner of the ancient Brus manor when it passed to John Hill at an uncertain date after 1669 but before 1688. It would appear that Christopher Hunter would be the vendor, and it may very likely have been so. But as early as 12 April, 1652, when the old Robert Hunter had been alive, there was drawn up an indenture between Robert Hunter, the elder, of Thornton, gentleman, Bethell Hunter, son and heir apparent of the said Robert Hunter, and Magdalen, the wife of the said Bethell, and Robert Hunter the younger, son of the said Robert and Anne his wife, all of Thornton of the one party, and William Ives of ffarmanby and Robert White of Thornton, gentleman, conveying all that messuage tenements etc. in trust for Robert the younger,[1] who had married Anne, daughter of Thomas Boyes, of Edston, co. York. Whatever was the actual result of this arrangement, Robert was dead, in or before 1688,[2] and by this time the manor had been transferred to John Hill.

There were evidently a few outlying pieces of land separated from the manor that the Hill family ultimately acquired. On 23 December, 1698, Anne Hunter, widow of Robert, and her son-in-law, Henry Crist,[3] and her daughter Hellen, wife of the said Henry, sold to John Kirkby the messuage where they all now dwell etc. and he, on 14 May, 1702, sold the same to John Hill II., together with one grass garth or hempyard 'to ye stinting upon Peaslands adjoyning on ye land late Robert Hunter's on the south.'[4] There were some other small parcels held by members of the Hunter family. Christopher Hunter had a son called Robert, born in 1674,[5] and married one, Dorothy, who died on 18 October, 1718.[6] On 5 March, 1732/3, this Robert Hunter sold to John Hill that 'flatt of arable called Hurrill flatt lying in Thornton Harrowcliff field' consisting of 7 acres, 'yielding and paying therefor the rent of one peper corn at the feast of St. Michael the Archangel.... if the same shall be lawfully demanded.'[7] And finally on 26 May, 1756, a certain Robert Hunter of Lamberhurst in Kent appeared upon the scene. It is probable that he was the son of the aforementioned Robert, born in 1713, and married to one, Susanna. They, together with Francis Walmesley of 'Bridlington Key, yeo-

---

[1] G. F. G. H.
[2] Christopher Hunter seems to have lived for many years. His wife Katharine died 31 July, 1681; he died 8 October, 1717.
[3] Henry Crist was buried at Ellerburn 28 November, 1727, *cf.* Ellerburn Registers.
[4] G. F. G. H. *Cf.* for hempyard, Ch. I.
[5] Buried, aged 74, 20 October, 1748. A mortuary of 10s. was paid.
[6] C. R.
[7] G. F. G. H.

man and Catherine his wife,'[1] and Matthew Rymer 'of Bridlington Key, officer in the Customs, and Dorothy his wife'[2] of the first part, and Roger Atkinson of the second part, sold several arable lands 'and balks lying in ffarfield in a part called Highfield, part of Thornton Common called the Brow on the north and the road to Wilton on the south' and 'an intack called Woofnest End'[3] and other lands, to the aforesaid Roger Atkinson.[4] These lands, as already stated,[5] passed to Richard Johnson Hill in 1788.

Thus it may be concluded that the whole of the Gospatric-Brus-Gresham-Hunter manor passed into the hands of the Hill family, which has continued to hold it to the present day.

[1] Francis Walmesley married on 31 January, 1748/9. Catherine, born 3 August, 1705, daughter of Robert Hunter, born 5 May, 1674, son of Christopher Hunter. Francis Walmesley, with his brother-in-law Danby Hunter, born 21 March, 1716/7, was executor for 'Mrs. Elizabeth Hunter Spinster' aged 91. They paid a mortuary at her burial on 11 February, 1761. *Vide* C. R.

[2] Dorothy was the daughter of Robert Hunter. She was born 24 August, 1708.

[3] To-day Woofnest or Woolness or Woolnest is a lane turning east off Hurrell Lane south of the railway bridge. The first use of the word that I have found is 10 December, 13 Jas. I. when John Spenlay sold to John Gill, carpenter 'a broadland from the 'halfland' unto the Woolnest sike' 1 a. 2 r. *Vide* G. F. G. H. In 1670 Christopher Bradley had a 'close' in 'Woolness.' In the Rate Books of 1869 'Wool Nests' is said to be in the hands of John Baker.

[4] G. F. G. H.

[5] *Vide* Ch. XI.

CHAPTER THIRTEEN.

The Torbrand-Todeni-Lambert-Robinson Manor

'I followed my Duke ere I was a lover,
To take from England fief and fee;
But now this game is the other way over——
But now England hath taken me!'

KIPLING, 1906.

THE manor of Torbrand or Turbrand, which is described in Domesday Book as consisting of one carucate for geld and land for half a plough, passed, like much of Torbrand's other land elsewhere, to Berenger de Todeni.[1] It was surmised by the late Professor Edward Freeman, that Torbrand was 'perhaps the same person as Turbrand, who slew Uhtred, by whose son Ealdred, he was himself slain. Carl the son of Turbrand afterwards had his revenge and killed Ealdred. Turbrand, Carl's eldest son, lived at Settrington....and was slain by order of Earl Waltheof in 1073.'[2] As to the identity of the Norman interloper, it should be noted that Randolph de Toeni or Todeni was lord of a vill of that name, near the Seine, and had a son Robert, who after the Conquest, held 78 manors with his headquarters at Belvoir. He married Adela de Mowbray, and died 4 August, 1088, leaving three sons. The first, William de Albini, became the ancestor of the Dukes of Rutland.[3] The second, Berenger, married Albreda, became lord of many manors, including that in Thornton, and died without issue. The third was Nigel de Albini, who married Gundreda de Gournay, and had a son Roger, born in 1125, and who took part in the Battle of the Standard in 1138, at the early age of thirteen. This Roger

---

[1] Domesday Book. V. C. H. *York.*, II. on Domesday Book says that Liedtorp was in Thornton Dale. No reason is given. It does not appear to the present writer to be very likely, as the Thornton area is known to have been very seriously ravaged, whereas Liedtorp obviously had not, for it was worth more in 1086 than it had been in 1066.

[2] Freeman, *Norman Conquest* IV., p. 525. But this should be compared with MSS. of the Duke of Rutland, Hist. MSS. Com. IV., p. 106.

[3] Skaife, *ut supra*, pp. 92-3.

married Alice, daughter of Walter de Gand, the founder of Bridlington Priory in 1114,[1] and he himself founded both Newburgh Priory and Byland Abbey. He adopted the name of his grandmother's family and became Roger de Mowbray. He succeeded to some of the possessions of his uncle Berenger, amongst which was this manor in Thornton, but he probably never lived in the village as he made his headquarters at Hovingham.[2] The manor in Thornton descended to his son, Nigel, who married Mabel, daughter of the Earl of Clare. Their son, William, married Agnes, daughter of the Earl of Arundel. They had two sons, Nigel, who died in 1228, and Roger, who married Roesia, daughter of the Earl of Gloucester. This Roger is mentioned, in 1284, as holding of the King-in-chief three carucates of land in Thornton for the fourth part of a knight's fee, and that William Wyville holds of Roger and that the 'heirs' of Roger Morant hold of William Wyville.[3] These so-called 'heirs' of Roger Morant may have been a certain 'Ascilia Moraunt' of Thornton, from whom, as 'Acilia Moraunt' on 6 August, 1275, Alan de Kingthorpe held by knight service, 8 bovates and 8 acres of land worth yearly £6. 2s. 0d.[4] She it was who, also, on 25 April, 1276, claimed wardship over the lands of a minor in Ellerburn.[5] She was obviously a descendant of Roger Morant, probably daughter or granddaughter, but whom she married, if indeed she ever married, has eluded research.

As to the Wyvilles they had been tenants of the Mowbrays at least since the early part of the reign of Henry III. This is shown in an action by William Wyville in 1279, against the abbot of Rievaulx about property in Thornton and entered in an Assize Roll of that year. The descent of the land is traced from a certain William, whose son Richard, died leaving two daughters, Amfelisa, who died without issue, and Eustachia, the mother of the plaintiff.[6] Richard Wyville was the first lord of Slingsby, and died in 1225. His great-great-grandson, Sir John, died in 1301, having married Maud, and leaving a son, Sir William II.[7] He married Agnes,[8] daughter of William Lascelles of Sowerby, and their child was Sir William III., who died in 1334.[9]

---

[1] Walter de Gand or Gant died 1139.
[2] Eastmead, *ut supra.*
[3] Cal. Feud. Aids, VI., p. 82.
[4] Y. A. S. Rec. S. XII., p. 158.
[5] Cal. Inq. Ed. I. II., No. 200.
[6] Y. A. S. Rec. S. XII., p. 46.
[7] 'The tradition is that betwixt Malton and this toune (Slingsby) ther was sometymes a serpent that lyved upon prey of passengers, which this Wyvill and dog did kill where he received his deathes wound.'
[8] She died 1306.
[9] Y. A. J. III., p. 177.

It was, probably, on the death of this William Wyville, that John de Percy of Kildale, grandson of the already mentioned Arnald de Percy, who died in 1323/4,[1] became the tenant of this manor, holding from a member of the Mowbray family,[2] and which manor it is definitely stated was *formerly* held by the Wyvilles.[3] John de Percy continued to hold until his death in 1382/3. He had married before 1365 Alicia, daughter of John Meynell, widow of Sir Walter Boynton,[4] and their son John succeeded as lord of the manor.[5] He married one, Elizabeth, and died about 1428, his widow survived him for at least ten years.[6]

Since the days of Ascilia Moraunt, however, there are no references to any resident holders of the manor. But suddenly, in 1428, it is stated that the tenant of the manor, as of the fee of Mowbray, which John de Kildale formerly held,[7] was 'Matildis Lamberd.' Whether the family of Morant had merged by marriage into the family of Lambert, no proof has yet come to light; but for the next century, the Lamberts were in occupation. Robert Lambert succeeded Matilda, during the latter part of the fifteenth century; and he, in turn, was followed by his son Nicholas, who died seised of 5 messuages and 100 acres, in February, 1543/4.[8] His son Roger or Robert had been born in 1540/1, and married one, Grace, of what family is not known. They disposed of their Thornton property to Henry Robinson in Hilary Term, 1566/7.[9]

It was by this conveyance that the Robinsons came to be the holders of the third manor in Thornton. Henry Robinson married Agnes, daughter of a certain Greaves, Lord Mayor of York, and as there was a conveyance in trust to Christopher Maltby,[10] in Hilary Term, 1573/4 it is probable that the marriage took place about that time. They had three children, Henry, John, afterwards the rector, and William, a citizen of York.

---

[1] John de Mowbray was hanged at York after the battle of Boroughbridge in 1322.

[2] Cal. Feud. Aids, VI., p. 258.

[3] V. C. H. *N.R.* II., p. 495, suggests that the Gospatric and Torbrand manors are here confused. The present writer prefers to differ and thinks that John de Percy probably held both.

[4] Whitby Chart. Sur. Soc. LXIX., p. 303. Cal. Pat. R., 1401-5, p. 297.

[5] John de Percy on 29 June, 1392, received four bovates of land and 2/3 of 2 tofts in Thornton, the escheated holding of John Halscarth who had been outlawed for felony.

[6] Guis. Chart. Sur. Soc. LXXXVI., p. 229n.

[7] Cal. Feud. Aids, VI., p. 312.

[8] V. C. H. *N.R.* II., p. 495.

[9] Y. A. S. Rec. S. II., p. 330.

[10] Ibid. V., p. 44. This man must have been the son of 'Christofer Maltebi' who had been a husbandman in Thornton and who made his will on 8 October, 1548, and it was proved on 9 May, 1549. *Cf.* Y. A. S. Rec. S. XI., p. 114.

From later information it seems clear that the eldest son, Henry, became lord of the manor, and after fighting for Charles I., died in 1649. It is also clear that the Lambert holding had not passed in entirety to a single owner, because in Norden's *Survey*, for the lands of Lambert, John Robinson paid to the Honor of Pickering, probably on behalf of his brother, Henry, 2s. 2¼d., William Skelton paid 9d. and Christopher Boyes paid 4½d.[1]

John Robinson became rector in 1609,[2] and living as he did in Thornton, he may have thought it wise to increase the family property as his brother was without an heir of his body. John married, secondly,[3] before January, 1620, the daughter of William or Christopher, Ives of Gilling. Children began to come with regularity,[4] and so he invested money in land for himself and his offspring. As early as Michaelmas Term, 1618, he acquired from Sir Richard Cholmley a water corn-mill with land in Farmanby.[5] On 11 August, 1626, Hugh Grande of Kingston-upon-Hull, transferred to him certain property in York, but it is not easy to estimate the amount.[6] On the following 20 February, James Harton of Ruston,[7] in 'Pickering Lithe,' and Alice, his wife, sold, for £400 to 'John Robinson, Person of the Rectorie or Church of Thornton,' certain messuages, 5 crofts, now enclosed, containing 2 acres, a garth, and 6 oxgangs 'with the granges'[8] 'within the territories or lordship of ffarmanby & Thornton'[9] and late in the occupation of Stephen Milnes, of Thornton,[10] and William Boyes, blacksmith.

The main story of John Robinson's life in the village has been told in a previous chapter. That he suffered much at the hands of the Parliamentarians for his own loyalty and for the loyalty of his brother is very evident. As early as 3 February, 1649, he begged to

[1] Norden's *Survey*, 1619. MS. Copy. G. F. G. H.
[2] *Vide* Ch. IX.
[3] *Vide* Ch. IX.
[4] C. R. Susanna, 30 September, 1620, buried 25 February, 1625/6. Henrie, 3 November, 1622, buried 5 May, 1650. Johadan, no date, buried 29 March, 1623. John, 1623/4, died before Samuel, but no date. 'Samuwell' 3 April, 1625, no date of death. 'Dedymus', Samuel's twin, 3 April, 1625, buried 13 April, 1625. Jayne, 1 October, 1626, married William Blanchard, citizen of York. Rosemond, 26 April, 1629, buried 2 March, 1631. Richard, 22 July, 1634, buried 17 August, 1635. Jehoadan, 1 August, 1641, married Henry Slee, 17 May, 1668.
[5] Y. A. S. Rec. S. LVIII., p. 114.
[6] G. F. G. H.
[7] James Harton was lord of the manor of Ruston.
[8] Barns.
[9] G. F. G. H.
[10] In Norden's *Survey*, Stephen 'Mylles' paid 8d. to the Honor of Pickering for 'Eglesfield lands.' He was probably the son of Ralph Milnes, who flourished c. 1587. *Cf.* Y. A. S. Rec. S. VII., p. 80. Stephen 'Mills,' Farmanby, 'gent,' was on the second pannel of the Jury at Quarter Sessions at Thirsk on 3 April, 1611. *Cf.* N. R. Rec. S. O.S. I., p. 214.

compound, being sequestered for adhering to the forces raised against Parliament,[1] and on 23 May, he was fined £78. 6s. 0d., based upon the value of the lands he held in the Marishes.[2] On 13 May, 1650, he petitioned for freedom from sequestration both as regards the first and second war. He stated that he had compounded a year before for his elder brother's, (Henry's), estate, valued £50 per annum which had descended to him, but that owing to the oversight of his solicitor, his discharge was only taken out as regards the first war, whereas he had paid the fine for both wars. He desired that the rents received since the discharge might be restored to him. Although an order for discharge was entered, John Robinson did not, as yet, escape from the clutches of his enemies; and again on 30 July, petitioned to compound, being again sequestered 'for the old delinquency committed in his poverty and youth.'[3] The outcome of this last appeal was that on 3 September, 1650, he was fined at 1/6, £150. But even now the Committee for Compounding seemed to lust for more because, on 13 May, 1651, the Secretary wrote to the County Committee, saying 'We thank you for your notice of blotting out and altering Robinson's estate, and you are desired to certifie when you have any jealousy that further inquiry may be made.'[4] After this, so far as can be ascertained, John Robinson was left in peace, though unfortunately posterity remains without any knowledge of the exact sum he paid in all. But if he were still in debt for the Marish land,[5] and if he had to pay considerable sums as fines, there can be little doubt that the Robinson family, like hundreds of others after the Civil War, was seriously crippled. The later story of their property seems to point to this conclusion.

After John Robinson's burial, on 1 February, 1656/7,[6] he was succeeded by his only surviving son, Samuel, who was baptized 3 April, 1625, and who married Helen, daughter of Robert Hunter, lord of the second manor in Thornton, on 13 September, 1654.[7] She died on 7 October, 1669, leaving several children.[8] On 15

---

[1] Cal. Cttee. of Comp., p. 1906.

[2] *Vide* Ch. XVII.

[3] This must have been a mere phrase for he cannot have been less than 65 years of age in 1650.

[4] Cal. Cttee. of Comp., p. 1907. 'Jealousy'=Suspicion.

[5] *Vide* Ch. XVII.

[6] C. R. The will of John Robinson, of 'Thorneton,' widower, was proved by his only son, Samuel Robinson, in 1657. *Cf.* Y. A. S. Rec. S. I., p. 183.

[7] C. R.

[8] The children were James, bapt. 19 December, 1656; John, bapt. 7 November, 1658, described as of Thornton, and in 1707 as clerk of Whitby; married Magdalen; there were also Jane, Magdalen and Helen. The latter died an infant 28 April, 1667.

February, 1663, there was an indenture drawn up between Samuel Robinson of 'ffarmanby' and Robert Hollis of New Malton, gentleman, William Ives of 'farmanby' and Robert Hunter, of Thornton, gentleman, on consideration of a marriage between Samuel Robinson and 'Ellen' Hunter, sister of the said Robert.[1] Samuel Robinson covenanted to the said trustees all his lands 'in the Townshipp, Tounefields, precincts and territories of Thornton, ffarmanby,' to uses etc., and to his heirs male.[2] This was probably a late form of settlement in the interest of Helen and her children. The pinch may have already been making itself felt, and even though Samuel married again, after Helen's death, Melior Hird,[3] before 1673, his affairs could not have been very prosperous. It was in that very year, that there seems to have been the first sale to John Hill, the new landlord of the main manor.

On 14 April, 1673, Samuel Robinson and Melior his second wife sold to John Hill for £86. 13s. 0d.[4] the one-rood-breadth oxgang 'called Attaget in ffarmanby,' a 1 rood broadland lying in 'Atiesdike,' extending from the 'Candike to the headland,' and 1 rood in each of the following :—'Spelgate' 'from Roxby Lane to the gate called Stiffegate in Langlands extending from headland to headland':[5] in 'Munklands'[6] from the 'Moordike': in 'Low Fausa' [?]: in 'Between Townes,' extending from the headland belonging to the vicar of Ellerburn:[7] in 'little holgate,' extending from 'the beck or river'; and near 'a water-sewer called the syme': and near 'Boodhills'.[8] This was the beginning of the gradual dispersion of the property. It may be presumed that Samuel Robinson was dead by 1683, for in that year, his three children, John, Jane, and Magdalen, made over to Mrs. Anne Hollis of Kingston-upon-Hull,[9]

---

[1] These Roberts are very confusing. This is Robert born in 1618 who seems to be the prominent person instead of his brother Bethell.

[2] G. F. G. H.

[3] She was a widow and was by birth a daughter of Thomas Fairfax, who was buried at Ellerburn, 1680. She was baptized at Bossall, 11 December, 1641.

[4] G. F. G. H.

[5] I have not been able to identify these.

[6] Still so named on west of Whitby Road.

[7] Near where the new Vicarage of Ellerburn now stands, but not the site.

[8] This name seems now to be lost. It was an enclosure about a ¼ of a mile due west of Charity Farm. Norden's *Survey* says 'Enquire of a parcell of lande adjoyninge to Thornton Ox carr called Budells.' The jury replied 'There is a parcell of grounde nere Thorneton Carr called Bowdhills contayninge 32 acres, whereof Robert Hunter holdeth 20 acres and Sir William Sandes 12 acres.'

[9] Probably their cousin by marriage. Their mother's sister, Mary Hunter, had married 'Macabysse' Hollis of Hull in 1633. *Cf.* C. R.

a capital messuage in 'ffarmanby.'[1] In 1685 a little bit more of the old holding passed out of their hands when Jane and Magdalen Robinson of 'ffarmanby' and Thomas Robinson, yeoman, conveyed to John Hill the 'land' called 'Hurrell' lying between Hill land 'on ye east and the land of Christopher Hunter, gent[2] and Hungrellway on the west and extending from the close of Larban flat on the north and the aforementioned way on the south.'[3]

The eldest son of John Robinson, 'clerk of Whitby,' had become a sailor, and is referred to as 'mariner of Scarborough.' He had married at an unknown date, one, Jane. On 28 January, 1691/2, he, his wife, his father, his mother and Thomas 'ffarside, gent' are declared to be 'co-partners,' and to hold a portion of the property, before the death, and another after the death, of Melior, the widow of Samuel Robinson. The property consisted of a capital messuage or 'Hall,' orchard, garths, 'the Walks,' four closes occupied by Abraham Medd, 'West Carr,' occupied by Anthony Hunter, 'East Carr,' occupied by John Boyes, and 'Low Broats,' occupied by Robert Hunter. Besides these there were seven houses, 'Broats Close,' 'Small Broats,' 'Herry Dy,'[4] 'the Ings,' commonly called 'Honey Pott,'[5] occupied by William Boyes, 'Hill Dykes in West Field,' three Roodbreeds and other lands. These, or the main part of them, including 'Clay Pitts' were mortgaged to John Hill.[6] On 7 and 12 April, 1706, when the mansion house was definitely called 'Robinson Hall,' John Hill made a part purchase, but on the rest the mortgage continued. The property had now been divided into two parts. On 25 September, 1721, one moiety was transferred to trustees; and in 1729, there was a lease and release of the second moiety to John Hill.[7] The Robinsons, however, as late as 1 March, 1733, exercised some hold, for the Rev. Thomas Robinson of Broxburne, Herts., and Mary his wife, leased to Matthew Robinson of London for one year, 'the Close' and 'Broats'; but by 6 December,

---

[1] By an endorsement on this document dated 24 July, 1702, the transaction was proved to be a mortgage. There had been intermediate renewals as in 1691 when John Robinson 'in ye right of Jane his wife' and of John Robinson, afterwards clerk of Whitby, in right of Magdalen his wife, and Melior wife and relict of Samuel Robinson, renewed the agreement. N.B. John Robinson, clerk, took the oaths to William and Mary at Richmond 22 July, 1691, and again as clerk of Whitby to Queen Anne on 10 July, 1705. *Cf.* N. R. Rec. S. O.S. IX., p. 36.

[2] Here is the solution of the present 'Hunter's Lane.'

[3] G. F. G. H.

[4] Herry Dy is still so named and is the field between 'The Lodge' and Maltongate. *Cf.* Ch. VI.

[5] Honey Pot is still the name of a field between Maltongate and the Beck, near Summertree Bridge. I am indebted to Mrs. Richard Hill.

[6] G. F. G. H.

[7] Ibid.

1734, all the Robinson property passed to John Hill II.; and a later abstract of title stated that this completed the purchase from the Robinson family.[1]

Since this date to the present time, this, the third of the manors of Thornton, has remained in the hands of the Hill family, concerning whose holding of the other two manors reference has already been made.[2]

[1] Ibid.
[2] *Vide* Chs. XI., XII.

CHAPTER FOURTEEN.

The Ellerburn-cum-Farmanby Manor.

'*A lord might well have a manor of which the soke lay in another manor external to his fief.*'

PROF. STENTON, 1910.

AT first sight, from the references in Domesday Book, neither Ellerburn nor Farmanby were necessarily manors in the eleventh century. The record definitely states that 'to the manor of the King in Pickering belongs the soke of Elreburne. In Elreburne Gospatric[1] had 3 bovates of land for geld. In Elreburne the King has one carucate.'[2] As to Farmanby there is the statement that 'the soke of Farmanesbi'[3] also belonged to Pickering. From many later records, however, there can be little doubt that Ellerburn-cum-Farmanby was as much a manor as any of the others already discussed.

The meaning of the name 'Ellerburn' is clear but curious. In this district, by all the rules, it should be 'Ellerbeck,' but it is not. In any case it means 'The stream of the alders'; but the question does arise, why, from the earliest times has 'burn' been substituted for 'beck'? In no other connection, in all the documents referring to the civil parish of Thornton, has the 'beck' ever been called a 'burn.' But it matters not, for there to-day, as from the distant ages, is the stream, beck, or burn; and there, until very recent years were the alders; but the clogging-trade has played havoc with what nature supplied so lavishly in the past.[4] As to Farmanby,

[1] *Vide* Ch. XII.
[2] Domesday Book. Stenton, *Types of Manorial Structure in the Northern Danelaw*, p. 52 says 'If a thegn of 1066 holding a manor of which the soke belonged to some great estate, forfeited his land, it might well be that the land in question should appear in Domesday merely as sokeland of the larger manor to which it was jurisdictionally subject.'
[3] Domesday Book.
[4] The last of the cloggers, for it is a dead industry, is John Raw, who in the season, before the Great War, worked up the valley and with his simple and yet ingenious cutting instrument, fashioned swiftly and deftly the sole of the clog, from logs of alder. These embryo soles were carted down to Thornton, and piled in what looked like Gargantuan honey-combs, in his garden, to dry; and were then transferred to Lancashire for the cotton-mill hands. Alder wood was regarded as the best for these clogs. It was hard for wear, and yet pliable enough to give to the toes, which after a short time made an impression, and left the apparently resisting and solid wood, quite comfortable to the foot. *Cf. Yorkshire Post*, April, 1929.

the name is obvious enough, though hardly so picturesque as that of her sister—Farman's settlement[1]—Farman or Farmann, was an ancient Norseman, and he settled on the west side of the Beck. For the sake of the historian it is a pity that he, or his descendants, did not keep that stream as a clear boundary, because to-day, and from records it is shown to be the same for centuries, the dividing line between Farmanby and Thornton is inextricable.[2] The very fact that they are so united and interwoven, early in history, and that the manor house of Ellerburn from the earliest times was in Farmanby, which to the non-initiated means the same as Thornton, shows that the division between the two is of immense antiquity and lost in the mists of the past. On the other hand it must be recognized that there has been handed down, from generation to generation, a remarkable knowledge, and each inhabitant seems to know, by instinct, whether their dwelling is in the ecclesiastical parish of Thornton or within the pastoral care of the vicarage of Ellerburn.

In very early times Ellerburn was a mesne lordship of the Hospital of St. Leonard of York, and under that Hospital the two resident tenants were Norman Bushell and Osbert.[3] There were, however, other freehold tenants as well, for about 1200, Rosedale Abbey, held by the gift of Roger de Laistor, two bovates in Farmanby, and one toft with a croft, granted, at much the same time, by Ralph Bardolf.[4] And that there were other small freeholders is seen by the fact that, on S. Clement's Day, 23 November, 1234, at York, Juliana, daughter of Maud, quitclaimed to Henry, son of Geoffrey, in exchange for 15s. sterling, for 3 acres of land

[1] A. H. Smith, *ut supra*, p. 89.

[2] In my ignorance, for many years, I imagined that the Beck was the boundary from a certain point to a certain point. In more recent years I have learnt that this is not so and that Thornton and Farmanby, united in every common interest are also completely interlocked geographically, so that it is impossible to explain why this house is in Farmanby and that house is in Thornton. The difficulty existed in the old days of tithes and is referred to in the Church Terriers. Exch. Dep. Mich. 12 Jas. I., No. 2 shows that as early as 1614 the towns of Thornton and Farmanby had no boundary and lay so close that they could not be distinguished. There is one farm-house in Maltongate, formerly occupied by the Gamble family and now by Thomas Darrell where a thick oak beam across the living room marks the division between Thornton and Farmanby. The Beck is in fact no definite boundary though obviously it seems to be the 'natural frontier.'

[3] V. C. H. *N.R.* II., p. 438.

[4] Dugdale, *Monasticon* IV., p. 318 edit. 1846. Roger de Laistor made a gift 'de duabus bovatis terrae in Farmaneby, illas scilicet quas Rogerus Racine tenuit cum omnibus pertinentiis et libertatibus et aisiamentis ad eandem terram pertinentibus in bosco, in plano, in pratis et pasturis.' Ralph Bardolf made a gift 'de uno tofto cum crofto et aliis pertinentiis suis in Farmaneby in liberam, puram et perpetuam elemosinam.'

and a moiety of a toft in Formodeby (Farmanby).[1] Alan Hert, son of Thomas Hert of Farmanby also held a small portion which he granted to Sir Nicholas de 'Hastingis,' about 1275, for a sum of money paid '*in mea magna necessitate.*' This conveyance was witnessed by several local persons such as John Kampyun [Campion] of Thornton, Adam de Rouceby, Walter de Rouceby, William de Thormoteby of Pickering, Astinus, son of Elias of Farmanby and Robert de Cliff of Thornton.[2] Another small patch in Farmanby belonged to Astinus, son of Elias and he leased it on 14 April, 1275, for six years to Alan Percie. The witnesses were again local, for in addition to Sir Nicholas de 'Hestinge' there were Alan son of Andrew, John Campion and Adam de 'Roxeby.'[3] In the reign of Edward I., the Knights Templar,[4] also, held a small portion of land here, and from them Alan de Kingthorpe,[5] was the holder of one toft. But his main property in this manor when he died, was held, partly from St. Leonard's Hospital, consisting of 6 oxgangs in Ellerburn and 4 oxgangs in Farmanby; and partly, from Ascilia Moraunt,[6] consisting of 20 tofts, a water-mill, a capital messuage situated in 'Thorneton,' which should be, more probably, 'Farmanby.'

An inquest was held on this property on 28 April, 1276, and it was the same that Philip de Wyleby, late Escheator beyond Trent, had taken into the King's hands after the death of Alan de 'Kynthorpe,' understanding that all the lands were held of the King in-chief. It was alleged, however, by Ascilia Moraunt of 'Thorinton,' that Alan held of her the capital messuage of the manor of 'Ellerburne,' together with seven bovates of land in 'Thorinton,' whereby the custody of the land ought to be hers until the lawful age of the heir. A further inquest was held to investigate the truth, and in the presence of Peter de Gaolya, Ralph de Loketon, Nicholas de Dale, William son of Thomas, Richard Archebaud, Philip de Alvestayn, [Allerston], William son of Robert, John son of Oda, Roger Kockerell, John son of Robert, Alan son of Andrew, John Campyun [Campion], and Adam de Rouceby, it was decided that Alan did hold by knight's service nine carucates making one knight's fee, of Ascilia 'Morant.'[7]

---

[1] Y. A. S. Rec. S. LXVII., p. 15.

[2] Hist. MSS. Com., Rawden Hastings MS. I., p. 193.

[3] Ibid.

[4] In 1322 the 'Minister's Accounts' of the Forest of Pickering refer to lands of the Templars at Farmanby and Ellerburn, which came into the hands of Thomas, Earl of Lancaster; but they do not specify the lands. *Cf.* N. R. Rec. S. N.S. IV., p. 202.

[5] *Vide* Ch. XI.

[6] *Vide* Ch. XIII.

[7] Y. A. S. Rec. S. XII., pp. 170-1.

Alan de Kingthorpe had outlived his son Geoffrey, and his heir was his granddaughter, Petronilla or Parnell, who, according to one authority,[1] sold the manor of Ellerburn to William Yeland for £100.[2] It is certain that on 31 July, 1299, there was a grant, and as this document afterwards passed into the possession of the Hastings' family,[3] it may be surmised that William Yeland held the manor for a short time. The grant, however, did not state that the sale was for £100, but said that it was by 'Petronilla, daughter and heir of Geoffrey de Kinthorp, son and heir of Alan de Kinthorp, to her kinsman William de Yelande, son of John de Yelande, of her whole Manor [of Ellerburn] together with all her tenement of "Tanetoun" in "Pickering Lythe," and a *cultura* called "Micting-haker" together also with the homage and service of John of Stodelay and his heirs, for all the lands and tenements held of her by him in "Slenkesby" [Slingsby] in Ryedale.'[4] This being so then Ellerburn and Farmanby must have been divided for a time for the latter was, at the end of the thirteenth century in the hands of Nicholas de Hastings; and by 1316 it is definitely stated that the lord of the manor of 'Farmanby-cum-Ellerton' [Ellerburn] was the heir of Nicholas de Hastings.[5]

The family of Hastings was an important one and had much to do with this district, exercising considerable power in Allerston, Ellerburn, Farmanby, and Roxby, being brought into the neighbourhood by marriage with an heiress. It has already been shown that the Norse thegn Gospatric sprang from Bishop Aldun or Alden, who lived at the beginning of the eleventh century.[6] Gospatric had four sons, Gospatric, Alan, Dolphin, and Uchtred. The last is commonly known as 'de Alverstone' or 'de Alvestane' or 'of Allerston.' He was succeeded by his son Thorfin and he, in turn, by his eldest son, Alan, who married Alice, daughter of Roger Despencer, and died before 1231. Their child and heiress was Helen, who married Hugh de Hastings and brought with her the family property of Allerston.

---

[1] V. C. H. *N.R.* II., p. 469.

[2] For the family of Yeland *vide* N. R. Rec. S. N.S. II., *passim.*

[3] Hist. MSS. Com., Rawden Hastings MS. I., p. 190.

[4] Ibid.

[5] Cal. Feud. Aids, VI., p. 177. V. C. H. *N.R.* II., p. 438 says 'In 1318 Hugh de Hastings of Dalton probably guardian of the heir of Nicholas de Hastings, conveyed the manor to William de Yeland and Katharine his wife and the heirs of William (Feet of Fines, 12 Ed. II., No. 44), and in 1328 Katharine, widow of William de Yeland, Hugh de Yeland and William his brother were concerned in a suit with the Dean of York about 60 feet of land in Ellerburn' [De Banco R. East., 2 Ed. III., m.17].

[6] *Vide* Ch. XII.

The descent of the family of Hastings, or rather of that branch that was connected with Allerston, Farmanby, and Roxby, has been most difficult to trace. The older genealogists, like Henry Nugent Bell,[1] have tried to find the earliest known ancestor in a certain Robert de Hastings, in the reign of William the Conqueror, 'port-reeve of Hastings,' of whom the late J. H. Round has scornfully said that he was 'an official unknown to History.'[2] The first, apparently, authentic ancestor was William or Walter[3] Hastings, who like his son, or grandson,[4] Hugh, was steward to Henry I. This Hugh married Erneburga, daughter of Robert de Flamville.[5] Their son was another William who married twice. His first wife, Maud Banaster and her descendants are not of interest to the present story.[6] His second wife is said by some to have been Ida, daughter of Henry, Count of Eu;[7] and by her (or by someone else), he had two sons, Thomas and John. The son of Thomas was Hugh, the already mentioned husband of Helen de Alvestain. He died before 1203, leaving an heir, Thomas, whose widow, the Lady Amice, long survived him and had as part of her dower the manor of Allerston. Their eldest son was another Thomas who succeeded to the Hastings' estates in Westmorland, at some unknown date in the reign of Henry III.;[8] while their second son was Sir Nicholas de Hastings,[9] Lord of Allerston.[10] He married Emmelina, daughter of Walter de Heron,[11] and she was alive as late as 1297. Nicholas and Emmelina had five sons, the eldest was Hugh, the next three were Henry, Nicholas, and Richard of whom little is known, and the last was Edmund who is dealt with under the 'Manor of Roxby.'[12] The eldest son, Sir Hugh de Hastings, received from his father, Sir Nicholas, as shown in a confirmatory grant of 20 October, 1287, the capital Manor of Farmanby and six bovates of land with two 'ovenames' which Sir Nicholas had had of the gift of Ralph 'Bardelf.'[13] Sir Hugh, who died in 1302, was succeeded by his son, another Sir Nicholas,[14] who married one, Agnes, and like all his family risked

---

[1] Henry Nugent Bell, *The Huntingdon Peerage*, p. 2.
[2] J. H. Round, *Studies in Peerage and Family History*, p. 63.
[3] Walter is the modern accepted version.
[4] *Cf. Book of Fees*, p. 132.
[5] Dugdale, *Baronage I.*, p. 574.
[6] They are of importance as being ancestors of a branch of the Hastings which died out in 1389, but this line had nothing to do with this district.
[7] But this is very uncertain.
[8] Hist. MSS. Com., Rawden Hastings MS. I., p. 201.
[9] V. C. H. *N.R.* II., p. 422.
[10] He was dead by the year 1284.
[11] Some authorities deny this.
[12] *Vide* Ch. XV.
[13] Hist. MSS. Com., Rawden Hastings MS. I., pp. 193-4.
[14] He had a brother Hugh, *vide* N. R. Rec. S. *N.S.* 11., pp. 103-4.

much as a poacher in the Forest of Pickering.[1] His son, Sir Ralph[2] of Allerston, Farmanby, Thorpe Basset, Slingsby, and Sledmere,[3] as has been shown, was Keeper of Pickering Castle, tried to annex Howldale, fought at Neville's Cross and died of his wounds in 1346.[4] He had married Margaret, daughter of Sir William de Herle of Kirby, Leicestershire, who, after the death of her brother, brought considerable estates to the Hastings family. Presumably under Sir Ralph de Hastings, his relative William, son of Edmund and the Lady Beatrice[5] Hastings, was a *tenant* of lands in Farmanby in 1334.[6] Sir Ralph's son, Sir Ralph, sheriff of Yorkshire in 1377 and 1380, remained lord of the manor for many years; and married, secondly, Maude, daughter of Sir Thomas Sutton,[7] who outlived him for ten years, he dying in 1397. His eldest son, and lord of Farmanby, was executed for taking part in Scrope's rebellion in 1405; and he was succeeded by his brother, Richard, born about 1380, and who was fortunate in obtaining the restitution of the family estates which had been surrendered to the Crown. He died, without issue, in 1437, and the property passed to his younger

[1] N. R. Rec. S. N.S. II., p. 114. Probably died in 1316.

[2] *Vide* Ch. II.

[3] Hist. MSS. Com. *ut supra*, p. x, says 'In 1307 when he must have been very young, his father gave him the manor of Thorpe Basset in Yorkshire, which he had just acquired in fee farm from Ralph FitzWilliam, baron of Greystoke (Lord FitzWilliam) (Dugdale's authority for this is a manuscript belonging to the Earl of Huntingdon). In 1329 he received a charter of free warren in his demesne lands of Allerston....(Cal. Char. R. IV., 117). In 1343 he purchased from William Wyvill the manors of Welford in Northants., and Slingsby and Sledmere in Yorkshire. (*Cf.* V. C. H. *N.R.* I., p. 559).'

[4] *Vide* Ch. II.

[5] *Vide* Ch. II. This does not agree with Hist. MSS. Com., Rawden Hastings MS. I., p. ix, because I find that on December 2, 1336, William is definitely stated to be son of Edmund, not as Nugent Bell says in *The Huntingdon Peerage*, p. 10, brother of Sir Ralph. Nor is the younger Edmund of Roxby son of William, because William is never shown to have anything to do with Roxby, and if it is the same William who is alive in 1359 Edmund de 'Hastinge' is called lord of 'Rouceby' and is the first witness to a grant of that year and 'William de Hastinge' is the second. It is clear from all that has been written on the subject that the pedigree is a complete tangle from about 1284 to 1360. But I should suggest that Edmund, son of the first Sir Nicholas, married the Lady Beatrice and died before 1301. She died before 1334 as a widow of long standing. Her two sons were William and Edmund (called senior in 1338 and was alive in 1347) and that this Edmund had a son, Edmund of Roxby (called junior in 1338 and was alive in 1381). *Vide* Ch. XV. It should also be noted a certain Nicholas is declared to be the son of 'William de Hastynges of Thornton' on 5 February, 1392. *Vide* Ch. XI.

[6] N. R. Rec. S. N. S. III., p. 41.

[7] Hist. MSS. Com., Rawden Hastings MS. I., p. xi, says 'Poulson (*Hist. of Holderness* II., p. 20) on the other hand says that he married Alice, sister and heir of John de Meaux of Aldborough in Yorks' and this view is taken by the modern historian of Sutton-in-Holderness (Thomas Blashill, *Sutton in Holderness: the Manor, the Berewic and the Village Community*, ed. 1900, p. 111).

brother, Leonard. About 1424, Sir Leonard Hastings[1] married Alice, daughter of Thomas, Lord Camoys, and by her had a son, William, born about 1425.

William Hastings, the first member of the family to be created a peer, was certainly the most prominent in national history, up to this date. He acted as sheriff both in Leicestershire and Warwickshire; but more particularly did he win fame as a very loyal and ardent Yorkist in the Wars of the Roses. He held numerous official posts, was created a baron in 1461,[2] and earned the gratitude of Edward IV., first in assisting him to escape to Holland in 1470; and, secondly, by his splendid gallantry at the battles of Barnet and Tewkesbury in 1471. On the accession of the infant, Edward V., he was bitterly opposed to the influence of Lord Rivers, and also made the mistake, as far as his own life was concerned, in refusing the overtures of the crafty Duke of Gloucester, afterwards Richard III.[3] The result was, that, most unjustly he was executed on 13 June, 1483. During his lifetime he had founded a chantry in the Royal College and Chapel of St. George at Windsor, and for this reason he was buried there. He had married Katherine, daughter of the Earl of Warwick, who survived him till 1503. Their child, Sir Edward Hastings, was born in 1466, and married Mary Hungerford, Baroness Botreaux,[4] sometime before 1481. On 20 October, 1506, he procured a licence in Mortmain by means of which he granted the manors of Farmanby and Esthallegarth and 26 messuages, 2 tofts, 2 mills, 2 dovecotes,[5] 20 gardens, 200 acres of land, 60 acres of meadow, 80 acres of pasture, 100 acres of wood, furze and heath, and 26s. of rents in 'Farmanby, Thorneton, Elleborne, Pykering, Easthallegarth and Thurkelby....for the soul of William, late Lord Hastings,' to the Dean and Canons of the

---

[1] He died 1455.

[2] Complete Peerage VI., p. 370.

[3] *Cf.* Sir Thomas More, *Edward V. and Richard III.* edit. 1789, pp. 28-9, and Shakespeare, *Richard III.*, Act III. Sc. iv. Lord Hastings is mentioned in the *Paston Letters*, edit. 1900, Vol. II. pp. 110, 112, and III. *passim*. Fuller in his *Worthies of England*, I., p. 581 says 'The Reader needeth not my dimme Candle to direct him to this illustrious person.'

[4] She died as the widow of Sir R. Sacheverell in 1534.

[5] I do not think that there are any signs of manorial dovecotes in Thornton to-day. There is a good specimen at the Low Hall, Brompton: but they are more numerous in the south of England than in the north. A *columbarium* is commonly associated with manorial privileges. These pigeons were a curse to the farmer. In 1813 it was estimated that there were 20,000 'dovecotes' in England and Wales, each, on an average, containing 100 pairs of old pigeons.

Royal free Chapel of St. George in Windsor.[1] A year later, on 8 November, 1507, he died,[2] and was buried in Grey Friars, London.

There must have been a fair amount of freehold in Farmanby which did not pass with the manor to the Dean and Canons of Windsor. As early as 1334 the Dean and Chapter of York had possessions in the two villages that encouraged them to claim 'to have common pasture for themselves, their men and tenants of Formandby, Kingthorpe and Ellerburn in the woods, moors and pastures of the same townships....and....to be quit of pannage[3] in the Mast season....to be quit of lawing of dogs[4] and *puture*[5] of all the officers of the forest; for themselves, their tenants of Farmandby to have housebote[6] and hedge-bote[7] and underwood to inclose their curtilage and the town ditch,[8] and to collect nuts,[9] for estovers[10] in the wood of Farmandby. And a like right for themselves, their men and tenants of Ellerburn....They claim to enjoy the rights....by virtue of a grant made by King Henry I. to Archbishop Gerard of York....it is found that the Dean and Chapter have enjoyed the rights in accordance with their claims.'[11] Whether they sold their lands has not been ascertained, but in 1494, there is evidence to show that 'Rauff Westrop one of the Kynges tenauntes' had 'by a wryt of ryght in the Kynges Courte ....certan landes and tenements within the townes of Thorneton and Fermanby.'[12] These must have been the lands conveyed by a son or grandson of 'Rauff,' James 'Westrope,' gentleman, in 1565, to Edmund Skelton, and at that time, included '6 messuages, and 4 cottages with lands, in Thorneton and Formanby.'[13] Sir Richard

---

[1] Cal. Pat. R. 1494-1509, p. 308. In anticipation of this there was a grant on 1 November, 1504, by Thomas Frowyk knight and Thomas Jakes, to Edward Lord Hastings of all advowsons, donations, nominations, and patronages of all churches belonging to the following premises (which premises the said Thomas and Thomas together with Reginald Bray knight and Thomas Shaa knight, now deceased, had recovered in Hilary Term 1502 against the said Lord Hastings) the Manors of Farmanby and Esthalgarth with the appurtenances, and everything as enumerated above. *Cf.* Hist. MSS. Com., Rawden Hastings MS. I., p. 194.

[2] Henry Nugent Bell, *ut supra*, p. 36.

[3] *Vide* Ch. XVI.

[4] *Vide* Ch. XVII.

[5] *Puture* equals a drinking. On this idea Sir Edward Coke says that the foresters claimed all victuals and drink for themselves, servants and dogs, and called this privilege *puture*.

[6] *Cf.* Neilson, *Customary Rents.*

[7] Ibid.

[8] Mr. R. Turton suggests 'that this was the ditch round the common field, on the bank of which a hedge appears to have been made.'

[9] *Cf.* Cox, *ut supra.*

[10] *Vide* Ch. I.

[11] N. R. Rec. S. N.S. III., pp. 155-7.

[12] Ibid. II., p. 213.

[13] Y. A. S. Rec. S. II., p. 317.

Cholmley obtained some freeholds in Farmanby about 1522.[1] His successor 'the Black Knight of the North,' purchased from William Robson and Isabel[2] his wife, 8 cottages in 'Thorneton and Farmanby in Pickering Leth,' in Hilary Term 1573/4.[3]

In the meantime as to the actual manor of Farmanby granted to the Dean and Canons of St. George's Chapel, Windsor, very little history can be found for the early sixteenth century. Their first tenant was James Thompson but he ceased to hold in 1542,[4] and on the 3 November, of that year, 'the scite of the manor of Farmanby' was leased to 'Stephen Holforde of Westminster,'[5] for 40 years paying as James Thompson had done. It was agreed that 'he will dwell there at Farmanby in the parish [?] of Pycheringe-lygge all the said term'; and to him the Dean and Canons granted the office of 'their Baylywicke Rentegatherer and Keeper of their woods on the manor of Farmanby and elsewhere in the county of York: he is to make his accompt and payment to them at Windsor or Leighton Buzzard, before All Saints every year'; and he is to have the leasing of the tenements of Farmanby and any of the Dean's property in the county of York.[6] By 1564 one of Stephen Holforde's employers, Sir John Gresham, was dead,[7] and Holforde may himself have been so, or left the neighbourhood. For whatever reason the Dean and Canons of Windsor leased[8] on 5 May, 1567, 'Farmanbye *alias* Farnhambye in Pykrynglygge and Esthall garthe to Nicholas Broke and George Harvey for 99 years at £29.[9] But this arrangement was very temporary.

Sir Richard Cholmley once again came forward and bought out[10] Nicholas Broke and George Harvey, and on 10 November, 1572, he purchased the previous lease for 93 years more at £29 rent at Michaelmas, i.e., for Farmanby £17, for 'Easthallgarth' £7; and for the wood, £5. In the lease is a clause by which all the tenants, before 1572, were to be bound according to the custom of the manor, and if rent were overdue there was to be a fine of 20s. a month up to Lady Day, then re-entry.[11] It was probably this fresh insistence on

---

[1] N. R. Rec. S. I., p. 227.
[2] *Vide* Ch. XII.
[3] Y. A. S. Rec. S. V., p. 76.
[4] D. and C. of W. XV., 18, 15.
[5] *Vide* Ch. XII. He must have been a kind of land agent and man of business.
[6] D. and C. of W. XV., 18, 15. The document is signed by 'Stephen Holford.'
[7] *Vide* Ch. XII.
[8] D. and C. of W. XV., 18, 16.
[9] Signed by Ny. Broke with seal crest, G. 'Harvy.'
[10] D. and C. of W. XV., 18, 17.
[11] Signed by Richard 'Cholmeley.' According to D. and C. of W. the farmer was Francis Hildesley.

ancient rights that roused the neighbourhood against the Black
Knight of the North. It would seem, both from the history of
Farmanby and of Roxby, that the Cholmleys were never popular,
and on 15 June, 1573, there was some question, by ill-wishers, as
to their lease of lands from the Dean and Canons of Windsor. It
is stated, however, in a pleading to 'Sir Ralphe Sadlier, Knt.,
Chauncelor of the Duchie of Lancaster' that, although Her Majesty
had 'diverse messuages, lands tenenements [*sic*] and hereditamnts'
etc. 'in Thorneton Formandby and Kynthropp,' they are now in
the hands of Sir Richard Cholmley, 'of Rockesbye,' including 'these
parcells called the Black Buske, the Wood end and Brackendell.'[1]
A year and a half later, on 24 January, 1575, Sir Richard Cholmley
defended his holding by saying that he understood that the Dean
and Canons of Windsor 'weare lawfullie seased in their demeane as
of Fee of and in the Mannor of Farmanbye al[s]. Farmhambie, as in
....the said parcell of grounde called Black Buske[2]....and that
the said parcell of grounde called Brakendell[3] ys and by like tyme
haith beyn parcell of a spring or woode grounde called Netherhedd,'[4]
and that he leased from the Dean and Canons 'the said mauner of
Farmanby al[s]. Farmhamby.'[5] Nevertheless, whatever his excuses,
it is clear that in 1581, Sir Richard Cholmley had tried to play
the tyrant with the result that there was an action, which is
recorded as 'William Cornewalles,[6] William Wivell, William Skelton
and others, Freeholders, *v.* Sir Richard Cholmeley, knight, Farmer
to the Dean and Chapter of Windsor concerning Common Pasture
for Cattle in Skythewoode and Langoudale, called woods, Boddam
Close and Dearham Meadow or Hagges and other specified lands
in Thornton, Farmanby, Ellerburn, Pexton Moor and Pickering
Lythe.'[7]

Neither this action nor the death of the Black Knight in May,
1583,[8] prevented the son of Sir Richard, 'Frauncys Cholmeley[9] of
Roxbie in the county of York, Esquire and Johane his wife,' taking
up the lease as in 1567 and 1572, and inserting a clause that they
'will keep the court leets and send up court rolls on parchment.'

[1] N. R. Rec. S. N.S. I., p. 217. *Cf. Ducatus Lancastriae*, III., p. 492.
[2] I cannot trace this. Buske = Bush.
[3] This name seems to have disappeared. I find on the map of 1796
that it was on the north side of Greengate Lane, then called High Lane and
on the east of Howldale.
[4] Nether Head was on the east of Howldale, the second enclosure in
from the Pickering Road.
[5] N. R. Rec. S. N.S. I., pp. 218-9.
[6] *Vide* Ch. XI.
[7] *Ducatus Lancastriae* III., p. 199.
[8] C. R.
[9] Signed 'Frauncys Cholmeley.'

They agreed that every twenty years a terrier was to be made, and that there should be certain restrictions as to the cutting of wood.[1]

In the latter part of the sixteenth century the Cholmleys seem to have ceased to be tenants of the Dean and Canons, for on 22 August, 1592,[2] that Collegiate body let all its manor of 'Farmanby *alias* Farnhanby' or, in other words what had been leased in the three previous leases,[3] to John Atkinson of York 'publique Notarie,'[4] and he, in turn, sublet to Francis Newton, Robert Parkinson, Richard Watson, William Horsley, Roger Todde and William Sollett. The tenants do not seem to have been entirely satisfied with the state of affairs. It was probably the old question of timber, and in 1613 two letters were sent to the Dean and Canons, when Maxey was the Dean, concerning the state of the woods.[5] Perhaps the tenants were not so wise as they thought, for by their correspondence they had called attention to themselves. Everybody at that time was feeling the pinch, largely produced by the marriage policy of James I., for his daughter Elizabeth, but whatever the cause on 29 December, 1613,[6] an assessment was made by Richard Watson and others for a contribution to be given to the Dean and Canons of Windsor their landlords by the tenants of Farmanby at 6s. 8d. for every oxgang of land, a sum which made the total of £20. 13s. 11d. So far one can imagine the chief tenant was John Atkinson of York.

The great change, however, came in the history of Farmanby and, ultimately, in that of Thornton when, on 9 May, 1620, 'Thomas Hill[7] of Hilltop in the county of York, Gent.' leased from the Dean and Canons 'Farmanby, nr. Pickering-leig and Easthallegarth in the parish of Swayne for 21 years at £29.'[8] This Thomas, is almost certainly the first of the Hill family to have anything to do with Thornton, and it is probably owing to this lease that Thornton became familiar to them. His early connection with the place does not seem to have been wholly happy either with the sub-tenants of

---

[1] D. and C. of W. XV., 18, 18.

[2] G. F. G. H.

[3] D. and C. of W. XV., 18, 19.

[4] John Atkinson was still alive on 12 July, 1598, as he wrote to the Dean and Canons on that date. *Cf.* XV., 18, 37.

[5] D. and C. of W. XV., 18, 19.

[6] Ibid. XV., 18, 21.

[7] Signed either T. or F. Hill, Seal of arms. The document is witnessed by Gregory Baker, John Darknall, Giles Beb.

[8] This reference to the parish of Swayne is very difficult. According to the V. C. H. II., pp. 423, 468, Easthallgarth was a manor within Pickering. I have some doubts as to this after reading 'in the parish of **Swayne.**' I must acknowledge that I have failed to find this parish. There is a Hallgarth in Pickering to this day, but not an Easthallgarth. There is 'Swine' near Beverley.

Farmanby, or with his landlords. In the first case, on 6 November, 1620, an agreement had to be drawn up between Thomas Hill and the tenants as to controversies concerning their leases;[1] and in the second there seems to be some difficulty as to the chief tenant's rent, which perhaps had arisen from a complaint of the tenant's on 29 October, 1622.[2] A document of 15 November of that year states that whereas on 9 May, 1620, the Dean and Canons let to 'Thomas Hill of Hilltopp,' Farmanby, and Easthallgarth, and specified if the rent were not paid re-entry would ensue they appoint Thomas Frith and Thomas Horn, B.D., their attorneys to demand the whole rent due.[3] On the 24 November, Thomas Frith did demand the £29, in the south Porch of the Chapel, 'and there continued for about half an hour before sunsetting and after sunset demanding, and no man tendered or payed any such rent for the same.'[4]

It does not appear, however, from documentary evidence, that Thomas Hill was deprived, and the fact that 160 trees were felled in 'Brackendale parcell of the manor of Farmanby' in 1623 was a fresh cause of annoyance to the sub-tenants, and, possibly, an act of the chief tenant which drove them to write to the Dean and Chapter complaining about the spoiling of the woods. It would seem from later events that Thomas continued to hold the chief lease until his son John succeeded him.[5]

In the meantime a part of the manor, including 'Netherhead' was sub-let to Richard 'Hardinge,' which he demised on 31 March, 1632, to his son Richard. Then followed the sequestration of all Church lands in the Civil War, and on 6 December, 'in the year of our Lord God according to the computation of the Church of England, One thousand six hundred fiftye and nyne,' an indenture was signed between Robert Hollis of Kingston-upon-Hull, gentleman, and Richard Parkinson of Pickering, in which it was stated that 'whereas Sir John Woollaston Knt., Robert Titchbourne, Thomas North, Marke Hildesley, Stephen Estwick, William Robson, Thomas Arnold, and many others did, by indenture, on 28 September, 1654, 'for the consideration therein expressed, being Trustees for the sale of Deanes, Deanes and Chapters' Commons and Pasture lands, grant bargain aliene and sell unto Maccabeus [Hollis], of Kingston-upon-Hull, of the one part, merchant and William Popple of Kingston-upon-Hull, alderman....among divers and severall other lands, all that Hagg or parcel of woody

---

[1] D. and C. of W. XV., 18, 4.
[2] Ibid. XV., 18, 37.
[3] Ibid. XV., 18, 4.
[4] Witnesses thereto, Gregory Baker and Robert 'Mountagu.'
[5] *Vide infra.*

ground....and all that part known of the name of the Nether Head.' William Popple bequeathed all his rights, in the said 'Maunor of Farmanby,' to Maccabeus Hollis[1] and he, by will, bequeathed to his son Robert. This Robert, in consideration of £8. 8s. 0d., paid by Richard Parkinson, handed over his rights in the manor and Hagg, and at the same time sold 'Nether Head' to Robert Harding.[2] The two purchasers were destined to rue bitterly their bargains for with the restoration of Charles II. in 1660 all Royal and Ecclesiastical lands[3] were returned to their rightful owners, and once more, the manor of Farmanby came under the control of the Dean and Canons of Windsor.

As soon as possible the Dean and Canons resumed their relations with the Hill family,[4] and on 30 June, 1663, released to 'John Hill of Normanby[5] in the county of York, Gent.,' the manor. It is stated that he is possessed of the interest of the lease granted 22 August, 1592 (obviously through his connection with Thomas), of which 2½ years have yet to run; and 'Whereas they have now leased Farmanby and "Esthallgarthe"[6] to John Hill for £30, they agree that no rent be paid until Lady Day 1665.'

A part, however, of Farmanby must have been free from the jurisdiction of the Dean and Canons as shown by a curious lease executed on 12 July, 1669. Frances Halliburton of the parish of St. Olaves [?] let to John Hill of Normanby, York, 26 oxgangs of arable, meadow, and pasture, 'situate lying and being in ffarmanby ....which sometime were lands of the late Lord Latimer,' with all their appurtenances for 'the full time and terme of ninety-nine years and eleaven months, if Lucy Withy poole of Cireencester in the County of Gloucester, spinster shall soe long live....tending and paying therefore yearly and every year during the said tenure unto the said ffraunces Halliburton or her Executors....if the said Lucy Withy poole shall soe long live, the yearly rent or sum of fifty pounds of Lawful money of England at or in the dwelling

---

[1] Maccabeus or 'Macabyse' Hollis had married Mary Hunter in 1633.

[2] G. F. G. H.

[3] 12 Car. II., c. 12. *Vide* Sir R. Lodge, *History of England* (Longmans), p. 10.

[4] D. and C. of W. XV., 18, 22.

[5] Known in this book as John Hill I., and this shows that he owned the manor of Normanby before he purchased the manor of Thornton. *Vide* Ch. XI.

[6] This cannot be quite true for other documents of the Dean and Canons of Windsor show that twenty-eight days later, Easthallgarth, co. York, was leased to Timothy Eman of New Windsor, gent. His daughter was Elizabeth Eman of Beverley who took the lease in 1695 and renewed on 11 May, 1702, when it was witnessed by Christopher Tadman, Frances Tadman and Francis Broxholme. *Cf.* D. and C. of W. XV., 18, 38, 42, and 43.

house of the said ffraunces Halliburton aforesaid in or upon the feast day of St. Martin the Bishop....and Pentecost by even and equal portions....if it shall happen the said yearly rent to be behind and unpaid in part or in all by the space of twenty days next after either of the said feasts,' then Frances Halliburton may enter and distrain.[1]

In addition to these 26 oxgangs, John Hill, soon after he had become the lord of the main manor in Thornton, on 30 December, 1671, released from the Dean and Canons their property in Farmanby; and, as already shown,[2] partly owing to his initiative Farmanby was enclosed as early as 1678. As tenants, the Hill family had to supply Terriers from time to time, as for example when John Hill the younger[3] of Farmanby, gent., took on the lease on 7 July, 1682, for 21 years at £30.[4] He renewed this on 25 January, 1689,[5] on 16 December, 1696,[6] and on 25 November, 1702.[7] Presumably the addition of the necessity of Terriers had been forgotten, for in the lease of November, 1710,[8] there were more stringent terms, and a fine of £20 was to be exacted if the terrier was not made and the Court Rolls not kept. No doubt this is why there is for the year 1710 'A survey or Terrier of the mann[r] of Farnhamby &c in Poss: of Dean & Canons.'[9] This gives a list of the tenants and cottages, including 'a close on Roxby Hill called "Great Anham" a meadow Close next adjoyning & also a little close part of Pannierman Pool Close.'[10] It states that at Ellerburn there was a 'Fulling mill,' and a cottage with a little hemp-yard,[11] and some closes called 'Mineacrs.'[12] In the Highfields there was a close called 'Muncklands';[13] and in the Westfield, a close called 'West Wandles.'[14] There was also 'a Parcell of Coppice ground near Ellerburn called the Ellars,[15] a barren sandy bank call'd Skeathwoods[16] in the possession of Richard Marshall.' Then follows 'a call Roll for the Mauno[r] of

[1] G. F. G. H.
[2] *Vide* Ch. VI. *Cf.* Correspondence D. and C. of W. XV., 18, 37.
[3] D. and C. of W. XV., 18, 23.
[4] Ibid. XV., 18, 24
[5] Ibid. XV., 18, 25.
[6] Ibid. XV., 18, 26.
[7] Ibid. XV., 18, 27.
[8] Ibid. XV., 18, 28.
[9] G. F. G. H.
[10] *Vide* Chs. VI., IX.
[11] *Vide* Ch. I.
[12] At Ellerburn.
[13] Probably named from having been Abbey property on the west of Whitbygate.
[14] *Vide* Ch. VI.
[15] Still so called.
[16] I have not been able to verify this; but I imagine it to have been where now there are decaying stumps on the hillside east of the Paper Mill Pond.

Farnhamby with the names of all persons that doe suite and service to the Court Leet & Court Baron of the Dean & Canons of the free & Collegiate Chappell of St George within her Majesties Chappell [*sic*] of Windsor.' The names mentioned are, Skelton, Horsley, Egglesfield, Marshall, Kirkby, Boyes[1] and Champley.[2] Another Terrier was made on 14 May, 1711,[3] 'and another ye 26th Nov. 1717.'[4] But these are much the same as that of 1710, though the names of a few tenants differ, but most of these have been dealt with elsewhere.[5]

The Dean and Canons of Windsor continued to hold Ellerburn-cum-Farmanby, having as their tenants the different members of the Hill family,[6] who were not only tenants in the ordinary sense, but under numerous agreements were to act as if real lords of the manor. The leases, from time to time, refer to a capital messuage in Farmanby, and the lessees are enjoined to 'keep or cause to be kept any manner of view of frankpledge, Leets, Law days or Courts in and upon the said manor....as farmer or farmers to the said Dean' etc. The lease of September, 1752, entered upon by John Hill III. just before his death, was renewed by Captain John Hill in January, 1760. This again was renewed by him in December, 1766. At Michaelmas, 1775, the Dean and Canons leased to George Robinson, of Welburn, Esq. as a trustee under the will of John Hill III., on behalf of John Johnson [Hill], who died in 1776. In 1782 Josiah Maynard, as trustee renewed the lease for Richard Johnson Hill, and seven years later, Richard Johnson Hill himself was the sole lessee. At his death, in 1793, he left all his affairs in trust, and Dr. John Johnston and the Rev. John Ward renewed the lease at Michaelmas, 1797. Owing to Dr. Johnston's[7] death, the Rev. John Ward renewed alone in 1803, but in 1810, and in 1817, Richard Hill was lessee.[8] During this period a letter from the Rev. J. Gilby, stepfather of Richard Hill, dated 30 July, 1814, shows much anxiety about the fine on the renewal of the lease. The agent of the Dean and Canons wanted to increase it enormously, 'an alarming statement for you.' John Gilby, however, managed, by negotiation, to keep it down, as shown by a letter

---

[1] Probate of the will of William Boyes of Farmanby, 19 May, 1720, and probate of will of Henry Boyes of the same, 23 February, 1721. *Cf.* Y. A. S. Rec. S. LXXIII., p. 36.
[2] G. F. G. H.
[3] Ibid.
[4] Ibid.
[5] *Vide* Ch. VII.
[6] D. and C. of W. XV., 18, 29-35.
[7] I think that he lived at Hedon, near Hull, about 1780.
[8] G. F. G. H.

dated 25 September, of the same year.[1] Fresh arrangements were made at the time of Richard Hill's second marriage to Jane, elder daughter of James Walker, Esq., on 3 August, 1819; and the lease of the Farmanby manor was assigned to the Rev. John Gilby and John Lockwood Esq. After many years, on 1 May, 1869,[2] the trustees assigned to the Rev. John Richard Hill, and previous negotiations having been made with the Deanery, the property, of which the Hill family had so long been the tenants passed into their ownership.[3]

[1] Ibid. *Cf.* D. and C. of W., 1 November, 1817, XV., 18, 37, stating that the Court Rolls will be sent in by Richard Hill.

[2] J. L. W.

[3] The acreage of the Deanery Leasehold in 1868 was 1159 a. 2 r. 27 p.

CHAPTER FIFTEEN.

The Manor of Roxby.

———

'The arch is gone, the stream is dried;
. . . .
Here's nothing left of ancient pride,
Of what was grand, of what was gay;
But all is changed.'

GEORGE CRABBE, C. 1800.

IN the Danish period, a Norseman, at some unknown date, must have settled on the top of the western hill that rises from the level of Thornton Beck, and, having established himself, the farmstead came to be known by his name as Routh's By,[1] contracted, as time went on, into Rozebi, Rouceby,[2] and Roxby. In 1086 'the soc of Rozebi' belonged to 'Pickeringa.'[3] After that for one hundred years Roxby disappears from all records, except for the fact that there were two brothers, Gamel and Gospatric resident there about 1158.[4] Thanks to the Assize Rolls between 1199 and 1215 fresh names begin to emerge. Walter de Rouceby was charged with having unjustly disseised Peter, son of Juliana de Thornton, of his free tenement in 'Rouceby' and of half an acre of land with appurtenances. Walter having appeared at the assize[5] acknowledged the disseisin and was committed to gaol, though Peter, somewhat generously remitted his damages.[6]

Geoffrey de Waghne was the chief tenant in Roxby in May, 1242, and he covenanted with Peter de Hedon as to the thirteen bovates, of which Roxby apparently consisted, with 6 acres of land and a messuage in Selgarbing or Selfgarding, [wherever that might be], and a messuage in Thornton.[7] The matter was settled on 25

---

[1] A. H. Smith, *ut supra*, p. 90.
[2] Still pronounced by many, locally, as 'Rousby.'
[3] Domesday Book.
[4] Rievaulx Cartulary, Sur. Soc. LXXXIII., p. 135.
[5] This was a case of *novel disseisin*. *Cf.* The Assize of Northampton, c. 5 and Magna Carta, c. 18. The writ of *novel disseisin* was abolished 3 and 4 W. IV., c. 27.
[6] Y. A. S. Rec. S. XLIV., p. 65.
[7] Curia Regis R. 123, m.3.

June, of the same year, by Final Concord,[1] at Westminster before the Justices. The right of Peter, as of the gift of Geoffrey, was acknowledged, and he obtained in demesne all homages, services of free men, wards, reliefs and escheats when they may occur, to wit the homage and service of Robert son of Walter, Alan of 'Whytegate,' Roger of Apelton, Robert son of William of 'Fermaneby,' Adam son of Roger, John son of the parson of Thornton,[2] and their heirs for all their tenements held by Geoffrey in 'Rouceby' to hold to Peter and his heirs of Geoffrey and his heirs, paying yearly a penny at Whitsuntide, and doing to the chief lords of the fee [The Honor of Pickering] for Geoffrey and his heirs all other services due. In exchange Peter gave to Geoffrey 2 bovates in Waghne[3] and 14 marks of silver.

By this time, the already mentioned family of Hastings of Allerston was getting a hold upon Roxby destined to last for nearly three hundred years. Nicholas de Hastings, in 1247, granted to his younger son Henry a capital messuage 'in Hundegate in Thornton,'[4] together with two oxgangs in 'Rauceby' [Roxby] with remainder to two younger sons, Edmund and Nicholas,[5] 'all which he had from Peter son of Peter the clerk of "Edun"[6] also all his land of "Selfgerding" in Roxby' and other lands saving the capital manor of Farmanby.[7] By 1284, Edmund Hastings had succeeded and was stated to have held four oxgangs in demesne;[8] and, in 1302, he held under Roger Bigod, Earl of Norfolk, thirteen bovates for the eighth part of a knight's fee.[9] As a working proposition these thirteen bovates seem to have been broken up. Edmund apparently held four in demesne, while two each were held by William de Everley,[10] Alan Pye, Matthew Gower and the heirs of Alexander de

[1] Pollock and Maitland, *ut supra*, II., p. 409, and Reeves, *ut supra*, II., p. 225.

[2] John was the son of Gilbert, parson of Thornton and Ysolda his wife.

[3] Wawne between Beverley and Hedon, E. Riding.

[4] Where could this have been ? Is it the forerunner of 'Dog Kennel Lane' ?

[5] V. C. H. *N.R.* II., p. 495.

[6] The editor of Rawden Hastings MS. suggests that this may be 'Eden House' north of New Malton. It is, of course 'Hedon' in the East Riding.

[7] Hist. MSS. Com., Rawden Hastings MS. I., p. 193.

[8] V. C. H. *N.R.* II., p. 495.

[9] Cal. Feud. Aids, VI., p. 81. 'Rowcesby. De feodo comitis Marescalli sunt in Rouceby xiij bov. terre de baronia quarum vij car. et di [et] j bov. terre faciunt f. un. m. quarum Edmundus de Hastyngs tenet de eodem Rogero [Bigod] in dominico et servicio iiij bov. terre; Willelmus de Everle ij bov.; Alanus Pye ij bov.; Matheus Gower ij bov.; heres Alexandri de Rouceby ij bov.; Stephanus Wotte j bov.... Et residuum dicti feodi in Hoton Baldolf.' *Cf.* also Feud. Aids, VI., p. 136.

[10] William de Everley in a deed of 1313 is said to have had a wife, Margaret, late wife of Seman son of Godfrey of 'Siwardebi' (Sewerby). He was of Ugglebarnby and Forester of Whitby Forest. For his poaching adventure, *vide* Ch. II.

'Rouceby'; and one was held by Stephen Wotte. The Hastings' family, such as Nicholas, Hugh, Edmund, Ralph, and the Lady Beatrice, like most of the gentry of the period, were in no sense too superior to poach within the bounds of the royal forest.[1] By 1334 the chief representative of the family, Sir Ralph Hastings of Allerston, had become Constable of Pickering Castle, and his cousin Edmund had become acting forester for Petronilla or Parnell de 'Kynthorp' who was, herself, 'forester-in-fee.'[2] This position of forester-in-fee needs some explanation.

As far back as 1198, and perhaps a great deal further, Alan, son of Geoffrey, held in 'Kinthorpe' three carucates by the 'serjeanty of the forest,'[3] valued at 30s. Alan's son, Alan, in 1219, is stated to have held the position and property, then valued at 42s., by serjeanty; but the commissioners asserted that they did not know by what service; which is somewhat strange, as it might have been imagined that everyone would have known that the service was that of 'forester.'[4] In 1226, the value of Alan's land had again risen and it was rated at 60s.,[5] but in 1241-2, Alan de 'Kintorp' and Walter Boye(s) paid 40s. and 120s. for three years arrears.[6] The whole question of the relationship of the land and the serjeanty came to a head when Roger, son of 'Stephen de Kynthorpe,' was accused of the murder of Astinus, son of 'John de Thorneton,' and grandson of Gilbert the parson.[7] This necessitated on 23 October, 1252, an inquisition as to whether the six bovates of land in Kingthorpe, whereof Roger, son of Stephen, held four, and William, son of Gamel held two, were of the King's serjeanty or not, and by which of the King's predecessors the rent

---

[1] N. R. Rec. S. N.S. II., p. 114. This is shown by the entry 25 August, 1336, that certain men came 'with bows and arrows and killed a hart' (in Haughdale) and were caught in the act by Edmund 'Hastynges' acting as forester for 'Parnell de Kynthorp, forester-in-fee.' They were taken to Pickering Castle and delivered to Ralph Hastings, who was the Constable, and each fined 13s. 4d.

[2] Petit-Dutaillis, *ut supra*, pp. 158-9 says 'there were in most of the large forests one or more *forestarii de feodo*....who....saw to the preservation of the vert and the venison, and executed the decisions of the itinerant justices. They possessed certain rights over the Forest. Some but not all, paid a ferm to the King. They were not always bound to obey the warden. Some, without doubt, had been enfeoffed by the King, and owed submission to him only.' Turner, *ut supra*, pp. xxiii-iv does not deal very fully with the foresters-in-fee. Their warrant for jurisdiction was generally 'nisi antiqua tenura.'

[3] Cal. Book of Fees, I., p. 4 says 'Alanus filius Galfridi tenet in Kinthorp per seriantiam foreste iij carucatas valencie carucatarum,....xxxs.'

[4] Ibid., p. 248 says 'Item Alanus de Kintorp tenet tres carucatas terre per seriantiam nesciunt per quod servicium, valet xlijs.'

[5] Ibid., p. 256.

[6] Great Roll of the Pipe, p. 25.

[7] Cal. Pat. R., 1247-58, p. 155. *Cf.* Ch. ix.

of the six bovates was assigned to serjeanty.[1] Before the matter was decided, most fortunately for himself, Roger received a royal pardon, for the judge, Roger de Thurkill, found that the death of Astinus was due to misadventure.[2] The jury, however, gave a verdict as to the property on 22 December, 1252,[3] and it was decided that the six bovates were of the King's socage of Pickering, 'and the rent of the same was assigned to the said serjeanty of the King.'[4]

This decision, undoubtedly, established the serjeanty which had in previous years been fully recognized, and when Alan died in 1275 at the inquest *post mortem* on 6 August,[5] it was stated that he[6] 'held of the Lord Edmund [Crouchback, Earl of Lancaster[7],] three carucates of land with the appurtenances in Kynthorp, by the service of keeping the forest of Pykering, and it is worth, with the mill, 12s. and three pounds of cumin [*cymini*] and one pound of pepper.'[8] Alan, many years before, had married Petronilla, daughter of John de Crackalle, and by her had a son, Geoffrey, who died in his father's lifetime. He, however, had left a daughter, born about 1267, and she was the heiress of her grandfather, and as such 'forester-in-fee.' In 1316 she was described as Lord of the manor of 'Kynthorp,'[9] and, at some period before this, married Roger Mansergh, who, as her husband, acted for her as forester-in-fee, although this did not prevent him poaching with 'greyhounds, bows and arrows' on Sunday, 7 October, 1321,[10] for which he was declared an outlaw in 1334; but as he had died in February, 1323,[11] the sentence fell rather flat. His inquest *post mortem* stated that he held, of his wife's inheritance, certain tenements which were held of the King in-chief as of the Honor of Pickering by the serjeanty of being the King's forester in Pickering Forest and

---

[1] Y. A. S. Rec. S. XII., p. 35.

[2] Cal. Pat. R., 1247-58, p. 155. *Cf.* Ch. iv.

[3] The jury, as usual, was composed of many local characters :—William Malecake, senior, Thomas de Edbistone, Peter de Neville, William Malecake, junior, Thomas de Pikeringe, Richard le Brun (of Thornton), Adam de Rouceby, Robert son of Walter, John de Neuton, junior, Robert de Brunton, William son of Matilda de Pickering, Roger de Kirkedale in Edbristone, Alan Hert of Farmaneby, John son of Reginald of Thornton, Walter de Rouceby, Hugh at the gate of Pickering and John de Castre.

[4] Y. A. S. Rec. S. XII., p. 35.

[5] Cal. Inq. Ed. I., II., No. 111. *Cf.* Y. A. S. Rec. S. XII., p. 158.

[6] It was also stated that he held land in Ellerburn, *vide* Ch. XIV.

[7] Cal. Inq. H. III., p. 56, shows that Henry III. had granted Pickering to his younger son.

[8] Cal. Inq. Ed. I., II., No. 111.

[9] Cal. Feud. Aids, VI., p. 177.

[10] N. R. Rec. S. N.S. II., p. 101. The '1324' is here a misprint for '1321.'

[11] Ibid., pp. 101, 243.

paying to the King £1 yearly, 'half at Easter and half at Michaelmas.'[1]

Once again, the widowed Petronilla or Parnell was forester-in-fee in her own right; but it was practically impossible for a woman to fulfil the task, especially as she was about 56 years of age; and so, Edmund Hastings, her neighbour at Roxby, came to her help and acted for her. How far he was disinterested it is a little difficult to say. Roger and Petronilla had had a daughter, Alice, aged at the death of her father in 1323, eleven years.[2] The astute Edmund saw, in that mercenary age, an heiress to a property closely abutting upon his own.[3] The kindly help offered to the widowed mother may have been with the direct intention of winning the hand of Alice. Whatever the incentives, Edmund did marry the heiress, and after the death of Petronilla,[4] became himself lord of Kingthorpe and forester-in-fee. Petronilla was, however, alive as late as 1338, and between 1334 and that year appeared many times before the Justices for forest offences.[5] She claimed to have '*escapes*'[6] in Blandesby and in Dalby from Easter to Michaelmas. This was disallowed.[7] She also claimed housewood, drywood, nutgeld,[8] and pannage. The two former were refused; the two latter allowed; but she was amerced 3s. 4d. for making false claims. It was, then, by the marriage of Edmund Hastings and Alice Mansergh that the Kingthorpe and Roxby properties were united, and references to Kingthorpe cease for one hundred and fifty years. As the property of Kingthorpe is not in the civil parish of Thornton from this point it passes, except incidently, out of the present story.

---

[1] Inq. p.m. 16 Ed. II., No. 20, says, 'dicunt quod idem Rogerus tenuit die quo obiit de hereditate prefate Petronille quondam uxoris sue quedam tenementa in Kynthorp que quidem tenementa una cum predicta bovata terre tenentur de Rege in capite ut de honore de Pikering per serjanciam essendi Forestarius Regis in foresta de Pikering et reddendo Regi per annum xxs. ad terminos Pasche et Sci Michaelis.'

[2] N. R. Rec. S. N.S., II., pp. 242-3.

[3] Not that the premises were worth much *vide* Ibid., p. 242.

[4] Ibid. IV., p. xli.

[5] *Cf.* Ibid. II., pp. 171, 185; III., pp. 42, 82, 89; IV., pp. 31, 42, 49, 54, 64, 65, 67, 126. Her son-in-law was not exempt, for on 31 March, 1338, he was fined 2s. for hunting hares in the forest. *Cf.* Ibid. IV., p. 66.

[6] *Cf.* Neilson, *ut supra*, p. 79 ' "*escapium*" was "money paid for beasts escaping into forbidden enclosures." ' This was generally a large fine.

[7] After many postponements, in 1336.

[8] The hazel was sufficiently abundant in the Forest to make the nut-geld, or licence to gather nuts, an item of importance in the Forest Account. *Cf.* Cox, *ut supra*, p. 73. In modern times Dalby nutwood has been destroyed by order of the Duchy of Lancaster. When the present writer was a boy he has been on happy nutting parties to this wood, then under the control of the Rev. John Richard Hill, as Deputy of the Duchy.

Once again, in 1346, the heir of Edmund Hastings is said to hold in 'Rouseby' thirteen bovates of land for the eighth part of a knight's fee.[1] This still referred to Edmund, husband of Alice, as he was alive, at least as late, as 1347. Their son was another Edmund, who had a lawsuit with the Prior of Malton in 1368, concerning lands which the Prior held in 'Kynthorp and Pykeryng-lithe.'[2] This Edmund was alive in 1381, and with his son Nicholas, together with their chaplains, John Kyng and John de Brighton, witnessed a release on 7 March, 1381/2, by Agnes de 'Rouceby,' widow of Alan, to John de 'Rouceby,' 'staying'[3] in 'Pikerynglith,' of all the lands which she and John had in Thornton, Farmanby, etc., and which had come to her by hereditary right on the death of William Thornton, her brother.[4] Both Edmund and Nicholas Hastings were alive on 4 July, 1390, when they witnessed a release by William King and Margaret his wife to William Campioun and Richard his brother of all their right in a little land in Roxby.[5]

It is not clear when Nicholas succeeded his father at Roxby, nor when he married one, Joan; but that he was married before the Octave of Trinity, 1373, is seen by a Final Concord when a decision was given for Nicholas and Joan his wife, on payment of 100 marks as to 1 messuage, 9 tofts and 13 bovates of land in Thornton for part of which they agreed to pay 'one rose at the nativity of St. John the Baptist' and do all services due to the chief lords: and for the rest, to pay to John de Cotorn and Alice his wife an annual sum of 26s. 8d. during their lives.[6] Nicholas Hastings was certainly alive as late as 1395. He was followed by his son Edmund, who was declared in 1428, to hold the thirteen bovates in 'Rouseby' on the same service as his grandfather.[7] He married Agnes,[8] daughter of Sir Thomas Sutton, widow of Sir Ralph Bulmer. It is evident that, like his predecessors, he had his own private chaplain in Roxby Castle,[9] and that these chaplains were not always satisfactory, for on 3 November, 1442, Thomas

---

[1] Cal. Feud. Aids, VI., p. 258. Sir Ralph Hastings in his will, dated 2 December, 1346, speaks of Edmund Hastings as his nephew, he was, more probably, his cousin. *Cf.* Test. Ebor. Sur. Soc. IV. I., p. 20.

[2] The Prior was evidently at cross purposes with the family as Sir Ralph 'Hastynges' brought an action against him in 1372 concerning a plea of debt. *Cf.* Y. A. S. Rec. S. XVII., p. 124.

[3] '*Manenti.*' It may mean 'dwelling.'

[4] Y. A. S. Rec. S. L., pp. 192-3.

[5] Hist. MSS. Com., Rawden Hastings MS. I., p. 193.

[6] Y. A. S. Rec. S. LII., p. 172.

[7] Cal. Feud. Aids, VI., p. 311.

[8] She was declared to be 40 and more in 1415.

[9] Or at Kingthorpe where in early days there seems to have been some kind of chapel. A very tattered document of the late seventeenth century refers to the remains of a chapel. J. L. W.

Doune '*capellanus*' who had been sued for the debt of 40s., and not appearing before William Babyngton and his fellow justices, was outlawed and then received a pardon.[1] Edmund was succeeded by his son William, and he in turn by his sons Edmund[2] and John. The elder died without issue and John, who married Isabel, daughter of Sir Ralph Babthorpe, of Hemingburgh,[3] had as his heir another Edmund.[4]

This, the last of the Edmunds, was appointed by Richard III. on 15 July, 1483, Seneschal of the royal demesne and Master Forester of Pickering.[5] These offices were again settled upon him by Henry VII. on 30 September, 1485, and 19 February, 1487/8.[6] As this man's son, Roger, became 'forester-in-fee' in 1489, and as Brian Sandford is mentioned as Seneschal of Pickering on 4 July, 1489, it may be presumed that Edmund had died; and that his son only received the hereditary forester's office and none of the other royal appointments.[7] At first, the new Seneschal was on good terms with the Hastings' family, and, in 1489, 'by the gefte of the stuard [Brian Sandford] to my Lady Hastings a oke to the valor of vij loode of woode,'[8] but the friendship evidently declined. Probably Sir Roger Hastings disapproved of being deprived of his father's emoluments, and very likely chafed at being restricted within the forest as a mere forester-in-fee. Whatever the cause, by 1494, tales had been told, and Brian Sandford and his future successor, Richard Cholmley, were commissioned to investigate the trespasses in vert. Amongst the principal offenders they found the two foresters-in-fee, Lionel Percehay and Roger Hastings.[9] But the Commission of 22 February, 1494/5, went considerably further than the investigation of mere petty offences such as wood-stealing. The King wrote 'we be credibly enformed that oure game of dere and our woodes....beene greatly hurted and wasted ....We not willyng the seid mysdedes to remayne unpunysshed, nor our....tenants....to contynue in theire seid troubles.... charge you....to procede ferther to the good order, direction, reformacion and appeasyng of every of the premisses....and if the seid persones be wilful and frowerd....al such wilful persones

---

[1] Cal. Pat. R., 1441-6, p. 117.
[2] This Edmund is probably the incorrectly named 'Edward Hastynges' of 'Rowesby' who witnessed a grant of Sir William, afterwards Lord Hastings on 12 May, 1460. *Cf.* Hist. MSS. Com., Rawden Hastings MS. I., p. 294.
[3] Burton, *Monasticon*, p. 437.
[4] *The Genealogist*, N.S. XXIII., p. 95.
[5] N. R. Rec. S. N.S. I., p. 113.
[6] Ibid., p. 117.
[7] Ibid., p. xxiv.
[8] Ibid., p. 162.
[9] Ibid., p. xxiv.

to appere before us and our Chauncellor of our seid Duchie at our paloys of Westminster.'[1] Apparently Sir Roger Hastings was a 'wilful and frowerd' person, and he was accused of much poaching, for example, one hind on 5 December, 1489, one stag on 15 July, 1491, one hind on 7 November, 1491, two does in Blandesby Park on 1 December, 1491, one doe on 4 January, 1492, one doe on 16 July, 1493, another on 31 December, 1493, and two more does on 8 June, 1494.[2]

At the inquiry it was stated that Sir Roger Hastings held three carucates of land in 'Kynthorp' of the King by Grand Serjeanty, and paid 20s. per annum and owed reliefs and homage for the same. There was much wrangling over this, the point being as to whether Sir Roger really was a forester-in-fee. The jury then asserted that both Sir Roger and Lionel 'Pershey' claimed in right of their fees two stags and two bucks in summer, two hinds and two does in winter, and this they declared was not to be allowed; but that they had a right to have one course, twice a year, at the sufferance of the Master Forester. Sir Roger at once replied that he made no such claim as the one urged by the jury, and that what he did claim was, one deer, called a 'scadde,'[3] in summer and one, called a 'Hyrsell,' in winter. The jury rejected this explanation, and said that Sir Roger and Lionel 'Pershey' went far beyond this, demanding from every deer slain in the Forest the two shoulders, and from every deer killed in Blandesby Park, the entrails.[4] They decided that this was not just and that the two foresters-in-fee had only a right to the left shoulder and that the rest was the perquisite of the Master Forester. In addition, the servants[5] of Sir Roger were charged with poaching offences similar to those of their employer.[6]

The first trial was treated as null and void; and a fresh trial was ordered in 1495, no longer in the presence of Brian Sandford, for he had left the district; but before two new officials, Sir Thomas Wysteley and Nicholas Knyfton, together with Sir Roger's old enemy, Sir Richard Cholmley, who, at the moment, held all four of the principal offices of the Honor, Receiver, Seneschal, Constable and Master Forester.[7]

It was from now onwards, for more than a hundred and fifty years, that the Cholmley family was the most important in the

[1] Ibid., pp 125-6
[2] Ibid., p. 148.
[3] Scad=carcase: but the reading according to Mr. Turton is very doubtful and the word may be 'stadde.'
[4] These were the 'humbles' or 'umbles,' and so the origin of 'humble-pie.'
[5] *Vide* Ch. IV.
[6] N. R. Rec. S. N.S. I., pp. 152-3.
[7] Ibid., pp. xxiii-iv.

neighbourhood. This Sir Richard was a soldier of fortune whose immediate ancestors had not been conspicuous in national history, but who were of good stock, through the female line, being descended from Robert FitzHugh, Baron of Malpas, who held the manor of Cholmondeley in Cheshire in 1086. Sir Richard had won some prominence under Henry VII., and on 30 January, 1488, was Chamberlain and Treasurer of War at Berwick-on-Tweed.[1] Four years later, when war with Scotland was imminent he was made one of the Guardians of Durham.[2] Then followed the trouble with James IV. over the Perkin Warbeck question, and Sir Richard was appointed with Sir Thomas Darcy, a commissioner for the settlement of disputes upon the Border.[3] He had already, by this time, transferred his home from the county of Chester, and taken up his abode at Cottingham, near Hull, from whence he corresponded with Henry VII.'s notorious minister, Sir Richard Empson. It may possibly have been owing to Empson's influence that Sir Richard was sent to assist in superintending the decaying interests of the Forest of Pickering. He came well supported, for he brought with him two brothers, Sir Reginald, a priest, and Sir Roger. Like his descendants Sir Richard seems to have been strong-willed and obstinate, clever and cultured, ambitious, passionate and easily led by women.[4] When he died, in 1522, he had no legitimate descendants, but left an illegitimate son, Sir Roger, who became Chief Baron of the Exchequer and Lord Chief Justice.[5] Sir Richard's right heir was his brother Roger.

When Sir Richard Cholmley found himself in complete possession of power at Pickering in 1495, he introduced far stricter rules in the Forest than there had been for many years. Presumably he resided at Pickering Castle, and continued to bait Sir Roger Hastings of Roxby. He accused him of hunting the King's deer in Staindale under colour of hunting foxes,[6] and this, added to all that had gone before, goaded Sir Roger into a condition of ungovernable rage. This state of affairs was not helped by the fact that about the same time Sir Roger was at violent loggerheads with one of his tenants, Ralph Joyner, and the bitter quarrel with the Cholmleys

[1] Rolls. Ser. LX., p. 234.
[2] Surtees, *Durham*.
[3] Rymer, *Foedera*.
[4] N. R. Rec. S. N.S. I., pp. xxv-vii.
[5] He was the founder of Highgate School in 1562. He married one Christina, and left, at his death in 1565, two daughters, Elizabeth, who married Sir Leonard Beckwith, and Frances who married Sir Thomas Russell of Strensham.
[6] N. R. Rec. S. N.S. I., p. 170. 'In Standall infra Forestam....venavit ad vulpes, et sub colore illo venavit ad ferinas domini Regis.'

came to be bound up with this lesser dispute already described.[1]

The passionate, lawless, and ambitious characters of so many men at this time, and, in particular, of the members of the Cholmley family, make it most probable that Sir Richard Cholmley had from the first determined to oust Sir Roger Hastings from Roxby and Kingthorpe. He played his cards well, and presuming that in the early days of the reign of Henry VIII. he had already a mortgage[2] on the property, his future acquisition must have seemed a certainty. The Cholmleys obviously had the goodwill of their sovereign, as shown when Sir Richard's brother Roger obtained the reward of gallantry, being knighted after the battle of Flodden in 1513. In the same year their old enemy, Sir Roger Hastings, died,[3] leaving a son Francis, who, in 1520, conveyed the manors of Roxby and Kingthorpe to Robert 'Constabyll de Flamborough, Knt' William 'Cunstabyll de Hatfeld, Knt.' Thomas de Brodester, clerk, and Richard Belerby, chaplain,[4] and from whom they had certainly passed, after Sir Richard Cholmley's death in 1522,[5] when Sir Roger Cholmley, his brother, was described as 'of Roxby.'[6]

Little or nothing is known of Sir Roger's residence at Roxby Castle. Early in the sixteenth century, probably between 1515 and 1519, he had married 'Kateren,' daughter of Sir Robert Constable of Flamborough, and before her husband's death, on 28 April, 1538,[7] she had presented him with five[8] children; Richard, of whom later, John who was slain in his youth, Roger, of whom there is little to record; Margaret, and Anne.[9] Margaret married first, Sir Henry Gascoigne, and Anne married Henry, fifth Earl of Westmorland. Anne died before her sister, and after Gascoigne's death, the Earl of Westmorland[10] married his deceased wife's sister: a most astounding act, even allowing for greater laxity in Elizabethan times. Presumably the marriage took place in Hilary Term, 1560/1, and

---

[1] *Vide* Ch. IV.

[2] It is evident that Hastings was in financial difficulties in 1504. *Cf.* Camden Society, *Plumpton Correspondence*, p. cxiii.

[3] Hastings late of 'Rowcebie' was said to have had land in Lockton escheated from John Chapman who was 'Outlawed of ffelony 20 January, 10 Hen. VII.' G. F. G. H.

[4] Y. A. S. Rec. S. II., p. 36.

[5] N. R. Rec. S. O.S., IV., p. 131.

[6] Ibid.

[7] Y. A. S. Rec. S. LXX., p. 62. Foster, *Pedigrees of Yorkshire*, says he died in London.

[8] There may have been another son, Marmaduke, for the C. R. for October, 1542, records as baptized 'John [? Johanna or Joan] Cholmley daughter of Marmaduke Cholmley.'

[9] She is sometimes called Jane.

[10] He was born 1525. *Cf. Letters and Papers of Henry VIII.*, IV. ii., p. 4891.

certain lands in Thornton, together with the advowson[1] of Thornton Church, were to remain after the decease of the Earl to 'Margaret Gascoigne late the wife of Henry Gascoigne, Knt. deceased, now Countess of "Westmerland",' and after her death to his lawful heirs.[2]

Sir Richard, or the great 'Black Knight of the North' as he is generally known, succeeded his father at Roxby[3] and probably made it the headquarters of his active life.[4] He was twice married; first to Margaret, daughter of William, Lord Conyers of Hornby, by whom he had six children, Francis, Richard,[5] Roger, Margaret, Jane, and Elizabeth: secondly, in or before 1555,[6] Catherine, the daughter of the Earl of Cumberland,[7] by whom there were one son, Henry, and two daughters, Katherine and Anne, the latter of whom married Ralph Salvin or Salvayn.[8]

'The Black Knight' took some part in the Scottish war of the reign of Edward VI., and was knighted, in 1551, at Musselburgh Field.[9] At the same time he was still the all-important official of the Forest of Pickering, though he does not seem to have managed the property any more wisely than the old Sir Richard, in the reign of Henry VII. In fact the long list of charges brought against him, 'read like a repetition of the charges against his predecessors.'[10] Nor does he seem to have been any more successful than Sir Roger Hastings in keeping his servants in order, for his dependants, John Keddey and Richard Maltby of Thornton, were charged with having 'gaulled, hurt and maimed as well by large bowes as crosse bows' the deer of Her Majesty.[11] His outstanding act of scandalous character, however, far outweighed anything done by other

---

[1] *Vide* Ch. IX.

[2] Y. A. S. Rec. S. II., p. 245.   He died August, 1563.

[3] *Cf.* Charlton, *ut supra*, p. 303, and Young, *ut supra*, pp. 829-38.

[4] Leland, I., p. 14, edit. 1745, says 'This *Chomeley* hath a House....at Rollesley (Rottesby) [Roxby]: and *Cholmeley's* Father that now is, was as an Hedde officer at Pykeringe, and setter up of his name yn that Quarters' Leland is wrong in saying that at Wilton there was 'a Manor Place with a Tower longging to *Cholmeley*.'

[5] The C.R. says for 11 October, 1569 'Mr. Rich. Chomlay married Tomysyn Thankard.' She was presumably the illegitimate daughter of Thomas de la Riviere or 'Dallriver' as the *Memoirs* call him. Her sister probably married Richard's brother Roger. They were both set on one side in the Cholmley succession.

[6] Y. A. S. Rec. S. II., p. 185.

[7] She survived her husband many years and died in 1598.

[8] Their son 'Ralph Salvane' was baptized in Thornton Church on 3 May, 1590, *vide* C. R.

[9] D. N. B.

[10] N. R. Rec. S. N.S. I., p. xxviii.

[11] Ibid., p. 213.

Seneschals. A mere enumeration of a few oaks stolen here,[1] or a little poaching done there, are nothing as compared with the astounding charge that 'S[r]. Rychard Cholmley did send Gyles Raunde and George Rand, two masons, to the Quenes Castell of Pyckeringe, whenn he builded his gallerye at Roxbye to polle [pull] downe the chefe stones of the Masoun work owte of one house in the same Castell called the King's Haull, and took owte of the pryncypall and cheffest Toure....the stones of the stayres ....and....caused xiiij wayne lodes of the same....to be caryed by his Tenantes to his owne house at Roxbye....S[r]. Rychard had owte of the Quenes Castle of Pycheringe two lodes of slaytes givinge to him by the late Erle of Westmoreland.'[2] Thus it was to the detriment of the royal castle that Sir Richard Cholmley increased the splendours of his private house. Roxby Castle reared its proud head over the village of Thornton and stood as a formidable place of defence along the Pickering road, and its keen-sighted sentinels would easily detect any hostile movements in the 'low country' of the Marishes. By the irony of fate all is changed. There is not a single stone of Roxby left and Pickering Castle still stands as a beautiful ruin of mediaeval military architecture.

'Sir Richard Cholmeley of Rockesbie' did not stop at robbing his sovereign. He was ever trying to increase his estates, as for example on 15 June, 1573, when the question arose as to his lands in 'Thorneton, Formandby and Kynthropp,' including certain 'parcells called the Black Buske, the Wood End and Brackendell.'[3] Actions were brought against Sir Richard concerning these lands in 1575[4], and as far as Kingthorpe was concerned, he answered that he held three carucates by the gift of Queen Elizabeth in Grand Serjeanty;[5] and that the Kingthorpe Beck, 'so farre as yt dothe adjoyne oppon the said manner unto the midstream.... by all the tyme of mannes remembrance haith bene parcel of the said manner.'[6] Further action was taken against him by Sir Henry Gate, knight, concerning rights of forest and chace;[7] while, as shown elsewhere, he had litigation with the inhabitants of Thornton.[8]

---

[1] It is also charged against Sir Richard that he built a new barn at Roxby out of money belonging to Queen Elizabeth. *Cf.* N. R. Rec. S. N.S. I., p. 209.

[2] Ibid., p. 207.

[3] *Vide* Ch. VI. *Cf.* N. R. Rec. S, N,S, I., p. 317, and *Ducatus Lancastriae* III., p. 492.

[4] Ibid., p. 32.

[5] *Mr. Ayloffe's Book of Demises.* MS. G. F. G. H. *Cf.* N. R. Rec. S. N.S. I., p. 9.

[6] Ibid., p. 219.

[7] *Ducatus Lancastriae* III., p. 54.

[8] *Vide* Ch. IV.

About 1580, Sir Richard seems to have enlarged the estate immediately abutting on the south side of the Castle, for he obtained the right to 'certain parcells of land call'd Hornum[1] *alias* Hornum gieft in the fforest of Pickering....and to build thereupon.'[2]

It is impossible to imagine that the 'Black Knight' was a lovable character. His great grandson, Sir Hugh Cholmley, says of him, 'His chief place of residence was at Roxby....(now [1651] almost demolished) where he lived in great port, having a very great family—at least fifty or sixty men servants about his house ....This Sir Richard was possessed of a very great estate, worth at this day [1651] to the value of about £10,000 a year....He died in the sixty-third year of his age at Roxby....and lies buried in the Chancel of Thornton Church of which he was patron, May 17, 1579.[3] He was tall of stature, and withal big and strong made, having in his youth a very active body, bold and stout; his hair and eyes black and his complexion brown, insomuch as he was called the great black Knight of the North; though the word *great* attributed to him not so much for his stature as power and estate and fortune....He was a wise man and a great improver of his estate which might have prospered better with his posterity, had he not been extraordinarily given to the love of women.'[4]

Sir Richard's eldest son by his first wife, Francis,[5] married Joane Bulmer, but died three years after his father, without issue, and, therefore, in 1586, Henry,[6] son of the second wife, succeeded. At first he lived at Whitby with his mother, Catherine, but after her death in 1598, he returned to Roxby Castle. By this time he had long been married to a Roman Catholic, Margaret, daughter of Sir William Babthorpe, and their son,[7] Richard, was

---

[1] So called to-day.

[2] Rev. A. H.

[3] Sir Hugh Cholmley was four years wrong in his reckoning, 'Sir Richard Cholmelaye Knight, was buried the xvij of Maye, 1583', according to the C. R. It is impossible to know why tradition has produced the legend that the recumbent figure in the Church is that of the Tudor Knight. *Vide* Ch. IX.

[4] *Memoirs* of Sir Hugh Cholmley, p. 7.

[5] According to Foster, *Pedigrees of Yorkshire*, III., Francis was buried in St. Mary's, Beverley, 28 April, 1586.

[6] A seventeenth century MS. [J. L. W.] shows that Henry Cholmley evidently felt the pinch caused by his father's extravagance. 'Henry Cholmeley of Whitby Esquire sold all his lands and tenements [in Pickering] unto John Lyghton and Ralph Hodshon two old Batchelours of Pickering who sold the said lands and tenements to the then tennants of this land and tenements by Indenture bearing date the tenth day of January 1586 [1586/7] to be holden of the Honnor and Mannor of Pickering.'

[7] They had a daughter Dorothy who as 'Doritie Cholmelaye' married on 5 November, 1601 'Nichelas Busshill.' This was Nicholas Bushell of Bagdale Hall, near Whitby. Their son Brown Bushell was a parliamentarian and became a royalist and was executed at Scarborough in 1651. Their daughter Mary married, 1639, Henry Tempest of Tong.

born in 1580. Henry was knighted at York, on 17 April, 1603, and his son Richard was also knighted at Windsor by James I., on 9 July,[1] of the same year.[2] It would seem that Sir Henry was not well-to-do, and this is very likely after succeeding to such a person as 'the Black Knight,' and also because of compositions he had to pay owing to the prosecutions of his Papistical wife. The numerous conveyances of lands in Thornton and Farmanby,[3] in 1607, 1609, and 1613,[4] give the impression that much of the estate was heavily mortgaged when Sir Henry died at York from a fall from his horse, in 1617.[5] Many years before this, probably in 1599, Henry's son, Richard, had married Susan, daughter of John Legard, of Ganton,[6] and they had three children. Hugh, of whom later, Margaret, who married Sir William Strickland of Boynton,[7] and Henry, born 1608/9, who married Catherine, daughter of Henry Stapleton, of Wighill, Esquire. Henry was in later life a Parliamentarian and took up his residence at West Newton.

'Mr. Hew Cholmelaye sonne to Mr. Richard Cholmelaye was christened the xxvij daye of Julye' 1600.[8] He himself writes 'I was the first child of my dear mother, born upon the 22nd of July, being a Tuesday and on the feast day, commonly called Mary Magdalen's day, in the year of our Lord God, 1600, at a place called Roxby....near to Thornton....the chief seat of my great grandfather, and where my grandfather, Sir Henry Cholmley, then lived ....At three years old, the maid which attended me let me tumble out of the great chamber window at Roxby, which (by God's providence) a servant waiting upon my grandfather at dinner espying, leaped to the window, and caught hold of my coat, after I was out of the casement. Soon after I was carried to my father and mother, who then lived with her brother Mr. John Legard at

---

[1] Metcalfe, *Book of Knights*, p. 143.

[2] Charlton, *ut supra*, is wrong in saying that they were both 'knighted by King James at his first coming into England A°. 1603 at a place called Grafton, in Northamptonshire.'

[3] *Vide* Ch. IX.

[4] Y. A. S. Rec. S. LIII., pp. 69, 112, 217.

[5] Young, p. 830, Henry Cholmley was buried in St. John's Church.

[6] Burke, *Peerage*, 1915, p. 1217, says 'John Legard, 3rd son of Ralph Legard of Anlaby, by Isabel his wife, dau. of Sir Piers Hildyard, of Wynestead, settled at Ganton, E. R. Yorks. He m. dau. of Robert Franke, of London, and had issue.'

[7] Burke, *ut supra*, p. 1904, says 'Sir William Strickland, 1st Bart. of Boynton, M.P. for Hedon 1640-53, and for E. R. Yorks. 1654-6, was created a Baronet 30 July, 1641. Sir William was a person of consideration during the protectorate, and summoned to the 'other house' as *Lord* Strickland. He m. 1st June, 1622, Margaret, dau. of Sir Richard Cholmley, Knt. of Whitby in Yorkshire, and by her (who d. 1629), had four daus.'

[8] C. R. He must very soon have lost a faithful friend for the Burial Register records, without giving any name 'old nurse of Roxbye was buried ye 6th of March 1602/3.'

Sir Hugh Cholmley 1600 - 1657

Photo by kind permission of Major George R H Cholmley and Mr Hugh J N Cholmley

his house at Ganton, nine miles[1] from Roxby, where I continued for the most part until I was seven years old; then my father and mother going to keep house at Whitby I went with them, and beginning to ride a little way by myself, as we passed over a common called Paston moor [Pexton] one of my father's servants riding beside me, I had a desire to put my horse into a gallop; but he running away, I cried out, and the servant taking hold of my arm, with an intention to lift me from my horse, let me fall between both, so that one of them, in his gallop, trod on my hat; yet by God's protection, I caught no harm. The next year being 1608, upon my very birthday....I escaped as great, if not greater danger than this; which was, that at my father's house at Whitby ....there was a great fierce sow, having two pigs near a quarter old....lying close together asleep....I being alone, out of folly and waggery, began to kick one of them; in the interim another rising up occasioned me to fall upon them all, and made them cry; and the sow hearing; came and caught me by the leg....and dragged me half a score of yards, under the window, now called the larder....from the leg she fell to bite me in the groin with much fierceness; when, the butler carrying a glass of beer to my father (then in his chamber) hearing me cry, set down the beer on the hall table, and running out, found the sow passing from my groin to my throat.'[2]

After these youthful adventures, life, for a time, was fairly quiet. Hugh[3] went regularly from Whitby or Roxby to school at Beverley,[4] and passed from there to Jesus College, Cambridge. Leaving the University in 1618, he entered Gray's Inn. Four years later, on 10 December, 1622, he married Elizabeth, daughter of Sir William Twisden, of East Peckham, Kent;[5] and this was probably the occasion of the conveyance in trust of the manors of 'Whitbie, Roxbie and Kinthorpe' and elsewhere to Ralph Bovey and William Cragge, gentlemen.[6] There is no doubt that Sir Richard still held the castle of Roxby for he is recorded as paying to the Honor of Pickering for Roxby, Kingthorpe and lands in Thornton £5. 12s. 4d.;[7]

[1] These were the old British miles and not the measurement of 1760 yards per mile which had not yet been introduced as a *customary* mile, although for many years a *statute* mile. *Vide* Sir H. G. Fordham, *Studies in Carto-Biblioeraphy*, p. 26.

[2] *Memoirs of Sir Hugh Cholmley.*

[3] Young, *ut supra*, p. 830 calls Sir Hugh, 'this ornament of the Cholmley family.'

[4] While at school he had some kind of dangerous fever, and being visited by his mother, she caught it and died.

[5] D. N. B.

[6] Y. A. S. Rec. S. LVIII., p. 201.

[7] MS. Copy of Norden's Survey, G. F. G. H.

and apparently, 'the Thornton parte amounted unto xiijs. vd. ob. which is divided as follows, vizt. 16 oxgangs (5d. or 6d. each) cottages and messuages.'[1]

It has already been suggested that the Cholmley estates were heavily mortgaged and the family embarrassments were not lessened by the fact that Sir Richard Cholmley III. had most costly law suits with Sir Thomas Posthumous Hoby of Hackness.[2] Nor could Hugh's life have been entirely free from expense to his father as he represented Scarborough in the House of Commons in the last parliament of James I., and in the first two of Charles I.[3] These expenses[4] at length necessitated the sacrifice of the family home at Roxby, which place, says Sir Hugh, without giving any date, 'since I was married was sold by my father and self, towards the payment of his debts.'[5] After the death of Sir Richard in 1632, matters might have permanently improved had it not been for the national disaster that fell upon the country. In any case Sir Hugh writes about 1635, 'Having mastered my debts, I did not only appear at all public meetings in a very gentlemanly equipage, but lived in as handsome and plentiful a fashion at home as any gentleman in all the county of my rank. I had between thirty and forty in my ordinary family.'[6]   Sir Hugh's cost of living would probably be even greater after 1636 when he records 'I was made Deputy-lieutenant and Colonel over the Train-bands within the hundred of Whitby Strand, Ryedale, Pickering Lythe and Scarborough Town.'[7] His first great success in these offices was in 1637, when he smartly captured some pirates at Whitby and sent their captain to York. For this action he was heartily thanked by the Privy Council.[8] In 1639 he had to muster his men for the Bishops' War, and he writes 'About June the King sent down his army into Yorkshire, and himself came to it in August. The Earl of North-

[1] N. R. Rec. S. N.S. I., p. 43.

[2] Young, *ut supra*, p. 830. *Cf.* D. M. Meads, *ut supra*.

[3] D. N. B.

[4] It is sometimes said that the Cholmleys, owing to their property at Whitby, had speculated in the new alum industry introduced by Sir Thomas Chaloner in 1600. Certainly the neighbourhood of Whitby was rich 'with allome veines'; *cf.* Drayton, *Polyolbion* Pt. II., p. 146. But had they engaged in this trade before the Civil War it would have been a breach of royal monopoly. It was probably not until after the Restoration that this family took up the industry. Canon Atkinson, N. R. Rec. S. O.S. III., p. 137 says that the story of Chaloner's introduction of the alum trade is 'an absurd fable.'

[5] *Cf. Memoirs, ut supra*, and *vide infra*.

[6] *Memoirs, ut supra*, p. 56. It is not surprising that at some period before the outbreak of the Civil War he had had to borrow money as is shown by the Cttee. of Comp. 1645. *Cf.* Y. A. S. Rec. S. XV., p. 13.

[7] *Memoirs, ut supra*.

[8] Ibid.

umberland, was General from whom I had a commission. Divers of the Colonels of the Train-bands, with their regiments, were called to march with the King....amongst which I had been one, but at that time I had caught cold and a dangerous sickness in raising and training my whole regiment together on Paxton [Pexton] Moor,[1] near Thornton, where one Hallden, a stubborn fellow of Pickering, not obeying his captain, and giving me unhandsome language, I struck him with my cane and felled him to the ground. The cane was tipped with silver, and hitting just under the ear had greater operation than I intended. But either the man was ill, or else counterfeited so, to be freed from service; which I willingly granted, and glad when he was well; but it was a good monition not to be hasty in the like or any other provocation, for passion doth not only blind the judgment but produceth other ill effects.' Henry Cholmley, brother of Hugh, led the trainbands in his place, but when he reached Durham, he was ordered to return. Sir Hugh, himself, was well enough to sit in the Short Parliament in April, 1640, as Member for Scarborough; and in November, 1641, he sat in the Long Parliament, and being in London was very anxious about the advance of the Scots into Yorkshire. This, he wrote, 'did not a little disquiet my mind and thoughts for my dear wife and children; the snow being so great I could not possibly remove them so soon as I desired....but at the latter end of February [1641/2], as soon as the ways were passable, I had her and all my family in London.'[2]

Events were now hastening on with great rapidity towards the outbreak of the Civil War; and isolated as was this district, it was nevertheless destined to see something of the coming and going of Cavaliers and Ironsides. Sir Hugh Cholmley showed himself one of the most active of local leaders. He was by no means a King's man, as he had proved by refusing to pay ship-money in 1639, for which he was slighted by the great Earl of Strafford,[3] 'with some scorn' says Sir Hugh, 'which my nature could ill-digest.'[4] The differences between the King and many of the northern gentry were very extreme; but it is evident that Sir Hugh Cholmley and Sir John Hotham were particularly disliked by Charles I. If this had not been so, he would hardly have told them that 'they had

---

[1] It is curious that he should have drilled his men on Pexton Moor having sold Roxby and Kingthorpe some years before.

[2] *Memoirs, ut supra.*

[3] As a matter of fact Strafford brought about the loss of all his official posts in the north.

[4] *Memoirs, ut supra.*

been the chief causes and promoters of all the Yorkshire petitions, and if they ever meddled or had a hand in any more he would hang them.'[1]

It is not altogether surprising, therefore, to find that the moment the Civil War broke out, Sir Hugh raised a regiment for the Parliament, and commanded it at Edgehill in October, 1642. It is impossible to refrain from wondering whether any of the tenants at Roxby or at Kingthorpe followed their former landlord to take part in that ghastly struggle, which practically marked the opening of ten years of bloodshed. Sir Hugh, shortly after joined Fairfax in his endeavour to coop up the royalists in York. But this was not for long, and he must have engaged in actions of his own, as at Guisborough on 16 January, 1642/3, or again, as Lord Fairfax wrote, on 26 January, 1643/4, 'In the North Riding Sir Hugh Cholmley hath carried himself very bravely giving several defeats to the enemy near Malton.'[2] This would certainly give the impression that Sir Hugh's headquarters might still have been at Roxby; and if that were so, troopers must have passed up and down Marishes Lane and Maltongate with messages and news either for their leader or sent by him to his beloved wife;[3] but what documentary evidence there is, though it is very slight, is in favour of Roxby being no longer in Cholmley hands.[4] Suddenly Sir Hugh changed his mind and deserted the parliamentarians for the King. It is said that the landing of Queen Henrietta Maria at Bridlington determined this. At any rate after being received by her at York, and kissing her hand, he openly declared for Charles I., on 20 March, 1643/4.[5] He at once came under the orders of the Marquis of Newcastle, who, appreciating his value, gave him 'the command of all maritime affairs from the Tees to Bridlington Bay, and he became one of the most formidable enemies of the trade of the parliamentarians.'[6] He must have rejoiced in his post for it kept him in a neighbourhood familiar to him by long residence in his homes at Roxby and Whitby. Then followed the colossal royalist disaster at Marston Moor on 2 July, 1644, and after that fatal disgrace the King's forces were either shattered or scattered. Sir Hugh at once threw himself into Scarborough Castle which he

---

[1] D. N. B. *Cf.* A. M. W. Stirling, *The Hothams*, I., p. 37.
[2] Rushworth, V., p. 125.
[3] Young, *ut supra*, p. 837, says that when Sir Hugh was in Scarborough Castle Lady Cholmley was staying in London, but sailed to Whitby and joined him at Scarborough.
[4] *Vide infra.*
[5] *Mercurius Aulicus.* Mar. 25. 31.
[6] D. N. B.

determined to hold stoutly for Charles I. In February, of the next year, the town of Scarborough was taken by Sir John Meldrum, who converted the parish Church into an artillery battery, and pounded away at the Castle; but Sir Hugh's men, not to be deterred, rushed down upon St. Mary's Church, stormed it, destroyed the choir, and returned unharmed to their stronghold. Starvation, however, began to play its part, and on 22 July, 1645,[1] Sir Hugh was obliged to surrender, when his officers and men were so weak that some were carried out on litters, and some needed the support of a friend on either side.[2] Meantime the battle of Naseby had been fought and lost, and Sir Hugh, seeing the game was up, retired into exile at Rouen. After the execution of the King on 30 January, 1648/9, he returned to England and compounded for his estates. It is hardly likely that he ever came again to Roxby, for by this time it had long been out of his hands, and the parliamentarians had allowed it to fall into a dilapidated condition.[3] The fine old castle, with its orchards and fishponds,[4] and with its great gallery built from stolen masonry, had started on that downward course that has, to-day, left nothing but grassy mounds and ridges. In 1651, Sir Hugh was imprisoned for eight weeks on suspicion, at Leeds, and it was during this time that he wrote for his two sons the '*Memoirs*' which were intended 'to embalm the great virtues and perfections'[5] of their mother. She died on 18 April, 1655, and he followed her to the grave two years later, on 30 November, 1657.[6]

When Sir Hugh returned to England after exile, his estates[7] were so seriously embarrassed,[8] that he realized the impossibility of ever repurchasing Roxby and Kingthorpe; and henceforth members of the Cholmley family were no more seen in the village of Thornton.

The discovery of the name of the actual purchaser of the Roxby estate from Sir Richard and Sir Hugh Cholmley long evaded all research. By good fortune, however, there came to light[9] a very tattered and almost illegible manuscript belonging to the Duchy

[1] Sir Hugh's birthday.
[2] J. S. Fletcher, *A Book about Yorkshire*, p. 163.
[3] *Memoirs, ut supra.*
[4] The position of these can still be seen and are marked on the Six-Inch Ordnance Map.
[5] D. N. B.
[6] Ibid.
[7] Part of the terms of the surrender of the Castle at Scarborough was that Lady Cholmley should have Sir Hugh's house at Whitby, which had been seized as barracks for Parliamentary soldiers. In July, 1652, Sir Hugh states that he came with his family 'to a comfortable meeting at our own house at Whitby.'
[8] He had to compound for his remaining property by a payment of £450.
[9] J. L. W.

of Lancaster, called 'A Survey of the severall Townshipps and grounds....Lying within the Hono^r. of Pickering.' In this midseventeenth century document Roxby was described as 'a single messuage....a mile[1] east from Pickering in the Lordship of Thornton and ffarmanby of which the Lord Lumley is chiefe Lord. It was once a very' (here the manuscript is completely worn away, but the missing words were probably) 'fine house of the family of Cholmley.' The manuscript then states 'of whom the Lady Cary bought it.' The question is 'who was this Lady Cary' for it is not a name that had hitherto appeared in the story of Thornton? In the same document 'the Lady Cary' is said to have bought, from the Cholmleys, the manor of Kingthorpe,[2] and part of the manor of Cropton from a certain 'Mr. Horseley the chief lord....but decayed in his estate.' No date was given as to any of these purchases, but there is reason to suppose that the sale of Roxby must have taken place after December, 1622, when Sir Hugh Cholmley married,[3] and before June, 1630, when, the only possible Lady Cary or Carey died and was buried at Stowe in Northamptonshire at the age of 84 years.[4]

Elizabeth, youngest daughter of John, fourth and last Baron Latymer, and lord of the main manor in Thornton, was born about 1546. She married before her father's death, in 1577, Sir John Danvers of Dauntrey, Wiltshire. He died 10 December, 1594. She married secondly, in 1598, Sir Edmund Carey,[5] sixth son of Henry Baron Hunsdon,[6] and thus came to be known as the 'Lady Cary.' By her first marriage there were many children: amongst whom were Anne,[7] Eleanor,[8] Elizabeth,[9] Katherine,[10] Dorothy,[11] Charles, Henry, afterwards Earl of Danby, constable of Pickering Castle in 1628 and an ardent royalist, and Sir John the celebrated

[1] Roxby is about two miles from Pickering.
[2] The manuscript says 'Kinthorpe. Is a Hamlett or Village in the Parrish of Pickering and doth appear by the ruines of some old buildings to have beene much bigger than it is now for the chappell garth shows the Rubbish of an old chappell, as Smithy garth and Cutter garth doe seeme such [here worn away] as were used there. Some say there is a mannor house and a Court kept there by the Cholmleys once Lords thereof from whom together with Roxby it was purchased by the Lady Cary. It is hard dry and stony ground.'
[3] *Memoirs, ut supra.*
[4] *Cf.* Baker, *Northamptonshire* I., p. 448, and Aubrey and Jackson, *Wiltshire Collections*, p. 217.
[5] D. N. B.
[6] First cousin of Queen Elizabeth.
[7] Married Sir Arthur Porter.
[8] Married Sir Thomas Walmseley.
[9] Married Sir Edward Hoby of Glos.
[10] Married Sir Richard Gargrave of Nostel.
[11] Married Sir Peter Osborne.

parliamentarian.[1] The last was born about 1588, and was knighted by James I. Like his elder brother Henry,[2] he had a great taste for gardening and is well known for his Italian gardens at Chelsea.[3] He was member of Parliament for the University of Oxford in 1625, 1626, 1628 and 1640. On the outbreak of the Civil War, he was a Colonel in the Parliamentary Army; and three years later was elected member for Malmesbury. His real fame or infamy, however, rests on the fact that he signed the death warrant of Charles I. The fact that he was a regicide,[4] no doubt, made him particularly prominent among the Commonwealth men, and he was a member of the Council of State from the death of the King to the time of Cromwell's acceptance of the office of Protector.[5] It was to this man that the Roxby property and other estates passed for a time.

Immediately after the death of her first husband in 1594, Elizabeth Neville, Lady Danvers settled her main property of Danby on her eldest son Charles with remainder to her second son, Henry, with remainder to her third son, John. Charles never succeeded for he was beheaded in 1601,[6] during his mother's lifetime. Henry, Earl of Danby, inherited in 1630, but as he died without issue on 20 January, 1643/4,[7] was succeeded by his brother Sir John Danvers in the properties of his mother. It was stated at the time that 'after the death of his brother ....he proved him to have been a malignant, and by Parliamentary proceedings overthrew his brother's will, outed his sister Gargrave[8] and Sir Peter Osborne[9]

---

[1] *Vide* pedigree in Aubrey and Jackson, *ut supra,* p. 217.
[2] Founded the Botanical Gardens in Oxford.
[3] *Vide* Peter Cunningham, *Handbook of London,* p. 114.
[4] Canon Atkinson in F. Y. in M. P., p. 300, makes a bad mistake when he says 'that Sir John was one of the goodly band of noble and faithful gentlemen who impoverished themselves' in supporting Charles I. Canon Atkinson had evidently never read Lord Clarendon's *History of the Great Rebellion*, Bk. XI. s. 237, where Clarendon says of Sir John 'and having, by a vain expense in his way of living contract a vast debt, which he knew not how to pay, and being a proud, formal, weak man, between being seduced and a seducer, became so far involved in their counsels, that he suffered himself to be applied to their worst offices, taking it to be a high honour to sit upon the same bench with Cromwell, who employed and contemned him at once; nor did that party of miscreants look upon any two men in the Kingdom with that scorn and detestation as they did upon Danvers and Mildmay.'
[5] D. N. B.
[6] Aubrey and Jackson, *ut supra*, p. 217.
[7] G. E. C. *Peerage III.*, p. 18. On his tomb in Dauntsey Church there are the words, 'Full of honour, woundes and daies, he died at his howse in Cornbury Parke, in the county of Oxford, in the yeare 71 of his age.'
[8] Katherine, who married Sir Richard Gargrave. Hunter, *South Yorkshire* II., p. 213, says that Sir Richard 'could once ride on his own land from Wakefield to Doncaster: [20 miles] but was at last reduced to earn his bread by travelling with pack-horses.'
[9] Husband of Dorothy Danvers.

of the estate, and hath it.'[1] Whatever the truth may be, by 1651 Sir John Danvers was entered as a freeholder of Roxby paying the Honor of Pickering 6s. 5d.;[2] and 'for certaine Lands in Kinthropp for which he paieth the yearely Rent' of £1. 12s. 6d.[3] He did not, however, live long to enjoy the estates, for he died in 1655; and Roxby Castle[4] passed to his widowed sister, Eleanor Walmseley, though why is difficult to say, as Sir John Danvers had several children of his own.

Thanks to the already mentioned tattered manuscript,[5] it is possible to obtain some slight information concerning the estate when in Lady Walmseley's hands. 'The house is now soo farr gone to decay that it would be [hole] lost husbandry to putt it' in a state of repair. The names of only two tenants are ascertainable, those of Robert Smith and Thomas Skelton, though no doubt there were several others, but the marginal list which contained the names has completely perished. The tenants occupied the following sections of land :—'the garth,' 'the orchard,' 'the flatt of Cõmon arrable before the gate,' 'beast gates in Cow and Ox Carr,'[6] 'arrable cõmonly called Clodds,' 'upper Dunhill meadow,'[7] 'Lower Dunhill mead,' 'the Oname mead,'[8] 'Rempland Syke,' 'Stonye Close,' 'Abbots Crooke,' 'West Close,' 'North Close,' 'Benson Close,' 'Middle Syke,' 'Moore Close' and 'one close nigh the moore close he hath for repairing the highway.' In all, the estate was 273 ac. 3 rd., and the rents arising were £78. 1s. 4d. The manuscript then states, 'The Tennants of Roxby have the Liberty of Thornton Cõmon or Moor which is of a vast Extent. There are about Roxby Inclosures above one hundred old decaying Ash trees, and about the house a matter of twelve Load of old Timber and boards which were part of the floors & outhouses.' There is also the interesting additional note that 'the Inclosures about Roxby house....are incidentally worth soo much as they are' because the Township of Pickering has a great deal of arable common and very little enclosed land. But if ever Pickering 'be inclosed it will make a

---

[1] Quoted in Aubrey and Jackson, *ut supra*, p. 226.
[2] *MS.* Copy of *Parliamentary Survey*, 1651. G. F. G. H. *Cf.* N. R. Rec. S. N.S. I., p. 76.
[3] Ibid.
[4] From this period Kingthorpe splits from the Roxby ownership, and passed into the hands of the family of Fothergill. Miss Harcourt succeeded Thomas the last of the Fothergills, and married Dr. James Thornhill Ashton. She is the present (1929) lady of the manor.
[5] J. L. W.
[6] Still called Cow Carr and Ox Carr.
[7] Now known as Dunkhill on the north and south side of Westgate near Broadmires Crossing.
[8] The same as Aunum or Hornum, north of Dunkhill and east of the old Fish Ponds.

considerable abatement in the rents....The Moore Close seems the cheapest being soo vast a quantity of land [132 ac. 1 rd. 31p.], and lying low.' It might by 'dividing into lesser parcells be somewhat improved, but it lyes low in the Marrishes far from [?] any Habitation and is ill fenced and a harsh, cold, unfertile [?] soil.'

The owner of this 'unfertile soil,' Eleanor Danvers, had as already said, married Thomas,[1] son of Sir Thomas Walmsley of Dunkenhall, Lancashire. Their son, Sir Thomas, married Juliana, daughter of Sir Richard Molyneux and had a son, Richard, and a daughter, Anne, who married Sir Thomas Osborne, later Earl of Danby and Duke of Leeds. Richard Walmseley married Mary, daughter of Bartholomew Fromonds of Cheame. He is definitely stated to have held under the Honor of Pickering five oxgangs of land and vert closes called Roxby Closes, paying to the Honor 6s. 5d. Unfortunately this manuscript is not dated,[2] but the payment must have been previous to 1679 as Richard Walmseley died that year. His family died with extraordinary rapidity: his eldest son, Thomas, died in Paris in 1677, Richard, in Rome, in 1680, Charles, at St. Omer, in the same year and his widow, in Paris, in 1687. The youngest son of this Roman Catholic and unfortunate family, was Bartholomew, who married Dorothy, daughter of John Smith, and died in 1701, leaving two children: Francis, heir of Roxby, born in 1696, and Catherine, born in the next year. Francis died without issue before 1718, and the property passed to his sister who had married Robert, the young Lord Petre,[3] who died a few months after marriage, from smallpox, on 22 March, 1712/13. Their child, Robert James, Lord Petre, was born posthumously on 3 June, 1710, and his mother for many years acted as guardian. It is recorded that on 15 January, 1717/8, she had to register her estates as a Papist, and she appointed Thomas Starkie of Preston in Lancashire, gentleman and John Morilden, of York, gentleman, as her attorneys.[4] On 6 October, 1719, she had again to register, and it is stated that 'in the township of Thornton cum Farmanby [there were] a mess^ge with its appurtenances, let to Fr. Hodgson, from year to year, at £29. 10s.: several closes let to John Nicholson at £40: a close, called 'Bothon Close,' let to James Waters at £5. 10s.: a close called 'Benson's

---

[1] Died, 1641.
[2] MS. vellum folio of the accounts of Pickering, G. F. G. H.
[3] Born 1689.
[4] N. R. Rec. S. O.S. VII., p. 252. She married secondly, 2 April, 1733, Charles, fourteenth Baron Stourton, and died 31 January, 1788.

Close,' let to Robert Barker at £3. 0s. 0d.: two closes called the Carrs let to Will. 'Boys' at £4. 10s.'[1]

The Roman Catholic and Jacobite, Robert James, Lord Petre, married on 2 May, 1732, Anne[2] daughter of the celebrated leader of the 'Fifteen Rebellion,' James Ratcliffe, Earl of Derwentwater. He died in 1742. His son, Robert Edward, born in 1742, and his grandson Robert Edward, born in 1763,[3] ninth and tenth barons Petre held Roxby, but the latter, though owning as late as 1796,[4] appears to have conveyed the property, soon after, to the trustees of Richard Hill, and since then the historic site[5] of the old castle has remained in the hands of the Hill family.

[1] Ibid., VIII., p. 80.
[2] Or Mary. She died 31 January, 1760.
[3] Died 29 March, 1809.
[4] G. F. G. H.
[5] Eastmead, *ut supra*, p. 329, writes, in 1824, 'nothing now remains but inequalities on the surface to indicate where this once splendid mansion formerly stood.' A short time before the Great War, a barn was destroyed on the western slope of Roxby, and it was discovered that it had been built out of the material of the castle, some Tudor window jambs being found in the masonry. This fact was told to the present writer by the late Rev. Arthur Hill.

CHAPTER SIXTEEN.

The Manor of Dalby.

'*It stood embosom'd in a happy valley.*'

BYRON.

'*For Arcady is here, around,*
In lilt of stream, in the clear sound
Of lark and moorbird, in the bold
Gay glamour of the evening gold.'

JOHN BUCHAN.

THE earliest owner that can be found in Dalby is, the already mentioned Gospatric; and, his lands, consisting of two carucates,[1] and marked in Domesday with the manorial M, passed into the hands of William the Conqueror. From that reign to modern times the ownership of the little settlement in the valley (dael-by),[2] has always been in the possession either of the Crown or of members of the royal family. It is clear, however, that as late as 13 May, 1251, Dalby was not regarded as part of the manor of Pickering, for it was then definitely stated that the men of the King's demesne of Pickering had no pasturing for any beasts in Dalby.[3]

It was, indeed, this pasturing or agisting[4] that was the main value of Dalby as far as the proprietors were concerned. After the death of Edmund, Earl of Cornwall, lord of Pickering and Dalby, on 1 October, 1300, it was recorded that 'In Dalby Hagg there is meadow in places worth £1 a year; the agistment of Dalby and the

----

[1] Domesday Book.
[2] A. H. Smith, *ut supra*, p. 88.
[3] N. R. Rec. S. N.S. I., p. 1 and Y. A. S. Rec. S. XII., p. 28.
[4] Manwood, *ut supra*, c. II., s. 1. says concerning Agistment, 'The taking in the beasts and cattle of every person being an inhabitant within a forest that may for their money have common herbage there for such beasts as are commonable within the forest; and this manner of taking in of cattle to pasture a forest by the week or by the month or otherwise is called agisting of beasts or cattle, and the common of herbage that they have there for their beasts is called agistment. But it is to be understood that agistment is most properly the common of herbage of any kind of ground or land or woods or the money that is received or due for the same.'

adjoining dales is worth £3 a year.'[1] The value evidently increased because in 1309, for 'cattle and sheep agisted in Dalby Hagg' the returns were £7. 1s. 2d.[2] Thirteen years later, however, in 1322, there was a very considerable falling off, as the 'Minister's Accounts of the Issues of Pickering Castle' show that for thirty-four weeks the cattle and sheep agisted in Dalby only produced 6s. 10d.,[3] though in 1342, the fees had again risen to £1. 10s. 4d., after thirty acres of meadow had been withdrawn for 'sustaining the Lord's cattle there.'[4]

It would seem that in the early fourteenth century Dalby was more of a loss than a profit to its royal owners, for the expenses were far in excess of the average agistment fees. In 1325, for example, the Accounts show that '1 qr. 5½ bushels of maslin[5] for livery of the Keeper of the demesne meadows and Dalby dales for 20 weeks from the 14th March to 1st August' cost £1. 5s. 2½d.;[6] while 'mowing 47 acres in Dalby meadow for the sheep, tedding the grass, cocking it, carrying it and stacking it in the barn,' cost £1. 14s. 1½d.[7] This is stated to have been a very high price for labour owing to persistent rainy weather. If this is so, then the weather in the next year must have been worse still, for the expenditure, for the same work, was £3. 18s. 4d.[8] On the other hand the fines arising from unagisted beasts found in Dalby demesne may have helped to make up for the annual agricultural loss. At the Great Eyre of 1334 and 1335, a very large number of men were accused of this forest offence. Thus John Hert, William Latimer, lord of Thornton, and Alan, the late reeve, were all charged,[9] for unagisted pigs valued at 2s. apiece,[10] while the forester himself, John de Neville, was fined 6d. for having his pigs

---

[1] N. R. Rec. S. N.S. I., pp. 228-231.
[2] Ibid., II., p. 18.
[3] Ibid., IV., p. 199. Probably due to the Scottish Invasions.
[4] Leather bound MS. folio of about 1650 stating that the material contained was 'From the Reeve & Bayliffes Accompts,' G. F. G. H.
[5] Maslin was a mixture of wheat and rye. The allowance to the under-forester was about 6 lbs. a day.
[6] N R. Rec. S. N.S. IV., p. 203.
[7] Ibid., p. 208.
[8] Ibid., p. 218.
[9] Ibid., III., pp. 49, 50, 68.
[10] The price of pigs fell later, for in 1349, 'a good fat pig' sold for 5d. Neilson, *Customary Rents*, pp. 72-3, says 'Pannage was paid annually at Martinmas according to the number of animals agisted. The ordinary rate was a penny for a pig over a year old, that is to say, a year old on the last Holy Cross day, a halfpenny for a half-yearling or for a pig just separated from its mother. Little pigs and sows were often free.... *Retro pannagium* which is especially common in descriptions of royal forests, was the pannage paid for the agistment of swine after the termination of the ordinary season, that is to say, after Martinmas.'

unagisted under colour of his office.[1] John de Roxby was also
charged for allowing ten stirks,[2] total value £1, to wander in
Dalby 'Hay.'[3] Sheep, too, were also found, and these, each valued
at 1s. proved to be the property of Peter de Sarterye, of William
son of William son of Ivetta of Ayton, of William Hastings son of
the Lady Beatrice,[4] and of the Preceptor of Foulbridge,[5] for which
the Prior of the Hospital of St. John was responsible.[6] Colts, valued
at 1s. 6d. apiece were caught galloping about and were proved to
be the property of Geoffrey de Lith, of William the forester, of the
late vicar of Ellerburn, and of Robert del Clif of Thornton.[7] A horse,
valued at 3s. 4d., belonging to Richard de Wrelton, was also
impounded by the under-foresters, and its owner charged.[8] And
another horse, again valued at the same sum, belonging to John
Prest of Ebberston, was restored to its owner on his undertaking
to produce it when the Justices came into the Forest. He managed
to get Richard, late forester of Dalby, to be his surety, but as both
failed to appear before the Justices in 1335, he 'was in mercy' and
must pay the value of the horse to the lord,[9] who happened, at
this moment, to be Henry, Earl of Lancaster.[10] And last, but not
least, several men, including Richard Russel and Robert Wygan,
both of Farmanby, were fined the very large sum of £6 for allowing
24 oxen to pasture in Dalby meadow.[11]

These agistment amercements, however, were not the only
means of adding to the somewhat meagre revenues of the Dalby
property. Heavy fines were also exacted for the stealing of timber.
At some period, previous to 1334, Adam Skelton, Keeper of the
Forest, 'sold one hundred and seven dry oaks in Dalby Dale,' to
different persons, and, to that old rascal, 'William Latimer two oaks
in the demesne woods of Dalby.'[12] As Adam Skelton was dead at
the time of the Great Eyre, 'those holding his land are to answer
for him,' and there can be little doubt that the fines would be
very severe indeed.[13] On a smaller scale there were other cases,

[1] N. R. Rec. S. N.S. III., p. 68.
[2] A young ox or heifer.
[3] N. R. Rec. S. N.S. III., p. 50.
[4] *Vide* Chs. II., IX.
[5] Little is known of this Preceptory which belonged to the Templars
until 1308 and was then transferred to the Knights Hospitallers. It was
near Yedingham and had some property in Allerston and Wydale. *Cf.*
V. C. H., *York*, III., p. 258.
[6] N. R. Rec. S. N.S. III., pp. 54, 55, 56, 58.
[7] Ibid.
[8] Ibid., p. 58.
[9] Ibid.
[10] 1281?-1345.
[11] N. R. Rec. S. N.S. III., pp. 38, 47, 68.
[12] Ibid. II., p. 140.
[13] Ibid.

John White, for example, possibly the ancestor of the family still in the neighbourhood, was sufficiently daring to take the bark of an oak in Dalby demesne. The value of it was 4d.; but he was beyond human justice in 1335, for he was dead; not so, however, Henry 'Cokereell,' who had been more deeply implicated, for he it was who cut down the oak and carried it away. He was fortunate in being allowed to pay for his misdemeanour by a fine of 4s.[1] Had Thomas Sturmy or his bail been alive, in 1335, they, too, would have been fined for 'taking a green oak in Dalby,' but in this case, both parties were dead and so 'proceedings against them are stayed.'[2]

Among other items of possible profit, at this period, there seems to have been a somewhat mysterious 'Colliery.' Information as to where it was situated, and how long it had been worked, is now probably lost for ever; but that it was not a very paying concern may be seen from the fact that in 1342, 'one Colliery'[3] in 'the Demesne,' only produced an annual return of £1. 6s. 0d.; and that, in 1351, even this small sum had disappeared, for the 'Accompts' state 'ffor one Collyery in the Demesne of Dalby *nill* ....from the defects of the works.'[4] Still smaller sums were obtained, first, from the sale of Alders, but, in 1342, the entry was 'nill for none sold';[5] secondly, 'ffor the Turbary of Water Moore sold in grosse' which produced 4s.;[6] and thirdly 'ffor the Hermete Close demised to the fforesters there etc. 25th of Edw. ye 3d at 2s. p ann.'[7]

This entry of the 'Hermete Close' arouses interest. Much has been written[8] about the famous Richard Rolle as a Hermit at Thornton, and though it is extremely unlikely that he ever had anything to do with the parish of Thornton, yet the neighbourhood did undoubtedly have in the early fourteenth century a hermit known as William of Dalby as has already been shown.[9] The fact that the 'Hermete Close' was let for 2s. to the forester in 1351 is fair presumption that the good William had departed this life;

---

[1] Ibid., pp. 38, 39, 47.
[2] Ibid.
[3] V. C. H. *York*, II., p. 340, says 'in the North Riding the thin and inferior seams of the Jurassic coal, as for example at Cloughton, may have received some intermittent attention in the 14th century, but there is little or no evidence on record.' There were iron-works near Dalby in Levisham Wood as early as 1255. *Cf.* Pipe R. 39 Hen. III. m.16.
[4] Leather bound folio, *ut supra.*
[5] Ibid.
[6] Ibid.
[7] Ibid.
[8] *Vide* Ch. III.
[9] *Vide* Ch. III.

and all knowledge of the exact spot where he dwelt would have been lost had it not been for the fact that there are from time to time references in documents to the site. In 1560, the 'Hermitage' was still being let at the old rent of 2s.[1] Again in 1619, in 'Norden's Survey' there are the words 'The Hermitt Close in Dalbie demised to Thomas Whitwell there arrented at two shillings p ann.';[2] but what is much more important for the tracing of the site, is the statement, later in the Survey, that Christopher Tucker, who is said to be a copy holder, held a 'close nere Dalby called Keldhousegarth *or* heremite close of the yearlie rent of ijs. contayninge about 6 ac. which he holdeth in peace.'[3] This so-called Keldhousegarth was held by Mrs. Dutton as copy hold land in 1651, for the same rent;[4] by Thomas Dutton, 'gent,' for 2s. on 6 April, 1657,[5] and three years later 'The Hermitage,' as it was still sometimes called, was let to John Wilson at a similar rent.[6] In 1717 it is stated to be copy hold leased by a man called Carpenter.[7] A survey of 1722 says that Keldhousegarth 'lyes near Ellesbourne (the house is down) containing abt. 4 acres, now belongs to Mr. Jas Boys of Thornton in his Own Occupation. All of it said not to be Copyhold.'[8] From that date to comparatively recent times the place has been known as Keldhousegarth.[9] This name has now disappeared and the little that remains of buildings is marked on the Six-Inch Ordnance Survey as 'Harwood House.' The character of the base stones, hidden as they are in bracken and nettles, is such that they might well be some of the stone foundations used by William of Dalby more than six hundred years ago.[10]

In the fifteenth century, what are now known as High and Low Dalby did not exist. The farming rights were not divided. Towards the end of the century, one, John Eure[11] had the lease of the parcels in Dalby and Langdon, and during his tenure, Henry VII. appointed George Bukton, forester of the district on 4 October, 1487.[12] This man must have been well aware of the trespass of his superior, Brian Sandford, Seneschal of the Honor,

---

[1] '*A Perfect rentall*' etc. MS. G. F. G. H.
[2] N. R. Rec. S. N.S. I., p. 19.
[3] Ibid., pp. 30, 44. The earliest reference I have found to the word 'Keldhousegarth,' is in a document of the late sixteenth century.
[4] For Mrs. Dutton, *vide* Ch. V.
[5] J. L. W.
[6] N. R. Rec. S. N.S. I., p. 103.
[7] A Mr. Watson's Account, 1717. J. L. W.
[8] G. F. G. H.
[9] James Green, retired gamekeeper, has helped me much here.
[10] Mrs. Richard Hill has been of great assistance in finding this and other sites.
[11] N. R. Rec. S. N.S. I., p. 120.
[12] Ibid., p. 118.

who on 14 June, and on 12 November, 1489, 'Slow a Brokett[1] in Dawbye.'[2] On the expiry of John Eure's lease, on 29 September, 1492,[3] there seems to have been a slight gap in the tenure, for the next lease dates from 29 September, 1493, but it was not signed until 20 March, 1494. The tenants were clearly relatives of the forester, for they bore the name of John and Robert Bukton, and they agreed to pay the old rent of £11 per annum with an increase of £1.[4] There is something rather suspicious about this Bukton family, for among the many charges brought against Sir Richard Cholmley, there is one that he had put 'into his office, to kepe the wodes of Langdon, John Bukton, son of William Bukton of Haknase [Hackness], whereby the seid wode ys mynshed and hurt and by the same Bukton daly sold and karyed away to Scarysbourgh.'[5] Whether these misdemeanours were a cause of a new lease, it is now impossible to say, but the Bukton lease must either have been surrendered or forfeited almost immediately as on 2 July, 1495, 'the Herbage and Pannage &c of Dalby and Langdon were let to 'Sir John Pykering and Richard Chomley, esqrs.' for fourteen years from the following Michaelmas, at the old rent of £12, plus an increase of £1. 6s. 8d.'[6]

It was just about the time that the Buktons disappeared that Sir Richard Cholmley allowed his brother Roger 'to put in his office Thomas Belendine of Farmanby to kepe the wodes of Dalby.' Unfortunately exactly the same complaint is brought against Belendine as against John Bukton, and the woods are said to be 'destroyed.'[7] In 1523 the 'Herbage and Pannage' with the house called 'the Sheepcoate,' that is the later 'Low Dalby Farm,' was demised to Roger 'Cholmeley,'[8] and remained in Cholmley hands until the reign of Elizabeth, the lease being renewed to Richard Cholmley on 22 February, 1542.[9] About twenty years later, oaks were still being cut in Dalby, and apparently the Earl of Westmorland gave orders that 'servene okes in the woodes in Dawby' valued at 8d. per oak, should be given to Cuthbert Chilton;[10] and, at very much the same time, William Metham 'felled and caryed

---

[1] A Brokett or Knobbe was a Hart of the Red Deer of the second year.
[2] N. R. Rec. S. N.S. I., pp. 159, 160.
[3] Ibid., p. 120.
[4] Ibid.
[5] Ibid., p. 178.
[6] Ibid., p. 120.
[7] Ibid. II., p. 202. It should be noted that Belendine is not a local name.
[8] *A Perfect Rentall*, etc., *ut supra*.
[9] Ibid.
[10] N. R. Rec. S. N.S. I., p. 208.

awaye in Dawby sixe Timbre trees of oke,' but this was for 'the reparinge of the Quenes nether mylne of Pyckeringe and by warrant of John Braddell, Surveyor of the Quenes woodde there.'[1] After all these cuttings, however, trees were still left at this time, because 'there ys in the hagges of Dawby forty Timbre trees of oke.'[2] It was about this period, though the exact date is not clear, that the agistment of Dalby was let to Thomas Coleby for twenty-one years;[3] while the twenty-four acres of Dalby Hagg proper were demised to Robert Barneston.[4] The wrongdoings of Sir Richard Cholmley and his confederates continued to be very marked. In October, 1580, there was a suit between the plaintiff, John Brograve, Esquire, the Attorney-General of the Duchy, on behalf of the Queen, and 'Thomas Brockett, gent' concerning the 'Herbage, Pannage and Pasture, called Dalby and Dalby Rigg Intacks.'[5] An inquisition was held at Pickering, and, on 30 January, 1580/1, Brograve wrote to Sir 'Raffe' Sadler, Chancellor of the Duchy, saying that 'the said Thomas Brockett[6] hathe inclosed foure intacks in a place called Dawbye conteyning by estimacion foure acres, being of the Quenes Maties. demeynes, and hath sett three haystackes in a certain place called Dawby Privett [?][7] and Sotherbrough[8] contrary to the assize of the fforest.'[9]

By this time documents make it clear that there are three things being leased: the agistment, the Herbage and Pannage, and the Hagg. Thus in 1582, the agistment was leased to Sir Richard Cholmley for £13. 13s. 4d.[10] Four years later the Herbage and Pannage was granted to Maurice [or Margaret] Bartley [or Barkeley].[11] The latter lease evidently led to legal friction, for in 1588, there was a suit between the plaintiff, the Attorney-General of the Duchy, by Henry Cholmley and others in right of Thomas 'Colby' and Margaret 'Barkeley,' against, amongst others, William Metham, 'a notorious trespasser,' and Thomas Brockett, 'concerning Land with Herbage and Pannage at Dalby and Langdon.'[12] Shortly afterwards, but at an uncertain date, there was a further suit

---

[1] Ibid.
[2] Ibid., p. 210.
[3] Rev. A. H.
[4] Mr. Ayloffe's *Book of Demises*, etc. MS. of G. F. G. H.
[5] *Ducatus Lancastriae*, III., p. 90.
[6] Edward 'Brokett' son of Thomas 'Brokket' was christened in Thornton Church 1 January, 1575/6.
[7] Another reading is 'Dawby Britoe.'
[8] Now spelt, on Six-Inch Ordnance Map, 'Sutherbruff'; it is the third rigg on the east side of the Beck as one goes up-stream from Ellerburn.
[9] N. R. Rec. S. N.S. I., p. 221: and Rev. A. H.
[10] Rev. A. H.
[11] N. R. Rec. S. N.S. I., p. 83.
[12] *Ducatus Lancastriae*, III., p. 167.

between Robert Hunter, of Thornton, and Richard Dutton, Thomas Dutton and James 'Wynchecombe,' concerning a disputed title to lands and tenements called 'Keldhousegarth, Dalbye, or Dalbye Riggs and Langdon.'[1] Whether Richard Dutton had settled down at Dalby because it was an ideally peaceful spot, in which, he, as a Roman Catholic would not be troubled, is impossible to say; but, if this had been his intention it was evidently rudely frustrated, for on 6 September, 1591, he and his wife[2] were charged as recusants 'for not receying the holie communion at Easter last.'[3] In 1595, the wood and underwood called 'Dalby Hagg' was demised to a certain Robert Younglove for twenty-one years at a rent of £1;[4] but this still further complicated affairs for he assigned the lease to Thomas Dutton;[5] and matters were made no easier by the fact that Richard Dutton died at this time. Henry Cholmley, as Richard Dutton's administrator, brought an action against Thomas Dutton, John 'Winchcombe,' William Preston and others, concerning an intrusion on ground called 'Dalbye hagg,' and for wrongful possession of messuages and lands, and with waste and spoil of woods.[6] Thereupon Thomas Dutton, because of the assignment of Younglove's lease, brought a similar action against Katharine and John Dutton,[7] and, it must be said in favour of Thomas Dutton, that he had, in October, 1598, paid £1 rent for 'the hagg' to the 'graves' of Pickering.[8] As far as Dalby Hagg was concerned the difficulty seems to have been got over by it being demised on 10 December, 1597, to Henry Cholmley for £1 per annum.[9]

From a document of 1651, however, it appears that the Bartley or Barkeley lease of 1586, continued to hold good until a fresh indenture was drawn up on 11 January, 1603/4, by which Ingram 'Frizer' had granted to him by James I., the Herbage and Pannage of Dalby, 'all which Lands (by diverse meane Conveyances) came to the hands of Tho: Pudsey Esq. after whose death it came to the hands [of] Philippa Pudsey[10] his Relict.'[11] In 1619 'The widow of

---

[1] Ibid., p. 504.
[2] *Vide* Ch. V.
[3] Y. A. J. XVIII., p. 219.
[4] *Mr. Ayloffe's Book of Demises, ut supra.*
[5] *Ducatus Lancastriae* III., p. 371.
[6] Ibid., p. 369.
[7] Ibid., p. 371.
[8] N. R. Rec. S. N.S. II., p. 11.
[9] *Mr. Ayloffe's Book of Demises, ut supra.*
[10] One of Mrs. Pudsey's labourers at Dalby was a Peter Metcalf, who, on 12 April, 1611, had to appear before Quarter Sessions at Pickering, for brewing contrary to the assize. *Cf.* N. R. Rec. S. O.S. I., p. 223.
[11] N. R. Rec. S. N.S. I., p. 83.

Thomas Pudsey, gent,' is said to hold 'by a lease, one ferme house called Dalbye ferme, the house being very ruinous, with a garden and garth, containing by estimation 3 ac. 2 r. 0.';[1] for which she paid 13d.[2] The reason for the ruinous state was given by the Jury, at the time of Norden's *Survey* at Pickering, when they say that there was also 'an auntient fayre barne of five bayes[3] taken down and caried away, about 8 yeares since by one Richard Dutton[4] then fermer thereof.'[5] In addition to this there were 1,683 acres,[6] of which 1,500 acres were 'open heath and moorish groundes being sometimes with the moste of the rest an agistmente': 42 acres were newly enclosed, and the rest were Dalby Haggs, Herbage and Pannage.[7] Of these Haggs, Norden writes 'the Princes haggs lynge at Dalbie being of late cutt in 3 or 4 yeares a hagg, maketh the last cutt wood at the seaven yeares ende so younge that it is spoyled therbye. Theis haggs are called Littiegate,[8] Haygate,[9] and Lowehagg.[10] All which haggs if they were duly preserved might yelde his highnes good profite,[11] wood now growing scarce in the forest.'[12]

Mrs. Philippa Pudsey assigned her rights on 16 April, 1624, to William Darcy, Esq. During the period that he held this property, Sir John Walter,[13] on 16 November, 1626, at the command of the King, granted to William Popell, of Kingston-upon-Hull, the Low Spring Hagg and Rishesty *alias* Haygate Hagg for thirty-one years.[14] He, however, on 31 July, 1628, transferred the Haggs to William Darcy, who assigned them with the other property,[15]

---

[1] Ibid., p. 46.

[2] Ibid., p. 45.

[3] For the meaning of this word, *vide* Wright's *Dialect Dictionary* I., p. 195.

[4] The will of Richard Dutton was proved 31 October, 1637. *Cf.* Y. A. S. Rec. S. LXXIII., p. 45.

[5] N. R. Rec S. N.S. I., p. 38.

[6] Jacobean acres must have been larger, for in the late seventeenth century there were more than these.

[7] N. R. Rec. S. N.S. I., p. 46.

[8] Marked on Six-Inch Ordnance Map as 'Lidygate Way.' It means the 'steep road.'

[9] The same name to-day.

[10] Marked on One-Inch Ordnance Map as 'Low Wood.'

[11] Norden's advice was not taken. Dalby wood became famous for nuts; but a modern Duchy has forgotten the old 'nut geld' that was worth something even to a Duke, and since the Great War the Nut wood has been destroyed and larches planted.

[12] N. R. Rec. S. N.S. I., p. 28.

[13] Sir John Walter, 1566-1630, educ. at Brasenose College, Oxford. Attorney-General, 1613; Chief baron of the Exchequer, 1625· ordered not to act as a Judge 1630.

[14] *Mr. Ayloffe's Book of Demises, ut supra. Cf.* N. R. Rec. S. N.S. I., p. 84.

[15] Ibid., p. 85.

on 8 December, 1633, to Thomas Hassell of Stonegrave and William Ives.[1] The latter assigned to James Brooks and Thomas Fairefox [*sic*] on 14 March, 1633/4 for the use of Henry Robinson son of John Robinson of Thornton. Henry Robinson assigned to Henry Thompson, alderman of York, and Richard Seaton of Foulworth on 18 July, 1649. They assigned on 9 February, 1650/1, to Ralph Hassell, who took one moiety and Beatrice Hassell, widow of Thomas Hassell, who took the other, and together they paid £10. 13s. 4d.[2] At last, then, in 1651, there is for the first time, the modern division into Low and High Dalby.

This document of the Commonwealth period is of considerable interest as it gives certain pieces of information about the two properties which show how very little change had been made in the picturesque valley from the days of the Civil War to those of the Great War. Low Dalby fell to the share of Mrs. Beatrice Hassell[3] who held, 'all that messuage knowne by the name of the Coatehowse,[4] conteyninge a Kitchen on the west end of the said howse,' a buttery, milkhouse, 'a faire Roome called a Parlour' and 'three chambers above stayres.' Outside was a barn and farm buildings, 'the scite of which conteyneth one Acre more or less.' She also had four acres in Keldale, and a hemp garth of one acre, besides 'Sumer Close,' 'Highgate Ing' [Haygate Ing], 'Low Ing' and 'Long Low Lands' comprising in all twelve acres. There was a Paddock of two and a quarter acres, Dalby Hagg of forty acres and sheep pasture on 'Southerborough Rigg,' in Flaxdale, on 'Coatrigg,' 'Hareboroughrigg' and in 'Snyverdale' and 'Sybdale.' Her tenant was John 'Boss' [Boyes], who held 'all that messuage' 'Flaxdale End' which consisted of two rooms open to the roof, 'Tupp Close' and three parcels of arable of four acres, known as 'Flaxdale End Closes,' and bounded by a sheep-pasture,[5] which in 1651, belonged to Lord Lumley or his assigns. In all Mrs. Hassell held 935 acres, 3 roods, and 38 perches, for which she paid the rent of £5. 6s. 8d.; but it was estimated that in addition to the rent it

[1] Probably of Farmanby.

[2] *MS.* Copy of Parliamentary Survey, July, 1651. G. F. G. H.

[3] From a seventeenth century document (J. L. W.) it would appear that on 29 November, 1660, Thomas Hassell 'Merchant Taylor and Citizen of London' became tenant for twenty-one years 'to commence after the Expiration of one other lease of Eleaven yeares, then in being.'

[4] It was in earlier days 'Sheepcote house,' and in 1660 'a Messuage called the sheepcoat.'

[5] This was no doubt Whitecliff Rigg and Flainsey warren, which have in recent years passed into the possession of the Forestry Commission.

could be made worth £69. 6s. 0d. On the property there were 870 standells[1] and old dottrells[2] worth £14. 5s. 4d.[3]

Ralph Hassell's moiety[4] was, what is now known as, High Dalby; and his share was 1,010 acres, 1 rood, 23 perches, for which he paid £5. 6s. 8d., though again it is stated that the property might be improved to be, with the rent, worth £77. 13s. 0d. His house portion was known as the 'Ing next the Low Ing,' and his two tenants for this part were James and Christopher Todd. A part of the land was called 'Bouchard' or 'Dutton Close,' and this was bounded on the south by Mrs. Hassell's Paddock, on the west by Dalby Hagg, on the north by the highway leading from the Hagg to the Beck, and on the east by Dalby Beck. There were evidently more houses at Dalby, than ever again until after 1924, for there were other tenants such as William Gilbanke[5] and his relative, Richard Gilbanke,[6] the latter having a two-roomed house, and a barn, called 'Sibdale End House,' and two closes up the hill 'known by the name of "the Hill before the Door."' Another tenant was a nameless widow, who had a cottage of two rooms open to the roof, and 'Hollow Closes' which were situated under the west end of Clenfield Rigg, and on the east side of the Beck. Most of the Hassell property lay on the south side of 'The Highway that leadeth to Hackness'[7] and bounded on the east by the Beck.[8]

Such were Low and High Dalby nearly three hundred years ago, and many of the old names can still be found on the Six-Inch Ordnance Survey. It is to be presumed that Ralph Hassell was succeeded by his son, Thomas, who on 19 April, 1664, was chosen one of the Chief Constables for Pickeringlythe.[9] These Hassells were not, of course, owners, and it was possible for the Crown to let to anyone from whom in turn the Hassells might hold, so that as early as 1661, after the restoration of Charles II., and as the Honor

---

[1] When a wood was being felled there was a practice of leaving single trees called standards or standells, as they were regarded as too young and thriving to be taken down.

[2] *The New English Dictionary* says a dottrell was a 'doddered tree.' Apparently this means a tree fit only for burning.

[3] *MS.* Copy of Parliamentary survey, *ut supra.*

[4] In the early part of the reign of Charles II. this moiety was held by William Clemment. J. L. W.

[5] *Cf.* C. R.

[6] It was one of these tenants who as 'a Dalby yeomn.' had to appear at Quarter Sessions at Kirkby Moorside on 17 January, 1655/6, 'for shooting at a quicke [living object] contrary to the Statute' [2 Ed. VI. c. 14] *vide* N. R. Rec. S. O.S. V., p. 203. Richard Gilbanke was at Dalby as early as 1648, as shown by the Church Registers.

[7] This reference puzzles me. It must have been a track leading to Hackness Gate.

[8] *MS.* Copy of Parliamentary Survey, *ut supra.*

[9] N. R. Rec. S. O.S. VI., p. 77.

of Pickering had been settled on Queen Henrietta Maria, as part of her Jointure, it is not surprising to find that Elizabeth Howard, 'one of the Maydes of Honor attending the said Queene,' paid 20s. for 'Dalbie Hagg,' and £14. 13s. 4d. for the Herbage and Pannage of Dalby and Langdon together with 'Le Sheepcote' and the right of folding sheep.[1] These rights[2] of Miss Howard probably date back to a period previous to the Civil War, possibly to 4 May, 1641.[3]

Members of the family of Hassell were still tenants in the late seventeenth and early eighteenth centuries, in the persons of two ladies, a Mrs. Mary Lassells, probably a relative of Mrs. Beatrice Hassell, and a Miss Jane 'Hassle.'[4] But another document, dated 19 April, 1705, shows that the Dowager Queen Catherine of Braganza demised Dalby and High Moor on Wheeldale Rigg to Mary Lassells and Thomas Lassells under the yearly rent of £10. 14s. 0d.[5] By this time, however, High Dalby, at any rate, had been sub-let to the family of 'Body'[6] or 'Boddy' who long continued to farm there. John 'Body' was the first and the reference to him would lead one to suppose that he had resided for some time when he died in 1681.[7] He was succeeded by Robert Body who was alive in 1719.[8] Another John Body was tenant in 1722,[9] and probably the same 'Boddy' is stated to have owed his rent on 20 April, 1739.[10] His successor was another Robert 'Boddy'; and in 1751,[11] and as late as 1755,[12] the tenant was Francis Body. There was an Edward 'Boddy' resident in 1816, another Robert in 1825 and another Edward in 1830,[13] and another John from 1866 to 1886, after which the farm passed into the hands of the Hoggarths and Brewsters who held it in the early twentieth century; and is now occupied by John Arthur Coulson.

Low Dalby was farmed by Thomas Robinson in 1718[14] and the

---

1 '*faldagium.*'
2 N. R. Rec. S. N.S. I., pp. 100, 101.
3 Ibid., p. 67. *Cf.* V. C. H. *N.R.* II., p. 466.
4 *MS.* 'Accounts of the Honor of Pickering.' G. F. G. H.
5 G. F. G. H.
6 A tattered seventeenth century document (J. L. W.) shows that a James Boddy had five acres of copy-hold in the Hole of Horcum in October, 1656, that a Robert Boddy had the same in May, 1658, and that a Robert Boddy had ten acres in the same in October, 1666.
7 C. R.
8 A James 'Body' was a horse dealer in 1733 and with Richard Harding sold John Hill III. a 'Halifax mare' for £10. *Cf.* Sam. Tetley, *ut supra.*
9 G. F. G. H.
10 Letter of Sam. Tetley in Normanby Papers. J. L. W.
11 'A Rentall of the Honor and Manor of Pickering.' J. L. W.
12 He was Churchwarden at Thornton this year.
13 C. R.
14 G. F. G. H.

farm was still held by his widow as late as April, 1739.[1]   Flainsey
Warren or Flansey Warren was tenanted by John Robinson at a
rent of £63. 8s. 0d. in 1743.[2]   It was at this time that John Hill
III. as direct tenant of the Duchy, spent certain sums on doing
up the farm and stocked it at remarkably low prices as has been
mentioned elsewhere.[3]   Between 1756 and 1758, and perhaps
for longer, George Brown is described as 'of Dalby';[4] and at some
period, between 1780 and 1812, it was occupied by Robert Champley
and Anne his wife.[5]   In 1824 Thomas Cross was the farmer at Low
Dalby.[6]   He was succeeded by Hesle Poad Robinson who was there
in 1834.[7]   In 1843 Thomas Cross, senior and John Cross[8] leased the
premises.[9]   Low Dalby Farm in 1853 was said to consist of 2294 a.
1 r. 16 p. and was rented at £625. 7s. 2d.   Its portions included much
more than was in the true limits of Dalby, such as, Longlands
Close, Crofts below the Wood, High, Low, Great, and Highgate
Ings, Wood Close, Low and High Wood Warren, Moiety of Turf
Moor, Harrowcliffs, Wandales, High, Middle and Low Hurrell,
Keldhousegarth, Harland's Closes, Low Warren, North part of
Ellerburn Warren, Pexton Moor, Whitecliffe Rigg and Flainsey
Rigg.   Members of the Cross family remained as tenants till the
end of the nineteenth century, when, after the death of 'Old' John
Cross, as he was familiarly known, the tenancies have been of a
more rapid and far shorter duration.[10]

To-day the Dalby valley is still glorious, but changed and
changing.   As one gazes up the dale from a point above what are
now the new waterworks of Thornton, but once beloved under the
name of the 'Springs,' where the 'Grass of Parnassus' showed its
lovely white,[11] or if one were fortunate, one could find the 'Sundew'
and the 'Butterwort,' there is a view that is not what it was.   The
Riggs have still their graceful curves;[12] one can, as yet, see the

---

[1] Letter of Sam. Tetley, *ut supra*.
[2] G. F. G. H.
[3] *Vide* Ch. VI.
[4] Churchwarden in these years.
[5] Memorial in Thornton Church.
[6] G. F. G. H.
[7] Ibid.
[8] C. R. shows John Cross of Low Dalby died 1869.
[9] G. F. G. H.
[10] Lawrance Jackson held Low Dalby at the beginning of the twentieth
century, and was followed by Frank Avison.
[11] I am glad to say that there were quantities of this pretty flower at
the lower end of Sand Dale in 1929.
[12] Dalby Warren, Sand dale and Heck dale are composed of conflicting
combinations of soil and have distinct lines of vegetation running along the
hillsides.   *Vide* Fox-Strangeways, *Jurassic Rocks of Yorkshire*, pp. 339, 482.

remains of the ancient rabbit-types,[1] but the brilliant browns, coppers, and reds of the autumn bracken are fast disappearing; the purple heather is being cut away; the old meandering self-guided 'Springs' are now forced into rigid beds. And all across the hills are lines that look as if some giant had combed the land with a superhuman comb. In a sense it is true. The giant 'State' has combed away the bracken and the heather; swept away the sandy rabbit and the black rabbit[2] which seldom, if ever, intermingled, and, even, the moorland sheep with their startled eyes and twisty horns, the progenitors of which had been there since time immemorial.[3] All have gone. The effect upon the eye of a comb, is merely because thousands and thousands of tiny conifers have been planted in straight rows, so that, in a generation there shall be more pit-props. The glory of the valley is rapidly vanishing: the deep gloom of one of England's largest forests is its immediate destiny. And then, when the axe-man comes to convert the trees into money —a land of devastation. Happily those who in mediaeval days hunted the deer, hereabouts, happily the old hermit of Dalby, can never know; but those of us who have loved every inch of what it was, look forward with dismay to the blow that must come, if we live to see those sun-clad heather slopes, first mile after mile of dark masses of trees, and afterwards—a waste of decaying stumps.

[1] These rabbit-types were stone lined holes, covered with a trap-door, in the corner of small walled enclosures. Leading to the hole, through the wall was a drop-board over which the creatures must pass, and when the board 'tips up' they were precipitated into the hole. Towards autumn and in the winter the rabbits were fed with turnips, and often during frost and snow with branches of trees, i.e., '*garsell.*' The chief season for trapping was between 5 November and 25 December. At the beginning of the nineteenth century Dalby was regarded as one of the principal rabbit warrens in Cleveland. Several thousand rabbits were sold, mainly to the hatters of Scarborough and York at 1s. to 2s. a couple.

[2] The black rabbits, now shut out from the growing forest, are still to be seen near the 'Shoulder of Mutton' Plantation.

[3] *Cf.* F. Elgee, *Moorlands of North East Yorkshire*, p. 252.

Thornton Marishes.

'An amphibious place
Unsound, of spongy texture, yet withal
Not wanting a fair face of water weeds,
And pleasant flowers.'

WORDSWORTH.

'All the cuntre maykythe exclamacions of thys abbot
of Rievax uppon hys abhomynable lyuing and
extorcions by hym commyttyd also many wronges to
divers myserable persons don.'

DR. LEGH, Commissioner for the
dissolution of Monasteries.

IT is probable that 'the Marishes,' as they are commonly known, had been in the hands of a Norse family for many years before the time of the Conquest. In 1086 Domesday Book records that 'In Chigogesmere Torfin had 1 manor and 2 bovates'; but that the soke of 'Chigocemers' belonged to the manor of 'Pickeringa,' and that in 'Chigomersc' the King had 1 carucate and 2 bovates and that the Count of Mortain[1] had the same[2] which had previously belonged to Torfin.[3]

No material as to the history of 'the Marishes' seems to exist between Domesday Book and the reign of Henry II.; but in 1158 or 1160,[4] a grant was made of this territory by the King to Rievaulx Abbey, and it might be presumed that the mesne-tenant was a descendant of the 'Torfin' of Domesday Book. The wording of the charter is of very considerable interest, for not only does it give many local names, but it endeavours to define the boundaries

---

[1] Brother of Udo of Bayeux, and half-brother of William the Conqueror. Died 1091.

[2] Domesday Book.

[3] For family of Torfin vide Ch. XIV.

[4] Dugdale, *Monasticon*, V., p. 282, quotes 'Anno ab incarnatio Domini M.C.Lviij dedit nobis rex Henricus secundus vastum subtus Pickering, in escambium pro Steintonia quam nobis dedit Walterus de Gant ad abbatiam construendam ibi.'

of the property. In the first place 'Thorphinus de Alveston,'[1] or 'Torphin' of Allerston and his nephew, Geoffrey, gave evidence, and the other witnesses were, Thorold of Newton, Gilbert of Ayton, Ralph Lovel of Gristhorp, William, son of Norman of Ebberston, Asktell Malelak (Mauley), Gamel of Ruston, Theobald of Marton, Gamel of Roxby, Gospatric his brother, Richard, son of Roger of Thornton, 'Eugenaldus' of Wilton, Theodore of 'Sexendall,' Theodore, son of Payn of Wykeham, Thor, son of Asce of Snainton, Roger, son of Ukk of Ruston, Hugh, son of Walthevy of Ruston, Stephen Maungevylayn,[2] Walter Bardulph, (probably of Farmanby), Ulfrik of Kingthorp, Richard son of Angot, Richard of Galmeton (?), William, son of Ketell, Richard son of Rollemylans (? Rollevylain),[3] Stephen, son of Gamel of Pickering, Robert of Bonefield, Walter, son of Arnald of Aslakby, William, son of Roesy, Lucas of Newton and Godfrey of Newton. The charter proceeds to state that 'the waste from Allerston Beck to Takryvelyng'[4] belonged to the King, 'that is to say, up the course of Midsike from Allerston Beck to the boundaries between Theokmers[5] and Thornton, thence along these boundaries back to the Midsike so that the whole of Theokmers is included in the waste, thence along the midsike to Kyptoftsik[6] and so by Kiptoftsik unto the Costa and on the other side of the Costa to Takryveling. Between these boundaries Eustace, son of John had half a carucate of land and a meadow in Edyuemersk,[7] from which meadow hay could be carried every year. He paid 4s. a year for it to the King's soke at Pickering.'[8]

This grant was renewed in 1174, by Henry II.;[9] and Robert de Ros, Peter de Surdevalle and his brother William, and William Fitz Levock, all surrendered any claims that they might have either to Theockemarais or Loftmarais (i.e., Allerston Loft),[10] in

[1] 'Torphinus de Alvestain dedit nobis unam carucatam terrae in Alvestain [Allerston] cum pertinentiis suis.' *Cf.* Dugdale, *ut supra.*
[2] *Vide* Ch. IX. Dugdale, *Mon.* V., p. 282, spells the name 'Mangevilain.'
[3] *Vide* Ch. III.
[4] *Vide infra.*
[5] It should be noted how quickly the Chigogesmere, Chigocemers and Chigomersc of 1086 has become about 1160 Theokmers, or in 1174 Theokemarays, Theockemarais, or 1190, Theokemarais, or 1244, Kekemareis, or 1301, Kekemarrays, or 1322, Kekmarreys, or 1335, Kekkes marsh, or 1538, Kekmaresse, or 1611, Keckmarris. The word does not seem to appear after this date, and the district is known as 'the Marishes.'
[6] *Vide infra.*
[7] This equals Edue's marsh from O.E. woman's name Eadgifu and mersc. *Cf.* A. H. Smith, *ut supra,* p. 86. In the time of Henry II. 'Ediumersc' was said to be near 'Pons de Houm' i.e., Howe Bridge: it is, what in later times was known as 'Castle Ings.'
[8] N. R. Rec. S. N.S. IV., pp. 120-1.
[9] *Cart. Rievaulx,* Sur. Soc. LXXXIII., pp. 149-50.
[10] Ibid., pp. 131-2.

the same year.[1] But the really important confirmation, giving further details of the territory is that of Richard I., between 1189 and 1199. The charter reads as 'Scil., quicquid est inter Alvestainbeck[2] et Tackerivelingam[3] in longitudine praeter pratum de Ediumersc—per has scil., divisas: A loco ubi Alvestainbec cadit in Derewentam sicut eadem Derewenta currit usque ad locum ubi Ria[4] cadit in Derewentam,[5] et inde usque ubi Costa cadit in Riam, et inde per Costam ad Tackeriveling, et inde per Tackeriveling usque ad fossatum monachorum[6] et inde per idem fossatum sicut currit Lund et cadit in Costham, et inde per Costham contra aquilonem sursum usque ad locum Kiptoftsic[7] cadit in Costham, et inde per Kiptoftsic sicut tendit usque ad Midsic,[8] et inde per Midsic usque ubi Tornetunebec[9] cadit in Midsic, et inde per Thornetunebec contra aquilonem usque ad fossatum quod circuit campum de Theokemarais,[10] et inde per idem fossatum usque ad Blastam,[11] et inde per siketum quod ibi est usque Midsic et inde sicut Midsic descendit in Alvestanebec, et inde sicut Alvestanebec descendit in Derewentam.'[12]

In 1244 there must have been some considerable disagreement between the Abbot of Rievaulx, Adam de Tilletai, and William de Vescy,[13] as to the pasture of Edumersc. The fences had been broken down and William de Vescy was annoyed. But on 22

---

[1] The charter is witnessed by Ranulf de Glanville who is stated to be 'Sheriff.' He was 'Sheriff' in 1174.

[2] Allerston Beck.

[3] Unknown, but evidently the western limit. It may be Tranmore Hill and the present Ackland Beck passing through, what is called on the map, Lund Forest, which may be the ancient Lund.

[4] The river Rye.

[5] Howe Bridge.

[6] Friar's Ditch. If the 'ditch' was made by the monks of Rievaulx it is curious that it should have acquired the name of 'Friars.'

[7] Probably Toft Drain or Toft Swang Drain.

[8] Midsyke drain, 2 miles, S. of Pickering.

[9] Thornton Beck.

[10] The Theokmarais *campus* abutted on Wilton, and is the equivalent of Thornton Marishes.

[11] Of Blasta no trace seems to have been left; it was probably not far from the angle formed by the incidence of the modern Carr drain flowing between Thornton and Wilton with the Friar Dyke which is the north boundary of Loft Marishes and literally descends into Allerston Beck. *Cf.* 'Bastam's ditch' in late seventeenth century, mentioned in purchase by John Hill I.

[12] *Cart. Rievaulx,* Sur. Soc. LXXXIII., pp. 127-8, 136. This charter was confirmed in much the same words by Henry III. in 1252. *Cf.* N. R. Rec. S. N.S. IV., p. 76, and Cal. Char. R. I., p. 398.

[13] William de Vescy was Justice of the Forest north of the Trent as early as 1237. On 23 June, 1315, it was decided that his widow, Isabel, had a meadow called Edith mersch, dower of the inheritance of the said William, of the Earl of Lancaster as of the Honor of Pickering, by service of 4s. fee yearly. *Cf.* Cal. Inq. p.m. Ed. II.

March, 1244/5, an amicable agreement was reached between the disputants, and it was decided that 'if it should happen that the Cattle of the Abbot should....enter the meadow....and graze there....the damage is to be viewed by a brother or brethren or a shepherd or shepherds of Kekemareis Grange,[1] and by a servant or servants....or reeve of William de Vescy....But if the Abbot refuses to make good the damage so proved then it shall be lawful for William to distrain....so that the Abbot's animals.... belonging to the Grange and so distrained are not to be led outside the King's fee in the Wapentake of Pickering.'[2]

At the beginning of the fourteenth century the Marishes, though low lying and boggy, were by no means uninhabited. The Lay Subsidy for 1301, shows 'Kekermarays' assessed at £1. 18s. 7d.[3] while the whole of Thornton for the same year was £5. 11s. 4d.[4] These marsh-dwellers would consist, either of a few free tenants, or of the villeins of the Abbey of Rievaulx under the guidance of a granger. This man was not always above suspicion as far as forest offences were concerned, and on 4 December, 1322, the lay brother, Austin Stalwardman, granger of Kekmarsh was a receiver of a hind knowing it to have been poached.[5] Such an incident, how-ever, did not militate against his active duties on behalf of the Abbey, and it is clear that his labourers must have done some work in 1335, for the Castle Authorities at Pickering bought 'six cart loads of hay....at Kekkemarsh and carted them 9 miles to Blansby Park for 17 mares, 7 three-year old colts, 5 three-year old fillies, 5 two-year olds, 6 yearlings, and 10 foals, and the deer in the Park, about 1,300 by estimation.' The sum paid for all this hay was 15s. that is 2s. 6d. a cart load, including cartage.[6]

The property was by no means of small value, for not only were there the profits of farming, but the abbot, William de Langton, had the right of building houses and sheep-folds without inter-ference from any forester.[7] He also claimed to be quit 'in his manors of Marreys *scilicet* Loftmarreys, Lund, Neusted and Kekmarreys

---

[1] Apparently not yet called Newstead Grange, but very soon to be.
[2] N. R. Rec. S. N.S. IV., p. 188.
[3] Y. A. S. Rec. S. XXI., p. 61.
[4] Ibid., p. 60.
[5] *Vide* Ch. II.
[6] N. R. Rec. S. N.S. IV., p. 227.
[7] Ibid. III., pp. 90, 94.

of the lawing of dogs,[1] and of all other assizes of the forest except those relating to game and hare-hunting.' The inquest found that 'from time immemorial presentments have always been made at the Attachment Courts,[2] with regard to the dogs of the abbots in the manors of ''Marreis,'' not being lawed, and at times the officers of the forest have gone there to view the dogs, but neither the Abbot nor any of his predecessors ever paid a fine or made a composition for not lawing them. Even though they were fined, sometimes by bribing the Keeper of the Castle, or his lieutenant[3] and sometimes by their goodwill, they never paid the fine.'[4] One would imagine that this last sentence was a complete confession as to acceptance of the principle of lawing on the part of the abbot. Apparently, however, the Justices did not think so, for the question was postponed till October, and again postponed till February, 1336, and again till May of the same year, and, as far as history records, was never decided.

The Abbot did not limit himself to this privilege with regard to his dogs; he had a much more personal interest in sporting rights, and brought forward a claim to 'free-fishing in the Costa from the spot where the Friardyke [Friar's Ditch], above Belyvause,[5] falls into the Costa down to the spot where Le Lowndyke[6] falls into the Costa.' He was ready to prove that he and all former abbots had from time immemorial fished in the stream between the boundaries mentioned as a common of fishing *appurtenant* to the geldable land of 'Kekmarreys et Neustede.'[7] In this case he was more successful, for after an inquiry it was decided that he was

---

[1] Manwood, *ut supra*, says 'The mastive being brought to set one of his forefeete upon a piece of woode of eight inches thicke and a foote square, then one with a mallet setting a chissell of two inches broade upon the three claws of his forefoote at one blow doth smite them clean off.' Mr. Turton writes 'The fine for keeping an unexpeditated dog within the forest was 3s. It is, therefore, clear that the *hungill* was not a payment made in order to avoid expedition. More probably it was a fee to the forester, or perhaps, to be more accurate, a bribe to induce him to do his work impartially and skilfully which in course of time from long continuance became perpetual, and was regarded as a right.' *Cf.* N. R. Rec. S. N.S. I., p. xxxiii.

[2] *Vide* Ch. II.

[3] A splendid confession to make before the Justices of the Forest.

[4] N. R. Rec. S. N.S. III., pp. 136-8. That these bribes were really a very serious thing is shown by the accounts of the Priory of Malton. The Priory paid between 1243 and 1257 to the officials at Pickering as bribes £94. 14s. 3d. *Cf.* V. C. H. *York* III., p. 253.

[5] In the N. R. Rec. S. N.S. the word 'Belyvause' is misprinted and spelt 'Belynause'. In modern times it is represented by Bellifax Grange. *Cf.* Carfax in Oxford. The exact spot where the abbot started his fishing can easily be seen on the One-Inch Ordnance Survey.

[6] This is probably the 'Lund' of the charter of Richard I.

[7] N. R. Rec. S. N.S. III., pp. 139-40. Between 1367 and 1370 the Abbot of Rievaulx again claimed all liberties in his manor of Kekmarays. *Cf.* Cal. Char. R., 1367-70, p. 213.

right. But it must have annoyed him very considerably to hear that the Prior of Malton,[1] claimed to fish from the Costa 'to the stream which flows passed the houses of the monks at Keke-marays'[2] in the direction of Pickering.

The abbot does not, however, with all his privileges, seem to have been able to protect his under-tenants, for by the time of Edward III. there were under-tenants, the Marishes having been broken up into varying sized holdings. One of these farmsteads is to be found in the word, read by some as 'Calwsthotes' in the Lay Subsidy of 1327,[3] but which is really 'Calveschote' or, as known a few years later 'Calfcote' and remaining such for centuries. The unfortunate occupier of this, Robert de Sunley, was seized in the summer of 1347 by the myrmidons of William de Kirkby, Keeper of Pickering;[4] nor, was he alone, for in the same July, Adam de Selley Bridge, at Selley Bridge, had also been dragged away with others and taken to Pickering Castle, and kept there until they all compounded for £4.[5] The Keeper had already extracted, extortionately, £1 from Robert Hert of 'Derholme' in the Marishes, and had threatened that if he did not pay he would indict his son, John Hert.[6] It is satisfactory to find that the Keeper was convicted ultimately on his own confession; and it is to be trusted that the tenants of the abbey remained in peace. There is only one change of tenancy in the next century left on record, and that, at an unknown date, when John Chaloner occupied 'Selybrig,' made his will there on 12 August, and died some day previous to 16 September, 1455.[7] Happy is the country that has no history, and so, probably, happy were those in the Marishes. They were well off the main roads, they were probably well protected by marsh and stream from marauders. No great or violent disturbance, even in the Wars of the Roses, could have affected them, and one day must have been very much like another.

Changes, however, were destined to come. At some time, early in the sixteenth century, the estate was leased to a tenant, who sub-let it to others, and thus made what he could out of it. This system was very common in a day when there were no other forms of investment, and it relieved the supreme landlord of dealing with smaller tenants. On 10 October, 1524, Abbot William

[1] Ibid., p. 162.
[2] If this means 'Newstead Grange' the exact piece of water is rather difficult to determine.
[3] N. R. Rec. S. N.S. IV., p. 140.
[4] Ibid., p. 178.
[5] Ibid.
[6] Ibid., p. 172.
[7] Y. A. S. Rec. S. VI., p. 35.

of Rievaulx leased to Robert Hunter,[1] from 1523 for thirty-one years 'Newstede' in the Marishes for an annual rent of £21. 10s. 0d.[2] Robert Hunter renewed his tenure on 10 August, 1534, when Abbot Roland leased to him 'the Grange of Newstede in lez Marres, Calfcote and Cowhouse Yng from the Invention of the Holy Cross, 1535, for a term of forty-one years at a rent of £31.'[3]

The whole Marish property, not only within the parish of Thornton, but also in that of Pickering, was now broken up. The Abbots had evidently found it uneconomic as a grange, and saw greater advantages in letting separate portions to individuals. Thus for example on 24 May, 1533, Abbot Edward leased to Robert Herryson the 'new house in the Marres in the New House Lathe,' at a yearly rent of £7. 6s. 8d.[4] In 1538, Robert Hunter acted as rent collector for Rievaulx Abbey,[5] and he paid over the following various sums :—£9. 3s. 4d. for one tenement and pasture called 'Selley Brigge,'[6] leased to Sir Roger Cholmley: £10 for one tenement called 'Dereham' with meadow and pasture called 'Dereholme,'[7] leased to Sir Ralph Evers: £5 for one tenement called 'Yowe Cotte' leased to Robert Seloo and Richard Raysyn, 'with certain pastures called Kekmaresse in the tenure of William Adames,' together with the already mentioned Newhouse let to Robert Herryson: £21. 10s. for two messuages with pasture called Westede let to Robert Hunter:[8] £41 for Loftmaresse,[9] let to William Burton and Ralph Burton: £10 for one tenement called Londe, let to Ralph Bawde: £4 for one tenement with certain pastures called 'Bellyfaxe,'[10] let to[11] Edward Blyeton.[12]

Such was the situation in the Marishes, with regard to the property of Rievaulx Abbey, when the awful crash came. Little did anyone think, even in 1536, that this great abbey, with its

[1] *Vide* Ch. XII.
[2] *Cart. Rievaulx*, Sur. Soc. LXXXIII., p. 354.
[3] Ibid.
[4] Ibid., p. 352.
[5] Ibid., p. 326, where it is shown that Robert Hunter was allowed expenses.
[6] Still known as such and situated in the parish of Thornton. It means 'the Bridge by the Willows.' *Cf.* A. H. Smith, *ut supra*, p. 90.
[7] Marked on the One-Inch Ordnance Survey as 'Deerholme Grange,' a mile west of the modern Marishes Road Station, and not in the parish of Thornton.
[8] Note the discrepancy: it is £21. 10s. 0d. in this list, and in the lease of 1523, but it was £31 in the lease of 1534.
[9] Allerston Loft Marishes, not in the parish of Thornton.
[10] Bellifax Grange, four miles due south of Pickering on the Malton Road.
[11] *Cart. Rievaulx*, Sur. Soc. LXXXIII., p. 325.
[12] This makes a sum of £100. 13s. 4d. Dugdale, *Mon.* V., p. 285 quotes from the account of 1540 and shows that the total sum (probably less expenses) arising from the Marishes was £88. 3s. 4d.

abbot and twenty-three monks, and its income of £278 per annum would follow so quickly in the wake of the lesser ones. But Yorkshire had been ablaze with the Pilgrimage of Grace, and Henry VIII. was not the man to forgive lightly. In 1539, the order went forth for the dissolution of the greater monasteries, and Rievaulx fell with the rest.

It is obvious, from the next documentary evidence, that most of the tenants holding in 1538, continued to hold under the Crown, when granted by Henry VIII. on 12 November, 1542, to Edward, Archbishop of York,[1] and when Philip and Mary, in the second year of their reign, regranted the Marishes to Nicholas, Archbishop of York, 'Dereham' Grange was still in the hands of Sir Ralph 'Evans' i.e., Evers; Newstead Grange and all messuages, lands, and tenements 'yt known by the names of Newsted Calfecote and Cowhouse Yng lying in the Marsh,'[2] were occupied by Robert Hunter; while the Grange and lands 'called Lofte Maresse & half of Calfecote lyeing in the Marshe' were held by William and Ralph Burton. The 'tythes of ye same lying in the pish or pishs of Thornton, Pickering and Allerston, and late bel[onging] to the Mon[aster]y of Ryvalles'[3] were to go to the Archbishop.[4]

It may be presumed that members of the Cholmley family continued to hold Selley Bridge from 1538 onwards, because in 1611, the jury at Quarter Sessions in Pickering, on 12 April, of that year, presented 'John Cholmley, gent[n]. fermer of the marrish called Keckmarris for not repairing of *two yeat steades*[5] belonging to the same farme uppon the Marrish Moore whereon no man can well passe but in great danger.'[6] Two years later, in Michaelmas Term, 1613, 'Henry Cholmley, knt. and Margaret his wife, Richard Cholmley, knt. son and heir apparent of the said Henry, Henry Cholmley, gent. and John Cholmley, gent. conveyed to William Thorneton Esq. and Robert, gent. his son and heir apparent '2 messuages and lands in le marrishes *alias* Sellibridg Marishe in Thorneton and Pickering.'[7] The conveyance was probably in trust for another, as in 1637, James Angell was stated to be the owner

---

[1] L. & P. Hen. VIII. XVIII. (1) g. 226 (66).

[2] This may be what is now called Low Newstead Grange, roughly in an angle between the Derwent and Thornton Beck, and in the parish of Thornton.

[3] This is somewhat strange because tithes were paid from four of the Marish farms to the rector of Thornton in the eighteenth century. *Vide* Ch. IX.

[4] Small white vellum volume, named '*Pickering Honor*' G. F. G. H.

[5] Canon Atkinson says 'site or place of the gate across the highway.'

[6] N. R. Rec. S. O.S. I., p. 222.

[7] Y. A. S. Rec. S. LIII., p. 214.

of 'Sollybridge Marshes.'[1] This property, about that date, ought to have passed into the hands of the already mentioned Rev. John Robinson, Rector, and lord of one of the manors in Thornton.[2] But owing to his 'delinquency' it is difficult to determine whether it did so or not; but, probably not. The charge against him is in much the same words as with regard to his Thornton property,[3] but, in this case, he is said to have an 'estate of the moiety of Selly-bridge Marshes worth yearly 40ll. out of which he craves allowance of 10ll. p. Anñ, a rent charge to Christopher Ive for his life, who is living, 100ll. debt to George Conyers, gent. borrowed by the compounder and by him lent to the Parliament upon the public faith,[4] 500ll. charged upon the said moiety of Sollybridge Marshes upon the original purchase from James Angell in 1637, the whole land being sold for 1800ll. whereof 800ll. was paid in hand the other 1000ll. to be paid 18 Sept. 1642, or else the conveyance to be void, the said 1000ll. was not paid and so the said debt of 500ll. lies upon this moiety.'[5] It is clear that there had been some rather mysterious dealings with this Selleybridge property, for on 27 August, 1651, Richard Culme, aged seventeen, grandson of Richard Culme of Common Leigh, Devon, prayed the Commissioners for Compounding for 'the benefit of his grandfather's composition for Sellybridge Marsh in Thornton and Pickering, co. York, with £60 a year, originally conveyed by James Angel to Philip Culme, peti-tioner's great-uncle, who died 10 years ago. On his grandfather's composition, letters of suspension of the sequestration were promised to be conveyed by Mr. Darley, M.P. to the County Cttee but miscarried.' This petition was granted.[6] In 1668 Barney Mawe of 'Sellibridge in ye Marishes in ye parish of Thornton' demised the property to Michael Dawson of the Marishes of Pickering, and the latter was bound to pay tithes of Corn and Hay from the land.[7] What then happened to the Sellybridge property has (so far) remained a mystery.[8]

As to Newstead Grange the Hunters clung to it generation after generation. There was Robert Hunter, collector for Rievaulx: there was Anthony 'of the Marish' baptized 6 January, 1575/6 and buried at Thornton 7 May, 1637; he was succeeded by his son

---

[1] *Vide infra.*
[2] *Vide* Ch. XIII.
[3] Ibid.
[4] It is difficult not to suspect John Robinson as something of a trickster.
[5] Y. A. S. Rec. S. XVIII., p. 207.
[6] Cal. Cttee. Comp., p. 1161.
[7] Document kindly shown to me by Arthur Kitching, Esq.
[8] In 1928 it was farmed by Johnson Beswick, and owned by Collingwood Jackson.

Roger,[1] baptized 17 January, 1609/10, and buried 28 April, 1659, and entitled 'of Newstead Grange'; then came 'Anthonie of the Marishe,' baptized 19 March, 1654/5, married one, Frances, their daughter being Barbara, baptized 24 May, 1681.[2] But long before this date the circumstances of the family had been changing, and as shown elsewhere,[3] money was becoming scarcer, and some time before the outbreak of the Civil War some financial arrangements had been made with Mr. Tobias Swinburne.[4] This fact is disclosed once again by the composition fees paid by royalists to the usurping Government. The northern commission wrote to the central authorities on 25 February, 1645, 'In answeare of a letter from you we have informed o[r]selves of the Crymes and estate of Mr. Toby Swinburne....and doe certifie that he listed himself in the Prince's troope when the King first raised his guard at York and went with him to Edge hill where he was hurt....ffor his estate he hath nothing w[th]in the Northridd., But a lease for three lives (whereof two is dead) of the fourth pt of Newstead Grange in the Marris of Pickering of the yearly value of fortie pounds (ultra reprizes). We further certify that we are informed he hath taken the oath of the fift of Aprill in the Citty of York where he dwells.'[5]

At the beginning of the eighteenth century 'the Marishes' were divided into at least four farms. In 1708 there were, Newstead Grange proper,[6] Sugar's farm, where James Boyes[7] held four closes, and two other farms without specific titles.[8] A year or two later Newstead Grange was tenanted by John Gibbins, who died on 7 February, 1727, and must have been a man of some importance as he paid a mortuary of 10s.[9] He was succeeded by Robert Baker who was buried on 22 June, 1741, and who also paid a mortuary

---

[1] One wonders whether he was the unnamed 'gent[n] of Newstead Grange' who 'with four yeom[n] of the same' made a forcible entry into a house in 1652. *Cf.* N. R. Rec. S. O.S. V., p. 109.

[2] These dates are taken from the Church Registers of Thornton.

[3] *Vide* Ch. XIII.

[4] Tobias Swinburne was the son of Henry Swinburne, LL.D., Judge of the Prerogative Court of York, by Helena, daughter of Bartholomew Lant. He, himself, was LL.D. of Oxford in 1652, and was buried in York Minster on 28 January, 1656.

[5] Y. A. S. Rec. S. XV., p. 142.

[6] It is difficult to know whether William Holder of Newstead Grange, who was buried on 14 October, 1714, was a farmer or a labourer. *Cf.* C. R.

[7] Church Terrier.

[8] Marshall, *ut supra*, p. 183, thinks that at the end of the eighteenth century the Marishes were badly looked after and suggests the introduction of Marsh Mills to pump out the water. He says 'the whole expence would be inconsiderable when compared with the improvement of converting perhaps two or three thousand acres of unproductive fenny ground, into arable meadow and pasture lands of five or perhaps ten times its value.' His suggestion was not carried out.

[9] *Vide* Ch. IX.

of the same sum.[1]   From some period, before 1777,[2] to 1816, William Harrison farmed Newstead Grange, and was succeeded by Stephen Burden, who died aged 75, in 1855.[3]   As early as 1831 a portion of Newstead Grange was leased to Thomas Cross and in 1839 to Joseph Robson[4] and then to John Robson who died aged 48 in 1850.[5]

In 1777, John Ripley[6] had what is now called Low Newstead and Robert Skelton held the Sugar's farm of 1708, afterwards called Staines Farm.   John Parke, William Harding of Pickering and Richard Todd, junior, held Frank's farm, possibly what is now Willow Grange.   A fifth division was known as 'Low Farm,' and held by William Bacon, whose name, now, is probably attached to 'Bacon's farm' just outside the Thornton parish boundary.[7]

From the middle of the nineteenth century the much sub-divided Marishes seem to have passed through many hands.   The Archbishop's property was taken over by the Ecclesiastical Commissioners and partly sold.   In 1890, Philip Abbey had a hind at Low Newstead, William Brisby, was at Charity Farm, now occupied by J. A. Robinson, Charles Grayson and Charles Pratt were described as of the Marishes, Thomas Brisby was at Willow Grange and John Wilson Spanton at Fir Tree.   George Warwick was at what is now a ruin, and which was leased from the Ecclesiastical Commissioners[8] by Major Preston; while Thomas Pearson was said to have held Newstead Grange, and Thomas Robson was still at 'Newstead, Farmanby',[9] William Walker had Todd Bridge Farm and Joseph Coulson was at Summertree Bridge.   In 1928 Joseph Sedman owned 'High Newstead,' Philip Abbey Hall owned 'Low Newstead,' the so-called 'Derwent Farm' was in the possession of Stephen Robson,[10] and 'Fir Tree' in that of Simon Hardy.

While writing the above Simon Hardy, a fine example of a Yorkshire farmer, has passed away, and with his passing we conclude the story of the Manor of the Marishes and that of the civil parish of Thornton.

[1] He was buried near the Church porch, and there is a neat brass let in to the side of the box-tomb stating the facts given above.
[2] Church Terrier.
[3] C. R.
[4] Ibid.
[5] Ibid.
[6] Church Terrier.
[7] Ibid.   Bacon's farm practically divides Thornton and Pickering Marishes and in 1928 was owned by Mr. Beale.
[8] Purchased from the Commissioners by Simon Hardy.
[9] And in 1910.   Thomas Robson, aged 71, died February, 1913.
[10] Information given by R. A. Scott, Esq.

L' Envoi.

And so FAREWELL to all my readers, but more particularly, perhaps, to my many friends in Thornton-le-Dale. In times of happiness and of sorrow they have ever been kind and courteous. I have endeavoured 'to show clearly what is true and accurate' as to the story of our village. I may have failed in that (for which I ask forgiveness); but, assuredly for Thornton-le-Dale and its inhabitants my affection will never fail.

APPENDIX A.

The Inhabitants, 1140-1540.

1140-1200.

Thornton. Roger of Thornton, Richard his son; Robert and Ralph sons of Walter (? Bardulf); Thorold, Ashetin his son; Alan of Thornton or the Forester, Alan and John his sons; Geoffrey of Thornton, Alan his son, and Alan I. and Alan II. his sons.

Ellerburn-cum-Farmanby. Walter Bardulf; Norman Bushell; Osbert.

Roxby. Gamel and Gospatric his brother.

1200-1245.

Thornton. Gilbert the parson, Isolda his wife, William and John of Thornton their sons, Alan and Astinus sons of John of Thornton; Juliana of Thornton, Peter her son; William the lame man; Reginald of Thornton, John and Walter his sons, Robert son of Walter; William and Robert the Millers, William son of Robert; Roger Brun, Isabella his wife; Richard le Brun; Roald, Andrew his son; Roger Racine; William de Swyntone; Walter Blaber; Gamel, William his son.

Ellerburn-cum-Farmanby. Hugh Bardulf of Farmanby, Ralph his son; Nicholas de Yeland of Ellerburn, Eustacia his wife; William of Farmanby, Robert his son; Reginald of Farmanby, Alan his son.

Roxby. Maud, Juliana her daughter; Geoffrey, Henry his son; Jordan of Roxby; Walter de Rouceby; Alan of Whitegate; Roger of Appleton, Adam his son; Alan, Roger his son.

1246-1301.

Thornton. William de Everley; Ascilia Moraunt; John, Alan his son, Emma his sister; Andrew, Alan his son; Alan, Stephen his son; Alan of Thornton, Cecily his daughter; Alan the Chaplain; Alan Pye; Alan Marshal; Hugh Brun; Hugh Luthre; Robert de Caishliffe; Robert del Clyff; John de Cliff; Henry, John his son; John, Isabel his wife, Adam their son; Thomas de Amcotes; Mathew Gower;

Peter Gower; Richard Gower; Ivo de Joueby, Robert his son; Thomas Joueby, Joan his wife, Robert their son, Nicholaa and Joan their daughters. William Lovel; Nicholas Lovel; John de Barton; John de Hutton; Henry Chamberlayne; Alan, John his son; Hugh the Smith; Simon and Hugh the Millers; John the Carter; John the Fisherman; Richard Russell; John Westing; Thomas Burton; Geoffrey the curate; John de Kynthorp; Henry, Agnes his wife; Thomas Percevall; Tun, Hugh his son; Amicia, Richard her son; Roger Fuziby; Alinot, Robert his son; Walter, Astinus his son; Richard, John his son; John Itory; Astinus Spark; Mon Spark; Hugh, Adam his son; Isolda, Robert her son; Reginald, Astinus his son; Roger, Alan his son.

Ellerburn-cum-Farmanby. Thomas Hert, Alan Hert his son; Nicholas Hert; William Hert; (all of Farmanby); Elias of Farmanby, Astinus his son; John Campion; Robert Campion; Alice Campion; Richard Campion, Alan his son; Juliana wife of Alan Campion; William de Yeland, Alan the curate; Alan, William his son; Hugh, John his son; John Norrays (? Marrays); John Rudde; Richard Squier; Alan Hunter; Robert the Shepherd; Mabel, Stephen her son; John Oxhird; Roger Oxhird; Edmund Hastings; Lady Beatrice Hastings; Richard de Newton; Simon de Wytten; Robert Ladell; Robert, Geoffrey his son; Reginald the Cook; Reginald de Speton; Beatrice daughter of Reginald; William the Weaver; John de Caldham; Isolda *ad caput ville*; Thomas de Holme; Richard of the Marishes.

Roxby. Adam de Rouceby; Walter de Rouceby; Robert de Rouceby, Alexander his son.

1302-1327.

Thornton. Russet de Thornton; John Burmer; Ralph Rook; Henry, William his son; Ralph Raffat, Adam his son; Alan of Thornton, John his son; William de Bergh, rector; Hugh de White-nere; Robert de Bordesden; John the Smith; Nicholas Welum or Wylom; William Itory; John de Wyntryngham; Hugh (? the vicar); Roger Brun; Geoffrey de Kynthorp; William de Everley II.; Bartholomew the Carpenter (?); Rachel of Ellerburn; Robert the Smith; John Boyes; John de Hawkesgarth.

Ellerburn-cum-Farmanby. John, Alan his son the neat-herd of Farmanby; William Page; Richard Russell, *junior* of Farmanby; John Hert; Henry Wytens.

Roxby. Edmund Hastings.

The Marishes. Austin Stalwardman.

1328-1354.

Thornton. Robert Bruyn (? Brun); John Smythe; Robert Sparke; Alan Campion; Ralph the Weaver; Robert, William his son; Alan, John his son; Reginald of Ellerburn; Matilda, Robert her son; Robert de Clif; Henry Rippelay; John Brettsby; Austin the reeve; Alan the reeve; John de Everley the rector; John de Ampleforth the rector.

Ellerburn-cum-Farmanby. Edmund Hastings; William Hastings; Robert de Wygane; John Marshall; Thomas de Caldeham; Thomas de Bachy of Farmanby; Robert Tan of Ellerburn; William Stut of Ellerburn; Eldred of Ellerburn; William Yeland, Catherine his daughter, Katharine his wife.

Roxby. Alan de Rouceby.

The Marishes. Alan de 'Selley Bridge'; Robert de Sunley; Robert Hert, John his son.

1355-1405.

Thornton. Alan Campion; William Campion; Richard Campion; Robert Greteheved; Walter Lofthous; John Barkere; John de Cotorn, Alice his wife; John Halscarth; Thomas de Barton; William Dodemor; Sir Richard Malton, rector.

Roxby. Edmund Hastings; Edmund Hastings II.; William Hastings; Nicholas Hastings, Joan his wife; John de Roxby; John Kyng; William King, Margaret his wife; John de Brighton.

1440-1500.

Thornton. Richard Barwgh I.; John Kirkby; Alexander Botcher; Emmot Forster; John Lytell; Rauff Westorp; William Byrdsall; Richard Smothinge; John Stabbey.

Ellerburn-cum-Farmanby. Sir Robert Sawdane; Thomas Belendine.

Roxby. Ralph Joiner; Sir Roger Hastings, Francis his son.

The Marishes. John Chaloner of 'Selybrig.'

1501-1540.

Thornton. George Champay (Champley), John Champlay; William Champney (Champley); Richard Norram; Christopher Atkinson; Ralph Grimston; Emma Grymston; William Grymston; Richard White; John White; Dionessa White; Richard Barghe II.; Gefferey Barghe; Martin Bargh, Peter Bawrgh; Richard Barugh III.;

Sir Richard Bartholomew; Anthony Hunter; Robert Hunter; Roger Hunter; Christopher Hunter; Lewes Honter; Brian Spofford; Robert Smythe; John Smyth; John Smythe; Richard Prystman; John Presmande; George Prestman; Thomas Allane; Oliver Robinson; John Bakar; Sir John Pynder; William Robson; Joanna Robson; William Robson, *junior*; James Robson; William Jackeson; William Johnsone; William Thompsone; William Milborne; Thomas Mylborne; Robert Lethe; Christofer Maltebie; John Wilson; Richard Owston; Geoffrey Todde; Robert Tode; James Tod; Thomas Batson; Thomas Browne; John Guddeyll.

Roxby. Sir Roger Cholmley; Marmaduke Cholmley.

The Marishes. Robert Hunter; Robert Herryson; William Adams.

APPENDIX B.

The Hill Family since 1761.

RICHARD JOHNSON HILL b. 1761, m. 22 August, 1785, d. 28 July, 1793, left by Eliza (b. 21 November, 1757) his wife, dau. of John Johnston, M.D. of Beverley (b. 19 August, 1727), a son, Richard Hill, J.P., D.L., of Thornton Hall, co. York, educ. at University College, Oxford, b. 4 June, 1786, m. July, 1807. 1st, Anne (b. 1781) younger dau. of Rev. Luke Yarker, J.P. of Leyburn Hall, and by her (d. 15 July, 1815) had issue :—

I. JOHN RICHARD.

II. RICHARD LUKE, b. 1810, d. 1812.

1. ELIZA, b. 21 February, 1809, d. unm. 22 March, 1883.

RICHARD HILL m. 3 August, 1819, secondly Jane (b. 1796) elder dau. of James Walker of Springhead and Beverley, Esq., and sister of Sir James Walker Bart. of Sandhutton; and had by her (d. 1890) further issue :—

III. JAMES (Rev.) of Normanby, M.A. of the University of Durham, b. 9 May, 1820. Rector of Normanby, m. October, 1848, Mary Anne, eldest dau. of the Rev. Luke Yarker, J.P. of Leyburn Hall, and d. 1893, leaving a son—

REGINALD JAMES (Rev.) educ. at Rossall, M.A. of Exeter College, Oxford, Rector of Normanby and Lee on the Solent, b. July, 1849, m. 1901 Constance Mabel, dau. of Rev. William Wright of Bournemouth. He died February, 1929, leaving one son—

Arthur John Reginald, b. 1902. Lieu. R.E.

IV. JOHN, b. July, 1821, m. 1863, Mary Elizabeth, eldest dau. of Rev. John William Bower, Rector of Barmston, co. York, J.P. She died 1877. He died 1906 having had two sons and three daughters—

(i) JOHN R., b. 20 March, 1869, m. 1901 Helen Hall, and has

(a) John Robert, b. 1902.

a. Emily Eugenia, b. 1901.

(ii) ROBIN, b. February, 1871.

i. EUGENIA, b. 21 November, 1864, d. August, 1893.

    ii. Mary E. S., b. 21 December, 1865.

    iii. Jane, b. 31 December, 1866, d. 13 June, 1915.

V. Thomas, b. September, 1822. Chief Constable of the North Riding, late Capt. of N. Y. Rifle Militia and sometime of the 24th Regiment, m. 1858, Frances, dau. of Thomas Stubbs Walker of Maunby Hall, co. York, Esq., and d. 5 November, 1899, having had issue—

    (i) Alan Richard Hill-Walker, V.C. of Maunby Hall, co. York, Major 2nd Batt. Northamptonshire Regiment, adopted the name Walker, b. 12 July, 1859, served in South Africa and India, m. 1902, Lilias, dau. of the late Thomas Walker of Maunby Hall, and has issue—

        (*a*) Gerald Alan, b. 1903. Lieu. Northamptonshire Regt.

        (*b*) Thomas Harry, b. 1904. Lieu. R. N.

    (ii) Cecil, C.B. Brig.-General, R.E., b. 25 October, 1861, m. 1893, Edith, d. of Charles Lambert, Esq., and has issue—

        Cecil Vivian, B.A., of Brasenose College, Oxford, Lieu. R.F.A., b. 1893, m. 20 October, 1925, Rosemary Isabel, dau. of Basil Maxsted Esq., of South Cave, E.R.

    i. Maude, b. 1860, d. 13 November, 1925.

VI. Gowan, b. 1824, d. 1824.

VII. Robert, b. 1826, d. 1826.

VIII. Robert, b. 15 May, 1831, m. 1877, Caroline, dau. of Col. Macdonald, Staff Officer of Pensioners, Toronto, Canada. She died 1914. He died 6 October, 1907, leaving two sons—

    (i) Lionel George, b. 23 January, 1879, m. 1911, Millicent dau. of Colonel Hill of Reading. He was killed in action at Zillebeke as Captain of the East Yorkshire Regiment, 17 February, 1915, leaving one daughter—

        Zita Olive.

    (ii) Vivian, b. 29 July, 1881.

IX. Henry, of The High Hall, Thornton, J.P., b. 11 May, 1835, m. 1870, Fanny Delabere (d. 12 February, 1921), dau. of Rev. Henry Pixell, M.A. He died 27 April, 1907, leaving one son—

    Gerard Robert, educ. Eton College, M.A. of Balliol College, Oxford, barrister-at-law and Counsel to the Treasury, b. 19 February, 1872, m. 10 September, 1903, Dorothea, 2nd dau. of the late Edward Gordon

Place of Skelton Grange, York, Esq., and has issue—
(a) (Peter) Leonard Arthur, b. 3 November, 1904. Lieu. R.A., and 13th D. C. O. Lancers.
(b) Gerard Henry, b. 5 April, 1908. Lieu. R. A.

2. JANE, b. 1825, d. unm. 15 September, 1915.
3. MARY, b. 1827, d. unm. 13 August, 1896.
4. HARRIET, b. 1829, d. unm. 3 August, 1915.
5. LUCY, b. 29 January, 1830, m. December, 1857, Rev. Edward W. Heslop, M.A. of Queen's College, Oxford, Rector of Thornton. She died 2 March, 1860. He died 8 December, 1899, leaving two daughters—
   i.   MARY KATHERINE JANE, b. 26 September, 1858, m. Richard Arthur Scott, J.P. She died 15 January, 1913, leaving one daughter—
        Dorothy.
   ii. MARGARET LUCY, b. 6 February, 1860.
6. ALICE, b. 1833, d. 1834.

MR. RICHARD HILL, d. 5 January, 1855, leaving his eldest son John Richard (Rev.) of Thornton Hall, M.A. of University College, Oxford, J.P., D.L., Rector of Thornton, b. 29 October, 1811, m. 29 June, 1842, Harriet, dau. of Joseph Robinson Pease of Hesslewood, E.R., Esq. He died 21 December, 1896. She died 5 November, 1899, having had issue—

I.   RICHARD.
II. WILFRED, b. 9 March, 1848, d. August, 1848.
III. ARTHUR (Rev.), M.A., of University College, Oxford, b. 25 August, 1849, d. 20 January, 1923.
IV. EDWARD JOHN, b. 9 April, 1855, Lieu. R. N., m. 2 July, 1884 Florence Laura, d. of J. R. Forman, Esq. She died 17 March, 1917, having had one child—
     ISABEL BLANCHE, b. June, 1887, d. December, 1891.
V.   HERBERT, b. July, 1858, d. May, 1860.
1.   ANNE ELIZA, b. 22 March, 1845, m. 6 February, 1865, Walter James, third son of William Marshall of Patterdale Hall, Cumberland, Esq. She died 29 August, 1876. He died 6 February, 1899, having had issue—
     (i) WILLIAM, b. 18 November, 1866, m. 13 October, 1896, Lenore Muchley. He died March, 1929, leaving—
          (a) WILLIAM M., b. November, 1903.
          (b) GODFREY H., b. April, 1905.
          (c) JOHN R., b. August, 1912.
          a. MARY L., b. July, 1897.

b.   Johanna, b. February, 1899.

(ii) RICHARD, b. 7 November, 1867, m. December, 1899, Gertrude Temple, having—

    (*a*)   RICHARD T., b. 1900.

    (*b*)   WALTER R., b. May, 1902, m.?   Adeane having—

        a.   Heather, b. 1927.

        b.   daughter, b. 1929.

(iii) GODFREY (Rev.), M.A., Trinity College, Cambridge, Rector of Thornton, b. 25 May, 1869, m. 10 June, 1914, Zoe, dau. of Rev. C. H. V. Pixell of Stoke Newington.

  i.   VIOLET A., b. 13 August, 1870, m. 22 August, 1894, U. Lambert, Esq.   She died 13 October, 1894.

  ii.   ELLEN H., b. 14 August, 1872, m. April, 1899, M. J. S. Rutherford, Esq., having—

    (*a*)   IAN M., b. May, 1901.

    (*b*)   WALTER S., b. July, 1908.

    (*c*)   WILLIAM, b. 1905.

    a.   MARION V., b. 1900.

2. CATHERINE HARRIET, b. August, 1846, d. May, 1847.

3. BERTHA MARGARET, b. March, 1852, d. July, 1852.

4. MARY ELLEN, b. September, 1853, d. 31 March, 1900.

5. LOUISA, b. September, 1856, d. March, 1857.

6. HARRIET, b. June, 1861, d. November, 1922.

The eldest son—

RICHARD HILL, of Thornton Hall, educ. at University College, Oxford, Hon. Major late Yorkshire Militia Artillery, J.P., D.L., b. 14 May, 1843, m. 5 September, 1872, Evereld Ellen, dau. of the late Rev. George Hustler, late of Weald Manor, Oxon, Vicar of English Bicknor, Glos.   She died April, 1906.   He died 1 April, 1906, leaving—

  I. RICHARD.

  II. GEORGE FRANCIS GORDON, now of Thornton Hall, J.P., b. 26 March, 1885, m. 25 February, 1911, Monica dau. of John P. Crosland, of Scarborough, Esq., and have had—

    (i)   JOHN RICHARD GORDON, b. 29 June, 1916, d. 4 January, 1917.

    i.   EVERELD MONICA.

  1. EVERELD CONSTANCE, b. 5 June, 1873, m. 1895, P. Stanton of Birtle, Manitoba, Canada (d. 1930) and has issue—

    (*i*)   HARRI, b. 1895.

    i.   MAY, b. 1898.

    ii.   CONSTANCE, b. 1913, d. 1917.

2. KATHLEEN CHARLOTTE, b. 10 November, 1876, m. April, 1910, Clement G. Briggs, son of Archdeacon Briggs of Rochester.

The eldest son—

RICHARD HILL, J.P., Lord of the Manors of Thornton and Ellerburn-cum-Farmanby, Major 3rd Batt. A. P. W. O. Yorkshire Regiment, b. 14 November, 1877, m. 16 August, 1911, Gertrude Mary, dau. of the late Edward Rymer of London, Esq. He died 17 February, 1915.

APPENDIX C.

A grateful record of the names of all those who served in His Majesty's Forces in the War, 1914-1919.

ANDERSON, W.
AVISON, E.
APPLEBY, W.
BAKER, C.
BAKER, J. F. A.
BALDWIN, C. L., *M.C.*
BALDWIN, J. E. A., *D.S.O.*
BALDWIN, D. M.
BALDWIN, S. F.
BARNES, A.
BAXTER, J. R.
BEAUMONT, R. H.
BEAUMONT, W. H.
BELL, H.
BELL, T.
BETTS, R.
BIELBY, J. A.
BOYES, D.
BRADLEY, ALFRED
BRADLEY, ARTHUR
BRADLEY, W.
*BREWSTER, J. T.
BRIGGS, C. G.
BURGESS, J. R.
*CHARLES, T.
CHARLES, H.
*CLUBLEY, B.
CLUBLEY, E.
CLUBLEY, F. C.
COATES, G. L.
COCKERILL, W.
COCKERILL, WM.

*COULSON, HERBERT
COULSON, H.
CROFT, A.
CROFT, W.
CROSS, A.
CROSS, J. R., *M.M.*
CROSS, M. W.
DARRELL, E. J.
*DENNISON, M.
DENNISON, R. F.
DENNISON, W. R.
DICKEN, H. S., *M.M.*
*ELLIOTT, G.
ELLIOTT, J.
EVERS, H.
FRASER, J. H.
*GARBUTT, A. R.
GARBUTT, W. T.
GRAYSON, E.
GRAYSON, E. H.
*GRAYSON, G. W.
GRAYSON, H.
GREEN, C. J.
GREEN, J. T.
GREEN, R. J.
HALDER, J.
HARDACRE, R.
HARDY, H.
HARDY, R.
HARRISON, E.
HART, E. C.
HART, R.

HART, R. G.
HESLEWOOD, A. G.
HESP, F.
HILES, A.
*HILL, E.
HILL, ERNEST
HILL, G. F. G.
*HILL, RICHARD
*HILL, ROBERT
*HILL, W. H.
HOLGATE, G.
HUNTON, F. J.
INGLE, J.
JACKSON, T.
JEFFERSON, R.
JOBSON, J. E.
JOHNSON, M.
JOHNSON, R.
KITCHING, L.
LAKIN, E. W.
MANBY, E.
MANBY, M.
MARSHALL, G. A.
MAW, J. S.
*McFADDEN, J.
MERCER, C.
METCALFE, J.
METCALFE, J.
MILNER, A.
MILNER, E.
MORLAND, A.
MORRILL, E. J.
MUDD, W.
MYERS, G.
MYERS, J.
*MYERS, J. W.
NELLIS, R.
ORRAH, J.
PAMLEY, T. R.
PATEMAN, H. T.
PATEMAN, R. T.
PATTISON, W. S.

PERCY, E. C.
PESEL, H. G., *M.C.*
*PICKERING, F.
PICKERING, J.
PIERCY, G. W., *M.C.*
PREST, R.
RAW, H.
REVELEY, A. J.
*REVELEY, H. H.
REVELEY, T.
REX, A. R.
*REX, H.
REX, H. S.
REX, H. W.
RICHARDSON, H.
RILEY, J. W.
ROBINSON, A.
ROBINSON, C.
ROBINSON, G.
ROBINSON, W.
ROBINSON, WM.
ROBSON, J. N.
ROGERS, G. E.
*ROGERS, G. R.
SELLERS, E.
SHAW, M.
SIMPSON, R.
SIMPSON, W. P.
SKELTON, T. F.
SMITH, G. R.
SMITH, W. F.
SMITH, W. H.
*SMITHIES, T. N.
SNARY, G. W.
STINGSON, G.
*STRANGEWAYS, E. R.
STURDY, G.
STURDY, J.
THOMPSON, A.
THOMPSON, E.
THORNTON, C. S.
VENTRESS, G. E., *M.M.*

WALKER, H.	WEBSTER, W.
*WALLER, J. R.	WHITE, B.
WALLER, M.	*WHITE, W.
WARD, W.	WILSON, C. W.
WATSON, E.	WOOD, J.
WATSON, P.	WOOD, R.
WEBSTER, J.	*WOOLFE, F. B.
*WEBSTER, J. R.	WRAY, R. S.

* This sign denotes those who laid down their lives for their country, an whose noble service is commemorated in the Church of Thornton Dale.

APPENDIX D.

The First Parish Council, 1894.

The Thornton Parish Stakes.

The Parish Stakes are over, and a story of the past:
It was a splendid race—the pace throughout was fast.
Seventeen competitors went to the starting post,
A ten-to-one chance some of them had not at the most.
The course it was a long one, and the going very rough,
The winners must for certain be made of rare good stuff.
The 'Bookies' too were present, in fact they were in force—
All of them were eager to lay 'gainst any horse.
'Strong-arm'[1] was first favourite at two-to-one upon,
For this horse in his training had gone both well and strong.
The odds against the 'Doctor'[2] at the same time were not great
In his paces he was very good, his fencing was first-rate.
'Post-horse,'[3] too, was fancied by critics not a few.
'Farmer,'[4] trained in Maltongate was also well-backed too.
Of the other runners I really have not space
To tell how they were fancied for the Thornton Parish race.
The start it was a good one, they all got well away,
It soon became quite evident that all could never stay.
The people whose perception to bias did not yield
Made up their minds there could not be but eight left in the field
The first jump was a 'Slag-heap' just into Hunter's Lane;
'Lord John'[5] refused at this one, which caused his backers pain.
The obstacle that bothered many horses in the race
Was a quarry known as 'Musdale'—here the 'Builder'[6] made the pace
Pulling himself together, with one gigantic bound,
He landed very neatly upon the 'Flint-stone' ground.

[1] Samuel Armstrong.
[2] R. Arthur Scott.
[3] Alfred Garbutt.
[4] Thomas Norrison Marr.
[5] John Elliott.
[6] William Barnes (Senior).

The next fence was a big one—into 'Allotment Field,'
The 'Doctor' went full at it and made its timbers yield.
A 'Steam-roller' was seen passing; this made the 'Farmer' go
And took him many lengths ahead as all of you do know.
'Strong-arm' took the 'Water-jump' with a headlong stride—
The other seven came along but at it never tried.
A 'Limekiln' caused the 'Post-horse' to run out of his course,
In other points he shewed himself a very well-trained horse.
The 'Cleric'[1] and 'Sir Charlie'[2] now first appeared in view,
And in what way they all ran home I'll now describe to you.
The 'Doctor' came in first of all, with 'Strong-arm' close at hand;
The 'Farmer' and the 'Builder' a dead-heat next did land.
A little distance further off 'Lord John' did then appear,
But to place the sixth and seventh is most difficult I fear,
For neck and neck together the other three came in.
And now the Stewards have to say of those three, *which* did win.
A word of warning ere I close to those it may concern,
Don't trust a local tipster, if the winner you would learn,
With such-like men the wish is always father to the thought,
For this race has shown clearly their opinion is worth naught.

[1] Rev. Arthur Hill.
[2] Reuben Charles.

R. A. S.

THORNTON DALE IN THE TWENTIETH CENTURY

by Keith Snowden

Since the coming of the railway Thornton Dale's population had declined. The number of inhabitants, including Ellerburn, was 1,258. Young people were moving out to find work. In 1903, Oxlee Grabham's magic lantern shows came to Thornton Dale with a lecture on 'the advantages of emigrating to west Canada instead of finally emigrating to an English poor house'. It has been estimated that one third of the population 'weren't doing too badly', including freeholders, professional people and a growing body of 'annuitants', sometimes listed as 'private persons'. Yet there were many for whom poverty was a daily fact of life with little to fall back on except charity when times were hard.

The story of Thornton Dale in the twentieth century, like many other villages and small towns, was one of gradual improvements in health, housing and education punctuated by large events on a national scale which intruded into everyday life and took men off to war or to distant factories.

The North Riding County Council became responsible for education in 1902. A Grammar School enquiry was held at Pickering, the result of which led to the building of a new, larger school in Middleton Road, Pickering.

Thornton Dale schoolchildren were given a holiday on May 25th, 1900 to celebrate the Relief of Mafeking, during the Boer War. The new century found the Primitive Methodists in good strength and their new chapel was opened in 1901, on the corner of Roxby Road and Pickering Road. Mr T. Anderson, the schoolmaster, bought the old one in Whitbygate, and converted it into a house where he lived for a number of years, before moving next door into *Ebor Cottage*. A later occupant of *Chapel House* was Ronald Garnett, the ornithologist, who is buried at Ellerburn. A Methodist mission at Thornton Dale netted fifty new members in 1903.

A Charabanc convoy stops in Thornton Dale.

For the Coronation of King Edward VII, the schoolchildren were given a holiday from June 23rd to 27th. Coronation mugs were distributed to the children on July 4th.

Following a further restoration, *St. Hilda's* church, Ellerburn was reopened in 1904. The first restoration had been a century earlier. The lychgate was added during the later work and the carved reredos were completed four years later. New waterworks were constructed in Thornton. Part of the new system was a windmill above the northern end of the village and George Elliott was responsible for its satisfactory operation.

The Evolution of an English Town[1] was published in 1905. In this book Gordon Home gave a rather poetic description of the village at that time: *The first point of interest as one goes to Thornton-le-Dale from Pickering is the grass-grown site of Roxby Castle, the birthplace of Sir Hugh Cholmley, and the scene, as we know, of those conflicts between the retainers of Sir Roger Hastings and Sir Richard Cholmley. The position must have been a most perfect one for this ancient manor house, for standing a little higher than the level ings and carrs of the marshy land, it was protected from the cold northern winds by the higher ground above. From the top of the steep hill west of the village, Thornton Dale has almost an idyllic aspect, its timeworn roofs of purple thatch and mellowed tiles nestling among the masses of tall trees that grow with much*

---

[1] Published as *The History of Pickering* by the Blackthorn Press.

Chestnut Avenue in the 1900s. Before cars and tarmaced roads. The village postman is on the left.

Thornton Dale as Gordon Home would have seen it.

luxuriance in this sheltered spot at the foot of the hills. The village is musical with the pleasant sound of the waters of the beck that flows from Dalby Warren and ripples along the margin of the roadways, necessitating a special footbridge for many of the cottages.

The Wesleyan Methodists opened their new, chapel in Maltongate on July 3rd, 1909. Methodism was growing and hand-in-hand with it, Liberalism. There were those villagers who dare not vote other than the squire would want them to - that being, of course, Conservative. With the Ballot Act of 1872, electors could record their vote in secret. In 1905, a by-election was called with the raising to the peerage of E.W. Beckett, the Conservative member. Mr. Noel Buxton won the seat for the Liberals.

On May 20th, 1910, severe flooding affected the area. Ellerburn valley was swamped and the beck flooded houses on Beck Isle and in the village streets.

George Hill, Lord of the manor, removed his family from *Thornton Hall* to *The Lodge,* in Roxby Road, for a time, before occupying *High Hall.* About that time, all the thatch was removed from *The Forge,* and it was re-roofed with French pantiles.

It was in 1911 when Jimmy Green found the fragment of an ancient chariot wheel on Pexton Moor. Jimmy Green was a celebrated gamekeeper and a great naturalist and was often visited by the gentry who desired to know more about their countryside. Ranging the entire estates, Mr Green was constantly alert and observing natural activity, and he could tell where a rabbit had been caught by the soil on its feet. He was not

Maltongate in Edwardian times. Note the thatched rooves.

popular with all the villagers however, for some accused him of laying poison and killing their dogs.

In 1914, Mr Thomas Anderson retired from the headmastership of the village school. He did, however, go to Marishes to teach for the first two years of the war. Mr. Anderson had completed forty-five years service and was succeeded by Mr. Parratt. Although retired, Mr. Anderson played an active part and continued to administer the Yorkshire Penny Bank, which he had introduced at the school.

During 1914, the Baldwin family came to *Thornton Hall.* They also had property in Levisham. In the following year, Captain Lionel Hill was killed at Ypres, in his thirty-seventh year. A memorial dedicated to him was placed in *All Saints* church.

It was an exciting day for the schoolchildren in 1916, when an aeroplane landed in the vicinity. Many of the children played truant to see the machine, which was piloted by Captain John Baldwin of *Thornton Hall.* He was later to become an Air Marshall and was knighted.

The War To End All Wars ended in November 1918 and the village had lost twenty-six of its young men. A War Memorial Tablet was placed on the front of the *Hill Memorial Institute* recording the names of the fallen. Another memorial, the following year, was the Institute clock. A small tablet on the building recorded, *This clock is given to Thornton Dale in memory of Henrietta Priestman of Brook Cottage by her daughters Edith and Ida M Priestman in the year of peace 1919.* This clock ceased to work in the late twentieth century and was replaced. Another clock is also a war memorial; the one in *All Saints* church tower was provided by public subscription as a thanks offering for peace after the Great War and was dedicated in November, 1920. Squire G.F.G. Hill rebuilt the flour mill and enlarged it, calling it *Victory Mill.* Harry Burgess. whose mill at Kirby Fleetham had been worked by water power and used a stone grinding wheel, introduced more modern techniques to Thornton and became famous for his *Gold Medal* plain flour, produced in *The Mill By The Stream.*

Eddie Slater came with the Burgess' as a boy of sixteen and lived in High Street. He remembered an old ale house, *The Fox and Hounds,* which was kept by Arthur Robinson, whose family held it for a great number of years. It had only a six day license and only sold beer and stout; no spirits, but it was very popular with the local people. Mr. Slater remembered some of the characters about the village. There was a man who kept the keys to the village stocks. Some visitors would ask to be

Thornton Dale Football Team in the 1904-5 season.

Photo: John Garbutt collection

Trying out the Stocks

locked up in the stocks to have their photographs taken. If the stockskeeper felt that way he would leave the prisoner locked up for a while, until he had drunk a pint of beer. Another character was William 'Putty' Appleby, who was a chimney sweep. He also had some land in the south of the village where he grew grain, which he used to thresh in the *Buck Inn* yard; at the same time carrying on his trade as a sweep. He was a good sweep, but not always punctual and housewives would get vexed, as they had to keep their fire grates clear until after he had been. When they berated him, he would say, 'Oh Well, I'm here now. You'll soon have a fire going again.' If Putty was having a particularly busy time, he would stay in his black until the week-end and then wash and change.

Eddie Slater married the daughter of Alf Thorsby, one of the village wheelwrights, who was a perfectionist. Another wheelwright was Dick Wray, who as a woodcarver, executed the reredos in Ellerburn church.

John C. Barnes, son of William the builder, opened his *Roxby Garage* in 1919. His brother, Harold later ran a taxi business.

John Wood was the bellman and gravedigger and an unfortunate victim of arthritis. On one occasion he dug a grave and could not get out of it before the funeral procession arrived. His sister, who lived in Chestnut Avenue, used to make toffee, which she always placed in her window. She also had a large cat which would sit in the window. What with the heat of the sun and the hairs of the cat, one could imagine the toffee would not be too appetising.

Frank and George Skelton had a farm and sold milk. It was not bottled in those days; you would take your own basin and George would measure it out with a ladle. Frank was also a huckster and would run to Scarborough with a flat cart.

Thornton Hall had a bell which was rung at noon each day and at 11 a.m. on Shrove Tuesday, for the pancakes to be prepared.

Wilton School was closed in 1924 and the children then attended the Thornton school. Mr. Parratt took some of the children to the Wembley Exhibition of 1925, and J.H.S. Baldwin of *Thornton Hall* paid all their expenses. December of that year brought extremely heavy snowfalls, the worst for thirty years. A rapid thaw meant serious floods, when hundreds of acres of land below the village were swamped and farms entirely isolated. By that time there was a daily motor bus service to Scarborough the *Blue Bus* being operated by Abrahams and Gibbins. Harold T. Cooper ran a daily service from Pickering to Thornton.

A Thornton Dale wedding in 1910.

Photo: John Garbutt collection

Thornton Dale waterworks were enlarged in 1928. The following year brought more disastrous floods.

A second religious and historical pageant was held at Pickering in June 1930, organised by the Pickering Rural Deanery. Parishioners from Ellerburn performed in the first scene, while those from Thornton played in the sixth scene. By that time the United Automobile Services Ltd., had been formed and they were running the buses.

There was a Parliamentary By-election in 1931, when David Lloyd-George, the Liberal leader, came to speak in support of J Ramsey-Muir, who was opposing the Conservative H. Paul Latham.

The local Tories had stretched a banner right across the Square. As the car carrying Mr. Lloyd-George and the candidate arrived, some lads, with expert timing, cut the banner which fell under the wheels of the Liberal car as it came to rest. It was said that if old Mr. Garbutt could have caught those boys, he would have shot them. Elections were a lot more fun in those days.

Following the General Strike of 1926, there was a great increase in the number of unemployed. At Low Dalby a camp was established in 1933, to train men for the forestry. Most of the trainees were out of work miners from the North-East of England. They fitted into the social life of the village, and when Thornton *Village Hall* was opened in 1935, gave concerts there. A Mr. Pinfold, who was a very good pianist, produced the entertainment.

George Hill converted the former *Poor House* and the *French Woman's House* into a dwelling and called it *The Old House,* moving his family from the *High Hall* in 1933. The following year his daughter, Evereld, married Anthony Dudley Smith. A familiar figure in the village was Charlie Myers who had a little fourteen-seater bus with which he ran a service to Scarborough for the Market Day, and to Malton when they had two Market Days. He also ran an evening service to Pickering for the cinema. Mrs. White had a cafe in Maltongate at *Roxby House;* and there were four butcher's shops: Robinson's in Pickering Road; Mattie Cross' at The Square: Tommy Bell's in Whitbygate and E. & J. Cross' in Maltongate, who were successors to A. Hill. Alfred (Allie) Garbutt had the Post Office and lived there into his nineties. When Allie retired he was succeeded by his son, Noel, who was a very good water colour artist, and some villagers are fortunate to have some of his beautiful landscape pictures. Ted and Charlie Rogers had *The Forge,* carrying on the family tradition as smiths.

Market Day 1910.

Photo: John Garbutt collection

Baden Balderson came to Thornton and opened his *Welcome Cafe* in 1937, after a short spell at the *Castle Cafe* in Pickering. Before that the *Welcome* premises were a sweet shop, kept by a Mr. Ingle, who was the leader of the brass band and a plumber by trade.

Thornton had a very successful football team at that time, and the schoolchildren were noted for their prowess in sporting events. They did well in the Ryedale Sports, which were held at Kirkbymoorside. Mr. Parratt, the headmaster, suffered a series of nervous breakdowns and had to resign in 1938. In the same year, Mrs. Hayes took over the bakery in Maltongate, which had been in the Wardle family for many years, and was of ancient foundation.

It was still the custom to ring the Curfew Bell; a ritual that had survived the centuries, but would end with the coming of the Second World War, when all the church bells in the country were silenced.

As well as its hard core of local inhabitants, many of whom are the descendants of long-standing families, Thornton Dale has long been a place for other people to retire to. Some of these *incomers* have been people of distinguished service. One such was Arnold Rowntree, who came to *Brook House* in 1939. 'A finer gentleman never walked the streets', a villager told me, 'He was a true Quaker and democrat.' Arnold Rowntree was first cousin to Seebolme Rowntree, the famous sociologist, and a nephew of Joseph Rowntree, the founder of the chocolate firm. He was Liberal M.P. for York from 1906 to 1919. One meal time a tramp called at his house in York. Mr. Rowntree invited him in and sat him down to dine with the family and their servant. Arnold Rowntree died in 1951 and his widow lived on at *Brook House* for another fourteen years, to be followed by her son, Richard S. Rowntree, who resided there until 1968, when he moved to *Kingthorpe House*. Some Rowntree office employees also made Thornton their home.

Before ending the inter-war period, mention should be made of Mr. J.T. (Dot) Green, who had an ice cream parlour on Chestnut Avenue, next door to the *Welcome Cafe*. Dot had been a cricketer for Yorkshire and kept a collection of souvenir bats and balls, which had been autographed by some of the great players of his time. He used to make his own ice cream and he also had a billiards room at the rear of his premises, with three tables, where the local lads would play in the evenings. Dot's mother had a cafe in Whitbygate. Next door to Dot Green's was Daddie Pickering's sweet shop. He also sold dishes of hot peas.

Sunday School Outing to Lockton Pastures, 1905.

Photo: John Garbutt collection

The moment the Second World War started on September 3rd, 1939, plans were put into operation for the evacuation of children from the large towns and cities of strategic areas. The village school was opened the following day for informal instruction of Hull children, of which 31 were present. By the end of the month the school rota had swelled to a total of 184, consisting of 130 North Riding pupils, 34 Hull evacuees, and 20 private evacuees.

The Stobart family had followed the Baldwins in occupying *Thornton Hall*. There was a small army camp built nearby and during the war *Thornton Hall* was used as an officers mess.

Mr.T. Philip (Pop) Horner was appointed as headmaster of the village school in 1942. A Bachelor of Science, he was the first master to carry qualifications.

A new experience for villagers was to be able to see films in the *Village Hall,* projected on portable equipment, using 16 millimetre safety film.

In 1944, Sergeant Thompson of the North Riding Police visited the village school to alert the children to the dangers of the 'Butterfly Bomb.' This was an anti-personnel device which looked like a fruit tin with wings attached. The slightest touch could detonate the bomb, and the Germans dropped them in cornfields to prevent farmers getting their harvests. In that terrible war, ten young villagers gave their lives in the armed services. Happily, Thornton Dale did not suffer any bombing.

During the early 1940s a Youth Club was formed by a Methodist minister. Wilf Garbutt. then a schoolboy, was a member and recalls that it first met in an attic room above the *New Inn.* Some forestry-workers and Mrs. Doris Shaw-Baker were leaders. The *New Inn* was held by Mr. and Mrs. J. Riley from 1937 to 1954. Mrs McNeill, their daughter, says there was no Youth Club held in the pub, but it was in the chapel schoolroom.

POST WAR THORNTON.

After the war, some of the businesses began to change hands. Ted Hayes returned from the R.A.F. and took over his mother's Maltongate bakery. Ted worked a long day, rising early in the morning - as is a baker's wont - and then, after baking, setting off in his van to sell and deliver his goods for the rest of the day, leaving his wife, Marcia in charge of the shop. Ted ran the business until 1974, then closed it down.

Thornton Dale Station with Tom Wright in 1920.

Bill (Flash) Pickering, one of Daddie Pickering's sons, started a taxi business and also grew cultivated mushrooms, which he sold to hotels in Scarborough. Bob Fletcher, an estate agent, took over *Thornton Hall* and ran it as a country club. In 1947 Harold Barnes bought *The Forge,* as Ted and Charlie Rogers were retiring. The blacksmith business had been in their family for seventy-three years. Mr. Barnes opened the following year as a coppersmith, antique and gift shop. He soon found the antique side of his business too time-consuming, so he gave up antiques, continuing at *The Forge* for fourteen years.

Peter Barnes took over the running of his father's business at *Roxby Garage.*

Thornton had some breeders of fancy rabbits, such as Geoff Hill, George A. Barnes, and 'Huckster' White.

Pickering Rural Council built the Castlegarth estate in 1948. Some local girls had married servicemen from other parts of the country, and some of the village men who had been in the armed forces, had married girls from elsewhere, so the new houses came as a boon to them.

In 1949, Arthur Slater opened up the disused limestone quarry. The passenger rail traffic was closed down in the following year, although the line to Pickering was kept open for the carriage of the quarry stone.

George Hill, the Lord of the manor, died in 1953 and was succeeded by his daughter, Mrs. Evereld Dudley Smith.

Following the death of Harry Burgess, who was the county councillor. a by-election was held in 1954. Since the formation of the Division in 1889, there had been only one contest. In 1895 the district was divided and the Thornton-le-Dale and Rosedale Division was formed. The seat had been held by Colonel Scoby, until his elevation to the Aldermanic bench in 1904. He was succeeded by Samuel Baker of Wilton, who was followed by Richard Hill of *Thornton Hall.* When Mr. Hill retired, J.R. Twentyman of *Kirkbymisperton Hall,* replaced him. Mr. Twentyman became an alderman and John Parkinson held the position until his death in 1944. Harry Burgess, the miller, had served since that time.

There were two candidates for the contest, one being Sir Franklyn Gimson, of *Applegarth,* who had been a prominent man in the Colonial Civil Service. He was the Hong Kong Colonial Secretary from 1941 to 1945, and as Senior British Government Officer under the Japanese, was a tower of strength to those British subjects overrun by the Nippon invasion. From 1946 to 1952 he was Governor and Commander-in-Chief of Singapore.

Photo: *Bob Hill Collection*

The overflowing of the Beck was a regular occurrence.

Sir Franklyn's opponent was Lieutenant-Colonel Anthony Dudley Smith, the husband of the Lady of the manor. A member of the Northumberland Fusiliers, he had served many years abroad with his regiment, retiring in 1945, after which he took a Foreign Office appointment as British Resident in Germany. The Colonel won the election with 870 votes to Sir Franklyn's 180, going on to serve until 1965.

The Thornton Dale Players performed their first three-act play in the *Village Hall*. Entitled *The Happy Prisoner,* the play was produced by Margaret Elwin. Those taking part were Trotty Blackburn, Edith Whittaker, Mrs Easton, Mildred Beal, Irene Hill, Francis Croft, John Mills, Bernard Grayson and Ken Arundale. *The Thornton Dale Players* developed as an offshoot from the *Women's Institute*.

The license of the *Fox and Hounds* public house was transferred from William Robinson to Mr. W. Desmond Appleby, who kept it for about five years, then it finally closed.

Johnnie Mercer kept a gentlemen's outfitters shop on Pickering Road. A member of the Parish Council, he was also a tireless worker for the *Village Hall,* which has a tablet as a memorial to him.

Roye Manthorpe, a native of Lamberhurst, Kent, met Mary Warriner, of Thornton parish, while they were both in the R.A.F. He married her and came to live in Thornton in 1946. He founded a branch of the Royal Air Force Association. For over twenty years 'Mannie' ran Bingo sessions in the *Village Hall* in aid of local charities. Roye died in August 1997.

In 1954, the publicity film, *The Story of a Grain of Wheat* was produced for Burgess' by Air Commodore H.G. Crowe, who had taken up residence at *Ganstead* in 1946. He had been keenly interested in cinematography for twenty-nine years. Air Commodore Crowe was a veteran airman of the Royal Flying Corps, for which he volunteered in 1917. He was posted to No: 20 Squadron in France, where he served as a gunner and observer in the two-seater wood and fabric aeroplanes of the time, displaying a great aptitude for reconnaissance work. His duties also included navigation and photography. The following year he was promoted to Lieutenant. Lt Crowe and his pilot had several narrow escapes from death, including an encounter with three Fokker triplanes of Baron Richthofen's Squadron and were shot up, but managed to limp back to their base. On leaving No: 20 Squadron, Lt. Crowe was awarded the Military Cross. These Great War experiences led to a long and

The Thornton Dale Players presented 'Spring and Port Wine' in 1977.
M Beal, C Brown, C Hill, L Bromley, C Baxter, C Robshaw, I Hill, R Vasey

distinguished career in the Royal Air Force, in which he served on the Indian North West Frontier, gaining the C.B.E. and other campaign and Victory medals. He was even decorated by Chiang Kai-shek, the Republican President of China. During his service in India he was promoted to Air Commodore and before retiring served as Acting Air Vice Marshall.

Mrs. Adelaide Daphne Hermione Oliphant, the widow of Rear Admiral Laurence R. Oliphant of *Miller's Hill,* received fatal injuries in a motor accident. Mrs. Oliphant was seventy, and was a sister of the late Lord Middleton. While at *Miller's Hill,* she briefly entertained Princess Grace of Monaco, the former film star Grace Kelly.

At that time Thornton Dale could lay claim to a good record for longevity. In one area of less than one hundred yards, the combined ages of seven inhabitants totalled 618 years.

Mrs. Priestman died in 1955 at her home in Peaslands. She was eighty-five and the widow of Edgar Priestman, a native of Thornton Dale, who moved his business to the West Riding, and went to live in Bradford. Mrs Priestman returned to Thornton in 1947.

Another of the villages oldest inhabitants, James Webster, of Westfields View, died at the age of eighty-nine. He had spent virtually all his life in the village.

At a Pickering Rural Council meeting in August 1955, Councillor Leo Wood complained of the limestone dust problem caused by Slater's quarry. He asked that pressure be brought to bear on the company to alleviate the trouble. After some months of negotiation, Mr. Slater promised to make some improvements to the plant, at a cost of £4,000.

A grand old man of Thornton Dale died in 1956. William Richard Wilson, of *East Lynn,* was ninety-two and the last surviving member of the original Thornton Dale Brass Band, which he had joined as a euphonium player, when a boy of seventeen. He still had the instrument at the time of his death.

Mrs Elizabeth Mouncey, of Brook Lane, died at the age of eighty-one. A native of the village, she had lived in the same cottage all her life, with the exception of one year. On leaving school she obtained a post as a student teacher at the village school, under Mr.T. Anderson. She left to take up an appointment in Leeds, but returned after a year to nurse her parents. Later she married Mr.E. Mouncey, who predeceased her by a few years.

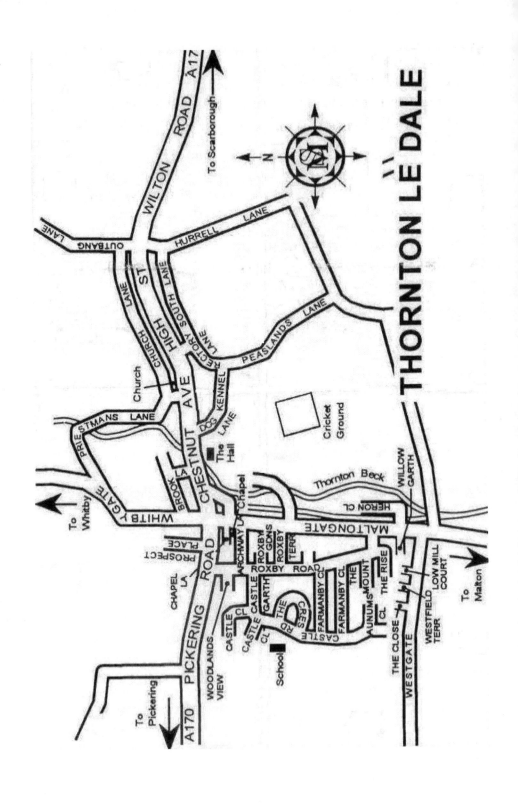

Mr. James Evers died in High Street in 1956, at the age of ninety, having lived and worked in the district all his life. Although he was born at Marishes, his family had been associated with Thornton Dale for some considerable time.

Bill (Flash) Pickering opened an ice cream parlour and built an extension in 1959. In the same year Wilfred Pickles came to Thornton Dale with his popular radio show, *Have A Go*. At that time the County Council had produced millstone signs for the village and dropped the -le- from the village name. Wilfred made reference to this in his introduction. In describing the village and its surrounds, he said they offered some of the most beautiful walks in the world, particularly on Ellerburn Road, where he said the four wooden benches had been responsible for more marriages than any other single factor. Those taking part in the programme were, Jack Pickering (Jack of all trades), Mrs. Bradbury (eighty-four), Francis Croft (Long distance lorry driver), Mrs Molly Gray, and Dick Wray (Wheelwright), who said in his young days, he had seen more people waiting to go into the local inns at six a.m., than went in during the day now. Butcher John Robert Cross, who had the shop in Maltongate, before being succeeded by Geoff Hill, died in 1963, aged sixty-three.

By that time the limestone quarry dust problem had grown to such an extent that a *Thornton Dale Quarry Nuisance Committee* had been formed. The Rural District Council was pressing the quarry owner and he threatened to close the quarry if the council persisted, pointing out that he employed 68 local men.

Ashley Burgess, who had succeeded his father at the flour mill, ceased to mill flour in 1963 and went over to the production of animal feeds and pet foods.

An interesting person who retired to Thornton Dale was Sir Oscar Moreland, who lived at the *High Hall*. He was H.M. Ambassador to Japan from 1959 to 1963. Educated at King's College, Cambridge, he joined H.M. Consular Service in 1927, serving many periods in the Far East. He was a member of the Leeds Regional Hospital Board from 1965 to 1974. Lady Alice Moreland was the daughter of the Rt. Hon. Sir F.O. Lindley, P.C., G.C.M.G., and was keenly interested in the preservation of wild flowers on the roadsides.

Josephine Butler came to Thornton Dale in 1968, because she wanted somewhere quiet to write her book, *Churchill's Special Agent,* recounting her wartime experiences as a spy in Nazi-occupied Europe. When I spoke to her she said she was writing a new book, *Dirty Tricks.*

The High Street in 2009.

Doubt has been cast on some of her stories, but what is certain is that she spoke excellent French including several regional dialects, due to a pre-war medical career in Paris. Part of her wartime career as a decoder has not been challenged. From 1968 to her death in 1992, Dr. Butler was a leading local worker for charity, especially cancer relief.

A building craze started in the late 1960s. A small estate at The Rise was followed by Farmanby Close, the first stage of which was completed in 1970. Some of these private houses were bought by local people, but mostly there was an influx of new residents.

Harold Barnes retired from *The Forge,* which was bought by Terry Besau in 1971. The blacksmith equipment went to the *Beck Isle Museum* at Pickering. Terry Besau extended the premises to include a restaurant, which he ran for a number of years.

Joe Thompson, who ran a riding school at the *Hall Hotel* stables, died in 1977 and the stables were taken over by George Morley of High Marishes.

Sir Franklyn Gimson died in 1975. He was a Knight of St John and a Bachelor of Arts. He had served as a churchwarden at *All Saints* church for twenty years, and in his memory the pulpit was repositioned in 1978. Lady Gimson was a former organist at the church, and a daughter of the late Canon Ward.

Other new estates were built Aunums Close in 1975, to be followed by Castle Close and Castle Road, with a new village school adjoining, to replace the old one.

Sir Oscar Moreland, G.B.E.., K.C.M.G., C.M.G., died on May 20th, 1980, at the age of seventy-six. Lady Alice lived on for some time at the *High Hall,* before moving to Easingwold.

Air Commodore H.G. Crowe, C.B.E., M.C., J.P., died on April 26th, 1983, aged eighty-five. He had been a valuable addition to the village life, having served as churchwarden, a school governor and a Justice of the Peace, as well as a trustee for the *Alms Houses.* Mrs. Crowe was also active in the community and was a member of the Darby and Joan Club, and a member of the Naturalist Trust in Ellerburn. After her husband died, Mrs. Crowe left the village. Simon Cowe, a musician with the long-standing popular Northern group *Lindisfarne,* came to *Ganstead* having married a great niece of Air Commodore Crowe.

John Spence, the Conservative member of Thirsk and Malton, and after the boundary changes, the Ryedale Parliamentary Constituency,

The Beck and Beck Isle Cottage.

resided at *Greystones* (the former *Ellerburn Vicarage*), until his sudden death in 1986.

THORNTON DALE TODAY.

IN 1987 the Thornton Dale Parish Council officially resurrected the Victorian *Thornton-le-Dale*. A new Thornton Dale has been added to the old one. It is not conspicuous from the main thoroughfare, but to the west of the village there is a brick-built concentration of housing estates. Other parts of the village, such as Church Lane and South Lane, have had individual houses built in what were orchards and paddocks; *infilling* the planners call it.

Local trades have declined; there is only one grocery shop and one butcher shop. Now there is a conglomeration of cafes and gift shops. Bill Balderson has enterprisingly extended his *Welcome Cafe* to take in the old Flash Pickering premises and neighbouring properties; all geared to serve the great influx of visitors at weekends and during the tourist season.

The mill no longer grinds, but is the headquarters for a larger animal food organisation.

Even beside the beck new housing has sprung up, for at the end of Maltongate there is Heron Close, a small estate of artificial stone houses.

The Rowntree Trust renewed earlier links with the village when they built a small estate of warden-attended flats, known as Roxby Gardens. Robin H. Barnes took over the joinery and undertaker business of his erstwhile master, Dick Wray, in Roxby Road, but joined into a larger firm of funeral directors. His son, Michael is a joiner in his own business.

Quarrying has long ceased and the site is now the Ryedale District Council's rubbish tip. *The Hall* is now a curious mixture of a residential home for the elderly and a public bar.

The Wardill Brothers shop continues to flourish under the guidance of descendants of that family, John Garbutt and Helen Ward, the children of Wilf Garbutt, who died in 2007. Wilf, known to locals as 'Fiff', like the factotum of old, was keenly interested in village affairs, representing Thornton Dale ratepayers on Ryedale District Council and Thornton-le-Dale Parish Council as well as numerous committees.

The evening of December 11th, 1999 began with the switching on of the Millennium Clock on the *Hill Institute.* Mr. A Dudley Smith, the chairman of the Millennium Committee, presented a cheque to Wilf

350

Photo: Colin Dilcock

Thornton Dale Show, 2009.

Garbutt, who received it on behalf of the parish council and then introduced Miss Monica Priestman, whose family presented the original clock to the village, and she then switched on the clock. Matthew Airey, who was the winner of a Christmas competition organised by the school, then switched on the Christmas lights. He was assisted by Father Christmas, who had arrived in one of Brian Turnbull's vintage cars.

In the hundred years outlined in this chapter, the population of Thornton Dale has grown from 1,258 to 3,311. The average age of its inhabitants is 47, yet a quarter of these are classed as long-term unemployed. Of those in employment, 26% are in agriculture and forestry, 19% in manufacturing and 17% in wholesale and retail. There are 122 holiday homes, a high percentage of the village's stock of housing.

Voted in a newspaper poll many years ago, as the prettiest village in Yorkshire, Thornton Dale retains its charm for all to see. May its personalities, past and present, and its natural beauty remain for ever part of our local heritage.

INDEX

Abbey, Philip, 111, 308.

Abbots Crooke, 281.

Abolition of the House of Lords and .
Accounts of the Honor of Pickering,
102, 295.

Acklam, 218.

Ackland Beck, 300.

Ackworth, Friends School at, 106.

Adam, son of Isabel, 200, 204.

Adam, son of Roger, 261.

Adames, William, 304.

Adderstone, the, 2, 19, 213.

Addison, Sir Roger de Coverley, 55.

Adelaide or Adeliz, 197.

Aella, King of the Angles, 3.

Agistator and agistment, 13, 284-7,
290.

Ainderby Steeple, 38.

Airey, Matthew, 352.

Aiskew, 34.

Aislaby, 76.

Alan of Allerston, 247.

Alan brother of Alan, 13.

Alan the capellanus, 185, 199.

Alan the fisherman, 19.

Alan the Forester, 12, 159.

Alan the Smith, 117.

Alan son of Andrew, 246.

Alan son of Geoffrey, 13, 159, 262.

Alan son of John, 13, 199.

Alan son of John the neatherd, 15.

Alan son of Reginald, 13.

Alan son of Torfin, 247.

Alan of Thornton, 15.

Alan of Whytegate, 261.

Albemarle, Countess of, 6, 197-8;
earls of, 197-8; fee of, 197-8.

Albini, Nigel de, 236; William de, 236.

Albreda, 236.

Aldborough, 249.

Aldun, bishop of Durham, 227, 247.

Allanson, Francis, 176; Frederic, 112;
George, 109, 111; James, 119; John,
176; Simpson, 111; Thomas, 112;
William (c. 1734), 109, 118; William

(senior), 178; William 255. (junior),
118-9.

Allayne or Rowlynson, Thomas, 52.

Allen, Miss H. E. Writings ascribed to
Richard Rolle, etc., Ch. III passim.

Allen, William, 105.

Allerston, 16, 21, 45, 46, 61, 66, 100,
101, 118, 130, 150, 157, 185, 189, 13,
217, 246, 247-9, 262, 286, 299, 300,
304-5.

Allerston, Helen de, 248.

Allerston Loft, 299, 300.

Allerton Wapentake, 30.

Alum trade, 275.

Alverstain, or Alvestayn, John of, 200;
Philip, 246; Robert, 200.

Amcotes, Thomas de, 26, 27, 160.

America House or Chester Villa, 79.

Amneys, the Rev. Burton, 155.

Ampleford or Ampisford, John de, 163.

'An Exhortation to all People to
consider the Afflicting Hand of God,'
88.

Ancient Petitions, 228.

Anderson, Henry, 95; Thomas, 128,
140, 329; Mr T 324.

Andrew, Joseph, 116.

Angell, James, 305-6.

Anne, Queen, 75, 90, 126, 175, 218,
242.

Anti-Corn-Law League, 106.

Antigua, 177-8, 221.

'Antiquary, the' (1886), 79.

Antiquity, 3, 4.

Appelby or Appulby, Isabella, 156; Sir
William, 156; William 'Putty', 332.

Appilton, Rev. William, 163.

Apple Garth Lane, 92-3.

Archaeological Journal XXVI, 197;
LII, 2; LXXI, 3.

Archebaud, Richard, 246.

Archer, William, 13.

Arches, Ivetta de, 197; Osbert de, 197.

Armour, 50, 53, 54.

Armstrong Samuel, 111, 323; Samuel

T., 112.
Arnold, Thomas, 255.
Arundale, Ken, 342.
Arundel, Earl of, 207, 237.
Ashby, William, 18.
Ashton, Dr. J. T., 281.
Aslakby, Arnald of, 299.
Astinus, son of Elias, 246; son of John
  of Thornton, 42, 262-3.
Atiesdike, 241.
Atkinson, family of, 98; Annas, 98;
  Christopher, 98; James, 176; John (of
  York), 254; John (c. 1733), 113;
  Kateran, 98; Marmaduke, 167-8;
  Richard, 98; Robert, 98; Roger (c.
  1731), 98, 176, 178, 255; Roger (c.
  1780), 99, 224.
Atkinson, Canon, 79, 148, 275, 305;
  Forty Years in a Moorland Parish, 2,
  4, 9, 26, 61, 67, 128, 206, 208, 280.
Attachment, Court of, 14, 21, 302.
Attaeet, 241.
Aubrey and Jackson, *Wiltshire
  Collections,* 279, 280.
Audus, John, 81.
*Aunums or Aunam, Anham,
  Ofnam,Ovenam, Hornum, etc.,* 92, 95,
  159, 183, 207, 249, 272, 281.
Austin of Pickering, 15.
Avicia, d. of William le Gros, 198.
Avison, Frank, 296; Messrs., 112.
Ayloffes Book of Demises, 271, 288-2.
Ayton, 206-7, 217, 286; Gilbert of, 299.

Babthorpe, Isabel, 266; Margaret, 266;
  Sir Ralph, 266; Sir William, 272.
Babyngton, William, 266.
Bachy or Backy, Thomas de, 19.
Back Church Lane, 107, 118, 145.
Back Lane (South), 151.
Backgammon, early game of, 41.
Bacon, Roger, 160, 161; William, 308.
Bacons Farm, 308.
Bagdale Hall, 272.
Bainbridge, Rev. H. P., 179, 193.
Bainton, 167.
Baker or Bakar, family of, 107-8;

Benjamin, 111; Christopher, 78;
  Gregory, 254-5; John (c. 1530), 108;
  John (c. 1675), 78; John (c. 1780),
  81; John (c. 1809), 183; John (c.1849),
  111, 235; Mary M., 128; Richard, 87;
  Robert, 307; Roger, 107-8; Samuel (c.
  1780), 81; Samuel (c. 1849), 111, 180;
  William, 81.
Baker, *Northamptonshire,* 279.
Baker, *Unhistoric Acts,* 74.
Baker, Samuel, 340.
Bakewell (?) 77.
Balderson, Baden, 336; Bill, 350.
Baldwin, Capt J, 329, 332.
Ballard, *The Domesday Inquest,*6, 9.
Banaster, Maud, 248; Ralph, 19.
Banke or Bankes, or Banks, Easter, 69;
  Jayne, 19; Margrett, 69; William, 87.
Bannockburn, battle of, 204.
Barde, Robert, 209; William, 209.
Bardelf, or Bardolf, or Bardulf,
Hugh, 159; Ralph, 159, 245, 248;
Walter, 299.
Baring-Gould, *Yorkshire Oddities,* 189.
Barkeley or Bartley, Margaret, 290;
Maurice, 290-1.
Barker, John, 176; Richard, 115, 124;
  Robert, 283.
Barkere, John, 46.
Barking, co. Essex, 105, 219.
Barlow, Dr., Bishop of Lincoln, 133.
Barmston, 191, 314.
Barneby Bossall, 46.
Barnby, William T., 112.
Barnes, George (c. 1867), 119; George
  A, 340; H. W., 184; Harold, 332, 340,
  348; Henry (1930), 112; John
  (c.1743), 110; John (c. 1860), 122;
  John C, 332; Peter, 340; Robin, 350;
  Thomas (c. 1830), 119-20; William (c.
  1860), 119; William (senior), 322 332.
Barneston, Robert, 290.
Barnet, battle of, 250
Barney, Mrs. Anne, 95; Rowland John,
  95.
Barnsley, 215.
Barrow, G., *Geology of North*

354

118, 176; Richard (d. 1909), 95, 121, 180; Robert, 81; Thomas, 61, 114; William, 176.

Birdsall, 127.

Bishopthorpe, 41.

Bishops War, the, 70-2, 275-6.

Blaber, Walter, 12.

Blackbourne, Thomas, 63.

Blackburn, Trotty, 342.

Black Busk or Buske, 253, 271.

Black Death, the, 39, 44, 163.

Blackstone, Commentaries, 150, 154, 209.

Blanchard, William, 239.

Bland, Brown, and Tawney, English Economic History, Select Documents, 7.

Bland, Mrs. H., 81.

Blandesby, or Blandsby Park, 51, 56, 264, 301.

Blashill, Sutton in Holderness, etc., 249.

Blasta, 300.

Blenheim, battle of, 75.

Blesdale, William, 210.

Blyeton, Edward, 304.

Blyth, Alexander, 230.

Boddam Close, 253.

Body or Boddy, Edward (1), 295; Edward (2), 295; Francis, 176; James (1), 295; James (2), 295; John (1), 295; John (2), 295; Matthew, 176; Robert (1), 295; Robert (2), 295; Robert (3), 295; Robert (4), 295.

Bogo, Nicholas, 46.

Boer War, 324.

Bohemia, Queen Elizabeth of, 254.

Bole, prebendal stall of, 165.

Bolebake, or Bolebec, Osbert de, 198, 200; Ralph de, 198, 200.

Bolingbroke, Henry of (Henry IV), 47; Henry St. John, viscount of, 75.

Bolton, Alfred, 119, 131, John, 107, 119; Richard, 119, 123, 138; William, 81, 120.

Bonefield, Robert of, 299.

Bonnie Prince Charlie, 76.

Boodall Carr, 217.

Boodhills, 241.

Boot or Booth Close Flat, 79, 83, 223.

Booth, family of, 178; John, 111, 124-5, 147; Thomas, 180.

Bothrode, or Boothroyd (2), 64, 114.

Bordesdene, Robert de, 16, 19.

Boroughbridge, battle of, 16, 36, 43, 204, 238.

Bosco, Sir Henry de, 202.

Bossall, 102, 241.

Boswell, Life of Johnson, 215.

Bosworth, battle of, 48.

Botcher, Alexander, 47, 114.

Botetourt, John de, 206.

Botreaux, Baroness, 250.

Bolton, 79; close, 282; Field, 84, 98, 100, 101, 148, 216, 219; Lands, 148, 216; Lane, 8, 9, 10; in West Fields, 79; Way, 100, 148.

Bouchard or Dutton close, 294.

Boulton, John, 180.

Bovey, Ralph, 274.

Bowden, Lincs., 166.

Bower, Elizabeth, 127; Richard, 121.

Bowes, John R., 112, 117.

Boyes, family of, 107, 258; Anne, 234; Christopher, 60, 120, 239; Elizabeth, 120; George, 186; Henry, 258; James, 176, 288, 307; Jane, 120; John (c. 1650), 293; John (c. 1690), 242; John (c. 1734), 109, 220; John (c. 1780), 81; John (c. 1807), 110; John (c. 1814), 111; John (c. 1830), 180; John, (d. 1896), 113; Peter (c. 1601), 188; Thomas (c. 1613), 120; Thomas (c. 1662), 234; Walter (c. 1241), 262; William (c. 1626), 117, 239; William (c. 1690), 242; William (c. 1720), 258, 288; (?) (c. 1734), 87.

Boynton, 273.

Box, or Box Tree Farm, 94, 95, 112, 223.

Brackendale, or Brackendele or Brecondale, 79, 223, 253, 271.

Bracondell way (vide Greengate Lane), 93.

Brackton, 233.

Bracton, 'De Legibus Angliae', 6, 208.

Braddell, John, 290.

Bradford, 106; Lady Mills, at, 106; old corn mill in, 106; Ragged Schools at, 106; woollen trade in, 106.

Bradley, Rev. Christopher, 78, 100, 103, 169-73, 216, 235; Francis, 172; Gregorie, 172; Henrie, 172; John, 172; Robert, 172; Samuel, 172.

Bramley, Rev. H. R., 'The Psalter of Richard Rolle of Hampole', 31.

Brand, Wilfred, 231.

Bray, Sir Raynold, 50, 251.

Braybroke, baron, 202-3; Gerard, 209.

Bretigny, Treaty of, 207.

Brett, Thomas, 17, 202.

Brewster, family of, 295; Elizabeth, 128; John, 125, 128; Mary, 128; William, 119.

Brewsters Garden, 125.

Brian son of Alan, 202.

Bridgnorth, co. Salop, 110.

Bridlington, 232, 234, 235, 277; Prior of, 161; Priory of, 237.

Briefs in Thornton, 152-3.

Brigantes, the, 3.

Briggs, Clement G., 180, 318; J Jonathan, 110-11.

Bright, History of England, 44.

Brisby, Thomas, 111, 308; William, 111, 308.

Bristol, siege of, 214.

Broadmires, 223; close, 83; Crossing, 281; Drain, 82.

Broats, the, 79, 81, 83, 149, 150-1; close, 242; Low, 242; Small, 242.

Brockett, Edward, 290; Thomas, 290.

Brock Lane, 8, 83, 101, 111-2.

Brodester, Thomas de, 269.

Brograve, John, 290.

Broke, Nicholas, 252.

Brompton, 33, 50, 209, 229, 250; Low Hall, at, 127.

Bromsgrove, 223.

Brook Cottage, 106-7, 117.

Brooks, James, 293.

Brow or Browdyke, the, 85, 217, 235.

Brown, George, 124, 176, 296; William, 78.

Browne, Agnes, 53; Ann, 100; Cuthbert (1) (c. 1605), 53, 63; Cuthbert (2) (c. 1605), 53; Elizabeth, 53, 63, 78; Ellen, 53; John (c. 1600), 188; John (c. 1655), 189; John, of Hull, 157; Maud, 155-6; Robert, 155-6; Roger, 100-1, 216-7; Thomas (c. 1611), 60; Thomas (c. 1623), 53; William (c. 1590), 187; William (c. 1601), 188; William (c. 1700), 220.

Broxburne, 242.

Broxholme, Francis, 256.

Bruce, Robert the King, 43-4.

Brun, Hugh, 199; Richard, 263; Roger, 13.

Brunton, Robert de, 263.

Brus of Skelton Castle, family of, 17, 107, 154-5, 196, 228.

Brus of Pickering, family of, 228.

Brus, Adam de, 197; Adam de (2), 197; Agnes, 197; Elizabeth, 229; Joan, 156; Lucy, 203; Peter (1), 18, 29; Peter (d. 1272), 155, 228; Peter (3), 203; Robert, 209; Robert de, 6, 227; Robert de (of Pickering), 30; William de, 209; Sir William, 155-7, 229.

Bruster, Rev. Richard, 185.

Brymbleclif Wood, 17.

Brythonic dykes, 2.

Buchan, John, 284.

Buck Inn, The, 93, 123-4.

Bucke, Rev. George, 188.

Buckland, 'Reliquiae Diluvianae', 1.

Buffit, Close, 109, 110; Hedge, 148; Wood, 9, 110.

Bukton, George, 288; John, 289; Peter de, 208; Robert, 289; William, 289.

Bulmer, Joan, 265; Sir Ralph, 265; R. J., 139; Thomas, 123.

Bulmer, North Riding of Yorkshire, 89, 95, 112, 124.

Burden, Stephen, 308.

Burdett, John, 219.

Burgess, Messrs., 113; Ashley, 346;

Harry, 329, 340; Joseph, 106; Sarah, 106.

Burke, 'History of Commoners' III, 232; 'Peerage 1915', 209-11, 273.

Bulmer, John, 15, 161.

Burn, 'The Justice of the Peace', 65.

Burnett, family of, 118; Thomas, 118; William, 113, 118.

Burrow, Richard, 219.

Burton, Annas, 101; Ralph, 305; Thomas, 160-1; William, 305.

Burton, 'Monasticon,' 112, 266.

Burtons Close, 83.

Bushell, Dorothy, 272; Mary, 272; Nicholas, 272; Norman, 272.

Butler, Josephine, 346.

Butler, William, 186.

Buttercrambe, 61.

Butteroyde, Elizabeth, 64; Richard, 64.

Buttery, family of, 108, 184; John 105. (c. 1625), 78; John (d. 1707), 84; John junior (c. 1707), 84; John 112. (c. 1890), 111; Thomas (c. 1860), 180; Thomas (c. 1870), 117.

Buttery, Close, 83; Stub or Stubb, 100, 148, 217.

Byland, Abbey of, 37, 237; abbot of, 45; battle of, 43.

Byron, Lord, 284.

Caishliffe, Robert de, 199.

Calendar, Book of Fees, 159, 242, 262; Chancery Rolls, 201; Charter Rolls, 26, 198-9, 249, 300, 302; Close Rolls, 42, 199, 201, 202, 205, 209; Committee of Compounding, 170, 214, 240, 275, 306, 307; Feudal Aids VI, 27, 29, 155, 163, 185, 199, 200-1, 204, 209, 229, 237-8, 247, 261, 263, 265; Fine Rolls, 199, 205; Inquests post mortem, 205-6, 230, 237, 263, 300; Papal Registers, 163; Patent Rolls, 42-7, 112, 114, 157, 203, 205, 206, 207, 210, 211, 238, 251, 262-3.

Caley, John, 70.

Calf Coatgarth, 213.

Calfcote, 303-5.

Calvert, John, 187.

Calverts House, 102.

Cambridge, 'Alumni' of, 132, 135, 168-9, 174, 177, 215, 217, 233; Caius College, 138; Christs, 233; Clare, 178; Emmanuel, 100; Jesus, 141, 189, 274; Pembroke, 138; Peterhouse or St. Peter College, 141, 169, 172; Queens, 139; St. Catherines, 133, 138-9; St. Johns, 138-9, 168, 175-6, 222; Sidney Sussex, 132, 135-6, 139, 158, 173, 175, 217, 221.

Cambridge, Maud, Countess of, 210; Robert, Earl of, 210.

Camden, 'Britania,' 4, 48.

Campion, Campioun, or Kampyun, family of, 116; Alan, 19; John, 14, 17, 246; Juliana, 19; Richard (c. 1330), 19; Richard (c. 1390), 265; Robert, 19; Thomas, 116; William, 265.

Canada Allotments, 79.

Candike, 241.

Canon Ecclesiastical, 133.

Capes, 'History of the Church of England' 149.

Cary or Carey, Sir Edmund, 212; Sir Edward, 279; Lady, 279.

Carl, son of Turbrand, 236.

Carleill, Anne, 232; John, 232.

Caroe, W. D., 181, 184.

Carpenter (?), 288.

Carr, Charity, 148-9; dyke, 82, 214; Field, 100; Mr. Hills, 148; Low, 105.

Carrs, the, 9, 111, 148, 224; Farm, 112.

Castle Ings, 299.

Castle Levington, 203.

Castre, John de, 263.

Catherine of Braganza, 295.

Catley, Rev. Francis, 189; 'Jaine,' 189.

Cattle, T. S., 123.

Cawthorne, 3, 76.

Caulklands, 84, 86, 120, 148.

Cayley, Sir Everard, 127; Sir George, 136, 140.

Cecily, daughter of Alan of Thornton, 202.

Chaloner, John, 303; Sir Thomas, 275.

Chamberlain or Chaumberlayn, Alice, 204-5; Henry de, 204-5.

Chambre, Chambar, or Chamber, Dr. John, 165-7, 173.

Champagne, Count of, 197.

Champley, Champay, Champnay, or Champney, family of, 98-100; Anne, 296; George (c. 1539), 99; George (c. 1734), 109; John (1778), 178; John (c. 1790), 81, 100, 146; Minnie, 184; Robert (c. 1670). 78, 100, 216; Robert (c. 1711), 109; Robert (c. 1743), 110; Robert (c. 1780), 81, 100, 150, 296; Robert (c. 1807), 100, 110; Robert (c. 1895), 100; Robert (c. 1905), 184; Roger, 99.

Champleys Charity, 100; Garth, 110.

Chancery, Court of, 9, 78, 132, 135.

Chapman, Jane, 66; John, 269.

Charity Farm, 98, 112, 217, 241, 308.

Charles, I, 71-2, 118, 169, 214, 239, 275-8, 280; II, 79, 99, 100, 126, 172, 174, 214, 256, 294.

Charles, John, 120; Reuben, 120, 323; Mrs. Reuben, 123.

Charlton, History of Whitby, 4, 41, 112, 270, 273.

Chaucer, Geoffrey, 142.

Cheam, 282.

Cheesebeck, 210.

Cheesmarr, 213.

Cherry Garden, 91.

Chicksands, Beds, 189, 234.

Chigogesmere, Chigomersc, or Chigogesmers, 5, 6, 298; (vide Marishes). Chilton, Cuthbert, 289.

Chimyne or Chymine, John de, 161; William de la, 161, 200.

China Garth, 48, 219.

Cholmley, family of, 51, 253-4, 258, 267-8, 305; Anne, 269; Catherine, 272-3; Dorothy, 272; Elizabeth, wife of Sir Hugh, 274, 278; Lady Elizabeth, 171, 270; Sir Francis, 253, 270, 272; George, 139; Sir Henry, 65, 168, 272, 273, 290, 291, 305; Sir Henry (2), 273, 276; Sir Hugh (1), 65, 70-2, 96,

158, 171, 273-9; Sir Hugh (2), 158, 173; Jane 270; Joan, 253, 269; John (d. young), 269; John (c. 1611), 305; Margaret, 65, 158, 269, 270, 273, 305; Marmaduke, 269; Lady Mary, 158, 175; Sir Reginald, 268; Sir Richard (1), 49, 266-70, 289, 290; Sir Richard (2), The Black Knight, 119, 145, 158, 167, 251-2, 269-72; Sir Richard (3), 239, 270, 272-5, 278, 305; Mr. Richard, 270; Sir Roger (1), 49-51, 268-9, 289, 304; Sir Roger (2), 268; Roger (3), 269; Roger (4), 270; Mr. Roger, 270; Susan, 273.

Cholmley, Sir Hugh, Memoirs of, 65, 70, 158, 272-9.

Church Lane, 350.

Church Street, 111, 112, 124.

Chymney, Avery, 51; John, 21; Robert, 21.

Cirencester, 256.

Clare, Earl of, 237.

Clarendon Code, 66; 'History of the Great Rebellion,' 214, 280.

Clark, Francis, 134; Samuel, 128.

Clarke, Jane, 78; John (1675), 78; John (1701), 219; John (the Greek scholar), 134, 176; John W., 123; Joseph, W., 180; Mary, 219; William, 78.

Claudius, the Emperor, 3.

Claudus, William, 159.

Clavell, Robert, 133.

Clay, 'The Hermits and Anchorites of England,' 37, 38.

Clay Pit Lane, 92-3.

Clay Pitts, 242.

Clement VI, Pope, 163.

Clemment, William, 294.

Glenfield Rigg, 162, 294.

Cleveland, 45, 79, 107, 163, 208, 297; cottages in, 61.

Cleyburgh, 100.

Clif or Cliff, John de, 204; Robert de, 246; Robert del, 286.

Clifford, Lady Elizabeth, 270; Thomas, 210.

Clodds, 281.

Cropton, 76, 137.

Crosby, George, 110; John, 81.

Crosdale Head, 4.

Crosier, Edward, 223; Matthew, 81.

Crosland, John P., 226; Monica, 226.

Cross, family of, 108, 122; second
family of, 122; John, 140; John (c.
1843), 296; John of Dalby Deer in the
Forest, 210-11, 267, 270; (c. 1890),
111, 296; Tom, 122; Thomas (c.
1825), 180; Thomas (c. 1849), 111;
Thomas junior, 111, 296, 308.

Cross, E & J, butcher, 334.

Cross, Robert, 346.

Crosscliffe, 19, 66.

Crosthwaite, Bishop, 145.

Crowe, Air Com H.G., 342, 348; Mrs
Crowe, 348.

Culme, Philip, 306; Richard (1), 306;
Richard (2), 306.

Cumberland, Earl of, 270.

Cunningham, Alien Immigrants to
England, 115; Doctor, 98.

Curia Regis Rolls, 260.

Curtesy of England, 208, 229, 230.

Curtler, The Enclosure and
Redistribution of our Land, 10, 77, 80;
The History of English Agriculture, 8,
70, 87-8.

Cussons, John P. W., 113.

Customs, Commissioner of, 219, 220;
House of, 219, 220.

Custumals of Battle Abbey, 6.

Dalby, 2, 6, 18, 59, 110, 124, 141, 151,
162, 213, 260, 264; agistment of, 284-
5; attacks on property in, 45;
Coatehouse at, 293; Colliery in, 287;
Forester of, 18, 40, 162; Hagg, 284,
290-4; High, 2,112, 149, 162, 174,
288-9, 293-5; Low, 100, 103, 111,
149, 175, 288-9, 293-4, 296; Manor
of, 5, 7, Ch. XVI, passim; meadow in.
20, 286; nutwood of, 2, 83, 264, 290,
292; Princes haggs in, 292; Privett or
Britoe, 290; recusants in, 65; Riggs,
291; Rigg Intacks, 290; valley of, 37;

warren, 2, 296; William, hermit of,
36,
37, 39, 40, 187, 288, 297.

Dale Bank, 83; closes, 107.

Daile or Dale, Francis, 102; James, 59,
John 188; Nicholas, 246; Richard 59,
188.

Dalton, estate of, 38; family of, 24, 38;
John, 16, 30, 31, 35-8, 42.

Danby, 208-11; Henry, Earl of, 214,
279-80.

Danvers, Anne, 279; Charles, 279-80;
Dorothy, 279-80; Eleanor, 279, 282;
Elizabeth, 279; Sir John I, 212, 279;
Sir John II, the regicide, 214, 224,
279-81.

Darcy, Lord of Templehurst, 211; Sir
Thomas, 268; William, 292.

Darknall, John, 254.

Darley, Mr., 306.

Darell, Edward, 112; Thomas, 91, 94,
112-3, 245.

Dauntrey, Wilts., 279-80.

Dawson, Michael, 306; Robert, 71.

Deans flatt, 83; New Ing, 149.

Dearham Meadow, 253.

De Banco Rolls, 2 Edw. III, 247.

Declaration of Indulgence, 1687, 215.

Deer in the Forest, 210-11, 267, 270;
Brokett, 289; Fallow, 15, 16; Hart,
211, 262; Hinds, 16; Knobbe, 289;
Pricket, 16; Red, 16, 289; Scadde,
267; Soar, 51; murrain amongst, 42;
outbreak of, 56; `umbles of, 267.

Deerholme Farm or Dereholme, or
Derholme or Dereham, 110, 223, 303-
5.

Defoe, Complete Tradesman, 215.

Deira, Kingdom of, 3.

De la Hou, Alan, 42; Richard, 42.

Del Cliffe, Robert de, 17.

Delgovitia, 3.

Denham, Ann, 171.

Denham Farm, 78.

Denison, George, 78.

Dennis, Peter, 119; Robert, 119;
William, 139.

Dennison, Mrs., 123; William, 111.

Derventio, 3.

Derwent, the, 3, 26, 45, 81, 164, 300, 305; Farm, 308; Hounds, 126.

Derwentwater, Earl of, 283.

Desmond, Mr W, 342.

Despencer, Alice, 247; Roger, 247.

Devastation of William the Conqueror, 5, 6, 196.

Deyncourt, Sir Edmund, 202.

Dickinson, Henry, 217.

Dictionary of English History, 152, 205; of National Biography, 23, 45, 105-6, 133-4, 165-6, 173-4, 201, 203-4, 206-8, 211, 214-5, 230, 274-5, 277-9.

Dimans or Dinham Land, 110, 148.

Ditchfield, The Old Time Parson, 113.

Dixon, family of, 108, 122; Elizabeth, 108; George, 122; Jacob, 108; James (c. 1658), 171; James (c. 1675), 78; James (c. 1692), 108, 114, 216; John (c. 1780), 81; John (c. 1800), 107, 180; Margaret, 108, 220; Matthew, 108; Robert, 108-9, 176, 220; Stephen (d. 1768), 122; Stephen (d. 18181, 86, 110, 178; Thomas, 111, 122; William, 122.

Dobson (?) (c. 1717), 109; Jonah, 118; John, 87.

Docking, Norfolk, 140.

Documents in the possession (a) of the Dean and Canons of St. Georges Chapel, Windsor, 215, 252-9; (b) of the Rev. Arthur Hill, 52, 90, 272, 290; (c) of George Francis Gordon Hill Esq., 9, 13, 40, 56, 78-9, 81, 87, 96, 98-105, 108-10, 114-6, 118, 121, 126, 128, 131, 135-6, 189, 200, 214-5, 217-20, 224-5, 234-5, 239, 241-2, 254, 256-8, 269, 271, 274, 281-3, 285, 288-90, 293, 295-6; (d) of James Loy Whitehead, Esq., 85, 87, 91, 104-5, 115-6, 119, 121-3, 128, 135, 137-40, 220, 259, 265, 272, 278, 281, 288, 294-5.

Dodmer or Dodemore, Henry, 46;

Ralph, 46; William, 46.

Dodsworth MS., 198.

Dog Kennel Lane, 92, 118, 126, 261.

Dolphin of Allerston, 247.

Domesday Book, 5, 6, 24, 196-7, 227, 229, 236, 244, 260, 284, 298.

Doncaster, 211, 280.

Dor Croft or Dorcroft, or Dawcroft, 8, 79.

Dorset, Henry, Marquis of, 214-5.

Double Wall, the, 84.

Donne, Rev. Thomas, 265-6.

Dow, Bennet, 96; John, 188.

Doyle, Peerage and Baronage of England, 158.

Drayton, Polyolbion, 4, 275.

Drokenesford, Sir John, 202.

Dryden, John, 1.

Ducatus Lancastriae, 253, 271, 290-1.

Dudda, or Duddey, or Duddy, or Dodo Hill, 100, 107, 110, 217.

Dugdale, Baronage, 248; Monasticon, 28, 150, 245, 298-9, 304.

Duncombe, Charles, 136, 140.

Dunhill or Dunkhill, 281.

Dunn, Robert, 80.

Dunsley, Manor of, 102.

Durham, Archdeacon of, 31; Bishop of, 30; City of, 44; Dean of, 173; jurisdiction of, 32; University of, 193, 314.

Durrard, Rev. A. J., 193.

Dutton, John, 291; Katherine, 291; Richard, 65, 291-2; Thomas, 288, 291; Mrs., 288.

Dynham, or Dynam, or Dinham, or Denham, Anthony (c. 1675), 78; Anthony (c. 1712), 78, 84; Henry, 78; Robert (c. 1600), 188; Robert .(c. 1627), 78; Stephen, 78; Thomas .(c. 1641), 78; Thomas (c. 1675), 78;Thomas (c. 1707), 78, 84.

Ealdred, 236.

Eaman, or Eman, Elizabeth, 256; John, 109; Thomas, 176; Timothy, 256.

Easington, 177.

East Carr, 242.

East Field, 9, 100, 223; Allotment, 151.

Easthallgarth, or Esthallegarth, or Esthalgarth, 250-1, 254-6.

Eastmead, Historia Rievallensis, 73, 88, 91, 95, 131, 135-7, 176, 192, 211, 214, 237, 283.

Eastnewton, 174.

Easton, Mrs, 342.

East and North Ridings, Account of, 88, 111, 116, 119-24, 139, 192.

East Peckham, 274.

Ebberston, 2, 113, 118, 130, 185, 230, 286; Norman of, 299.

Ecclefield, or Eglefield, or Eglesfield or Aglefield, or Eggleford, or Hekylfield, family of, 98, 100-2, 258; Ann, 100; Brian, 100-1; Diana, 101; Elizabeth, 156; Eustace, 229; Francis, 100; Jane, 101; Joan, 156; John (c. 1440), 229; John (c. 1612), 100; John (c. 1855), 122; Miriam, 101; Peter,101; Richard (c. 1440), 100, 156, 229; Richard (c. 1595), 188; Richard (c. 1681), 101; Robert (c. 1440), 229; Robert (c. 1660),78-9, 101, 118; Robert (c. 1697), 101; Robert (c. 1790), 101; Robert (c. 1818), 121; Robert (c. 1844),101; Thomas, 100; widow, 101, 109; William (c. 1605), 54, 100-1; William (c. 1660), 101; William (c. 1678), 78-9; William Old Willie, 101-2, 122.

Ecclesfield or Eglesfield lands, 239.

Ecclesiastical Commissioners, 308; Courts, 71.

Ecgfrida, daughter of Aldun, 227.

Eclipse, the race horse, 222.

Edbriston, Thomas de, 200, 263.

Edgecote, battle of, 210.

Edgehill, battle of, 72, 277.

Edlingthorp, Henry de, 199.

Edmondson, Joseph, 106.

Edues marsh, 299-300.

Edward, I., 7, 43, 162, 199, 201-3, 211, 228-9, 246; II., 7, 16, 37, 39, 42-3, 116, 145, 202, 204; III., 44, 205, 303;

IV., 164, 250; V., 250; VI., 167;

Black Prince, 207; the Confessor, 6.

Egerton, Sir Richard, 213.

Ekkedale or Heckdale, 17, 296.

Eldred of Ellerburn, 22; John, 99.

Elgee, Frank, The Times, 1; Early Man in North-East Yorkshire, 3; Moorlands of North-East Yorkshire, 2, 26, 297.

Elizabeth, Queen, 54-5, 65, 90, 269-71, 279, 289.

Ellars or Ellers, 257.

Ellerbeck, 4, 244.

Ellerburn, or Ellerburne, or Elborne, or Elleborne, or Ellesbourne, or Elreburn, or Elreburne, 6, 23, 49, 59, 60-2, 78, 104, 110-1, 121, 136, 154, 170-1, 174-5, 177, 231, 241, 244, 250-3, 257, 288, 290; affray at, 62; Banks, 2; bleaching in, 83, 109, 113, 113-6; bubonic plague in, 67-9, 189; cattle plague in, 88; Church in, Ch. X. passim, 4, 26, 49, 83, 95, 102, 120, 160, 168; Church Registers in, 88, 95, 109, 115, 119, 133, 178, 189-93, 234; Church-yard in, 116; corn mill in, 112-3; Enclosure (1795), 82-3; le Bothone Close, in, 62; linen weavers in, 114; Ode to, 192; Old Vicarage of, 193; paper-making at, 115-7; population of, 89; priests house, in, 8; riotous conduct at, 49; Road to, 7, 92; smallpox in, 89; Vicar of, 82, 286; vicarage of, 93, 96; Warren, 110, 296; Wood, 2, 10, 26, 91, 125.

Ellerburn-cum-Farmanby, 11, 15, 43, 102; manor of, 5, 7, Ch. XIV, passim; Quakers in, 190; Tithes in, 183.

Ellicar or Elliker, the, 82, 151.

Elliott or Elliot, Frederick, 193; George, 112, 193; James, 110-1, 180; John, 110-1, 180, 193, 322; Mrs. John, 112.

Elliotts Banks, 110.

Ellis, James, 106; Mary, 106.

Elrington, Edward, 62.

Elwin, Margaret, 342.

Ely, 177.
Emma, daughter of John le Prevost, 42.
Empingham, lord of, 155.
Empson, Sir Richard, 211, 268.
Enclosure Act (1780), 9, 11, 79, 80, 96,
   110; (1795), 11, 80-83.
Enclosure Award (1678), 189; (1781),
   86, 105, 151, 223; (1796), 85, 137,
   213.
Engagement, The, 72.
Essex, Earl of, 197.
Eshton or Eston, Henry de, 200-1;
   James, 200; John (senior), 17, 18, 198-
   204; John (junior), 200; Juliana, 200;
   Richard, 200; William, 200.
Estovers, 10, 21.
Estwick, Stephen, 255.
Etherington, Richard, 171.
Eton College, 223.
Eu, Count of, 248.
Evers, Mr James, 346.
Eyre, John, 288-9.
Eustace, son of John, 299.
Everingham, Robert (d. 1246), 284;
   Robert (c. 1313), 284.
Everley, Alan de, 229; John de, 26, 27,
   162-3; Margaret, 261; Robert, 155,
   160; William, 14, 20, 28, 155, 199,
   202, 261.
Evers, or Eure, or Eyre, Sir Ralph, 50-
   1, 304-5; William, 20, 156.
Evers, George, 119.
Exchequer, Court of, 78; Depositions,
   172.
Excise Bill (1733), 76.
Exeter, 166; first Earl of, 212; Synod
   of, 165.
Eyre of the Forest, 14-22, 53, 285-6.

Fairfax, family of, 98, 102-3; Anne,
   103; Catherine, 102; Mrs. Catherine
   (c. 1693), 103; Cuthbert, 102;
   Dorothy, 102, Elizabeth, 102; George,
   102; Hungate, 102; Isaac, 78-9, 102;
   Jane, 102; Katherine, 102; Lord, 277;
   Lucretia, 103; Melior, 102, 241; Sir
   Nicholas, 102; Nicholas, junior, 102;

Sir Thomas, 71, 241, 277; Thomas,
   293; Thomas, junior, 102; Thomas, of
   Sand Hutton, 102.
Fairwether, John, 187.
'False Zeal and Christian Zeal
   distinguished'-A Sermon, 76.
Fanacourt, Bartholomew de, 204.
Far Field, 9, 148.
Farman or Farmann, 245.
Farmanby, or Farmanbye, or
   Farmondby, or Farmhambie, or
   Farmhamby, or Farnhamby, or
   Farnhanbye, or Farmeby, or
   Farmarneby, or Fermanby, or
   Formondeby, or Formanbye, or
   Formandby, or Faremanby, 9, 13. 15,
   18-22, 28, 42-46, 51, 53, 57-62, 65-6,
   71, 96, 100-1, 104, 108, 110, 119-20,
   154, 159, 184, 187, 231, 244, 246,
   249, 251-4, 261, 271-3, 282, 289, 293,
   299; cattle plague in, 88; corn-mill in,
   239; Cunnyngyerthe in, 51; enclosure
   award (1678), 51, 102; (1795-6), 78-
   83; four men of, 85; freeholders in, 77,
   101; gloving in, 59; linen weaving in,
   58; Manor of, 157, 215, 218; and vide
   Ellerburn-cum-Farmanby; 58.
   manorial courts of, 84-6; pinfold in,
   58, 86; tithes in, 149-50, 224; three
   fields in, 79; weaving in, 114.
Farmanby, Elias of, 246.
Farmanby Gate, 58; Ings, 100.
Farrer, Victoria County History,
   Lancaster, 6.
Farside, Thomas, 242.
Fawcet, Christopher, 171.
Fawcus, Lower, Middle and Upper, 79.
'Feet of Fines,' 215.
Ferrers, Sir Robert, 209.
Feversham, Lord, 91, 139-40.
'Final Concord,' 261.
Fine Roll, 56. Hen. III, 228.
Firmstone, Rev. Edward, 139-40, 192;
   William, 192.
Fir Tree Farm, 112, 308.
Fitton, Francis, 212.
FitzAlan, Elizabeth, 207; Richard, 207.

FitzDuncan, William, 197.
FitzLevock, William, 299.
FitzNeal, Dialogus de Scaccario, 18.
FitzWalter, Robert, 203.
FitzWilliam, Earl, 77; Ralph, 249.
Flainsey or Flansey Warren, 2, 110,
  293, 296.
Flamborough, 104, 269.
Flammarville, Agnes de, 228.
Flamville, Robert de, 248.
Flanders, 201.
Flattends, 148.
Flaxdale, 17, 39-40, 213, 293; End,
  293; End Closes, 293.
Fleta (Selden edition), 8, 13, 200.
Fletcher, A Book about Yorkshire, 278.
Fletcher, Bob, 340.
Flodden, battle of, 211, 269.
Flooding, 327, 334, 341.
Folkton, 216.
Folkyngton, Adam de, 42.
Foord, Miss, 122.
Forbye, John, 157.
Fordham, 'Studies in Carlo-
  Bibliography,' 274.
Forester in fee, 262-3.
Forestry Commission, 293, 297.
Forster, Robert, 176; Thomas, 176.
Forty-Five Rebellion, the, 75-6.
Forz, William de, 197, 200; children of,
  198.
Foster, Alumni, 176, 178, 191-3;
  Pedigrees of Yorkshire, 100, 102, 145,
  269, 272; Visitations of Yorkshire,
  100, 229.
Foster, Barbara, 87.
Fothergill, family of, 281; Thomas,
  281.
Foturer, John de, 20.
Foulbridge, 33, 35, 37, 286.
Foulis, Mark, 139; Rev. J.R.,
  136.
Foulworth, 293.
Fountains Abbey, 230.
Fowle, History of the Poor
  Law, 58.
Fowler, Coulson, 144, 180;

Hodgson, 144; Mrs., 144.
Fowler, Episcopal Registers of
  England and Wales, 165,
  185.
Fox, Charles James, 222.
Fox Farm, 223.
Fox, George, Journal, 67.
Fox and Hounds, the, 124.
Fox-Strangeways, Jurassic Rocks
  of Yorkshire, 296.
Frank, John, 113; Thomas, 111.
Franks Farm, 308.
Franke, Robert, 273.
Fraser, J. Horace, 105-7, 144.
Freehold Oxgang, 223.
Freeman, Professor Edward, 236;
  The Norman Conquest, 5, 236.
Freke, Robert, 212.
French wifes house, 95.
Friars Ditch, 300, 302.
Friends, Provident Institution, 106;
  Society of, 67.
Frith, Thomas, 255.
Fromonds, Bartholomew, 282;
  Mary, 282.
Fronstead, 219.
Frowyk, Thomas, 251.
'Fryer Dyke,' 213-4.

Gamble, family of, 108; Ann, 111;
  Benjamin, 111; Elizabeth, 66;
  George, 111; John, 111; Marie, 108;
  Robert, 66, 114.
Gamel of Roxby, 260.
Gand, Alice de, 237; Walter de, 237.
Ganstead, 92, 220.
Ganton, 179, 193, 217, 274.
Gaolya, Peter de, 246.
Garbutt, Alfred, 97, 123, 322, 334;
  Mrs. F. A., 96, 184; Herbert, 97, 145;
  James, 89; John, 350; Noel, 334;
  Robert, 123; Wilfred, 97, 123, 338,
  350; William, 123.
Gargrave, Sir Richard, 279-80.
Garnett, Rev. John, 133, 158, 175;
  Ronald, 324.
'Garsell,' use of, 297.

365

Greteheved, Robert, 45-6.
Grey, John, 124; John (c. 1613), 99; Nicholas, 132; Nicholas of Sinnington, 132.
Grey Friars, London, 251.
Grey Stone, or great, 148, 217 .
Greystoke, baron of, 249.
Grimes, Matthew, 107, 147.
Grindstonewath, 211.
Gristhorp, 299.
Grundon House, High, 79, 111; Low, 111.
Grundy, Dr. G. B., 80.
Gryme, Jane, 187.
Grymnesby, Simon, 205.
Guffick, John, 122; Richard, 117.
Guisborough, 277; Priory, 208; Chartulary of, 228-9, 238.
Guiseley, 168.

Hacker, John, 158.
Hackness, 4, 275, 289, 294; Gate, 294.
Hackney, 212.
Hagget, John, 186.
Hagg House, 94, 109-12, 233.
'Haia,' 20.
Haincliff, Beck, 15.
Haldane, Nicholas, 44.
Halidon Hill, battle of, 44.
Halifax, 106.
Hall, John, 81; Philip Abbey, 112, 308; Robert 124; William 116.
Hall Farm, 112.
The Hall, 350.
Hallden, a stubborn fellow, 276.
Halliburton, Frances, 256-7.
Halscarth, John, 238.
Hampole, 38.
'Hanaper' the Kings, 208.
Haram, near Helmsley, 172.
Harcourt, Miss, 281.
Harden, Thomas of, 154.
Hardforthlithe, 42.
Harding, John (d. 1794), 184; 238. Richard (c. 1756), 114, 295; Robert (c. 1655), 189; Rev. Samuel (senior), 191; Rev. Samuel (junior), 191;

William (c. 1777), 308.
Hardinge, Richard (1), 255; Richard (2), 255; Robert, 256.
Hardwick, or Hardwicke, Lord, 73; C., 139; John, 87; Thomas, 122.
Hardy, family of, 108; George, 113; Mary, 101; Simon, 112, 308; Symon (c. 1734), 88; William, 119.
Hardynge, Chronicles of, 41, 47.
Hare, Rev. J. C. F., 140.
Hareborough rigg, 293.
Hargreaves, Rev. Robert, 190.
Harland, family of, 108; Christopher, 219; John, 189; Robert (c. 1786), 178; Robert (c. 1807), 115; William (c. 1727), 176; William (c. 1734), 87; William (c. 1768), 115; William (c. 1780), 81.
Harlands closes, 296.
Harley, Earl of Oxford, 75.
Harold Hardrada, 5.
Harper, The Great North Road, 77.
Harrison, Mr., 123; William (c. 1780), 81, 178; William (c. 1816), 308.
Harrowcliff, 98, 148, 219, 234, 296; Field, 9; Lane, 92.
Hartley, Symon, 88.
Hartofft, 76.
Harton, Alice, 239; James, 239.
Harvey, George, 252.
Harwod, John, 51.
Harwood House, 40, 288.
Hassell, family of, 98, 103; Beatrice, 293-4; Catherine, 102; Isabel, 103; Jane, 295; John, 103, 233; Marv, 103, 233, 295; Philip, 103; Ralph (c. 1606), 62; Ralph (c. 1654), 103, 293-4; Samuel, 102; Thomas (c. 1606), 62; Thomas (c. 1635), 103; Thomas (c. 1705), 295; Rev. Thomas (d. 1706), 103; Thomas, of London, 293.
Hastings, family of, 6, 18, 43, 52, 145, 248; Agnes, 248; Alice, 264-5; Amice, 248; Lady Beatrice, 20, 44, 145, 249, 262, 286; Edmund (c. 1270-1300), 151, 202, 248-9, 261-2; Edmund (c. 1316), 21, 22, 204; Edmund (c. 1338),

18, 44-5, 264-5; Edmund (c. 1408), 209, 265; Edmund (c. 1460), 266; Sir Edward, Lord, 157, 250-1; Emmelina, 248; Erneburga, 248; Francis, 269; Francis, Earl of Huntingdon, 157; George, Earl of Huntingdon, 157; Helen, 247; Henry, 248, 261; Herbert (c. 1305), 15; Hugh (c. 1100-30), 247-8, 298; Hugh (c. 1300), 15, 18, 262; Hugh of Dalton, 247; Ida, 248; Joan, 265; John (c. 1200), 248; John (c. 1400), 266; Rev. John, 167; Sir Leonard, 250; Maud, 248; Nicholas (c. 1247), 261; Nicholas (c. 1290), 16, 18, 246-8, 261-2; Nicholas (c. 1318), 247; Nicholas (c. 1373), 205, 248, 265; Sir Ralph (1), 20-1, 44, 62, 247, 249, 262, 265; Sir Ralph (2), 21, 45-6, 249; Richard, 248-9; Robert, 248; Sir Roger, 48-51, 124, 185, 266-7, 270; Lady Roger, 49-50, 266; Thomas, 248; Walter, 248; William, first Lord, 156, 250, 266; William, son of Lady Beatrice, 20-1, 44, 248-9, 286; William (c. 1392), 205, 249.

Hastings, 'portreeve' of, 248.

Hatfield, 269.

Haughdale, 262.

Haverbergh, 162.

Hawdale, 213.

Hawise, wife of William de Forz, 197-8.

Hawkendale or Hirkendale, or Orchandale, 213.

Hawley, Major, F. H. J., 146.

Hawsome, Elizabeth, 109; William, 123.

Hawson, William (c. 1745), 176; William (c. 1807), 110.

Hawyke, Margaret, 155; Walter, 155.

Haxby, 178.

Hayes, Mrs, 336.

Hayes, Ted, 338, Marcia, 338.

Hayes, Thomas, 136.

Haygate, 292; Ing, 293.

Hayley, Mrs., 123. Head, Sir Thomas, 223.

Hebton Ursula, 65.

Heckdale, 17, 296.

Hedon, 258, 261, 273; Peter de, 260-1.

Helmsley, 57-60, 172, 174-5, 233; Robert de, 45.

Hemingburgh, 201, 266.

Henderson, History of Merton College, 166.

Henrietta Maria, Queen, 277, 295.

Henry I., 41, 163, 251; II., 24, 112, 298-9; III., 107, 160, 237, 248, 263; IV., 47; VII., 166, 211, 266-8, 270, 288; VIII., 166, 269, 305.

Henry, son of Geoffrey, 245.

Herbert, Captain S., 130.

Hereford, Earl of, 201.

Herle, Margaret de, 249; Sir William de, 249.

Hermit Close, 40, 287-8.

Heron, Sir Walter, 248.

Herry Dy, 93, 242.

Herryson, Robert, 304.

Hert, Alan, 246, 263; John, 285, 303; Robert, 303; Thomas, 246; William, 204.

Hervy, John, 209.

Heselerton, Sir John de, 202.

Heslop, Rev. Edward William, 97, 102, 130, 143-6, 178-9, 193, 316; Rev. John, 178; Lucy, 146, 316; Margaret Lucy, 48, 76, 179, 219, 316; Mary Katherine Jane, 130, 179, 316; Rev. William, 139.

Hesslewood, Richard, 119.

Hewet, John, 99.

Hick, Thomas, 85.

Hicke, Elizabeth, 63.

Highfield, E. G., 141

Highfield close, 224.

Highfields, 9, 79, 83, 108, 111, 216-7, 223, 257.

High Ings, 296.

Moor, 295

High Nursery, 92.

High Riggs, 79; Lane, 79.

High Street, 92, 126.

Higham Ferrers, 220.

Highgate Ings, 296.

Highway Acts, 56-8.

Hildebrand (Gregory VII), 159.

Hildesley, Francis, 252; Mark, 255.

Hildyard, Sir Piers, 273.

Hill, A, butcher, 334.

Hill, family of, 77, 98,109-12, 137,159, 177, 229, 257-9; since 1761, App. B, 314-8; Alan Richard (afterwards Hill-Walker), 315; Anne (b. 1677), 218; Anne (d. 1815), 146, 225, 314; Rev. Arthur, 76, 91, 94, 101, 113, 126, 144, 191, 226, 283, 316, 323 (vide Documents); Catherine (b. 1704), 218; Catherine (Miss Kitty and 'Mrs. Catherine'), 81, 121, 177, 221; General Cecil, 315; Edward, 143, 316; Elizabeth (b. 1687), 218; Elizabeth (dau. of William), 221; Elizabeth (wife of John II), 218; Elizabeth (wife of Richard Johnson Hill), 146, 191, 224; Elizabeth (wife of C. Webb), 178; Evereld Ellen, 184; 225-6, 317; 334; Evereld Monica, 226; 317; Fanny M., 113; Francis (farmer, 1890), 111, 180; George Francis Gordon, 78, 85, 180, 226, 317, 327, 329, 334, 340 (vide Documents); Gerard R., 82, 315; Gertrude Mary, 79, 99, 107, 113, 167, 226, 242, Harriet (d. 1915), 109, 316; Harriet (d. 1899), 146, 225; Harry (butcher, c. 1880), 122; Henry ('Mr. Harry'), 113, 140, 315; Henry (farmer, 1930), 112; James (b. 1695), 218; Rev. James, 140, 215, 314; Jane (d. 1915), 91, 109, 113, 316; Jane (d. 1890), 113, 146, 225, 259, 314; John I., 78-9, 100-1, 108, 132, 147, 215, 217, 234, 241-2, 255-7, 300; John II., 75-6, 98, 105, 126, 128, 132, 215, 217-9, 234, 242-3; Mrs. John II., 118, 120; John III., 75-6, 87, 91, 105,108,124, 158-9, 176, 215, 218-21, 295-6; John IV., 146, 148; Captain John, 177, 221-2, 258; John (b. 1681), 218; John (b. 1788), 224; John (b.1821), 127, 138, 314; John (a poor child), 116; John Johnson, 222, 258; Rev. John Richard, 94-7, 105, 113, 115, 125-6, 140, 143, 145-6, 151, 178-9, 183, 222, 225, 259, 264, 314, 316; Rev. John Samuel, 76, 88, 121, 176-7, 190-1, 221-2; Lionel, Capt, 329; Lionel George, 146, 315; Lucy, 109, 146, 179, 316; Martha (d. 1725), 221; Mary (d. 1896), 109, 316; Monica, 226, 317; Rebecca, 217; Rev. Reginald, 215, 314; Richard (b. 1694), 176-7, 218-9, 221; Richard (b. 1786), 82-3, 90-1, 101, 113, 119, 124-6, 138-9, 145-7, 178, 225-6, 258, 283, 314, 316; Richard (b. 1843), 184, 223, 225-6, 316-7; Richard (b. 1877), 86, 180, 226, 317-8, 340; Richard Johnson, 81, 98-9, 121, 126, 136, 146, 150-1, 191, 222-4, 235, 314; Richard Luke, 225, 314; Captain Robert (of Jamaica), 221; Robert (a boy), 217; Robert (farmer, 1930), 112; Robin, 127, 314; Sarah (wife of John I), 215; Sarah (d. 1682), 218; Sarah (d. 1723), 221; Sarah (d. 1757), 218; Thomas (c. 1620), 215, 254-5; Thomas (b. 1822), 138, 315; William (of Antigua), 177-8, 218-9, 221.

Hill, Dykes, 242.

Hill, Geoff, 346.

Hill, Irene, 342.

Hill-before-the-Door, 294.

Hilltop, in the parish of Wragby, 215, 254.

Hilton, Sir Robert, 46.

Hind, Ann, 88.

Hinderwell, History of Scarborough, 72.

Hindslackside Wood, 17, 18, 33.

Hipperley, 18.

Hird, Melior, 102, 241.

Hirst (? 1930), 112.

Historical MSS. Corn. Rawden Hastings MS., 21, 46, 88, 155-7, 204, 236, 246-9, 251, 261, 265-6.

Hobson, Roger, 188.

Hoby, Sir Edward, 279; Lady Margaret,

369

56; Sir Thomas Posthumous, 56, 275.

Hodgson, Anne, 65; Francis, 282;
Henry, 178, 180; John (c. 1765), 116,
177; John (c. 1818), 121; (c. 1793),
86; William (c. 1814), 111; William
(c. 1827), 115.

Hodgson, Miss G. E., The Sanity of
Mysticism, Ch. III, passim.

Hodshon, Ralph, 272.

Hoggard, or Hoggarth, family of, 108,
295; Ann, 88; Jane, 88; Mary 87, 110.

Hokelbardi, (Ugglebarnby), William
de, 28.

Holbeck Terrace, 96.

Holder, William, 307.

Holderness, first Earl of, 217; Lord of,
197.

Holdsworth, History of EnglishLaw,
64.

Holford, or Holforde, Barbara, 52;
Eleonora, 157, 281; George, 52;
Stephen, 52, 157, 231, 252.

Holgreaves, W., 113.

Hone Maydens Grave, 214.

Hollenheade, 63.

Hollinbourne, 177.

Hollis, Anne, 241; Maccabeus, 241,
255-6; Robert, 241, 255-6.

Hollow Closes, 294.

Holin, John de, 19.

Holmes, Robert, 122; William, 116.

Home, 'Evolution of an English Town,'
1, 41, 88, 95, 177, 190-1.

Hone, Manor and Manorial Records,
196, 199.

Honey Pot, 242.

Hopkins, Rebecca, 106.

Hopper, J. C., 124.

Horcum, Hole of, 295.

Horn, Thomas, 255.

Hornby, 279.

Horner, Philip, (Pop), 338.

Hornsey, James, 107.

Horrel, West, 148; vide Hurrell.

Horsley, family of, 98, 104, 258;
Andrew, 114; Christopher, 104, 187;
Francis, 59, 104, 187; Frank, 104;

Grace, 104; Helen, 104; Mr., 279;
Richard, 104, 109; Robert, 104, 114;
Roger, 59, 104, 188; Thomas, 104,
110; William, 187, 254.

Horstmann, 'Yorkshire Writers,
Richard Rolle of Hampole', 23, 27,
30, 37.

Horton, John, 78.

Hospital for Lame Soldiers, 233.

Hotham, Sir Charles, 183; Sir John,
276.

Hoton Baldolf, 261.

Houldsworth, John, 119.

Hovingham, 237.

Howard, Elizabeth, 295.

Howe Bridge, 299.

Howes, or tumuli, 2, 21.

Howldale, 2, 13, 18, 20, 79, 213, 249,
253.

Huddam, Rev. Roland, 165.

Hudleston, John, 157.

Hudson, George, 61; Richard, 61;
William, 61.

Hugall, Thomas, 193; Rev. William H.,
193. Huggate, 168.

Hugh, at the Gate of Pickering, 263; the
miller, 113; the smith, 117; son of
Walthevy, 299; the vicar, 162.

Hull, 193-4, 239, 241, 255, 258, 268.

Humphreys, William, 123.

Hundegate, 261.

Hungate, Jane, 102; Ralph, 102.

Hungerill gutter, 98.

Hungill, 302.

Hungrel Way, or Hungrellway, 92, 148.

Hunmanby, 223.

Hunt, Rev. Ralph, 186-7.

Hunter, family of, 74, 158, 231; Agnes
(c. 1494), 232; Ann (b. 1640), 233;
Anne, 234; Anthony (c. 1546), 52-3,
232; Anthony (c. 1634), 66; Anthony
(c. 1655), 307; Anthony (c. 1690),
219, 232, 422; Barbara, 307; Bethel,
103, 233-4; Catherine (b. 1705), 235;
Cecilia, 232; Christopher (c. 1546), 52;
Christopher (d. 1603), 232;
Christopher (b. 1646), 216-7, 233-4,

370

242;Danby (b. 1717), 235; Dorithe, 232; Dorothy (b. 1708), 235; Dorothy (d. 1718), 234; Elizabeth (c. 1734), 109; Mrs. Elizabeth, 235;Frances, 307; Helen (b. 1601), 233; Helen (Robinson), 233, 240; Helen (2), 234; Helen, 103; Rev. Henry, 133; Hildah, 65; `Kateran, 232; Katharine, 234; Magdalen, 233-4; Mrs. Maggy, 133, 175; Mary, 103, 233, 241; Robert (d. 1407), 232; Robert (c. 1494), 231-2; Robert (c. 1523), 304; Robert (c. 1534), 232, 305; Robert (c. 1544), 232; Robert (b. 1546), 232; Robert (c. 1570), 232; Robert (c. 1605), 54, 58, 60; Robert, junior, (c. 1616) 60; Robert (b. 1618), 72-3, 78, 170-1, 234; Robert (d., c. 1620), 232-3, 241, 291; Robert (d. 1653), 233; Robert (b. 1674), 234; Robert (c. 1711), 83; Robert (b. 1713), 234;Robert, of Wilton, 78; Robert, father of Helen, 240; Rev. Robert, 135-6; Roger (c. 1540), 52, 232; Roger (c. 1564), 53; Roger (d. 1583), 231-2; Roger (d. 1659), 58, 147.

Hunter, South Yorkshire, 280.

Hunters Lane, 242, 322.

Huntingdon, Earls of, 157; Francis, 231; Katherine, Countess of, 231; (vide Hastings).

Hunsdon, Baron, 279.

Hurrell, or Hurrill, or Horrell, 98, 242; Close, 105; flatt, 234; High, Low, and Middle, 296; Lane, 9, 61, 92, 148-9; West, 148.

Husband, Mrs. Elizabeth, 88.

Hustlar, John, 121; Thomas, 115.

Hustler, Catherine, 218; Elizabeth, 218; Rev. George, 225; James, 218; Sir William, 126, 132, 215.

Hutchinson, Christopher, 61; Edward, 132; Thomas, 78.

Hutton, John de, 16.

Hutton Bushel, 60-1, 68, 223, 233.

Huttons Ambo, 68.

Hyde, Rev. George A., 141; Rev.

Robert, 140-1, 179.

Ice Age, 1.

Ilkley, 182.

Impeachment, first case of, 207.

Imprisonment in the middle ages, 14.

Incendium Amoris, of Richard Rolle, 31.

Incrofts, 110.

Industrial Revolution, 84, 115, 117.

Ing Closes, 86.

Ing next the Low Ing, 294.

Ingdales, 79.

Ingle, Mr, 336.

Ingles Café, 96.

Ings, the, 100.

Inquest ad quod damnum, 206.

Inquest post mortem, Ed. II, 264; Ric. II, 206 (vide Calendar).

Insula, Adam de, 154, 160, 184; Roger de, 184; Sir Warin de, 202.

Ipswich, 213.

Irvin, Rev. Thomas, 138-9, 178, 192; Thomas, of Hackness, 138.

Itinerant Justices, 14-22.

Itory, William, 19.

Ive or Ives, Christopher, 168, 239, 306; Jane, 168; William, 168, 239, 241, 293.

Ivers vide Evers. Iveson, James, 56-7.

Jackson, Collingwood, 306; Edward, 110; Henry (c. 1724), 121; Rev. Henry, 187; John (c. 1770), 116; John (c. 1818), 121; Laurance, 296; Lucretia, 103; Richard (c. 1675), 78; Richard (c. 1727), 120; William (c. 1734), 122.

Jacob, Law Dictionary, 51.

Jakes, Thomas, 251.

Jamaica, 222.

James I., 53, 55-6, 59, 65, 99, 118, 254, 273, 275, 280; II., 216.

Jeffery, Elizabeth, 116; Honor, Intro., 324.

Jelly, Mrs., 144.

Jenks, Edward Plantagenet, 201.

Knights Hospitaller, 286; Templar, 246, 286.

Knyfton, Nicholas, 267.

Kylvyngton, John de, 37.

Kyng, Emmott, 188.

Kyploftsike, 299, 300.

Kyrkhous, le, 156.

Labron, Matthew, 96, 178.

Laistor, Roger de, 245.

Lamberhurst, Kent, 234.

Lambert, family of, 238; Grace, 238; John, 111; Matilda, 238; Nicholas, 238; Robert, 238; Roger, 238.

Lambert Lands, 239.

Lame Soldiers, Treasurer of, 71.

Lancaster, Duchy of, 13, 40, 50, 86, 93, 218, 263-4, 266, 278-9, 296; Blanche, Duchess of, 44; Henry, first Duke of, 44; John, Duke of, 44, 207, 209; Edmund, Earl of, 32, 195, 263, 284; Henry, Earl of, 44, 206, 286; Thomas, Earl of, 16-9, 36, 43-4, 162, 201, 204, 246, 300; House of, 43, 47.

Lanfranc, Archbishop, 159.

Langathoudale or Langatdale, 13; Wood, 20-1; vide Howldale.

Langdale, Yorkshire, 134.

Langdale, 16.

Langdon, 288-9, 291.

Langham, Simon, 144.

Langlands, 148.

Langley, Thomas, 132.

Langwith, James, 177; Rev. Oswald, 88, 147-8, 176-7, 191.

Landon Sandy Banks, 110.

Lant, Bartholomew, 307; Helen, 307.

Larban flat or flatt, 110, 242.

Lark flatt close, 110.

Lassells, Mary, 295; Mr., 77; William, 237.

Lastingham, 4, 72.

Latimer, family of, 202, 209; Elizabeth, 208, 211; John, sixth baron of first creation, 210; Thomas, 205; Thomas, of Warden, 205; Warin, 205; William, first baron, 16-20, 37, 47; William,

second baron, 17, 45-6, 202-5, 285; William, third baron, 206; William fourth baron, 207-8; William the Sheriff, 202.

Latymer, family of, 74; Anne wife of Richard, 211; first Baron of new creation, 209-10; second Baron, 210-1; third Baron, 55, 73, 211; fourth Baron, 211, 224, 279; Sir Thomas, 202; barony in abeyance, 212.

Laweys, William, 42.

Laming of dogs, 302.

Latham, H Paul, 334.

Lawson, Rev. Francis, 188.

Lay Subsidy Rolls, 14, 19, 22, 28-31, 232, 301.

Laybron, or Leybron, Rev. William, 165.

Laye, Captain, 113; Francis, 191; Rev. H. T., 191, 222; Nancy, 222.

Leaf, John, 114; William, 122.

Ledet, Alice, 202; Walter, 202.

Lee, William, 63.

Legard, Grace, 217; Sir John, 217, 273; Ralph, 273; Susan, 273.

Legh, Dr., 298.

Leicester, 106.

Leighton Buzzard, 166, 252.

Leberston, 230.

Leland, 270.

Le Neve, 164.

Leng, John, Bishop of Norwich, 133-4.

Lesley, Robert, 140.

Letters and Papers of Henry VIII, 269, 305.

Levisham, 130, 198, 200-1; wood, 287.

Lewes, Michael, 212.

Lewis, Topographical Dictionary, 90.

Lewiss Plantation, 92-3. Lexinton, Robert of, 154. Leyburn, 225; William de, 203.

Liedtorp, 236.

Linfoot, John, 123.

Lister, Edward, 61; Roger, 61.

Lith, Geoffrey de, 286.

Littiegate or Lidygate Way, or Lydegate, 13, 292.

'little holgate', 241.
Lloyd-George, David, 334.
Local Government order (1866), 89.
Lockton, 19, 70, 130, 137, 200.
Lockwood, John, 259.
Lodge, The, 96, 242.
Lodge, Axor, 188; Thomas, 59.
Lodge, History of England
  (Longmans), 256.
Lofthouse, Walter, 46.
Loftmarais, or Loftmaresse, or
  Loftmarreys, 299, 301, 304.
Loketon, Ralph de, 246.
London, 215, 230, 276; bubonic plague
  in, 68; Great Fire of, 152; Lord Mayor
  of, 46; prices (1633) in, 87.
Long, Jane, 115; William, 115-6.
Longburne, John, 191.
Longe, Katherine, 59.
Longlands Close, 296; Lands, 293.
Lord Hardwickes Marriage Act, 221.
Lords Ordainers, 204.
Lound-in-the-Wolds, 230.
Louthe, 46.
Lovel, Ralph, 299.
Lovell, John, 209.
Low Dalby, 334.
Low Fausa, 241.
Low Field, 79.
Low Hall, 7, 8, 109.
Low Hall Garth, 2.
Low Ing, 293.
Low Ings, 296.
Low Mill Garth, 1, 2.
Low Spring Hagg, 292.
Low Warren, 196.
Lowehagge or Low Wood, 292.
Lowndyke, 302.
Lowther, Sir Richard, 71.
Loy, Dr. Martin, 130.
Lumbard, William, 121.
Lumley, Castle, 214; Charity, 81, 104-
  5, 115-6, 121 2, 128, 131, 137;
  Charity in London, 131; family of,
  229; Grammar School, Ch. VIII,
  passim; Lady Elizabeth, 73-4, 131-2;
  Henry, 73; John, fifth Baron, 211,
214; John, 214; Viscount, 73, 131-2,
  214, 279-93.
Lund Forest, 300-4.
Lunn, Isabel, 88.
Luther, or Luchre, or Louther, Hugh de,
  199, 201.
Lyghton, John, 272.
Lyndwood the Canonist, 142.
Lyne, Audrey, 230.
Lythe, John de, 202; Robert, 110.
Lyttleton, Tenures, 199.
Lyverton, 208.

Macdowall, Rev. W., 193.
Mackereth, Rev. Charles, 192; Rev.
  George, 192; Rev. Mark Anthony,
  192; Rev. Michael, 136-8, 178, 192.
Mackley, John, 122.
Maitland, Constitutional History of
  England, 163, 196, 227; Domesday
  Book and Beyond, 7, 8, 9.
Malecake, or Malkake, Sir William
  (senior), 200, 263; Sir William
  (junior), 263.
Mallison, Thomas, 109; Widow, 109.
Mallisons Close, 109.
Mallory, Francis, 111.
Malmesbury, 280; William of, 6.
Malpas, Baron of, 269.
Maltby, Christopher, 238; Richard, 270.
Malton, 3, 4, 8, 57-9, 62, 68, 70, 72, 78,
  90, 128, 187, 214, 220, 229, 233, 237,
  241, 261, 277; Prior of, 45, 46, 265,
  303; Priory of, 45, 46, 198, 302;
  Richard de, 164.
Maltongate, 2, 7, 8, 33, 58, 79, 83, 86,
  91-6, 111-3, 122, 125, 151, 193, 224,
  242, 277, 304.
Mandeville, Geoffrey de, 197; William
  de, 197.
Mangevileyn, or Maungevylayn, or
  Mangevilam, Alice, 229; Joan, 155;
  Robert, 153, 228-9; Stephen, 28, 29,
  153, 299.
Mann, John, 121.
Manneser, John, 44.
Manor Farm, 111, 113, 178.

Mansergh, Alice, 264; Roger, 263-4.

Manthorpe, Roye, 342.

Manwood, Treatise of the Lawes of the Forrest, 12, 284, 302.

Map of 1729, 10, 26, 79, 83, 91-4, 105.

Marflitt, or Marflet, or Marfitt, family of, 108; James (c. 1763), 108, 177; James (c. 1780), 81; James (c. 1803), 178; John (c. 1900), 123; Robert (c. 1890), 111; Robert (c. 1930), 112; Thomas (c. 1734), 109, 176; Thomas (c. 1771), 100; Thomas (c. 1837), 108; Thomas (c. 1860), 122; William (c. 1747), 177-8.

Marishes, the, 5, 7, 19, 28-9, 72, 83, 111, 155, 170, 187, 217, 240, 371, 282, Ch. XVII, passim.

Marishes Lane, 33, 58, 77.

Marlborough, first Duke of, 75.

Marr, Herbert, 113; Thomas Norrison, 111, 322.

Marsden, Thomas, 117.

Marsh-mills for pumping, 307.

Marshall, family of, 110, 258; Agnes (c. 1460), 157; Alice (c. 1649), 71; Elizabeth, 68; Rev. Godfrey, 94, 105, 144, 147, 154-5, 161-2, 179-80, 317; Mrs. Godfrey, 147, 317; Henry, 69; John, (c. 1624), 64, 114; John (c. 1741), 101, 114; John (c. 1803), 178; Richard (c. 1649), 71; Richard (c. 1746), 110, 114, 257; Robert, 109; William (c. 1460), 155, 157; William (c. 1638), 69.

Marshall, Rural Economy of the West of England, 80, 307; Rural Economy of Yorkshire, 84.

Marston Moor, battle of, 277.

Martin, Peter, 13.

Marton, Theobald of, 299.

Mary, Queen, 53, 167, 305.

Masdales, 224.

Mason, James, 116; Miss, 122; Rev. Thomas, 146, 149, 158, 175-6.

Maslin, 285.

Matilda of Pickering, 263.

Mattie Cross', butchers, 334.

Mauley, family of, 45; Asktell, 299; Peter V, 203; Peter (c. 1366), 45.

Maunby Hall, 314.

Mauslacoate, 213.

Mautalent, John, 229; Mary, 229.

Maw, family of, 108; Harrison, 119; James, 176; John, 116; Robert (c. 1734), 109; Robert (c. 1818), 121; Roger, 171; Thomas (c. 1743), 110; Thomas (c. 1780), 81; William (c. 1655), 189; William (c. 1706), 176; William (d. 1766), 78, 118.

Mayman, John, 66.

Maynard, Fanny, 222; Harriet, 222; Josiah, 98, 136, 223-4, 258; Nancy, 191, 222.

Mayne, Sir Anthony, 132, 214; Sir John, 131, 215.

Meads, Diary of Lady Margaret Hoby, 56, 233, 275.

Meath, Archdeacon of, 166.

Meaux, Abbey of, 197; chronicle of, 197; John de, 249.

Medd, Abraham, 242.

Mediterranean Sea, 197.

Medley, English Constitutional History, 53, 57-9.

Meek, W. A., Recorder of York, 184.

Meldrum, Sir John, 278.

Melum Contemporar of Richard Rolle, 31.

Mercer, family of, 108; Charles, 122; John, 120, 123; Susannah, 123.

Mercer, Johnnie, 342.

Mercurius Aulicus, 277.

Merley, Matilda, 203; Sir Robert, 203.

Mery, John, 219.

Metcalf, James, 121; Peter, 59, 291.

Metcalfe, Book of Knights, 273.

Metham, William, 289-90.

Methodists, Primitive 324; Wesleyan, 327.

Meynell, Lord, 203; Sir John, 203; Nicholas, 203.

Mictinghaker, 247.

Middlefield, 9, 217.

Middleham Castle, 208.

Walter de, 228; William (c. 1280), 155; William of Kildale, 29, 32, 203, 226.

Perkin, Warbeck, 268.

Perrott, Andrew, 176; Martha, 176.

Pesel, Dr. H. G., 130.

Petch, Elizabeth, 69; Thomas, 176.

Peter, son of Juliana, 260.

Petit-Dutaillis, Studies Supplementary to Stubbs Constitutional History, 6, 13-4, 22, 48, 163, 262.

Petre, Lords, 83, 282-3.

Pexton Moor, 1, 2, 10, 71, 79, 151, 174, 213, 253, 274, 276, 296.

Philip II, King of Spain, 305.

Phyllyppe, James, 157; Ralph, 157.

Pickering, 1, 4-6, 20, 24-31, 33, 35, 37, 41, 46, 59, 60, 63, 89, 117, 124, 128, 135-6, 163, 189, 198, 200, 210, 218-9, 229, 230, 239, 244, 254, 263, 272, 279, 281, 302-4; attacks on property in, 44-5; castle of, 15, 30-1, 36-7, 41, 43, 47-8, 51, 72, 200, 202, 204, 206-7, 218, 249, 262, 268, 271, 279, 285, 301-3; church in, 26, 76; court-house at, 141; Forest of, 10, 12, 16-22, 43-4, 53, 107, 112, 159, 161-2, 210-1, 232, 246, 249, 262-3, 266-70, 302; Gamel of, 299; George Fox at, 67; Glacial lake of, 1; Grammar School at, 141; Haugh in, 20; Honor of, 40, 43, 50, 84, 124, 213-5, 218, 239, 261, 263, 272, 282, 288-9, 294-5, 300, 334; House of Correction in, 57; Knitting at, 57; Manor of, 284; Museum, 2, 147; Newgate of, 85; Quaker Meeting House in, 74; Spinning at, 57; three-fields in, 85; vicar of, 177, 184, 190.

Pickering Lythe, or Pickering leig, or Pickering Leth, or Pickering lieth, or Pickeringlith or Pickeringlithe or Pickerynglith, or Pikeringlight, or Pikerynglith, or Pyckeringelygge, or Pykeringlith, or Pykerynglith, or Pykeryng lithe, or Pykeryng-lythe, or Pykrynglygge, 2, 25, 45-6, 56, 63-4, 70-1, 99, 165, 198, 201, 205, 208-9,

211, 230, 247, 252-4, 265, 275.

Pickering, Bartholomew, 176; George (c. 1780), 81; George (c. 1807), 110; George (c. 1849), 111; George (d. 1927), 91, 115, 117, 125; George Edward, 123; John, 123; Sir John, 289; William, 111, 180.

Pickering, Bill (Flash), 340, 346.

Pickering, Daddie, 336.

Pickering Road, 9, 79, 84-5, 92, 94, 96, 120,122-3, 250, 271.

Pickering and Scarborough Railway, 90, 92.

Pickering and Whitby Railway, 90.

'Pickering and Thornton Mercury,' 128.

Pickles, Wilfred, 346.

Pikeringe, Thomas de, 263.

Pilgrimage of Grace, 55, 211, 305.

Pinfold, Mr, 334.

Pinkney, Robert, 109.

'Pipe Roll,' 12, 112, 197, 287.

Piper, John, 85.

Pippinhead, Reginald, 18.

Pixell, Fanny, D., 113, 315; Rev. H., 113, 179; Zoe M., 179.

Players of interludes, 61.

Plumer, or Plummer, Thomas (c. 1717), 88, 176; Thomas (junior), 176; Sir Thomas, 137.

'Plumpton Correspondence,' 269.

Poade, William, 176.

Pocklington, 132; School at, 172, 217.

Poll of the County of York, 1807, 77, 100, 104, 120, 123.

'Polling Register, 1929,' 108.

Pollock and Maitland, History of English Law, 6-8, 200, 205, 208, 227, 261.

Pontefract, 43, 47, 71, 204.

Poole, Mediaeval Reckonings of Time, 209.

Poor House, the, 94.

Poor Law, 56-8.

Popple, William, 255-6.

Population, 324, 352.

Porret, Richard, 113.

Porter, Sir Arthur, 279; John, 145.
Postgate, Christopher, 116; William, 109.
Poulson, History of Holderness, 249.
Pratt, Charles, 111, 308.
Prayer Book, Elizabethan, 55.
Preglacial Man, 1.
Prest, John, 286.
Prestebi, 5.
Preston, 282; Agnes, 59; Major, 308; William, 60, 186, 291.
Preveran, Mr., 128.
Prideaux, Directions to Church-wardens, 65.
Priestman, or Preistman, or Prest-man, or Presmande, family of, 67, 81, 98, 104-7, 137; philanthropic works of, 106-7; Alfred, 106-7; Alice (Smales), 105; Alice (1685), 105, 219; Annas, 104; Arnold, 106; David, 105; Edgar, 344; Mrs Edgar, 344; Edward, 106; Elizabeth, 105, 219; Ellyng, 104; Ethel, 105, 107; Frederick, 106; George (d. 1544), 67, 104; George (c. 1642), 104; Hannah, 105; Henry Brady, 107; George Isabell, 104; Jane, 106; John (c.1598), 104; John (c. 1641), 104; John (b. 1647), 104; John (c. 1658), 67; John (c. 1684), 105; John (c. 1700), 67, 105; John (c. 1743), 87, 105; John (c. 1777), 148; John (c. 1780), 105, 113; John (d. 1807), 105, 107; John (son of Joshua), 106; John (b. 1815), 105-6; John (c. 1867), 113; Jonathan (d. 1816), 105, 109-10; Joseph, 107; Joshua (senior), 105-7, 109, 137, 148; Joshua (junior), 105-7; Mary (c. 1684), 104, 219; Mary (c. 1852), 106; Mary Ann, 106; Mehetabell, 104; Monica, 352; Ralph of York, 104; Rebecca, 106; Richard (b. 1653), 104; Richard, (c. 1700), 219; Roger, 104; Samuel (c. 1780), 105; Samuel (c. 1804), 106; Sarah, 106; Simon of Seamer, 104; Sissalaye or Sissalayne, 104; Thomas (c. 1678), 79; Thomas (d. 1699), 105; Walter,

106; William of Flamborough, 104.
Priestmans Carr, 79, 105; Farm, 105, 110; House in Farmanby, 105; Lane, 92, 107, 117; Plantation, 107.
Prospect Place, 92, 94.
Prowde, John, 188.
Pudsey, Philippa, 291-2; Thomas, 291-2.
Puritans, 61.
'Puture,' 251.
Pye, Alan, 261.
Pygott, Baldwin, 209.
Pynder, Sir John, 167.

Quarter Sessions at, Easingwold, 218; Helmsley, 57-60, 62, 66, 70; Kirkby Moorside, 59, 62, 71, 172, 174, 294; Malton, 57-9, 62-4, 70; Pickering, 59, 291, 305; Richmond, 60; Thirsk, 56-8, 61-3, 71, 239.
Quia Emptores, Statute of, 202, 228.

Rabbit types, 297.
Raby Castle, 24, 30, 32.
Raffat, Adam, 15; Ralph, 15.
Ragby Castle, 110-2.
Raimes, Rev. J. M., 193-4.
Raleigh, Sir Walter, 108.
Ralph, son of Peter Martin, 13; the weaver, 114.
Rampton, 191.
Ramsay, The Dawn of the Constitution, 161.
Ramsey-Muir, J, 334.
Rand, George, 119, 271.
Ranke, History of England in the Seventeenth Century, 170.
Ratclif, William, 187.
Ratcliffe, Anne, 283; Charles, 95; James, 283.
Rate Books, 193, 235.
Raunde, Giles or Gyles, 119, 271.
Ravenspur, 47.
Raw, family of, 108; John, 244.
Raysine, Richard, 304.
Read, family of, 108; Rev. Cutts Rudston, 136; Rev. Francis, 140;

380

Captain Herbert, 140; James, 81; John (c. 1711), 85, 176; John (d. 1926), 180; Philip, 176; William (c. 1724), 121; William (c. 1734),87, 109; William (c. 1743), 110; William (c. 1807), 81, 110.

Reade, Anthony, 171; Thomas (c. 1600), 188; Thomas (c. 1654), 171.

Readshaw, Thomas, 119.

Recusancy Laws, 56, 64.

Red Dyke, 2, 19.

Rede, Rev. John, 165.

Reevley, Matthew, 111.

Reeve Bayliffes Accompts, 285.

Reeves, History of English Law, 208.

Reformation, The, 55, 167-8.

Regarders of the Forest, 17.

Reginald, son of Walter, 159; of Thornton, 263.

Rempland Syke, 281.

Rentall of the Honor and Manor of Pickering, 295.

Repton School, 226.

Rex, Mark, 111; Thomas, 111.

Reynolds, Thomas, 109.

Riccal, 179.

Richard, I., 14, 196, 202, 300; II., 47; III., 250.

Richard, son of Roger of Thornton, 299.

Richardson, Rev. John, 168, 186-8; Robert, 122; Thomas, 124, 180.

Richmond, 60, 226; Shire, 30-33.

Rievaulx Abbey, 19, 28-9, 37, 144, 155, 237, 298, 304-5; abbot of, 27, 29, 32, 45, 300-4; cartulary of, 260, 299-300, 304.

Riley, Mr & Mrs J, 338.

Rillington, 90.

Ringrose Farm, 110.

Ripley, John, 176, 308.

Rishesty or Haygate Hagg, 292.

Rising of the Northern Earls, 55.

Rithard, Enos, 219.

Rivers, Baldwin de, 197; Isabelde, 197. Riviere, Thomas de la, 270.

Robert, the miller, 12, 112; the smith, 28, 117; son of Walter, 261, 263; son of William, 261.

Robertson, Dr., 129, 184; Robert, 118.

Robhow, 213.

Robin Hoods Bay, 1.

Robinson, family of the Rector, 74, 239, 242; present family, 108, 124; Agnes, 168, 238; Anne, 138; Sir Arthur, 171; Arthur, 119, 329; Benjamin, 119; Cisse, 187; Cyril, 122; Edward, 60; Elizabeth, 67, 117; George (c. 1890), 111; George (c. 1930), 112; Grace, 168; Harold, 101; Harriet, 222; Helen, 103, 233, 240; Henry, 68, 168, 170, 238-40, 293; Hesle Poad (c. 1834), 296; Hessle (c. 1849), 111; Hessle (c. 1930),112; Hessle Poad (c. 1890), 111; James, 240; James Albert, 112, 308; Jane, 240; Rev. John the rector, 54, 68-9, 72, 136, 168-72, 189, 238-41, 293, 306; John, 240-1; John (c. 1743), 63, 110, 296; John of Whitby, 242; Rev. John (c. 1784), 191; Luke, 170-1; Magdalen, 240-2; Marie, 108; Mary (c. 1720), 242; Mary, of Pocklington, 172; Matthew of London, 242; Melior, 102, 242; Rev. Proctor, 222; Samuel, 64, 78-9, 102-3, 168, 233, 239-242; Thomas (c. 1618), 63, 68-9; Thomas (c. 1675), 78; Thomas (c. 1718), 295; Thomas (c. 1734),95; Rev. Thomas, 242; Thomas the yeoman, 242; William (d. 1626), 117; William (c. 1650), 114; William of Scarborough, 171; William (d. 1671), 173; William of Kirby, 115; William of York, 238.

Robinson's butchers, 334.

Robinson Hall, 242.

Robinson, William, 342.

Robson, A. (1930), 112; Isabel, 111; Johanna, 231; John, 308; Joseph, 308; Stephen, 308; Thomas, 111, 308; William the bastard, 231; William senior, 231; William (c. 1654), 255.

Rockingham, Marquis of, 75, 222.

Rodheram, Rev. Robert, 155.

Reform Bills, 77.

Rodgers, Ann, 184; John, 111, 184.

Roger, of Apelton, 261; son of Stephen of Kingthorpe, 42; son of Ukk, 299.

Rogers, family of, 108, 118; Dawson, 118; Mrs. Dawson, Intro; Isaac, 115, 151; Michael, 118; Thomas, 115; William (c. 1700), 113; William (c. 1734), 113, 118;William (c. 1807), 110.

Rogers, Ted & Charlie, 334.

Rogerson, Robert, 66, 189.

Rol, Hugo, 27-8.

Rolle, family of, 28; Richard, Ch. III, passim; sister of Richard, 34-5; William 28, 31-3; William of Aiskew, 29-30; William of Yafforth, 29-30.

Rollevilain, or Rollevylain, Ricardus, 28, 299.

Rolls of Parliament, 161, 199.

Rolls Series, I, 165, 197; II, 13; LX, 268.

Rome, 282; ecclesiastical courts at, 42; doctrines of, 4.

Roodbreeds, 242.

Rook, Ralph, 15.

Rookwood, 94, 112.

Ros, Robert de, 299.

Rosedale, 76; abbey of, 99, 245.

Roseles, William de, 203.

Roses, Wars of, 47-8, 210, 250, 303.

Rostan, Robert de, 200.

Rouceby, Adam de, 246, 263; Agnes, 265; Alexander de, 161-2; Geoffrey de, 261; John de, 14-5, 19, 265; Walter de, 246, 260, 263.

Rouen, 197, 278.

Round, Family Origins, 27, 156, 212; V.C.H., Hants., 6; Hereford, 6; Studies in Peerage and Family History, 248.

Rowland, L. G., 2.

Roxby, or Roxbie, or Rouceby, or Rousby, or Rowoobi, or Rowcesby, or Rockesbye, or Rottesby, or Rollesley, or Rozebi, or Ruksby, 20, 42, 50-1, 60, 79, 183, 207, 247, 249, 253, 260-1, 269; castle of, 18, 45, 48-51, 93, 265,

269, 271-2, 281; Closes, 282; demesne of, 9; enclosure in, 51; estate of, 83; fields of, 96; Fish Ponds, 281; Gamel of, 299; Gospatric of, 299; John de, 286; Manor of, 5, 7, 248, Ch. XV, passim; Old barn in, 283; riots at, 50.

'Roxby,' 96, 120.

Rowntree, Arnold, 336.

Rowntree, Richard, 336.

Roxby Hill, 33, 42, 50.

Roxby, Lane, 241; Road, 93, 350; Terrace, 93, 95, 96.

Royal Exchange, The, 230.

Ruddock, or Ruddoke, William, 51.

Rupert, Prince, 214.

'Rushworth Papers,' 277.

Russel, Richard, 17-9, 286.

Russell, Frances, 268; Sir Thomas, 268.

Russet de Thornton, 202.

Ruston, 200, 239; Gamel of, 299; Ukk of, 299; Walthevy of, 299.

Rutland, Dukes of, 236.

Rutter, John, 146; John Champley, 100, 146.

Rye, the, 300.

Ryedale, 247, 275.

Rymer, Dorothy, 235; Edward, 226, 318; Gertrude Mary, 226, 318; Matthew, 235.

Rymers Foedera, 268.

Ryton, 233.

Sacheverell, Dr., 75; Sir R., 250.

Sadler or Sadlier, Sir Ralph, 253, Wilfrid, 180.

St. Albans, Abbey of, 150.

St. Helena, 147.

St. Hilda, 4.

St. Hildas Cragg, 16.

St Hilda's church Ellerburn, 325.

Saint Iles, 83.

St John, Viscount Bolingbroke, 75.

St. Leonards Hospital, York, 41, 245-6.

St. Margarets, Westminster, 166.

St. Omer, 282.

St. Pauls School, 133.

St. Peters School, York, 178.

St. Quintin, family of, 145; Beatrice, 145; Eleanor, 230; Sir John, 230; William, 145.

St. Stephens, Westminster, 166.

Salisbury, Earl of, 41.

Saltburn, 228.

Salter, Rev. H. E., 190; Registrumin Annalium Collegii Mertonensis, 166.

Saltersgate Brow, 4.

Salvayn or Salvin, Sir Gerard, 202; Ralph, 65, 167, 220.

Sand Dale, 83, 296.

Sand Flats, 2, 79.

Sand Hutton, 102, 136, 225.

Sandford, Brian, 266-7, 288.

Sandys, Elizabeth, 213, 214 (vide Lumley); Sir William, 131, 213-4, 241.

Savage, Geoffrey, 154.

Sawdane, Sir Robert, 49, 185.

Sawdon, 33.

Sawer, Elizabeth, 68; John, 68-9; Roger, 68.

Scafe, Miss M., 81.

Scalby, 135-6, 175.

Scales, Robert, 123; William, 115, 137.

Scampston, 202-3, 218, 232.

Scarborough, 1, 8, 41, 50, 89-90, 95, 96, 100, 104, 129, 134, 171, 212, 220, 224, 226, 229, 232, 272, 275, 289, 297; bombardment (1914), 5; bubonic plague in, 67; Castle of, 14, 41-2, 72, 197, 200, 277-8; destruction of (1066), 5; Roman station at, 3; St. Marys Church at, 278; Siege of, 278.

Scholefield, Rev. R. B. (senior), 137, 178, 192; (junior), 138-9, 178.

Schroeder, Annals of Yorkshire, 1.

Scoby, Col, 340.

Scoby, Mrs. Thomas, 184.

Scotland, Wars with, 43-4, 162, 203-6, 209-11, 268-70, 276, 285.

Scott, Dorothy, 130, 316; Rev. Douglas Arthur, 141; Rev. George, 130, 179; Julia, 179; Mary Katherine, 130, 179, 316; Richard Arthur, 97, 102, 126,

129-30, 141, 144, 179-80, 308, 316, 322-3.

Scott, The Lady of the Lake, 126; Marmion, 4.

Scrayingham, 164-5.

Scrope, Lord, 211; Rebellion of Archbishop, 269.

Seaman, Anne, 224.

Seamer, rector of, 43; vicar of, 103.

Seaton, Richard, 293.

Sedman, Mrs., 119; Joseph, 308; Thomas, 111.

Seebohm, English Village Community, 3, 6, 10, 80; Tribal Custom, 150.

Seive Dale, 2, 17.

Selden, Tithes, 149.

Selden Society, XIII, 12, 13, 17.

Selfgarding, or Selgarbing, or Self-gerding, 260-1.

Sellar or Seller, Edward (c. 1668), 147; E. (c. 1710), 99, 147.

Selley Bridge, 112, 303-6; William de, 303.

Selley Wray, 22, 83.

Seloo, Robert, 304.

Seman, son of Godfrey, 261.

Seres, William, 212.

Serjeantson, Rev. W., 179.

Settlement, Law of, 57.

Settrington, 3, 150, 200-1.

Seven, the river, 44.

Sewerby, 232.

Sexendale, Theodore of, 299.

Shakersty or Shakerstile, 14.

Shakespeare, 1, 47, 108.

Shaw, An, 61.

Shaw-Baker, Doris; Mr, 338.

Shawcross, Rev. Richard, 184, 192.

Shawe, John, 59, 186; Robert, 62.

Sheepcoate, or Sheepcote House, 289, 290, 293.

Sheffield, Miss, 129; William, 129.

Shepherd, or Shephard, Nicolas, 70.

Sherbrooke, P. C., 127.

Sherwood, George, 88.

Shinney, vide Chymney.

Ship Money, 276.

Shirburne, William de, 202.
Shotten, Thomas, 176.
Shoulder of Mutton Plantation, 84, 297.
Shrewsbury, Duke of, 75.
Shum, Rev. Frederick, 193; Madeline, 193.
Sibdale, or Sybdale, 293-4.
Sidgwick, Robert, 132.
Sidmouth, 225.
Sigrida, wife of Archil, 227.
Simon the miller, 113.
Simpson or Sympson, Henry, 78; Isabell, 65; Robert, 53, 119; Rev. Thomas, 139-40.
Singleton, Mr., 217.
Sinnington, 107, 131, 137, 203, 206, 208, 210, 212-4, 216, 219, 225; Hounds, 126-7; Manor of, 16; township of, 17.
Six-Inch Ordnance Survey, 8, 17, 40, 83, 90, 93, 148, 213, 278, 288, 290, 292, 294.
Skaife, Domesday Book of Yorkshire, 227, 236.
Skeathwood or Skythewoode, 33, 253, 257.
Skelton, nr. York, 107.
Skelton Castle, 29, 107, 203, 228.
Skelton, family of, 107, 184, 258; Adam, 286; Andrew, 54; Ann, 216; John, 176; Edmund, 251; Edward, 78; Frank, 332; George (c. 1807), 123; George (1930), 112, 332; Mrs. George, 77, 121; 'Henrie,' 129; John, 114; Rachel, 128; Robert (c. 1570), 86; Robert (c. 1675), 78; Robert (c. 1720), 176; Robert (c. 1769), 177-8, 308; Robert (c. 1815), 110, 180; Robert of Wilton, 61; Samuel (c. 1780), 81; Samuel (c. 1800), 100, 107; Thomas (c. 1675), 281; Thomas the eldest (c. 1675), 78; Thomas the younger (c. 1675), 78; Thomas the youngest (c. 1675), 78; Thomas (c. 1743), 115, 128, 220; Thomas (c. 1856), 120, 122, 180; William (c. 1581), 253; William (c. 1605), 54;

William the Churchwarden, 58, 60; William (c. 1620), 239; William (c. 1651), 58; William (c. 1662), 171; William (c. 1675), 78; William (c. 1696), 216, 219.
Skeltons dole, 100; Garth, 83.
Skipton, 198; Cicely, Lady of, 197; School of, 134.
Skirpenbeck, 163.
Slater, Eddie, 329.
Slater, Mr, 344.
Slavery, abolition of, 77, 105.
Sledmere, 249.
Slee, Henry, 188; Robert the elder, 78; Robert the younger, 78.
Sleightholme, William, 187.
Slingsby, 27-8, 247, 249; Sir Henry, 158.
Smailes, or Smales, or Smayles, family of, 108, 189; Alice, 104; Anne, 81; Christopher, 176; George (c. 1600), 188; George (c. 1616), 60; James (c. 1763), 177; James (c. 1780), 81; Jane, 78; John, 78, 121; Matthew, 115; Richard, 111; Robert (c. 1670), 66, 105; Robert (c. 1743), 176; Robert (c. 1814), 110, 122; Sarah, 66, 78; Thomas the elder (e. 1675), 78; Thomas the younger (c. 1675), 78; Thomas (c. 1785), 110; William (c. 1735), 176; William (c. 1787), 110.
Smith, A. H., Place Names of the North Riding, 5, 17, 30, 81, 149, 182, 207, 245, 260, 284, 304.
Smith, Anthony Dudley, 334, 342, 350
Smith, Mrs E.D, 340.
Smith, Sir T., The Commonwealth of England, 55.
Smith, family of, 108; Alfred, 111-2, 180; Anne, 103; Dorothy, 282; George, 111-2; James, 219; John, 282; Mary, 106; Robert, 281; Thomas (d. 1696), 176; Thomas, of Uxbridge, 106; Rev. William, 103.
Smithies, John, 125.
Smithson or Smythson, family of, 184; Ann, 216; Robert (c. 1734), 123, 176;

Robert (c. 1675), 78; Robert (c. 1780), 151; Robert (c. 1807), 110; Symon, 78, 216.

Smythe, John, 52; Robert, 52.

Snainton, 35, 51, 60, 118, 230; Asce of, 299.

Snyverdale, 293.

Sollatt or Sollett, Richard (c. 1490), 48, 124; Richard (c. 1675), 78; William (c. 1592), 233, 254; William (c. 1600), 118.

Somerset, Henry, 212; Lucy, 212; Thomas, 212.

Sothull, Sir John de, 202.

South Lane, 350.

South Milford, 141.

Southerbruff, or Sutherbruff, or Sotherborough, or Southerborough, Rigg, 290, 293.

Spacye, William, 233.

Spanton, John W., 111, 308.

Spavin, William, 66. Special Sessions, at Hutton Bushel, 60; at Snainton, 60-1.

Spelgate, 241.

Spence, John, 348.

Spencer, Bishop, 145. Spencer, Mrs., 144.

Spenley, or Splenlaye, or Spendley, Elizabeth, 117; Isaac, 117; John (c. 1618), 118, 235; John (c. 1833), 116; Roger, 117; William (c. 1719), 176; William (c. 1780), 81, 178; William (c. 1800), 107, 110, 119.

Spenley Close, 117.

Spofford, Rev. Brian, 167.

Springs, the, 296.

Squire Osbaldeston, His Autobiography, 223, 225.

Stafford, Anne, 210; Sir Humphrey, 210; Mr. Justice, 171.

Stainclyffe, Rev. James, 168. Staindale, 268. Staines, family of, 184; Mark, 176; Thomas, 191; William, 178.

Stalwardman, Austin, 19, 301.

Standard, battle of, 236.

Stape Cross, 35.

Stapleton, Archaeologia, XXVI, 197.

Stapleton, Catherine, 273; Henry, 273.

Star Chamber, Court of, 51-2, 231.

Starkie, Thomas, 282.

State Papers, Domestic, 67.

Statutum de malefactoribus in partis, 15.

'Staunnestoon,' 232.

Steel, Thomas, 124.

Steinton, 298.

Stenhouse, Mr., 229.

Stenton, Types of Manorial Structure in the Northern Danelaw, 5, 244.

Stephen, of Kingthorpe, 42; son of Alan, 199; son of Gamel, 299.

Stephens, Frank, 220; Mary, 220.

Stephenson or Stevenson, George, 90; John, 69; John (d. 1881), 118; William, 116, 118.

Sterling, The Hothams, 277.

Stobart family, 338.

Stockland, 18.

Stodelay, John de, 247.

Stoke, battle of, 210.

Stokeslay, Thomas, 156.

Stokesley, 189.

Stonegrave, 173, 293.

Stonehouse, Charles, 113; F. E. (1930), 112.

Stoneygate, 213.

Stonye close, 281.

Stopes, William, 39.

Storr, Christopher, 135; George, 129, 136; John, 136; John (c. 1807), 110; Robert, 128; Thomas, 136, 171; William (schoolmaster), 136; William (shoemaker), 121; William (c. 1740), 176.

Story or Storye, John, 58, 66; Margaret, 58; Margery, 171; Mary, 216; Robert, 58; William, 171; Valentine, 58, 172.

Stourton, Baron, 282.

Stowe co. Northants., 279.

Strafford, Earl of, 276.

Strangers Garth, 136-7.

Strangways, Sir Thomas, 132.

Streanaeshalch, 4, 5.

John (c. 1930), 112; Robert (c. 1605), 54; Robert (c. 1654), 234; Robert (c. 1890), 112; Robert (1) (c. 1930), 112-3; Robert (2) (c. 1930), 112.

White, Directory, 119-23, 125, 144.

White Cliff Quarry, 79; Rigg, 293, 296.

White, 'Huckster', 340.

White, Mrs, 334.

Whitegate, 216, vide Whitbygate.

Whitehead, James Loy, 85 (vide Documents); James Dove, 85.

Whitelock, William, 81.

Whitenere, Hugh de, 19.

Whiteways, 120, vide Whitbygate.

Whitgate, 108, vide Whitbygate.

Whitney, Professor J. P., 100; Mrs., 81, 100.

Whitwell, Thomas, 288.

Wickens, Rev. Dr., 223; Mrs., 223.

Widd, family of, 108; Richard, 120; Mrs. Richard, 123; Roger, 78; Thomas, 120.

Wighill, 273.

Wikes, or Wykes, Rev. Marmaduke, 78, 189-90.

Wilberforce, William, 77.

Wilberfoss, Priory of, 99.

Wiles or Wyles, Mary, 65; Michael, 110; Peter, 62; Richard, 62, 65-6; William, 62.

Wilfred, Archbishop, 3, 4.

Wilkinson, Rev. Christopher, 178; George, 78; John, 117; Margritt, 69; Matilda, 63.

Willerdale, 17.

Willerton, Alfred, 119-20; John, 119; William, 119.

William the Conqueror, 5, 6, 196, 227, 244, 248, 284, 298.

William III., 75, 90, 174-5, 189, 206, 216, 218, 242.

William, abbot of Rievaulx, 45; of Dalby, 36-7, 39-40; of Farmanby, 261; the Forester, 286; le Gros, 197; the Miller, 112, 159; the Shepherd, 19; son of Alice, 19; son of Gamel, 262; son of Henry, 15; son of Ivetta, 286;

son of Ketell, 299; son of Matilda, 263; son of Norman, 299; son of Robert, 28, 159, 246; son of Roesy, 299; son of Thomas, 246; son of William, 286; the Weaver, 19, 114.

Williams, Elizabeth, 223; Thomas, 223.

Williamson, Elday, 70.

Willoughby, Elizabeth, 211; Elizabeth wife of Robert, 211; Sir John, 210; Sir Robert, 211; Robert, Lord Broke, 211; Robert, Lord, de Eresby, 46, 208-9.

Willow Grange Farm, 112, 308.

Wilmott or Willmott, Hannah, 110, 183; William, 80, 95, 110, 183.

Wilson, Henry, 217; John, 288; Mr. (c. 1734), 123; Rev. Thomas, 133, 175, 189; W., 180; William, Richard, 344.

Wilton, 17, 18, 61, 99, 100, 108, 113, 150, 177, 194, 200-1, 213, 235, 270, 300; corpse road from, 79; Eugenaldus of, 299.

Winceby, 42.

Winchcombe, John, 291.

Winchester, Earl of, 43.

Windsor, Dean and Canons of St. Georges Chapel in, 78-9, 81, 83, 157, 215, 223, 250-9; vide Documents.

Wisperdales, 79, 110, 224.

Withipool, Sir Edmund, 213; Frances, 213; Lucy, 256.

Wivell, Roger, 70.

Wivelsby, Philip de, 198.

Wivelscombe, 166.

Wolds, the, 33.

Wood, family of, 108; John, 332; L. E., 123; Mary, 123.

Wood, Leo, Cllr, 344.

Wood End, 271.

Woodland Farm, 107, 112.

Woodstock, Assize of, 14.

Woofnest, or Woolnest, or Woolness, 148, 235.

Woollaston, Sir John, 255.

Worcester, Earl of, 212.

Wordsworth, William, 181, 298.

Worsley, Sir Thomas, 132; Sir William, 139-40.

Wotte, Stephen, 261-2.
Wray, family of, 108; Charles, 121; Dick, 332, 350; Richard, 96, 119; William, 119; Messrs. William and Son, 94.
Wrelton, 76; Richard de, 286.
Wright, Dialect Dictionary, 292.
Wright, Tom, 339.
Wydale, 286.
Wyerne, William de, 202.
Wygane, Robert de, 19, 20, 286.
Wyghton, Sir John de, 202.
Wykecliff, Christopher, 157.
Wykeham, 63, 68, 200; abbey, 41; Payn of, 299.
Wyleby, Philip de, 246.
Wyles, vide Wiles.
Wynn, Sir Rowland, 76-7.
Wysteley, Thomas, 267.
Wyvile, William, 27; William (c. 1329), 249; William (c. 1581), 253.
Wyvville, Agnes, 237; Amfelisa, 237; Eustacia, 237; Richard, 237; William (1), 237; William (2), 237; William (3), 237-8.

Yafford, 31, 34.
Yarker, Rev. Luke, 225, 314.
Year Books, Ed. III, 7.
Yedingham, 24, 135, 175, 224, 286.
Yeland, or Eland, family of, 247; Catherine, 16; Eustachia, 154; Hugh, 15-6, 43; Katharine, 247; Nicholas, 154; Ralph, 21; William, 15-6, 18, 21, 43, 202, 247.
Yeoman of the Guard, 232.
Yeoman, Robert, 116.
York, 3, 4, 6, 15, 17, 41, 43, 46, 66, 72, 90, 106, 168-9, 173, 215, 217, 225, 238-9, 273, 282, 293, 297, 307; Archbishop of, 41, 305; Arch-bishops Registers, Booth, 164; Corbridge, 160; Gerard, 251; Giffard, 155, 160-1; Gray, 154, 160, 184-5; Neville, 165; Kempe, 164; Wickwane, 155, 160; Archbishop Herrings Visitation Returns, 73, 135, 158, 176, 190;

Archbishops, Melton, 147; Thomson, 144; Thoresby, 38; Zouche, 38, 163; Castle of, 42, 60; Chancellor, 164; Consistory Court of, 203-4; Dean of, 20, 79, 184-9, 224; Dean and Chapter of, 251; diocese of, 24; Gotheramgate Church in, 233; Hospital of St. Leonard in, 41, 245-6; James I at, 55; Minster, 147, 176, 179, 216, 307; St. Peters School, 178; Vale of, 34.
Yorkshire Archaeological Journal, I, 70, 216; III, 237; V, 65, 216; VII, 156; XIV, 221-2; XVIII, 168, 186-8, 291; XIX, 5, 182; XX, 20; XXI, 166-7; XXII, 41, 203, 206, 228; XXV, 145; XXVIII, 145; XXIX, 203.
Yorkshire Archaeological Society Record Series, I, 103-4, 114, 240; II, 157, 211, 231, 238, 251, 269, 270; V, 212, 252; VI, 99, 104, 164-5, 232, 303; VII, 239; XI, 167, 238; XII, 11, 14, 237, 246, 263, 284; XV, 275, 307; XVII, 203, 265; XVIII, 169, 306; XX, 169; XXI, 22, 27-8, 113-4, 117, 161, 185, 206, 301; XXIII, 201, 228; XXXI, 198, 228; XXXIX, 201-2; XLI, 52;XLIV, 260; L, 265; LII, 155, 229,265; LIII, 158, 163, 273, 305; LV,107, 216; LVIII, 51, 63-4, 113,120, 233, 239, 274; LIX, 209, 229;LXII, 154; LXV, 232; LXVII,200, 246; LXX, 51, 269; LXXI,175, 177, 191; LXXIII, 54, 78,172, 175, 184, 258, 292; LXXIV,118, 162; LXXV, 73, 135, 158,175-6; LXXVII, 74.
Yorkshire Geological Society, XIII, 2.
Yorkshire, magistrates of, 216; political election (1734), in, 76; (1807), 77; Post, 163, 244; Wilfreds conversion of, 4.
Young, Sit C. G., 198.
Young, History of Whitby, 1, 3, 6, 9, 41-2, 95, 116, 120, 129, 137, 171, 273-5, 277.
Younglove, Robert, 291.
Ysolda, wife of Gilbert, 159, 261.

Also available from the Blackthorn Press

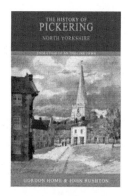

Home & Snowden, *The History of Pickering*

An updated version of Gordon Home's 'Evolution of an English Town'.

£14-95

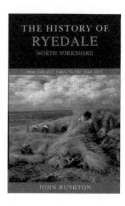

John Rushton, *The History of Ryedale*

A fully illustrated history of the District of Ryedale.

£25-00

Pat Nuttgens, *The History of York*

The complete history of the city of York from Roman times to the present day

£14-95

Available from all good bookshops or post free from the Blackthorn Press, Blackthorn House, Pickering YO18 8AL. Cheques made out to 'Blackthorn Press'. Or buy online at www.blackthornpress.com